CONRAD AIKEN

. . . .

POET OF WHITE HORSE VALE

CONRAD
AIKEN

Poet of White Horse Vale

· ·

EDWARD BUTSCHER

The University of Georgia Press

Athens & London

© 1988 by the University of Georgia Press
Athens, Georgia 30602
All rights reserved

Designed by Richard Hendel
Set in Mergenthaler Times Roman with Kabel display

The paper in this book meets the guidelines for
permanence and durability of the Committee on
Production Guidelines for Book Longevity of the
Council on Library Resources.

Printed in the United States of America
92 91 90 89 88   5 4 3 2 1

Library of Congress Cataloging in Publication Data

Butscher, Edward.
Conrad Aiken, poet of White Horse Vale.
Bibliography: v. 1, p.
Includes index.
1. Aiken, Conrad, 1889–1973—Biography. 2. Poets,
American—20th century—Biography. I. Title.
PS3501.I5Z59   1988   818'.5209 [B]   84-16275
ISBN 0-8203-0760-2 (v. 1: alk. paper)

British Library Cataloging in Publication Data available

In memory of Amy

And her untrodden ways

CONTENTS

. . . .

ILLUSTRATIONS

· · · · · · · ·

Never believe that you know

the last word about any human

heart.

Henry James

.   .   .   .

PREFACE

If we do murder to dissect or, like Audubon, for art's sake—and no honest biographer dare claim more than partial success for his autopsy—then the process must be as thorough as possible, however selective and speculative. Thus any biography of a writer worth doing and reading has to be a literary biography, intent upon limning the diverse influences that helped shape its subject's artifices. And those artifices must be confronted within the context of both their environment and their historical relevance.

At the practical level such a procedure entails a constant sifting of verbal debris for the materials to construct a prism capable of mirroring whole the shard realities of the "victim" and his vanished world. As a result, critics dismayed by the use of certain psychoanalytical vantages in my study of Sylvia Plath will be no less disturbed by this investigation of Conrad Aiken's life and imagination, since I remain committed to the notion that a modern biographer cannot afford to ignore insights garnered from other disciplines, whether psychological, philosophical, or from more impressionistic realms where specialists refuse to tread. The dynamic of human creativity is the sole legitimate focus for a discursive technique, which, like all criticism (*contra* Harold Bloom et al.), remains parasitic in nature and origins, if not ambitions.

Assuming such a paradoxical contraption could exist, a definitive biography lies outside my interests, though Joseph Killorin, friend and surrogate son of Aiken in his last years, is hard at work on what should prove an exhaustive, doubtless valuable recounting of the poet's passage through this vale of canceled checks. But questions of approach are beyond argument; the text alone must justify its weakest synapse. More important, the arrogance implicit in the biographer's task should never blind his or her audience to the built-in obsolescence of the genre, intrinsic ties to seemingly urgent current concerns.

I have tried, of course, to avoid parochial judgments and am egotistical enough to think myself equal to the substantial body of literature so conveniently manufactured for my benefit, literature which is still largely unappreciated. And yet the consciousness brought to bear upon the main chores of reconstruction and interpretation—evolving consciousness was the fulcrum of Aiken's entire career—is inescapably cultivated in the garden of my own era's cultural tropes. Ten or twenty years from now, if not sooner, that domain might be reshaped to reflect a *zeitgeist* radically different from the present one, making another biography plausible, even imperative. As Tennyson optimistically insisted at the start of *In Memoriam,* "Men may rise on stepping-stones / Of their dead selves to higher things."

Because the forced march of experience from birth to death appears most true to a developmental mode, the order of this book is generally chronological, except in the beginning. There, a more circular pattern prevails, an echo of the circular voyage Aiken liked to believe defined his progress as man and author, as "Poet of White Horse Vale" and as "Cosmos Mariner," a pattern of unceasing quest for identity and redemption that a second volume—covering the years from 1926 to 1979—will complete.

But in the end, art's obdurate struggle against death locates its arena elsewhere. A critical biography can merely affirm less pleasing revelations of real toads in real gardens.

August 1987   EDWARD BUTSCHER
Amagansett, New York

ACKNOWLEDGMENTS

．　．　．　．　．　．　．　．　．　．　．　．

Perhaps the pleasantest aspect of the biographer's task is the opportunity to thank all the people and institutions that provided so much of the essential information along the way, often creating friendships in the process.

Clarissa Lorenz Aiken was unstinting with her aid over an extended period of time, frequently tracking down obscure items and answering an endless river of pesky questions. And Conrad Aiken's three children were no less generous with their time and invaluable insights. Jane Aiken Hodge and her husband, Alan, opened their home to my wife and me and never denied requests for assistance: Allan's subsequent death represented the loss of a truly gentle, scholarly man. Joan Aiken and her husband, Professor Julius Goldstein, were also helpful and hospitable, maintaining the family's well-earned reputation for congeniality, and John and Paddy Aiken could not have been kinder than they were, submitting to a tedious interview, showing me Rye, and, in Paddy's case, providing several photographs.

One of the most enjoyable friendships to emerge from these research chores was that with Professor George Boas and his wife, Simone. George helped greatly with whatever questions arose in connection with Aiken and T. S. Eliot, both of whom he had known at Harvard, and exchanged letters with a gay erudition delicious to know and savor. His passing marked another major loss. Dr. Grayson P. McCouch, Aiken's friend since their prep school days together, and his wife, Margaret, were equally hospitable, despite the former's ill health. Dr. McCouch died on August 2, 1979, after a life of dedicated service to medicine and teaching.

Before his death, D. G. Bridson also offered valuable testimony through the mails, and his interviews with Aiken for the BBC are priceless for an understanding of the poet's later years. Robert La Zebnik, an unusually zealous Harvard student, was indefatigable in tracking down important documents, and Virginia L. Smyers, conscientious and kind, was similarly zealous in her pursuit of pertinent material, as was Carleton Kelsey of the Amagansett Free Library, who cheerfully secured every volume needed, whatever the cost in time and trouble. Writers Jane Mayhall and Ruth Herschberger kindly granted me interviews, and the latter generously gave permission to peruse her own batch of letters from Aiken.

Special thanks must go to Carol Krusen Scholz, now a dear friend, for sharing her Ph.D. thesis research with me and for performing many burdensome detective chores on my behalf. Novelist David Markson also deserves special mention for opening his apartment and mind to my investigations, assisted by his perceptive wife, Elaine, as well as for supplying several fine photographs. Professor Edward Huberman granted a helpful interview, as did Ruth Dadourian (née McIntyre), whose memory of the poet she knew during his adolescent and Harvard years was precise and acute, providing a significant record of a shadowy period in Aiken's life.

Other people who provided helpful data include Seymour Lawrence and Paul C. Metcalf. Metcalf, in particular, was refreshingly frank in his letters to me, which are rich in human detail. Aiken's fellow writers rarely failed to respond warmly to requests for aid, among them Mary McCarthy, Robert Penn Warren, Richard Eberhart, A. R. Ammons, John Hall Wheelock, Kenneth Burke, Josephine Jacobsen, Barbara Guest, and Stephen Stepanchev. Alfred Knopf replied promptly to a mail inquiry.

Despite illness and advanced age, which he gallantly refuses to recognize, Malcolm Cowley granted an extended interview, made his Aiken letters available, and responded to various questions with kindly patience. Professor Philip Butcher shared his specialist knowledge with me, and Professor Howard Hirt, with the aid of his wife, Muriel, relieved me of many research tasks in the Boston area.

And there is an inevitable honor roll of people who volunteered crucial bits of information or in other ways helped to make the biographer's path smoother: Lewis Turco, director of the Program in Writing Arts at the State University of New York at Oswego; John Unterecker; Steve Bassett; Janet Piper; Joseph F. Dillon III; Tony Kilgallin; Charles A. Wagner, executive secretary of the Poetry Society of America; Mrs. E. Clifford Nelson; Cryssana J. Bogner; Lewis Sckolnick; Arnold Gates, literary editor of the *Lincoln Herald;* Alan Wald of the University of Michigan; Robert Disraeli; Ralph Hickok; Willard R. Trask; Christopher Whelen; Clayton Hoagland, who shared his memory of Aiken and an article that he wrote for the *Literary Messenger;* Alvin V. Sizer, managing news editor of the *New Haven Register and Journal-Courier;* Catherine K. Harris; Dr. Henry Murray; Jean A. Hall; Russell A. Fraser, R. P. Blackmur's astute biographer; Robert Beum, print editor at the University of Mid-America; Jerre Mangione of the University of Pennsylvania; Sally Haskell; David Crosson, research historian at the University of Wyoming; H. C. Joslen; Eloise B. Bender; Gene M. Gressley; Laura Benet; and George Wallach.

As usual, the bulk of the documentary evidence came from a wide variety of libraries, staffed, for the most part, by a host of amiable experts. At the Huntington, Winifred E. Popp, Manuscript Department, Mary L. Robertson, curator of manuscripts, Virginia J. Renner, reader services librarian, and David Mike Hamilton, assistant curator of literary manuscripts, well deserve appreciation for their efforts on my behalf, and at the University of Texas's Humanities Research Center, Ellen Dunlap, research librarian, was particularly helpful. Other librarians who were generous with their time and skills include Diana Haskell and Elsa Lee Sink at the Newberry Library; Paul T. Heffron, acting chief at the Library of Congress, and his kind assistant, Charles Kelly; Harley P. Holden, curator of the Archives at Harvard University's Library, and his assistant, William W. Whalen; Carolyn A. Davis, manuscript librarian at the George Arents Research Library, Syracuse University; Richard F. Phillips at the Savannah Public Library; Elizabeth Stege Teleky, manuscript research specialist at the Joseph Regenstein Library; Alexander P. Clark, curator of manuscripts at the Princeton University Library; and Andrew Hubbertz, director of collection development at the University of Saskatchewan Library.

More personal thanks go to George Cohn and my colleagues at John Bowne and to those many students whose energetic aid freed me from countless professional chores, especially Paula Haber, Karen McKindly, Mary Morello, Balram Persaud, Debbie Hyson, Brigida Valesquez, Melissa Konikoff (peace personified), beautiful Sheela Battu, the Jennifer Ypes and Vandana Misra twins, and the charming, ever-efficient Wendy Chan.

Closer to home, perpetual gratitude belongs to Pudding, Miss Boo, Mrs. Podge and her errant son Pushkin, and to Paula, who keeps the menagerie functioning.

Special thanks to the Huntington Library and its librarian, Daniel H. Woodward, for permission to quote and reprint items from the Aiken Collection and to the Harvard University Archives for permission to reprint the photograph of the *Advocate* staff.

The author has quoted passages, for the purpose of illustrating his discussion of Conrad Aiken's life and works, from the following volumes: *Ushant: An Essay,* by Conrad Aiken, copyright © 1952, 1962 by Conrad Aiken, published by W. H. Allen and Duell, Sloan, and Pearce; *Blue Voyage,* by Conrad Aiken, copyright © 1927 by Conrad Aiken, published by Charles Scribner's Sons; *Great Circle,* by Conrad Aiken, copyright © 1933 by Conrad Aiken, published by Charles Scribner's Sons; *Conversation: Or Pilgrim's Progress,* by Conrad Aiken, copyright © 1940, by Conrad Aiken, published by Duell, Sloan and Pearce; *The Collected Short Stories of Conrad Aiken,* by Conrad Aiken, copyright © 1922, 1923, 1924, 1925, 1927, 1928, 1929, 1930, 1931, 1932, 1933, 1934, 1935, 1941, 1950, 1952, 1953, 1955, 1956, 1957, 1958, 1959, 1960, 1961, 1962, 1964 by Conrad Aiken, published by World Publishing Company and Schocken Books; *A Reviewer's ABC,* by Conrad Aiken, copyright © 1935, 1939, 1940, 1942, 1951, 1958 by Conrad Aiken, published by Meridian Books, Inc., and by Oxford University Press as *Collected Criticism: Collected Poems, 1916–1970,* by Conrad Aiken, copyright © 1916, 1917, 1918, 1920, 1921, 1923, 1925, 1926, 1927, 1929, 1930, 1931, 1932, 1933, 1934, 1935, 1936, 1940, 1941, 1942, 1944, 1945, 1947, 1948, 1949, 1952, 1955, 1958, 1959, 1960, 1961, 1962, 1963, 1967, 1970 by Conrad Aiken, published by Oxford University Press.

A man is a bundle of relations, a

knot of roots, whose flower and

fruitage is the world.

Ralph Waldo Emerson

. . . .

PROLOGUE

When Conrad Aiken died in the late afternoon of August 17, 1973, a few weeks after his eighty-fourth birthday, he was one of the country's best-known, least-read poets and men of letters. Honors had accrued late, for the most part, as honors tend to do for poets: the National Book Award in 1954, the Bollingen Prize in 1956, and the Gold Medal for Literature in 1969. In April of that last year Governor Jimmy Carter had proclaimed him Poet Laureate of Georgia, a dubious distinction that still seemed appropriate for a writer intent upon completing the broken arc (the *Great Circle*) of his art's quest for total reified consciousness. Having been born in Savannah to his parents' rich New England heritage, it was perhaps fitting that he die in a Savannah nursing home.

It was also fitting that he be buried in the same plot with his parents, William and Anna Aiken, in Bonaventure, Savannah's lovely old cemetery facing the Wilmington River, since their tragic destiny had been responsible for the abyss between him and other human beings that always defines the unconscious sea where solitary artists pursue their krakens. On a marble bench placed near the parental tombstone to mark his grave, the inscriptions COSMOS MARINER DESTINATION UNKNOWN and GIVE MY LOVE TO THE WORLD that bracket CONRAD POTTER AIKEN represent poetry's triumph over circumstance, a psyche raised to the level of myth. Not as massive as Walt Whitman's tomb to himself in a less impressive New Jersey setting, the Aiken marker is similarly heroic and deceptive. Though Aiken was never the equal of Whitman, whose example had helped free his generation from the weight of Europe's cultural monuments, *Ushant*, his Joycean version of *Leaves of Grass*, had sought to project, at a sharper Freudian angle, the myth of the redemptive poet upon the screen of a personal past as well.

Several years before his death, Aiken, punster and wry traditionalist to the end, wrote the caustic, balladlike "Obituary in Bitcherel," insisting, "Separate we come, / Separate Go. / And this be it known is all that we know."

Thus another orbit had been fashioned as Aiken, dismissing the Keats of his youth, duly alerted critics that truth was not necessarily the issue when poetry and biography struggle against the power of history. Alden Whitman, more prosaic obituary writer for the *New York Times,* preserved Aiken's casual detachment from his own demise: " 'I'm running out of time,' he said last summer. 'All things come to an end.' " But obsessions can only be deflected elsewhere, and the spider enigma behind art, behind specific forms and generic survival drives, remains cobwebbed in the fragments of a refracted self. "For all his poetry and short stories," Whitman wrote, "Mr. Aiken believed that *Ushant,* his autobiography in the third person and a continuation of *Blue Voyage,* provided the best clue to his life and personality. He saw *Ushant* not only as 'an autobiography of the creative spirit, but also as a candid self-revelation of my poetic wellspring.' "

Never as candid as its author professed, akin to Wordsworth's *Prelude* in that and other respects, *Ushant* did wrestle with the crucial traumas of childhood and their subsequent effects in an effort to articulate Aiken's sincere conviction that exposure and self-consciousness, reflexive artifices, were essential: "If it was the writer's business, or the poet's, to be as conscious as possible, and his primary obligation, then wouldn't this impose upon him the still deeper obligation of being conscious of his *own* workings, the workings of his psyche, and of the springs and deficiencies and necessities and compulsions, the whole subliminal drive which had made him a writer to begin with, and along with the work itself, to present, as it were, the explication—?" And yet simple endurance, the integrity of the ego, cannot tolerate too much reality. *Ushant,* which might be traced back to Rousseau, Wordsworth, Nietzsche, and George Moore, and which had an immediate analog in Joyce's *Portrait of the Artist as a Young Man,* ultimately emerges as a variation on Saint Augustine's conversion journey from the City of Man to the City of God, a secular variation in which the healing function of the imagination replaces deity.

What this meant in practical terms was a constant distorting of self and experience to simulate patterns of sin and salvation that embraced the abreaction process of psychoanalysis, a rational impulse toward catharsis without ever really risking a loss of the mask identity that literature supplied. Neither *Ushant* nor the autobiographical novel *Blue Voyage,* for instance, alludes to Aiken's sister Elizabeth, who went insane in her early thirties and spent the rest of her long life in a mental institution. And the Don Juanism conceded by *Ushant* as the leitmotif of an amoral sexual stance is phrased always in the grammar of love, mitigating the compulsive, often cruel extent of the misogyny governing its expression. In other words, "the profound psychological truth" about himself and the world that Aiken began to seek in *Blue Voyage,* which he began in the early 1920s, then claimed to have snared in *Ushant,* completed in 1951, was no less a myth than the "good grey poet" adumbrated by Whitman's persona.

Evidence of the failure of *Ushant's* telic quest, a failure of nerve, not art, can be adduced from the fact that its composition and publication did not perceptively alter Aiken's character. George Wilbur, psychiatrist and close friend since their Harvard years, had said in 1946 that "Aiken's personal life and his art have been seriously damaged over a period of years by a neurosis for which he refused to undergo treatment." Further, after *Ushant's* emergence, none of the inveterate ardor for acquiring mistresses appeared dampened, except by age. Of course, the question of whether the artist, unlike the physician, can heal himself through his art is moot and vast, though art mandates the discipline and emotive release that keeps clinical madness at bay. But Aiken was almost unique among his American colleagues in believing from the start that the dynamics of psychoanalysis could be integrated into a writer's metaphoric apparatus, that both writers and critics could benefit from a more scientific awareness of depth psychology.

As early as *Blue Voyage* he had asked: "Every man his own psychoanalyst?" In the same chapter, where his alter ego is grappling with the implications of Freudian theory in the context of his own gift and remembered childhood trials, a new type of artist is conceived surfacing, "a type in which there is an artist's neurosis, but also a penetrating intelligence which will permit, or permit only with contempt, the neurosis to work itself out." He rejects the notion of surrendering his poetic role, "suspecting my whole life would be deranged by it," but remains mired in the fundamental dilemma inherited from the Romantics, a pertinacious identity crisis, self-devouring consciousness: "My destructive speculations . . . were coming too close to a destruction of *myself.*" The consequence, to quote Carol Scholz, was that "Aiken's whole life and art were a long process of self-analysis, with himself as the psychoanalyst and also the patient."

If the treatment failed, at least the myth and the literature it generated succeeded well enough to grant him significant stature in the literary history of our century. *Ushant,* a durable piece of fiction, confirms this judgment. The idea of writing a third-person autobiography in a stream-of-consciousness mode probably had its inception around 1922, when the *Blue Voyage* experiment with very personal material began and when Joyce's *Ulysses* was a recent publication, but the novel made it superfluous at the time. Aiken later described how he "outlined and began *Ushant* in 1933, abandoned it as too difficult, resumed it only to abandon it again, but all the while adding notes both for material and design, made a third start in 1946, and finally finished it in 1950 and 1951." For his 1961 report to Harvard classmates on their fiftieth anniversary he would explain: "It's pronounced, you shant. The idea being that you set out to do something, and you think you know what it is, but you don't, and it hasn't come to be"—the title is a pun on *Île d'Ouessant,* a rocky barrier reef visible from Rye once believed to mark the edge of the world.

When in the fall of 1951 Aiken completed *Ushant,* sections of which had been typed in his office at the Library of Congress, where he was serving a second term as poetry consultant, he was relieved and anxious, anxious in particular about its reception by friends and relatives. On November 29 of that year he wrote to his brother Kempton Taylor: "Well, the queer, large and perhaps offensive book got itself done at long last, after these eighteen years—I began to see that here in the Library, between interviews and phone calls and committee consultations, it would drag on forever, and to no very satisfactory ending, so I up and took five days *en garçon* in NY, incognito except to a few friends for the evenings, and sat myself down to do or die. And I did, *and* died. In four days I added the requisite 22 pages to wind it up."

Aiken tried to anticipate and defuse natural fears about revealing family secrets, especially the strain of mental illness that had caused Kempton, a surgeon, voluntarily to forfeit the joys of fatherhood. "As you see," he wrote, "you and Rob [Robert, his other brother] figure only slightly, and briefly, in it—I thought that best for a variety of reasons; and Elizabeth I thought it simpler not to mention at all, or at any rate so thought until it was too late to do anything about it. Maybe just as well. But the family insanity is dealt with, and my own neurotic inheritance of it." To his old friend Maurice Firuski, owner of Cambridge's Dunster House Bookshop, he wrote kiddingly: "We think maybe we'd better be in New Zealand what time it comes out—it might be quieter and safer!"

Kempton's reply, meanwhile, was disturbing as it bared yet another nervous breakdown by a relative and intimated serious doubts about the advisability of placing the family skeletons on display, at the same time offering to finance Conrad and Conrad's wife, Mary, to a nostalgic Savannah weekend, Kempton having retired to Clearwater, Florida, with his own wife, Elizabeth. Although agreeable to the trip, Aiken was adamant in the matter of his autobiography's ostensible candor, indicating that "there are only three or four references to the family *petit mal,* or shall we say insanity, and as it's highly important to my own artist-exegesis and self-exegesis, I'm now more than ever inclined to let it rip. But let's talk about it—and at Bonaventure!"

Aiken had been back to Savannah only once since his youth, and that was in 1936, when too deeply involved in the dissolution of his second marriage to be touched by the city's ghosts. The April weekend with Kempton and the two wives proved that one could go home again, at least as a tourist, because,

Aiken wrote, "it was all quite staggeringly beautiful, I thought, and for me at least performed a sort of miracle of recapitulation and subsumption, so that what was *apparently* lost turns out to be no such thing, but a habitable reality in the very systole. I now *have* Savannah again." He had visited the house at 503 Whittaker Street opposite Forsyth Park, where he and his sister Elizabeth had been born, and, accompanied by Mary and a woman named Catherine, a childhood companion, the house at 228 Oglethorpe Street across from Colonial Park, site of so many vivid memories.

The thought of returning to Savannah to live was attractive, but as usual, in spite of public success, money was scarce, too scarce even to consider the possibility of completing, in virtual truth, the circle that had taken him from Savannah to Cambridge and Cape Cod and England and back again to the Cape, where the Aikens now owned a rambling house in Brewster. Aiken had to be content with the mythical voyage of spiral discoveries about literature and self that *Ushant* configured, confounding the past by floating it into the present and refusing terminal berths in either. If not totally honest, through conscious and unconscious design, the book was a valid summary of his life's relentless quest for the partial reality that literature illuminates and psychological knowledge reinforces. After all, the fluidity of its fictional technique, which depended upon reflexive awareness of the writer in the act of writing his story (and life), adhered to the self-conscious disguise that had enabled him to survive.

When Wallace Stevens, whose poetry had influenced Aiken's early work, read *Ushant,* he discerned necessary retreats behind figurative poses and wrote Aiken: "A book of this sort is subject to a variety of judgments. It need not be judged according to the conscious intentions of its author. What I found of special interest was that it exhibited the special focus of the poetic mind. For instance, one sees no one in the book without a mask of one sort or another. I don't intend that to be a comment but as a statement of fact. It is a question of focus"—a cautious analysis from a man not given to removing his own Janus mask as 1890s dandy and efficient insurance executive. In his response Aiken accepted the insight: "Yes, I found the mask imperative—nothing else could possibly have worked. As you say, focus was an inherent necessity, distance had to be kept, or *I* had to keep *my* distance, and this degree of stylization was the answer."

This subtle misconstruing of Stevens's comment, easing the emphasis away from implied falsifications of other people to the artist's inevitable poetic license, reflects the lacuna between fiction and autobiography that *Ushant* tries to span with an idealized portrait of the prodigal artist returning home to a Savannah of love and forgiveness (Saint Augustine *redux*) under the aegis visage of Grandfather Potter, "Teacher from the West," as "towards this as yet unseen face we rise, we rise, ourselves now like notes of music arranging themselves in a divine harmony, a divine union" (365).

It is the music of the spheres, an Elizabethan resolution to a modernist absence of resolutions, but the voyage from childhood's Savannah scenes to *Ushant*'s hymned synthesis of psyche and *res* requires another dimension also, the biographer's equally partial merger of fact and focus.

CONRAD AIKEN

POET OF WHITE HORSE VALE

POSSESSED OF THEM FOREVER

The biographical cycle might begin with a brief consideration of the human vortex, the whirlpool of human antecedents that produced Aiken's locally prominent parents, transplanted New Englanders who were (according to a *Savannah Morning News* reporter) somewhat mismatched: "Mrs. Aiken was a woman of unusual mental endowment, broad culture and remarkable attainments. Intellectually, the husband and wife faced each other, equals upon a high plane of mentality. In almost every other respect their characters were direct opposites." Anna's husband, Dr. William Ford Aiken, ophthalmologist, inventor, photographer, graduate of Harvard Medical School (Class of 1886), had "attained a reputation which extended beyond the confines of the state and the South" by his early thirties. He was the only son of William Lyman and Emily Potter Akin, spelling his name to conform to an older usage.

The Akins, who also had a daughter named Grace, were nominal Quakers of mixed New York and New England stock, Emily a farm girl from Glenville in upstate New York with little education and none of the social graces, the eldest of thirteen children. At the age of eighteen she had married a man fourteen years her senior, probably to escape the endless drudgery of raising a large brood of siblings after her mother's early death, and there is no evidence to deduce a love match in her precipitous choice of husbands. Quite the contrary. The man she married, who must have been drawn to her by the "libidinous" component his grandson detected beneath his severe façade, did not have much to offer beyond a respectable appearance and a rosary of respectable ancestors extending back to the colonial period, when John Akin, a Quaker, left Scotland to escape religious persecution and settled in Dartmouth, Massachusetts, in 1680.

The portrait of William Lyman Akin painted in *Ushant*—"stern, abstractly intelligent, puritanical but libidinous martinet" (102)—explains why marriage for Emily became "one long misery of despotism," why she, in turn, assumed a cloak of "defensive anger and bitterness" as a shield against her husband's slashing "condescension and contempt." Frustration was the keynote of the marriage, the frustration of an extremely intelligent, ambitious man, lacking in original talent, who settled for an uneducated, if attractive, younger wife and a career teaching mathematics and natural science at a private preparatory school in Manhattan, eventually assuming its principalship, but who yearned to participate fully in the creative ferment of the city's "minor literati," around whom he revolved like a mere satellite (105). Frustration fueled Emily's rage as well, the frustration of a woman with a keen mind and genuine capacity for love who was locked in the prison of her husband's rigid, loveless tyranny, whose own survival depended upon a constant discharge of answering fury. The birth of Grace, the daughter "she had hated," had done nothing to relieve the inner tensions energized by repressed emotions and needs, perhaps because her untapped store of love could not react to another female, too close, as it was, to sexual desire, competition. All of her unspent affection was lavished instead upon her beautiful son, whom she idolized as a compensatory golden boy, further traumatizing and alienating his sister.

William inherited his father's intellect, an impressive but treacherously double-edged weapon. Avid for knowledge, he was capable of brilliant flashes but also unstable, influenced by a distinct predisposition toward paranoia and the daily pressures of being raised in a divided home that was darkened by a loveless marriage but at the same time inexplicably brightened by a mother's doting attachment. For each parent, William seems to have represented an escape from and a buffer against the other, as well as a chance to project thwarted ambitions upon the world through his achievements. His success was their success, though whatever overt affection and encouragement he received undoubtedly came from his mother. And yet the love she so eagerly gave must have always been filtered through the contemptuous image of her created by her husband, the father he strove to emulate and please. Certainly the form his delusional paranoia eventually assumed, a profound distrust of his wife, had environmental roots in his father's grim puritanism and condescending distaste for the woman below his station he had married out of carnal weakness. Like his father, William would wed a woman much different from himself in temperament and values, albeit one whose family history was far more illustrious.

There was a strong Quaker element in Anna Potter's genealogy too, but its Calvinist harshness had been considerably humanized by the Unitarian revolt of her father, William James Potter, a shy, gentle, scholarly preacher who had been born in North Dartmouth, Massachusetts, on February 1, 1829, to William and Anna (née Aiken). This was the first junction of the Aiken and Potter lines, and the Aiken mother Reverend Potter named his only daughter after had been known in the family as a "memorable character" in a very positive sense, cosmopolitan and independent-minded. His antecedents included direct descendants from one Nathaniel Potter, "who died in Rhode Island some time before 1644," and connections with the energetic Delano (De La Noye) clan, French Huguenot immigrants who had engaged in shipping, whaling, and shipbuilding in New Bedford since the 1700s, often to their great profit. New Bedford was where Captain Joseph C. Delano retired in 1870 after an extremely lucrative career as a master of clipper ships and bought an impressive mansion with stables on two and a half acres of prime property, the sole stone structure of its kind in the village. Jane Delano Kempton, Aiken's mother's maternal great-aunt, lived not far away in a smaller wooden version of the same house. Captain Delano's strong-willed daughter Julia, who was destined never to wed, would take a special interest in the affairs of William and Anna Aiken and their children.

New Bedford was also where William James Potter was ordained minister of its First Congregational Society on December 28, 1859, after a year at the Harvard Divinity School and another year studying abroad at the University of Berlin. His decision to enter the Unitarian fellowship in spite of the family's long Quaker past and in defiance of his father suggested the will of steel that skeletoned his sweet surface, a firm commitment to a more sophisticated, antievangelical approach to religion that typified the age's progressive softening and demythification of Calvinist dogma. It was an approach that T. S. Eliot would reject as "decayed Protestanism" and his friend Aiken welcome as a sound shift toward a more universal humanist vision. Despite his "shy and retiring" nature, Reverend Potter's liberal ministry was marked by the steady loyalty of his flock, who appreciated the integrity and innate decency motivating his frequently unorthodox behavior. In 1863, the same year he married Elizabeth Claghorn Babcock, he was drafted into the Union army and accepted the call as a matter of civic duty, serving as an inspector of military hospitals until embarrassed government authorities finally appointed him chaplain to a convalescent camp at Alexandria, Virginia.

The admiration and affection accorded him by his congregation, because "he was so plainly honest and unselfish," was spotlighted in 1866 when he received a unanimous vote of confidence supporting his dramatic decision to cease administering the sacrament of holy communion. A year later, at about the time he had stopped referring to himself as a Christian because "to do so, he felt, would deny the universal religious fellowship he cherished as an ideal," Reverend Potter was dismayed when the Unitarian National Conference voted to limit its membership to "followers of Christ." Along with his friend Ralph Waldo Emerson, Reverend O. B. Frothingham, Colonel T. W. Higginson (Emily Dickinson's kind encourager and inept literary adviser), and several other notables, he helped to organize the Free Religious Association, which came into existence in 1868 with the express purpose "to promote the interests of pure religion, to encourage the scientific study of theology, and to increase fellowship in the spirit." Potter served as the organization's secretary for fifteen years and as its president for the next ten. In 1885, six years after his wife's death and three years before his daughter Anna's marriage, he published *Twenty-five Sermons of Twenty-five Years.* His *Lectures and Sermons,* the book Aiken would treasure, appeared posthumously in 1895.

A measure of Reverend Potter's ready compassion might be gauged from his becoming the guardian of his nephew William Hopkins Tillinghast, when the boy was orphaned at the age of eight, although Tillinghast was doomed to wed Grace Akin, William's neglected sister, who would make their conjugal life together a farce of nagged-at silences, earning him the title "Frightened Uncle" in *Ushant.* Wheels within wheels, Potters and Aikens intermingled with one another and with related families, with Delanos, Kemptons, Hathaways, Claghorns, Spooners, and other New Bedford connections, perhaps making the match between Anna Potter and William Akin's promising son almost inevitable.

After graduating from Harvard and being certified by the New York City Medical College, Dr. Aiken had gone to Germany for further study, returning in April 1887. The two journeys, father's and grandfather's, later coalesced in Aiken's mind as a mystical union between him and them when he first visited Europe in 1908. Having met at the Tillinghast wedding, William Aiken and Anna Potter probably pursued their interest in each other either at Duxbury, on the coast below Boston, or in the White Mountains of New Hampshire, which were family summering retreats. It was in the White Mountains that William proposed to Anna and was accepted, offering her a handful of goldenrod in the bargain, a romantic gesture that would acquire symbolic significance in Aiken's vivid imagination, as Joseph Killorin's research has shown. Though Anna was almost a head taller than her short, sandy-haired, boyish-looking beau—about five feet, seven inches, Aiken's eventual height—she was charming, vivacious, and obviously intelligent, attractive in appearance, with long, dark hair and dark eyes, her graceful social manners appropriate to the daughter of a highly cultured home. If less intense and intellectual than her husband, as well as less creative, she conformed to the era's sexist image of a proper genteel companion for a professional man.

Their engagement was shadowed, however, by the first serious signs of Dr. Aiken's frail physical and mental condition. Upon his return from Europe, the doctor established a private practice in upper Manhattan and was attached to the New York City Health Department, where he worked in the Eye, Ear, Nose, and Throat Infirmary as an assistant ophthalmologic surgeon. Like a delicate and complex machine, he soon found himself sputtering under the weight of fatigue to the point of "nervous prostration, followed by an almost complete, though temporary, collapse of his intellectual powers." It was subsequently decided that a warmer climate might be better for his vulnerable constitution, and plans went forward for him and Anna to reside in Savannah after their marriage, Dr. Aiken to serve first as an assistant and then a partner in the office of Dr. J. P. Houston, the city's elderly specialist in eye, ear, nose, and throat diseases. There is an unconfirmed family rumor that the move to Savannah was involuntary, the result of family pressure to remove a potential embarrassment before it materialized, which suggests that the strain of instability in the Akin line was indeed known about and feared. Accidental or planned, the young couple, both twenty-four at the time of the wedding ceremony, would be isolated twelve hundred miles away from family assistance.

The marriage took place at 1:30 on a November afternoon in 1888 at Reverend Potter's house in New Bedford, but the bride and groom did not set out for Savannah until early June of the following year, apparently living with Anna's father and brother in the interim. When they did depart on the two-and-a-half-day voyage along the coast, Anna was already seven months pregnant. Their ship was caught in a hurricane, floundering against the rocky shore off Cape Hatteras, and William and Anna were handed to safety with the aid of a human chain formed by the crew only a short time before a wave washed away the deckhouse where their cabin was located. But Anna suffered no ill effects, and she and her husband reached their new home, a Mrs. Heywood's boardinghouse, several days later. There, on August 5, 1889, their first child was born, a blue-eyed boy with the red hair of Reverend Potter. The proud father sent off a night telegram on his behalf to anxious grandparents in the North: "Arrived safely at six-thirty evening. Found Mother very comfortable. Conrad Potter Aiken."

For the further pleasure of the grandmother, William drew a rough caricature of his infant son for her as the baby sat in his diapers on the floor, a humorous pen-and-ink sketch in which the infant sports a single hair and tooth. With the retrospective insight of one who has himself confronted a son,

Dr. William Ford Aiken in 1888, the year he wed Anna Potter and a year before the birth of Conrad, their first child.

Aiken in *Ushant* discerns his father's mixed emotions: "The egoism of the ovum is only surpassed by that of the baby; and one unconsciously, or even consciously, begins at once to resent it. And in this crude caricature one could recognize all too easily the contention for mastery of the father's anger and pride" (33). The observation is shrewd because the father in question was Emily Akin's golden boy, torn always between her worship and her husband's stern demands for perfection.

Whatever William's feelings, Anna enshrined Conrad in her heart with the beatific permanence often reserved by mothers for first-born sons, a position that the arrival of three other children could never threaten. Furthermore, over the next five years, as the small family settled down first at 503 Whittaker Street, which formed part of the western boundary of Forsyth Park's twenty acres near the heart of the city, and then on South Broad, the relationship between father and son was warm in the extreme. Aiken's memory of him during these years would retain an idyllic cast. His father was, he said, "really a remarkable man, extraordinarily intelligent and gifted . . . he was really quite beautiful. And I remember once, or I'm told—this, I don't remember myself—that somebody asked me when I was five or six years old what God was like, and I replied that I thought God must be very like my father when he smiled."

The birth, in late May 1891, of his sister Elizabeth, the only sibling he would harbor much feeling for, at least in adolescence and through early manhood, apparently did not disrupt the honey flow of his relationship with either parent. One of Carl Jung's "islands of consciousness" rescued from childhood was a pellucid recollection of his mother rapidly drawing for him the pig she had learned to draw from her mother, as, book on her knee, "she would trace once more the twelve-cylinder pig, with the coiled watchspring tail and the tiny smiling eyes" (38). To Conrad, it was fascinating and yet horrible, as any visual variation on the normal is within a child's narrow eye, but the crucial role it was fated to play in his imagination was inextricably bound up with his later ambivalent attitude toward a mother judged unfaithful to him and his father.

The occasional derision of Anna Aiken in *Ushant,* in which she is damned at another point for possessing "that lacklustre quality in her character which was not exactly cowardice but which, except for a sheer fluke, would have made her, as she ought to have been, a typical small-town New England old maid" (43), cannot be understood apart from the convoluted psychological *gestalt* that underlay the book's artistic architecture, its poetic pith. Gaston Bachelard has isolated the manner in which our reveries lead us inexorably back to childhood, where the image, in absence of experience, "takes precedent over everything else," and when—as in *Ushant*—"this reverie of remembering becomes the germ of a poetic work, the complex of memory and imagination becomes more tightly meshed; it has multiple and reciprocal actions which deceive the sincerity of the poet." There is scant reason, in other words, to believe that the love between Conrad and his mother, who regarded him as her favorite, was anything but deep and mutually nourishing.

The closeness between them is implicit in an episode that happened when Conrad was about five or six, shortly before the birth of his brother Robert and after the family's removal from Whittaker Street. On a rare visit to Savannah in 1894, William's mother had remarked to Anna, "Do you realize, that son of yours, Conrad, isn't seen after breakfast until he comes home to supper?" A direct result was that Dr. Aiken escorted his son into Forsyth Park, determined to teach him how to read, "and he'd made a primer. . . . All done by hand and made into a beautiful little book with stitched back and all the rest of it. And I think there were illustrations too. Well, he sat me down on a bench in the park to teach me to read. And I just read through the primer in one flash." It seems that Conrad had already taught himself to read "while listening to my mother reading to me on my bedroom floor, and so I had learned to read upside down."

Besides the son's evident intellectual keenness, the incident encapsulates a tender, repeated tableau of mother and son sitting close together on the floor, engrossed in whichever magical book she was reading to him at the moment, as he studied the pages in front of her, an incident amplified by *Ushant*'s memory of the tiny poem—"One—two—three— / Out—goes—she!"— Anna ritually recited each night when she reached out to extinguish the gas flame, the same flame used by his father to demonstrate the circulation of the blood by holding the children's hands in front of it (42). If never the attentive mother she might or should have been, Anna was hardly indifferent to her children, especially Conrad, more careless than neglectful, keeping in mind that each child had his or her own black nurse or nanny, plus the presence of other servants when the family moved to a grander dwelling on South Broad Street in 1893. Death alone, in league with the poet's voracious desire for ontological design, would mangle and enlarge her somewhat frivolous features into a Medea mask.

Meanwhile, the family's fortunes were constantly on the rise. The Aikens were evolving into one of Savannah's leading couples, Anna's propensity for giving parties and making friends complementing her husband's steady expansion of his practice—Dr. Houston's death several years after their arrival left it entirely in his control—and ceaseless attempts to express himself in other fields. Dr. Aiken's restless, ambitious character, which *Ushant* accurately skewers as that of "the passionate amateur" (46), drove him to paint inadequate portraits, to compose unremarkable songs, to write respectable poems, to take arty landscape photographs with a pinhole camera made out of a soap-box, to organize the Savannah Camera Club, serving as its secretary and pres-ident at various times, as if competing with both his own father and Reverend Potter, and to become actively involved in a host of professional organiza-tions, such as the Congress of American Physicians and Surgeons, the Ameri-can Ophthalmological Society, the American Osteological Society, the Geor-gia Medical Association, and Savannah's Georgia Medical Society, in which he served as recording secretary for several years. In addition, he had replaced Dr. Houston as the Savannah Hospital's ophthalmic surgeon, and his con-science never permitted him to refuse patients who lacked money for treat-ment.

In *Ushant*, Aiken would record a poignant moment when his uncle, William Tillinghast, in trying to dissuade his nephew from turning into a shy, hen-pecked failure like himself, a college librarian buried in Harvard's Gore Hall, celebrated William and Anna's reckless, glittering lifestyle: "Your fa-ther and mother . . . took life with both hands, they met it and used it: they lived with their minds, that is true, for they were brilliant creatures, both of them; but they knew that that was not all there is to it, they were social, they were gay, they lived richly, even, in fact—which took courage—to living beyond their means—and not only economically" (123). The portrait paints true, if romanticized by Aiken's phenomenal, albeit heightened, memory. The letters of William Aiken that have survived and that his son later read at his grandmother's Watertown home while a Harvard student support this view of the marriage, particularly when considered in conjunction with *Ushant* and the *Annals of Savannah*, its news items detailing Dr. Aiken's achievements and the card parties, dances, birthday parties, and other social events attended or given by him and his vivacious wife.

The distance between the Aikens and their northern relatives was eased by annual excursions to Duxbury to escape Savannah's humid summer heat and renew family ties, first to Steele's boardinghouse and then, in the late 1890s, to the large cottage built by the Tillinghasts at Powder Point. And Dr. Aiken occasionally took trips to the North on his own, for business and social rea-sons, visiting his parents in New York or in Watertown, Massachusetts, where they bought a home in 1891 after his father's retirement. The *Savannah Morn-ing News*, for example, notes that he left March 2, 1891, for New York on the Atlantic Coast Line, the same year that Elizabeth was born and Conrad cele-brated his second birthday, and that he had been reelected recording secretary by the Georgia Medical Society. In a letter to his mother, written December 6, 1891, and mailed in time to reach her on her fifty-seventh birthday (December 8), Dr. Aiken regretted not having "the time and money to send you a hand-some reminder of the day, but I'll have to wait another year or two until

Conrad Aiken, age two, poses happily for the camera (1892).

business and domestic affairs are in a more settled state before I can do all I want to in that line." Finances were to remain troublesome despite an increasing practice.

Without doubt, the most revealing part of the letter concerns the doctor's agitation over a servant problem:

> These creatures are the embodiment of all that is careless and wasteful, heedless, destructive, mendacious and thieving. They have all the qualities which make for social degradation, all the traits of character which are organically criminal one might say. They are possessed with the Anti-Christ. I can not tell you how I abhor them, how every good tendency in me cries out against this evil. I never could endure poor work. It is to me the unpardonable sin; and here it is all one sees. Even the white mechanics are mostly infected with the same wantonness. They botch and mar their own work; destroy property, lie, are utterly deaf to commands or directions given, and are generally worthy of the torrid place which, let us hope, is in preparation for them!

This is the voice of hysteria, of a compulsive perfectionist, impelled by rigid puritanism to magnify human carelessness into mortal sin, a voice diametrically at odds with the Dr. Aiken who was sympathetic to human misery and indifferent to organized religion. It is, perhaps, the voice of a harsh father, a mimic form of self-condemnation, childish appeasement of impossible parental demands. It is also an ominous foreshadow of the voice that would transmogrify Conrad's childhood from Edenic security into *Paradise Lost*. The next letter home, exactly a year later, was written immediately after a return from a winter holiday, Dr. Aiken traveling on one boat and his "harem"—Anna, the children, and Mary Cray, Anna's close friend—on another. Emily Akin had apparently sent her son a "homily on economy" shortly before, and his response, defending the decision to give his family two vacations that year, points up his sharp consciousness of the mental and physical weaknesses he and his sister were prey to. "The kids were as rosy as apples when I found them at the dock," Dr. Aiken wrote. "Travelling has been a great expense to us, but I hope the good health we have thus give them full-sized bodies and sound healthy nervous systems, such as neither Grace nor I possess. . . . I never want to rob the children of any chance to become sturdy men and women. I had much rather let them go without education and even become mechanics and mechanics' wives. With health such people are happy and what else do we aim at I'd like to know?"

Further into the letter Dr. Aiken mentions that "gout has made me miserable for a week, attacking my feet and eyes. The latter have been too weak for reading or any work almost, but now stand the light better, and the head-confusion has greatly diminished." Debilitating pressures, self-imposed and hereditary, were obviously ever-present, and they must have intensified several weeks later when he took another trip north to see his father, who was ailing. The year 1893 was to be a bad one for both sides of the family; Reverend Potter had been forced by illness to surrender his preaching post and would be dead by year's end.

When Dr. Aiken returned home from another excursion north in early January 1894, he found Anna "on the brink of a severe illness, which however my timely arrival arrested." His wife also informed him that his father had died the day after he departed from Watertown, sad news confirmed by a glowing *New York Herald* obituary and a telegram from Emily Akin that Dr. Thomas Charleton, his best friend in Savannah, had hand delivered. However ambiguous his feelings about his stern father, the blow was heavy, and Dr. Aiken watched the hours pass during the time when he knew his father was being "laid away in the cold ground." A reporter for the *Morning News* would eventually claim that the doctor's father had taken his own life with a pistol, but William's letter to his mother on January 8 does not support the contention: "I shall always bless the otherwise sad fate that called me north for this one satisfaction, that I saw Father the last day he lived and left him seemingly so happy. . . . His whitened hair and beard surrounding his transparent face made him look like some delicate snow-wraith, ready to dissolve into the wintry air. . . . As the train carried me past the street I looked up wondering if I would ever see him in it again. I knew it must come soon, but it came more tenderly for him than I had dared hope."

The letter also implies that William Aiken had not been the easiest of men in life, his son discovering that in "his last days his character seemed to undergo a softening and purifying change, making him more lovable in many ways, and he himself loved much. I loved him fondly and he knew it which is even better to remember." One immediate effect of the loss was the return of a cough Dr. Aiken thought he had shaken off during the rough voyage to Massachusetts, though it might have been the result of a rougher return voyage "against head winds and heavy seas all the way down." More worrying was the familiar complaint of financial distractions: "Business is brisk but what with many patients and Anna's sickness, I have been unable to get out my bills yet and I fear money will be very low this month. Can you send me what we spoke of or shall I borrow again of Will?" His timid brother-in-law, who seemed to have resources beyond a librarian's modest salary, loaned him several thousand dollars during these years.

There is, to be sure, no certain way to fathom the psychological depth or precise extent of the negative impact his father's demise had upon Dr. Aiken's frame of mind, but at best it must have further loosened his always tenuous grip on self, accelerated his internalized Protestant ethic's implacable progress down the groove of frantic overachievement. A fascinating sidelight to his character's compulsive nature can be detected in a legal wrangle that developed between him and a George S. Haines, which had commenced in 1891 and was now brought to the attention of the justice of the peace court in the form of a suit against Dr. Aiken. In 1891 Dr. Aiken had decided to rent a row house on what was then South Broad Street opposite Colonial Park, eight or nine blocks north of Forsyth Park and closer to the Savannah River, the same house that the family would move into two years later. Why the house was rented at this time can only be a matter of speculation. Probably it was the consequence of Dr. Houston's death and Dr. Aiken's desire to have an office in a more respectable part of town, where a number of other doctors already had offices and residences. This would also explain his willingness to pay the high rent of $100 per month.

Haines was the previous tenant and claimed that Dr. Aiken had agreed to pay him $15 for some gas fixtures in the house, a claim the new tenant vehemently denied, offering to let Haines remove the fixtures. The suit would drag on for nine years before reaching Georgia's supreme court, where the decision went in Haines's favor. The small sum involved, the precious time and energy wasted over such a trivial matter, reminiscent of Elizabethan litigiousness, intimates the taint of paranoia that was to rot into actual psychosis by the end of the decade. Money and sex are inextricably bundled together in any advanced state of society, and Dr. Aiken's eventual breakdown would manifest its most blatant symptoms in a ferocious suspiciousness of his wife's fidelity and a concomitant conviction that his patients were conspiring to avoid paying his fees.

But Dr. Aiken's private mourning and minor legal hassle did not intrude upon the pampered tenor of Conrad's and Elizabeth's lives. Each had the undivided attention of a black nurse, the loving, if intermittently distracted, presence of a good-humored mother, and the fussy but kindly supervision of a father determined to provide them with a healthy environment. Domestic affairs were eased by the arrival of Lizzie Welkins, who proved to be a reliable housemaid, and the earlier hiring of a competent cook, a definite relief for Anna, who was again pregnant and concerned about her ailing, aged father. Reverend Potter's loyal congregation had reluctantly accepted his resignation at the end of the previous year only after he submitted it several times, but he had no intention of dying quietly in New Bedford. Instead, he commenced a national lecture tour, despite a "weakened constitution," buoyed by the prospect of a World Parliament of Religions, which he welcomed "as a partial fulfillment of his hopes" for universal religious fellowship predicated upon "the various ethical principles which constitute the only saving virtue in any religion." While in San Francisco, he wrote a letter especially to Conrad, earning him the title "Teacher from the West" in *Ushant*.

By summer he was back in New Bedford, and it was decided that the Aikens' annual trip north would include Conrad's first visit to his grandfather's home. There the four-year-old boy walked up the steep cobblestones of County Street to the brown, high-columned house that resembled a Greek temple. He would never forget his gentle, white-bearded grandfather taking him to New Bedford's Buttonwood Park, "that blessed scene under the trees . . . when the teacups and saucers had been made out of the little green acorns, grandfather tenderly stooping over them to work with the tiny pearl-handled penknife" (111–12). To an older Aiken in quest of a secular metaphysic, impressed by Reverend Potter's ability to absorb the truth of Charles Darwin without surrendering his faith in "a new earth and a new heaven . . . the seeds of a grander and more fruitful conception of Deity than of any which I had found in the old theologies," the scene would represent a laying on of hands, a wordless "implicit and transcendental exchange, subtle as ether between them" (112).

At the time, of course, the child was merely impressed by the benevolent reticence of a grandfather he was first meeting and would never see again, which was in pleasant contrast to the more frenetic behavior of his father and had the added weight of new surroundings behind it. But when Conrad returned to Savannah at the beginning of October 1893—because of her condition, Anna had either not accompanied the children north or had departed for home much earlier—it was to find his mother in seclusion after having given birth to a second son, named Kempton in honor of great-aunt Jane Delano Kempton. Although *Ushant* indicates that the family did not occupy the South Broad Street house that Dr. Aiken had rented until after the birth of Robert two years later, it is obvious that they had already moved in immediately before Conrad's return, if not earlier. With three children and several servants, the Aikens needed the room.

His mother's mysterious illness, coupled with the arrival of a sibling of his own sex, was enough to have made Conrad anxious. When he was also informed that he would be leaving the nursery off the master bedroom in a short while, given a room of his own like an adult, the entire episode acquired a traumatic quality. Though delighted by the prospect of grown-up privacy and independence—"that flattering overtone as of a newly found importance" (49)—he could not help but be upset as well because the room change gave outward expression to the gesture of maternal rejection suggested by the sudden appearance of Kempton. His mother had planted another son in the house, close to her, simultaneously banishing him to a physically detached sphere of existence.

It is curious that Aiken never admitted the circuit of maternal abandonment

Aiken's grandfather, Reverend William James Potter, in his New Bedford study (1890).

and parallel repressed hostility evident in the events surrounding Kempton's birth, although he was quite aware of the significant function they served for his imagination. This failure relates, I believe, to the partial blindness he tended to exhibit when confronting the ambivalent specter of his mother. What he did remember and use poetically on more than one occasion was an incident that occurred soon after his return from New Bedford. Unbidden, he entered Colonial Park across the street and picked a clover for his mother, placing it in a glass of water. Later his father allowed him to bring it in to Anna, who was still in bed, the room hushed and dark, blinds drawn and folding doors open to shield the nursery (Conrad's former domain) where Kempton slept: "For see, he brings you now his fourleafed clover / who is already (as you bear again) your lover." In this poem, "The Clover," written fifty-six years after the fact amid excavations in the past for *Ushant* ore, the Oedipal attachment is patently conceded, but all hidden rage and hurt have been erased by myth, the transforming lyric abstractions of art, which insist upon a positive theme.

A house is the maternal archetype, is womb and first nest, the primal security symbol, glass, stone, wood, and plaster transmuted by the alchemist-mother, not the father, into a "home," refuge from the daily discoveries of the self's limitations and the world's brute indifference to and distinction from the "I" a child is programmed to shape. The fine old house at 228 South Broad Street where Aiken was to forge his identity and his poetic persona was one of four attached gray stone dwellings known as Marshall's Row. It had been built in the 1850s on the former Marshall estate and incorporated the Greek Revival style common to the fashionable neighborhood surrounding it. Three stories high, its narrowness compensated for by its great length, the house had an entrance at street level that led into Dr. Aiken's waiting room and office and, behind them, the kitchen and maid's quarters. An exterior stair or stoop mounted to the front door of the second story, the residence's main or "first" floor, dominated by a long parlor or drawing room, where Anna Aiken did all of her entertaining.

The four bedrooms were on the "second" floor, the master bedroom and the adjoining smaller bedroom being used as Kempton's nursery located at the front of the house, the two others, including Conrad's, at the rear. His room gave him easy access to the back stairs, which led down to the pantry and through the kitchen to the yard. It was to prove a convenient means of escape in the years ahead, escape from the unknown intentions of an unstable father and the too-well-known intentions of a neighborhood bully. The walled garden, its latticed door leading to the fetid alley beyond framed by a peach tree and chinaberry tree of impressive size, was a haven in itself.

But it was the drawing room that captured Conrad's admiration. He often

Aiken's childhood house (to the left) on Oglethorpe Avenue East, Savannah.

spied on it and its adult occupants from a safe perch behind the curved banister of the front inside staircase, and he would remember the two chandeliers and the solid traditional furniture, the Victorian rocker, the morris chair, the long table against one wall, the grandfather clock, the desk and its lamp toward the rear, the four pictures on the high walls, one of which was Millet's *Angelus,* from Whittaker Street, as vividly as he recalled the plaster statue of Psyche standing in the back piazza. The hallway perch was in fact the scene of the sole recollected instance of Conrad overtly expressing the hidden fury inspired by the emergence of a rival. During one of his mother's tea parties for her lady friends, he had dropped Kempton's milk bottle from there (35).

Trees were extremely important to him, then and always, literal and symbolic ways, like Wordsworth's, of melding past and present into an aesthetic, spiritual whole, the unity of personal meaning and organic universal structure that poetry ordains. He remembered the palmetto leaves outside the windows of Mrs. Heywood's boardinghouse, and, in addition to the rear garden's peach and chinaberry trees, the new house offered two huge holm oaks out front, "one's first trees, the symbols therefore of all that was tree" (40), awesome extensions and reflections of the thrilling experience (retrospective or immediate) it had impressed upon Conrad's nascent consciousness as he sat often on the brick stoop that led to the second story.

Across the street in Colonial Park, so named because it had been a burial ground in the colonial period and still contained many ancient tombstones and crumbling above-ground vaults among the cypress trees and hanging moss, there was a stand of sapling cedars that would become a special retreat for him and other local boys, an improvised clubhouse and hiding place that he would later compare to Virgil's "sacred grove" in the *Aeneid,* which moved Aeneas to gloomy eloquence: "They weep here / For how the world goes, and our life that passes / Touches their hearts." In contrast to the park's lush greenness and anomalous white grave markers was the brick police station and prison building at its eastern corner, at the intersection of South Broad and Habersham streets, the barred windows of which were visible from the park benches.

Near the end of 1893 came another profound intrusion upon the ordinary unfolding of Conrad's days. Still ailing, the indomitable Reverend Potter had gone to Boston on December 21 to officiate at the wedding of his son Alfred ("Beloved Uncle" in *Ushant*) to Edith Van DuZee ("Aunt Sybil"). That night, after the couple had departed for a New York honeymoon, he died, "unnoticed and alone, there on the dark doorstep behind the Parker House" (111). The next day Anna learned of her father's death and was faced with the task of having to telegraph the news to her honeymooning brother. She decided to take Conrad with her to the telegraph office, which was farther uptown in the shopping district along Liberty Street, several blocks from South

Broad Street. Experienced in conjunction with the news of his grandfather's death, though death had no felt reality at the time, the walk through the warm, holiday-festive streets alone with his mother became "the first *continuous* scene which he could remember" (39).

The solemn strangeness of the event was peculiarly enhanced by the proximity of Christmas, Dr. Aiken having promised to take Conrad into Colonial Park on Christmas Eve to set off the Roman candles he kept piled in a corner of the waiting room, and by the "obvious formality" that had altered his relationship with his mother as a result of Kempton's arrival. He and his mother were dressed in their Sunday best, she in a "sharp-winged hat . . . which gave her a little the air of flying," as he remembered her, poised on the stoop above him, putting on and buttoning her gloves, before the two of them left together, proceeding through the streets of Savannah under tall trees toward the shopping center and the telegraph office, "where something, some message, was to be dispatched about grandfather to the Beloved Uncle" (38).

The memory of this walk, unique in its assumption of a new adult status (Elizabeth and Kempton having been deemed too young to accompany them), the memory of his mother telling him about Reverend Potter's death, as if he actually grasped the concept, was another lucid demonstration of the gulf that had yawned between him and Anna without his having done anything to cause it, except to grow older and bigger. But the Roman candles were set off as planned, and the unreal deaths of two distant grandfathers left no visible scars upon his parents. On March 15, 1894, Dr. Aiken scrawled a hasty letter to his mother, who was preparing for her trip south to see her three grandchildren, mentioning a receipt for $2,000, either a loan or a purchase made on his behalf, and stressing fatigue: "I have about as little vitality as a last year's cornstalk. That is the reason I neglect my correspondence so badly." There is also an allusion to possible in-law trouble: "Will seemed to think we had had some sort of quarrel but I have no knowledge of anything of that sort."

Enclosed with the letter was a note from Anna asking her mother-in-law to buy a yard of dark navy blue linen for her at McCutcheon's in New York on the voyage down: "I want it for sailor collar and cuffs for Conrad on his little blouse waist. The linen is the only thing that stands laundering, and I had been told that they keep it, at, I think, about sixty cents a yard." Aiken seems to have spent most of his Savannah youth dressed in a sailor suit of one sort or another, and the story "State of Mind" summons up a vivid image of him staring into the window display at the toy store on Liberty Street: "A small boy in a blue sailor suit, with a knotted silk tie, and spots of mashed potato on the blouse—and a round sailor hat on the back of his head—himself that small boy."

The visit of Emily Akin came to pass as expected, as did the admonition to the parents about their neglect of Conrad and Dr. Aiken's subsequent discovery in Forsyth Park that his son could already read. Reading was a major bridge between Conrad and his mother. Although Dr. Aiken fancied himself a poet in his spare time, keeping frantic pace with his musical and painting talents, it was his wife who was enthralled by literature, who had her own bookcase of classics, juvenile and adult, and read them faithfully to the children. One of her friends, a Mrs. Karow, has testified to Anna's zealous literary interests, remembering that later, after her friend's hearing had deteriorated, they used to exchange frequent letters "devoted to literary subjects." And her own mother, Elizabeth Babcock, had been, like Reverend Potter, an avid reader, as well as an amateur poet, so that the very act of reading was, for Conrad, a metaphoric repair and extension of the ruptured umbilical cord, along with being an exciting fantasy escape and, in time, at school, a congenial method of asserting his superiority and thus his identity.

One of his favorite books was a special edition of James Russell Lowell's *Vision of Sir Launfal* that his mother owned and that he would claim for himself, and Cousin Julia, "rich, fabulous, mannish" Julia, who had inherited the Delano mansion in New Bedford when her father died in 1886, sent him expensive illustrated volumes for Christmas presents—first Juliana Horatia Ewing's *Jackanapes* and then John Bunyan's *Pilgrim's Progress,* both of which he treasured. But the genuine first book, his first creative endeavor, was a newspaper serial by George Alfred Henty, noted children's author and novelist, which he cut from the paper each Sunday and pasted together, "in a deep sense feeling he was thus somehow *making* a book" (57). Like countless other children, he was also exposed to the "ghostly horrors" of the Lang fairy-tale volumes, instinctively reacting to the relished fear and satisfaction they produced, which was in some mysterious fashion fundamental to unconscious needs and anxieties.

Meanwhile, Dr. Aiken continued to overwork and expend his energies in too many different directions at once, most notably attempting to perfect various inventions in the optics field (his essay "An Improved Phoroscope" appeared in the October 20, 1894, issue of the New York *Medical Record*), and Anna resumed her active social life. The Aikens were by now members of the Cotillion Club and were welcomed completely into the upper-class reaches of the highly stratified, somewhat decayed southern city, where manners were still geared to the plantation mentality of the antebellum South and England's Edwardian ethos, regardless of difficult economic conditions, unabated prejudices, and sporadic outbreaks of violence among the lower classes, not to mention the bleak poverty endemic in Savannah's substantial black section. The pace was lazy and superficially genteel, which undoubtedly continued to madden the compulsive Dr. Aiken, but its semitropic languor could not totally conceal the seething undercurrent of brutality that would increasingly impinge upon Conrad's awareness after the following year, when he was more or less shoved out of the house's protective circle of love to roam the city's back alleys and dangerous waterfront at will.

Again and again, when looking backward for clues to the mystery of who he was and why, Aiken would emphasize that the crucial alteration in his childhood occurred at the age of six, the year 1895, when another brother, blondish and blue-eyed Robert, was born, and when the wonderful house, in the human guise of a "charming imaginative fibbing mother" and a "sensual analytic father," released him and turned against him. In a 1963 interview, in response to a question about his experiences after the first five or six years, Aiken replied, "Well, then both my parents lost track of me. I wasn't sent to school until the last year . . . in Savannah. I just ran wild." In *Blue Voyage,* the terrifying metamorphosis from "my romantic and beautiful childhood" to "my suffering and pitiful childhood" is more graphically depicted: "I was disliked and distrusted. I was cruelly beaten. I was humiliated. My pride and will were broken before I had come to my seventh year. I was in a state of continual terror. I sneaked in and out of the house, mouselike and secretive, my only purpose to attract as little attention as possible."

Slowly, spasmodically, yet with implacable inner logic, Dr. Aiken started to exhibit signs of mental illness that took the form of manic-depressive swings in mood, fitful moments of angry distrust directed at his wife and eldest son, whom he largely ignored, except when suddenly driven to correct or instruct him. Perhaps the two things children cannot abide above all else are erratic adult behavior and injustice, especially when fused, preferring consistent mistreatment to unpredictable changes in parental dispositions. And Conrad's problems were compounded by the foundational ambiguity of his attitude toward his "forgetful" mother, who had separated herself from him, produced two male rivals, and was now helpless to shield him from the inexplicable suspicions and punishments of a father grown "cruel." Worse, between the key ages of six and eleven, while struggling with the intrinsic treachery of language—"To speak is to simplify, to simplify is to change, to change is to falsify"—and inevitable interior conflicts generated by Oedipal competition for the mother's affection (always part of the individuation process, the search for a viable self), Conrad had to deal with both the unstable behavior of a frightening father and the more normal ordeals associated with adjusting to hostile, competitive contemporaries and Savannah's violence-prone back streets.

Not that he would have to look very far to find the savage reality the world everywhere tends to inflict upon a sensitive and intelligent child, who like Conrad tried "to imagine the feelings of suffering animals" and was un-

Conrad Aiken with his sister Elizabeth in 1895.

failingly kind to "birds, dogs, children, cats and mice." Next door lived Dr. William A. Duncan, a lover of seafood, and in the backyard abutting the Aikens' he kept a number of terrapins alive in tubs and bins of water. Their splashings and struggles could be heard throughout the night, and Conrad would never erase the memory of a black servant in the Duncan yard showing him how the big sea turtle in one of the tubs had to be prodded to force its head out for the ax. More searing was the carnage he witnessed one day from his own front stoop, as recorded in *Blue Voyage,* an actual murder: "*Bang bang bang bang bang,* and the man's felt hat falling off, and his head sinking down on his breast . . . while the murderer (a fireman whom I knew, who owned a monkey) stood there in his shirt-sleeves, unmoving, as if surprised at what he'd done."

But the isolated scenes of violence in Savannah streets and his father's surprising outbursts of indignation did not yet considerably alter the banal respectability of daily family existence. Nor should foreshadowed tragedies and a selective series of poetic impressions distort the ordinary aspects of Conrad's freedom, which he thoroughly enjoyed, however much he resented the lack of concern motivating it. His mother still read to him and the other children, now in a room on the upper floor that had been turned into a combined nursery and playroom for all of them; she still drew grandmother's pig on endless sheets of scrap paper on demand, and his father's abrupt flare-ups were still few and far between.

For the most part Dr. Aiken was able to maintain a humorous, somewhat pedantic attitude toward the welfare of the children, nicknaming the boys "High," "Wide," and "Handsome" in order of age, and referring to Elizabeth as "Kittums." He remained intent upon providing them with a healthy outdoor childhood, which included excursions to Tybee Beach, and all the cultural refinements and scientific knowledge he could supply from his own large store of learning and talent. He strove to master the violin, played an organ he had had installed in the house, teaching the children to sing along with him, and frequently talked about his inventions, particularly his repeated efforts to produce a cheap, simple ophthalmoscope for examining the eye. An episode involving his father that stood out in Aiken's mind was the decision to build a boat in their own garden, like Noah (45).

As could be expected, despite sending for blueprints, the plan led to naught, but Dr. Aiken never ceased striving to emulate a Renaissance household, to model himself after an idealized Renaissance man. In a December 5, 1896, letter to his mother, typed on a Blickensderfer machine he had bought and taught himself to use, he briefly chronicles recent events of the day: telephoning for coal, wiring the hospital to see "how two operations I did . . . the other day are doing," waiting the arrival of a patient, too many of whom arrive tardily ("People have no right to disappoint in that way"), having a Mr. Kinney over for dinner Thanksgiving," a "very happy day," and looking forward to Christmas: "I am going to get Conrad a $1.00 watch, warranted to keep good time for a year—how can they be made so cheap I wonder?" Also, with restrained pride, he notes that he has gotten himself "into politics in a mild way" by sending a letter to the mayor and board of aldermen

> suggesting that the city set apart a room in the city dispensary for the treatment of eye and ear cases, offering to give enough of my time to see them there. . . . There has never been anything done for these cases by the city. The city doctors have treated some of them to the damage of the patients, but most of them they have sent to me. I never got either money or satisfactory results out of the work. . . . So I determined to see what I could do in the way of starting a new charity. The idea seems to have been very well received by the public, and I am already the object of considerable interest, both as a public-spirited citizen, and as a rising politician! You may see me in the White House yet you see! Joking aside, I consider it a good cause, and I'm willing to do considerable work to make it a success.

Later, after hoping his mother's sixty-second birthday would "be a very bright one," he added: "You can reflect upon the fact that you have a very bright grand-son in Conrad. Do you believe it, he can almost read *this letter!* He read one I wrote to a patient day before yesterday, and I wrote him a story about a tailor which he read, even to the word 'counterfeiter'!" Another letter to Emily Akin the day after Christmas thanks her for a generous array of gifts she had sent down, as had the Tillinghasts: "Conrad's horse was the one thing he wanted to lug with him into the street as soon as he was dressed. With the paints he colored one of the pictures in the book before we knew that he had tried at all, and he did it very nicely, too."

The letter concludes with relief that, excepting Elizabeth's "incipient earache," the family had managed to escape the holiday season with no illnesses, and illness was a remorseless enemy, inescapably so among a family with children in an age not yet visited by miracle drugs. But Dr. Aiken's personal battles against physical complaints and fatigue could not have helped but assist his occasional slides into paranoia and delusions of grandeur, bouts of cruelty aimed at Conrad, who might have been a scapegoat for inchoate, unresolved conflicts with a dead father and the achievement ethic he had embodied and inculcated. There may have been a potential streak of sexual jealousy as well, as his son matured into a definite male presence, a possible rival, and his wife pursued the city's gay social life with lighthearted persistence. The very notion of unalloyed pleasure, mere entertainment, must have seemed like unregenerate lotus-eating to one with his Puritan soul and Victorian background.

Further insight into his mind and fragile health can be gained from a letter written to his mother the following year, on November 12, 1897, which refers to a severe sickness he had suffered during the family's annual trip north in August: "Your good letter the other day made me feel quite ashamed of myself for not having let you know before this late day that I am in very good condition again, considering what a wretched time of it I had with you all in Cambridge. I have been quite myself again, barring a considerable loss of weight, until about ten days ago, when I took cold and had a return of the cough which I had all last winter. Then suddenly that disappeared the latter part of last week, and I came down with another 'hay-fever' attack, but nothing like as severe as the August ones." He also alludes to his brother-in-law's securing a long-sought position, the librarian post at Harvard, believing that opportunities usually fall into the hands of such quiet men, "possibly because they have not made decided enemies by over-active participation in the little field of politics that each profession creates for itself. I know this to be true in medicine"—an expression of frustration, self-disgust? The closing lines are curiously divided in their vision of his wife: "Anna and the 'kids' are all very well, tho' I don't like A. as thin as she is. She, however, takes great stock in herself!"

When this letter was composed, Conrad was several months past his eighth birthday and not yet attending school, a reflection of parental neglect and his father's greater interest in his physical soundness, he being, like his siblings, frequent prey to a wide assortment of ailments. The relative freedom of his daily existence permitted him to test new emotional horizons, to detect gaps between inner and outer states. In *Blue Voyage* he recalled having spied a swift imprisoned in an abandoned house, running to locate a key, and opening a window to permit the bird to get out. The kindness to animals offers an invidious contrast to the mystifying outbreaks of cruelty from his usually benevolent father, as when "Martha," either the cook or a maid, was told to get rid of a kitten and instead of having it put to sleep abandoned it in the street. The night was stormy and Conrad lay awake in sympathetic despair over the kitten's imagined misery in the wet, windswept streets: "Good God it was a cruel thing to do—to take it in for a few weeks and then put it out in the streets like that."

It is easy to see that the boy's pity for the kitten and for every other unfortunate creature that came into his orbit, such as a dog he saved from drowning in the river, were his sensibility's initial forays into the world beyond self, his compassion for the kitten a psychic expansion of the self-pity instilled by a father's erratic behavior and a mother's apparent defection. It was not diffi-

Conrad Aiken at the age of six (1896).

cult, shifting from the animism of the ego's first response to phenomena, to empathize with vulnerable lower forms of sentience clearly similar in their helpless, dependent state to his own insecure feelings. The kitten's predicament, for instance—welcomed into a warm home, then inexplicably expelled, like Adam—paralleled his intense emotional reaction to the fearful alteration in his own family position that occurred after Kempton's arrival. The drowning dog, the ousted kitten, the swift "flapping against the curtains" of the empty house, the rats released each week on the grass of Colonial Park for local dogs to chase and rend as *sport*—they all preferred flesh and blood aspects of a victimized self he would never have any trouble recognizing.

The tragic central reality of Conrad's inner growth, which would make him the lyric poet he became, was that the next stage in his psychological development, the essential move from metaphoric expressions of self-pity into genuine love, never materialized. It was a move that would have been signaled by identifying with strangers, what Freud designated as the normal transcendence of the Oedipus complex into a desire for the mirror psyche (Jung's anima) in members of the opposite sex outside the family group. Like most artists, Aiken would remain frozen in a narcissistic phase that did not permit him to enter other consciousnesses, that kept him locked forever inside the child's shell of self, permanently deficient in sensitivity to the complex personalities of alien equals. And the narcissism, which is always constructed upon the quicksand of a fractured psyche, was innocent in its early, private articulation: "When I was a youth, I used to stand naked before a tall glass, or walk gracefully toward it, transported by the beauty I saw."

Contrast this beguiling Dorian Gray gesture of self-absorption with the qualifying "I have always been one in whose consciousness illusion and disillusion flashed simultaneously" and with the obsessive identification, before Poe, with the tale of the Ugly Duckling, Aiken's "favorite story," which he read over and over ("And as I read it I searched in my soul for signs of the wonder to come . . . that I might some day astonish and confound my cruel father, my forgetful mother"). It is hardly surprising that such a wounded, uncertain ego should have been enormously awed by exposure to the potent icon of Christ-on-the-Cross when he "went with his comrades to a Methodist Sunday School, which did not convert him to God but gave him a curiously deep fixation on Christ, due largely to gaudy post cards of Christ in the wilderness" and various crucifixion scenes. Far in the future, his fecund imagination, working through dreams and art, would integrate the crucifixion with his mother's prolific pig drawings to manufacture a pivotal allegory of a pig crucified by its own ceaseless awareness.

Conrad's freedom to roam Savannah's streets with bands of black and white companions was finally curtailed in his ninth year, the year the Spanish-

American War began and certified America's emergence as an authentic modern power with imperialist designs. Actually, it is hard to know precisely when he started school because he specified his ninth year in "Obituary in Bitcherel" but indicated it was during his last year in Savannah in the 1963 interview, which would have meant late 1899 or 1900. The earlier date is more likely, and the school he attended was private, Morton's School for Boys at 13–17 East Macon Street, near the shopping district and within walking distance.

School itself was a boon, a counterforce to the steady diminishment of self entailed in the fear inspired by Dr. Aiken; it allowed him to demonstrate his superior intellect and reading skills among contemporaries and with adult approval. Annie Waring, his "first and best of all teachers," slightly disguised as "Miss Baring" in *Blue Voyage,* made him blush one day in class when she announced that he would some day be successful. "He is intelligent, and he works," she said. The effect was electrifying: "Successful! What a blaze of glory . . . perhaps it was in this way that I began to associate knowledge with success; or mental skill of some kind." To enlarge his victory, to garner more admiration from a mother figure, he copied a drawing of Julius Caesar from the blackboard, and "this too she praised."

Another unexpected gift from school was an introduction to poetry. Rhyme words were written on the board, and the students were encouraged to write their own poems. Conrad did and proudly took his specimen to his father, who contrived to steal his glory and ruin the entire experience by revising it slightly and adding a pretentious Latin title, "Lex Talionis," which his son did not comprehend:

> The wild beasts' law is the law of might
>   And the law of might is Death;
> From the rising sun and the pall of night
>   Till the dawning day's first breath,
> The wild beast kills, till he in turn is killed—
>   For the law of the beasts is death.

Its Darwinian message was an ironic stab at a home truth, and Dr. Aiken's deed of pedantic possessiveness, almost childish in its egotism, resulted in Conrad not writing another poem for "several years." At about the same time he discovered Poe, a volume of his short stories—significantly "filched" from his mother's library—and frightened himself and the other children by reading them aloud to the latter.

Like fairy tales, Poe's appeal to the prepubic or early adolescent mind is irresistible, offering both manifest chills catering to rational fears of a transitory reality and latent reenactments of unconscious conflicts in which the immature ego can ventilate repressed drives, tireless angst. Death is rendered ultimately, paradoxically harmless by the stagecraft of a world that welcomes ghosts to the family table; sex is sublimated into chaste pursuits of unreal maidens and sensual mothers. More relevant, for Conrad the fantasy escape from an unbearable situation they energized was being voiced as Gothic horrors and unconscious hostility that related directly to his own existence. Echoing *The Arabian Nights,* another important tome in his childhood (and in the childhoods of many Romantic poets), Poe's contraptions of revenge, implicit incest, and motiveless injustice gave exotic formulation to and partial release from the negative feelings and bitter anguish he was unable to avow openly for a variety of reasons, not the least being parental disapproval and internalized Puritan prohibitions.

To the point, as counterpoint, Dr. Aiken's instability was gaining momentum, and there was increasing tension in the house, more quarrels between husband and wife. Illness again intruded to worsen matters. Near the end of 1898 Robert was stricken with scarlet fever, and as Dr. Aiken explained in a January 7, 1899, letter to his mother, that meant "putting him and Anna into the big room and sealing them in with paper pasted over the doors and the establishment otherwise of a perfect quarantine." A harrowing few weeks ensued that carved precious chunks of energy from the doctor's limited physical resources:

> Then I had to move my office as no-one would risk coming to the house. Next I came down with grip and was in bed three days myself. Then this Tuesday Anna broke out with the reddest case of Scarlet-fever I ever saw and I, just out of a sick bed, chased all over town all day and till midnight and after, hunting a nurse, while she and the sick baby lay in this prison with no-one even to keep the fire going or so much as give them a drop of water except when I could run in to do it. One time I had to leave them alone thus for five hours! Anna vomiting and having horrid chills and breaking out with the rash, and the baby screaming for lack for attention and the fire untended—just imagine it!

When Dr. Aiken returned home at last that night after his fruitless search for a nurse, it was to a deserted abode, "every servant gone home: I lay on the floor all night outside the door to answer their needs (fierce from my grip!) and when next day at about eleven Dr. Rollins found me a nurse I was a wreck." In the weeks since, Anna's fever had abated and Robert seemed past the critical stage, although the effects of the disease were often delayed and permanent. Anna, for example, was afflicted with a progressive deafness after her recovery, and Robert too, who had to be dragged around in a car for nearly two years for fear of heart complications, experienced a measurable degree of

Anna Aiken with Kempton and Robert, who is held by his nurse (ca. 1896).

hearing loss. Mother and youngest son were also forced to remain in their bedroom cell until the quarantine could be officially lifted, the red warning notice removed from the front door. Robert would not be able to recall much of the episode, of course, or his mother's reaction: "I remember up there, and I was also given some blocks at that time, and I suspect she played with me, but I don't remember her. The only recollection that I have, and I must have been about three, was of having a bath with her in a tub, and I remember reaching up and slapping her thigh . . . she was a rather tall woman."

He did recall looking out the front bedroom window and "seeing the troops that were bivouacked out along Oglethorpe Street"—the latter was to be South Broad Street's new designation after it was paved. The troops were Company K, Fourth Illinois, destined for a Cuba assault. For Conrad, the sudden appearance of the soldiers camped right outside the door, their pup tents laid out behind a green line painted down the middle of the street, was a continuation of the war excitement sparked by a recent visit from Uncle Alfred. A short, slight, dapper man who related easily to the children, his uncle had arrived by ship despite the perils of minefields, "and the battles of San Juan Hill and Manila Bay had been re-enacted, with lead and paper soldiers, and cardboard battleships" (197).

On the day of their arrival Conrad had brought the hungry soldiers a bag of animal crackers, and he was quickly adopted as company mascot, allowed to hang around their tents and share in their banter, given a bayonet to march with when accompanying them to mess in the courtyard of the prison. He would always treasure the time the men "lent me a bugle and four bayonets— we paraded three times around the square." An unanticipated bonus of the troops camping at Colonial Park was temporary relief from a minor reign of terror instituted against him by Charles Hogan, a tough storekeeper's son who lived at 204 Oglethorpe Street down the block, tagged as "Butch Gleason" in *Ushant* and *Blue Voyage*. A typical neighborhood bully, Hogan had pounced on Conrad's "Yankee" accent and heritage as justification for his attacks, perhaps goaded equally by his attendance at a private school and other evidence of affluence and social standing.

The relief came when Hogan and several of his rough cohorts, whose daily presence near the camp had kept Conrad "a prisoner in his own house" for weeks (89), spied him emerging one Sunday afternoon in the company of "Captain Davis." The Aikens had invited the officers of Company K to dinner, and Davis was in full uniform, including a sword at his side. Conrad's status immediately rose, and he was delighted to learn that "hostilities" had ceased. But it was Hogan, according to *Blue Voyage,* who caused him to lose some respect in the eyes of his closest friends among the soldiers when he convinced Conrad to take a cartridge from the tent of "Sgt. Williams" while he was away. The sergeant found the bullet in his pocket upon his return—Aiken thought the business "arranged" by Hogan—and expressed sorrow over his young friend's betrayal, handing him the cartridge as a present. Mortified, Conrad could say nothing and went home to store the bullet on his mantelpiece, determined never to touch it again.

The military authorities eventually decided that Company K should move out of the city proper and into the countryside, a blow to Conrad's grand adventure, but he and a few friends were given bayonets and marched alongside the soldiers as they departed. The band up ahead played Sousa, and the soldiers sang their own marching song, "Soup soupy, soupy, without a single bean." Later, recalling the incident, he would also remember the songs his mother sang to him, ballads, Negro spirituals, Civil War airs: "*Shoo fly, don't bother me . . . for I belong to Company G . . .* I remember her singing and laughing and singing again."

Several of the soldiers wrote to Conrad after the company sailed for Cuba, including "Sgt. Williams," who drowned off Havana. It was another small, unreal death to add to the secret store of losses mounting in the boy's mind to a staggering sum of nightmares that would darken his entire life. And yet death was a mere word, the core verbalization of Poe's extravagant allegories, which did not prevent him from playing amid the tombs of Colonial Park, occasionally digging up a few browned bones. More frightening by far had been the day when Conrad's father let him accompany him to the hospital to watch him operate to remove a patient's eye. Fear itself, excluding the terrors of combat with Hogan and similar frights connected with jostling for acceptance among rugged companions, was centered in the slight figure of his father, angel turned Lucifer behind rimless glasses and a mustache ill-suited to his youthful features. Dr. Aiken's "basilisk eyes, eyes that shot through you," seemed to burn away Conrad's being like a welding torch, "tearing out thoughts, blood, and vertebrae." One morning close to dawn Conrad had slipped out of bed to creep down the back stairs to let in a family cat and was surprised and scolded by his enraged father, who had almost shot him in the mistaken belief he was a thief: " 'Next time I *will* shoot you!' "

But Dr. Aiken remained in fairly firm control of himself through most of 1899. He was much too busy with his various projects and the Camera Club to pay close attention to any of the children, who again had the fun of a summer vacation at the Tillinghast cottage, where Conrad could play tennis with his cousin Harold, who was five years older, and where rabbits could be fed, chickens tended, and entertainments produced in a barn. On the trip home together in the fall—the parents had not accompanied the children to Duxbury, going off for a "honeymoon" trip of their own—fog and heavy seas forced the ship to anchor for a couple of hours at Vineyard Sound and then to pause again in New York harbor, this time for twenty-four hours, which at least gave them a chance to visit Manhattan, where Dr. Aiken bought Conrad a Kodak camera. The voyage took four and a half days in all, the ship not anchoring at Savannah until after midnight on Sunday, October 15, when her father had to carry Elizabeth, who "was very sick," off and home to bed.

Dr. Aiken's letter to his mother two days later is full of cheerful optimism and excitement over his photographic experiments: "Anna has stood the strain of moving wonderfully, and all our acquaintances pronounce us all looking exceedingly well. I find all the club members fully satisfied and delighted with the lens and camera, and interested in my pin-hole photos. Practice has begun in earnest and my perennial wonder where the winter's grub is to come from is already banished." His feelings for his wife are without a blemish of reserve, hinting at a manic peak: "Our little holiday certainly did A. worlds of good, and I hope we may be able to repeat it every year now that the children are getting bigger all the time." There is no record of Anna's reaction, but Aiken would remember with diamond precision a halcyon interlude earlier in the year when she and he were again alone, safe from adult and sibling rivals.

He had been sick for two months, and on a warm, sun-filled day she took him with her across the shell-paved street into Colonial Park. It was May, and Anna was still recovering from the scarlet fever that had kept her and Robert imprisoned in the upstairs bedroom. She sat on a bench under her parasol while Conrad lay in the grass not far away, near the place where he had found the clover for her during that previous confinement and near the small grove of saplings where he and his friends hid in a hut away from prying eyes. The memory was crystalline with light and love: "I made little houses out of dry twigs in the grass. The only moment at which I can *see* her—she sits there, absent-minded in the sun, smiling a little, not seeing the path and the cactus bed at which she appears to be looking . . . my mother sitting there with her parasol."

The spell was broken at last when Anna rose and stooped over her engrossed son to touch him gently on the shoulder, signaling their departure. "An angel stooped above me with wings of death, and a brow of cold clear beauty"—these lines from *House of Dust* blend mother and an actual tomb carving into a single harbinger of the death he really had no idea was hovering over them. Discarding retrospective analysis, why he remembered this tableau so piercingly cannot be detached from his sheer joy at having regained sole possession of Anna, however briefly, and the frustrated love for her that was assuming sexual proportions. Boy or girl, a child needs his mother more, not less, as he struggles to enter adolescence. The scene's deeper meaning emerged more fully a year later, when Conrad again spied on a party in the drawing room from his landing perch and observed a strange piece of family

*Anna Aiken with her four children (left to right: Conrad, Elizabeth, Robert,
and Kempton) and their nurses, Selena and Clara, in the Colonial Cemetery
(ca. 1896).*

drama acted out between his mother and father after the guests departed. He
had seen his father sitting on his mother's knee, with his arm around her, and
had heard him say, as he softly repeated, 'Yes, if you don't stop this insensate
round of party-going, with the inevitable neglect of your children, then there's
just one way to put an end to it: I'll have another child!' " (302)

The threat to produce another rival and the sight of his parents behaving like
children, shockingly revealing their sexual natures and relationship in the process, was probably less pertinent than the position of Dr. Aiken on his wife's
knee, the position that should have been Conrad's. Not only had the father
turned against him, ignoring or punishing him too severely for real and imagined wrongs, but he had now demonstrated his unfair competition for the
mother's love by claiming the son's role in her lap, in her arms. It was yet
another betrayal, though the anger it engendered toward Anna, unlike that
toward the fearsome Dr. Aiken, was repressed, eventually sublimated in the
reaction formations of literature, and thus never permitted overt disclosure,
potential release, resolution, as would happen to some degree when Conrad
rehabilitated the shade of his father with Emily Akin's aid at Harvard.

Literature was already at the nexus of Conrad's survival. Regarding boyhood writing efforts, Aiken could say, "I think that was what made it possible for me to exist." And he "devoured" books with a voracious passion for escape and meaning, self-magnification, whether pursuing heroic alter egos into the adventurous flights of *Under Two Flags* or sanctifying the madness of his own family matrix through the looking-glass injustices of *Alice in Wonderland.* He also investigated his father's taboo medical volumes in search of graphic illustrations of and verbal evidence for his mind's and body's burgeoning sexual awareness. The central figures that teased his young imagination most were, naturally, like Poe's haunted, often insane narrators, obsessed protagonists, gifted with an indomitable sense of mission capable of extraordinary endurance under the burden of extraordinary suffering in pursuit of some transcendental ideal, such as Christian's dreamed "Celestial City" or Sir Launfal's holy grail: "I so passionately longed to stand with something of Parsizal's mindless innocence, bearing on brow and palms the stigmata of that crucifixion."

Aided by subsequent immersions in Walter Pater and Matthew Arnold, the theme of a mystical, all-consuming quest, of poet as innocent (childlike) culture hero and Orphic martyr would govern his whole poetic career, despite the challenges of Freud, Darwin, and his own skeptical temperament. The very title "poet" had impressed itself indelibly upon his imagination when he opened Thomas Hughes's *Tom Brown's School Days* to feast upon the magical epigraph at the head of its first page: "I am the Poet of White Horse Vale, sir, with liberal notions under my cap." The word itself had been explained by either his mother or father. Next had come the school exercise with Miss Waring, Dr. Aiken's usurpation of "Lex Talionis," and a fallow period of silence, though he had previously experienced the thrill of manufacturing his first book from the Henty serial and penning a series of sermons with red ink, carefully lettered to simulate the printing in Reverend Potter's volume of sermons. The Hughes epigraph elevated him, gave vocational shape to his vague future. Writing verse was a family tradition, a pious avocation, and a weapon in the psychological guerrilla war waged against Dr. Aiken, eventually hardening into the resolution that "he must become like father in this, perhaps even to surpassing him" (108).

Like literature and poetry writing, school was another method of escape and asserting self-worth, and yet he was not above playing hooky. During one of these unofficial holidays he and a companion sneaked into the DeSoto Hotel, Savannah's oldest and grandest, and made their way upstairs to the roof, where they "stood looking over the city, even down into the schoolyard, where perhaps they had not been missed yet." There were other transgressions, ranging from having once stolen pencils from school desks through numerous gang fights to the time he lifted a book from the local bookstore

(90). A more serious incident developed when a policeman spotted him hacking down a sapling cedar to make a bow and arrow and roughly dragged him home by the sleeve, certain he was being arrested.

Besides reflecting the influence of tough contemporaries, these minor acts of delinquency were obvious calls for attention, but the response they were to elicit from Dr. Aiken as the century turned into 1900 was an increasing resort to violence, to harsh reprimands and beatings, done with a deliberateness worthy of the coldest Calvinist ancestor. Much worse to a prepubic sensibility, the punishments were more and more repeatedly meted out for illusionary crimes. Dr. Aiken's mental equilibrium was deteriorating rapidly under the prod of exhaustion and whatever genetic or chemical imbalance was already at work. Though always lashed to manic-depressive oscillations and hidden behind a cloak of calm efficiency, his paranoia began to dwell exclusively on Anna, who continued to fling herself into the city's gay social whirl, with or without his approval. The *Annals of Savannah* records that "Dr. and Mrs. W. F. Aiken gave a very delightful children's party on Friday for Miss Elizabeth and Masters Conrad, Kempton and Robert Aiken," printing a list of more than fifty children who attended.

Apart from his busy practice, Dr. Aiken's scientific researches and hopes for fame as an inventor were reaching a fever pitch, abetted by the approach of a solar eclipse that was due to occur in May 1900. He had patented, among other things, several improvements on the form of telescope in use for making observations of the sun and had managed to get himself selected as a member of the Barnesville corps, a government-sponsored group of scientists planning to observe and photograph the eclipse from Mount Washington. He believed that certain ideas adapted from his experiments with pinhole photography enabled him to formulate a reliable "theory as to the course of the corona," a theory of "shadow bands" that proved inadequate, as did the cheap and simple estigmascope he finally perfected and would write up in an October issue of the *Morning News*. In *Ushant,* Aiken, who accompanied his father on the trip to view the eclipse, remembered the latter invention well, which was "inexpensive, all right, but apparently beyond a point it wasn't good enough, or precise enough" (46).

Because of his age Conrad was the one toward whom Dr. Aiken directed his enthusiastic explanations of the various inventions. Besides being the only child permitted to go to Barnesville, he was the recipient of his father's eager descriptions of his work on perfecting a revolutionary parabolic lens for cameras and telescopes, which he was about to patent (46). In addition to frantic labors over his many inventions, Dr. Aiken continued to devote much of his spare time to the affairs of the Camera Club, which had held its "Winter Salon" in February with the doctor acting as chairman of the annual competitions. But the combined pressures of all these activities had weakened his control to the point that Anna was convinced he needed treatment.

By the time the family was ready for its annual trip north to deposit the children with the Tillinghasts at Duxbury, Dr. Aiken refused to budge and sent Anna and the children on ahead, promising to join them later. Once in Cambridge, Anna believed the situation serious enough to consult a physician on behalf of her husband and to appeal to relatives for aid and comfort. In Dr. Aiken's suspicious mind this was concrete proof that she was plotting to have him committed to an insane asylum, bringing out his deepest fears concerning the strain of madness he had always worried about inheriting. It was, ironically, the final swing of the pendulum, ensuring his last slide over the ledge of neurosis into psychosis, a paranoid depression fired with delusions of Anna's treachery. Nothing could dissuade him from this *idée fixe,* and attempts by his sister, his mother, and various Potter relations to convince him otherwise had no effect, except to instigate explosive scenes of recrimination and accusations of treason.

Cunning, of course, is part and parcel of the paranoid's covert defenses, and Dr. Aiken's September 27, 1900, letter to his mother upon his return to Savannah is redolent with apology and saintly goodwill:

> Everything is serene and full of promise of happiness for us in our winter's endeavor to make our house a satisfactory one. The spirit of our enterprise is to be charity and kindness dressed in the protective covering of courtesy and mutual helpfulness. In this spirit I want to recall all the unkind things that escaped me when overwhelmed with a somewhat natural resentment at my latest discovery that Anna, aided and abetted (as she says) by Grace and Will, had actually taken the step of seeing a doctor and giving Sissie a mass of perverted facts and putrifications with a view to making Sissie a tool in the hands of Anna for putting me in an asylum. Of course this is my view of the fact of Dr. Vickey's being supplied with copious notes and his declaration to Anna that I was "crazy as Hell." And my hot resentment expressed to you towards yourself for allowing me to almost fail to discover this outrage was truly natural.

The letter concludes with Christian reasonableness, his avowed intention to abandon "all resentments toward everyone, truly determining more fixedly than ever that only through great charity can good come out of it all. So I ask forgiveness for the pain I caused you, Mother." But a visit from Dr. Charleton, the family friend who lived a few doors away, indicated that Dr. Aiken had not surrendered his delusion regarding his wife's duplicity. Earlier, in June, after Anna informed the family of Dr. Aiken's erratic behavior, Alfred

Potter had written to Dr. Charleton inquiring about the condition of Dr. Aiken's health. Mystified and curious, Charleton, when next meeting his colleague walking down Oglethorpe, asked him how he felt and was told, "I haven't got time to answer that question. I'm in a hurry."

That night Dr. Charleton confronted Dr. Aiken in his office with the same question and received an even more startling reply: "Well, for an answer to that question, I shall have to refer you to my lawyer." Undaunted, Dr. Charleton characterized his friend's manner as "absurd," and Dr. Aiken finally unburdened himself, charging that "his wife had been persecuting him. That she had entered into a conspiracy with her relatives and physicians in the North to have him placed in an asylum and that he was permitted to have no peace of mind." Believing Dr. Aiken merely worn down from fatigue, Dr. Charleton suggested he join his family for a summer vacation, "and you will rid yourself of all of these absurd ideas." The advice was duly heeded.

Now, when Dr. Charleton visited Dr. Aiken, he found him "very much improved in health and strength, and apparently his normal self." Soon, however, Dr. Aiken demonstrated that the improvement was superficial, confiding that he had learned in the North about his wife's "cut and dried plan" to have him incarcerated. Again, the ingenuous Dr. Charleton simply told his colleague "not to permit himself to entertain any such ideas." Concerning Dr. Aiken's obsession, he would later admit: "On this subject, the man has been for some time perfectly insane. On every other subject he was perfectly rational." The question was why Dr. Charleton failed to recognize such an elementary symptom of paranoia and why he and Dr. Aiken's other physician friends in Savannah made no serious attempts in the months ahead to investigate the situation further, or at least to notify distant relatives of the doctor's persecution mania. Admittedly, there was little surface betrayal of inner discord— "Otherwise he was perfectly sane, and not in appearance nor conversation nor manner did he betray any indication that his mind was not altogether normal and performing in every way its proper function"—but Dr. Charleton's neighborly proximity to the tense Aiken household, and his ready welcome there, should have alerted him to his friend's worsening mental condition.

Though Anna was the primary target of her husband's suspicions, Conrad was the one to bear the physical brunt of his rages through the next six months. Elizabeth's sex saved her, and the other two boys, ages seven and five, under the care of their nurses, Selina and Clara, were still too young to attract notice. As the young man of the house, and Anna's favorite, he was the handiest scapegoat for his father's despairing fury, which expressed itself in the guise of self-righteous strictness toward what he viewed as a son's delinquent ways. Dr. Aiken also feared that the boy had become a tool in his wife's

plot to have him institutionalized. To prevent Anna from communicating with
the outside world, especially from writing to his mother or her own relatives,
he forbade her to leave the house alone and would not permit her to send or
receive letters, counting the sheets of note paper on her desk to make sure that
she was not disobeying him.

In *Blue Voyage,* Aiken preserves the dialogue between his father and himself that once ensued when he returned to the house from the post office with
two letters, entering by the rear garden to avoid a confrontation with Hogan
and several of his gang, whom he had spotted hanging around the front of the
house: " 'Where is the other letter?' 'There wasn't any other letter.' 'You
brought back three letters. Do you deny that you gave one of them to your
mother?' 'There was only two letters!' 'Why did you sneak in by the back
door?' 'It was because there were some boys I didn't want to meet—' 'Don't
lie to me! . . . Why did you come in by the back door?' 'It was because I saw
"Butch" Gleason.' "

Such relentless interrogations, frequently climaxing in a beating, were to
multiply; nor were the servants able to escape Dr. Aiken's intense scrutiny.
They later testified that his "insane suspicions of his wife were manifested in a
thousand absurd and unusual ways. He would not permit her, if he knew of it,
to hold any conversation with the servants, and when one of them left the
house, after speaking to Mrs. Aiken, the woman would find herself stopped
by him and compelled to submit to a rigid examination as to her purpose,
intentions and destination." Anna was a virtual prisoner in her own home, and
her natural, if insufficient, response was to try to convince her husband of her
affection and of his need for professional help, which only reinforced his
belief in her evil machinations to have him confined. Two letters from her to
him have survived in which, with "a kindly and quiet affection," she exhorts
"him to be careful of his health and to consult a specialist on the subject of his
nerves." Across one, Dr. Aiken scrawled, "See what Anna has done!"

As for Conrad, he remained "in continual terror," sneaking in and out of
the house to avoid his father's strange explosions of rage, and when he won a
gold medal at school did not bother to show it to him, concealed it, as if
punishing him for his unfairness. The most severe example of his father's
viciousness stemmed from a lie told about him by either Robert or Kempton
that culminated in his being bound to his own bedpost and whipped on the
naked back "with eight thicknesses of rubber-tubing." There was more than
one such flogging. And Aiken's oldest daughter, Jane, would recall "my
mother telling me how he told her these literally appalling stories about his
father tieing him up and beating him if he told lies."

Once again, as the winter of 1900 peaked, the delicate machine of brilliant
fits and starts that was Dr. Aiken had reached a critical juncture, similar to the

breakdown of 1886. This time, the gears were frozen into place by a delusional obsession that gave no sign of spontaneous remission. Once again,
fatigue and anxiety were greased by physical weakness, the onrush of influenza. The sole relief appeared to arise from the violence inflicted upon the
oldest son—potential rival, rebellious conspirator against an insecure
throne—including, at one point, holding the son's hand over a lit gas jet,
leaving a scar. To make matters worse for Conrad, it was about this time that a
neighborhood girl, whose house he had once visited, died from scarlet fever.
The same red quarantine tag that decorated her door had decorated theirs
during Robert's illness. In the short story "Strange Moonlight," which Aiken
labeled "autobiography," the girl's death could not quite achieve emotional
reality in Conrad's stunned mind, although its figurative value within the fictional sphere is abstracted into a musical symphony of variations upon the
moonlight theme and substituted for the more profound deaths awaiting him
on the supratextual horizon.

The other children were far less conscious than Conrad of the mounting
tensions warping the household into a peculiar shape. Either that or the instinctive defenses of their own embryonic psyches were shielding them from
the terrible knowledge, as Kempton suspected when viewing the Savannah
experience from the remote perspective of old age. He remembered very little
of his father, and of his mother would write: "I remember mother as dark,
beautiful, composed, soft-voiced and with a mole on her thigh at my eye level
as a small child. She looked very much like Joan Aiken [Conrad's youngest
daughter]. She had a fascination of hands and white gloves." Elizabeth's
memories have not been preserved, and Robert could scarcely recall his parents, particularly his father, Selina and Clara having a greater impact upon his
daily existence than they. He did recollect that Kempton's nurse had him bap-
tized on the sly at her Baptist church, the only Aiken offspring so knighted.

Kempton would get a letter from a relative who had known Anna well and
who, to quote Robert, "said she was a very charming person and was the life
of the party, so apparently she had the real gift of gab, I suspect." Robert also
retained a lucid image of the summer trip to Duxbury: "We'd be shipped up;
we came up by the old Savannah Line, ships that ran up shore, banana
boats . . . then at Duxbury, they were very good to us. They built us a little
playhouse, and this was the first time I remember playing with my brothers
and sister . . . [I] never played with them." Nothing afterward would linger
in connection with their autumn return.

Conrad was the exception. Though too young to grasp the psychological
dynamics of the changing relationship between his mother and father, "two
angelic people" whose fused "egotism" would feed the egotism fueling his
own art, he was sufficiently mature, sufficiently sensitive, to register as the

prime victim of its collapse. The beatings, which appear to have been relatively rare, however excessive, were secondary to the basic insecurity, the excruciating terror that Dr. Aiken's uncertain moods instilled, for, said Conrad, "I hardly ever forgot what it was to be afraid." And the helplessness of his mother, her absence from his daily rounds, transformed her into the guilty party, as Dr. Aiken's paranoid distrust of her became his. A climax was imminent, but the moment of recognition and consequent catharsis were impossible to achieve under the circumstances, making neurosis inevitable, which Aiken could recognize, if never neutralize.

Dr. Aiken's frantic intellectual activities were unaffected by his illness. His article "Dr. Aiken's Astigmascope," with relevant drawings, appeared in the October issue of the *Meyrowitz Bulletin,* and the February 16, 1901, issue of the *New York Medical Journal* would carry his piece "A New Portable and Inexpensive Ophthalmometer," along with a letter from him offering to be the magazine's representative during a proposed expedition by a U.S. Naval Observatory party to Sumatra to observe an eclipse: "Last May I served under Prof. Milton Updegraff who had charge of the U.S. party whose observation station was at Barnesville, Ga." His letter also describes a recent trip through Washington, where he called on Professor Updegraff, and his recuperating from overwork and influenza, with the result that "time is of no value to me just now."

Only the month before, in the middle of January, perhaps inspired by dawning knowledge of his madness and slide into depression, Dr. Aiken had attempted to commit suicide. Since he was now occasionally sleeping in the smaller room attached to the master bedroom, where Anna continued to sleep, it was easy to conceal his plan from his wife. He took a lethal dose of drugs, including morphine and atropine, left a note addressed to Dr. Keller, the coroner, on the mantelpiece, specifying what he had taken and how he wished to be buried, and lay down on the bed, still in his dressing gown and pants. But Anna was awakened by his abnormally heavy breathing and sent an urgent message to Dr. Charleton, who testified: "I summoned Dr. Waring [Anne Waring's father], who had treated the doctor some time before, and we soon had him in his normal condition again." Incredibly, Dr. Charleton also pocketed the suicide letter and returned it to Dr. Aiken somewhat later, "telling him that I hoped he would never make such a fool of himself again."

With naive persistence, as if common sense alone was a sufficient remedy, he also had both Dr. Aiken and Anna come to his office for a consultation, at which he advised the former to "go away for a two or three month trip, as he was evidently very much run down, nervous and out of condition. He accepted this advice and left very shortly afterwards, expecting to be away about three or four weeks." He did indeed travel by himself to Washington, as the letter to the *New York Medical Journal* confirms, but he canceled plans to continue on to New York and suddenly returned to Savannah, where he reinstituted his reign of terror and resumed quarreling with his distraught wife: "He would not permit any one of the servants to have even a scrap of letter paper, and when he saw one of them with a letter of any kind in her hand, he demanded that he be permitted to see it and enforced his demand. His wife's letter and note paper and envelopes he counted frequently, and with scrupulous care, and he required her to account for every sheet. Once when he could not account for an envelope, he quarrelled with her."

The arguments, "the extraordinary quarrels" (302), were now a permanent feature of Conrad's life, and he was also sent on "secret missions" by his father, which Kempton believed had something to do with spying on patients whom Dr. Aiken thought were conspiring not to pay their bills. It was true that many unpaid fees were listed in his ledger, which enlarged his anxiety, though the debts had been amassed through his own past generosity. More important, despair had again regressed into suicidal depression. This time, however, Dr. Aiken decided to take Anna with him. After his return from Washington he had gone to St. Mary's, a resort area on the Georgia coast, to make arrangements for a long vacation stay with the family, trying to implement Dr. Charleton's advice. Sometime after his second return, however, he turned on the gas jet in the master bedroom where he and Anna were again sleeping together, another destructive impulse thwarted by his wife, who awoke and shut off the flow of gas.

Conrad soon had his last private meeting with his mother, as detailed in *Ushant*. He had played hooky and spent the day cavorting with companions down at the docks, almost drowning under the Yacht Club pier. He returned home in a panic after sundown, still drenched, climbed the back stairs, and undressed in the dark of his bedroom, hoping to avoid detection and draping his wet clothes on the back of a chair. After slipping into bed he was surprised to see his mother enter and unconsciously place her hands on the chair as she spoke. Instead of saying goodnight, she asked "that when he had grown up, he would protect her, *wouldn't* he—?" Shaken and bewildered, he assured her that he would, hoping she did not notice the wet clothes under her hand: "But she had said nothing more, after the strange little speech; during which she had not really so much looked at him, as beyond him, and into the future. And then she was gone" (90).

Maybe it is significant that Aiken's three most durable memories of his mother—the walk to the telegraph office, the hours together in Colonial Park after his sickness, and this pathetic plea for help—present her as looking elsewhere, never at him. It might explain, or at least illustrate, the feeling of being deserted by his mother that Aiken forever nursed, while also illuminating why he deduced that the quarrels between his father and his mother were based upon a suspicion that Anna had been unfaithful to her husband. No evidence exists to warrant such a charge, which appears absurd in light of Anna's background and highly visible position in the community, not to mention the constraints put upon her movements by Dr. Aiken. She was not unfaithful, but it was crucial for Conrad to *think* she was, to have a rationalization for the guilt-ridden hostility he would always harbor against her in his unconscious.

But events were conspiring to grant superficial credibility to his conviction of his mother's infidelity. Dr. Aiken was busily writing philosophical pieces in his room adjoining the master bedroom, sketches for full treatises, epigrams, random *pensées,* all of which Aiken would later read. The most telling of these are an untitled page of prose and a poem called "Isolation." The prose paragraph eerily foreshadows the older Aiken who would peruse it, anticipating Freud and revealing an odd link between Conrad and his father in their instinctive identification with the Ugly Duckling fairy tale:

Work is the one thing left after the illusions of happiness are destroyed: in work one may at least find relief from the insistence of pain and wrong. But what use is there in attempting any work that is destined to be misunderstood either through the ignorance of those over whose heads the entire matter lies, or through the wilful misrepresentation of those whose plan of life is based upon one's downfall—who, while wiser than those others to whom one is only an ugly duckling, aim at working one's undoing by exploiting the incomprehensibility of one's results to the average mind to excite ridicule, or even to prove that the worker is a harmless hare brained fellow or even a dangerous paranoiac. Even the marks of fatigue that the worker shows may be made to furnish evidence of his dangerous condition. Moreover it will do very well to merely excite pity, commiseration and solicitude for his health among his well meaning but stupid friends to prevent their attempting to comprehend his work and in this way, by surrounding the worker with people that persist in treating him as an invalid or weakling to be cossetted—not an earnest thinker to be listened to—he will soon feel despair of obtaining an audience and lose his last grip upon life. It is all so easily accomplished, and the sympathy of the public is sure to be with such an astute plotter.

Dr. Aiken's paragraph of prose is a near-textbook example of delusional paranoia in operation, supported by unrealistic expectations and a swollen ego. The poem, which his son's Freudian expertise and unbanked anger caused him to designate "Intro-uterine reversion" in *Blue Voyage,* centers on the underlying anguish, reifying the angel of death motif essential to Conrad Aiken's art:

> When my naked soul shall feel
> Primal darkness softly steal
> Closer, closer, all about—
> Blotting all the light of living out,
>
> Like a garment soft and warm,
> Grateful to my shrinking form—
> Promise of the welcome sleep,
> Free of dreams and oh! so long and deep!
>
> When the mother angel, Rest,
> Gently folds me to her breast—
> How far off and dim will be
> All these joys and pains 'twixt thee and me!
>
> Naked then my soul shall feel
> Primal darkness softly steal
> Closer, closer, all about,
> Blotting all the light of living out!

This poem contains much that would organize Aiken's metaphoric assault upon the obsessional motives behind his own behavior, its salient tropes surfacing in his strongest works.

But the grimmer immediate truth was the final collapse of Dr. Aiken's props against a crumbling self. On the night of February 26, 1901, he and Anna argued without relief, Conrad hearing most of it from his bedroom diagonally across the hall, a quarrel that had commenced in the afternoon when something transpired "that again served to excite the dementia that lay latent always in Dr. Aiken's breast. All of that afternoon he kept his wife locked up in her room with him, charging her with imaginary offenses, imputing to her imaginary intentions against his liberty, all the time." As the morning of February 27 dawned, Conrad heard the quarreling renew itself until the "sound of their voices died away at last, and there was quiet, but the boy's strained nerves kept him awake."

It was about a quarter to seven when the taut silence was shattered, as reported in the *Savannah Morning News:* " 'One! two! three!' The first shot rang out, sending echoes through the house. 'One! two! three!' The second shot was fired, there was the sound of a body falling heavily, then silence,

Studio photographs of Aiken's parents, Dr. William and Anna (Potter) Aiken, taken shortly before their deaths in 1901.

deep and unbroken." Conrad slid out of bed and rushed into his parents' room. "He found the bodies still warm, and the weapon, a .45 caliber revolver, warm also. Then, as quickly as he could, he donned some stitches of attire and ran barefooted to the station house." Aiken's 1968 account is more specific, and more revealing: "I woke . . . in my bedroom at the back of the house, which was at the end of a passage from my mother's and father's bedroom, and heard them quarreling. And this reached a climax in which I heard my mother saying a reluctant 'Yes' to persistent questioning by my father, and then came my father's voice chanting 'One, two, three' and a pistol shot, and another pistol shot." That "Yes" from his mother affirmed, no doubt, subsequent belief in her unfaithfulness.

Aiken continued:

And so I got out of bed and went through the children's bedroom, where my sister and two brothers were in their cribs, and closed the folding doors between the nursery and my father's room, and stepped over my father's body . . . he'd sprung all the way across the room from the bed, and was lying on his face with his pistol still in his hand, and went to see if my mother was still alive—and of course she wasn't. Her mouth was wide open in the act of screaming, as I said, I'd heard the scream. So I closed the doors and got dressed. And told the children to stay in their beds and that the nurse would come up and take care of them, and went down to the maids' room in the basement, and woke them, and told them that there'd been a . . . a mishap, and that I was going for the police and would they go up and dress the children and bring them down, and keep them in the dining room. So I went to the police station which was only a block away from our house, and I told them about this.

Conrad's control was remarkable, as everyone would agree, an early demonstration of the stone façade he asserted to mask self-conscious fears. But most interesting was the instantaneous concern for his mother: he had stepped swiftly over Dr. Aiken to reach her body on the bed. Though there was a gaping wound in her temple and blood splashed against the pillow and wall above her head, she seemed alive, and in *Blue Voyage* he speculates that perhaps "she knew I was there, looking at her, and then walking softly, quickly away," imagining that she was speaking to him: "Run and wake Nanny. Shut the door into the nursery. Wind the clocks on Sunday morning. And say goodbye to this house and world for ever."

Patrolman Harry Lange was on duty shortly before seven o'clock when the barefooted boy of eleven entered the station house and said calmly, "Papa has shot mama and then shot himself." Lange asked, "Who's your father?" The answer sent him hurrying with Conrad at his heels across the street to 228 Oglethorpe, after notifying his sergeant, Walter Fleming, where he was going and why. Conrad followed the patrolman through the basement entrance and up the main staircase to the master bedroom: "With a degree of calmness and self-possession beyond his years and that under the tragic circumstances was almost weird, the lad indicated the room of his mother," where "the shutters of the windows were closed." But he refused to enter, and Dr. Charleton and Coroner Keller soon arrived. As they examined the bodies, "Conrad lingered outside the door, while the other children, Elizabeth, Kempton, and Robert, the last named but six years old, scarce realizing the extent of the awful calamity of which they were the innocent victims and from which they would be the greatest sufferers, cowered in terror and sorrow unrestrained, in the adjoining room, which they occupied. The two younger peered wide-eyed from the bedclothes in which they were huddled." All four children were taken to Dr. Charleton's house to stay until relatives could be telegraphed.

"The time of childhood is the time of imagination," Octavio Paz has written, and Conrad understood the awesome implications of that after "he had tip-toed into the dark room, where the two bodies lay motionless, and apart, and, finding them dead, found himself possessed of them forever" (302).

In childhood I must have felt with

the energy of a man what I now

find stamped upon memory in lines

as vivid, as deep, and as durable

as the exergues *of the Cathoginian*

medals.

Edgar Allan Poe,

"William Wilson"

•   •   •   •   •   •   •   •

THE VOCABULARY OF SELF

In one of his pessimistic aphorisms, Arthur Schopenhauer suggests that "as soon as our thinking has found words it ceases to be sincere or at bottom serious"—an insight that Aiken would rephrase in *Blue Voyage.* Schopenhauer then seeks a comparison in an apt family allusion: "When it begins to exist for others it ceases to live in us, just as the child severs itself from its mother when it enters into its own existence." Though astute, near enough a profound truth to startle, the aphorism does not extend down into the primitive reaches where philosophy and psychology join, into language as mother tongue, the mother's gift, an unbreakable bond that enables an offspring to fashion the series of selves that will permit survival in the world beyond her influence and control, beyond her love. Language per se had given Conrad the means to make a hostile, confusing array of events and beings amenable to his imagination, and thus a vehicle of some power, but the writing of poetry and the reading of books expanded the range of this miraculous medium to encompass experiences of public triumph among adults.

By killing Conrad's mother, Dr. Aiken had committed the worst possible offense a child can envision, and his poet-son could never erase his sin, even if, in time, he forgave it. Addressing his dead father in *Blue Voyage,* backed by a Freudian perspective, Aiken does not hesitate to ascribe the "horrified and lack-lustre restlessness which prevents me from loving one person or place for more than a season" to that crime. He is equally candid about crediting the mask that resulted—a stern facial immobility replicating a father's disapproving countenance—to the same tragedy, "my trick of unexpected reticence, my impassivity of appearance, my proneness to fatigue and indifference, the rapidity with which I tire of people." Attached to the sterile mask and obstinate pain was a permanent sexualization of his feelings into a satyr appetite for women as mere meat, totems of a mother who had to be simultaneously possessed and degraded, saved and punished, again and again, including a penchant for cunnilingus—"our little peculiarities . . . canyon yodeling. Pearl diving. Muff barking."

Along with oral and Don Juan compulsions would go a more generalized misogyny that Aiken never fully conceded and a concomitant drive to marry chaste maternal substitutes. Of more disturbing import was the time bomb that the destruction of Anna and her husband had planted in their son's psyche, a bomb as ambivalent in design as his reaction to her memory, desire for its insidiously appealing relief—"I will return at last into the womb of nothing!"—alternating always with fears of its implacable approach, an endless sequence of nightmares involving death and decay. The loss of a parent is, of course, the first death, bringing one's own end closer. The loss of both parents on puberty's doorstep ushers in doubts of the self's very reality. In the vacuum left behind by William's and Anna's violent demise, Conrad must have feared he was about to be sucked into their wake, snuffed out before he actually existed, though language and art alone might prevent this from happening.

But the immediate consequences of the February 27 explosion were not yet ready to be processed into such convenient and necessarily incomplete packages of rational analysis, as events transpired around Conrad with an adult logic too mysterious to comprehend. The holidaylike visit with the Charletons was enhanced by the attentions of solicitous neighbors. When Dr. Keller called together a coroner's jury the same afternoon of the tragedy in Dr. Aiken's own basement office, he decided that Conrad's testimony was unnecessary after being informed that the boy had been taken for a walk by some "kindly women." Buttressed by the physical evidence and statements from the servants and patrolman Lange, the six jury members did not take long to reach the verdict of murder-suicide with Dr. Aiken as the culprit.

The *Morning News* reported that one of the men on the jury stared at a child's glove lying atop the doctor's desk throughout the proceedings, finally commenting, "It is almost a pity that Dr. Aiken stopped with his wife and himself." Across the street in Colonial Park, workers were busy excavating old graves in quest of the remains of General Nathanael Greene, George Washington's most effective lieutenant. Robert remembered his nurse taking him to watch the men dig, and Aiken himself would never forget staring down at the men from the same bedroom where he had found the bodies as they successfully unearthed the general's skull. Another memorable sight was the bloody, bullet-torn mattress stuffed into the outhouse, where Conrad and a companion went to look at it, pretending to be searching for a lost kitten.

Uncle Alfred arrived the next day and immediately made arrangements for the funeral with the Henderson Brothers, a respectable local firm of undertakers, the family having decided that William and Anna would be buried in Savannah rather than transported back home, a curious decision in light of the absence of other relatives in the city, perhaps an attempt to conceal what was regarded as a scandal. But the funeral was an elaborate affair, befitting such prominent society figures. Alfred hired three carriages for the Aiken side of the family and four for the Potters, besides the two black-plumed hearses. Reverend Rob White, rector of Christ Church, agreed to preside over the services, which were scheduled for March 1.

Neither Kempton nor Robert retained any images of the ceremonies and actual burial of their parents in a common grave at Bonaventure, though Kempton did recall their prelude: "I remember the shooting clearly, and the endless talks preceding it, but I have no recollection at all of the funeral." Conrad was not so fortunate. In *Blue Voyage* salient bits and pieces of the well-organized ritual are resurrected with an etching's sharpness: the two caskets laid out in the beloved drawing room, where, unlike his siblings, he refused to kiss his parents: "The others were lifted up and kissed the dead face, surprised. Why did I refuse? Shyness and horror." And then the slow procession "through the streets crowded with the curious" to the cemetery, Spanish moss "hanging in long gray streamers," Reverend White sprinkling dust into the open grave. "And dust to dust. Then the shovels, more businesslike—My father. My father which are in earth. It was just over there he took my picture once, on the bluff by the river." At last came the ride back home to Oglethorpe Street, where police were needed to control the crowd of black and white onlookers.

The children remained in Savannah for another week while the family debated the question of their future. Dr. Aiken's estate was far from munificent. Though his accounts receivable ledger showed debts to him totaling $3,651.25, only $300 of this would be collected, according to the county administrator, and the doctor's own debts, bills due at Knight's Pharmacy, Joyce's butcher shop, and West's grocery store, came to $295.03. The entire contents of the house's eleven rooms were auctioned off but brought in only a few hundred dollars.

On March 5, Julia Delano arrived from New Bedford to take command, establishing her headquarters at the DeSoto and bringing news that Frederick Winslow Taylor, wealthy engineer and pioneer efficiency expert, husband of

Louise Spooner, Anna's cousin, was considering adopting the Aiken orphans. She had also convinced Jane Kempton, who had been extremely fond of Anna and her parents, to leave her small fortune to the Aikens and Potters. The problem was Taylor's cruel insistence that all four children adopt his name or he would refuse to accept responsibility and the family's contrary belief that at least one of them should keep the name Aiken, an honor that fell to Conrad as the oldest. Until the situation could be resolved, the children were to be taken to Cambridge, Robert traveling on to stay with his great-great-aunt Jane in New Bedford, while the other three boarded temporarily with the Tillinghasts at their small house on Garden Street.

The trip north was by train, a first for the children, and Aiken has preserved in *Ushant* a moving portrait of himself stepping down the high front stoop of the Oglethorpe house for the last time, "leaving the funeral wreaths and purple ribbons on the door behind him, a copy of *Jackanapes* in his hand, and the epigraph from *Tom Brown's School Days* in his head. 'I'm the poet of White Horse Vale, sir, with Liberal notions under my cap!' " (52). The epigraph was his now, if only in his imagination, the shield of purpose and a heroic guise saving him from stepping off into oblivion. But it had to struggle against the slings and arrows of an outrageous loss, the half-stifled scream of his mother in that instant before the bullet ripped into her brain: "I remember how for a long time afterwards I couldn't hear a door squeak on its hinges without hearing her scream. *TERROR!* I remember her face vividly. Very like mine, same forehead, same mouth." Poetry aligned him with mother *and* father to ward off the furious assault of self-doubt unleashed by their disappearance, though it was a mother's legacy mostly, the syllables shared on the nursery floor, not the ones stolen from him by a jealous father: "*Lex talionis.* Cruelty is inevitable."

Over the next year Conrad spent most of his time with the Tillinghasts either at Cambridge or at Duxbury, where he and his cousin Harold resumed their tennis matches and where his physical health steadily improved. His relationship with Harold's sister, Ruby of the "rich red hair," was less felicitous for she had inherited the Aiken penchant for instability. Conrad also grew very fond of another cousin, Ruth Tillinghast, a "darling" girl lamed by polio, but he could never abide the domineering ways of his Aunt Grace, "Aunt Deena" in *Ushant*—"termagant Aunt Deena, the unbearable Aunt Deena, Aunt Deena of the unsleeping intellect and the relentless vulgarity" (121). Uncle William did teach him much about wildflowers, however, a passion they shared at Duxbury and during botanical expeditions to the White Mountains, and his red-haired cousins supplied the companionship of peers denied him through the departure of his siblings, whether playing cards or putting on the amateur shows that had become a regular feature of their Duxbury summers together.

Kempton and Elizabeth were often with him as well, although the former briefly visited Robert in New Bedford, and Robert came to visit him at Cambridge—he remembered Kempton and himself constantly pestering Uncle William to read to them aloud and suspected that their teasing caused the brevity of his stay. But permanent separation was soon to come as the family agreed to let the three youngest children be formally adopted by Taylor, assuming his name and moving into his Allentown, Pennsylvania, home. He came to pick up Robert at New Bedford in November and a month later removed Elizabeth from the Tillinghasts. Kempton was not called for until the spring of 1902, after the Taylors had moved to Red Gate School in Germantown, Pennsylvania. the final adoption being legalized on June 15 in Philadelphia.

The effect on Conrad of this slow dismantling of his remaining nuclear family can be imagined—"I lost touch with them, and I was really homeless." It was bound to intensify the anxiety generated by his parents' deaths, forestalling any chance of transmuting repressed, contradictory emotions into healthy mourning, especially because the Tillinghasts were unable to provide a firm replacement for a mother's unquestioning love, a real home, what John Ruskin described in its ideal state as "the place of Peace; the shelter not only from all injury, but from all terror, doubt and division." Aiken himself, while at Harvard and cognizant of Pater, would use the distance of the essay form in "On Moving House" to articulate the trauma associated with the loss of a home: "A child of ten is like a little hermit-crab, very sensitive, who must depend for protection upon his shell. . . . The house is indeed his body in one sense, for it is the lodging-place of his soul: a soul still too sensitive and large for the tabernacle of flesh that is building around it. . . . What a hazardous enterprise comes to him at the age of ten, if he must tear himself out of that well-loved earth, and transplant himself to other and wholly unknown regions!"

Loss of home, not death, was the tragedy to be borne because death lacked sufficient meaning to weigh down Conrad's days of adventure in new or vaguely familiar surroundings. In the same essay, contemplating a loss of parents, Aiken would write with secret knowledge:

Even if he see them buried—which God forbid—and hear the 'earth to earth, dust to dust, ashes to ashes' in the grave-side voice of the preacher, and hear also the thud of the first shovelful falling upon the coffin, dreadful warning that he is never to see them again—even so, with all its dull panoply laid bare to the sun, death remains to him unexplained. He is prone to believe it nothing more than a curious dream, unnecessarily fantastic, out of which he will soon rise, as the sea-nymphs out of the dark caves under the sea. . . . The idea of irretrievable loss is a planet that never swims into his ken; for if people die, then no doubt they are angels; and to the child an angel is as real a thing as a mortal.

Most touching are the sentences in "On Moving House" that strive to drama-tize the eviction from paradise, Conrad's expulsion from his Savannah home: "Suddenly, with no volition of his own, he is torn out of his dark crypt and exposed to clouds of sunshine. His toys, his pictures, his books—the very treasures of his soul—are remorselessly huddled away in splintery boxes; his tiny room is devastated of all beauty, emptied even till it echoes, and the key of it given to the Captain of the Spiders and the Lieutenant of the Mice. Bare floor, bare walls, a dusty window,—that is all that remains to him of years of perfect happiness."

When asked directly in old age about the impact of his parents' deaths, Aiken seemed uncertain, saying at one point, "I was eleven, and I think in a way I . . . I've never gotten over it," and then, when prodded, "Oh I . . . I think it took me . . . fifteen years." In response to a specific query regarding any possible attempt to "forget the tragedy, and even to pretend it had never really happened," he was positive: "No. The only bad thing about it was that nobody would talk to me about it, and I never knew who knew about it and who didn't. At school, for example, I felt that they all must know about this, and I felt that . . . a little shame, you see, about this . . . that it was a sort of disgrace, that I had a black mark on me. I've never quite lived that down." Unguided by adult relatives, who mistakenly believed that silence was the kindest, surest method of relieving a child's grief, Conrad obviously found confirmation of his own guilt and anxiety in that silence, which exacerbated feelings of being "different" from his contemporaries, one of the heaviest burdens conformist adolescents can bear.

Not unexpectedly, a surface consequence was a period of "acting out," of misbehavior, that coincided with the natural rebellions and extreme mood swings associated with the onset of puberty and its host of hormonal and physiological changes. To make matters worse, at least in an immediate sense, the family decreed that Conrad would live for a while in New Bedford with Aunt Jane Kempton and her aged companion, Miss Martha Daggett, a former native of Martha's Vineyard. In *Ushant* and elsewhere Aiken has given the impression that he spent an entire year with his great-great-aunt, moving there straight from Savannah, but Robert has insisted that his brother did not set foot in the Kempton house until after November 1901, which means that

Jane Delano Kempton's New Bedford house, Aiken's beloved second home for a while after his parents' death.

Conrad probably lived in New Bedford from December 1901 to September 1902. After that, he would be residing with the Tillinghasts and attending school in Cambridge.

It was another case of shifting homes, further eroding confidence in a permanent nest, although the two old ladies were a perfect selection in their embodiment of the tender affection and moral certitude a motherless boy needs, yearns for, and a home that was humane and stable, full of unspoken love, genteelly old-fashioned. New Bedford itself, starting point for Ishmael's voyage in *Moby-Dick* and scene of Father Mapple's sermon, was then in its architectural prime, though the apogee of the whale industry had been reached in the 1850s, coinciding with the brief, glorious age of the clipper ships and their record-breaking runs around Cape Horn to the California gold fields. County Street, site of Aunt Jane's Victorian house, two blocks north of Reverend Potter's former home, which had been transformed into a private school, was "perhaps the most beautiful street in the world around the turn of the century," in Aiken's words.

Besides scores of relatives, the town retained its strong Quaker influence, reminding Conrad of his gentle grandfather, reassuring and welcoming him. Aunt Jane's house, "perhaps the most living and lived in, and loving, and loved, of all houses" (83), provided the center of maternal affection he desperately required, particularly because the sudden death of his parents had been followed by much uncertainty as to an ultimate home. Neither Aunt Jane, who celebrated her ninety-fifth birthday that year, an event attended by the entire family, nor Miss Daggett had had any experience with an active young male on the threshold of manhood. Jane's only child, a son named Alfred after her husband, had died at the age of three. But they treated Conrad with benign courtesy, making him an integral part of their old-fashioned world.

The pattern included the two old ladies' frequent games of cards and their winding the grandfather clock together every Saturday night, as well as watering the plants in the pantry-conservatory every morning "before one could sit down to breakfast" (99). Breakfast was served by "Irish Maggie," who had churned the butter from their own cow's milk, and sometime during the course of the meal the other servant, a coachman-gardener and distant relative, "mutton-chopped and grizzled," would appear in bowler hat to receive his instructions for the day, which usually included a leisurely carriage jaunt to nearby points of interest, after the family cow had been driven to pasture. On Saturdays and Sundays, when Conrad did not have to go to the local public school, he was allowed to accompany the coachman, sitting beside him on the high driver's seat of the carriage as they slowly drove behind the cow on the trip over paved streets and through busy traffic to the fields and woods further inland, much to the enjoyment of neighbors.

Aunt Jane ("Aunt Jean" in *Ushant*) was always the first down in the morning to read the *New Bedford Mercury* with her enormous magnifying glass. In *Ushant* (100) Aiken pays homage to her "goodness" and "classical beauty," though the latter is not confirmed by photographs, intimating the former's influence over the eye of its grateful beholder. He also confesses to the sober truth of Aunt Edith's tart characterization of him during this period as "a holy terror, and definitely something of a monster" (95). After her nephew's move to the Tillinghasts' in 1902, Aunt Edith would subtly endeavor to curtail his visits to the Potter residence for fear of his pernicious impact upon her own two children, Elizabeth ("Beautiful Cousin") and William ("Wild Cousin").

The precise forms that Conrad's misbehavior took have not been recorded, except for an incident described in *Ushant* in which he and a companion plundered a cherry tree for profit and were caught after a neighbor complained to Aunt Jane of the violation, much to Conrad's chagrin (97–98). Whatever his "crimes," they were undoubtedly minor and did not extend into his decorous home life, where he was learning proper manners—the need to excuse oneself before leaving the table, for instance—and basking in the sunny solitude supplied by the glassed-in cupola atop the tall County Street house, from which he observed the active harbor far below and in which he read through shelves of enticing old books and magazines, among them forty-odd volumes of *Harper's* "absorbed from cover to cover," and Hawthorne's *Our Old Home,* inspiring him with "a longing for England."

From his high observatory he could easily see across the river to Fairhaven, where numerous Aikens rested in its Rural Cemetery, and beyond, to Buzzards' Bay and the western coastline of Cape Cod and the Elizabeth Islands. The cupola, which was reached by a set of steep stairs from the cluttered attic, had become his holy place of study and refuge, its treasures complemented by those stored in the attic below, countless boxes of old letters he could peruse at will. But his favorite spare-time activity was haunting the docks, walking under County Street's parade of huge leafy elms past his grandfather's house to Union Street, then down Union's mile of steep cobblestones, passing the gray Congregational church, where busts of his grandfather and Emerson flanked the pulpit, until he reached the waterfront. There, amid the bustle of commerce, he and his cousin Edward Anthony, son of Mr. and Mrs. Benjamin Anthony, owners of the *New Bedford Standard,* "collected" ships in a series of notebooks purchased for the purpose, noting "the name and category and port of origin of every vessel larger than a yacht that had tied up there" (95). Another cousin, Steve Howland, owned a share in the *Frances Allen,* destined to be the last whaleship to sail from New Bedford, lost off Greenland a year later.

Equally memorable were the occasional visits to Cousin Julia's much grander stone version of Aunt Jane's house further inland, a genuine mansion of forty rooms located one block west of County Street on Hawthorn Street, named for the impressive English hawthorns lining its path. Again, it was the trees that exerted the strongest pull on his imagination (84), though the house's exotic furnishings—many gathered by Julia's father during his voyages around the world—had their own enchantment, such as the Egyptian watercolors and Chinese *kakemonos,* especially a rendering of *The Immortals in the Mountains of Eternal Youth,* gracing the walls of the sprawling library and drawing room. Of particular fascination to the active youth was the extraordinary marble-floored gymnasium that occupied the entire third floor, its parallel bars and flying rings affording him countless hours of sweaty pleasure.

It did not take long for New Bedford, which at first had struck him as merely cooler, more polite and quieter than Savannah, to feel like "home" (88). Savannah's lush shore began to recede, to seem "an alien place, another country," and his beloved Aunt Jane replaced in bold outline the mother he could never forsake or forgive, aided by Cousin Julia and her pragmatic, "forever up to date, forever on the go" ways (87). The two houses were as one in the assurance and practical affection, the loving routine provided him

Julia Delano's New Bedford mansion (ca. 1890).

by the kind female hearts that kept them stationary beneath his feet, aided by the town's gift of an extended family. The Anthonys, for example, besides welcoming him into their home and supplying the companionship of their son, considered adopting him and would eventually offer him the editorship of their newspaper.

Adoption was the real problem because legally Conrad remained without a guardian. It appeared absurd to expect a woman in her nineties to assume full responsibility for a boy entering his teens, and the family decided that either Uncle William or Uncle Alfred should claim him, whatever the difficulties or expense. Fairness dictated that Conrad choose between them. Accordingly, one Sunday afternoon William Tillinghast took his unsuspecting nephew for a leisurely stroll along Cambridge streets and explained the situation to him, asking Conrad which uncle he would prefer as a legal guardian. Caught off guard and reluctant to hurt the well-intentioned man at his side, he opted for the Tillinghasts, although actually preferring the Potters— "he felt it would be discourteous to say to [William] Tillinghast, in fact, I would much like to go and live with Uncle Alfred, which is what he would rather have done." Furthermore, Conrad was secretly furious at Aunt Grace, who bore the major blame as the power behind the throne for not having informed him of his siblings' permanent removal. "I'd forgotten my hatred of my Aunt Grace," he wrote three decades later, "for concealing from me the fact that my brothers and sister were being adopted." Still later, he complained, "my guardian uncle . . . took me in, but I never felt it was a home."

Leaving New Bedford, leaving Aunt Jane, Cousin Julia, and the house that would always remain, "in the deepest sense," his home, was enough of a blow to damage seriously the repair work done on his frail ego by the surrogate motherhood those two women had provided. To reside with a man he could not respect and a woman he hated in a modest Cambridge house, however lightened by the presence of Cousin Harold and the proximity of the Potters, must have made his life intolerable at times. But he would visit New Bedford during the summers and on certain holidays, and *Ushant* concedes that his aunt tried to make him welcome in her "Ladies' Home Journal monstrosity of a house" by setting up an attic room for him, with window seats and bookshelves (75). Though hardly the equal of the glassed-in cupola, his attic room did endow him with some measure of significance and the solitude he found essential.

More relevant, being forced to surrender New Bedford and Aunt Jane's most "lived in, and loving," house, including its carved jade and soapstones from China and his grandfather's wonderful books, especially *Twenty Thousand Leagues under the Sea,* did not lessen his escapist focus upon the kingdom of books given to him by his mother. Quite the opposite. Uncle William had an extensive library and books brought home from Gore Hall, where both uncles were librarians and where he was often allowed to roam among the stacks (92). Also, in 1902 he began carrying around a pocket edition of Poe's poetry like a precious artifact or Bible, writing his own imitations in private.

Nothing could completely neutralize the threat to self involved in the loss of yet another hearth, another mother figure—"new schools, new houses, new faces, too many of them; the stream too swift for anchorage" (91)—but literature continued to help him pile up barriers against the flood of *angst* seeking to overwhelm him. If in Savannah Poe's stories had partially relieved his fears and repressed thirst for revenge against parental sins, Poe's poems would soften the fall into loveless Cambridge shoals by satisfying his need for heretical postures, alter egos capable of abstracting the mother quest into hymns for beautiful dead heroines, subsuming Oedipal longings under Byronic attitudes. Poe and he were true offsprings of the Romantic revolution in England, self-conscious victims of a family romance in which a tyrannical father struggles to destroy a mother icon, Poe's "Alone" the memorial poem for their shared conviction of a special tragic destiny: "From childhood's hour I have not been as others were— / I have not seen as others saw."

And in Poe's melodious, albeit at times mechanical, laments for lost Lenores, Helens, and Annabel Lees, adolescent projections of chaste maternal substitutes, Conrad could both mourn (at an arranged distance) the ambiguously sensual mother he had been deprived of and expend some unconscious ire over her treachery by envisioning her in repeated deaths, fated sacrifices to his angry wish. In addition, like Poe himself, the concentration upon the intense sorrow of his predicament, his "Romantic agony," was ironic consolation, shoring up the narcissism that had to fight off extinction. The grand gestures of Werther-like suffering that Poe's lyrics and his own compositions endeavored to objectify were delicious in their very excesses, their conversions of death threats into vainglorious melodramas, as in the final stanza of "The Conqueror Worm":

> Out, out are the lights—out all!
>   And over each quivering form
> The curtain, a funeral pall,
>   Comes down with the rush of a storm;
> While the angels, all pallid and wan,
>   Uprising, unveiling, affirm
> That the play is the tragedy "Man,"
>   And its hero the Conqueror Worm.

Poe's tightening grip on Conrad's imagination derived as well from their common reaction, persistent and mysterious, to the sea and to dreams, their conjunction in intimating the presence of reality beyond mere consciousness— "dreaming dreams no mortal ever dared to dream before," to quote from "The Raven," or contemplating "The City in the Sea," where "Lo, Death has reared himself a throne." Savannah and New Bedford, particularly the latter, had indelibly impressed the sea upon Conrad's awareness so it entered his dreams, and Conrad's dreams were already soaked in death, images of death which he vividly remembered when awake, his unique blessing and curse. "I'm always dreaming about the sea," Aiken has his protagonist say in *Great Circle,* and he would write there and elsewhere about the pig nightmare worrying his sleep for years, the "pig with wings" being attacked by a ferocious dog, which will ultimately symbolize consciousness *in extremis* and has obvious links with Anna's endless drawings of pigs for her children.

Conrad's recall of his dreams in precise detail, as a storehouse for many future poems and tales, suggests how close conscious and unconscious energies flowed in his mind. "Dreams are the true interpreters of our inclinations," one of Montaigne's essays observes, and in 1900 Freud had already published *The Interpretation of Dreams,* the first scientific endeavor to construe the art that Montaigne believed was "required to sort and understand them." But conscious and unconscious states are never separate streams in any of us, as Jean Piaget has stressed. Conrad's total recollection of his dreams steered him toward psychological control, not its contrary. He was floundering in a dangerous identity crisis, but the capacity for remembering—and, later, exploiting—his colorful dreams helped him militate the crisis rather than simply affirm its existence, since the act represents the emerging psyche's determination to commandeer instinctual impulses and anxieties, an extension of the heroic persona borrowed from Poe. In time, in adulthood, he would even be able to manipulate his nightmares along Freudian lines to aid his exploration of the relationship between consciousness (self) and creativity.

In addition to Poe's verses, which he memorized, Conrad had the comfort of maintaining his foothold in the fantasy terrain shaped by more traditional adventure fare—*Ivanhoe, Calumet K, Tanglewood Tales, The Black Arrow,* and Sir Arthur Conan Doyle's *The White Company* and Sherlock Holmes stories—which tends to reconfirm William Hazlitt's comment on a youthful penchant, when discovering "our personal and substantial identity vanishing," to "strive to gain a reflected and vicarious one in our thoughts." The process was further abetted, in Conrad's snug attic retreat, by the introduction to Cambridge lions such as Henry Wadsworth Longfellow and Longfellow's locally celebrated contemporaries, Oliver Wendell Holmes, John Greenleaf Whittier, James Russell Lowell, and others. Though inferior architecturally to New Bedford, Cambridge possessed historical and literary charms that would prove more hospitable to his poetic ambitions and emerging cultural awareness.

Ushant describes turn-of-the-century Cambridge as "remarkably like a country village," generously nurturing art and tradition, feeding "one's sense of the past" (92). It was nothing like the "ugly manufacturing city" it had become by 1949, according to an Aiken memoir, but was still a town without automobiles and urban rush, where there were "horse-drawn watering-carts to lay the dust in the blindingly dusty streets of summer, board walks put down on the pavement every winter and taken up again every spring, sleighs and pungs in the snow, and the dreadful college bell reverberant over all." The Tillinghast abode, on Garden Street near the intersection with Shepard, lay only nine or ten blocks north of the Harvard Yard and the triangular, parklike Common (bordered on one side by Radcliffe buildings and on the other by the Harvard Law School), soon a favorite playground, home for Conrad to "the cannons, which he used to straddle," and "the baseball-field, where he used to strike out every time he came to bat."

Besides domiciling many of Harvard's leading professors, including William James, whose *Varieties of Religious Experience* had recently been published, and Charles Eliot Norton, ancient and retired but still holding his Thursday night Dante readings on Shady Hill, the Cambridge that Conrad quickly mastered over the next year or so, until he was sent to boarding school in September 1903, was an ideal environment for sanctifying his grail mission as nascent "Poet of White Horse Vale." To the west of Garden Street, beyond Concord Avenue (scene of his fateful walk with Uncle William) and Berkeley Street, stood the Longfellow House, a three-story mansion with white Ionic pilasters, and farther west, across Brattle Street, was Longfellow Park. In winter Conrad ice-skated on a shallow pond at the end of Concord Avenue or on the puddle lakes formed by rain between the Longfellow house and its neighbor, ever conscious of "skating here in the lamplit twilight where once a poet had lived" (91).

Down Brattle Street, nearer Harvard Yard, a granite slab commemorated the spot where the Village Blacksmith's "chestnut tree" once stood, and at the other side of the Common's triangular apex was the similarly honored birthplace of Oliver Wendell Holmes. To the north of the Tillinghasts', fronting on the Charles River, sprawled the verdant acres of famed Mount Auburn Cemetery, for many years the sole garden cemetery in the Boston area, its grounds "thickly wooded with rare trees and shrubs, landscaped with occasional ponds," giving rise "to a commanding hill, from which is a dreamy view of the winding Charles River, Cambridge, Boston, and distant hills." Among its notable denizens, who ranged in importance from Harvard dons (Louis Agassiz and William Ellery Channing) to a mere actor (Edwin Booth), were numerous writers such as Longfellow, Holmes, Lowell, and Julia Ward Howe, as well as Margaret Fuller and historians William Prescott and Francis Parkman. In *Blue Voyage,* Aiken alludes to a ritual he evolved after moving to Cambridge, probably in his late teens, entering Mount Auburn the night of every February 28 to cut himself with a razor and let a few drops of blood fall on an unknown tombstone (shaped like a lamb, not the angel figure remembered from Savannah) in deference to the loss of his parents. Even if done only once, the gesture signifies the compulsion to relieve repressed rage, guilt, and grief, sadly, in secret.

Added to the literary ambience created by the town's monuments to past authors was the presence in Cambridge streets of living writers and scholars. Conrad was awestruck when Dean Le Baron Russell Briggs of Harvard was pointed out to him, having enjoyed reading his two books of *Charades,* and he knew that many of the professors encountered on his visits to the college library were themselves writers. But the strongest boost to his budding literary career came when he began attending the nearest local elementary school, the

Peabody Grammar School, "a sturdy brick building of four stories" on the corner of Linnaean and Avon streets, a few short blocks from his new home.

Conrad entered Peabody's ninth and final grade, "a class of some 40 boys and girls," and apparently found it much more congenial than the New Bedford public school had been. A classmate, Richard C. Evarts, left an enchanting account of the school and of Conrad's role in class activities. In the literary sphere, Evarts, Conrad, a boy named Endicott Marean, and Henry Kittredge, son of Harvard's renowned Shakespeare and Chaucer scholar George Lyman Kittredge and one of Conrad's earliest Cambridge friends, decided to start their own weekly magazine, which they called the *Story Teller,* listing the Akvartean Publishing Company as its publisher:

> The name Akvartean was supposed to be a combination of the letters of our own names, but it is apparent that Conrad and Henry were short changed, although they were the most important and talented contributors. Conrad contributed both prose and poetry, and Henry contributed a continued detective story which his father told him in installments at breakfast. Sherlock Holmes had just returned in *Collier's Weekly* after everyone, including his creator, thought he had been disposed of, and we were fascinated by the stories. I would have thought that *The Story Teller* lasted for only two or three numbers; but there must have been more as the only copy I have been able to find is number 16. Its circulation was practically non-existent as most of the numbers were laboriously written in long-hand.

Not surprisingly, the creative efforts leaned toward imitations of Longfellow, Poe, and Nathaniel Hawthorne, as *Ushant* (92) admits, and Aiken recalled that he and Henry had composed the magazine in Professor Kittredge's study at his home on Hilliard Street while he was off lecturing. Another classmate was John Tunis, future writer of popular sports novels for teenagers, and the males in the class, among them John's brother Robert, Henry, Evarts, Norman Nash (later Episcopal bishop of Massachusetts), and two other brothers, Richard and James Gozzaldi, formed a neighborhood baseball team. Though always a weak hitter, Conrad had what was considered "a good fast ball" and became the "star pitcher" for the "Imps," as they were known, although Evarts is vague about opponents: "I don't recollect that we ever played any other team. . . . It seems to me that most of our activity consisted of playing scrub games ourselves and practicing the art of catching fly balls under the tutelage of Mr. Gozzaldi in the Gozzaldi back yard."

The school's staff and student body were above average, but its routines and curriculum varied little from those followed in thousands of other public schools before John Dewey's reforms descended: "We were drilled in spelling, arithmetic, punctuation, and English grammar; we also learned by heart pieces of prose as well as poetry." Each day commenced with a recital of the Lord's Prayer and the reading of a scriptural passage by the ninth grade room teacher, Charlotte A. Ewell, former principal of the Agassiz School, a "slim, straight-backed lady with white hair and a fringe . . . almost a prototype of that unsung heroine, the New England old maid." The class marched in to the weekly assembly "to the sound of a drum beaten with great vigor and skill by a classmate whose first name was Gordon," and singing was a regular part of the daily agenda. "There was no intensive instruction. . . . We were told how to read music, but I suspect some of us could never learn to carry a tune. So most of our singing was done by the class as a whole." Some of the boys, excluding Conrad, who loved the music but was not especially gifted as a singer, despite his resonant voice, were members of the choir that performed in the morning services at Harvard's Appleton Chapel.

Excepting Miss Ewell, the teacher who seems to have made the deepest impression on Conrad's class was Frederick Spaulding Cutter, Harvard graduate and Peabody's principal or master since 1889. He was held in great respect; a legend circulated "that what appeared to be round shoulders were really the bulging of powerful back and shoulder muscles, and that some boy had once seen Mr. Cutter lift an iron beam single handed," which, as Evarts testifies, "instilled awe and admiration in most of us to whom physical prowess outweighed intellectual attainments and was much more interesting and exciting." The girls, however, "all far and away better students than the boys," were less impressed. In addition to his administrative duties, Cutter was responsible for the ninth grade's scientific and mathematical education, giving the students "a preview of the mysteries of elementary physics and of algebra in preparation for high school" and performing "simple experiments in physics which entranced us."

Near the end of May, several days before Memorial Day, a pair of Civil War veterans visited the school: "They were probably in their sixties but to us they were ancient. They spoke not only without bitterness but with respect for their former enemies, and emphasized the evils of war rather than its glories." Miss Ewell's already considerable reputation was further enhanced when it was rumored that she was a relative of General Richard Ewell, one of Lee's officers. Of course, the major event for Conrad's class was graduation day, which entailed a great deal of preparation and drilling. Two reading selections had to be memorized, the speech of Brutus to Cassius the night before the Battle at Philippe in *Julius Caesar,* which begins, "There is a tide in the affairs of men," and a stirring passage from Daniel Webster's famed reply to Robert Y. Hayne, which concludes with "Liberty *and* Union, now and for ever, one and inseparable!"

At Peabody's June 1903 graduation exercises, the selections were recited on cue— "in unison distinctly and with appropriate expressions"—and the familiar ceremony unfolded without a stumble: "We were all dressed in our best clothes—most of the girls wore white dresses—our families attended, and we received our diplomas individually from the hands of Mayor McNamee." Soon thereafter, perhaps while summering at Powder Point, if not sooner, Conrad was told that he would be attending Middlesex Preparatory School in Concord, some twenty miles from Cambridge, boarding there and readying himself to enter Harvard in four years.

However much he might have resented the Tillinghasts, the prospect of four years in a dormitory with a host of strangers could not have enthralled Conrad, still suffering from the hurt of losing Aunt Jane's maternal sanctuary. He had only recently acquainted himself with Cambridge's highways and byways, spiritual and literal, with the nearby Harvard Botanical Gardens and Observatory, where he hunted flower specimens for his growing collection under Uncle William's approving eye, with the old Unitarian church across from the Common and its burying ground, and "the old gymnasium there, among the stables, and the huge book on physiology which they had all read in secret," and even with the dancing school, "misery of miseries," where he was supposed to acquire the social art required by his background. Garden Street had already become identified with significant signposts along his path to maturity and self-knowledge: "In this street once—you broke a watch-chain, wrote a valentine, threw snowballs at the feathered trees." And in the companionship of friends such as Henry Kittredge, witty, literate, and well-mannered, he had begun the awkward socialization process essential to the struggle against anhedonia that a wounded young ego must invariably confront.

Now Conrad would once again have to endure the painful experience of integrating himself in a crowd of potentially hostile peers, intensifying the shyness that was emerging as a permanent part of his character. The shyness (and its attendant narcissism) he continued to mask with his father's stern features and a pugnacious willingness to take affront. Needless to add, perhaps, being hustled off from yet another nest must have contributed more kindling to the fire of insecurity raging beneath his bold surface.

On the positive side, Middlesex was small, rural, located in a beautiful village sharing some of the same literary and historical associations as Cambridge, site of "the shot heard half-way round the world" and home, at various times and in various degrees, to Emerson, Hawthorne, Bronson Alcott, and other significant figures in the Transcendental pantheon. It was also new, having been founded by its headmaster, Frederick Winsor, in 1901 as a nondenominational boarding school aimed at readying its young charges for entry into Harvard and other Ivy League bastions of white, Anglo-Saxon man-

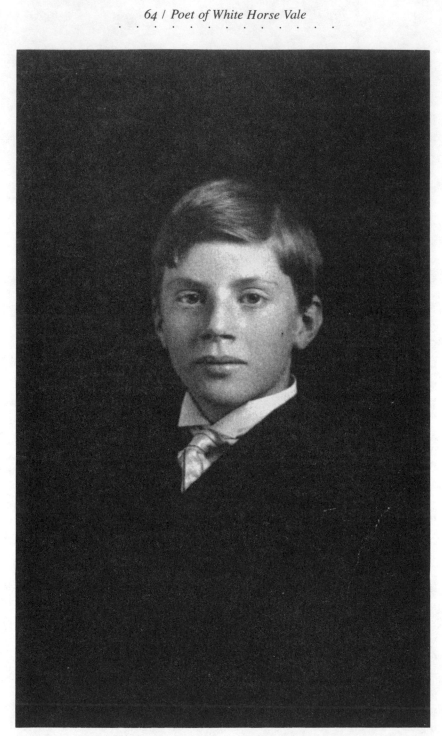

Conrad Aiken in 1903, the year he entered Middlesex.

hood. A former headmaster at a respected country day school in Baltimore and brother of the originator of the Winsor School in Boston, Middlesex's founder and leader was an ambitious educator who had managed to interest a number of people at Harvard in his project, among them Dean Briggs. He kept the lines to the university open through his contacts with its faculty, which meant that a high proportion of his first graduating class slipped easily into the Yard.

Sophisticated, efficient, and clearly shrewd, Frederick Winsor is an unknown quantity in the Aiken scheme because Conrad conceived a dislike of him that grew into positive hatred by the time he graduated in 1907. In *Ushant* the headmaster is dismissed as "god-impersonating," an epithet also hung on the school's baseball coach by *Great Circle,* referred to as "the Boss" (146) there and elsewhere with blatant contempt. But the boy who entered Middlesex in September 1903 was a self-conscious rebel, admittedly *"Farouche"* in his defiance of authority while residing in Cambridge, smarting from the wound of yet another rejection, still unable to accept his personal tragedy as other than a "black mark" that had to be concealed from his classmates. Instinctively and by protective design, he was the descendant of John Milton's Lucifer model ("I will not serve") that James Joyce's Stephen Dedalus and Thomas Mann's artist protagonists would soon limn for the new century, as is every psyche driven into creativity by the premature loss of parental deities. His brother Robert remembered that Aiken "didn't like to follow the rules unless he made them."

More pertinent, Grayson McCouch, a classmate of Conrad's who became his closest friend, though not close enough then for Conrad to reveal his past, always felt that Aiken never "gave Middlesex the credit it deserves" for the beneficial influence it exerted "on all of us," that "Conrad got a good deal out of the school" but had "come there after a shattering experience." Ruth McIntyre, daughter of a Cambridge physician whom Conrad would meet in his senior year, was less indulgent. She felt that people such as Winsor and Gig Gallagher, one of the teachers Conrad particularly despised—"detestable red-faced red-headed vulgar master (tuberculous, too)" is how *Blue Voyage* damns him—were beyond his comprehension, far too "sophisticated" for him to appreciate.

If little else, Winsor and his staff were guilty of enormous insensitivity, perhaps downright brutality, in their rigid handling of Conrad. They must have been acquainted with his family records and could have adopted a more enlightened attitude toward the rebellious air of sullen superiority beneath which he hid. Familiarity with the emerging field of psychoanalysis would not be needed to grasp the obvious underAsprings of Conrad's defiant behavior; these educators deserve whatever opprobrium Aiken chose to heap upon their memories. But overt conflicts with Winsor should not obscure the weightier internal struggle against an unfair fate and contradictory emotions tearing Conrad apart at Middlesex, since, as René Char has commented, it "is from lack of *inner* justice that the poet suffers most in his relations with the world. Caliban's sewer window behind which Ariel's powerful and sensitive eyes are angry."

In 1968, at the age of seventy-nine, Aiken wrote to McCouch about the "boss" and his pernicious effect upon a vulnerable younger self, repeating what he had recently told people soliciting money for the school: "Just said that we hated each other, and that this crimped my career" at Middlesex. Joseph Killorin, to whom the aged Aiken confided memories of boarding school life, has tersely summed up Conrad's four years in Concord: "He was an enthusiastic athlete and he formed fast friendships, particularly with Grayson P. McCouch ('The Old Bird'). But preparatory school . . . was overcast by loneliness; he was shy and he had no real family (his relatives never once visited him at school). He felt marked by the whisperings around him about his family tragedy." If none of his relatives visited him, which was devastating at holiday times, he did have summers at Duxbury and New Bedford to console him, and he kept in touch with Aunt Jane, his grandmother, and other relatives by post. The whispers were probably more imagined than real in his sensitive ears, a sign of the interior inferno of doubts and causeless guilt.

These inner flames flashed to the surface during the first year, when Conrad paid a visit to the Taylor home in Germantown. Robert and Kempton were playing catch when he arrived and asked him to join them, which he did. Robert, who "was catching right in front of the barn," shouted, "Let's see your fastball or something like that." Conrad reared back and fired with all his might. The baseball sailed easily through the flimsy glove of that era, striking his brother in the forehead and knocking him unconscious. Frederick Taylor came running from the house and "gave Conrad hell, said you had no business throwing a ball that hard at a kid that size." Conrad's future visits to the Taylors would be few and far between, though the next year the family moved to Boxley, an estate in Chesterwood, Pennsylvania, only three blocks from McCouch's home.

Taylor and Conrad would never have gotten along under any circumstances, even if Conrad could have conquered his rebellious rage. Like Winsor, Taylor represented another rigid authority figure, evoking memories of Dr. Aiken at his pompous worst. A muscular Christian in the Victorian mold, graduate of Exeter and the Stevens Institute, winner of the U.S. doubles championship in lawn tennis at Newport in 1881, he had worked himself up from gang boss to chief engineer at the Midvale Steel Company before leaving in 1889 to

establish a business organizing management procedures for various large factories. Patents for a hundred inventions were credited to him, and he was
cocreator of the Taylor-White process for treating high-speed tools, which
resulted in the award of a gold medal at the Paris Exposition of 1900. Eleven
years later two of his extremely successful books, *Shop Management* and *The
Principles of Scientific Management,* guaranteed his place in the history of
American industry as the father of modern efficiency techniques. Taylor
would transform Kempton and Robert into "a couple of nice stuffed shirts," to
cite a relative, and might have contributed to Elizabeth's eventual breakdown,
at least by maintaining his household in strict conformity with unbending
genteel mores.

Lacking siblings and a proper home, Conrad had little choice but to make
the best of Middlesex's advantages—"it became my home." Its size was a
definite asset—sixty or seventy boys at most, with four or five masters, and a
few converted farm buildings surrounded by rolling lawns and acres of
woods. He quickly achieved casual familiarity with his thirteen classmates,
aided by his skills at baseball and tennis, although he never made any of the
school teams. He bombarded the school's magazine, the *Anvil,* with submissions and had his first story, "The Making of the Trail," published in its
January 1904 issue. By his second year he would be the *Anvil*'s editor, contributing poems and stories with determined regularity.

In his first year he also began taking piano lessons but gave them up, a
decision he subsequently regretted, though he realized that his gift for im-
provisation on the instrument was modest (221). Poetry was more enticing
and seemed easier to do, though most of his energies were channeled into
sports, study, the *Anvil,* and the flower collecting that had evolved into a
deeply ingrained habit. In *Ushant* Conrad concedes that Middlesex—which
he contemptuously dubbed "Middleclass"—was "a necessity, a duty; delightful, novel, and even exciting," but he makes clear that "there had been
no room at the school to which he could now look back with anything like
affection or nostalgia" (72).

The nourishing core of the boarding school experience for Conrad resided
in the company of several sympathetic companions and attractive physical
externals, opportunities to explore nature and test the concrete self's growing
powers on football and baseball fields. Complementing scenic hikes and athletic joys was an evolving friendship with a handful of schoolmates variously
referred to in *Ushant* as "the five boys of genius" (72) and "the four geniuses
of Middleclass School" (185)—the discrepancy probably stems from the inclusion in the former group of Thomas McCabe, who was in the class a year
behind Conrad's.

First and foremost among them was Grayson Prevost McCouch, "the Old

Bird," born and raised in Philadelphia in comfortable middle-class circumstances, a solid, strikingly handsome boy with blondish hair and light blue
eyes, afflicted with a stuttering problem that caused him to speak with deliberate slowness. Kind and considerate, old beyond his years, fascinated by literature despite ambitions for a medical career, McCouch possessed in humane
abundance a quality of moral certitude that Conrad could respect in the same
manner that he respected the implicit ethical code of Aunt Jane's every word
and action. He was "the whole world's conscience," and Conrad ached for
certainty of any sort, even if unable to emulate his new friend's high standards
except in the sphere of literature, which would be his temple and his state.

Not as deep or as enduring, the appeals of the others had their own rewards.
Alfred V. deForest ("Avy"), for instance, "of the unforgettable Etruscan
beauty and nobility," nicknamed him "Candlepower" and would teach him
how to sail, being an expert yachtsman himself. And there was "Penny," who
crowned him "Noox," and "intrepid, enchanting Jack" (185), as well as less
close classmates Robert Wallace and "Charles, from Kinderhook" with his
"charming and luminous asymmetrical face, and his infectious love of
Shelley," generous "with his love, as of his gift" (145). If this description
sounds a bit homoerotic, it undoubtedly was and had to be, to some unconscious degree, in a society bereft of females—Middlesex's sole failing in
McCouch's wise eyes. But there are no intimations of the homosexual affairs
and cruel "ragging" that often characterized life at English public schools
because the community and school were not separated by a great distance, and
the community, that part of it involved, remained Puritan.

Meanwhile, Conrad had to wrestle with a demanding curriculum catering to
Ivy League requirements for proficiency in Latin and Greek, and a brief February 6, 1904, letter to his grandmother admits: "I wont [sic] stand as high in
my class this term as I did last, for my fourth french [sic] is pretty hard, and
today, in Latin Composition I probably failed. Caesar is going quite nicely."
Before the end he returns somewhat compulsively to the competitive theme:
"I am feeling rather down-hearted today; I am studying hard all the time these
days, but french [sic] and Latin Comp. are pulling me down. However I
probably won't drop more than three places." He also mentions a cabin he and
Wallace built in the snow-filled woods and notes sadly that "the club fellows
are going home this afternoon, except Alfred de Forest and I, so there will be
no meeting." But that night he was "going to a candy-pull at Mrs. Chase's,
and will probably have a very good time."

His grandmother had attained greater visibility in his life, and Conrad began visiting her little house on Common Street in Watertown, which contained
several of his father's effects, among them "the hidden leather portfolio of
father's poems and articles" (101). Though by comparison to Aunt Jane's and

Aiken's "fierce" paternal grandmother, Emily H. Ford Akin (ca. 1890).

Cousin Julia's grand dwelling her modest abode seemed "poverty-stricken," it contained the same careful clutter and Victorian furniture as theirs and emitted the same sweet sachet scent associated in his mind with the rooms of genteel old ladies. Emily Akin had bloomed like a suddenly released rose bush after her husband's death, losing many of her defensive thorns, energetically educating herself to appreciate the more refined advantages of culture, such as the paintings of Renaissance Italy, and appeared ready to substitute Conrad for her lost genius of a son, to the extent, if *Ushant* is to be trusted, of a near seduction.

Conrad needed the support and attention, just as he needed the heroic profile of his father she would eventually fashion for him. Middlesex was too often a place to escape from over the next four years, a starting and departure point rather than a destination or snug sanctuary. It was only from his school companions that he turned away on bicycle trips into Cambridge or Duxbury, along the Concord Turnpike, with any regret. "For in that period it was to 'the houses' that he moved, as by a compulsory tropism, to the houses and the dear people who lived in them, the 'family' " (72).

The insightful older Aiken in *Ushant* asks and answers the right questions about the restless quest for a permanent perch among these houses and his tendency never to stay too long in any one of them for fear of wearing out his welcome: "Was this one of the effects of having been orphaned, and further orphaned by the adoption of R. and K. by Cousin Ted [Taylor]? Was it all quite simply the need of, and search for, a home? a sustaining, but above all *uninstitutional,* locus of one's own? Yes, there was no doubt about it" (72). But he does not complete the metaphor, as he did elsewhere in his fiction, does not translate the hearth quest into a grail quest for his lost mother.

In the summer of 1904, which was spent at New Bedford, he was to lose another maternal replacement. Despite her ninety-seven years, Aunt Jane had decided with typical independence to carry a heavy valise up to the attic by herself and had tumbled back down the steep stairs. She was soon bedridden and delirious. Conrad was at her side while she raved, mistaking him for other male members of the family, for Uncle Alfred, her son, her husband, and, at last, her own father. When writing *Ushant,* avid for structure, Aiken remembered the bizarre experience as a moment of intense transitional paradox, of shifting roles. It had made him feel, "as never before or since, the queer ambiguity of one's existence within the *frame* of family, the simultaneity of belonging and of being, of group anonymity and individual identity" (96).

Apart from the patent absence of ego undercutting the experience, the importance of Aiken's words hinges upon the amalgamated identity achieved through clan history, its emotional links with the Romantic reverence for place—a worshipful yielding of consciousness to elegiac memory—epitomized by Wordsworth's personal poetic schemas, whether at Tintern Abbey or the grave of "We Seven," where memory, intensified by loss, seeks to fill the void left after the disappearance of the gods, of myth. The self is thus saved from dissolution by an obsessive deification of the very pain and place erasing its margins, as Aiken would attempt in casting Virgil's "sacred grove" enchantment over the scene in Colonial Park between Anna and him when she was recovering from scarlet fever. Aunt Jane's hallucinations provide, within *Ushant's* redemptive road map, a parade of visages for concealing the anguished reality of Conrad's fragmented psyche—grief for her fatal condition thereby also transfigured, lessened.

Conrad did not have to witness Aunt Jane's death on August 1, for he was packed off hurriedly to Duxbury, but he soon had to return, alone, for the funeral. He resented the solitary trip back to New Bedford, as well as being the sole child present, sitting in the front row beside Cousin Julia. It must have seemed like an extended session of déjà vu from Savannah: the folding chairs, the casket in the parlor, the inability to feel what should be felt. Resentment, however, was but a minor expression of the fury energizing internal engines— fury at the mother figure for dying on him again and fury at the injustice of a world in which death could wield such awesome, capricious power, so similar to that once wielded by Dr. Aiken.

Though real mourning had yet to occur, death continued to stain Conrad's awareness, separating him not only from relatives and friends but from life itself. Aiken's alter ego in *Great Circle* bemoans "this death business. This dying business. These coffins. These funeral parlors. These greasy undertakers, and the ribbons on the doors. . . . We're dying piecemeal. Every time someone you know dies, you die too, a little piece of you. . . . And the worst of it is that what's dead isn't buried: it rots in you." The mothlike fascination with extinction entered his consciousness most vividly during sleep. One of his recurrent nightmares was the "execution dream," in which he waited in the electric chair for the surge of fatal energy and was terribly aware of his ineffectuality when it came, his attempt to scream for "a deeper and more final intrusion" emerging as a faint, unheard murmur (36). Besides showing significant connections to the pig-with-wings image and a palpable delineation of Conrad's fundamental insecurity, the dream's sexual connotations are difficult to ignore, intimating a subsequent, mature yoking of life and death drives.

Externally Conrad's existence was minimally changed by Aunt Jane's demise. It involved financial gain, thanks to Cousin Julia's foresight in having earlier convinced Jane to write her will with the four Aiken orphans in mind. The estate came to $180,000, a considerable legacy in that pre-income-tax, preinflationary era. Half went to the Potters, and the other half was divided equally among Conrad and his siblings. Alas, Conrad's share of $20,000 would have to provide the funds for his education and other major expenses, whereas Taylor left the inheritances of his three charges intact, earning full interest. This would be further cause for resentment, though the capital from Aunt Jane's estate guaranteed Conrad a steady, albeit diminishing, income for many years to come, the means for pursuing a literary career without the need to resort to a second profession.

Although New Bedford seemed emptier, he passed several summer vacations with his cousin Edward Benjamin at Nonquitt, taking the little steamer that voyaged daily to there from Buzzard's Bay. In *Ushant* he recalled the shoreline's postcard beauty as well as "the pretty girls on the beach in their gay bathing-suits, and the delicious torments and heat-lightnings of adolescence" (95). Girls were naturally a constant topic at male Middlesex, the center of endless conversations and jokes.

The major problem for Conrad during his Middlesex days, excepting the inner torments associated with his parents' demise, revolved around the Christmas and spring recesses, which he frequently endured at Middlesex with the handful of other boys who had no place to go. He spent several vacations at McCouch's Chestnut Hill home, twice taking the opportunity while there to visit his brothers and sister at Boxley for an hour or two. Another Middlesex friend who helped him resolve the recess dilemma was Thomas Tonkin McCabe from the class a year behind his. McCabe's family, originally from Bloomington, Indiana, was affluent and cosmopolitan; the father often took his son on trips to Europe. Conrad's friendship with him is depicted in *Ushant* as "strange and in its way delightful," disapproved of by the doting mother, who thought Conrad "far too sedate" for her manly son (158). McCabe himself is drawn as "an extreme individualist, a most engaging nonconformist in all things," for whom "all discipline was abhorrent" (159–60). The portrait is somewhat contested by Ruth McIntyre, McCabe's girlfriend. Though conceding that her impressions were gained "through Tom," she believes that McCabe was simply "much more sophisticated than Conrad was, he lived abroad quite a bit . . . and he liked Dr. Winsor, and he used to, well, Winsor would ask him in to have dinner or something—they had that kind of relationship—and talk." McCabe was also "great friends" with Gallagher, the master Conrad detested.

Aiken, who would dub McCabe "Wild Michael" in *Ushant*, records a winter recess the two boys spent together climbing in the White Mountains, where the McCabes had a cabin, "a scatter-brained ascent, in midwinter, without proper equipment or precautions." Heavy snow forced them to seek shelter, which they miraculously found in a hut, where they read *King Solomon's Mine* until the storm abated. Despite antagonistic strains, the relationship with McCabe was a necessary relief from compulsive struggles with Middlesex authorities, as were most of Conrad's school bondings, predicated upon propinquity, class and ethnic similarities, and common interests in sports and (with a select few) literature. McCouch, who shared both interests, recalled that Conrad "never made a school team. He played baseball and just missed making the school team. He played tennis, never played football." McCouch also recalled a conflict between Conrad and the baseball coach, cursed in *Blue Voyage* as "the God-impersonating baseball coach who would never trust me with a chance on the first nine."

The Middlesex friendships were crucial stays, however temporary, against the continued confusion engendered by being bandied about from relative to relative. They were also more congenial extensions of the onerous social education Conrad had begun to acquire from Aunt Jane and other New Bedford relatives, such as Benjamin Anthony (*Ushant*'s "Cousin Lew"), who had provided "his first dress-suit" for "the dreadful little formal dinners" that were part of the New Bedford and Cambridge family scene (136). His legal guardians, the Tillinghasts, could apparently offer no aid in these matters, and it was McCabe who finally "taught him to overcome" the inadequacy in himself caused by their lack of taste (124). Proper breeding, knowing how to dress, what and how to eat, which language to use with whom, would be a hallmark of the surface Aiken in the years to come, regardless of circumstances, especially after the last layer of varnish had been applied by exposure to Harvard's class-conscious atmosphere.

Internal pressures were apparently relieved, at least sufficiently to permit intellectual growth and increasing emotional control, by the expenditure of physical energies in sports and occasional defiance of school faculty and school codes. Dreams, too, remained important safety valves when not recharging old anxieties. Sometime during his third year at Middlesex, Conrad had a minor operation, his first time under ether. It resulted in the "Columbus dream," which, like the pig-with-wings nightmare, was to recur. Aiken compared its main effect, a "sense of cosmic consciousness," to hashish trances, similar to later ether dreams in that respect. In the "giant" dream, he is a sailor with Columbus but falls overboard. At the sea's bottom he experiences "a sensation of sadness and remoteness and lostness," realizing he would miss the discovery of America: "I had stepped clear out of time and space, my consciousness was both before and after the event; I had become God." The motif—human awareness expanding into godhead—foretells a central obsession, and accompanying pangs of loss over his "own dissolving identity" summarize prevailing inner turmoil, aches of homelessness.

But the reading and making of literature, a mother's gift and father's secret rivalry, was the surest method for rescuing his psyche. "Words, and the rhythms of words, were the medium in which it seemed most likely, or at any rate most happily and magically" his nature could conjure "the equivalents of being, the equivalents of the still shadowy self" (92). A year or so before graduation, through the kind offices of his cousin Harold, Conrad met several editors of the Harvard *Advocate* and experienced "a foretaste of the excitement of the adventure to come" (144). His own compositions were keeping the *Anvil* afloat—six stories and eighteen poems published by November 1905—and he was gaining solid editorial experience.

The strongest poems Conrad wrote at Middlesex were gathered together in 1927 into *A Quarter Century of Middlesex Verse*, an anthology published by the school. The eight poems are impressive for their technical mastery, a subsequent trademark, and their relentless focus upon death and the sea, a combination congenial to his temperament and patterns inherited from Poe. They demonstrate, in every aspect, the ardent fascination with awesome natural forces one might expect from a literate American adolescent writing shortly after the turn of the century. Three of them—"The Storm," "The Sunrise," and "The Lightning"—are exactly what they say they are, verbal landscapes and seascapes, minor foreshadowings of an Imagist approach. In "The Lightning," where the iambic line is varied enough by troches and spondees to amplify a breathless assault, the climax configures lightning's inevitable aftermath: "Then rushes down with hiss and roar / A sudden burst of rain." And "The Sunrise" projects a similar narrowness of intent: "Then gleaming north and south, as still it grows / From morning's tiny prophesying spark, / Aurora's dawn casts o'er the sky its glowing mark."

"The Storm," however, merges cloud with war cloud, nature with man, extending the metaphor to a logical conclusion:

> Forward the army starts,
> Thun'ring in deeper parts,
> Lightning from armor darts,
>   Flashing a warning;
> Fiercely the storm winds blow,
> Up from the west they go,
> Whirling the blinding snow,
>   Veiling the morning.

Another sea poem is more successful, perhaps because it is more closely aligned with deeply absorbed Poe *mise en scènes* and a psychological need of Gothic images. "On a Derelict," which roughly emulates the sense of an English sonnet's structure, exemplifies Conrad at his youthful strongest, almost as strong as "Lex Talionis," the poem his father had appropriated:

As in a dream, from through the fog, there looms
    Thy shattered timbers, spectre derelict,
    Now chilled and worn by waves that e'er predict
Thy long-impending, ever-tempted doom.
Thy wretched form rolls through the dripping gloom;
    The hands of death thy skeleton have picked
    By gnawing waves thy shattered bow is licked,
While tow'ring o'er the cliffs, the breakers boom,
Thy hulk, now guided by no human hands,
    Drifts onward through the mist to find its death
Where sea-gulls cry and angry waters roar;
Straight towards the coast that knows no softer sands,
    It drifts, as steered by magic's fickle breath,
And breaks upon the cliffs and is no more.

Two other sea poems, "The Song of the Buoy" and "The Song of the Ocean," are equally adept at manipulating rhyme and meter, although less potently so, the former simulating the singsong bell's voice with playful precision:

    I swing and warn on surging flow,
    Midst jarring ice and driving snow,
    Still o'er the Death that breakers hide
    I moan and clang and drift and slide;
    Still to and fro I, warning, go,
    At sunset glow!

"The Song of the Ocean" is more ambitious, though it is unlikely that Conrad was as yet aware of Wordworth's and Byron's confrontations with the ocean, the ocean as archetypal mother, fecund giver and taker of life, so that his ocean is another personification of death alone:

    For Death is mine, with power vast
    Destroying at my will;
    The headlands sink, the fires die,
    There comes no answer to my cry—
    And all is still!

The identification here is with the sea that sailors fear, the sea that had swallowed the whaleship of Conrad's New Bedford cousin.

Aside from "Lex Talionis," the only poem in the anthology not about the sea or nature in upheaval is "In a China Jar," which was obviously instigated by explorations of Aunt Jane's attic. The rhymes are forced and oddly juvenile at times:

> The first one I read—
> (A candle I lighted!)
> The spelling was bad—
> But I was delighted

But the small narrative about finding two old letters in a Chinese vase, where a "Squat little God / Was perched on the lid," has undeniable charm. The first letter, from John to Mary, promises to meet his beloved by the church the next day, "if I can"; Mary's reply is tantalizingly incomplete: "I confess—" Conrad's closing stanza is aptly teasing and clever:

> Heaven knows where they are!
> But mine was the sorrow;
> And the god on the jar
> Nodded me a good morrow.

The eight pieces in the anthology present credible evidence that Conrad was a talented and sensitive teenager, several notches above his contemporaries in mastery of fundamental verse techniques. They also reveal inescapable links with the American Romanticism that best expressed his own obsessions. Their tyro character and borrowed imagery should not obscure the satisfaction their author must have derived from their engagements with death tropes. Allegorical frames for nature's unbridled power, for death's omnipotent sway, were at least edging him toward unconscious depths since fears of paternal forces in nature, the primal father, had unseen associations, tenuous and inarticulate, with Dr. Aiken and the shameful past Conrad was careful to conceal. Even as he advanced in control over his craft, establishing a "persona" in Jung's specific use of the term—an asserted self that performs in public until genuine—he was simultaneously closing upon the potential means for reconstituting the murky ghosts of his father and mother.

An integral part of his development, of course, was the rich formal education that Middlesex supplied. Learning Latin and Greek was an invaluable adjunct to Conrad's quest after the shield magic of words, if only for introducing him to Socrates, whom he would eventually enshrine as "the prototype of highest man" (220), and Virgil, whose *Aeneas* he had started decoding as a freshman. The latter reminded him of the little hut in Colonial Park surrounded by sapling elms near where his mother and he had had their momentous hours alone together: "I remember thinking about it . . . when I began reading Virgil. *Et vox in faucibus.*" Along with readings in significant Greek and Roman poets and Xenophon's exciting *Anabasis,* he was also encountering a variety of Latin prose styles, ranging from gossipy Suetonius and blunt Caesar to Cicero's elaborate periods. The highly inflected language did not come easy. In *Great Circle,* Aiken's protagonist thinks back to summers at Duxbury when, as a boy, he had to go to the village to "have my Latin lesson with Mr. Dearing," and *Blue Voyage* castigates "Mr. Greenbaum, the Latin teacher, who watched me through the crack of the door to see if I was cribbing."

Sophocles, or as much of him as a callow prep student could assimilate, exposed the heroic and tragic structural dimensions inherent in an existence forever victimized by mortality and painful moral choices, the fulcrum of a family dynamic in which past governs future, character, and fate as inextricable, predetermined paradigms. And Sappho's limpid lyrics and fragments had to have underlined poetry's eternal battle against finite horizons, prosaic reductions of experience. But Catullus, most "modern" of the Romans in speech and sensibility, was a Latin pupil's true friend, anticipating Aiken's own generation's war against florid Victorian models in the 1910s and 1920s: "The little boy had been reading Latin poetry again. *Odi et amo.*"

Added to these distant but relevant literary influences were the host of standard English and American authors from the nineteenth century that buttressed Middlesex's rigorous curriculum, though Conrad's interaction with the English Romantics—Wordsworth, Coleridge, Shelley, and Keats in particular—would commence in earnest at Harvard. Equally influential, if less detectable, were the countless books perused outside the classroom, currently popular adventure tales and novels such as *Huckleberry Finn* and *Alice in Wonderland,* devoured as children's fare and reconsidered later with adult care to discern subterranean architecture. O. Henry, for instance, a writer whom Conrad treasured, was in his heyday—*Cabbages and Kings* appeared in 1904—and Jack London's *Call of the Wild* had been a 1903 best-seller. The American novel of manners was in the refined hands of Edith Wharton, whose *House of Mirth* was published in 1905, a remarkable contrast to the reformist realism of Upton Sinclair's *Jungle* a year later. From England came the novels of Henry James's prime, *The Wings of the Dove* in 1902, followed by his most accomplished performance to date, *The Ambassadors,* in 1903. American poetry, alas, continued to languish, despite recent strivings for a peculiar free-verse merger of allegory and narrative starkness by Stephen Crane and the official recognition of Emily Dickinson's unique verses in Edmund Clarence Stedman's prestigious *An American Anthology* of 1900.

More important, for Conrad and for Western civilization, the early years of the twentieth century were witnessing extraordinary creative surges in almost every discipline on both sides of the Atlantic, surges destined permanently to alter man's perception of himself, his culture, and his world. The Freudian revolution was already brewing during Conrad's tenure at Middlesex, as was Jung's no less rebellious reorganization of the theoretical schema behind that revolution. Closer to home, Harvard's own William James and George Santayana had consequential books published in 1905, *Pragmatism* and *The Life of Reason* respectively, the same year in which Albert Einstein's *Special Theory of Relativity*, Freud's *Three Treatises on the Theory of Sex*, and Henri Bergson's *Creative Evolution* appeared on the Continent.

In America technological breakthroughs seemed more dramatic and more tightly bound to cultural expressions, which retained a staunch conservative bias. It is probably significant that in 1903, when Thomas Edison made *The Great Train Robbery* and Alfred Stieglitz started his pioneering *Camera Work* magazine, the first Ford factories were being built, the first radio message between England and the United States was exchanged, and the first Wright brothers' airplane flight took place at Kitty Hawk. If subtle and uncertain at the outset, the profound social changes these events foreshadowed had to have effected (then and later) the germination of the poet's aesthetic, the fashion in which he adjusted to the complicating of human awareness mandated at every level of experience. The new consumer society mushrooming around him was an irresistible threat to the ethnic and social group, the New England leisure class, that was his by birthright and education, to its historic domination of the "cultural hegemony" that had prevailed since the landing of the Puritans. The very success in literature of Aiken's New England generation would sound the death rattle of its national impact. It was no accident that Eliot's poetry of despair would come to epitomize its achievement, a vulnerable psyche deconstructing in tandem with satiric attacks upon the Old Order, Boston's and Cambridge's ineffectual Prufrocks.

These are matters of unknown substance and linkage, which could hardly have intruded with much weight upon Conrad's daily life at Middlesex, a bastion of the Old Order's most cherished boardingschool values. His concerns were necessarily more immediate and circumscribed. In his final year a major consideration was who to invite to the senior dance. The landlady or landlord of a Boston boardinghouse on Beacon Street, who knew Conrad and knew that he had no place to go during one of Middlesex's midyear breaks, invited him to room there for the week. Circumstances were in his favor because the only other boarders were a brother and sister and a pretty Cambridge girl named Barbara Leighton, the youngest of three sisters, who was attending Miss Winsor's School nearby.

According to Ruth McIntyre, a girlhood friend of Leighton, the brother and sister pair "were both boresome and homely," so "naturally Conrad talked with Barbara, and he invited her to the dance." Arrangements were made easier because McCabe had asked Ruth to the same dance, and the two girls

The Middlesex graduating class of 1907. Aiken sits in the first row at the far left with Avy de Forest directly behind him. Grayson McCouch is in the second row, second from the right.

traveled together through the snow to Concord by train. The boys met them at the station with horse-drawn sleighs and conveyed them to the dormitory, which had been turned over to student dates for the night. This was the initial meeting between Ruth McIntyre and Conrad. She had encountered his sister previously "at summer camp when we were kids, but I didn't know about the past." Camp counselors had told the girls not to talk about suicide to Elizabeth, whom McIntyre recalled as "a nice kid" who "looked very much like Conrad" but did not possess "an outstanding personality." In *Ushant* Barbara Leighton is given the sobriquet of "Anita," and her vivacity and animal energy are stressed, her love of dancing, the "long-legged, blue-eyed, giddy Anita" (169).

Ruth McIntyre's original impression of Conrad, with whom she danced a single dance, was too vague to recollect, but further acquaintance led her to observe: "He was a very strong personality, and I liked him . . . you'd know he was somebody," though "he was terribly shy, of course." The dance was a big success, the two couples enjoying one another's company, and afterward, "the four of us went around together quite a bit." Barbara soon became Conrad's ostensible girlfriend, at least someone from the right social background whom he could squire to dances, ball games, and other functions in the year immediately ahead—an attractive, acceptable date intelligently capable of appreciating his wit and growing erudition. Indeed, it would not be difficult to convince himself that he was in love with her.

In June 1907, when Conrad's class of fourteen graduated, he and eleven of his classmates knew they had been accepted into Harvard—a foregone conclusion in his case. One of the two boys not going to Harvard, Avy deForest, had been accepted by MIT, which meant his friendship with Conrad could be maintained. And yet, whatever happiness Conrad experienced at escaping from the "boss" and his minions was immeasurably dampened by a cruel and humiliating prank played upon him earlier. As a result, the rancor against Winsor and Middlesex would endure for a lifetime, Aiken writing with bitterness from his deathbed to McCouch, the school's loyal defender: "What would you think of a school where in your senior year you were waylaid in the Headmaster's house by two characters, known as Face Godfrey and Gid Gallagher, upended, you pants ripped off, given the water cure, and then dumped on the floor."

This, too, like the heavy emotional baggage carried north from Savannah, was a part of the burden, the secret shame and rage he had to cart to Harvard, where the quest for the "vocabulary of self" would assume different dimensions, confront different faces, but never lose its obsessive drive.

As in a supreme dramatic crisis
all our life seems to be focused
in the present, and used in
coloring our consciousness and
shaping our decisions, so for
each philosopher poet the whole
world of man is fathered
together.

George Santayana

.   .   .   .

STEP BY PRECARIOUS STEP

When Conrad Aiken entered Harvard in the fall of 1907, he was entering the oldest, most prestigious, often snobbiest college in the country. It was also, at every level, literature-oriented. Van Wyck Brooks, who had graduated a few months earlier, along with his good friends Maxwell Perkins and Edward Sheldon, the popular dramatist, remembered that he had been initially attracted to Harvard because he supposed "it was the college for writers. It was intensely literary, as it had been for three hundred years,—it was even more literary in my time than before." This recent intensification of the school's literary climate might be traced back to the middle 1880s, when George Santayana, with the aid of several classmates, founded the *Harvard Monthly* as a serious alternative to the aged *Advocate* and the lighthearted *Lampoon*. The *Monthly*'s impressive list of editors would include Bernard Berenson, William Vaughn Moody, and John Hall Wheelock, a senior during Aiken's freshman year.

In the 1890s three brilliant students—Trumbull Stickney, George Cabot Lodge, and Moody—plus Santayana, by then an instructor in the philosophy department chaired by William James, achieved a national reputation as the "Harvard Poets," conservative in practice and vision but noetically liberal, conscious, like Henry Adams and Harvard itself, of the modern world's corruptive materialism and fated doom. Another poet, Edwin Arlington Robinson, the first American poet after Whitman and Dickinson who can be termed "modern" (a view shared by Aiken), was a special student at Harvard between 1901 and 1903, returning for a year in 1907 to work in President Charles Eliot's office.

The class a year ahead of Aiken's could count among its number T. S. Eliot; John Reed, future journalist, communist sympathizer, and author of *Ten Days That Shook the World* (1919); Heywood Broun, nascent columnist, liberal crusader, ultimate organizer of the American Newspaper Guild; Alan Seeger, the minor poet who "cut himself off almost entirely from the real world" (as Aiken subsequently described him) and who was doomed to achieve unenviable romantic stature by keeping his rendezvous with death in World War I as part of the French Foreign Legion; and Walter Lippmann, an ambitious, patrician, "owlishly solemn youth," who founded the school's Socialist Club. Though enlivened by the presence of Robert Benchley, Aiken's class could boast no similar roll of prominent names, and few of these gifted sophomores had much effect on him. His contacts with people such as Reed and Lippmann were minimal and casual. Lippmann, in fact, despite a common concern after 1909 for promulgating the revolutionary ideas of Freud, he did not find congenial at all: "There was no rapport and they rather disliked each other."

But Aiken felt immediately more at home in Harvard's familiar, tradition-drenched milieu than he had ever been at Middlesex, which is not surprising. His father and grandfather had been Harvard graduates, his Uncle William and Uncle Alfred still functioned as librarians there, and he had the supreme advantage of coming from the proper WASP, New England background and of being escorted into its hallowed precincts by close Middlesex companions such as McCouch, although he lived alone in the Yard the first year, at 14 Grays Hall. His Cambridge friend Henry Kittredge also entered that year, and he maintained close contact with Avy deForest and Barbara Leighton, the latter still at Miss Winsor's School but often available for dates and rural strolls, with or without the additional weight of McCabe and Ruth McIntyre. Consequently, what might have proved a daunting experience for a shy, non-affluent freshman in an institution where exclusive clubs held sway and the exhibition of strong emotions was frowned upon became instead a pleasant, stimulating swim through a sea of official indifference and formal reserve—aided, always, by the kindly McCouch and company. "At once," Houston Peterson would write of him, "he began the quiet process of sliding through, majoring in English and 'sitting in' occasionally on advanced language courses for tonal inspiration." One language course he took for credit was German B, but he never mastered the language and later switched to Spanish.

Aiken's ability to "slide through" from the beginning of his Harvard career, though his marks were usually respectable, was a product of the college's tendency to ingore its burgeoning freshman population. Freshman advisers were "overburdened instructors" with little time for or interest in their charges, and the college itself was benignly neglected by the university and had been since the installation of Charles William Eliot as president in 1869. A former chemistry professor afflicted with a glacial manner and a genuine zeal for reform, President Eliot evinced scant sympathy for the humanities, giving the impression that "cultivation was for women," and remained determined to reverse the trend that had culminated in the college being the hub around which the university revolved.

President Eliot's modernization project consisted of implanting at Harvard the contemporary notion that a university could and should be a legitimate center for original scientific research, which meant a greater concentration of funds and administrative attention on research facilities and graduate matters. No serious attempts were made to alleviate the undergraduate housing problem, which worsened as the nineteenth century drew to a close and the student body grew from 1,077 undergraduates in 1887 to over 2,000 by 1907. Outside of the elitist club system, which thrived under Eliot and was at its peak during Aiken's tenure, a student living in the Yard, the mostly walled twenty-two and a half acres of college property in downtown Cambridge, survived under rather bleak conditions. Unless he belonged to a restricted club or could afford to dine at one of the many boardinghouses bordering the campus, he had to partake of "the meals served on a vast and savorless scale at Memorial Hall," the huge, gray gingerbread structure built in the early 1870s to honor the school's Civil War dead.

More discouraging yet, none of the dormitories in or out of the Yard possessed common rooms, and socializing, again excepting the clubs, revolved around Union Hall, founded in 1901 as a democratic "house of fellowship" for the "unclubbed" (*sans* bar), where various campus groups and all the major student publications had their offices. It was in the Union's auditorium that Van Wyck Brooks first encountered America's newest literary hero, Jack London, the "Kipling of the Klondike," still in his twenties, who lectured passionately on socialism "with his open shirt and the shining face of a sailor boy fresh from the sea." But for culture-hungry undergraduates like Aiken, who wished to associate more intimately with students of a similar bent outside the frequently hectic offices of the *Advoate* and the *Monthly,* the two most potent magnets were the literary clubs, the Stylus and the Signet, both of which leased space off campus.

The Stylus, described by Francis Biddle, who wrote for the *Advocate* and had a "nodding acquaintance" with Aiken, as a "casual, friendly little club," rented rooms on the ground floor of a frame boardinghouse at 41 Winthrop Street. Run with cheerful propriety by an Australian widow, Mrs. Atchison (known as Mrs. Amy to club members), and her son Percy, who kindly supplied hot buttered toast or crumpets and tea to members who "weren't too late," the house had been the favorite haunt of Perkins, Brooks, Sheldon, and Wheelock a few years before, Perkins and Brooks boarding there together in their senior year. Wheelock, of course, was still in evidence during Aiken's freshman period, though their friendship was slight, and several members from earlier classes continued to attend club meetings in an honorary capacity, among them Harold Bell and Pierre de Chaignon La Rose. Bell was a typical Harvard aesthete and played the role with languid relish. The recipient of a large inheritance, he had himself chauffeured around Cambridge and Boston in a long open Mercedes and manufactured reams of "lifeless, overflowing sonnets in the manner of Oscar Wilde." La Rose, class of 1896 and Santayana's friend, was somewhat different. Although also given to affected mannerism and speech, he had been a Harvard instructor and was now designing fine books and residential interiors; he had presided over the redecoration of the Boston Art Museum. But to Brooks and others, La Rose personified "the Pre-Raphaelite aestheticism and the dilettantish Catholicism that flourished at Harvard" since at least the 1890s.

Aiken made only occasional visits to the Stylus, but it was important to him as a convivial oasis where literature and ideas could be discussed, dissected, fought over, in an almost noncompetitive fashion. The Signet, founded soon after the turn of the century, was probably even more important in this respect, as well as more fertile in a practical way, drawing heavily on the staffs of the *Advocate, Monthly,* and *Lampoon.* However shy and superficially cavalier about his educational progress, Aiken was calculating enough to understand that the future commercial success of his chosen career as a writer might depend upon crucial contacts initiated at Harvard. More pertinent, the Signet was the club preferred by T. S. Eliot, whom he would meet near the end of his first year, and he would sense Eliot's innate genius, his aura of preordained distinction, from the outset of their relationship. Located in "a pleasant house on Brattle Street," the Signet had the further advantage of a small but select library that catered to the literate undergraduate taste for Pater, Arnold, Wilde, Santayana, and Joseph Conrad, which confounded the prevailing faculty deification of Thackeray and Tennyson.

The two clubs were also the sole "places where students and teachers did meet and talk with any sense of freedom and pleasure." Benjamin Apthorp Gould Fuller ("Bag" in the Yard, "Ap" in his own circle), for instance, a popular young philosophy lecturer, often attended Stylus meetings, and Henry's father, George Lyman Kittredge ("Kitty"), "seldom failed to turn up to scrutinize new members" at the Signet. Other professors who bothered to establish any personal liaison with their students outside the classroom were Santayana; Briggs, dean of the faculty of arts and science and teacher of English 5, an advanced composition/creative writing course; Charles Townsend Copeland ("Copey") of English 12 renown; Barrett Wendell, Shakespeare and American literature specialist; and the history department's Roger Merriman ("Frisky"), whom Biddle recollected as "ebullient and popular." Their humanity helped narrow the chilly gap between student body and staff that had hardened into a Harvard reflex.

Despite being underpaid—a full professor earned $4,000 per annum, which had been a factor in William James's original decision to popularize his theories—and looked down upon as provincial by Boston society, unless Bostonians themselves, the Harvard faculty was an extremely impressive lot in their intellect, achievement, reputation, and diverse personalities. Perhaps because of President Eliot's remoteness, the college's imitation of Oxford and Cambridge mores, and their own alumni status, faculty members were permitted a great measure of individual freedom, to the point that eccentricities, on and off the dais, were the norm. Brooks claimed that the professors "were actors often and characters all the time."

The English and philosophy departments were particularly well endowed with talent and larger-than-life personalities. Since his appointment as an instructor in physiology in August 1872, William James had put his indelible imprint of cosmopolitan openness upon the philosophy department and the college as a whole, not to mention his unique contribution to the forging of pragmatism, that most American of doctrines. Though forced by failing health to resign in February 1907, James "was still around," Aiken recalled, when he entered Harvard, "and you felt his presence very much." Initially expected by President Eliot simply to provide education in physiology and hygiene to the great unwashed undergraduate population, James had relentlessly expanded his and his department's scope over the years, a relatively painless process in an era when divisions among the social and physical sciences were ambiguous and psychology was in its infancy as an academic discipline. He also gathered together under his direction perhaps the finest, most varied group of philosophers ever concentrated in a single college, a staff that was, for all intents and purposes, the founding fathers of American philosophy. Its members extended from Santayana and Ap Fuller to Josiah Royce, George Herbert Palmer, and Hugo Münsterberg, the latter having been persuaded by the tireless chairman to leave Germany in 1892 to take charge of the psychological laboratory that James had established shortly before.

The eclectic character of the philosophy faculty was a testament to James's refusal to impose his personal dogmas on subordinates and his belief that students should be exposed to as wide a spectrum of ideas as plausible within the confines of academia. As he wrote in an April 2, 1900, letter to Palmer, after commenting on the recent "great event" in his life, reading Santayana's *Interpretations of Poetry and Religion,* "If our students now could begin really to understand what Royce means with his voluntaristic-pluralistic monism, what Münsterberg means with his dualistic scientificism and platonism, what Santayana means by his pessimistic platonism . . . what I mean by my crass pluralism, what you mean by your ethereal idealism, that these are so many religions, ways of fronting life, and worth fighting for, we should have a genuine philosophic universe at Harvard."

The ideational microcosm envisioned by James did exist for Harvard students in the first decades of the twentieth century, thanks to his labors, at least for that precious handful seriously curious about its complex manifestations. Biddle remembered that James and Bliss Perry, who taught comparative literature, "in their lectures gave us a sense of the unbounded domain of the intellect which most undergraduates distrust and avoid, and left us stirred with increased curiosity." The elective system, another of President Eliot's double-edged reforms, which gave students the opportunity to avoid the classics and follow their own inclinations "virtually unconcerned with anything that did not amuse" them, held sway, so that a professor's idiosyncratic classroom performance or the intrinsic abstruseness of his subject matter commonly determined the size of his course's registration rather than strict career and intellectual needs. Santayana's classes, for example, were repeatedly under-enrolled, smaller than seminars.

In lecture methods, none of the philosophy teachers could match the histrionics generated in Irving Babbitt's French classes or by certain notorious members of the English department. Ironically, they leaned far more toward formal presentations than Socratic dialogues. Royce had the habit of sitting "immovable" before his audience, his delivery "continuous, even, unfailing, composed," not unlike the quiet approach of the frail and nearsighted Palmer, whose course on ethics (Philosophy 4) was "one of the most famous and popular" on campus, or Santayana's low-keyed style of exposition. Biddle recalls: "Santayana was a seductive lecturer, but he was not easy to follow without rapt attention because his style was so exact, so elusively simple, his sentences so emptied of every unnecessary word, that if your attention wandered you were lost. The class was comparatively small, the interest and silence concentrated and expectant." To Aiken, in grateful retrospect, "Santayana was the real excitement for me at Harvard," a view shared, no doubt, by many of the more sensitive undergraduates. *The Sense of Beauty* (1896) was almost a required text for the literary clubs and student publication staffs.

Since his own undergraduate days in the years between 1883 and 1887,

Santayana had always been Harvard's "odd man out," the eternal alien (Spanish on his father's side) in thinking and behavior, which was the source of his main strengths and weaknesses. He adopted an attitude of proud satisfaction toward his rebel stance, though it probably had behind it the defiant anhedonia of a rejected child: "I had disregarded or defied public opinion by not becoming a specialist, by writing pessimistic, old-fashioned verses, continuing to range superficially over literature and philosophy, being indiscernibly a Catholic or an atheist, attacking Robert Browning, prophet of the half-educated and half-believing, avoiding administrative duties, neglecting the intelligentsia, frequenting the society of undergraduates and fashionable ladies, spending holidays abroad." His delight in opposition, in a witty detachment from passionate extremes and current pieties, made him an invaluable antidote to both the school's Anglo-Saxon bias (excepting its beloved Dante) and yearning backward glances at Elizabethan England and its students' necessarily antithetical enthusiasm for the French Romanticism of Baudelaire and Rimbaud and Kipling's muscular neorealism. Even Brooks, who would link Santayana to Eliot and Babbitt as chief authors of a dangerously aristocratic and reactionary surge in early modern literature, "could not deny that, wandering alone, a stranger and exile everywhere, Santayana lived the true life of the sage."

For Aiken, who was to take two years of philosophy at Harvard, mostly with Santayana, the impact of this lizard-tongued sage was potent and lasting, if unavoidably more conceptual than technical: "Santayana was a philosopher without a philosophy. He was a skeptic, a critic of philosophy, and a poet of course, and a wonderful preacher—marvelous teacher. And I think it was his lectures on Goethe that most influenced me in the direction of becoming deliberately a philosophic poet. He himself stressed the value of the philosophic poet as providing a greater height from which to see things, and a great space in which to spread them." It was the Platonist who gently urged, "Let us live in the mind," not the poet who had smugly, perhaps sardonically, announced, "We poets at Harvard never read anything written in America except our own compositions," who was to help shape Aiken's mature aesthetic, its meditative bias and focus on consciousness as lyric means and end, the philosopher whose definition of "animal faith" would be seen by a much older Aiken as a fit analogy for his own mythless, Kantian notion of religion. The course mentioned by Aiken was Philosophy 6, a half-year class on Lucretius, Dante, and Goethe, the materials from which Santayana would mint *Three Philosophical Poets* (1910)—as essential to Aiken as Arthur Symons's *The Symbolist Movement in Literature* was to Eliot.

Whether philosophy or poetry, the books that Santayana produced were but a trickle in the veritable stream being unleashed on Cambridge and its environs by creative faculty members. Significantly, many of these were not the texts and discipline tracts anticipated from thrifty professionals; they were, instead, authentic efforts at original composition. As Brooks observed, "All the professors, whatever their specialties might be, seemed to be in addition men of letters." Besides its pedagogical contributions, the philosophy department also displayed a catholic willingness to thicken further the college's dense literary atmosphere. Josiah Royce had once written a forgettable (now forgotten) novel; Münsterberg published a collection of poems in the late 1890s under the name of Hugo Terberg; George Herbert Palmer translated *The Odyssey* and put together a definitive edition of his namesake's poetry; and Santayana continued to manufacture his passionless but surefooted sonnets with fair regularity.

The English department was peculiarly remiss in producing literary works, though Barrett Wendell had committed two novels before *Cotton Mather: The Puritan Priest* (1891), *William Shakespeare: A Study in Elizabethan Literature* (1894), and *A Literary History of America* (1900), his critical magnum opus, which would achieve a fifth edition by 1909. Wendell, who taught American literature as a semester course, epitomized his department's paradoxical mix of scholarship, personal dedication, professional conservatism, and highly individualistic classroom demeanor. His attitude toward American literature, condescending but not without shrewd strokes of discernment, invariably encompassed invidious comparisons with England's superior output, reflecting a schoolwide contempt for the present tense and clime. According to Biddle, Wendell's lectures were punctuated by his "mourning the onrush of the Socialists who were destroying the values with which Bostonians, he insisted, had endowed the country."

As a teacher, Wendell gave the impression of a stage Englishman, his manner nervous, his voice high-pitched, his mood excitable, as he cataloged the vices of the contemporary scene and the virtues of Elizabeth's immortal age in language extravagant enough to qualify as Elizabethan or wandered, with equal confidence, into foreign territory. Amy Lowell had the unfortunate experience of auditing his Shakespeare course in the early 1890s, an experience that left her less than overwhelmed: "We learned everything about the plays . . . except the things that mattered. Not once . . . were we bidden to notice the poetry." If he had ever learned of her reaction, Wendell would have merely been confirmed in his conviction that women did not belong at Harvard, that their presence was too distracting to the undergraduates. When the college announced that additional classes would be open to coeds in 1899, he had protested vehemently, arguing that a "purely virile" environment was a prerequisite for serious education.

At the other end of the departmental scale was Charles Townsend Copeland, who, like Wendell, believed in personal contact with his students, but who, unlike Wendell, suffered a lack of respect from the administration, which looked askance at his past as a newspaper critic and his stubborn refusal to write learned treatises. More damaging, beyond not having the foresight to have been born in Boston, Copeland let his relations with undergraduates become too familiar for official approval. He had the habit, not dissimilar from that practiced at Oxford and Cambridge, of drawing a circle of disciples around him: "Every Saturday night, in his chambers in Hollis Hall, he held get-togethers with himself seated in an armchair in front of the fire and his students sitting on the floor around him. He pleaded the cause of literary art, read approvingly or contemptuously from a wide range of literature, and listened to his students read from manuscripts of their own composition." To journalistic students Reed and Broun, Copey was a welcome lifeboat in their struggling passage to successful magazine careers, a vigorous exponent of "that lean, sinewy quality which distinguished American prose from its English ancestry."

A "small, waspish, and bitterly witty man," Copeland emulated and frequently exceeded his colleagues' zest for classroom dramatics and acid epigrams, as in his assault upon fornication: "The sensation is momentary, and the position ridiculous." Students with a more literary inclination (and more social assurance) were critical of the shallowness they detected under Copeland's Chesterton-carved façade. After bemoaning the shabby treatment accorded Copey "by the university to which he devoted a life of admirable teaching," Biddle admits that his own visit to Hollis Hall to drink chocolate with the professor was uninspiring: "I thought him stuffy and affected, and did not return after my first experience." Brooks, too, followed by Eliot and John Dos Passos, responded negatively to Copeland's theatrical techniques and rigid prose formula, his emphasis on locating the correct phrase, a Kiplingesque vividness and the like, judging him "wilful and stubborn."

In his memoir Santayana, who was rarely benevolent toward colleagues, painted Copeland with cool severity: "An artist rather than a scholar, he was a public reader by profession, an elocutionist; he could move his audiences by declaring, with disciplined voice and restrained emotion, all the most touching or thrilling popular selections from the Bible to Kipling." Of greater import, Santayana recognized his colleague's singular benignity to the "forlorn and disinherited" among the students, which lessens, to a degree, the stringency of Brooks's charge that Copeland surrounded himself with "good-looking" apostles, favoring surface over substance. In any event, he stimulated "countless students in and out of class," as Biddle concedes, and it is hard not to admire a man who rejoiced in having eluded the "Ph.D. death rattle."

Politically, Copeland betrayed his cherished credo of iconoclastic realism by lining up on the "right" side of the tracks with the bulk of his department in deploring liberal causes, as if they presaged Visigoth hordes battering down Harvard gates. This attitude might have contributed, in a minor way, to Aiken's own tart dismissal of the Copeland magic. Having long heard about Copey and his exciting English 12 workshop, he was determined to enter the class as soon as possible and managed to sneak in despite his freshman status. The consequent disappointment was near total: "Pyrotechnics and show-manship tried to make up for genius, as if they ever could." It may have been an instance of steel arrogance versus steel ego. "Brilliant reader, not a pro-found teacher. Vain," was the ultimate verdict of the impatient Aiken, who resented Copeland's endeavors to "impose a kind of pattern of his own on you—the choice of the right French word, that sort of thing." At year's end, sensing his pupil's dissatisfaction, the professor asked, "Do you think this course has benefitted you?" Caught off guard, the unhappy freshman replied, "Well, it has made me write often." Copeland could only rejoin, "Aiken, you're a very *dry* young man."

The teacher whom the students seemed to have unanimously esteemed was Le Baron Russell Briggs. Elevated to "seraph" in *Ushant,* Dean Briggs was the genuine article, neither a failed writer using his position as an ego prop nor an abstracted scholar at rest upon his economic base, but a teacher who viewed his profession as the raison d'être of his busy days, having devoted several books to the subject and taken on additional duties as part-time presi-dent of Radcliffe in 1903. Although his English 5 writing class, as celebrated as Copey's English 12, was too advanced for even Aiken to penetrate before his junior year, Briggs also taught a freshman course in eighteenth-century English literature. Aiken's affection for Briggs went deep, suggesting a desire for a father substitute. His thumbnail sketch vibrates with the energy of an adoring eye—"tall and a little shabby, chalk-marks on the back of his jacket, from his habit of leaning against the black-board, smiled with all the wrinkles of that homely but beautiful face."

Brooks and Biddle also fell under Briggs's spell, Brooks recalling his habit of quoting Donne to freshmen, his familiarity with and sustained feeling for Donne as the poet "who preeminently 'made the far-fetched worth fetch-ing.'" It was through Briggs that T. S. Eliot discovered Donne, a prime liter-ary and religious model, and Lyndall Gordon, the most persuasive interpreter of Eliot's Harvard years, has affirmed that two teachers alone "broke into his private world and touched a responsive growth: Irving Babbitt who helped him to become truly cultivated and Dean Briggs." Several years later Dos Passos was similarly enchanted. Briggs, he said, "had an old-fashioned schoolmaster's concern for the neatness of the language, a Yankee zest for the shipshape phrase, an old-fashioned expression, and a sharp nose for sham and pretense which was neither old nor new fashioned but eternally to the point."

Kittridge, who taught Shakespeare during Aiken's first semester and would encounter him at the Signet, was in the same mold, if never as popular as Briggs. With his ubiquitous cigar and air of stern reserve, backed by an omnivorous set of literary references, "Kitty" was another native Bostonian and Harvard alumnus who felt at supreme peace with his vocation and environs and who enjoyed carrying his eccentricities to their humorous extreme, a slender, gray-suited, white-bearded, quick-stepping figure around whom anecdotal legends accumulated like cotton candy. Brooks tells of the time Kittridge tumbled off the dais and immediately cracked, "At last I find myself on the level of my audience."

Bliss Perry, former professor at Williams and Princeton and editor of the staid *Atlantic Monthly* since 1899, could not have been more different in temperament and outlook from departmental colleagues than he was. Serene and cheerful, he appeared immune to the Puritan pessimism and passive detachment of Henry Adams's and Harvard's condemnation of the new age's mechanical tastelessness. His sunny vision, perhaps because nurtured elsewhere, remained limited, if sane, and he himself a somewhat distant but benevolent personage to the undergraduates in his well-attended classes.

Distinguished faculty members from other departments who aided in creating and maintaining the fertile intellectual milieu of Aiken's Harvard were Frederick Jackson Turner, commanding historian of the American West, who would arrive in 1910; Edward Kennard Rand in the classics, a favorite of Brooks and translator of Boethius; Abbott Lawrence Lowell, Amy's brother, originator of a unique "Government" course; Frank William Taussig, author of the widely respected *Tariff History of the United States* (1896) and editor of the *Quarterly Journal of Economics;* and Eliot's high priest, Irving Babbitt, the French department's scorcher of liberalism in life and literature, architect of the "new humanism," a "curiously inhuman" doctrine that was "all for authority and formalistic discipline as against the Jeffersonian vision he connected with Rousseau."

In apparent perpetual revolt against his father, an Ohio doctor who had been zealously radical in precepts and choice of friends, the influential Babbitt brought to a frantic pitch Harvard's elitist rejection of the impure modern world and modern literature, its distaste for experimentalism in the arts and liberal political ideologies. Like Copeland and Wendell, he perceived his country as in imminent peril of sinking under a flood of decadent, anarchistic ideas from abroad. With missionary fervor, Babbitt strove to reverse the Romantic revolution birthed by Rousseau and smuggled into England by Blake and Coleridge, where it seemed exploited beyond the bounds of decency by the corrupt Keats, Shelley, and Byron. However typical of the college's conservative stance, Babbitt was *sui generis*. Abetted by an encyclopedic memory and imposing manner and platform presence, he declared himself the implacable enemy of subjectivity in any form, of sentimentalism and thoughtless emotionalism, which included naturalism and its offshoots because they too tended to stress content over technique.

Paradoxically, Babbitt's civilized humanism, the watchwords of which were "decorum—restraint—the will to refrain," was defended by its founder in the classroom with all the partisan fanaticism of the most excessive Romantic. Brooks, who appreciated the brilliance of his teaching even though sweeping aside his credo, has recorded a common Babbitt performance as "tossing and goring the writers he disliked." He described Babbitt as "another Dr. Johnson in his grunts, blowings and gurgitations, roaring his opponents down, harsh and abrupt in manner and voice." Brooks also found him "as indifferent to novelists and novel-writing as to painting and to music," but had to throw him a memorial salute for having introduced him and many others to "the writings of Renan, Taine and, above all, Sainte-Beuve."

Aiken was impervious to the Babbitt doctrine and could not have taken kindly to an authoritarian personality so intent upon dominating his listeners. More relevant, Aiken's favorite authors, commencing with Poe and excluding the Elizabethans, were nineteenth-century Romantics and Victorians, ranging from Keats ("probably the most lasting influence on me . . . which was a pretty deep poison for many years") to Browning ("very, very much"), Tennyson, Arnold, and Francis Thompson, logical extensions, in his mind, of the lyrical impulse first ignited in Savannah and fanned by Poe and by such Cambridge idols as Longfellow. The poems he had published in the *Advocate* and *Monthly* during his freshman year are heavily indebted to these poets for much of their language, themes, and technical mannerisms. "The Wind," which appeared in the *Advocate* a mere month after his arrival on campus, largely due to the editorial liaison arranged the year before by Harold, is a solid case in point:

> How sad it whispered about the door,
>   Like a little child lost in the dark of night!
> Whimpering low to itself, and anon
>   Pattering round with feet so light,—
> Running its fingers along the walls,
>   Feeling in fear for the door of Light!
> Till at last, as the clock struck the midnight twelve,
>   With a little cry of last despair

> It fell in a huddled heap on the floor,
>   And buried its face in its tangled hair;
> And quick little sobs seemed to shake at the door
>   Like the faltering words of a child's first prayer.

Obviously appealing to a sense of lostness and homelessness that reverberated with special force for Aiken, the poem's central personification, wind as "a little child," is a clever stroke, if hackneyed and sentimental. The feel of Poe is strong here, and "The Wind" would have been at home in any nineteenth-century anthology. Smooth and professional, it evinces Aiken's already developed talent for operating comfortably inside traditional forms, the twelve lines internally structured into two sestets, which are reinforced by their rhyme schemes, as pervasive alliterations mimic wind sounds throughout.

A topical poem, "The Spirit of Christmas Eve," for the December *Advocate* is a playful piece of occasional verse cloyingly suited to the child-spoken season that must climax in formula heartiness:

> Then here's to the Spirit of Christmas Eve—
> With warm good-will, and the eyes that gleam,—
> The god of cheer and the Christmas dream—
> A toast to the Spirit of Christmas Eve!

If nothing else, the poem is a reminder that Aiken began his heavy drinking at Harvard and bore his adolescent love of Christmas into adulthood like a sacramental talisman of absent family life.

"Autumn," Aiken's sole contribution to the *Monthly* for the year, phrases its Keatsian theme in the stilted language and spent imagery that had come to epitomize Romanticism's attenuated realm of petrified, prettified nature— "the rugged upland," a cricket making "music faint and shrill," some implacable "silvery mist." It searches, in the first of two stanzas, for Pan to arrive and "sing the world to rest!" The second stanza is not much better but offers a brief glimpse, again, at the obsession with allegorizing a melancholy child figure:

> Did I hear a plaintive piping
>   Far up on the stark hillside?
> Did I hear a little sobbing sound,
>   Or was it a child that cried?
> A figure moved in the moonlight,
>   A gay little laugh, wind-flung,
> Rang echoing on the frosty night—
>   Answering, Pan had sung!

Though perhaps not so intended, this precious exercise can be read as an exuberant reply to that ancient Greek in Petrarch's tale who learned from Egypt's dark shore that Pan was dead, absorbed by crafty Christian dogma. It intimates the way in which Pre-Raphaelite imitations, screened through Romantic fathers, often preserved classical structures as ivory tower retreats from unpleasant modern truths. The 1890s, when undergraduates had first cultivated "that mixture of wit, exquisiteness, and boredom" which heralded a Harvard trademark, were alive and flourishing among Aiken and his school contemporaries, who were dedicated to burning with gemlike flames at the altar of art.

In "Francois Villon," Aiken used (and misused) Browning's dramatic monologue to reassert the artist as saint, as priest, as society's nonconformist hero of beauty. Villon is presented awake beside a drunken, sleeping companion, nagged at by the "bitter cold" and snow. His pockets are empty, and the walls around him, "So desolate, so bare," at least do not mock him with a "laugh of silver." What to do but "mill a verse" for Christmas? Sleep ends the night and the sentimental poem:

> O sleepy, sleepy eyes! Will verses keep?
>> Aye, think of roast-fowl, then,—Lights! Christmas spread!
>> Ah, what a vision! (*Smiles—nods low his head*)
> O! Verse, d' I say? Aye—(*murmuring, falls asleep*).

However saccharine, "Francois Villon" emphasizes Aiken's youthful commitment to a deification of the artist (replacement for lost religious energies) and is the initial indication of his subsequent discovery of Browning's worth as a viable means for moving poetic language closer to the vernacular.

This deification locates a more effective voice, that of Matthew Arnold, in "The Potter," the strongest, least cluttered poem written during his freshman year. Its relative success might derive, in part, from the pun upon his grandfather's name. He was officially Conrad Potter Aiken, a third name being almost mandatory at class-conscious Harvard, and signed all his college work as C. P. Aiken, which permitted the divinity of the artist/potter to incorporate his own persona more directly. It was a minor point, to be sure, but the sort of self-dramatization encouraged by an aesthetic planted in the Pater-Santayana matrix of sacred artisans. The opening lines, which deftly erect a basic iambic meter and quiet mood of step-by-step accretions, presage a fairy-tale economy: "With fingers white, the potter smoothed his clay / And set his pots in order on the shelf."

The fragile products of the potter's careful, contented labors invariably experience widely divergent fates, bearing "blossoms gay" or choking "cobwebs" or a "spark" or simply "shattering" at birth. The second stanza, a sestet to the previous stanza's octave, projects something of a sonnet's corpus in its curve away from semirealistic detail and into the Arnoldian region of Greece-shadowed allegory:

> And thus, beside a still and twilit sea,
>> Or on the shore, beneath the watching stars,
>> Bends the Great Potter over sea-gnawed clays;
> Toiling, alone in gray infinity,
> He shapes the frail-walled souls of men, or mars,—
>> And breathes in every cup a moment's blaze.

Albeit indebted to clichés and forced rhymes, an allegiance to the nineteenth century's poetic *zeitgeist*, "The Potter" still manages to demonstrate Aiken's firm grasp of basic verse principles. Its iambic line is varied by several line-commencing dactyls, its Keatsian compounds saved for the climax and doubling as sound effects ("sea-gnawed" and "frail-walled") to complement the assonance ("shore," "alone," "shapes," "breathes") that stresses the poem's hushed atmosphere. In addition, the organic emergence of a summary "moment's blaze" neatly echoes and enlarges earlier references to those pots, serving as censers, which "conceived a spark."

At the notional level a dialogue between Aiken and Arnold is implied in which the former seems to accept the bleak message of the latter's "Dover Beach"—that the age of faith is indeed over, the modern world naught but "a darkling plain"—while also offering a more modest, stationary artificer than "The Scholar Gipsy." Though hardly a permanent poem, "The Potter" convincingly betrays a growing control of manner and means and is another exhibition of the influence Harvard's aestheticism was exerting on Aiken, positive and negative. Culture is a rarefied, artificial sharing of inherited classical allusions and attitudes in "The Potter" and these other freshman compositions, couched in the diction of a mandarin sensibility, but the discipline of mastering traditional techniques, in conjunction with the focus on the magnified responsibility of the creative spirit in a world bereft of certitudes, was leading Aiken into a dawning comprehension of his craft's demand for verities of self and *res*. In time would come the understanding that the huge vacuum left behind by the loss of faith and the consequent evolution of poet into godhead, which paralleled a personal psychological situation since the trauma at Savannah, must sooner or later entail an examination of self *as* self, consciousness in reflexive flight.

For now, the wrestle was with the mundane public problem of writing poems that sounded and looked competent, that is, sounded and looked like the poetry written by pale descendants of Keats, Shelley, and Victorian offspring. A prime specimen is "Sunrise," which can be quoted whole:

> The silence of night is stirred from the sky,
> > And, blinking, the stars pale away, one by one;
> Life turns in its bed with a wakening sigh—
> > Earth raises her head; is the weary night done?
> Arise! For the day comes faster, more fast,
> > Like a song bursting silence, a smile in the eye—
> A whisper! And lo, the darkness has passed;
> > A finger of light feels the sky.

Except for the trace of an erotic undercurrent in the last line, also founded on a derivative image, the entire poem lacks originality in metrics and imagination.

Aiken, however, like innumerable novices before him, had resigned himself to the concept of assaulting his Muse with brutal regularity. "I compelled myself all through to write an exercise in verse, in a different form, every day of the year. I turned out my page everyday, of some sort—I mean I didn't give a damn about the meaning. I just wanted to master the form." When added to the writing already being done for Copeland in English 12 and elsewhere, these exercises were bound to flag in inspiration, to ape the writers surfacing amid the flotsam of an intelligence busily engaged (in and out of class) with expanding its literary horizons. "I wasn't much of a student," Aiken would remember, "but my casual reading was enormous."

"Wireless Messages," last of the published freshman poems, shows how perplexing (and essential) it was to weld a nineteenth-century style to the technological phenomena increasingly intruding upon contemporary consciousness. Intrigued by the miracle of Marconi's communication system, Aiken's thoroughly American imagination glibly transformed the invisible signals into "wings of thought" but caged them with an outmoded language:

> We slip betwixt the continents,
> > We pour across the world;
> Swifter than meteor's hot-breathed rush,
> > Or bolted lightning hurled;
> High, high, above the shrunken earth
> > We soar and float and glide,
> Whispering down the truths of men
> > To listeners far and wide.

The rest is a very astute, frequently inventive manipulation of the governing conceit in similarly Romantic terms, climaxing in an italicized apostrophe, which repeats the first stanza's pattern:

Brothers we are to the night,—
Falling, again we rise;
Brothers we are to the whirlwind
That blasts and sweeps the skies;
Brothers we are to the dawn—
Swift to the sky it springs;
Children we are of destiny—
We whisper the truth it brings!

Of such indigestible olios are undergraduate magazines composed, and to view them as more than apprentice dips into a learned sublime would be to miss their point and charm.

Whatever their objective weight, the poems were of inestimable assistance to Aiken's psyche. That feeling of isolated alienation, of being different to the extent of painful self-consciousness, which had shadowed his Middlesex days, was considerably relieved by his immediate acceptance as a poet worth publishing. The mantle of authorship, he discovered early, was a sign of divine election at an establishment where literature set the tone, and Harvard's rampant exclusiveness was no bar to his adjustment to college life. He had been writing, of course, before the tragedy of his parents' deaths, "was in orbit, so to speak," from childhood's later years, but devotion to his vocation was beginning to acquire more concrete value "because I could take pride in it, and it made me friends, particularly at Harvard."

Despite his shyness and his abhorrence of most formal group activities, which did not prevent him from taking Barbara to several dances and football and baseball games, access to the *Advocate* and the two literary clubs generated a widening circle of friends among the school's intelligentsia. The latter, a vague coterie of the high-minded, distinguished itself sharply from the social elite associated with the expensive dormitories located along Mt. Auburn Street, known as "the gold coast," where maintaining a gentlemanly C average with minimum effort and getting selected by one of the "final clubs"— Porcellian, Fly, and Dicky—were major concerns. Aside from Middlesex comrades, several of whom were being phased out of his life, and casual intimacy with Wheelock and Biddle, whom he did not really like, the friends Aiken made his first year at Harvard were usually chosen with care, deliberately pursued not only for their compatible personalities and common interest in things cultural but for their potential as sources of future aid and comfort. In *Ushant* he speaks candidly about "a selective shedding of friends . . . that had not always done him credit" (145).

Aiken's Harvard relationships were not, of course, solely motivated by calculation and expedience. Human nature and the normal academic situation of undergraduates thrown together in a random mass—less random in a scholastic enterprise ruled over by free elective procedures and an undemocratic club system—inevitably conspired to bring about accidental acquaintanceships. Some, as that with Harry Wehle, were bound to mature into deeper ties; others evaporated at graduation. In the last category might fit a huge undergraduate from San Francisco named Otis McAllister, a disciple of Eastern thought who claimed to have developed extraordinary intuitive powers via its meditative processes. Intrigued in spite of himself, Aiken listened for hours as McAllister elaborated on the Indian theory of reincarnation, which entailed (in his version) spending the thousand years between each human spell on earth inside a series of multicolored purgatories that pointed toward paradise's perfect white light. It was serious business to McAllister but much less so to Aiken, who retained a Darwinian faith in the "blind physical laws of a senseless Nature" and would delight in his campus designation as a "cheerful pessimist," the tag later applied by classmate Myron Williams.

Naturally, the new friends who were crucial to him were those students who fed an increasing hunger for mastery of his art, who seemed to own the subtle recipes of thought and expression that synthesized his era's cultural inheritance. These included Wehle, known as "Silk Hat" Harry ("Heinrich" in *Ushant*), native Kentuckian and nephew of Louis Brandeis, "whose love of music and painting . . . first aroused in him a curiosity about those arts" (144), and William Tinckom-Fernandez (*Ushant's* "Tinck"), aspiring writer from an Anglo-Indian background, frequent lively presence at *Advocate* conferences and punches, and one of the few with whom Aiken exchanged poems and stories.

Another important companion, first of Aiken's new friends at Harvard, was Paul Mariett, "the genius of his time" at the school (144). A product of Phillips Exeter Academy, where he had won a senior composition award and the Marshall Newell and Prentiss Cummings prizes, Mariett projected a striking combination of physical and intellectual vigor. Walter Lippmann, who knew him well, evoked his vivid personality in an introduction to *The Poems of Paul Mariett:* "Paul enjoyed life. He had, it seemed, no listless pleasures. When he ate it was with tremendous relish; a book was something to be attacked and beaten till he had subordinated it. . . . Languages, Paul seemed to learn with no trouble at all. . . . With his music, and his languages and literatures, he was a peculiarly learned undergraduate." Aiken recalled Mariett improvising "Debussian variations on the dark piano in the dark corner" of the Signet's reading room (134).

But without doubt, the student destined to exert the greatest impact upon Aiken's life and career was Thomas Stearns Eliot of St. Louis ("Tsetse" in

Ushant acid), whom he encountered near the end of his second semester. Casting a bemused eye back at that momentous meeting in later years, Aiken would describe Eliot with mingled affection and lingering reserve as "a singularly attractive, tall, and rather dapper young man, with a somewhat Lamian smile" (the apt last adjective did not sit well with its punctilious victim). Eliot was already a sophomore but not yet a member of the *Advocate* staff, though familiar with many of the magazine's members and contributors, and the casual introduction occurred outside the *Advocate* offices on the top floor of the Union Building. A punch was being served at the nearby *Lampoon* office, and Eliot came reeling drunkenly out into the corridor as Aiken and Wehle were passing on their way to the *Advocate*, which had recently sent Aiken his "shingle," notification of election to its board. Catching sight of the handsome, smiling, red-haired stranger, Eliot immediately embraced him in an uncharacteristic gesture of goodwill. Well aware of Eliot's inveterate disdain of emotional display, Wehle remarked, "And that, if Tom remembers tomorrow, will cause him to suffer agonies of shyness."

Extreme shyness was indeed a quality both young men possessed in generous measures—the breathless self-consciousness often magnified by sensitivity and enormous, albeit insecure, egos—but Eliot's method of combating its deleterious social effects was a bit different from Aiken's habitual retreats into the company of a few select souls and tentative forays into larger gatherings with Barbara. Afraid of missing "varieties of experience" that might prove useful, however distasteful or frivolous, Eliot went out of his way to adopt the superficially correct behavior of Harvard's upper crust, rooming on the gold coast, becoming a thorough clubman, attending the countless balls and teas and punches thrown by the college or by Boston's busy social matrons for undergraduates with the right connections. It was, of course, easy for him to experiment thus because his family credentials, originally New England, were impeccable. Relative of President Eliot and grandson of John Greenleaf Eliot, financial genius and Unitarian minister of note, Eliot was deemed proper enough to be invited anywhere.

In her otherwise perceptive study of his maturation process, Lyndall Gordon concludes that Eliot had been gifted with "a remarkably happy childhood," an absurd judgment that probably owes more to a lack of contrary information than to corroboration. The exterior serenity of Eliot's formative years should not obscure what their sad consequences—a highly repressed and infantile personality with a possible homosexual component, prickly sadomasochistic defense mechanisms, and the constant threat (eventually realized) of nervous breakdown under the weight of a severe identity crisis—intimate about hidden psychological damage. The youngest of seven children, the "baby" of the family, Eliot was doted upon by his adored mother, wor-

shiper of Emerson and cheerfully didactic poet, who shielded him from all
activity because of his delicate physical condition, the result of a congenital
double hernia (perhaps a touchstone childhood wound, literal and symbolic,
which festered into the prepubic obsession with and revulsion from death
and decay that permeated Eliot's vision). And his father, who must have endured much frustration squatting under the umbrella shadow of his own father's success, appears to have been more absent than not in a biographical
context; his name rarely surfaces. In an unpublished memoir, Henry Ware
Eliot rails against the idea of sex education for the young and piously hopes
that a cure for syphilis, God's most efficient weapon against sins of the flesh,
is never found or it might become necessary to "emasculate our children to
keep them clean."

Aiken's brief initial contacts with Tom Eliot in the short time before summer recess, which entailed a few shared meals at Memorial Hall and discussions at the Signet house or in the *Advocate* offices, were generally literary in
tone and substance. Eliot and he talked mostly about the poems they had
written or were writing, the authors they most admired, and the dreadful state
of modern literature in America. Eliot passed on his tip about fighting fire with
fire in the social sphere, conceding a common problem with shyness, and the
friendship was launched, though Eliot's reserve held firm. From Aiken's vantage, another invaluable ally had been recruited for the determined campaign
to explore the terrain of his chosen profession and to assert his identity as a
writer of distinct promise and seriousness in a fiercely competitive battle zone.
He could, almost at once, appreciate the original mind and self-confident
drive at work behind Eliot's erudite remoteness, the prim mask worn to protect a wary and vulnerable sensibility.

Aiken's public advances during his freshman year were enhanced by a
steady improvement in his relationship with his grandmother, Emily Akin, at
whose small Watertown house he was welcomed with increasing frequency.
More important, their new closeness encouraged her to restore Dr. Aiken's
image in his eager eyes, as she permitted him to peruse his father's written and
photographic remains, the leather envelope of pictures, poems, essays, and
letters from Savannah she had lovingly preserved. The "portfolio of writings," which he secretly studied when his grandmother went shopping,
proved central to a shared desire to rehabilitate the man Aiken still blamed for
the loss of his mother and still yearned to please.

In *Ushant* the alliance with his grandmother to restore Dr. Aiken's tarnished
genius, which presumably covered several years, culminates in his discovery
while at Harvard that "the staining sense of guilt and shame had been myste-
riously exorcised, was no longer there" (103), and that "now he could bring
his friends here from Harvard—the Old Bird first, as obviously and always

the most understanding" (106). The truth is here, a finding of a second home with his grandmother and an identification with Dr. Aiken, especially "the taking over of the father's role as a writer," which was complemented by the knowledge that his great-grandmother Potter had also written poems (107). But the undoubted relief garnered from resurrecting his father's image, restoring an ideal other self, and sanctifying his persona as writer in a family hierarchy did not, could not, alleviate the major neurotic anxieties undermining his identity quest because it did not encompass any similar effort at rehabilitating his mother.

Instead, as narrated in *Ushant,* the identification and overt competition with his father's ghost—a healthy psychological impulse—actually entailed another denial of Anna Aiken's reality, another assault upon her integrity. Inspecting his face in a mirror, comparing it to the sepia photographs of his father, Aiken saw (or thought he saw) that the paternal "character had simply been softened, and sensualized," by the Potter inheritance (106). To complete his transformation into Dr. Aiken's replacement and eventual superior, he practiced a deliberate tightening of mouth muscles until "the young face . . . had deliberately stiffened its upper lip, and learned how to mask itself as that of the father. He had acquired not only a second character, but a protective disguise as well" (107)—numerous people would testify to the "impassiveness" of his features. Besides representing a further rejection of the mother, the adoption of the father's visage took no cognizance of the intense hostile feelings he had long harbored against Dr. Aiken, beyond admitting to a normal rivalry.

In general, however, the changed perception of Emily Aken and her tragic offspring was a positive element in Aiken's maturation, gave added support to his choice of a poetic career, and reinforced his sense of the freshman experience as a giant step forward in his search for a viable self. A series of playful letters to Barbara Leighton has survived, and though many are undated, they provide several instructive glimpses into his social evolution. A number of them deal with various rendezvous arrangements, usually to attend a ball game. Despite his shyness, which could cause him to lapse into an embarrassing silence when confronted by Barbara's mother or a stranger, he did ask Barbara to various dances, once begging her to teach him the "Boston," a local variation on the waltz. Occasionally they were accompanied by Thomas McCabe and Ruth McIntyre, although some letters hint at an undercurrent of contempt in Aiken's attitude toward the latter pair—he apologizes at one point for referring to them as "Platonic Ruth" and "Laconic Tom." Apologies, in fact, are a familiar theme in the correspondence, indicating a tendency to strike out verbally at her friends and her Victorian notions of propriety.

As for sex, it must be assumed that Aiken had to depend upon masturbation and wet dreams, considering the rigid code of their time and place, particularly since Barbara was several years younger than he and still a student at Miss Winsor's. More relevant, his girlfriend was at least introducing him to the mating rituals of middle-class and college society, and he was proud to have an attractive female at his side when attending Harvard functions. In one letter he speaks discouragingly about having to take his sister Elizabeth, who would visit him in June, to a baseball game but concedes it was better than going in the company of a male.

Other aspects of Aiken's first year can be gleaned from the autobiographical *Great Circle,* which suggests that he attended freshman coffee parties at the very dancing school in Cambridge where he had been sent by the Tillinghasts earlier and that he entered the Institute of 1778, the large first club from which the final clubs drew their members, as an "honorary." There is one telling admission of the loneliness that could seize him, an allusion to his solitary room at Grays Hall: "In that lighted room up there, as a freshman, I carved my initials in the window sill, meanwhile saying over and over to myself, *'tu pupila es azul, y quando lloras.'* " In spite of such moments and whatever qualms he had about shedding certain Middlesex friends, he was elated by the prospect of spending the summer in England, "Ariel's island," his first trip abroad. Better yet was the satisfaction of knowing the year at Harvard had lived up to expectations, that "step by precarious step, from the illegal entry into Copey's English 12 to the printing of the first bad poem in the *Monthly,* it had all come about as planned" (144).

For a sensitive young man with some knowledge of American literature, a maiden voyage to England would be an exciting stroke of good fortune. For a sensitive young man with considerable knowledge of American and English literature, an impelling desire to write, and a year spent among Harvard's rabid Anglophiles, such a voyage could be nothing less than a cherished fantasy brought to fruition. Aiken's plan was to spend as large a chunk of each summer vacation as possible away from the Tillinghast domicile. For the first expedition he intended to familiarize himself with the rustic splendors of the Lake District, favorite stomping grounds and lyric haven from urban corruption for Wordsworth, Coleridge, and other poets near his heart, then head north into Scotland. London must wait for next year.

Before that, however, certain social amenities had to be observed. At the school year's end, it was traditional for Harvard seniors to give little parties or "spreads" for relatives and friends, usually at a Boston hotel, if financially feasible. The Taylor family came into town for a weekend to grace the spreads of Edward Clark (a Taylor cousin) and Harold Tillinghast, with Aiken naturally attending the latter's. Since the Taylors had an entire weekend at their disposal, Aiken asked for and secured permission to take his brother Robert, now age thirteen, on a trip to Concord to tour the grounds of Middlesex. Many decades later Robert could no longer remember details of the incident, including his brother's reaction to the tranquil pastoral scenes of so much recent misery and joy, but that Aiken took him there at all suggests a need to confirm that the past was indeed past, that a difficult period of adjustment had been transcended. Perhaps he found a sense of peace with himself, along with the prosaic awareness that childhood settings are always much smaller than recollected, though he never forgave or forgot either the school or the headmaster for their violation of his naive dependence upon them as home and parental replacements.

In any case, the sea beckoned like a mother, as did Ariel's siren island, another maternal analog destined to coddle and rebuff him with equal power. It was July 11, 1908, at six in the morning, when he and a classmate named Ernest Oberholzer ("Ebo") arrived in Quebec after a wearying train ride and boarded the S.S. *Empress of Great Britain.* They were given an inside room for four on the fourth deck, one deck above steerage, but a dollar tip to the steward got them switched to a comfortable outside (porthole) room for two on the same deck. The ship sailed at four in the afternoon, permitting them to explore the city first, which proved disappointing, except for a swim in the St. Lawrence. Despite fog and occasional slowdowns caused by icebergs, the voyage proved smooth and pleasant, as well as exotic, once the young men became familiar with the wide variety of human types and nationalities clustered together in the lower decks. One day Oberholzer, a talented musician, played his violin on the lower deck with cheerful abandon, drawing an admiring audience of first-class passengers above, who threw coins down to him during the performance. Embarrassed and angry, he gathered up the coins and gave them to two deck boys, which endeared him to the steerage crowd below. Aiken was surprised by the cleanliness of his fellow passengers, particularly a contingent of Swedes, and intrigued by their diversity, ranging from a tall Hindu seeking an audience with the king to regain some lost lands to a pretty Cockney girl "who confided to Ernest that she would like to marry me, if she wasn't already."

After docking in Liverpool, they wasted little time in purchasing bicycles and escaping the city's industrial dreariness, steering toward Windermere and the Lake District at a pace of about thirty-five miles a day. Along the way they dined in fields, often on buns bought at local bakeries, and washed themselves and their clothes in convenient streams. Aiken reveled in exploring "the island of Goose Green in *Jackanapes,* and the customs office in Hawthorne's *Our Old Home,* and the poet of the White Horse Vale" (59). From Windermere, where they tarried a week, the two friends bicycled farther north to the tiny hamlet of Troutbeck, then northeast until they reached Keswick on the

Greta River, snug amid the Cumbrian Mountains, the attractive town where Charles Lamb had passed his holidays when Coleridge was residing at Greta Hall.

While in Keswick, in August, Aiken penned a long letter to Mrs. Benjamin Anthony, Edward's mother, which she published in the family newspaper, marking the poet's first appearance in print outside a school publication:

> We are both so enchanted by the whole region that I don't know whether we'll ever get out of it. We have circled about and about on our wheels, finding one delightful place after another, valleys, lakes, falls and mountains. We have dreamed dreams on Wordsworth's seat and moved quickly through his 'Dove Cottage'; we have spent delicious minutes in the Ruskin Museum at Coniston, a beautiful little mountain village, and have looked with a kind of awe at the slender shaft that commemorates his life, his works, and his death. But I think, on the whole, we care less for these things than for the beauty of the place—and are rather inclined to run away from anything resembling an art gallery, or a Gothic cathedral. We like to see a quaint old village, with up and down cobbled streets and thatched roofs, and a peaceful church with a slanting graveyard; or a fine range of barren mountains, with a fertile valley beneath—cut by the hedges into many different-hued fields of green, like a great, smooth, green patchwork quilt.

This is public performance, to be sure, but its polished surface mirrors the truth of Aiken's love for countryside terrains and reveals—aside from the professional style—a precocious ability to adapt to "foreign" environments. After further exploration of the Keswick area, Aiken and Oberholzer continued their journey northward into Scotland, through Penrith, Carlisle, where they visited an impressive cathedral, Melrose, Peebles, Edinburgh, Stirling, and Kinross. At Persey Bridge, in the middle of Scotland, the two young men had a furious row and parted company. The cause of the quarrel is unknown, but Aiken could be a trying friend and his pride and shyness made it almost impossible for him to initiate reconciliations.

He returned alone to the Lake District and settled down for the rest of his vacation at Troutbeck, specifically at a small, homey inn located near the village bridge, with a stone chapel perched on the wooded hillside above it. The family that owned the inn, the Dixons, treated him as one of their own, offering a hearth warmth he could not resist. He passed his stay investigating the rugged beauties of the wild Troutbeck Valley. Every mountain within reasonable distance was conquered, and besides reading Shakespeare and a "little red volume" of Wordworth's verses, he consumed a 25-cent copy of Francis Turner Palgrave's *Golden Treasury,* romantic lyrics for a romantic idyll.

But romance needs sex, or at least the implication or promise of sex, for its poetry to recapture the desire that once fueled somatic passages into idea and language, and this Aiken discovered in a concealed passion for the inn-keeper's daughter.

Pictured in *Ushant* as "exceedingly attractive" (64), she was twenty-four or so to his nineteen years and probably more cognizant of his infatuation than he suspected. Aiken yearned to lose "his oh so troublesome virginity" and imag-ined her appearing suddenly in his room at night to seduce him. The fantasies were sharpened by his accidental intrusion upon a "couple copulating under a tree, on the far side of Lake Windermere" (65). He had pedaled into view on his bike too quickly for them to make more than an ineffectual stab at conccal-ment, and he sped past, face averted in shame. The guilt that the scene in-spired seems extraordinary, telling much about the Victorian mores that had nurtured him, the Boston-prim world in which proper girls were beyond car-nal approach and improper girls beyond the pale.

Ushant speaks of "those fevers of longing which had tormented him for seven years, or eight, or nine, and the guilt and shame which were the inevita-ble accompaniments," fevers that had now gained a concrete image. But the innkeeper's dark-haired daughter never did sneak into his room, and he de-parted from Troutbeck in early autumn with fantasies intact and a firm deter-mination to return the following summer.

• • • • • • • • • •

THE ONLY, THE INFINITE,
THE MAGICAL WELL

Back at Harvard in September 1908, Aiken had the sophomore's pleasure of familiarity with the lay of the land to ease him into a school routine, leaving him more time for his own reading and writing and bull sessions with his circle of budding intellectuals at the *Advocate* and the two literary clubs. Mc-Couch, he, and several others formed their own parlor enclave, the Monticure, which gathered irregularly to read aloud from works of literature thought worthy, though Aiken, like Eliot, also enjoyed ensconcing himself in the Union library and devouring several books at a sitting.

Friendship with Eliot was resumed, broadened, and deepened. They shifted from casual discussions of purely literary topics into a closer relationship in which the almost instinctive Harvard reserve of mocking, languid, high-toned indifference worn by the "imperially slim" Eliot with Richard Cory's deceptive elegance could be undercut somewhat by word games, sports talk, school gossip, frequent resorts to barracks humor, childish buffoonery. Aiken noted that "as the friendship, or kinship, developed—for in a way I became his younger brother—it widened to take in everything. And we met on very, very many quite frivolous occasions. . . . We developed a shorthand language of our own which we fell into for the rest of our lives, whenever we met, no holds barred." The comic strips soon to come into vogue would also unite them, especially the antics of Krazy Kat, who became part of their private language, as would "King Bolo," Eliot's invention, an imaginary African monarch they delighted in abusing with scatological rhymes that reek today all too strongly of the racism and adolescent vulgarities endemic to the prep-school mentality of the period. Punning, constant kidding, a taste for alcohol—Aiken's capacity for liquor was and would remain astonishing—were abetted by daring invasions of Boston's seamier neighborhoods to take in burlesque shows.

Meanwhile, Aiken, Eliot, and Tinckom-Fernandez maintained their habit of exchanging work and ideas, and Eliot had an outburst of verse writing sufficient to get him elected to the *Advocate* board by January 1909. The forces that drew Aiken and Eliot together were strong enough to blind them to fundamental differences of temperament and attitude that would eventually generate a great deal of disguised hostility as well as divergent aesthetic stances. Aiken, for instance, maintained his rebellious disdain for formal requirements, being expelled from Professor Charles Grandgent's Italian 10 class— "The Works of Dante, particularly the *Vita Nuova* and the *Divine Comedy*"— for absenteeism while in the middle of enjoying the *Inferno*. He also took Spanish 5, an advanced course, although he was "without the slightest previous acquaintance with Spanish" (208). Eliot, on the other hand, ever the grind, the perfect pupil, would achieve his B.A. in three years, followed in a year by the A.M. His junior program covered a survey of Latin poetry, classes in Latin literature and the Roman novel, two broad comparative literature courses, Santayana's advanced "Ideal of Society, Religion, Art and Science in Their Historical Development," and Dean Briggs's English 12, which perhaps spurred his poetic outburst.

The two friends obviously clashed over pedagogical philosophy, their contrary conceptions of the free-elective system. President Eliot had finally stepped down (under some pressure) after almost forty years of dedicated leadership and undeniable success in metamorphosizing Harvard from a rather parochial contraption of clerical and classical manufacture into a sleek modern university. He would be succeeded in January 1909 by another Brahmin, Abbott Lawrence Lowell, who immediately set about shifting administrative attention back to the college, seeking to curb the narrow-minded influence of the clubs and providing more and better undergraduate housing. A primary aim was to scrap the abused elective system and to restore a roughly classical curriculum in the form of required credit distributions among major and minor fields of study. In this enterprise he had student Eliot's and most of the faculty's enthusiastic approval, if not Aiken's.

To Eliot, neglect of the classics and students plotting their own programs (presumably with official guidance) smacked of chaos; it could never produce well-read, well-rounded graduates such as were sent into the world by superior European and British universities. Aiken, however, reveled in the opportunity to sample, practically at will, whatever courses he thought might benefit his literary ambitions. From any objective standpoint both were right; it is difficult to envision an effective college syllabus that does incorporate generous portions of free choice and compulsory, demonstrable mastery of various disciplines ancillary to the undergraduate's main subject area. But their opposite views illuminate the submerged fissure, which would widen over the next few decades, separating their perceptions of self and the structures that fashion its expression.

Eliot and Aiken came from similar Unitarian backgrounds and were intimately familiar with Emersonian notions of transcendental activism and of the individual's paramount importance in fashioning his own intellect and psyche as the ultimate measure of history and society, which are seen as malleable. For Aiken, the Unitarian movement away from the Puritans' Calvinistic sense of sin, of human culpability, toward a greater concentration on the concept of free will as an elemental factor in the affairs of men and God was an external formulation of his personal rejection of religious dogma and its theocratic trappings. As a compulsive rebel against authority and authoritarian figures, he felt most comfortable with the Unitarian trend toward increasing theological and personal freedom and was proud that his grandfather had been Emerson's friend and a leading nonconformist preacher. He would also loan Eliot a copy of Reverend Potter's sermons; Emerson had characterized Eliot's grandfather as "the Saint of the West," which foreshadows *Ushant*'s sanctification of Reverend Potter as "Teacher from the West."

But Eliot, "the quintessence of Harvard" (Brooks's uncomplimentary phrase) in his elitist aesthetics and unspoken contempt for the masses, could abide neither his mother's sunny Emersonianism nor his grandfather's broad interpretations of the Unitarian creed. As is clear from a batch of poems that he wrote in November 1909, he had an obsessive appetite for Royce's "Absolute," for salvation through immersion in a higher or ideal reality, which entailed a concomitant, childlike disgust with the physical operations of his own body, plus a fin-de-siècle fascination with sin—exaggerated, sensual, putrifying sin, à la Aubrey Beardsley. His excessive fear of and enchantment with death and decay—again, the childhood clutch rusted into place—dominated his reveries and appeared linked, out of sight and intellect, to some degree of inversion. Gordon has accurately noted that in each of the poems written in 1908 and 1909, "a woman manages to humble a man in a different way." The poems owe much to Poe's Romantic caricatures of females as saintly and satanic extremes and to Harvard's Pre-Raphaelite taste for such an attitude.

To take an admittedly reductive psychological position, it might be said that Aiken and Eliot (skeptics by nature) both sought an ideal father in their lives and minds, a prototypical self to emulate, confront, and measure themselves against. Aiken, perhaps because his quest was grounded in a later stage of development, rejected any older male who attempted too strongly to impose his will and ideas upon him. He also developed a more socially acceptable, if no less neurotic, sexual identity that would petrify into a persistent Don Juan syndrome, in which the compulsive search for the mother is characterized by the sadistic urge to punish women but little ethical revulsion—quite the contrary—toward the sex act per se. Congenial, liberal, nondoctrinaire Dean Briggs became his surrogate father; Eliot also admired Briggs but could never deify him as a genuine paternal idol. Eliot's father had to be stern, certain, extraordinarily erudite and European, and had to promote a credible system of Platonic beliefs (some version of the "Absolute") that could subjugate experience and the modern world's formless corruption; he had to be, in other words, Irving Babbitt. Eliot functioned as Babbitt's loyal disciple while at Harvard, following him into a wide-ranging study of Western and Eastern thinkers and of Pali and Sanskrit.

And yet it would be a mistake to stress too heavily the very real differences separating the two young men because their literary visions, their search for fruitful analogs, were still being nourished by many common springs. There were, for instance, the Elizabethan and Jacobean dramatists, perused with devotional zeal at Harvard and often performed by various undergraduate theatrical groups; the English Romantics and their Victorian descendants; Pater's and Arnold's cultural critiques; Santayana's precepts of beauty and the poet's epic philosophical task; and a consciousness, less formalized, of Dante's supreme stature (according to Aiken, Eliot was never without his pocket copy of Dante after 1910).

The single most significant literary bond between Aiken and Eliot remained, however, a vague but always intense shared conviction that what passed for contemporary poetry was inadequate to the convoluted demands of their egos and the new century. They also felt a corresponding dissatisfaction with their country's naive impotency, decried in the writings of Henry Adams and Henry James, whose *American Scene* had been published the year before, and best summed up by Santayana's tart observation that the "moral and intellectual atmosphere everywhere in the United States seemed to be uniform: earnest, meagre, vague, scattered, and hopeful." The "hopeful" category fit Aiken better than Eliot. In this year Eliot would read Arthur Symons for the first time and locate his basic voice in Jules Laforgue's experimental style, and Aiken discovered Whitman. Neither Whitman nor the French Symbolists were strangers to Harvard, having been introduced in the 1890s, when Santayana and his cohorts publicized Whitman's virtues on campus and *M'lle New York* and the *Chap-Book* (founded by two Harvard undergraduates) bloomed briefly among the originals of the small avant-garde magazines, singing the praises of Poe, Whitman, and the Symbolists. The respectability of French literature had been certified by Henry James's locally heralded return from abroad in 1905 to lecture on Balzac at Sanders Theatre (Memorial Hall).

Aiken had been impressed by the verses of Trumbull Stickney, which appeared in 1905, a year after Stickney's early death from a brain tumor, and he introduced Eliot to them. Though they are the accomplished, elegiac, sparsely elegant verses typical of the Harvard Poets' traditional praxes, Aiken's familiarity with them, coupled with his respect for Santayana's preachments, indicates that the turn to Whitman was logical within a Harvard context. Bliss Perry had written a book on Whitman in 1906, and near year's end George Rice Carpenter's *Walt Whitman* (a title in the English Men of Letters series) would be reviewed by the *Advocate*.

Whitman struck Aiken like an Arctic wind of limitless release after his labors inside the overheated parlors of inherited lyric forms and formulas: "I came down with a bad attack of Whitmanitis. . . . He was useful to me in the perfection of form, as a sort of compromise between the strict and the free." But he could never really accept *vers libre* as a legitimate alternative to conventional metrics, which came easily to him, as did rhyme schemes. None of his poems published in the *Monthly* and the *Advocate* during his sophomore year reflect Whitman's influence. Perhaps whatever free-verse exercises he did write—and he continued to grind out a poem a day—were subsequently discarded.

The poems that saw print vary little from those published the previous year. Their prevailing tone is late Victorian, as is the clinging to archaic diction ("ye," "doth," and "ere"), their major technique adamantly formal, playing with caesural placement and the like. Beyond expected Christmas whimsy, their subjects are deliberate, good-natured responses to the great themes of beloved Elizabethan and Romantic forefathers, as in "Mutability," which mocks, with affection, Shelley's familiar ode:

> Ye futile trollers of song
> Do ye know that life must depart?
> Your brains will be cobwebbed ere long—
> To the deuce with laborious Art!

Shelley's poem swoons into a tragic climax—

> Whilst yet the calm hours creep,
> Dream thou—and from they sleep
> Then wake to weep

whereas Aiken plays archly with the poet's self-deception:

> To-morrow in heaven we dine,—
> To-day we'll be merry on Earth.
> (What say ye? A penny a line?
> Ah, sing then, for all ye are worth!).

The self-consciousness of all the poems emphasizes the aesthete ambience that governs the direction and pose of almost everything Aiken and his class-mates wrote. "When I was at Harvard," Wallace Stevens remembered, "it was commonplace to say that all the poetry had been written and all the paintings painted," a situation that prevailed through Aiken's residence and after: "Scorning athleticism, a few students gathered at the Stylus Club, where they quoted Huysmans and composed Wildean sonnets. . . . Like Santayana, they sought liberation from the 'straitened spirit' of the late-Victorian bourgeoisie by tasting beauty in its many guises. Chalice and crucifix, Buddha and *ka-kemono*, all became relics in the cult of aesthetic experience." It meant, in effect and method, writing poetry about poetry or writing poetry about writing poetry, a logical progression from Pater's elevation of the poet to a priestly function and a thematic aorta in the body of twentieth-century verse.

The most overt enshrinement of this mannered impulse in Aiken's soph-omore poetry occurs in "The Burmese Sculptor," which glances back at "The Potter" and forward to the Keatsian "To a Marble Head":

> Under a bamboo thatch, in leafy shade—
>   'Tis very hot without—he toils away,
>   With ringing out and mallet's rhythmic play,
> And a smoke of powdered marble round him sprayed.
> *Clinkety-clink* the biting chisel goes,—
>   The work is nearly done, save for the face;
>   Pressing his lips, the sculptor leans to trace
> The smiling mouth, wide eyes, and faultless nose.
> Silent and placid, now, the thing must squat
>   Like a marble cobbler, peaceful and at ease—
>   Nay, I would swear the fellow's going to nod!
> When, flinging aside his chisel, reeking hot,

Sudden the sculptor falls upon prone knees
In babbling prayer,—the image is his god!

The clever construction, a double vision of the Buddha squatting like the "marble cobbler" who has just created him, preserves a refreshing cosmopolitanism despite the melodramatic denouement. It underscores Aiken's cynical detachment, confessedly incomplete, from his own plunges into Harvard's crimson sea of aesthete postures, even as he conformed to its taste for heavy ironies.

The narrative facility on display in "The Burmese Sculptor" is also a trademark of the sophomore short stories Aiken had published in undergraduate journals. Their most prevalent quality, however, is a superficial amalgamation of Poe's Gothic imagination (minus instinctive psychological insights) and O. Henry's reliance on trick endings. They are plot stories, professionally adept, possessed of a distinctly English aura and social focus—the summer journey to Ariel's island had left a definite impression.

A telling example is "Rabbit," in which the narrator, an outsider, is taken rabbit hunting by his local host, who is obviously upper class, identified only as "Jenkins." At the outset a mere quiver of foliage results in Jenkins firing carelessly into the underbrush, killing a three-year-old boy. Followed by the shocked narrator "with hanging head," the self-assured host carries his small victim down to a tent and gypsy wagon in the valley below them, where they encounter the boy's older sister and father, who look "entirely primeval." Jenkins explains the accident to the father and slips him a gold sovereign before walking away. He informs the narrator that they are Gaelic, "old clan people, so often intermarried that their brains are gone." Unperturbed, he returns to shooting their dinner. The final paragraph ruins the story's commendable terseness by belaboring the narrator's sensitivity: "Jenkins went off, the gun cracked, and he came back holding up a rabbit by the hind legs. He started to smile. He was surprised to find me squatting on the ground, and blubbering like a child."

Set in Scotland, the tale is an efficient unidimensional comment upon English-bred indifference to the lower orders, but an admirable economy of means suffers from Aiken's inability to know when to halt, to restrain a penchant (evident also in the poetry) for yet another explanatory twist. In spite of authentic scenic touches, the story is unreal because Aiken is intent on effect, not truth. "The Wallet" is set in America, presumably Boston, but the main character is a "little clerk" named Wordsworth, a "gray-haired, blue-eyed little German," who is Dickensian in his poverty. On the way from work, delighted by the sight of passing automobiles, still relatively rare, he is bumped into by a short, solid, curt man whose wallet falls at his feet. The wallet contains three thousand dollars. He chases after the man and sees him disappear into a brownstone. His moral quandary at this point is scarcely genuine because honesty is integral to his cliché existence, but his creator takes the opportunity to let him meditate longingly on the power that money represents in the human cosmos, a subject of concern to Aiken (and Dickens):

> Into how many beautiful things it might be converted! Into his mind swam a gleaming vision of a pulsating automobile—then out again, leaving a trail of fire. He smiled with delight, thinking of the omnipotence of this sum of money. At its bidding, a beautiful house could rise; it had but to speak, and he would be clad in purple and gold. The chill apartment could be cast away like gray ashes, Felix would be well, Marie would wear fine clothes and keep a maid-servant. It was like intoxication, thus to dream. A childlike smile was on his gray lips, he caressed the three notes as a baby strokes a kitten.

The twist must come and does with predictable bleakness: "The wallet? O-o-o-h! The sour-faced maid composed herself grimly, took it, and slammed the door in Wordsworth's face." Anticlimactically the little clerk, "frightened at the idea of being late for supper," totters away down the street, "still fumbling at the collar of his coat with trembling fingers." Virtue has again been confounded, though Aiken, who would never be a political writer or being, does not follow up the social ramifications of the plight of the poor clerk, who has run against the human wall the rich surround themselves with to keep such characters from their doors. Nor does he attempt to hone the moral question raised by Wordsworth's unusual honesty, content to settle for an O. Henry dash of bitters amid some sentimental tears. The realist revolt initiated by William Dean Howells and plotted into savage despair by Stephen Crane and crusader novelists such as Frank Norris had not yet penetrated Harvard's mauve fog as far as Aiken was concerned, at least not to the extent of his contemplating any abandonment of the pleasures gained from tooling simple but efficacious art machines.

In "The Cat and the Mouse," framed by Poe's revenge fantasies, especially "Hop Frog," the protagonist is another victim, a small, deformed Jewish jeweler who has decided to terminate his misery by committing suicide with poison, which he has purchased under the pretense of needing it to kill pesky cats. As he returns to his shop he ponders the relief poison will bring: "One sip—and everything in the visible, or the audible, would slowly pale, dim, and swirl away like vapor. In a twinkling he would whizz off from the earth leaving the crippled ugly body behind him, and in the promised land would move on an equal footing with all immortality." He is totally alienated from "an abominable world" that "had spurned him and ground him underfoot from the moment he had been born." Aiken makes little of his Jewishness beyond giving him the name Meyrowitz but must have intended and appreciated—there is a reference to Christopher Marlowe's *Jew of Malta*—the extra social value of linking his suffering outsider to a minority group grudgingly tolerated at Harvard and elsewhere.

Meyrowitz muses on the irony of his pretense that the poison was for cats, creatures Aiken loved, and the secret rancor he has nurtured for humans: "Animals he had compassion for, they knew no better; but men he despised utterly." This is a far cry from clerk Wordsworth's timid daydreaming or the soft collapse of the narrator in "Rabbit." The victim figure has crystallized into a monster of hatred, hardened by persecution, like Shakespeare's Venetian moneylender, who will tear his pound of flesh from the novice thief who breaks into his shop shortly after he has downed the poison. Meyrowitz proceeds to play "cat and mouse" with the frightened felon, making noises behind a curtain until the thief falls to the ground in a faint. Thinking him dead, the jeweler crawls toward him, but his prey suddenly leaps up and races for the door: "Meyrowitz, quick as a cat, caught one of his ankles in a freezing grip and the man fell heavily to the floor. The little jeweler was on him like a flash and laced icy fingers round his neck, laughing softly; but there was no need of it; the poor robber was dead." Forsaking Poe's immoral triumph, Aiken has the jeweler also die, concluding with a scene of two mice disappearing into the shadows when a policeman's fist hammers on the shop door.

Once more, story as story has predominated at the expense of realism and characterization, but the sly manipulation of the "cat and mouse" idea does not entirely suffocate stirrings of interest in the abnormal psychology of a man pushed into murderous excess by inequitable circumstances, a hatred for humanity that must be concealed. Although simplistic, lacking Poe's archetypal ken and the Elizabethans' flair for wrenching outer violence into inner truth, "The Cat and the Mouse" is pertinent to understanding Aiken's tentative exploration of action fiction as a means of partially venting unadmitted rage while mastering the mechanics of a resistant craft. Biographical factors made him a lyric poet, foundationally tied to self-as-subject; yet he retained almost enough curiosity about other people to want to broaden lyric consciousness into a prose vehicle.

Vengeance would naturally be the most fecund theme for such a psyche, as it had been for Poe, along with an absorption in the elusive, evanescent boundary between fantasy and reality. Both themes surface in another English tale, "The Murderer," which takes place in a private club, where the villain, Thorpe, like Jenkins, apes the upper-class bully. His victim is the club's butler, William Saucer, "very knock-kneed and small, and topped by an abnormally large red head." After an insult from Thorpe, Saucer retreats to the pantry and has his "good spirits" restored by the sight of the wine shelves. A man of imagination, he wonders how many elephants might get soused on the wine kept by the club, and this leads into his daring to take a sip himself. Soon he is drunk and scheming to murder Thorpe with a kitchen knife. What happens next—a drunken sleep, waking to recall his plan, entering the room and raising the knife only to have his tormentor awake at the same instant—is bound to prove a dream, a fantasy revenge: "Thorpe rose with a hideous deliberation and slowness, turned around in a leisurely manner, stepped nearer, loomed larger, then swelled enormously like a bubble—and burst into a thousand sparks."

That it was merely a dream is confirmed by the sight of Thorpe in the next room, "snoring steadily and deeply in the arm-chair." Aiken's final sentences, echoing the climax of "Rabbit," are lugubrious: "Saucer crumpled to the floor like ash. Then, huddled in a black little pile, he began to weep." The ashes image had been milked twice previously, a poet's thrift and possible Shakespeare allusion, and nothing can save the story from its stock plot and flat characters, from juvenile dependence upon the creaking gears of a dream's sleight of hand. The subject of dreams must have been crucial to Aiken, however, because he continued to remember his dreams with awesome frequency and suspected a fecund relationship between them and artistic creation. Though not yet capable of integrating the creative process with more profound mysteries of personality, of consciousness at the mercy of unconscious forces, he was familiar enough with Coleridge's three "nightmare" works—*The Rime of the Ancient Mariner,* "Kubla Kahn," and "Christabel"— and similar excursions into the fantastic to sense a convergence, an aesthetic lair, that was the source of both dream and self.

Jay Martin has claimed that in "Rabbit," "The Wallet," and "The Murderer" Aiken "used his protagonists as scapegoats for his own tensions, and thus lavished his sympathy upon the characters whose downfall he was preparing," which is accurate and perceptive but a bit misleading. The tensions released through these stories could not have been substantial. Their conscientious distance from raw experience leaves minimal room for much interaction between the frustrations and weepy anguish of his cartoon characters and Aiken's ferocious internal war against an unjust past. But Martin is right to focus on the victim-persecutor core of these slight stories in connection with their author's emerging psychological profile. However deliberate are the choices of an apprentice writer, they cannot avoid limning a few of the more prominent features of a private self, sublimated emotional peaks and valleys. Aiken was removed from his pathetic heroes—their diminutive stature excepted, which reflected bedrock insecurity and anxieties about his own height—but as "The Cat and the Mouse" convincingly shows, the dialectical kinetics governing their development, which went from unearned injury through repressed fury into art, drew a gross outline of his psyche's deepest operations.

This evolution is why Poe remained a key element in these stories and in their author's literary development. The following unsigned commentary in the January 26, 1909, issue of the *Advocate* elicited Aiken's approval:

> Having briefly finished with celebrating the tercentenary of Milton we are now come to that lonely and ill-starred genius, the "only Ishmael" of American literature—Poe. It is curious how consistently we disavow Poe, and exalt Whitman, for instance. Both were revolters: yet through the magazines the one is exalted, while the other is hunted. So much for the wonderful consistency of the Puritan temperament. With the passing of the Puritan, and the evolution of the future American type of national character, we shall hope to see poetic justice, at least, done to Poe. (130)

After offering up Poe and Abraham Lincoln as fit future subjects for the annual Garrison Prize poem, the editorial observes that "it was very good to hear the respective tributes paid by Prof. Bliss Perry and Mr. Copeland to Poe's genius." Besides affirming that Whitman and Poe were alive and well at Aiken's Harvard, these remarks elucidate the pervasive awareness on campus of the decline of the Puritan ethos and the spreading aesthetic fallout of that decline.

Poe and Whitman formed an ideal fulcrum (Romantic "madness" plus iconoclastic method) for any rebellion against the "Genteel Tradition" that had replaced the energetic Puritan drive toward salvation with a studied concentration upon manners and mannerisms, conventional techniques, but the relative isolation of Harvard, which mirrored Protestant Boston's isolation, from teeming immigrant ghettos and other working-class groups made the ambition that much harder to formulate. But the spirit of revolt, if muted, did exist: "During the years 1906–1910 the Harvard Yard was both the Citadel of social conformity and upper-class manners and the seedbed of social and political dissent." And the same two undergraduates who founded the *Chap-Book* had in 1894 published *Crumbling Idols,* Hamlin Garland's naturalist manifesto. To official Harvard and many of its professors, however, the shift toward literary realism seemed of a piece with the political radicalism they feared and loathed.

In the poetics sphere Aiken, Eliot, and the handful of undergraduates not seriously infected by the college's aesthete malaise were desperate to locate a voice for what they believed had to be a new style of verse, a more inclusive, less rigid style capable of combining Romantic inclinations and backgrounds with the vibrant currents being emitted by their culture's social, commercial, and technological upheavals. They intuited that the search for a modern poetry, like Wordsworth's a century before, would be initially linguistic, an assault upon the ornate phrasings and archaic diction distancing contemporary poetry from the living language, the changing language, kept at bay by Harvard's insular necrophilia—Copey had dubbed the Yard "Plato's cave." As Aiken recalled, "It was . . . perhaps the most creative period of American slang," crude and bigoted but humming with inventiveness: "How delighted we were with the word 'dinge' for negro!" The problem was a paucity of native models to lend support to Poe's and Whitman's earlier antiestablishment perspectives. "At a time which may be symbolized by the figures 1910," Eliot later wrote, "there was literally no one to whom one would have dreamt of applying. One learnt something, no doubt, from Henry James, and might have learned more."

Eliot believed the relative lack of contemporary resources had been a positive factor in his own growth: "I think it was rather an advantage not having any living poets in England or America in whom one took any particular advantage." Thomas Hardy was not yet known as a poet in America, and Eliot scorned the "Celtic twilight" lyricism of William Butler Yeats, as did Aiken, despite its popularity among the same students enchanted by an 1890s soulful "art for art's sake" lushness. Brooks remarks that the taste for Pater extended to Yeats, "whose vogue was just beginning and whose poems we scribbled all over our lecture notebooks." Eliot also spurned the plain-speech innovations of Edwin Arlington Robinson, after having read an article about him (with relevant quotations) in the *Atlantic Monthly* and deciding "that wasn't my cup of tea at all." But Robinson was extremely important to Aiken, who lacked Eliot's language skills and erudition, as was Emily Dickinson. It was a metaphor of Robinson's (in Aiken's memory) designating a syringe "a slight kind of engine" that triggered many of their literary discussions: "Was it poetry? Argument everywhere. How could Eliot and Aiken avoid it? They didn't."

Aiken would remember 1908 as the pivotal year for their exchanges. He would also remember that "for the next five years, this was their constant concern. They exchanged poems and discussed them. How to find a new poetic language?" In *Children of the Night* (1897), which contained several sturdy character sketches, including "Richard Cory," "Cliff Klingenhagen," and "Reuben Bright," and in *Captain Craig* (1902), Robinson had used lessons learned from poets as diverse as George Crabbe and Paul Verlaine to combat the orthodoxies of "the little sonnet men" (the Harvard Poets) by refining the reformist-motivated naturalism of Emile Zola and his American adherents into a more sensitive poetic and psychological field, radiating a prosier speech and centering upon a series of small-town personalities. His revolt against the Genteel Tradition—named by Santayana and epitomized by his own scrupulous, fatalistic sonnets—was, for Aiken, a natural extension of the shift to the vernacular already accomplished by Robert Browning, a book of whose poems he had borrowed from the Signet library and never returned.

Eliot could accept Browning reluctantly and selectively, as could Cambridge and Boston proper, where the Browning Societies still thrived, but it was inevitable that he would reject Robinson's gloomy, uneven, albeit technically sound verses; their monotonous orchestration of understated desolation was too narrow to represent the variety of voice and subtlety of emotion he believed a modern poetic must possess. The metaphysical poets, particularly Donne, were infinitely more relevant in this respect, thinking and feeling as seamless articulations of a complicated, divided self—a "dissociated sensibility" was a crippling malaise from the start—and the Renaissance dramatists, especially the Jacobeans, whom he, Aiken, and the rest of Harvard adored. Thus, while Aiken was pursuing his Whitmanesque line and pondering the example of Robinson as "maybe the earliest of the modernizers," Eliot stumbled upon *The Symbolist Movement in Literature* in December at the Signet and was intrigued by the brief section devoted to Laforgue. The few tantalizing quotes and Symons's account of his short, tragic life sent him on a hunt in the Cambridge bookshop specializing in foreign-language material, where he happily uncovered a three-volume edition of Laforgue's works. Soon he was writing deliberate Laforgue imitations.

It is evident that Laforgue's impact on Eliot decisively separated his maturing aesthetic stance from Aiken's, regardless of their common quest for a modernist mode. Buttressing Petronius, Donne, and Baudelaire, Laforgue offered Eliot a pliant method for voicing both his intense lyric and satiric impulses, as well as for introducing the vulgate into a sophisticated mosaic of contrasting dictions. By demonstrating that extreme shifts of tone and language could be accomplished without visible or intrusive narrative transitions in a sort of miniature symphonic arrangement—shifts that contributed additional ironies through their dramatic juxtapositions—Laforgue freed Eliot from dependence upon the traditional approaches employed in the long poems of Romantic and Victorian predecessors. But Aiken had had little French and would always lag behind his friend in the mastery of experimental idioms. More pertinent, Aiken lacked Eliot's genius. Also, talented and dedicated though he was, Aiken's grasp of modernist methodologies was circumscribed by a contradictory taste for conservative techniques, which persisted even in the face of a sincere desire to expand the inherited horizons of his art.

Consequently, the fraternal relationship between Aiken and Eliot was unequal from the very beginning. Although unable to emulate Aiken's surface *joie de vivre* and liberal, humane pragmatism, Eliot was ever the older brother, sometimes "stern" with reference to certain intellectual areas and his friend's poetry, which he would treat roughly over the years. That Aiken, who resented authority figures and brooked no serious opposition from comrades, should have catered to Eliot as he apparently did suggests a symbiotic bonding in which he was willing to endure much to retain the goodwill of his peculiar classmate. Repeatedly Eliot's "waspishness" manifested itself in rebukes and acid rejoinders, and repeatedly Aiken maintained his equilibrium, though he was not above chiding Eliot in a kidding manner or mocking him behind his back. For instance, Aiken viewed Eliot's perpetual physiological discomforts (perennial bouts of constipation) with wry amusement and noted the discrepancy between Eliot's adolescent flippancy about sex and his fastidious revulsion from it. Aiken subsequently became convinced that his friend had suffered from impotence through most of his difficult life.

Also divisive was a less certain split in their attitudes toward America. United in their dissatisfaction with their country's materialism, aversion to experimentalism in the arts, and paradoxical progressivism and reactionary worship of the past, they reacted differently. Aiken, like Eliot, would flee the United States on occasion, yet it was always toward England, the mother country, not an alternative. Eliot was already mulling over the possibility of an exile's existence in Paris, of transforming himself into a prototype of the European cosmopolitanite he thought superior to native imitations.

In an *Advocate* review of Brooks's *The Wine of the Puritans*, a short meditation on America's cultural inadequacies in dialogue format, Eliot reveals his own discontent: "This is a book which probably will chiefly interest one class of Americans (a class, however, of some importance): the Americans retained to their native country by business relations or socialities or by a sense of duty—the last reason implying a real sacrifice—while their hearts are always in Europe." He praises the book as "a confession of national weakness," which he calls "a wholesome revelation," and he almost makes a personal statement: "The reasons for the failure of American life (at present)—social, political, in education and in art, are surgically exposed; with an unusual acuteness of distinction and refinement of taste; and the more sensitive of us may find ourselves shivering under the operation." Not only was Eliot shivering, he was studiously ignoring those native authors—Whitman, Dickinson, Robinson—whom Aiken found most relevant in their attempt to inaugurate another literary renaissance in America.

At levels that did not involve competition, the friendship advanced. Eliot permitted few contemporaries to venture near the invisible barbed wire strung around his personal life, and Aiken's frequent exception certified an authentic emotional congruence. In Aiken's company, Eliot relaxed as he did in no one else's. Their joint adventures in Boston burlesque houses or at "Buckingham and Brattle Hall dances and at the Signet," along with dips into the Boston *Transcript*'s comic parade of "Krazy Kat, and Mutt and Jeff, and Rube Goldberg's elaborate lunacies," relieved many internal pressures. And their diverging literary visions were not yet far enough apart to precipitate open warfare. Aiken, for example, believed that James Thomson, minor nineteenth-century poet and Harvard favorite, was underrated, in particular his *City of Dreadful Night,* and that poem's transmogrification of London into a nightmare scene would influence *The Waste Land,* perhaps because Thomson and Eliot owed a large mutual debt to Dante.

Aiken's life was brightened by a highly successful sophomore year. He had published prolifically in the undergraduate journals, far surpassing Eliot in that aspect of their literary competition, and was elected to the presidency of the *Advocate* near the end of the second semester. He had also gathered several more friends, including William Taussig, his first roommate, who was the son of the economics department's leading professor and whose comfortable Belmont home would always be open to him in the years ahead. The tall, lanky Taussig enjoyed adopting "the languid posture of the enervated" and was not generally interested in things literary, but he was amiable and generous, an easy, intelligent companion appreciative of Aiken's witticisms. Another new friend, also a freshman, was George (Jake) Wilbur from Iowa, described by a woman who knew him later in life as "a shaggy-haired, homespun type, blunt, laconic, attractive to women, a real man." Wilbur was determined to pursue a medical career, and Aiken's friendship with him would grow more intimate with their shared discovery of Freud and Wilbur's consequent decision to become a psychiatrist.

Yet another freshman to swing into Aiken's orbit was Myron Williams from Springfield, Massachusetts, student of German and Latin and future English teacher, whose sensitivity and care for literature proved congenial. But the freshman whose friendship would endure the longest, rivaling that with Mc-Couch, was Gordon Bassett, a native of Cape Cod, born in Woods Hole but living in South Dennis. The two met in Spanish 5, Bassett, who had a gift for languages, rescuing Aiken from his impetuosity and serving as his "mentor" in Spanish. Part of Bassett's charm lay in his down-to-earth directness and his sense of humor, abetted by a tendency to rely on salty slang, which amused Aiken, though he was equally attuned to the "good Bassett's" innate sharpness.

When added to the array of companions who were already integral facets of his Harvard days—McCouch, Tinckom-Fernandez, Eliot, Mariett, and Wehle—and such casual acquaintances as Waldo Peirce and Thomas McCabe, these new friends guaranteed that college would continue to be one of the happiest periods in Aiken's life. And Barbara Leighton, in spite of occasional misunderstandings and apologies, enhanced the experience immeasurably. He had taken her to several of the winter dances at Buckingham School Hall and Brattle Hall as well as to several football games. In the spring of 1909 he also escorted her to an *Advocate* tea to meet Edward Sheldon and actress Minnie Maddern Fiske, who was starring in Sheldon's hit play *Salvation Nell.* They were among the few young people present, the rest being professors' wives and such, including his Aunt Edith.

In June and early July, his schoolwork completed, Aiken was free to loaf, read, and visit the Potters before embarking upon a second trip to England and Scotland. He buried himself in Sophocles and wrote to Barbara, who had to depart for camp in Eliot, Maine. He also bought *The Blue Bird (L'Oiseau blue),* the "fairy play" by Maurice Maeterlinck, Belgian poetic dramatist and essayist who would receive the Nobel Prize in 1911. Enthralled, he shipped it off to Barbara, repayment for a purple tie she had given him, probably an early gift for his birthday. Meanwhile, McCabe, one of his few Harvard comrades still around—Eliot had gone to his family's summer home in East Gloucester—fancied himself in love with Ruth McIntyre and harped on his beloved's virtues with sentimental persistence until Aiken felt he knew Ruth as well as Barbara did.

The voyage to the British Isles by steamer was enlivened by the company of Harry Wehle, Julius Clark ("Jules"), Harvard graduate, reporter on the *Boston Record,* and eventual music critic for the *Transcript,* and four other young men. The seven planned to walk through Scotland, but rain forced them into train travel and local ambles, except for a full day's hike among the Trossachs, Scotland's "Lake District." The beauty of the countryside again thrilled Aiken. By July 23, when the group was staying at the Old Waverley Temperance Hotel in Edinburgh, he was writing Barbara of a temptation to spend the winter in London or Paris, engaging in real work instead of loafing at school. It was pure fantasy, though he did threaten to inform his uncle (William Tillinghast) about the project. Daydream or not, the notion of living abroad was alluring, although he jokingly protested in the letter that the gravest objection to the scheme was its interference with his date to take Barbara to the Signet dance the following semester.

The next day Aiken and Wehle set off south on bicycles, intending to pedal all the way to London, where Clark was to rendezvous with them and guide them to and around Paris. For some reason, their plans were changed, and Aiken's subsequent letter to Barbara eight days later was written at the Dixons' Sun Hotel in Windermere. They still meant to see London, but Paris and Clark were apparently canceled. In the interim, Aiken took pleasure in exposing Wehle to the wild and varied landscape he had explored the previous summer, along with introducing him to the Dixons. His secret passion for their daughter Alice was unabated, but Wehle's presence turned the improbability of a seduction into an impossibility. After a brief stay they pushed on to London.

A sidelight of the letter to Barbara, which is largely devoted to a joking sympathy with her chores as counselor and awe over her proficiency at executing them, is his response to her enthusiastic espousal and defense of the Bahai philosophy. He admits to being a lover of everything Catholic, confirmation that he was hardly immune to the influence of Harvard's aesthetes. With jocund defensiveness, he further concedes problems with long-term relationships and a misogynist character, expressing surprise at how well he and Harry had adjusted to each other. The sojourn in London, two weeks or so, cemented the friendship between the two.

Fate appeared to be walking in his footsteps when Aiken secured lodgings for them at Saville Place in Grey's Inn, the same small brick building where his Uncle Alfred had boarded years earlier, run by the same sweet spinster who had brightened his uncle's time there. The city itself, then the biggest in the world, ravaged his senses. Although unaware of the artistic ferment beginning to agitate various parts of the rigidly subdivided metropolis, of Ezra Pound's recent arrival from Italy to search out Yeats, or of T. E. Hulme's founding the "forgotten school" of Imagism, he was getting a hurried but thorough art education course. Under the knowledgeable eye of Wehle, who would cap his career by becoming curator of paintings at New York's Metropolitan Museum of Art, Aiken started to acquire an appreciation of painting and sculpture, visiting the Tate, the British Museum, and the National Portrait Gallery and developing a particular attachment to the works of Rodin and Whistler.

According to *Ushant,* in the British Museum an elfin Irish homosexual approached the innocent Wehle and clung to him like a parasite, chatting urbanely all the while, until the bewildered undergraduate treated him to dinner at a Soho restaurant and then brought him home to the flat to meet Aiken, scandalizing their elderly landlady. No less innocent than his roommate, Aiken was mesmerized and disturbed by their guest, "the small, soft, cherubic Hawkins . . . neat, tiny, precise, but under all that nicety so amusingly and confessedly 'dangerous,' so eager to corrupt!" (126). When Hawkins, pleading the lateness of hour, asked to stay the night, which resulted in his sharing the double bed with Wehle, neither young man suspected his real motive, another sign of their era's and their country's strict mores. In the morning Aiken was shocked to learn from Wehle that Hawkins had attempted to embrace him during the night.

Though he had heard of homosexuality, "vaguely, tangentially," Aiken was dumbfounded by Hawkins, by "the first horrifying revelation" of its existence. Once convinced that sexual conquests were out of the question, Hawkins presented no difficulties, showering them with advice and salacious accounts of his sex life. What troubled Aiken, who viewed homosexuality with intense dislike, "an almost animal revulsion"—such homophobic feelings are not surprising in the context of his upbringing and psychological history—was the inherent contradiction in the situation, the fact that inversion "could produce quite admirable, if almost invariably somewhat unhappy and frustrated, human beings" (127), including great artists such as Michelangelo and Whitman.

Aiken's sexual education remained unfinished, however; his fantasy about the innkeeper's daughter stealing away his virginity had not disappeared but had been magnified into a near-conviction. He was sure that, in secret, Alice was throbbing with a reciprocal passion, and thus he and Wehle separated, Aiken scurrying alone back to the Troutbeck Valley. But Wehle's absence and the passage of time had neither altered Alice's sisterly distance from Aiken nor diluted his own shyness. His summer habits resumed: mountain climbing, bicycle riding, much poetry reading, and rousing daydreams about the grand seduction scene in his room that never materialized. To worsen matters, Alice mentioned one morning that another American was staying at the inn and asked if he would mind meeting him.

The other American turned out to be a traveling automobile salesman from Detroit, armored with the appropriate cap, gloves, goggles, and long duster (66). He had been as far north as Glasgow and Edinburgh and was now killing time until his ship sailed from Liverpool. It was as if he had stepped into life from every traveling salesman story ever told, an early version of the Ugly American in his coarseness, his loudness, his arrogance toward foreigners. To him, England was a backward country that resisted his pioneer efforts at introducing its citizens to the joys of motoring, a place where proper English, plain speaking, was rare.

Aiken cringed under the raw impact of the man's colorful vulgarities, his naked commercialism, the naive assumption that his student countryman shared his philistine prejudices. Fascinated in spite of himself, however, he listened attentively to the lurid descriptions of erotic conquests in France and America, pretending to an equal worldliness. They spent the day together, driving to Carlisle for lunch, then touring east toward the Pennines before returning to the inn for the usual choice between beef or lamb for dinner. The salesman was relentless on the topic of sex. At dinner he broached a scheme of their using his car that very night to try picking up some local girls, copying a highly successful technique employed in America.

Although apprehensive and embarrassed by the salesman, Aiken agreed, his sexual appetite too keen for him to refuse. They sped off at twilight to distant Ambleside, where girls were encountered strolling along the roadside in ones, twos, and threes. Predictably, the approach of the huge car and the cheerful offer of a lift from a stranger clad like a spaceman did not elicit much conversation. Frightened speechless, the girls fled into nearby fields or simply ran away.

But the salesman would not quit, shifted the field of their endeavors to Grasmere, where they met with similar rebuffs and alarmed flights into the underbrush. Fearful that one of their victims might have notified the police, Aiken found his anxiety increasing with each fruitless episode. It was not only the specter of public disgrace that haunted him; he could not help but speculate on what would happen if a couple of girls did enter the car and submit to their advances. His lack of experience would reveal itself in the most humiliating fashion, both to the girl and to his crude compatriot, whose opinion had weight solely because of his own self-conscious vanity. And yet, lodged beneath the fears pulsed the driving need to complete his initiation into the "sacred mystery" of sex. It was not to be, at least not this summer. His companion surrendered to the darkness at last and angrily drove back to the inn, his disgust with England more vocal than ever.

Before his departure for America, the salesman told Aiken about an adventure with a French girl crossing the Channel, which caused him to consult an understanding French doctor. The doctor gave him a tube of ointment that proved miraculous, eradicating his problem in several days. In appreciation of Aiken's recent partnership, he left him an untouched tube of the wonderful salve, which Aiken lacked the courage to refuse. During the ensuing week, his last, Aiken was obsessed by the presence of the tube, but, inexplicably, could not bring himself to throw it away. Instead, on the day of his leaving he dropped it into the bottom drawer of his dresser, hoping that Alice, when she cleaned the room, would either not notice it or assume it had been left by a later guest—a vain hope indeed, since the modest-sized inn's summer season was almost over.

Why had he not tossed the tube away? Why had he, in a panic, dropped it into a drawer rather than take it with him? In *Ushant,* Aiken expressed mystification, saw his behavior as "characteristic of his lifelong stupidity and incompetence, the panicky indecision in any crisis . . . perhaps an aspect of the family *petit mal*" (69–70). But Aiken's candor is suspect, though his hysteric tendencies could very well have had a genetic brace to bolster their environmental shaping, because his retrospective comments are precisely that, retrospective, no longer devoid of psychoanalytic hypotheses. He must have guessed that the abandoned tube was a blow at Alice for her failure to consummate his fantasy, or, on an elemental plane, an unconscious wish to communicate his sexual identity to her. Conscious or not, the act was, after the fact, self-abasing, and it grew more so as his rich imagination envisioned its most dire consequences, to the extent that back in America he became convinced he could never return to Troutbeck.

The normal, if chaste and often stressful, relationship with Barbara Leighton was preferable to such torturous imaginings. Their dating resumed without a hitch, except for inevitable petty misunderstandings, and he took pleasure in introducing her to the work of Francis Thompson, sending her a copy of the latter's remarkable *Essay on Shelley,* purchased in London, as a gift and in penance for some letter of his that had distressed her. When she replied with enthusiasm, he recommended Thompson's poetry, specifically "The Hound of Heaven," "A Carrier Song," "Dream-Tryst," and "To Monica Thought Dying," promising more gems from the collection of Thompson's lyrics he had bought in London—he remembered reading them fondly while crisscrossing the city on the tops of buses. Perhaps influenced by Aiken, Barbara alluded to attempts at acting and writing, and he defended the value of all the arts with a reference to Plato's theory of the purging effects of emotion, probably intending an allusion to Aristotle's *Poetics.*

School too offered the consolation of familiar faces, though the Harvard he returned to in the fall of 1909 for his junior year was in the midst of many changes, real and cosmetic, under President Lowell's suave, energetic leadership. Large dormitories were being erected, and plans were going forward rapidly for a new presidential mansion, designed by a Lowell relative, as more land was purchased in Cambridge for further expansion. Internally, the elective system was slowly passing into history, and toward the end of the year the inadequate adviser setup would be humanized by putting qualified seniors in charge of individual freshmen, a change cheered on by an *Advocate* commentary. As its president, Aiken would write the great majority of the magazine's articles and editorials.

But *la plus ça change, la plus c'est le même chose,* and another *Advocate* later lamented the college's continued inferiority to the graduate schools, remarking that older, distinguished faculty members who died or retired were not being replaced by teachers of equal reputation. Time and again in the course of the year, the magazine attacked the dependence in most undergraduate subjects on the inefficient, easily abused lecture system, in which professors addressed large classes and careless assistants were left to handle crucial group work and papers. Sports and social events dominated the scene, however, and the more affluent students continued to find it simple to obtain their C's with the aid of bought notes, paid tutors, and the like. In one editorial, certainly written by Aiken, who was taking Briggs's English 12, the

Advocate complained because courses in composition, like English 12 and Copey's 5, in which "more work is done per man than in many a course in Literature, and more thinking," were not credited toward a degree with distinction. Other editorials were lighter in concern and tone, discussing the disgraceful conduct of the Polo Club on one occasion and the unfairly high cost of using the college tennis courts on another, a sore issue with Aiken, who used the courts frequently.

A matter for deeper thought, never confronted directly by the *Advocate,* lay in an unaltered attitude toward literature, the aesthete pose keeping Harvard above the mainstream of American life and letters. A bright alumnus named Malcolm Cowley, who would enter the college a few years after Aiken's departure, has described a subsequent situation that devastatingly reproduces the same time-machine unreality of Aiken's school experience:

> The Harvard Aesthetes of 1916 were trying to create in Cambridge, Massachusetts, an after-image of Oxford in the 1890s. They read the *Yellow-Book,* they read Casanova's memoirs and *Les Liaisons Dangereuses,* both in French, and Petronius in Latin; they gathered at teatime in one another's rooms, or at punches in the office of the *Harvard Monthly;* they drank, instead of weak punch, seidels of straight gin topped with a maraschino cherry; they discussed the harmonies of Pater, the rhythms of Aubrey Beardsley and, growing louder, the voluptuousness of the Church, the essential virtue of prostitution. They had crucifixes in their bedrooms, and ticket stubs from last Saturday's burlesque show at the Old Howard.

Cowley also perceived that the aesthete mode was merely a studied reversal of the restraint preached by Eliot's admired Irving Babbitt, whose vaunted humanism—"poise, proportionateness, the imitation of great models, decorum and the Inner Check"—was, in turn, merely the student virtues rephrased in loftier language, such as "good taste, good manners, cleanliness, chastity, gentlemanliness (or niceness), reticence and the spirit of competition in sports . . . virtues often prized by a leisure class." Of course, as Cowley knew, the authentic artist transforms any material into artifice, but the two major currents, both derived from "penthouse garden" notions of the world, were bound to affect the construction and depth of those artifices and the lives generating them. How many Harvard graduates of the period, Cummings, Lippmann, and Dos Passos, for instance, eventually confounded the radical youth and style of their art by ripening into elitist conservatives, or, like Eliot, by totally severing experimental method from reactionary content? Even Cowley and Aiken, who remained generally true to a liberal perspective, would always regard themselves—in speech, in subtle condescensions, in unvoiced social assumptions—as preordained spokesmen for the white, Anglo-Saxon consciousness at the heart of American culture.

But Aiken, with lapses, was sufficiently sensitive to detect and combat the dangers of social and political isolation, the persistent smug egotism, that Harvard passed on to its sons and that he funneled into literature. Wallace Stevens phrased the dangers slightly differently: "Harvard feeds subjectivity, encourages an all consuming flame and that, in my mind, is an evil in so impersonal a world." Stevens, not ironically, was an ageless Harvard aesthete in his own poetic stance and conservative opinions and lifestyle. When Aiken sat down to investigate and sanctify the cycle of his past in *Ushant* four decades after graduation, he would insist "that it was not Harvard that was the center of his life while he was there, but the places to which he could escape from Harvard" (72).

Aiken's homelessness, the painful gulf between him and his contemporaries engendered by his parents' deaths (and fueling his writing quest), prevented him from being taken in by the artificial atmosphere doming Cambridge and Boston like a Giotto halo. His compulsion to rebel was never simply the youthful, transitory spasm of a peer member who accepts the group's superiority even as he defies its edicts; it was the reflex action of a permanently dislocated psyche that had come to grasp that every attitude and conviction has a dishonest (self-deceptive) base in private need. Rational education or discourse were not untenable, only suspect and incomplete. In a mature novel he would chide the "smugness and hypocrisy" of Cambridge and Boston; for now, he was a member in good standing of the college, despite a propensity for cutting classes, and of the select nucleus of talented, ambitious undergraduates seriously dedicated to achieving modernist literary goals. This nucleus was enlarged by the arrival of Hermann Hagedorn, former *Advocate* editor, who had graduated in 1907. After marriage, European travel, and a year teaching at Columbia, Hagedorn had returned to the English department as an instructor, assisting Wendell and giving a composition course. A slim, dark, handsome man of limited intellectual reach and generous impulses who identified with the revolutionary artistic aims of Aiken, Eliot, and their cohorts, Hagedorn had met Pound in Europe and in 1938 would write the first biography of Edwin Arlington Robinson.

Tinckom-Fernandez had not met Pound but had encountered his verses, and during Aiken's junior year he introduced him and Eliot to *Personae* (1909) and *Exultations* (1909). Aiken was mildly interested, but Eliot, working his way through Laforgue to a new voice, found his medievalisms quaint and "touchingly incompetent." And yet Pound's very existence, a significant catalyst in the poetic ferment coming to a boil overseas, his example of flight to elude American crassness, affected the collective consciousness of the Signet group. For Aiken, maintaining a staunch loyalty to nineteenth-century British models, even minor figures such as Thomson, John Davidson, and William Ernest Henley, the acquaintance with Hagedorn supplied another, more contemporary embodiment of a growing naturalist dimension.

Aiken reviewed Hagedorn's recent collection of poems from Houghton Mifflin, *A Troop of the Guard*, in the January 12, 1910, issue of the *Advocate*. The review is impressive for both its cold-eyed candor, a refusal to let friendship soften critical terms, and its patent knowledge of the naturalist impact upon American verse: "As a herald of the 'new poetry'—the poetry that probes to a beauty in railroads, massed cities, swarming tenements—Mr. Hagedorn is not altogether in character. In these longer and more turgid poems, at the beginning of the volume, he approaches even to the 'barbaric yawp' of Whitman; and his metres, though brutally irregular, are not electrified by dynamic motives. There is a spirit in them, but not clarity: he should mark them with some of that simplicity that marks his songs." Aiken's preference for Hagedorn's traditional lyrics, reflecting the conservative bias of his own poetry, for all its varying experiments, allows him to conclude with a sincere note of praise for "his sweetness of song and his fervor." Some twenty years hence, Edmund Wilson would declare that the "literary history of our time is to a great extent that of the development of Symbolism and of its infusion or conflict with Naturalism," and it is clear that Aiken was commencing to ingest the validity of that observation, albeit slowly, a bit reluctantly. It is also clear that Aiken's assumption of a modernist guise would never include abandonment of his strong commitment to conventional techniques, which is why he reacted positively to Robinson's marriage of the vernacular to inherited forms.

It might be well to comment briefly on this business of students reviewing students, teachers reviewing students and vice versa because it bears on the fiercely literary milieu at Harvard. Such a practice, which still prevails at Oxford and Cambridge, exemplifies the manner in which contentious interaction among a set of evolving sensibilities can be overbred into preciousness, a wary striking of pretentious poses and exaggerated delusions of self-importance. Sterility may ensue, budding careers be distorted or abridged, when this greenhouse environment, which tends to favor retreats into safe scholastic nodes and infringes upon the tyro's freedom to make silly mistakes, to take extreme risks in an art in which self must confront its secret visages. Though not harmful to an Eliot, with his internalized and durable injunctions against confessionalism in any sphere, or to an Aiken, who relished dissent, its intimidating encouragement of unequal infighting must have stymied or delayed more than one emerging talent.

Since measurements of the injury inflicted are impossible, the question remains moot. The process did inculcate a sense of literature as a vital tradition, prefiguring the embattled literary scene awaiting Aiken in his chosen profession. It also made him a better critic, whatever its negative influence on his poetic progress. That progress was given an enormous push soon after his return from England by a series of historic talks delivered at Clark University in Worcester, Massachusetts. With several colleagues, Sigmund Freud had been invited by G. Stanley Hall to lecture on his psychoanalytic theories as part of the university's twentieth anniversary celebrations in 1909. Freud gave five talks in all, followed by Carl Jung's and Sandor Ferenczi's papers, and among the distinguished audience were the ailing William James and James J. Putnam, professor of neurology at Harvard. Despite a lukewarm reception by the press, the lectures were a turning point for Freud's American reputation. Many previously hostile members of the scientific community were converted, including Putnam, who would introduce A. A. Brill's translation of *Three Contributions to the Sexual Theory* the next year. Legend has it that even James, dismayed by his Austrian colleague's eccentric dream theories, said good-bye to Freud with the words: "The future of psychology belongs to your work."

For public consumption, Boston had the benefit of the *Transcript*'s daily dispatches on the event between September 9 and 12, although "the other Boston newspapers did not consider Freud's presence in the United States to be worthy of notice." In the September 12 issue of the *Transcript* a discussion of and lengthy interview with Freud left scant doubt as to his respectability. He was referred to as "the most eminent neurologist of Europe" and "one of the greatest, if not the greatest, of psychotherapists." Previous editions had dealt with Freud's ideas about repression—regarded by its discoverer as the cornerstone of his entire edifice—and unlocking the enigmas of dreams that "preserve infantile inclinations, give 'the inside of the unconscious life,' and may frequently, if not always, be interpreted." Ferenczi's lecture was titled "The Psychological Analysis of Dreams," and it may have been the tantalizing references to dream interpretation that caught the attention of Aiken, a *Transcript* reader.

There are numerous reasons why in the period between Freud's visit and the 1920s the techniques and vocabulary of depth psychology so thoroughly infiltrated the country's intellectual climate, many having to do with the unflagging necessity for a younger generation to flail away at the restrictive vestiges of their parents' Puritan heritage, as well as a national propensity for public self-scrutiny. Later, like the Marxism of the 1930s, Freudian dogma would be embraced as another substitute for absent spiritual energy, a means of endowing a shrinking secular self with drama and significance. For artists, the appeal of psychoanalytic doctrines was almost irresistible, Freud himself having made frequent mention of the assistance received from imaginative works in unmasking and formulating some of his basic concepts. More to the point, the very language of Freudian discourse, its relentless metaphorical duality, reflected the figurative dynamics of literature and art, a further level of symbolic meaning.

For Aiken personally, whose search for self and salvation was no less urgent than Eliot's, if at a tangent to his friend's mystical bearings, the special topic of dreams and their hidden wellsprings exerted a hypnotic power. His own elaborate dreams cried out for elucidation, and he was American enough in his bones to react positively to the scientific aureole emanating from Freud's disciplined approach to them. The difficulty was linguistic, his weak command of German. Freud's masterpiece, *The Interpretation of Dreams,* would not be translated by Brill until 1913. Yet, as Carol Scholz's research indicates, the solution was near at hand, and soon after the Clark lectures "McCouch and Aiken were reading Freud's *Traumdeutung* together, McCouch's knowledge of German being superior to Aiken's. They tried to interpret their own dreams, and, according to Grayson McCouch, Aiken was much more successful in such interpretations than he. This was the beginning for Aiken of a lifelong interest in psychoanalytic theory, which he followed closely as it changed and developed."

Jake Wilbur, a slower convert to Freudianism but more devoted than McCouch, also aided Aiken's entry into the field, translating for him, bringing new information to his attention, and engaging him in long discussions about its pertinence to life and literature. His love of reading undiminished, Aiken was never content to limit himself to the leader's texts and sought relevant books and articles: "I swallowed Freud early . . . and then I pursued the thing in every direction." He consulted Jung, Ferenczi, Alfred Adler, and Ernest Jones, and he doggedly perused the six volumes of Havelock Ellis's *The Psychology of Sex,* the final volume of which was published in 1910. They complemented and amplified, at times paradoxically, the philosophical vision shaped by James and Santayana, whose *Three Philosophical Poets* was published that year by the Harvard University Press.

The lure of William James, like the lure of his brother's impressionistic psychological novels, resided ultimately in his humane openness to experience, his rejection of narrow formal and theological boundaries to sensual reality, which also assumed an underlying epistemological optimism—Freudian in this respect at least, diametrically opposed to the apocalyptic despair of a Henry Adams, more in line with Emerson and Reverend Potter. But Santayana had the additional attraction of his own peculiar brand of Romantic irony. He was the philosopher who could, with much justice, announce: "It may be conceit on my part but I think I was the only free and disinterested thinker among the Harvard philosophers. The others were looking in philosophy either for science or for religion." And yet Santayana was convinced that any serious consideration of the universe had to discern a "supernatural element" in its composition, which explains his equal appeal, though temporary, to more mystical-oriented salvation seekers such as Eliot.

Reading the essays on Lucretius, Dante, and Goethe he had heard in class, especially drawn to the introduction, in which their author insists that poetry "is not poetical for being short-winded or incidental, but, on the contrary, for being comprehensive and having range," Aiken felt that he had discovered a plummet for poetic markings of Freudian depths: "It really fixed my view of what poetry should ultimately be. . . . That it really had to begin by *understanding,* or trying to understand." The actual synthesis of philosopher-poet and Freudian investigator of an unconscious self was still nebulous, however, as his remorseless poetry writing, "all the way from free verse, Walt Whitman, to the most elaborate villanelles and ballad forms," stayed yoked to nineteenth-century models, Decadent in intention but Romantic underneath. That winter he had the honor of reading Shelley aloud to a small cadre of undergraduates, including McCabe, brought together each week in his rooms by Santayana (145).

In spite of Eliot's terse dismissal of the Promethean poet as a "fool," Aiken's love of Shelley was unshaken, and the personal contact with Santayana's subtle mind and caustic wit was as stimulating as ever, if occasionally disconcerting. For instance, considerable praise was lavished upon Anna Hempstead Branch, especially in Boston, her book-length narrative poem on the biblical *Nimrod* having recently pumped more abstract philosophizing into the city's dense literary haze. Never immune to inferior rhetoric when shackled inside Romantic formulas, Aiken fell under her spell and, in a fit of enthusiasm, loaned Santayana her books during one of their weekly reading sessions. The consequences were salutary when he returned them at the next session and dubbed her "Miss Twig" with a grin. Enthusiasm for Branch waned and would eventually disappear.

Something else Santayana said that winter clung to Aiken's selective consciousness, perhaps because it placed such an awesome weight on the under-developed psyche of a college junior with bold literary aspirations. After one of the readings, in the midst of a general discussion about Shelley's maturation, Santayana mentioned that "it was probable that the individual's 'range' of thought, or imagination, his reach, or capacity, was already adumbrated by the time he was twenty-one" (248). In retrospect, Aiken had the wisdom to wonder why, if this were true (and it seemed plausible), he had been unable to evolve his final aesthetic, "the consistent view," while at Harvard, and the further wisdom to perceive his younger self's confusion and immaturity. The slow translation of Freudian constructs into comprehensible tenets with Mc-Couch's and Wilbur's assistance was dismantling the pact with the past that his psyche had engineered, challenging the validity of the tool, his writing, most instrumental in keeping the pact secure. Intimating obscure foundation faults, the findings of psychoanalysis "appeared all too damningly to discredit the artist or writer completely: it had been difficult, in that esurient shadow, to keep up one's *amour-propre,* and difficult, too, and frightening, in such a situation, to venture further with one's own speculations and explorations" (248).

Regardless of expertise, self-analysis is always a perilous business, particularly before all the pieces have been located. Writing was Aiken's saving ritual, as well as his most successful mask, a paternal replica. The act itself served as release, as control device, as plastic extension of a fully absorbed deification of the creative function. Any blows delivered against the heroic statue of the poet erected in his imagination threatened fragmentation. Literature conceived of as neurotic wish-fulfillment, when not qualified by a more exhaustive familiarity with Freud's and Jung's crucial concessions to the artist's uncharted role outside psychoanalytic mechanisms, is naturally frightening to a sensitive, narcissistic individual schooled to respect an enlightened scheme of human progress, however indebted to Romantic synapses.

Though America's cultural consciousness was to adopt Freudianism as a new religion and pseudo-intellectual parlor game with revivalist passion, the young Aikens throughout the land had to confront the terrifying abyss suddenly yawning beneath their feet, plunging them into the inferno of their own strange minds, where reason had no more substance than tissue paper in restraining whatever primitive forces were governing their behavior, their arts, their politics, their philosophies, even their love choices. As therapy, depth psychology promised confession, catharsis, absolution, and sanity; yet its fundamental vision was harrowing, deterministic in the extreme. But the organism is always greater than the sum of its intellect, and Aiken was rescued by his youth, the physiological optimism of a healthy body that had no past or future death to slow down its enjoyment of an eternal present tense. He wrote his playful, self-conscious imitations of the lyric paragons museumed in *The Golden Treasury* and began, at least in his prose, to transmute, piecemeal, Freudian dynamics into surface conflicts.

Being in Briggs's class for the year helped, not only for the practical bonus of the professor's shrewd critical comments but for the habitual reassertion of serene self-confidence and stationary Socratic values he also incarnated, the good-natured *arete* Harvard offered at its best: much Donne mixed in with an American love of sports and a New Englander's steady cultivation of an inquiring mind as God's highest praise. The solid liberalism bred out of a Puritan pursuit of excellence by Unitarian radicalism, which Aiken admired in his grandfather, manifested itself in the classroom through a constant emphasis on independent study and student-teacher interactions. Like an effective editor, Briggs was not intent upon imposing the restrictions of a single ideal style or of using his platform for ego trips. The students were asked to write "more or less, what we wanted to," brought their papers to class, submitted them, and Briggs selected one of their poems, essays, or stories to read aloud at the start of each session. Discussion followed, then Briggs's personal evaluation or reaction, and the last ten minutes were given over to writing a short critique of the paper read.

It was a simple but efficient system, primarily because of its organizer's kindly tact and keen eye for self-indulgences. Although publishing in the *Advocate* with regularity, secure in his recognition as a literary light on campus, Aiken appreciated the enduring benefits bestowed by a teacher impervious to the vanity rife among his eccentric colleagues in the English department. Briggs, "perhaps the most universally loved officer of instruction and government that Harvard ever had," quoted Donne, made small, nonwounding jokes, exhorted every student to engage in team sports, and corrected the papers of his charges with wit and dispassionate insight. In later years Aiken was never reluctant to praise the affection and concrete aid rendered by this rare man.

But the work published during his junior year does not exhibit much improvement over the admittedly competent work of the previous two years, even though evidencing a curious thematic split between the poetry and the prose. The poems are all of a piece in their familiar adherence to a nineteenth-century logos, Robinson to the contrary. The fascination with the ambiguous relationship between artist and art, seen earlier in "The Potter" and "The Burmese Sculptor," was now extended into " 'Le Penseur,' " "Le Reveur," and "Orpheus." The first two obviously had for their inspiration Aiken's summer encounter with Rodin's powerful figures. In forty-nine lines of adroitly varied iambic pentameter that eludes blank-verse prosiness through a series of slant rhymes, repetitions, end-line alliterations, and a few masculine rhymes, " 'Le Penseur' " permits the statue to have his say, after a brief introduction by the sculptor, which is the best part of the poem:

> I made a statue; out of formless marble
> I fashioned him to image in my brain
> With smooth, white muscles, cunningly, and brow
> Unluminous with mind. I made him sit,—

> This thing uncouth,—and wrestle with his thoughts;
> And then I dreamed I heard him stir, and cry,—
> Baffled and hopeless in his quest for truth,—

Then follows a Shelleyan plea by the statue, a human figure freed by art, for an escape from the devouring consciousness of his new brain, a yearning for marble's sleep to erase the world he did not make. In light of the havoc wrought by Freud in Aiken's mind, it is no wonder such a plea triggers a reply from the dreamer—a ceaseless circling return to Poe's "dream within a dream" construct for a child's stance—in "Le Reveur," a dramatic monologue, in which the sculptor voices his godlike rage against the statue's whine:

> Bring me the chisel . . .
>
> . . . .
>
> . . . and I will smite
> Such master-stroke as never Phidias smote
> Among his Parian marbles; feel such bliss
> As God once gloried in, when out of dust
> He fused a beautiful man and laughed to see!

His rhetorical probing of the sculpture, which has become a symbol of mankind, could be a nightmare interrogation of Aiken by Freud:

> Under my chisel dost thou writhe and burn
> In anguish, like a sleeper stirred from dreams?
> For thee is everything so profitless,
> And life so filled with pain? And art so weary
> Of feeling with dull fingers after truth?

Aiken had no answer, except the poem itself, the reply lifted from Pater and Arnold, which meant the artist accepting divinity, cultural heroism. The poem must therefore conclude in the act of transforming the statue into a carbon copy of his own sacred image: "What if it pain him, or he long to sleep? / Hot is the impulse, now—bring me the chisel!" In "Orpheus," the mythic musician is talking to us from inside old age, "old as any toad," brought low by "frail human spirit, dust-perfume / Which gods bestow on mortals!" He is about to meet his preordained destiny, to be torn to pieces by the Maenads as he sings a dirge for Eurydice, "for her I loved." Archaic and precious, the poem manages to avoid achieving Browningesque animation despite clever pacing and a deft manipulation of sounds. But Aiken's desire to capture this specific melancholy moment in the Orpheus legend suggests how deeply he was agitated by Freud's rewriting of dream (hence mythic) sagas, how desperate to reaffirm the potency of the creative office.

With "Polyphemus" he also did some rewriting of his own, using the cyclops to play off against Tennyson's "Ulysses." By speaking from the consciousness of the one-eyed giant defeated by the crafty Greek, who was the aging voice of besieged but unyielding mankind in Tennyson's verse—"Made weak by time and fate, but strong in will"—Aiken could again exercise his preoccupation with victims, articulate the ultimate outsider, the monster, as Mary Shelley had done in *Frankenstein, or the Modern Prometheus.* Polyphemus is a human creation, an artifice of Homer and Tennyson and (as mythic antagonist) of Freudian caveman. Whatever compassion is elicited for Polyphemus is also, in the end, the essential self-pity of a poet shorn of rational faith and divine imminence. Blindness is a pith image because it is the worst fear imaginable for one who loves the word, who controls reality with language on the page. In this milieu the savage deed at the poem's climax, Polyphemus rending the faultless ram with bare hands, seems almost reasonable because the ram had been an element in Ulysses' escape, the sly hero, who "wove a darkness for me with his brain." A similar hostility was harbored against Freud.

Dreams, dreaming, and the dreamer were recurrent verse motifs, often linked with the theme of mutability, and in his prose Aiken was more apt to confront the Freudian dilemma directly. A story called "Corpus Vile," an adaptation of Dickens's *A Christmas Carol,* has a needy poet, Simon Plangian, for its protagonist. Sick, cold, and homeless as a Christmas Eve tide of rain and snow soaks him, he remembers happier Christmases past, when he could, like the children now eyeing him, "gaze out of the windows at the shivering passers-by." Taking shelter in a doorway, he is called into a warm house by a "dark, bearded man, with something fierce and supernatural in his face," perhaps Freud himself, who takes him inside, introduces him to two companions, and gives him a loaf of bread and a carafe of wine to eat and drink, promising him a feast after he talks to them a while. He tells his story of failure, of vain poetical ambitions, of sickness and loss of work, of the death or distancing of all relatives, of starvation, while the three men listen attentively, "as if they were conducting an experiment in a laboratory."

The wine and exhaustion, assisted by a clock (hypnosis), induce a trance, and one of the men gives him three suggestions: "Cleopatra's barge . . . the walls of Troy . . . Christmas Eve." The result is three dreams as Simon flies first to the Nile, where he plays a lute and sings to Cleopatra on her barge, futilely trying to warn her of a bleak future with Antony and the asp; second, to besieged Troy, where he vainly attempts to warn Andromache about the wooden horse; and last, appropriately, to his own childhood home on Christmas Eve, which is explicitly Aiken's Savannah home: "By an open fire stood three children, each holding a stocking, and talking feverishly. . . . With a sort of hunger he glanced at the familiar things in the room, grimly making an inventory of them—even the toy music-box, and the little glass penguin on the mantelpiece." Just as Santa Claus is about to enter the room from behind a Christmas tree, he is awakened by the doctors (now identified as such) and asked to write down his dreams, which he does. Their joy is plain: " 'A perfect experiment!' cried the man with the chill blue eyes—'the *motif* obeyed in all three cases—!' "

What happens next is extraordinary. It demonstrates the genuine rage Aiken nurtured against Freud at this point in his career. When questioned about the promised feast, Simon is informed that it "was all a fake," a false bait to get him involved, and he is unceremoniously given his hat and coat and hustled back into the street. Once outside, in agony, he realizes that he had merely served as the *corpus vile* for a weird experiment, had been dissected and cast aside. To all intents and purposes the story's sad, bitter climax has been reached, but this is the Christmas issue of the *Advocate*. Aiken knew that a happy ending was required. Thus Simon discovers a generous check in his coat pocket: "Christmas Eve—Christmas Eve!"

Jay Martin says that "Corpus Vile" constitutes "Aiken's first explicit self-investigation as he moves, in Plangian, from his generic to his specific past to discover that it is impossible to change history; one must simply, as he later argues in his play *Mr. Arcularis,* understand and accept it." However valid in thematic outline, this generalization takes insufficient cognizance of the relationship between the story's latent and manifest content (to borrow Freud's very pertinent terms), which tend to deny the presence of much "explicit self-investigation," unless hidden motives and fears are considered. The movement from the generic (poet) to a specific past (childhood home) is indeed the central mechanism in a linear plot, but the story's main energy, and it is not a potent work, wells from an inner frustration with the psychic damage inflicted by a Freudian apparatus. The scientists are arch villains, despite a slapped-on coda of joy, the story built around the insidious impact of psychoanalysis on imagination, keyed to *The Interpretation of Dreams.* In the one certain autobiographical scene, for instance, the Aiken children have been reduced to three, conforming with Freud's treatment of that number as fundamental to fairy tales, dreams' truest literature.

Literature abounds, from Dickens through Virgil to Shakespeare, never history alone. The lesson that Aiken preaches is not simply the impossibility of altering the past, including his own, but the way in which artistic praxes must now incorporate a Freudian system. At its emotive base, "Corpus Vile" is a deliberate, furious assault upon the loss of innocence embedded in any acceptance of Freudian language to describe the poet's task and self-anger against the intrusion of science in a realm previously thought safe from its calculated probes, plus a personal cry of pain over the psychic cost to Aiken's posture as a writer. It is interesting, from a biographical vantage, that the sole "real" dream is interrupted before Santa appears, before the father enters the picture. Even as readings in Freud and other analysts began to provide him with material for his fiction, Aiken sensed that the new science would eventually force a perilous confrontation with the traumatic scene of his parents' deaths and his repressed reaction to them and it, which explains Simon's role as a male Cassandra in the invented dreams. Logically, if the third dream had not been aborted, he would have had to play a similar part. The query then becomes: what would he have warned his childhood self about?

Of course, the introduction of psychological factors can be excessive, but the obvious Freudian allusions, to the extent of inserting the hypnosis method —Freud had already abandoned the practice himself—invites it. Besides, Aiken was to emerge as one of the first American writers consciously to employ Freudian and Jungian concepts in his work, which puts an additional burden on his biographer, who must chart their appearances, relating them to the more traditional methods and referential systems also being used, often simultaneously. The intriguing enigma, and literature thrives on mystery, would be to discern where deliberate and unconscious manipulation part company. In "Corpus Vile," for example, all seems conscious, the intentional construct of a highly intelligent mind laboring to synthesize Freudian theory and well-absorbed habits of craft, except, perhaps, in the shift from the victims of prior stories to the poet-as-victim in this case. I doubt that Aiken was fully aware of the shift's precise meaning, although in some fashion he had to have intuited the serious danger and richness of potential material available as poet-persona stepped closer to its protagonist mask, its imaged or willed self.

Other stories from the same year are not nearly as revealing or as good. "By the Hermitage Walls" is a brief tale about "Crazy Sue," a descendant of Wordsworth's female vagrants, who has lost her husband to an epidemic and lives with her infant in "a deserted slave-hut" outside of town, wherever that may be. Another victim, she lives off the land, but several boys playing at soldiers intrude, which precipitates a selfless gesture: she leaves the baby she loves for them to find and take home. They do so and march off, under the command, significantly, of a "red-headed lad." The anticlimax is a slight variation on the anticlimaxes of earlier tales: "And poor Sue sat down on the bank, her feet in cool water, and wept bitterly." "The Huntsman" fares little better, though more complexly plotted, an offspring of the convention of a character rushing to meet his inescapable destiny. Mark Lukens, the hero, is a Fatalist with a capital F: " 'It was Fatalism that made me a wholesale chemist, out of a pasty-faced clerk selling "Drugs and Spices" in a penny pharmacy. It was Fatalism—bless it!—that kept me a solid old bachelor, as I am to-day. And Fatalism will send me grinning to my grave!' "

The huntsman of the title appears at the inn where Lukens is staying and engages him in a game of cards for high stakes, five pounds a game, with a ten-game limit, after Lukens informs him of his defiant philosophy: Fatalism as a species of optimism, the belief that "man is the victim of circumstances . . . fate is preordained," a sour idea for most to swallow, but one that he deems fortuitous and exciting. During the game Lukens detects his opponent cheating, but cheating to lose. After losing every hand, the huntsman plunges a knife into the table and declares, "I am your Destiny. I am that Fatalism which has been toiling around you, spreading the net for your feet." As in a Poe fiction, Death has arrived in disguise to confound rebellion and philosophy, but Lukens is unperturbed: " 'I am ready, now. Strike me, and be done.' "

Both stories date from early in the semester, before Freud, and they reflect the English terrain and victim-figures of previous stories, with the dramatic switch at the end of "The Huntsman," where Aiken appears determined to negate the defeatism motif scoring all his college compositions. Though neither convincing nor touching, and based once more on flat characters, "The Huntsman" at least marks the manner in which a personality like Aiken's— youthful, vibrant, irreligious, attuned to contemporary currents, among them Spencer and Darwin—might shape, for the moment, a consoling secular philosophy, sheer Nietzschean will, out of the despair generated by knowledge of human insignificance. If still unrealized as *felt* experience, the only experience ensuring comprehension—and Aiken saw himself as a "cheerful pessimist"—the notion of transcending fate through acceptance of irresistible forces was an initial advance in a progressive acceptance of consciousness as godhead and destiny: plural, circular, contradictory, yet evolutionary. A future has to be assumed for fiction and existence to persevere.

Much more important is the essay "On Moving House," published in the *Advocate* a month after "Corpus Vile." The sequence is relevant because the essay emanates from the story's brief Christmas memory, a personal contemplation of the past that illustrates how Freudian doctrine (partial at this stage) and selective autobiography could be mixed to attain a surer grip upon existence's symbolic layers, nearer truth. In *The Interpretation of Dreams,* Freud quotes K. A. Scherner's analysis of a dream and its images, which included the human body "pictured by the phantasy of the dream as a house," and further on speaks about the unreality of death to a child, particularly the death of parents. A footnote to the latter reads: "To my astonishment, I was told of a highly intelligent boy of ten, after the sudden death of his father, who said: 'I understand that father is dead, but I can't see why he does not come home to supper.' "

Aiken, of course, had been a highly intelligent boy of eleven when his parents died, and homelessness had been a perpetual ache (and fictional signature) ever since. The philosophy behind "On Moving House" is that championed by the Fatalist in "The Huntsman," an exalted version of "whistling in the dark," converting the dross of mourning into golden opportunities: "Loss, or deprivation, is a salutary misfortune which the gods visit upon us with great wisdom; by this means they teach us all that is best in life; and by lopping off this or that bough and cutting away our lovliest flowers, they make us all the more sensitive to the sun that heals our stumps, and train our spirits to a greater profusion of bloom and far sweeter fragrance." Closer to William James and/or Unitarian optimism than to Santayana, this constitutes a brave formula of pragmatic adaptation to profound psychological injuries. When a threat to the psyche is involved, the imaginative faculty does, in general, seek healing reversals of polar oppositions, a form of protective rationalization. Aiken's struggle to deal with the anxiety-producing material of *The Interpretation of Dreams*, which undermined his persona as poet and instigated a flow of painful childhood recollections, prodded him into writing a personal essay—in itself unique, a sign of unease—that agrees with Freud's statement about a child's incapacity for comprehending oblivion, using a child "not yet ten" for his own example: "At such an age, death is to him an anomaly, an impenetrable mystery."

But personal experience had taught him that death's unreality, an absence or apparent absence of healthy mourning, can be connected to the terrible fears (separation anxieties) stirred up by the loss of a home, house-moving insecurity, which is "something real, intimate, and tangible." House and body are halves of a metaphor, he concedes, because the house "is the lodging-place of his soul: a soul still too sensitive and large for the tabernacle of flesh that is building around it. As he grows older his own body becomes hardier and stronger, and the house less important as an asylum; and some day he will leave it never to return. But what a hazardous enterprise comes to him at the age of ten, if he must tear himself out of that well-loved earth, and transplant himself to other and wholly unknown regions!" Aiken alights upon the hermit crab for his central analogy, which enables him to evoke the crucial difference between a crab adapting unsentimentally to a larger shell and a child "torn out of his dark crypt and exposed to clouds of sunshine."

The peculiar reversals here—sunshine as enemy, former life as death— unwittingly reveal the gap between the author's actual despair and the rational gaiety he is working hard to project as the affirmative consequences of losing a home, a mother, a self. True emotions surge to the fore at last in paragraphs of unrelieved desolation: "Bare floor, bare walls, a dusty window,—that is all that remains to him of years of perfect happiness. . . . For the wrath of God has been visited upon this fair land, and has left it only a necropolis, a city of the dead: where only the ghosts of things shall whisper among cobwebs, and the mice scamper in the walls, and the doors rattle a little on their hinges, as if crying to be open."

There is an allusion to Wordsworth's "solitary reaper" along the way, and Wordsworth's entire aesthetic campaign to retool sensual, amoral nature (via creative principles) into a divine dynamic to replace missing godheads might have contributed as much to Aiken's essay as Pater and Freud, if only as a model for how the human imagination can metamorphosize the most adverse circumstances into positive semantic nodes of apprehension. Aiken's version of resurrection and salvation emerges in the final two paragraphs, commencing "Thereafter comes the Adventure" and developing a parallel with Sinbad the Sailor discovering "new streets, new trees, new houses, new sunlight" as he finds in nature the soothing melodies of Wordsworth and of Coleridge's (and Shelley's) pantheistic Aeolian Harp. "He trembles to new and undiscovered arias of nature. . . . He is as sensitive to the inaudible melodies of the Universe as the Lyre that listens in heaven to the silver vapors that mount to it among the stars." He admits to the spirit's moments of "inexpressible sadness" but insists that such a "state of things cannot endure for long."

Aiken possessed enough insight, social and Freudian, to realize that the poet does not, like a "normal" child, ever mature, ever abandon the past and its sorrows, but surmounts the problem by accenting a slick-magazine vision of the artist: "Were it to continue, and steep that frail soul in the spilth of all loveliness, then the soul would remain forever a child, forever sensitive, and become what we call a poet or a composer." Leaving aside the slush language, which is not typical of his undergraduate prose and connotes insincerity as well as genuine agitation, the urge to convert unacceptable emotions into Pollyanna optimism has caused him to front, in public view, pieces of his own history never uncovered before, though still at an arranged distance. And the deeper self-deception behind "On Moving House" does not obviate its value (to him and the reader) as a tentative exploration of a semiconfessional mode. At the end of the essay he has sufficient candor to permit a blade of dolorous truth to slip between obese lines: "But the effect of that change will lie in his soul always, even as the golden delta at the mouth of a river: and islands rise from the waters, and trees grow on the islands, and birds sing in the trees."

That older Harvard aesthete, Wallace Stevens, who was intimately familiar with the "acute intelligence of the imagination, the illimitable resource of its memory, its power to possess the moment it perceives," would offer the prescription for enduring unendurable reality that applies to "On Moving House" and Freudianism, a paradigm of the universal creative process: "Resistance to the pressure of ominous and destructive circumstances consists of its conversion, so far as possible, into a different, an explicable, an amenable circumstance." Successful or not, and for the time being it allowed Aiken to continue his diet of psychoanalytic texts, the process is comparable to the act of faith many Victorian writers, Tennyson among them, had to will for themselves in order to bind divided egos into functioning wholes. To be cynical, the tension that accrues is wonderful for the poet's task, if harrowing, as *In Memoriam* can attest, but Aiken, still a novice in poetry and psychology, could not yet feed such tensions into his work.

Ironically, Aiken's essay was followed in the pages of the *Advocate* by Eliot's Laforgue-inspired "Spleen," a foreshadow of "Prufrock." The last stanza proffers an amusing yet melancholy portrait of the aged self trapped inside Eliot's lithe young body:

> And Life, a little bald and gray,
> Languid, fastidious, and bland,
> Waits, hat and gloves in hand,
> Punctilious of tie and suit
> (Somewhat impatient of delay)
> On the doorstep of the Absolute.

Aiken was impressed by the poem, conscious of its superiority to his own less urbane verses, but its satiric acidity and religious trajectory were not congenial to his temperament or philosophical set. Eliot, who would strategically bend Freud to suit metaphysical purposes and who already knew, unlike Aiken, that "we have all to choose whatever subject matter allows us the most powerful and the most secret release," was having an arduous year, his last at Harvard, as he steeped himself in Dante, merged "the study of Laforgue together with the later Elizabethan drama," and made the decision to spend the next year in Paris, finding himself and writing. It was a decision that irked his parents and contributed to a brief hospital stay near the end of the second semester.

Aiken and Eliot maintained their vocational partnership, shared poems and ideas, though Eliot was on the brink of major expression. They also shared the social scene as before, to a degree, and welcomed the appearance of moving picture houses in Boston, Aiken embracing films with an almost indiscrimi-

Harvard Advocate *staff in 1910. Aiken is in the center of the second row,
Eliot to his right in the first row.*

nate love that was to persist for the rest of his life. Their pleasure in mocking
the pretensions of Boston's upper crust located a perfect foil in Adeleine (or
Madeleine) Moffat, whose drawing room behind the Boston State House was
the frequent locus of teas for acceptable Harvard students. Aiken was harsh on
her, "our deplorable friend . . . the *precicuse ridicule* to end all preciosity
serving tea so exquisitely among her bric-a-brac," and Ruth McIntyre, introduced to her salon by McCabe, described her as a "tall, flat, arty woman"
who "wore long dresses, with long sleeves and wooden beads." In *Ushant* the
verdict is equally sharp but also intent upon attacking McCabe and Eliot, a
critical perception of Eliot in a toadying association with Madeleine, "who,
like another Circe, had made strange shapes of Wild Michael and the Tsetse"
(186). The reference to an early Eliot poem on Circe and to the complex
interaction between the shallow lady and the sensitive, reflective young protagonist of "Portrait of a Lady"—based on Moffat and well begun in November— implies that Aiken understood that his two cosmopolitan friends, for all
their disparagement of the lady, were drawn to the aristocratic cultivation of
the arts she tried so pitifully to simulate.

The rebellion against obsolete poetic forms that Aiken and Eliot were busy
launching never fully extended to their attitudes concerning more exclusive

social forms. They attended the teas and dances that Boston society offered as bridges to its refined Beacon Hill ghetto of "high serious" culture, but Aiken was never bewitched by the intrinsic snobbism of their presumed superiority, not recognizing minor reflections of the identical snobbism in himself. Neither was Eliot at the intellectual level, although, like Henry James, he was most at home when installed at the right club or in the right sitting rooms and would never dream of refusing to observe the rules of leisure-class decorum and custom, however inane. Chosen to write the Ode for the Class of 1910, he complied without qualm or hesitation, and on June 24 read it at Sanders, after attending the huge garden party for seniors in the Yard, then listened to "the Orator speak of the debt a Harvard man owed to the community and of efficiency as the quality to be cultivated above all others." The Ode is typical of its genre, nothing else, its second (and final) stanza summarizing what was expected to be summarized:

> Yet for all of these years that to-morrow has lost
>   We are still the less able to grieve,
> With so much that of Harvard we carry away
>   In the place of the life that we leave.
> And only the years that efface and destroy
>   Give us also the vision to see
> What we owe for the future, the present, and past,
>   Fair Harvard, to thine and to thee.

The dwindling of his junior year reminded Aiken not of debts to Harvard but of emptying halls, a period of farewells and change. Barbara, who accompanied him to baseball games and on rural walks, had graduated from Miss Winsor's—he bought her a bouquet of roses for the occasion—and was entering Radcliffe in the fall. Their relationship, still riddled by the parries and thrusts of contrary natures, did not alleviate the dreariness of contemplating Eliot's departure. Nor did it pillow the shock of Tinckom-Fernandez's expulsion for cutting too many classes. Incredulous, patently shaken, the small, dark student with the precise British accent and the contagious enthusiasm asked Aiken to stroll around Fresh Pond with him, "that classic Cambridge walk," as soon as he learned the worst, weeping as he tried to convey his anguish.

Another, more tragic farewell involved Paul Mariett, who was finishing a year during which he won the second Bowdoin Prize, had a story published in the *Atlantic Monthly,* and completed all the requirements for a degree, planning to devote his senior year to taking philosophy courses. Near the start of the second semester he had met Aiken and a few others in the Yard and stopped them to indicate a peculiar pain and lump he had developed in his back. The lump was malignant, cancer of the spine, and he would spend the greater portion of his senior year in the hospital and in his Cambridge home as an invalid wracked by increasing agony.

In *Ushant,* where literature must hold sway, the farewells signaled that the "literary *milieu,* at Harvard, had for the time being, with those absences, become stagnant."

Thou are young, and desirest child
and marriage. But I ask thee: Art
thou a man entitled to desire a
child?
Art thou the victorious one, the
self-conqueror, the ruler of thy
passions, the master of thy virtues?
Friedrich Nietzsche,
Thus Spake Zarathustra

· · · · · · · · · ·

SEX AND ART, YES

While Eliot went back again to the sea-cooled shores of Cape Ann before invading Paris, Aiken left Cambridge early in July 1910 for the muggy heat and airless tenements of Manhattan's Lower West Side. Though he was partially motivated by fear of embarrassment if he returned to Troutbeck and Alice, who must now know of his carnal urges, the choice of New York City for a summer vacation was not without canny literary foresight. Boston had rigidified into that front-parlor state in which social rituals replace original gestures of protest and rebellion, its decline as an artistic center evident to all but its most fanatic residents. The larger, cruder metropolises of New York and Chicago were attracting the new ideas (native and European) and their innovative supporters, who would soon bring about a cultural revolution unique in American experience. The New England Renaissance had been too local and British, its most profound effects—Emerson's covert radicalism, Hawthorne's severe moral criticisms, Dickinson's experimental poetry—not yet fully integrated into the nation's consciousness.

New York's city as city, as opposed to Boston as preserved town, offered the advantage of social fluidity, of indifference and mass, neighborhoods elastic and isolated enough to constitute separate but cross-fertilizing kingdoms, cheap places to live and relative freedom from Establishment interference, plus a steady supply of talented, uncorrupted, ambitious young immigrants (internal and foreign). Money had its prime function, too, the excess that such growing cities tend to accumulate and lavish on culture as justification for its acquisition—money and the energy it emits around its edges, making possible the emergence of counterenergies, the intermingling of generational antagonisms, aesthetic experimentalism, political dissent. Areas like Greenwich Village, once staid and secure, were crumbling under the onslaught of Italian immigrants, which, in turn, because of lower rents and middle-class flight, would generate a magnetic pull on apprentice artists and writers, much to the disgust of resident Italians.

The process is endless and invigorating, and it needs a genuinely urban setting for success—or, in later stages, the uncomprehending indifference of rural remoteness. America, as unrealized ideal and haven for Europe's revolutionaries and hungry masses, was ripe for the renewal of pure self-interest that such a process can inspire at the creative level, self-interest in the sense of self-scrutiny from angles previously thought oblique or dangerous. Art follows trade, feeds off commerce's droppings, even as it denies the philistine values inherent in that commerce. The cultural explosion that would soon transform America from a European province into a distinct world entity, paralleling events in the political and economic spheres, garnered its gunpowder from the interior trade routes that took the products of the Midwest into Chicago and the products of the East Coast into New York. Neither simple nor consistent, the pattern was almost inevitable. A Vachel Lindsay and a Floyd Dell would have to leave the countryside to seek their fortunes (and like spirits) in the Stockyard City, as Stephen Crane had earlier left New Jersey for the throbbing arteries of the Bowery. That Crane also had to flee New York under the pressure of corrupt policemen was a sign of the historic process running against the rocks of entrenched conservatism, another contrary flow that would cause many of Aiken's generation to do likewise a decade hence.

Though not yet familiar with Baudelaire and enamored of Boston's quieter ways, Aiken felt the lure, the deliciously sinful vibrancy of rawer cityscapes through acquaintance with the works of Whitman, Henley, and Davidson. As a young poet intent upon transferring naturalistic methods to his own verses, he was bound to respond to New York's ceaseless flow of traffic and people, the exotic sights and smells of constant human transitions, human extremes, as he and Eliot had responded to the slum neighborhoods of Boston. Determined upon a career in journalism, Tinckom-Fernandez had drifted to Manhattan after his expulsion and settled in a seedy lodging house on West Twenty-third Street, off Tenth Avenue, an old block long known as "London Terrace." Operated by a brawny Scotswoman and her drunken husband, the house attracted many writers and a number of British actors, two of whom were in residence when Aiken arrived. It was a kind of "Grub Street dormitory," in the words of Van Wyck Brooks, who had also recently come to room there after his return from England.

Brooks recalled that the house had "three big trees in the front yard, with a cast-iron fountain and a bench, and, within, the kind of furnished rooms that O. Henry so often described with half-broken chairs and the odors of mildewed woodwork." Rates were reasonable, however, and Aiken was glad to have Tinckom-Fernandez and Brooks around to remind him of Harvard's relative aesthetic proximity—a reminder enhanced by contact with Alan Seeger, who had graduated in June and who also believed residence in Manhattan necessary for his writing ambitions. Across the street was the saloon where they could buy a nickel beer and feed abundantly at its free-lunch counter, a favorite haunt of Edwin Arlington Robinson when he lived in a brownstone down the street eight years before. J. B. Yeats, well-known painter and father of the poet, who had come to America to lecture that year and decided to remain, was a frequent visitor and droll raconteur, aged but still young in energy and spirit. "I *am* the Great Yeats!" was his emphatic retort whenever asked if he was sire to the great W. B.

A favorite dining place and general hangout was the Petit Pas, a French restaurant several blocks away, where the painter could often be found. Aiken records in *Ushant* an evening when the death-obsessed Seeger had swept into the restaurant in typical histrionic fashion "with the announcement that war was beautiful, and old Yeats had sprung at him like a mastiff" (198). After dinner at the Petit Pas, Aiken, Brooks, and Fernandez liked to stroll down to the Battery to watch the Staten Island ferries berth before taking the subway back to their dirty, ovenlike rooms, where damp sheets and bedbugs made sleep near impossible. The heat and grime were part of it, of course, necessary ingredients of the Bohemian existence Aiken could only play at enjoying, another form of slumming, as he sought to process the city scene first encountered the previous summer in London.

Like most such numbing exposure, however, the "revel" proved chaotic beyond his control. An autobiographical short story, "The Orange Moth," captures the adolescent flavor of the experience and the sense of futility Aiken endured when attempting to render it into art: "It was wonderful, living in a dirty boarding-house in the great city. The vast multiplicity thrilled him and made him melancholy. There it was, so close to him, so immediate, yet he could do nothing with it! Some poison in his brain turned it all to dullness, to mud—no, worse than that, a kind of lifeless simulacrum, a mechanical formula—as soon as he tried to touch it." In essence, the city's cry for a realistic response was being muffled by his Harvard distance, the lingering haze of aesthete remoteness surrounding his every feeling and thought. Significantly, the protagonist in the story is seen attempting to write about "Beauty," that fondest of Romantic topics and rallying flag for the 1890 Decadents, with a volume of DeQuincey's ornate prose perched near at hand and sentences of Pater drifting through his head. Under the circumstances, failure was a foregone conclusion, and the tale's climax, an "actual" dream in which the hero closes his blank book on an orange moth and opens it to find that "in purple, a poem of extraordinary beauty was written there," points up his ultrarefined callowness.

But the summer was hardly wasted or tedious. Although he did not lose his embarrassing virginity, remaining a naif in the sexual sphere, Aiken took pleasure in New York's more banal charms: the chiming bell at Madison Square, eating at a Child's, the six o'clock whistle and resultant traffic jams, reading the foreign magazines at Brentano's, visiting the museums and sending picture postcards to Barbara and Cambridge relatives, and venturing to the Palisades for a swim and lovely river views. If nothing else, Manhattan illustrated the paradox at the frustrated core of his writing ambitions, his personal preference for the quieter, more civilized precincts of Boston in perpetual conflict with an awareness of the creative quasars pulsing beneath New York's restless streets.

In contrast, the summer of Aiken's urban initiation was also the summer of William James's death. Having voyaged to Lamb House in Rye, England, to comfort his younger brother Henry, whose despair over the paltry financial rewards gained from the New York edition of his collected works had culminated in a severe depression and psychosomatic illness, he then traveled on to Paris, Lucerne, and Geneva before returning to Lamb House for a rest. A dangerous heart condition had worsened under the strain of travel, and he yearned for home. Accompanied by his wife and brother, James sailed from Liverpool for Quebec and from there went straight to his Chocorua residence, where he died in the early afternoon of August 26, a Friday. The following Monday his body was taken to Cambridge and modest but impressive services were held at Harvard's Appleton Chapel, causing Henry James later to write that the college, "meagre mother, did for him—the best that Harvard can." As requested, his body was cremated and his ashes buried in Mt. Auburn Cemetery beside his parents.

Henry was to remain in America for a year, his last visit, dissatisfied as ever with the thinness of sophisticated cultural life in his native land, though he thought New York less drab than sterile Cambridge. His feelings about America, once as ambivalent as those about William, were congealing into final negative shape during that difficult year of adjustment and have been effectively summarized by his assiduous biographer, Leon Edel, in a pertinent

sketch of the era's gross national product: "Everywhere in America he de-
plored the lack of ritual, the absence of standards. Above all he saw great
affluence, great waste, and he was disturbed by the life of the rich who seemed
to have no sense of *noblesse oblige*. He was revolted by the growth of advertising and publicity; and it seemed to him that a great national selfishness
existed in America from which all kindness had been banished." The sketch is
precisely that, biased somewhat by Henry's inability to see beyond an unhappy past and acute class consciousness, which clashed with his dead brother's love of America's raw vitality and rich terrain, but near enough a consensus intellectual perception to underscore a generational disgust with rampant
American materialism that Aiken and Eliot tended to share.

After his return to Harvard for his senior year, Aiken began to receive
letters from Eliot detailing the excitement he was experiencing in Paris as he
attended a dazzling series of lectures by Henri Bergson, a new idol for him,
and explored the literary scene, albeit from a distance. His sole contacts were
with Jacques Rivière, an editor of the influential *Nouvelle Revue Française,*
Rivière's brother-in-law, Henri Alain-Fournier, and his single French friend, a
medical student named Jean Verdenal. The letters inevitably mentioned au
courant writers and books unknown to him, such as Charles-Louis Philippe's
Bubu de Montparnasse and Paul Claudel's *Connaissance de l'Est,* and instigated a slightly valedictory mood. Not that he was depressed, merely feeling a
bit left out, perhaps jealous of Eliot's access to Europe's modernist ferment
and missing Mariett's vibrant presence. Academically, his senior year was
emerging as his best yet. He was cutting classes less, earning superior grades
in all his courses, was a member of the class tennis team, had resumed his
enthusiastic discussions of Freud's ideas with McCouch, and continued to edit
and write poetry and editorials for the *Advocate*. Further, he was still dating
Barbara, though not as often.

Aiken's brief memoir of the period recollects that "now things were on an
even keel, he was happy in Thayer Hall with his roommates Taussig and
Wheeler, and he even had a Freshman *advisee,* attached to him by the Dean's
office, a brash young Irishman from East Boston, who viewed his advisor with
a mixture of amusement and suspicion. All seemed to be going beautifully."
True or exaggerated, a serene surface did not obliterate antagonistic undercurrents. The psychological turmoil generated by Freud's disturbing revelations
had been given additional dimensions by acquaintance with Darwin's *Origin
of the Species,* assimilated at last, and Nietzsche's *Thus Spake Zarathustra*
and *Beyond Good and Evil,* both of which were available in English translations. Aiken probably had read Herbert Spencer's *First Principles* as well,
since it was popular at the Signet.

Nietzsche was more poet then philosopher—akin to Santayana in that respect. His great appeal lay in his ferocious secular optimism in the teeth of enormous odds, a deliberate effort to overthrow the pessimistic asceticism of his once-beloved Schopenhauer by adapting evolutionary doctrines (Lamarckian) to a philosophy of relentless human progress, which was supposed to eventuate in supermen, creatures far above mere Christian ethics—feminine, *ergo* weak—and the fear inspired by a god's demise. His stance is rebellious and adolescent, antithetical, at every turn. It offers epigrammatic reversals of established norms that justify their irrational truths as strokes of impressionistic insight, not deduced principles, and so are more in tune with Freudian dynamics and philosophers like Bergson, who answered the challenge of biological determinism with poetic elaborations upon a "creative" evolutionary process that posited expanded human consciousness at its acme.

This was heady stuff for Aiken, who was soon to label himself a "Nietzschean" to the extent of assuming the validity of a poet-philosopher's highest function as Nietzsche's "Yea-saying" sage, melding Nietzsche with Santayana. But he rejected any optimistic interpretation of "the development of the human race as the *summum bonum*." He would take pride in claiming he was "a yea-sayer who found nothing to say yea to." Realistic, arrogant, cynically defiant, he could hide his secret insecurity behind nothing more substantial than a vague, sentimental belief that life itself was beautiful and good, which meant, again, a resort to the physical pleasures, the immediate anticipations and dreams of a young mind and body savoring their own growth and instinctive operations.

When taken seriously, poetry permits few evasions, however—"One can play the fool everywhere else, but not in poetry," says Montaigne—and it is significant that Aiken, always the prolific acrobat at the brink of glibness, found himself in a relatively dry spell. Although once more enrolled in Briggs's English 5 for the year, he had only four of his poems published in the *Advocate* during the first semester, and they dwell obsessively upon the relationship between art and artist.

Perhaps in reaction to the contractions of self implied by Freudian and Nietzschean tapping of unconscious energies, Aiken aligned himself even more firmly with Romantic models, with Shelley and Shelley's more contemporary shadow, Francis Thompson, and especially with Keats, whose brilliant "Ode on a Grecian Urn" had enshrined the potency of the creative act as destroyer— paradoxical, mysterious, yet human—of time and mortality, preserving youth as youth (unrequited striving) forever:

> When old age shall this generation waste,
> Thou shalt remain, in midst of other woe

Than ours, a friend of man, to whom thou say'st
   'Beauty is truth, truth beauty,'—that is all
   Ye know on earth, and all ye need to know.

In his own "To a Head in Marble," the last poem published in the *Advocate* (February 17, 1911) and the last unit in the series of similar efforts that had commenced with "The Potter," Aiken offers a parallel structure that is also a tribute. Its first stanza, which would reappear, altered, in some sixteen years as setting for the first prelude in the masterful *Preludes for Memnon,* yokes Keats's ode form and theme to Poe's nihilistic "The Raven":

   Tumultuous is the midnight, with no stars;
      The elm-trees, burthened deeply with soft snow,
   Mourn for the spring, for Youth's gay-tongued guitars,
      And dream of loves that blossomed long ago.
   Tumultuous is the midnight; at my pane
      The voiceless snow makes ceaseless whisperings,
      Yearning to tell of strange and demon things,
      But yearning still in vain;
   While I, envisioned, turn a starry page,
   And read the glories of a buried age.

It is the witching hour, and the snow, recurrent symbol in Aiken for the menace of madness and lack of meaning (Poe's terrifying white nothingness), is kept at a safe distance by the warm room and the retreat into literature, reading about the "glories of a buried age." The "whisperings" at the window "to tell of strange and demon things" could issue from psychoanalytic depths, which threatened Aiken's generation and him personally with the demolition of Romantic poet-worship and with incipient irrationality, the dreaded petit mal. If too derivative for much success, the poem is pellucid in its brave attempt to slam down Freud with the club of Keatsian aesthetics. "Starry page" summons memories of the sonnet that begins "When I have fears that I may cease to be," as it proceeds for seven more stanzas to address "Thou virgin head, with forehead sculptured smooth," until a final stanza claims victory, adding Shelley's rhetoric to the melodious clamor:

   Blow on, thou wind, and fall forever, snow!
      Ye sombre elms, still nurse your dreams of spring;
   Thou canst not touch this Soul of long ago
      Oh haggard mistral! with thy cruel wing.

> Thou voiceless sleet that frettest at my pane,
>> To human ear thy words can never come,—
> Thy demon warnings are forever dumb,
>> Thy yearnings are in vain;
> This night will pass, its storm remembered not;
> To-morrow dawns, this darkness is forgot.

Keats, who wrote in "Sleep and Poetry" that poesy "should be a friend / to sooth the cares, and lift the thoughts of man," is thus hero and maker, antidote for death and Freudian science. But as Aiken also knew from reading the letters, his celebration of the poet—of Wordsworth's mythmaking imagination and ego—was never blind to the actor's need for "negative capability" on the poet's part, the ability to suspend a biographical psyche in favor of an alternative, antipodal self—Yeats's "anti-self" or Lionel Trilling's "opposing self." And the poem is an anachronistic reassertion of a Romantic persona the author can no longer credit, a shout of defiance from a dead throat, simultaneously banishing Poe's mindless raven and Freud's primitive id.

Of the other three poems, "Sea Change" is the most effective. Stepping off from Shakespeare's song for a drowned father, it swims down, like many mythopoetic quest descents, to the bottom of the sea, where "the old Mage sits / And ponders there with all his wits," a father figure who is chillingly altered:

> He is ancient as the sea,
> Little cold blue eyes hath he,
> Wan is every finger-nail,
> His fingers too and lips are pale,
> And hoar as sea-rime is his hair.

He sits in a chair made from the bones of dead men, like Conrad's Kurtz in *Heart of Darkness,* while the ocean around him fills, at dusk, with the music of lost souls, "an elfin melody," each "voice like a silver bell" of "those who found an ocean grave." The harshest irony resides in the evil of "the sweet mermaids," relatives of Keats's lamias and "*belle dame sans merci,*" who, at noon, lure men to destruction with their physical charms and siren songs, "then, with fingers cold as ice / They'd snatch the body in a trice." After gnawing away the flesh of their victims, presumably male, they cast the bones aside to let the fish and shifting sands finish their work. A mage (father as wicked magician, not Prospero) completes the sequence, gathering them up to "strew his green sea-breathing wall."

In the end, processed by sea creatures and sea myths, safe from the "troubles of that world of men / Which thou shalt never see again," the victim becomes the mage, the son becomes the father:

> Thou art very old and wise,
> Thou hast little chill blue eyes;
> Hoary are thou as the sea,—
> Now thou hast felicity;
> Monster of the deep thou art,
> Slow and oozy beats thy heart!

By design or not, and the structure is marvelously suggestive, "Sea-change" mates Gothic impulse and fin-de-siècle decadence with classic legend and literature to convey a home truth about the manner in which a fundamental human relationship between parent and child—Aiken's earlier identification as poet with his father springs to mind—can project its own mythic drama and anxieties. Its Shakespearean crux is enlarged and deepened by possible debts to Arnold's "The Forsaken Merman" and Tennyson's "The Kraken," a fierce, magical poem that resists surface sense unless filtered through a Jungian schema: the search for a whole self the psyche must undertake if it is to mature and attain health.

There is no need to force such readings, and Jacques Lacan's ideas about the "absent father" in a literary text appear relevant as well, but the poem invites complex responses, and it originated at a time when its author was struggling with the overwhelming material of the new depth psychology. Nor can the background be ignored, the ambivalent attitude toward the dead father and related fears of the family's strain of madness. As for the sexual hatred, hatred impelled by insecurity, the personal element is enriched by literary antecedents, Keatsian inheritance blended with conventional 1890s postures and a strong dose of friend Eliot's poetic misogyny. The latter factor (and influence) was writ larger in "The Doubters," where retreat is once more a paramount concern:

> Fly from the Present, ye whose hearts are pure:
> For she, though rich in caskets full of gold
> Is cruel as green-eyed Circe was of old,
> Whose strange sea-loveliness was but a lure.

Eliot had written of Circe earlier, and her attractiveness for Aiken might have been enhanced by an uncertain courting of Barbara, but the flight from the present world is the same flight from contemporary realities that powered "To a Head in Marble," the same panic desire to flee the acid sea of self-diminishing undertows set in motion by Darwin and Freud. Loss of belief is explicit in the poem's very title, and its second stanza changes the Homeric tale to encompass a likely reference to H. G. Wells's *The Island of Dr. Moreau* (1896), in which science and scientist are depicted as immoral ravagers, by having the men turn not merely into swine but into "panthers, and pythons human eyed." The last stanza, in which Aiken speaks as Ulysses— "let us steal away before she snares / Our spirits too"—reconfirms that escape must be temporal, literary: "Come, we will steal away into the Past."

The last of the four poems, actually the first printed, "To a City Evening," is also constructed around the notion of escape—in this instance, from an urban scape, though the retreat has its own traditional allusions to display:

> Far from the city let me now be blown—
> I am unhappy in this sombre street;
> A little while, and autumn moons are flown,
> The panes will rattle in December's sleet;
> Oh let me dream, and let my dream have wings;
> So I may wander far
> To that green island where Calypso sings
> Her ave to the star;
> To drowse at even in music-haunted woods
> Where dryads faintly laugh, and Pan the Piper broods.

More sleep and less thinking is the answer, and Aiken, like Wordsworth in "The world is too much with us" sonnet, would love to return and be a "Pagan suckled in a creed outworn," restoring the innocence of the mythical systems (classical and Christian) that Freud was disassembling and science had disallowed. He is aware, however, that in the "breathless woods," where "dream" and sleep's "forgetfulness" would take him, his poem's plea is Romantic wish, nothing more: "Oh let them quaff, who thirst, of slumbers deep:— / Spirit away their souls, now, as they smile in sleep!" Death lurks beneath such pleasant thoughts, as it does beneath the lush scenery of Keats's *Endymion*.

Regardless of their competence and the evidence they supply that Aiken had not yet abandoned the nineteenth century, the poems vent a persistent urge to flee, whether into the past or into the past's literary artifacts and less unsettling visions. And his overt happiness has to be accepted as a superficial condition that hid interior unease. The initial sign of trouble came in December 1910, when he was named Class Poet, a position of great honor at literature-conscious Harvard but one that involved writing a poem for the graduating class, which then had to be read aloud in Sanders Theatre during the last-day exercises, as Eliot had done the year before.

To someone of Aiken's shyness, the prospect was unnerving. An *Advocate* editorial from the previous year, when he must have already suspected that the post would be his, stresses his distaste for the public aspect of the honor:

> Why are we saddled annually with a Class Day Oration, a Class Poem, and a Class Ode? These things are highly unpleasant ordeals for the unfortunate individuals whom the Class has singled, and they certainly provide no occasion for joy to the Class who must listen, and the others who must listen with them. . . . We think it would be a great deal more sensible if the Class Poet and the Class Orator were only, as the papers say, 'thinking parts' in the great play of Class Day. The honor would in no degree be impaired, a deal of pain would be saved on all sides, and no doubt the Class Poet and the Class Orator would willingly dispense with the glories of Sanders Theatre.

His growing dismay about the task was not solely the result of shyness or the inner restlessness exhibited in the poetry. Though the class poem had filled him with horror, there was also a principle at stake, a genuine professional dilemma for a young man who believed that graduation would signal the start of a writing career. His concept of poetic integrity, which was to remain unshaken through future decades of struggle and neglect, caused him to rebel against the "ignominy of having to write such a poem. This would be a falseness to himself that he could never live down" (148). Unlike Eliot, he simply could not grin and bear it for Mother Harvard.

He needed a reasonable excuse to act the rebel and evade the burden of either writing the poem or resigning without cause. The convenient excuse arose, appropriately, in his composition class with Briggs, where, as a special project, "enthralled by the short stories of Gautier, he decided to translate one of them, 'La Morte Amoureuse,' into a poem in English, and, as this would require a complete Romantic absorption, in the deepest and most dedicated sense, he decided on the only possible course—to cut all classes until the thing was done. He did so, ignored his roommates and other friends, lived underground for two weeks, cutting every single lecture, and got the poem done." The consequences were predictable. Within the month he was summoned to the office of Dean B. S. Hurlbut for disciplinary action. The dean's punishment was firm but fair: he was to lose his Irish freshman and be put on probation for the rest of the semester, which meant automatic expulsion should he cut another class.

Never one to bear reproof from above lightly, Aiken protested with vigor that the sentence was excessive because his project had been a creative endeavor. The dean's calm reply was to ask if the culprit, who he knew played tennis, approved of serving with his foot over the line. Instead of retorting in kind, Aiken stood up and denounced the unfairness of the reprimand, declaring his intention to resign from the college. He carried out this threat and was soon besieged by requests to reconsider his foolish action. Uncle William was vehement in trying to dissuade him from throwing away his degree so close to graduation, as was Uncle Alfred, and McCouch begged his friend to swallow his pride. Even his old nemesis Frederick Winsor, concerned about Middlesex losing the distinction of having produced a Harvard Class Poet, intervened and asked his friend Dean Briggs to have a word with his recalcitrant student.

Briggs was quick to oblige and requested that Aiken remain a moment after class one day. His speech on this occasion, which Aiken impertinently interrupted in mid-flight when he heard rustling in a trash basket and exclaimed that a rat was in there, has been preserved intact, probably polished with loving retrospective care, in *Ushant* (146–47). After touching upon ethical considerations, Briggs switched smoothly into a more practical sphere and discussed the negative effect Aiken's resignation would have on his writing ambitions and character, not forgetting to compliment his progress to date. At the end, in a gentle rebuke, he also noted that it was a mouse, not a rat, in the trash basket.

Like most such pieces of avuncular advice delivered to the young, it was lost on Aiken, who was already plotting how to reach Rome and the ground hallowed by his adored Keats, how to connect with Eliot in Paris and share in the excitement of the literary scene there. The decision to run away, to defy convention and authority, brought a feeling of exhilarating liberation, intensified by the realization that he would not have to write or perform the inane Class Poem. A measure of Byronic melodrama was injected by the simultaneous (and not unanticipated) swan song of his highly proper romance with Barbara Leighton. The final meeting of the unsuited pair took place at Fresh Pond and was fittingly concluded amid a sudden downpour. It climaxed with their sitting miserably side by side on the wet front seat of an open streetcar as it slowly circled back to Harvard Square, unable to think of anything to say to each other: "The imaginary love had reached its inevitably imaginary end in an imaginary heartbreak" (149). Impetus was thereby given Aiken's flight, further romantic justification, since painful disjunctions of this nature seem to demand dissipation, sea voyages, much drunken brooding, the grand tour of tears in the footsteps of Keats, and his own reluctant escape from Fanny Brawne.

The poem blamed for Aiken's resignation, "The Clerk's Journal: Being the Diary of a Queer Man," which had been submitted to Briggs on January 9, 1911, is the first modern poem he ever wrote, a startling contrast to the *Advocate* poetry in its using, at last, the vernacular freedom suggested by Browning and Robinson, particularly the latter. Aiken would always be proud that this versified tale of a clerk's brief fling with a beautiful waitress preceded

"The Love Song of J. Alfred Prufrock" and possibly had an effect on Eliot's development. Actually, the timid clerk protagonist, so popular with the nineteenth-century Russian writers they both read, had already surfaced in Eliot's Laforgue imitation, and it is unlikely that "The Clerk's Journal" exerted much influence on his Paris-stationed comrade-in-arms, except as it confirmed the value of realistic urban touches and unheroic central characters. Eliot maintained to the end that Aiken had no discernible impact upon his own work, and Aiken did concede the opposite, that, initially, "Prufrock stained us all," had "a tremendous influence on me."

More relevant, the satiric rage and complex moral ambiguity essential to Eliot's art were never part of Aiken's admittedly inferior poetic equipment or congenial to his temperament. He had not learned from Laforgue the advantage of shifting voices and sensibilities to expand the lyric's range, to convolute its levels of perception and experience; later, as Aiken concentrated more and more on the stream-of-consciousness technique, he would not be interested. In "The Clerk's Journal" he did accomplish a breakthrough in his poetry that partially freed him from the nineteenth century, and the poem itself contains a number of felicitous lines, including

> The dreary sempiternal way
> My desk's arranged, the nervous clink
> Typewriters make, day after day!

that could have left a faint impression on Eliot's sensitive retina, although the presence of "sempiternal" explains Briggs's admonition that the author did not always stay with the vocabulary of his clerk.

The final stanza is worth quoting for the evidence it gives of Aiken's spurt of aesthetic progress:

> These were a part of love, of me,
> Mazed in a mighty harmony.
> Now, they are notes that clash and jar,
> Like sullen chimney-pot and star.
> That harmony is all run wild—
> Music without a thought or theme,
> Like the scattered jargon of a child. . . .
> Or voices in an ether dream.
> It was so fabulously sweet!—
> And I go on with tired feet—
> And life is paved with cobblestones.

A Romantic conformity still clings and hinders conviction, but note the "sullen chimney-pot" and the "ether dream," which might have seeded Eliot's etherized sky, and the puissant metaphor at the end, phrasing in "cobblestones" with natural ease, plus the music tropes—a leitmotif for him in time, shared with Eliot and the Symbolists—and the Miltonic irony of "Mazed in a mighty harmony," where a single noun transformed into a verb does extraordinary spadework. If not Eliot's match, Aiken had, in a single surge, come near enough to touch his thin shoulder.

He must have sensed this himself as he prepared for a voyage to Italy. But the people who cared about him and feared the ruin of a promising future, viewing his capricious journey as a Rimbaud-like flight from bourgeois respectability into sordid destruction, had not given up. Relatives and friends prevailed upon Thomas McCabe, who had the money and adventurous inclination, to accompany him. As a result, when Aiken set sail from New York for Naples in March 1911 on a small, squalid steamer, McCabe was with him, and he was glad of the company. The two young men were used to each other, despite temperamental differences, though Aiken, recalling the recklessness of his companion on that almost disastrous trip to the White Mountains, was a bit apprehensive. Nothing, however, could dampen the ebullient release of pent-up tension that the cold, rough spring crossing represented to him.

The itinerary Aiken had devised was firm but leisurely: to explore Naples and Capri, move north to Rome and Florence and Venice for extended stays, and then on, through Switzerland, to France and a summer rendezvous with Eliot in Paris and McCouch in London before paying another visit to the Troutbeck Valley. Along the way he intended to learn Italian, which he hoped would come easily to him because of his Spanish studies with Gordon Bassett. McCabe and he labored together over Italian texts on the steamer's deck in between readings of Chaucer. In combination with his greater fluency in the language, McCabe's urbanity and self-assurance were distinct assets once they disembarked at Naples, and his common knowledge of home friends and country a definite comfort. But McCabe, justifiably or not, was worried about the dangers they faced as comparatively affluent strangers in a strange land— worried to the point that he purchased a pistol as protection against potential bandits.

The pistol, which intrigued Aiken, was to cause their eventual split, land McCabe in jail, and lead to Aiken's acquiring his first important British friend. He himself was fortunate not to have been arrested after accidentally firing a shot into his hotel bed while in Naples. Another incident occurred in Capri, which they reached ahead of schedule during an aborted trip to Paestum. McCabe went off to have lunch with some rich acquaintances who owned a villa there, impolitely leaving Aiken to his own devices. Irritated and lonely, he wandered down to a deserted beach and decided to pass the time by trying out the revolver on various objects strewn across the sand. The sound of the gunshots immediately drew a large, silent crowd of natives, who seemed awed by the spectacle. Self-conscious under the gaze of alien eyes, Aiken forced himself to continue, as if a circus performer afraid to disappoint his audience. He halted only when the ammunition reached near bottom and was fortunate that none of the several policemen in the crowd intervened. Apparently they were convinced that anyone so openly contemptuous of the law must be connected with high officials.

Naples's "cacophonous and deafening streets" (181) were exotic, and the city offered him an opportunity to hear Titta Ruffo in its grandiose opera house, though he preferred Capri's quieter beauties, but Aiken was impatient to reach Rome. He went on ahead by train alone, his eagerness to see the Italian capital enhanced by a desire for a temporary separation from McCabe. Though he would insist in an April letter to McCouch that McCabe and he "get along pretty well together" in spite of their different ways and that "one or two tiffs is the total of bloodshed," he also conceded that "he irritates me with his 'sentimental Tommy' and play-acting at times." Rome, in any case, as frantic as Naples but far more impressive, reduced all arguments to squabbles. McCabe rejoined him, and they set about, sometimes together, often not, examining the city's array of cultural treasures.

They stayed at Muller's Hotel Bavaria in the Piazza di Spagna, which was convenient for Aiken's frequent visits to the Spanish Steps, to Keats's death room and the Keats Memorial Library housed in the same small building, where he donated his early Moxon copy of the poet's poems and was, in return, permitted to read and write there without restrictions. In *Ushant* a detached future self perceives the moment as climax and ebb: "The identification with Keats had . . . reached its bathetic and pathetic apogee" (158). No amount of nostalgic reading or Roman antiquity could alter the fact that "The Clerk's Journal" had been written, that the Keatsian reply to Freud's challenge carried in the last *Advocate* poems had been put aside like a childish thing, although poetic influences are never erased entirely; Aiken's love for Keats as man and mind would remain steadfast. The Protestant Cemetery was also visited, final respects paid to Keats, Shelley, and the Romantic rebellion they had embodied with such graceful, spendthrift thoroughness.

The impact of Rome upon Aiken's imagination was staggering, as he trudged with pilgrim stubbornness from work of art to work of art, staring up in amazement at Michelangelo's Sistine Chapel ceiling or, like Byron's Childe Harold, musing on the grand ambitions and tragic flesh-and-blood limits of mankind as he contemplated the Colosseum's ruins. But the pervasive religious drive behind the paintings and the architecture, the remorseless Catholic mythology and ritual, was not something he could really imbibe, despite his aesthete sympathies and personal fascination with the image of crucifixion, with the idea of a god's violent demise. Freud, Darwin, Nietzsche, and Pater, in league with his own skeptical reflexes, ruled out salvation as a metaphysical quest, a postmortem possibility, and his new Freudian perspective caused him to peer beneath the painted surface of the Renaissance—the museumed Renaissance of secular aesthetics—into the artist's mind, where religious ecstasy fed off the sublimated fat of thwarted sexual energy. Every curve of flesh, every hint and tantalizing thrust of voluptuous breast and thigh, shaped the dialectic of "sex and art" (185), reminding him that he was still a virgin.

The dialectic was unsure in its terminology and its applications, but the need to relieve himself—Freud's ultimate definition of pleasure—from the pressure imposed by his virginal state was not. The skill of artists dead for hundreds of years seemed to conspire to mock his aching physical hunger. In a cold April rain, after having downed a bottle of Lacrimae Cristi on the lip of Mount Vesuvius, he explored the ruins of Pompeii with solitary completeness and would recall especially a fresco "which showed the young Roman's penis so emphatically outweighing the heap of gold on the other side of the balance" (167). And yet, fastidious from shame, he could not bring himself to respond to the urgings of prostitutes in dark doorways, perhaps also frightened of foul play or remembering the humiliation suffered in his junior year, when a "slattern" under a Cambridge streetlight derided his boyish appearance and "carolled at me, 'Does your mother know you're out?' "

The absurdity of his condition—a virgin at age twenty-one—was brought home to him at the Borghese Gardens, where he was scheduled to meet McCabe one morning. As usual McCabe was late, and Aiken sat on a bench under a purple Judas tree to await his arrival. While there he slowly worked his way through a volume of Alessandro Leopardi's poetry for the first time, with the aid of his Italian-English dictionary, and was disturbed by the sight of a Franciscan monk parading back and forth in front of him. Though presumably deep in meditation, the monk obviously found the Anglo-Saxon stranger intriguing. At last he plopped himself down beside Aiken and began communicating with him in a weird mixture of Latin, English, Italian, and Provençal French.

The gist of the monk's speech had to do with his observation that the many young Englishmen he had encountered always manifested "an extraordinary beauty, and an extraordinary appearance of innocence" (163), like Aiken at this precise moment. He bluntly asked if the gentleman was himself a virgin. The directness of the personal question flustered Aiken into answering truthfully, much to the monk's astonishment.

Their odd conversation eventually wandered into other pastures, including a discussion of Leopardi, whom the monk regarded as a great poet, albeit, naturally, "a pessimist, and misguided," but Aiken's mind was elsewhere. If *Ushant* is to be trusted, the monk's calm attitude toward sex had abruptly freed him from the taboos of his genteel upbringing, shown him the ridiculous nature of the guilt his culture associated with the sex act, to the extent that he was now determined to shed his virginity before returning to America. The monk, however, had merely completed the education begun by such writers as Freud and Havelock Ellis, adding a religious seal of approval to the adult attitude encouraged by their scientific detachment.

In the meantime, Aiken, angry over McCabe's rude stand-up, returned to the hotel for lunch. His meal was interrupted by a summons to the phone, where an Italian lawyer informed him that his friend had been arrested and would probably have to serve two weeks in jail and pay a small fine. McCabe had appeared at the Borghese Gardens on time but stopped in its print shop to buy some pictures. An altercation ensued when a guard accused him of taking more prints than he had paid for, causing McCabe to erupt and break the poor man's jaw with a single punch. To complicate matters, realizing he had no permit for the pistol in his pocket, McCabe tried to dump it out of the paddy wagon on the way to the station and was caught in the act. To Aiken, the mess seemed typical of McCabe's hasty, violent character, and he was far more irked than concerned. Without hesitation or regret, he accepted McCabe's advice to proceed ahead to Florence alone, leaving a curt note as to which hotel he intended to occupy. It was the beginning of the end of their erratic, often tense relationship.

Ruth McIntyre, not always a disinterested witness because of her affection for McCabe, claims that the flight from Rome, abandoning a friend in the lurch, was all too typical of Aiken's self-centered personality, which rings true and tallies with his admitted tendency to run away from unpleasant situations. And McCabe, who, Ruth reports, had grown weary of Aiken during the course of their Italian sojourn, was an anxiety-inducing comrade under the best of circumstances. The sundering of their friendship had been foredoomed by a basic dichotomy between their characters and social attitudes: McCabe's extroverted swings in mood and behavior versus Aiken's shy, sometimes na-ive self-consciousness, an adventurer's aristocratic egotism versus the poet's quieter but deeper egotism—a dichotomy that was bound to increase in sever-ity during extended close contact.

A complete rupture was still not envisioned, however, when Aiken boarded the train for Florence. He did not relish traveling alone among people whose language was not yet within reach, and his insecurity was given a jolt when he broke a leather strap by mistake and then could not force the window shut. A fellow passenger, irritated by the smoke pouring in the opening, called in a huge Italian from the next compartment, who easily closed the window and muttered "*Poco bravo*" contemptuously at Aiken before departing, so that his "paralyzing shyness had been re-intensified a hundredfold" (169). But Florence more than compensated, and the two weeks without McCabe were devoted to continuing his education in Italian art. He had secured lodgings in a Lungarno *pensione* where the only other male boarder was a tall, young, reserved, somewhat saturnine Englishman whom Aiken lacked the courage to approach or speak to at meals.

Fra Angelico's *Coronation of the Virgin,* Piero della Francesca's striking portrait of *Federigo da Montefeltro,* Ghiberti's doors at the Baptistry, Masaccio's frescoes in the Brancacci Chapel, Giotto's frescoes in the Bardi Chapel, Pietro Perugino's *Crucifixion* in the Santa Maria Maddalena dei Pazzi (a favorite), Brunelleschi's Foundlings Hospital and Pazzi Chapel—everywhere Aiken turned, his eyes and imagination were flooded with a bewildering series of Renaissance styles, early and late, high and low, alike, always, in prescribed subject matter, yet so different in execution, the use of line and color and light variations intimating how any content can be absorbed and reformulated into an original composition by authentic talent. Modern aesthetics, the urge to make it new, must have appeared distant indeed under the onslaught of living art history. It was appropriate that he now chose to have his precious copy of Palgrave's anthology bound in Florentine leather and embossed with gold lettering. Ruskin and Pater had prepared him, of course, with the language of appreciation, but verbal images from other tongues and ages can never wholly translate visual experience into private forms, possible tropes.

Though he was not given in later years to make direct use of his Florentine expedition, except for the recurrence of a crucifixion theme, the ambience surrounding his exploration of the city had to have solidified the conviction that art, human creativity, was man's noblest achievement, a view altogether congenial to a Harvard student. Meanwhile, the week-long silence between the English stranger and himself at the *pensione* was finally broken. The pistol, which Aiken had picked up at the police station in Rome, was the catalyst. A cleaning woman found it under his pillow while making his bed and ran into the dining room, upset and angry, to inquire about its presence. Aiken could not understand the stream of agitated Italian, and the stranger kindly translated. Embarrassed, he promised to remove and discard the gun, which he did later in the day, and Aiken and the stranger were soon engaged in amiable conversation, exchanging autobiographies and discovering common passions for art, music, and literature.

The stranger's name was Martin Donnisthorpe Armstrong, and he very much conformed to an American's notion of an upper-class Englishman in speech and appearance, in the easy correctness of his manners, and the light touches of erudite wit. Several years older than Aiken, Armstrong possessed the sophistication of a McCabe, with none of that gentleman's penchant for violent extremes, and his shyness was almost the equal of Aiken's. His personal credentials were impeccable in every respect, including a maternal grandmother, Elizabeth Wordsworth, who had been the Lake Poet's cousin, and a degree from Pembroke College, Cambridge, where he had, oddly, majored in mechanical science. After spending two years working in an architect's office in London, he had fled to Italy for a year to devote his attention to a study of pre-Renaissance and Renaissance art.

Aiken was enchanted by his new companion, the first respectable Englishman he had ever encountered and potential entrée to London's literary regions—Armstrong was bent on a writing career, and they read their poems aloud to each other. Generally ready to submit himself to an older man with knowledge beyond his own, or a contemporary like Eliot who clearly commanded genius, Aiken had little trouble in falling under the spell of Armstrong's charm, breeding, and superior experience, as he "was taken to see the great Perugino triptych, and the Michelangelo *abbozzi,* and everything else" (172).

The education gleaned from Armstrong over the next few weeks, uninterrupted by McCabe's sullen arrival, was more than aesthetic, encompassing subtle points of etiquette and British cultivation no amount of American imitation could duplicate. For Aiken, "it was precisely the final course in 'English,' " (172) that he had been seeking since Cambridge and New Bedford relatives began inculcating various social codes. Besides, Armstrong was easy to like, to relate to, and proved generous with his time and instruction, chatting learnedly, with many witty asides, while accompanying him on their long walks to San Gimignano, Settignano, the Certosa, and Fiesole, Walter Savage Landor's final home. Aiken would recollect with special vividness their climb to the top of Monte Scenario's stone parapet and sipping the cordial the monks made from native pine trees.

His growing closeness with Armstrong considerably widened the gap between him and McCabe, and their arguments became more heated. McCabe still rankled under having been, he believed, selfishly deserted at a critical moment, and Aiken expressed less and less patience with what he considered McCabe's high-handed mannerisms. When charged with abandoning his erstwhile friend to a dangerous jail in a foreign country, Aiken retorted by quoting from the Apocrypha: "Travel not by the way with a bold fellow." In *Ushant* (158) this scene is credited with commencing the end of their odd yet stimulating friendship. A distinct coolness pervaded their behavior toward each other, and the emotional estrangement was formalized by McCabe's announced decision to travel ahead by himself to Venice and book a room at a very expensive hotel, which he knew was beyond his schoolmate's means.

When Aiken arrived a day or more later, after having agreed to call upon Armstrong in London, he did so at midnight and by canal steamer, registering at a *pensione* on the Grand Canal, where McCabe came to join him the next morning. McCabe made known his intention to foreswear accompanying Aiken into the dull placidity of Switzerland and France, implying that these countries were safe enough for his companion to traverse without his protection. His warrior soul thirsted for challenges, more exotic vistas, which meant penetrating the mysterious East, the Balkans, and Constantinople via the famed Orient Express. Like a marriage of opposites reaching its natural termination, when the partners can once again relax and enjoy—at a safe psychological remove—the qualities in the other person that drew them together in the first place, Aiken and McCabe found themselves frequently sharing daily plunderings of Venetian riches with something of their former camaraderie.

A Viennese art teacher staying at the *pensione* told them that the works of Venice's Giovanni Battista Tiepolo, which she was presently engaged in studying, deserved their attention, and they complied, tracking down every Tiepolo the city had to offer. They also enrolled at the local Berlitz school to further their Italian and had a competitive but harmless swim off the beach at the Lido. Their eventual parting was casual and friendly, though both realized a sincere rapprochement was unlikely.

While in Venice, Aiken also managed to get embroiled in another minor romance that only served to frustrate, and thus quicken, his unappeased sex drive. In the interest of economy he had moved out of the *pensione* into lodgings with a family named Ghezzo. The old ladies of the house, impressed by his intention to write literature, brought a cup of morning chocolate to his bedside each day. He then ventured forth daily for his two hours of Italian lessons at the Berlitz school with a pretty signorina. Vivacious and bright, she teased him about his interest in Tiepolo, a minor artist, for the pleasure of seeing him blush, which he did easily.

The signorina lived alone with her mother in another part of town and walked to work—he was too shy to ask her name—but their relationship rarely shifted from literary to personal grounds, except when she questioned him about his background and college life. He had purchased a Tauchnitz edition of Oscar Wilde's fairy stories, which she adored, and memorized one each day for her benefit. (In Rome, Tauchnitz volumes of Maurice Hewlett's short stories, *Little Novels of Italy*, and Richard Whiteing's novel *No. 5 John Street* had been his main literary fare.) Inescapably, his thoughts drifted in the direction of seduction, but he feared its practical consequences, revelation of his inexperience and the awkwardness of her seeking marriage. Further, he simply did not know how to go about altering the tone of their involvement from congenial contemporaries in a teacher-pupil bind to that of lovers.

Flight, again, was the safest course, though he toyed with the idea of writing Eliot, McCouch, Armstrong, and Uncle William to inform them that he was remaining in Venice indefinitely.

Once decided upon retreat, he lacked the courage to tell her frankly of his departure plans, which suggests that he realized she did expect more from him than he was emotionally willing to yield. Sex was his sole aim, and conscience or love did not figure into his scheme of things. On the last morning he sneaked into the school when she was not present to pay the manager but then had the unpleasant surprise of her opening a classroom door to confront him in the act of counting out the money. She stood there, "silent, confused, hurt, incredulous—he would never forget the look of pain and shame—and he had then walked past her, too diffident to explain—for how could he ever explain?—simply murmuring, or mumbling, the words, 'Grazie—e 'rivederci!'" (180).

Her anguished reaction, which Aiken has preserved with the artful candor of old age and old guilt, leaves scant doubt that the unresolved pattern, the dialectic of "sex and art" seen in many prior and later flights from women, was not merely the cruel either/or dilemma of a young poet marching toward self-awareness and technical mastery but tokened an unconscious compulsion to punish the frail effigies of a faithless, inadequate mother as well. If explained, in part, by generic youth's callous attitude toward any females withholding their bodies, the abrupt dumping of his little Italian teacher was also Aiken's reflex method of exacting vengeance upon the lost woman who had first failed him, upon a scapegoat figure incarnating an unjust, menacing world. As distant sex object and potential source of embarrassment, she was an apt target for the inner rage that characterizes every artist's alienation from reality. Shyness contributed its portion of difficulty too because it prevented him from making the overt advances that might have resulted in consummation, although his sensitivity would have left him vulnerable to a serious attachment he did not want and probably feared. In addition, she was a foreigner, remote in language and culture from the Anglo-Saxon boundaries of his rearing, a fabulous creature in that respect, hardly proper marital material.

From Venice, Aiken resumed his journey north to Milan, where he was enraptured by Leonardo Da Vinci's *Last Supper,* which reminded him of the long table at the *pensione* where he and Armstrong first met, and had the unsettling experience of hearing an insane woman in the hotel bedroom adjoining his scream out, "Help! Help me!" throughout the night, ashamed of himself for not making inquiries, imagining that she was being whipped. Physical cowardice was another flaw he had to confront in himself, though he was inclined to blame Dr. Aiken. He did not linger but headed straight for Como through the orchards above Bellagio, pausing at Como only long enough to take an icy swim in late spring waters. McCabe had assured him that the St. Gotthard Pass into Switzerland would already be free of snow this time of year and the chalet at its summit open for tourists. He was wrong in both instances, increasing Aiken's animosity toward him. Snow was there in abundance, and the chalet was deserted and locked, forcing the exhausted climber to walk with improper shoes all the way to Göttingen, many miles distant.

Though wet and tired, he was at least in Switzerland and, after recovering from his ordeal, hiked deeper into the picturesque countryside, stopping at Lucerne. The highlight of his extended stay in Lucerne was the discovery of Hans Holbein the Younger's *Dance of Death,* three paintings on large wooden panels, which fascinated him with their grotesqueness and their almost medieval focus upon death's vulgar triumph, so different from the same artist's subtly realistic portraits done later in England. To reach the Holbein triptych from his lodgings, he had to cross a crooked wooden bridge, which became routine: "Day after day he used to walk to and fro over the bridge, to look at them, and finally left with an elaborate set of reproductions which he expected to convert into a long philosophical poem." Death was a topic bound to attract a young imagination schooled in Poe, English Romanticism, and fin-de-siècle morbidity, but Aiken was not yet ready for the ambitious undertaking he envisioned. He would not actually attempt such a poem until 1913.

For the moment he was in transition, physically and mentally, contemplating the crumbling of familiar deities and the birth of new ones. While in Venice, to supplement his excursions into Wilde's unique fairyland and ongoing bouts with the Italian of Dante, Foscolo, and Leopardi, he had bought copies of Wells's *New Machiavelli* (1911) and Matthew Arnold's *Collected Essays* in three volumes. Narrated by a politician who had forfeited his successful career for an erotic impulse and stropped into razor bitterness by self-pity, the Wells novel struck a responsive chord. Arnold's cool, judicious, occasionally sententious autopsy on Shelley's and Keats's swollen literary corpses—the former deemed "a beautiful *and ineffectual* angel, beating in the void his luminous wings in vain," the latter ranked with the greatest in promise, if not always performance—contributed further to a growing uncertainty about his own poetic touchstones.

Wells's rebellious support of sexual liberty suited Aiken's mood, and at Interlaken, his next resting place, he finished *The New Machiavelli* and tried once more to notch his first conquest. The intended victim, a pretty blond Swiss girl called "Elsa" in *Ushant* (182), worked at the hotel where he was staying and was its sole guest this early in the season. She flirted back after he initiated matters by remarking upon her single status, avowing she should have a husband and ten children. She leaned against his shoulder when serving him, climbed stools frequently to show off shapely legs, and he reacted with growing boldness, alluding to his evening habit of a stroll along a wooded road to the nearby mountain. Later in the week he summoned sufficient nerve to tell her the number of his room, mentioning that a nocturnal visit would not be unwelcome, but her reply was coyly noncommittal.

A week passed with no change in their routine of giggling flirtations and unrewarded nightly vigils. Like Alice, Elsa obviously had no intention of sneaking into his room, and, equally sure, her interest in him was strictly as a potential husband. He had climbed every mountain within sight, visited the nearest glacier, and was again eager to escape, to join Eliot in Paris. He arranged to leave by morning train but neglected to inform Elsa of his plan. As in Venice, the departure episode was embarrassing. The manageress rebuked him by implication, stressing Elsa's sadness at his leaving; then he had to face Elsa herself, to tip her for her services. She was indifferent to the wad of notes pressed into her hand and said good-bye without expression.

Another flight, another betrayal. Guilt is emphasized in *Ushant,* Elsa's voice entwined with the voices of other female victims: "None were truly lost, they were still there, and still, in the heart and mind, could exert their magic, their magnetism, and the more magic and magnetic for his acknowledged sense of having abandoned them, his sense of guilt" (185). Guilt of this order, lyrically indulgent, Wellsian with self-pity, has no serious power to wound; the protective schizophrenic detachment from experience that made Aiken a writer would always (or almost always) insulate him from both total collapse and commitment. His love for any woman in the years ahead could never be more than a child's unsteady love, passionate and generous at times, circumscribed and punishing, vulnerably self-deluding.

The train arrived at Gare de Lyon at midnight. His French poor and his abnormal shyness intact, Aiken avoided the buses and subway, walked the long distance to the *pension* behind Notre Dame where he had reserved a room by following the directions on a map torn from his Baedeker. The next day he called for Eliot at 9 Rue de l'Université "for the first time to the *patisserie* and then *sirop de fraises* and soda at the sidewalk cafe" (157). They talked of the past year in Paris and Cambridge and of mutual friends as they ate their strawberries and cream, and Eliot revealed his intention to return to Harvard in the fall to study philosophy and Sanskrit. He spoke with enthusiasm of Bergson, the philosopher praised by William James for defying the traditional system-making propensities of his colleagues, and alluded more than once to *Bubu de Montparnesse,* Charles-Louis Philippe's novel, strangely romantic and naturalistic in its delineation of a gorillalike pimp and the lower-class hades he occupies. Eliot himself had spent many nights wandering through slum neighborhoods in search of lurid sin, a sick, distant,

fastidious observer alive with repressed passions and Puritan distaste. He was
in the process that summer of writing "The Love Song of J. Alfred Prufrock"
and one of the "Preludes," which marked his emergence as a major modern
poet, one now capable of phrasing the tensions of his own divided psyche in
the abstract grammar of a fluid lyric disguise.

Aiken no doubt shared his own breakthrough as represented in "The
Clerk's Journal," and he would always remember Eliot reading aloud a poem
in the attic of his boardinghouse, which resulted in a haunting, cinematic
dream: "Invariably it began with the poem, the cadences of the poem heard in
the bare Parisian attic, and just as invariably then, like a camera, it dollied up
to the high little window, and, all sound and rhythm falling away, became
nothing but the unearthly beauty of an unearthly evening sky" (186–87).
"Prufrock," which Aiken believed was partly modeled on his Uncle Alfred,
convinced him of his friend's unique talent, but the quality of the dream, the
repetition of which indicates subterranean significance, might be read as an
unconscious awareness of the threat embedded in Eliot's superior powers. Did
he, perhaps, fear being swallowed up before he had begun?

There is no verifiable answer, yet the question is, in a way, its own reply,
existing as an image, recurrent, of frustrated song, empty beauty. Consciously, it did not matter very much because the joy in finding a lost brother
and teacher was intense, sufficient. When he learned that Eliot would be back
at Harvard for the next year, that made his own return easier to bear—apparently Uncle Alfred had convinced him, if he needed convincing, to reenter
school in the fall and graduate in 1912. It did not take him long to become
ensnared by another pretty young girl dedicated to ushering him down an
aisle, an American girl staying with her mother at his *pension*. She seemed
quite receptive to his advances, or so she pretended, and he christened her
"Hots" (187), more in hope than candor.

She and her mother took Aiken in hand, showing him around the city, but
once again he had to flee suddenly, though on this occasion out of humiliation
over the threadbare state of his single pair of trousers. He cross the Channel
alone but, for a change, did not burn his bridges; the two ladies would visit
London in a few days and resume the relationship. Aiken sensed in the
daughter's growing boldness an authentic chance at last to slake his yearnings.
After taking an early train from Newhaven, he located the address in Beau-
champ Place that Martin Armstrong had given him and dropped in for breakfast, catching his new English acquaintance by surprise. Armstrong was "already at breakfast, in his charming little digs, with the handsome young peer's
son, who was on his way to India" (175). The suggestion is that he and the
peer's son were dismayed by his intrusion because of a homosexual liaison,

and Aiken specifically identifies Armstrong as a bisexual elsewhere in his fictionalized autobiography.

Although Armstrong probably was bisexual, a fate difficult to avoid after being subjected to the blacking factory of England's public school system, Aiken uses the fact to discredit the essence of the man, linking it to his lack of originality in all aspects of the arts, which Armstrong pursued with intellect and erudition but never mastered to the extent of producing a memorable piece of literature. But the denigration of Armstrong's character has to be weighed with the knowledge that *Ushant* dates forward to a time when its author still harbored hostile feelings against a former friend, whom he thought had betrayed him in an unforgivable fashion. Not that the final judgment is necessarily unsound regarding Armstrong's paucity of original talent, but it is deliberately manipulated to belittle the genuine character of the person who had much to offer in the way of wit, warmth, and truly civilized taste, a person who paved Aiken's path into literary London, as he admitted in *Ushant,* and who was unfailingly generous in lavishing time and money on his American chum.

For example, Armstrong, despite whatever discomfort Aiken's unannounced arrival had caused, set about immediately to secure lodgings for his visitor, which he did at Trevor Square. The rooms were clean and reasonable, and McCouch soon appeared to share them with him. The night of McCouch's coming, with Avy deForest in tow, was to prove momentous to Aiken's frustrated sex life. The affair with the American girl was progressing rapidly, although during their recent meeting in a private hotel sitting room he had perceived a glint of calculation in her seductive embrace. But he was convinced that their next rendezvous would be the crucial one and daydreamed constantly about her naked body. After the champagne reunion with McCouch, deForest, and McCabe at the Gourmet restaurant on Wardour Street, Aiken and his companions walked outside and met "Irene Barnes," an attractive prostitute, and her escort, standing beside a pavement artist busy at work with his blue and green chalk (188).

The meeting was casual, full of banter on both sides, and ended in a congenial parting, with Irene's companion taking her for a cab ride in the park and Aiken seeing his schoolmates to their lodgings. But the obsession that had been torturing him with increasing urgency since his landing in Italy, aided by the champagne and memories of the American girl, drove him back to the spot outside the restaurant. Though a prostitute, Irene had an innocent air, a young, fresh beauty that belied her experience, experience that would compensate for his lack of skill. He searched desperately for her among the crowds that circulated through Leicester Square, determined to find her, worried only that she might still be with her latest customer. But she was alone when he encountered her on Shaftesbury Avenue and smiled at him in recognition. She took his arm and led him to a small hotel off Tottenham Court Road, where she expertly introduced him to the art of love in a little gaslit bedroom.

Because it was the first time for him, or because very few men can be given a woman's intimacy without feeling a compulsion to reciprocate in the language of courtship, Aiken repeatedly told her of his love. Irene burdened him with her life story, told him of her mother and brother in Australia, to whom she sent money without identifying its source, and of her father serving with the army in India, whose brass ring, inscribed "good luck" in Islamic, she gave him as a memento of their meeting. She also outlined a plan to save enough money to join her family in Australia and find herself a husband. It sounded plausible and endearing, but Aiken did not intend to get more involved than he was. When she asked if he would take her to a seaside hotel for a summer reprieve—it was still June, and he had mentioned that he was on holiday from school—he vaguely agreed, lying with half-meant ease. He left a gold half-sovereign on the windowsill beside the bed when he departed, knowing he would never see her again.

Since he already planned to return to Harvard, despite heated denials and grumblings, the summer had indeed become a vacation, and he and his school friends, along with Armstrong, planned to use it to discover London and explore the rest of the country. There were expeditions to Wales and to the seaside resort at Clovelly with McCouch and deForest, *sans* Irene, and another journey to Troutbeck to stay at the Dixons' inn and to have the pleasure of exposing Armstrong to an enchanting part of his own native land which he had never visited before. In *Ushant* he recalls the evenings when Armstrong played Chopin's *Mazurka* on the inn's "tinny piano" (193), which provides a lyric counterpoint to Mariett's relentless playing of Debussy at the Signet.

After returning from Troutbeck, Aiken haunted Leicester Square night after night in hopes of spotting Irene. In his evolving imagination, the experience with Irene and Irene herself were central, celebrated in *Ushant* for having taught him "love," giving him, "with her love, and with her father's ring, his heart, his life, and his courage" (190). Besides a prominent place in *Ushant* and an unsuccessful long poem, she was destined to appear in his first novel, *Blue Voyage*. But poets are liars by nature and learning: the quest for Irene was primarily motivated by a distended penis, a muscle desire to possess her again, the priestess of his sexual initiation. A touching scene occurs in *Ushant,* in which Aiken meets "Wounded Face" on a train from Windermere to London, a man who had had his face virtually blown off during an explosion at the foundry where he worked and who had undergone fourteen futile operations—he is headed toward his fifteenth. Horrified by the man's muti-

lated visage, he schemes how to go about removing himself from the compartment they share, but his pity and self-consciousness prevent him from leaving
when the man goes for tea. His return—he brings an extra cup for his traveling companion—precipitates a conversation in which he explains his predicament, engendering shame in Aiken for his plans to escape. He offers the man
a piece of chocolate cake and gives him directions for locating the hospital in
London he is seeking.

In *Ushant*, however, Aiken must be Wordsworth and St. Augustine, pos-
tulating the incident as another turning point in his ethical and literary progress: "The offer of chocolate could make no amends for that profound betrayal, that meanness, that violation of humanity—yes, the very sense of
one's humanity, of 'belonging,' which Irene had all simply and all humbly
revealed to him" (194). Without such a structure, confession is worthless to
the serious artisan, who knows that linguistic order must constantly emit a
corresponding moral and aesthetic syntax if it is to achieve climax and meaning, capture positive attention as an effective stay against chaos, random flows
of atoms. Though mostly free of nineteenth-century Christian assumptions,
Aiken would never lose his view of art as philosophy and moral statement,
literature as an Arnoldian "criticism of life." Thus the lesson of "Wounded
Face" was the young artist's discovery that, thanks to Irene, "perhaps, now,
at last there could be a little love" (194).

The lesson is not false in an ordinary sense, but the future, the many Irenes
to come, the mistresses and wives Aiken would betray repeatedly in the dec
ades ahead, diminish the sincerity of his retrospective construct, which is
vulnerable, always, to nostalgia. His second wife would note that "nothing
could rouse him to compassion or even sympathy, whether it be friends' emotional disturbances or some illness." Literature aspires to virtue, Aiken as-
pired to virtue, and the courage behind his career-long examination of his
deepest self leaves little doubt that, whatever the cost, he meant to drill down
to the very heart of his existence. But the organic brilliance of *Ushant* resides
in its quest for the figure in the carpet, the "consistent view," a revised history
of individual consciousness on the trail of an ambitious art that would illuminate and illustrate mankind's mental evolution, thus legitimizing the stance of
its creator as subject. It has to distort, for architectural reasons, the unruly
materials of a life too complex for very much moral scaffolding.

The Aiken who addresses us from the pages of *Ushant* is not a Marcus
Aurelius erecting a rock barrier of Stoic sanity against invasions of barbaric
deaths and spirit-sapping materialism, content to rest secular meditations
about the cosmos and man's niche in it upon the harmonies orchestrated within an integrated, rational psyche. He is, rather, the artist near the end of his
creative existence, hands buried in the entrails of his art, seeking a system of

emotive nodes that will reify (and justify) the shape of that art. Not that *Ushant*'s perceptions are inferior to the perceptions of Aurelius's *Meditations* or similar classical texts; they are merely different. For modern man, Aiken's simulated autobiography—simulated in governing fable—probably has more to offer than a series of sagacious epigrams delivered before the true extent of human evil was known. But the biographer has to walk with care among Aiken's runes and ruins because their language is ever the language of invention, not reportage.

Comments on Irene provide the case in point. *Ushant* insists upon transmogrifying her dainty, girlish figure into a mature reincarnation of Dante's Beatrice, using Jung's vision to do so: "Had she become its *anima* [England's], and had he, with the gift of that unwithholding love, at one and the same time recovered his lost mother and escaped from her? The *freedom* to love was at last unlocked in him" (193). The design of this passage is appealing yet should not obscure the ordinary sins of the flesh it is laboring to transcend, as literature must, the reality of Aiken's carnal appetite; Anna's ghost had not yet been staked to rest. However crucial Irene's role in his development, his behavior toward her did not vary measurably from the behavior exhibited toward Elsa or the Venetian language teacher and later toward countless other females. The sole unique feature was her instrumentality in introducing him to sex, which cast a sentimental glow over her in his mind that would brighten with time.

A highlight of Aiken's London summer, to which *Ushant* devotes almost three pages, was meeting at breakfast in a Guildford Street boardinghouse with "the queer little top-hatted, frock-coated, Unitarian-minister-and-clairvoyant, from California" (130). According to Aiken, who retained a weakness for such displays in defiance of his normal skepticism, the minister instantly recognized his ambition to be a writer and invited him to his room after breakfast for a palm-reading session. In the dark little room he managed to manufacture the most astonishing predictions regarding Aiken's future:

You have, I think, a streak of genius, maybe a little more than that, maybe a little less—the ability, perhaps, without quite the perseverance or devotion—no, it's not quite that either. You have the vision, the primary requisite: you will be a true seer: it is, I fear, in the communication that you will fail. You will always tend to rush at things somewhat prematurely: you will see beyond your years, ahead of your maturity, so that continually, and unfortunately, the immaturity of your expression, a certain glibness and triteness, will tend to spoil your excellent ideas, leaving them to be adopted and better expressed—better organized, because better understood—by others. (130–31)

There is more, all of it remarkably presentient, including a prophecy of compulsive infidelities, an uncontrollable sex drive. But, once more, it is imperative to remember that when transcribing this reading Aiken had already survived the foretold experiences and as the poet saint must mythify himself as carrier of consciousness into the empyrean of godhead, validating the spiral ascent of his autobiography's circular voyage. Again, it is not a question of accuracy. The California mystic might very well have been sensitive enough to his new friend's strong character to make shrewd generalizations about a future course, generalizations apt to remain steadfast in Aiken's mental mirror. But the architecture of his revelations, its seamless relevance from start to finish, cunningly incorporating admitted flaws, that is, "glibness and triteness" plus an overactive sex gland, dovetails too neatly with the telic pattern of *Ushant*'s confessional march to salvation.

Aiken reveled in the flare of larger meaning such a man ignites in the soul of a narcissist, particularly a Romantic-bred narcissist like himself. He and the minister became intimates, shared outings, taking long walks and rowboat rides together, with him at the oars as his top-hatted companion "discoursed of clairvoyance and clairaudience" (132). It is interesting that the author of *Ushant,* so given to psychoanalytic interpretations, never probes the sea shadows behind this odd pair of boated strangers perhaps to perceive another conjunction of father and son, a lost Stephen Dedalus eager to have the omniscient father bring light (insight) to a chaotic world of primeval forces (unconscious), like Shelley's Prometheus.

Instead, tying off the tapestry of consciousness's expanding power, he weaves the episode into a scene at summer's end, when his own gift for prophetic awareness—dream-based, to be sure—was confirmed in dramatic fashion. Three times during the summer he had dreamed that the ship he was booked on to sail home from Glasgow, a small, battered steamer named *Ultonia,* had been wrecked in the fog and sank. A day after writing about the dream in a letter to Uncle William he read in the newspaper of the *Ultonia*'s actual sinking in a thick fog. It seemed to authenticate both the minister's unique talents and his own importance, although *Ushant* remarks simply that, as a consequence of the scary event, "on another ship, and at an earlier date, he had set sail without seeing the little man again"—the father's small size reiterated, like the victim protagonists of the *Advocate* tales. In contrast to the minister's conventional seer function, Aiken's miraculous dream warning— probably true but not exceptional in an age of sea voyages—has the extra value of originating in nightmare, the source of his most disturbing fantasies, poetic images. He had, the year before, argued with McCouch "that *fear* should have its place in the motivation of the dream, just as much as the wish, or desire" (174), anticipating Freud's revision of his own theory. Such a profound glimpse into the future from the perch of a magically recurring dream hinted that the struggle to assimilate and neutralize depth psychology now inclined toward conquest.

Certainly he was a contented young man when he returned to Cambridge in the fall of 1911, to the reassuring prospect of Harvard reunions and Eliot's momentary arrival. Of his friends who had graduated in June, Bill Taussig was spending a year in business school and available, McCouch had entered the University of Pennsylvania's medical school, where he would eventually specialize in neurophysiology, and kept in touch through the mails, and Harry Wehle was doing "a little newspaper reporting in New York" before trying his hand at agriculture and would return to Harvard to take a few courses in fine arts as prelude to a job with a Minneapolis museum. Paul Mariett was confined to a Cambridge hospital, writing his last short stories, "as he watched the crews at practice on the Charles, and waited to die" (174). His suffering would end on March 14, 1912. But Gordon Bassett, Jake Wilbur, and Myron Williams were still around to keep Aiken amused.

His virginity safely disposed of, Aiken began to strive for and attain a more balanced accord with the people immediately at hand and to resolve several problematic relationships. He had thoughtfully brought a Medici print of the *Origin of the Milky Way* from London for his Uncle William, and that retiring gentleman was duly grateful. In the months to come he would also fall into the occasional habit of taking his uncle, who had once been to Heidelberg and acquired a taste for German beer, to Marliave's or Jacob Wirth's restaurant in Boston for dinner, followed by the theater or a concert.

The emotional balance represented by Aiken's move toward an accommodation with the timid, kindly, professorial uncle, whom he had secretly resented for being his legal guardian, found a parallel in an improved fellowship, a more equal friendship, between his Uncle Alfred and himself. Despite Aunt Edith's earlier reproach and fears of his pernicious influence, the Potters had always welcomed him into their comfortable brick home on Fayerweather Street and treated him with casual fondness as a close family member. Now, he and Uncle Alfred moved nearer to a father-son stance: "The wonderful alliance had really, and forever, been joined" (79). In the process, binding them tighter, Aiken discovered that his scholarly, highly respected uncle led a double life and had been for years: he kept a mistress on the side and spent frequent evenings away from home, drinking and partying. In spite of his demanding position at the library, where he had been assistant librarian since 1904, Uncle Alfred assumed a Parisian dandy role during his nocturnal prowls among Boston's less savory clubs and bars. Aiken's brother Robert recalled with amazement his uncle's ability to consume enormous quantities of alcohol, stay up until the early hours of the morning, and yet appear, fresh and immaculately groomed, at his desk on time each day.

The Potters started having Conrad over for dinner on a regular basis, and he began to regard their parlor and his chair there in front of the fire (below a painting of him done by Aunt Edith) as somehow attached to the attic room at the Tillinghasts', an extension of home, *his* home. And that concept, above all, was the rock upon which his emotional balance rested—a simple outgrowth of physical and mental maturity, on one hand, and a psychological acceptance of the pleasure duplicity could supply, on the other. Along with reconciliations with Cambridge relatives came the knowledge that the schizophrenic dispassion of the artist, already his by birthright and by virtue of a disrupted family network, had the merit of permitting him to establish an effective, if not necessarily healthy, distance between the angry, wounded, defiant self that created and the social persona at large. He was indeed, like his uncle, "beginning to lead a double life: bi-lingual, bi-focal, he was deliberately learning to be two slightly different persons . . . a secret dualism that profoundly suited him" (134). The uncle's influence was negative in this respect, bestowing the moral sanction of an admired paternal figure upon his obsessive sex drive, "that animal, that feral hunger" stalking his future with "years of sex-obsession," rapist in intensity, "the unappeasable desire of the nympholept" (141).

The abnormal element in all this, a validating of Otto Rank's conclusion that "the great works of art were bought at the cost of ordinary living," does not eradicate the perfectly normal maturation phenomenon taking place as well. Aiken had experienced physical love, and he was twenty-two years old, handsome and in good health, sufficiently reflective to realize that multiple selves are fundamental to any social adaptation, any rational intercourse with people from whom one seeks affection and acceptance. He was glad to be back amid familiar scenes and faces, especially Eliot's grave mien, pursuing a course of action that had a definite, widely approved goal, one not too remote from literature itself.

There were new authors to be discussed and dissected and debated about over rum punch at the *Advocate* offices and in the libraries of the Union and the Signet, old and new authors—Henrik Ibsen, Leo Tolstoy, Ivan Turgenev, George Bernard Shaw, Maurice Maeterlinck, and the French poets, whom he was to approach seriously for the first time under Eliot's prodding, swallowing *The Symbolist Poets* in a single gulp. He seemed more at peace, though the saving perspective, the dualistic perspective, of his new self-knowledge was linked, as always, to the unsettling awareness of the threat to sanity lodged in his unconscious: "He knew those days, those weeks, when the interior balance was perilous, when chaos had come again, and the machine of consciousness, and of controlled living, was all but vanquished. On these occasions he had learned to absent himself as much as possible from all social contact, for the slightest unusual pressure was likely to produce unhappy or embarrassing consequences" (165). If not a perfect or permanent solution, such withdrawals had the advantage of protecting him from a destructive tendency to rupture bonds of friendship over minor matters, to spill his bile on those closest to him.

He understood and accepted that he would never be able to function well in large groups, that he was at his witty, intellectual best in homey circles of intimates who could appreciate his gifts without putting undue strains upon his mask. Later he would also understand and accept that literary friends can be the most dangerous and egocentric, and he would narrow his clutch of close friends—excluding Eliot and a few others—to artists and psychiatrists, like Wilbur, and old school chums, like McCouch and Bassett, who posed no consistent threat to his own need for center stage. He did not become a dove of silent benevolence during his final year at Harvard. Robert has described his oldest brother as "a charmer, there's no question about it," but also "impulsively as mean as they come. You'd cross his bow sometime and either get rammed or veer off awful fast." Even taking into account contrary lifestyles and subsequent periods of hostility between the brothers, the assessment has too much confirmation from other sources to be denied.

What fascinates is the sustained absence of this truculence in Aiken's relations with Eliot. Determined to secure a Ph.D. in philosophy, the latter had returned already perceptibly Europeanized. "He made a point, for a while, a conspicuously un-American point, of carrying a cane—was it a malacca?—a little self-conscious about it, and complaining that its 'nice conduct' was no such easy matter. He had taken a room in Ash Street, installing in it a small stove and a Gauguin *Crucifixion,* brought from Paris. The suggestion that the latter was a kind of sophisticated primitivism brought the reply, with a waspishness that was characteristic, that there 'was nothing primitive about it.' " Obviously Eliot was still embroiled in fabricating his own persona, further refining his mask as cosmopolitan intellectual to counter the fractured, oddly passive psyche exposed in "Prufrock." But Aiken rarely challenged Eliot's persona directly and accepted the snappishness and the critical absurdities it engendered, such as Eliot's remark that he preferred his Ibsen straight when queried about Anton Chekhov's plays.

He continued to admire Eliot, to appreciate the dry humor and affected elegance of the man and the mask: "There was something of the actor in Tom, and some of the clown too. For all his liturgical appearance . . . he was capable of real buffoonery. . . . Manners . . . he had them. He did things with an enviable grace." Charlie Chaplin had made his first movie, and his films and the Mack Sennett comedies became another tie between them, supplementing their unremitting love of comic strips and American slang. They were never closer. Eliot had decided to take up boxing, perhaps another exercise in character building, and Aiken recalled the experience with amused warmth: "The boxing lessons . . . took place at a toughish gymnasium in Boston's South End, where, under the tutelage of an ex-pugilist with some such monicker as Steve O'Donnell, he learned not only the rudiments of boxing, but also, as he put it, 'how to swarm with passion up a rope;—his delight in this attainment was manifest . . . it was our habit to dine together after these gymnastic afternoons, usually at the Greek restaurant in Stuart Street, a small, dirty, and wonderfully inexpensive establishment which was in fact half restaurant and half pool-room."

The long, lazy dinners at the Parthenon, after Eliot's sessions with O'Donnell (possible model for "Sweeney") were naturally centered around literary and philosophical matters, though Eliot accused Aiken more than once of using terms he did not comprehend—he was already deep into Francis Herbert Bradley's neo-Hegelianism. Eliot's enthusiasm for Bergson had not yet abated and was passed on to his somewhat reluctant companion. He was also loud in praise of Charles-Louis Philippe and Charles Vildrac, and of Maeterlinck's mysticism, but expressed little interest in Aiken's hero, Nietzsche, about whom he would later write: "Confusion of thought, emotion, and vision is what we find in such a work as *Also Sprach Zarathustra*." And yet Aiken's attraction to Nietzsche's poetic negatives was not completely at a tangent to Eliot's quest for a rational metaphysic to replace the lost Absolute, causing him to rate the *Bhagavad-Gita* as "the next greatest philosophical poem to the *Divine Comedy* within my experience," since Nietzsche's stress on the "Will to Power" and supermen saviors was articulated within the grammar of an "Eternal recurrence of all things," which sounds Indian and demonstrates Emerson's appeal for the German iconoclast. And Zarathustra's comment on the creative act is not far from Eliot's view of the matter: "Creating—that is the great salvation from suffering, and life's alleviation. But for the creator to appear, suffering itself is needed, and much transformation."

The separation between Aiken and Eliot remained most pronounced in the precocious maturity of the latter's poetic skill. Now that he had finished "Prufrock," Eliot's self-confidence as a poet was considerable, expressed by a voice totally his own, however indebted to Laforgue and similar French sources. Aiken's introduction to French verse, Symbolist and Parnassian, actually dates to near the end of the academic year: "I hadn't really got around very much to the French poets at that time. I'd heard something of them from Eliot naturally, who came back from Paris full of Vildrac and Laforgue; but it wasn't until I'd read Symons on the Symbolists somewhat later, that I got into

it at all." To Houston Peterson he gave the impression that his French education— "Verlaine in 1911, a little of Rimbaud; Baudelaire, Malmarmé, Vildrac
and Laforgue somewhat later"—exuded a "general aroma" he enjoyed inhal-
ing, smelling in the dimly translated texts "the possibility of a freer rhyming
free-verse, a more flexible and moving technique than he had previously
thought of." But he was more drawn to Spanish and Italian poets; Leopardi's
Pensieri offered its own version of freely rhyming *vers libre,* as did Eliot's
"Prufrock," of course. He was also charmed by contemporary British poetry,
the mildly rebellious Georgian traditionalists encountered in London and epitomized in his friend Martin Armstrong's tepid work, to a degree that Eliot
would have thought peculiar.

Eliot and he reverted to their habit of exchanging poems and literary ideas,
which was nourishing for Aiken in and of itself. Further, Eliot later affirmed
that Aiken convinced him to excise an entire page from "Prufrock," an indication of the faith vested in his friend's critical acumen, despite any reservations about his poetic and philosophic abilities. Aiken would shrewdly compare their relationship to the ambivalent intercourse between Hawthorne and
Melville. Eliot was still enthralled by the neohumanism of Babbitt, though
that conservative pedagogue would have been dismayed by his Gauguin, and
by Josiah Royce's preachings of human life as a manifestation of the "Absolute," reality as an "Eternal and Absolute Mind and Will," while sharing
Aiken's high regard for Santayana, who had spent the summer teaching in
California. There, on August 25, he had delivered his famous address "The
Genteel Tradition in American Philosophy," as fully important as Emerson's
Harvard lecture "The American Scholar," at least in the sense of defining the
suffocating effect of a genteel phase and the heroic oppositional impulse toward democratic vistas and experimental, developmental pragmatism cham-
pioned by Whitman and William James.

Santayana's speech also isolated the growing contemporary revolution that
was quickening the pulses of various talents among Aiken's generation: "On
the one side came the revolt of the Bohemian temperament, with its poetry of
crude naturalism; on the other side came an impassioned empiricism." Almost
in desperation, for California was overwhelming him, the philosopher's final
plea, as old as Socrates', was for the life of the intellect, "for by the mind only
do we exist as men. . . . Let us therefore be frankly human. Let us be content
to live in the mind." Santayana soon had the opportunity to do precisely that
because of the death of his American mother. Besides severing his last genetic
link with the United States, her demise and generous legacy left him free to
abandon Harvard and pursue the life of the mind abroad. When Aiken graduated in June 1912, Santayana had already escaped, never to return, foreshadowing the exodus to Europe of many of the country's thinkers and artists

over the next decade or so, including Aiken, intermittently, and Eliot, permanently. The immediate impact of all this upon Aiken's poetry is moot because none of the verses written during his tardy senior year have survived in their original form. If nothing else, the belated introduction to ninetenth-century French poetry, in which the loathing of existence so congenial to Eliot's *angst*-ridden stance was a persistent motif amid contrary streams of surreal spontaneity and classical revivalism, abetted his subsequent determination to vindicate Pater by bringing his verses nearer the condition of music.

In the personal arena, Aiken's familiar routines had experienced a major alteration that autumn when he met and fell in love with Jessie McDonald, a strikingly attractive graduate student concentrating in literature at Radcliffe. The precise details of the meeting are somewhat in doubt. Aiken apparently always claimed to have made her acquaintance during one of his regular walks around Fresh Pond, but Ruth McIntyre remembers it differently. According to her, a friend and fellow student of Jessie's—"we were taking a graduate course, English 39, I think it was, with George Pierce Baker"—Aiken spotted Jessie in the streets of Cambridge and was struck by her beauty, "the prettiest thing you ever saw, bright red cheeks, blue eyes, black hair." His shyness and the Victorian-shaded mores of the time prevented a direct approach, though he learned she was Canadian, had graduated from McGill University, and was now at Radcliffe for a master's degree in English, boarding in a house off Brattle Street not far from Ruth's residence. He also figured out her schedule and usually managed to be walking up Brattle at the moment she was walking down Brattle to the college.

Aware of Aiken's predicament, Ruth and a few sympathetic girlfriends decided to invite the two to a dance, where proper introductions could be engineered. The results were satisfactory: "I don't think they danced at all; I think they probably left immediately." The stroll around Fresh Pond came later, several of them, since it was the custom on Sunday morning for friends and lovers slowly to circumscribe its tree-shadowed banks, enabling curious Cambridge to discover who was having dinner with whom. Jessie's fresh beauty, attested to by contemporary photographs, was matched by brains, common sense, and good humor. Ruth deemed her "very intelligent" and "lots of fun," though "she wasn't a strong personality like Conrad, but everybody liked her, and she had a good time in life, I think." Aiken's brother Robert was also impressed: "She was a very able, nice gal . . . she was short and she had beautiful coloring; she was dark, dark Scotch, but really . . . had the coloring, red cheeks, she was awfully pretty, and she was smart." For Aiken, of course, aside from the mandatory resemblance to his mother, her attractiveness was greatly enhanced by her knowledge of and interest in literature—she had mastered several languages. As her daughter Joan has ob-

Jessie McDonald as a graduate student, shortly before she met Aiken in 1911.

served, "She was extremely well read and continued to be so to the day of her death . . . she had all this education, and she had a very keen sort of critical mind."

Jessie McDonald was the next to youngest of eight siblings in a solid middle-class family, probably the brightest of the children. Her father, a successful Montreal accountant, had returned to Scotland to acquire—in the words of Jane Aiken Hodge— "a sort of certified as sound-of-wind-and-limb bride, extorted the poor woman to Canada, and a very hard time she had of it, I always suspected." Jessie's ambition was modest enough— a teaching post somewhere in the United States—but her achievements at McGill and Radcliffe and her drive to continue her education in America certainly imply a personality stronger than the one limned by Ruth. In any event, as the year wound down, marriage became the great unspoken topic at the back of both their minds. To Aiken, her suitability as a marital prospect was augmented by what he judged her lower-class background, sturdy peasant roots, potential corrective to the mad genes he believed had run amok among the branches of his own family tree.

By spring of 1912 he was writing of his infatuation to McCouch: "When I begin to think I'm passionately in love and in need of immediate hugging, I go and walk with this marvelous child and find that I'm perfectly happy and contented just with her companionship." Marriage appeared imminent, though Aiken hesitated. In later years he often told his daughter Joan that her mother knew of his reluctance, was putting pressure on him, "and finally she applied to some teaching job . . . in the Midwest somewhere, and after they'd had a date gave him this letter to post as he went downstairs, saying this is the application for my job." The ploy worked. In the letter to McCouch he admitted, "I think I should only fall in love with her if someone else started wishing for her, or she threatened to go away, or if in any fashion I should be deprived of the pleasure of seeing her." He proposed and was accepted shortly before he graduated with his A.B. in June.

Aiken's second senior year thus ended with quiet satisfaction, a dramatic contrast to the previous year and his entire Harvard tenure, which had been distinguished by numerous highs and lows, significant achievements and increasing acceptance varying with rebellious gestures and many traditional undergraduate pranks, the latter fueled by notorious beer parties and gin binges. His second wife has written: "I had heard rumors of college capers involving Conrad and the editors of the *Hound & Horn,* Varian Fry (expelled for a year after putting up a For Sale sign on President Eliot's grounds) and Lincoln Kirstein (the wealthy poet-scholar addicted to the ballet)." Another antic in which Aiken had been a fellow conspirator during his abbreviated first senior year, when rooming at Hollis with Taussig, had been the attempt to gag the

Harvard bell, "deliciously thin, melancholy, which he had reviled so often, which rang rising hours, morning prayers, lectures, recitations, Thursday vespers, Sunday evening chapel." The futile effort had been launched on a freezing January night, its failure caused by the immediate freezing of the water in the pail of tar brought along to glue the knocker into place.

Such schoolboy pranks reflect the assimilation actually achieved over five years, the progress from freshman year, "fraught with physical dangers, mental torture, inferiority complexes, etc.," through the sophomore experience, "the most priceless of all," and junior class blues, "seared with multifarious duties and a waning play spirit," to the tensions of senior status, "surfeited with teas and small speeches and the worry of grabbing a *summa cum laude* in June." Along with memories of all-night card games and "peerless beer nights" went less happy recollections of the tears shed in Grays Hall, where his initials decorated a windowsill. More lasting were the friendships made with such people as Bassett and Eliot and the aesthete spirit of the college that would forever stain his literature, a spirit fortunately diluted by exposure to the humane influence of minds on the order of James and Briggs, which encouraged a liberal, energetic vision of literature and life at odds with the elitist, conservative bias permeating the air behind "the walls of Troy," Copey's name for the iron fences penning the Yard.

Graduation was a cinch, unpressured by the need for a public performance and in pleasant contrast to the bitterness surrounding Aiken's departure from Middlesex. Only a wedding ceremony remained. The original plan was for the marriage to take place in Cambridge that summer, after an extended visit with the McDonald clan at their summer home in Quebec. But the family had a highly emotional impact on Aiken, especially Jessie's mother and five sisters. His daughter Jane recounts how "he talked . . . about how he went up to Canada for the first time . . . and just fell in love with the whole family. It must have been quite extraordinary for a familyless young thing like him to get up there and find five ravishing likenesses of his fiancée. . . . He also used to talk about how he fell for my grandmother, with whom he became very good friends, and my Aunt Marian, who was most like my mother, in appearance at least." Soon he was addressing Mrs. McDonald as "Mother."

On July 29 Aiken wrote McCouch to apologize for a change in plans, "for various reasons, chiefly that it saves Mother a great deal of trouble and worry." Jessie and he had decided to be wed "down here at Cap a l'Aigle on the 25th day of August." The Tillinghasts and Potters could not have been too thrilled by the new arrangements. After the ceremony the couple did pay a brief visit to Boston before sailing to Liverpool on September 6 for a lengthy European honeymoon.

The whole machinery of life,

and the minds

of every class and kind of men

change beyond recognition every

generation. I don't know that

"progress" is certain. All I know is

that change is.

Rupert Brooke

. . . .

THE EVOLVING PATTERN

Surveying the treacherous past from the safety of a prestigious post in Washington, D.C., many years later and marriage, at last, to a woman who accepted the maternal function assigned her, Aiken could afford to see the honeymoon trek of 1912 with Jessie as marking "the beginning . . . of things that would *never* be finished, poems, loves, lives, books" (57). There is no reason to believe that the young couple had anything but a happy journey from Liverpool to the Troutbeck Valley of his recent summer idylls, where Jessie played the same piano played by Martin Armstrong in the shadowed hotel room (56).

Aiken would always recall with romantic nostalgia "the magic of that particular autumn," shared walks amid rain showers to Bowness, Ambleside, Grasmere, Kirkstone Pass, and the subsequent leisurely Paris jaunt before settling down in London for an English Christmas. Necessary adjustments to a marital state were made easier by Jessie's ingrained domesticity and cheerful disposition, her good-natured sense of the practical acting as a reassuring balance to his flights of fantasy and egotism. Money helped, too—the income from his inheritance and a legacy from her father, which enabled them to travel abroad in relative comfort and to contemplate a life of creative activity together free from the need to earn their daily bread.

For a writer, especially a writer molded by Harvard's elegant, Anglophile

183

vision of art, the situation was ideal. Aiken responded by turning out reams of narrative and lyric verse, filling notebook after notebook with his small penciled script, to the amazement and admiration of his wife, who often typed the material for him. The newest deity in his literary pantheon, and in London's as well, was John Masefield. This adventurous self-made man had run away to sea as a boy, wandered around America surviving on menial jobs, labored as a journalist for the *Manchester Guardian* after his return to England in 1900 at the age of twenty-two, and soon began publishing a string of well-received novels, plays, and poetry and short story collections, most of them based on his sea experiences. In 1911 his *Everlasting Mercy,* a vivid long poem in relentless octasyllabic couplets about the brutal life and ultimate religious conversion of Saul Kane, a small-town ruffian, had become an immediate best-seller, followed a year later by the almost equally popular *Widow in the Bye Street.*

Aiken read both works with intense approval, relating at once to their colorful amalgamation of traditional techniques, harsh naturalism, and reformist thrust and ignoring their heavy-handed didacticism. Masefield appeared to epitomize the dream of his own poetic ambitions at the time, a quest for a naturalistic language and scene set within a conventional frame. If unable or unwilling to admit the inherent limitations of Masefield's modest talent, he was wise enough to sense that it represented the most visible sign of the growing revolt among England's younger generation. *Georgian Poetry, 1911–1912,* edited by Edward Marsh, had recently been published. Initiated by a group consisting of Marsh, Harold Monro, Rupert Brooke, John Drinkwater, Wilfrid Wilson Gibson, and Monro's friend Arundel del Re, the anthology was intended as a defiant gesture against the Establishment's loyalty to a Victorian ethos and elevated speech and against the imperialist smugness typified by Kipling. It was, in effect, a continuation of the Romantics' century-earlier struggle to infuse English poetry with the lexicon and personae of ordinary existence, as well as the natural outgrowth of a steady shift toward Jamesian impressionism and the social realism exploited by the novels of Wells and Hardy and Shaw's satiric plays, although most of the poets numbered among the contributors to the five Georgian anthologies that would be published between 1912 and 1922 relied mainly upon conventional formulas. Among these were poets such as those in the founding circle, plus W. H. Davies, Lascelles Abercrombie, Walter de la Mare, Masefield, and Aiken's London acquaintance Martin Armstrong.

Adamantly opposed to the Georgians' technical conservatism was another London cluster of younger writers and artists loosely orbiting around Pound, T. E. Hulme, F. S. Flint, and Ford Madox Heuffer, founder of the *English Review* in 1908. The *Ripostes* of Pound was also a recent publication, concluding with "The Complete Works of T. E. Hulme," five *Imagiste* poems, identified by Pound as the consequence of Hulme's "forgotten school" of 1909, an allusion to a small coterie of obscure poets who had met weekly under Hulme's guidance at the Eiffel Tower, a Soho restaurant, to discuss a new poetic of "dry and hard" severity. Hulme, however, was primarily an aesthetician and art critic; it remained for Pound in 1912 to transform his friend's doctrine—a merger of Symbolism and classical purity—into a bona fide literary movement with all the furious energy at his command. Besides possessing a knowledge of and antenna for poetic excellence second to none in its catholic grasp of fundamental principles, Pound was ever the master tactician, and "like Zola (or, later, Tzara and Breton) . . . recognized that the *avant-garde* functioned best, made its mark, when it performed as a campaign, or when its writers operated as a cadre."

Among the contending forces of rebellion jockeying for power in London salons, galleries, coffeehouses, and editorial offices, Ezra Pound was unique in the influence he exerted as he infiltrated journal after journal to showcase his own work and the work of disciples and to lay down the hard laws of modernism: "The mastery of any art is the work of a lifetime." Since his arrival from Italy in 1908, and despite his twenty-seven years, Pound had made a strong impression upon older, well-established writers such as Yeats, who was then forty-seven, and Heuffer, thirty-nine, publishing *Personae* (1909), *Exultations* (1909), *Provenca* (1910), *The Spirit of Romance* (1910), *Canzoni* (1911), *Ripostes* (1912), and the translation of *The Sonnets and Ballate of Guido Cavalcanti* (1912), all of which proclaimed a fascination with metrical experiments and the literature of medieval Provençe. Though raised and educated in Pennsylvania, he was intensely cosmopolitan in his conviction that English-language verse had to adopt a European consciousness—one of Arnold's cherished goals—if it were to escape from under the burden of English Romanticism's ornamental and didactic excesses, whether exampled in Wordsworth's cluttered moralizing or in the culminating vagueness of the starchy Victorians, excluding Browning and certain Pre-Raphaelites.

Besides the *English Review,* Pound found a congenial outlet in the *Poetry Review,* which Monro had started at the beginning of the year with the reluctant support of the ultraconservative Poetry Society to forge "a weapon of criticism" to counteract the baneful dominance of reactionary elders, in particular Kipling and Alfred Noyes. Stressing criticism over original poetry, Monro was concerned with creating an audience for verse necessary to any contemporary purgation of the past: "Poetry is uninteresting to-day in that degree only that it is remote from life . . . it must be fundamental, vital, innate or nothing at all." Five poems by Pound were printed in the second number of the magazine, along with his assertive "Prolegomena" and

"Credo," clearly defining the point at which he and Monro parted company. Monro welcomed contributions from many of the Georgians, kindly reviewed Edmund Gosse's old-fashioned *Collected Poems,* and avowed in the initial issue, "We admire sincerity more than originality." In contrast, Pound insisted upon judging technique "as the test of a man's sincerity" and viewed the Georgians as a stumbling block to an authentic revolution in their avoidance of technical experiments and hostility to Hulme's Imagism. He also persuaded Monro to give one of his promising epigoni, Richard Aldington, then barely in his twenties, books to review and in general strove to heighten what he regarded as the editor's insufficiently radical fervor.

Besides several English magazines, the journal destined to become the single most important conduit for Pound's campaign to drag poetry into the twentieth century was *Poetry,* which Harriet Monroe, a middle-aged spinster and former art critic, had established in Chicago. The first issue of *Poetry* appeared in October 1912, that crucial year, a month ahead of schedule to outflank a similarly named periodical being readied in Boston. It contained poems by Pound, Helen Dudley, Arthur Ficke, Grace Hazard Conkling, and Emilia Stuart Lorimer and the posthumous "I Am the Woman" by William Vaughn Moody—not a very impressive list, excepting Pound. But the magazine's unique financial structure and dedication to discovering new voices, based on the principles of paying for every line and publishing nothing but poetry and poetry reviews, guaranteed that it would emerge as the leading organ for the age of poetry dawning across America.

Harriet Monroe seemed an unlikely catalyst, a lean, short-haired, schoolmarmish woman of extraordinary determination and an uneven but always open taste, as her own turgid, overwrought style evidenced, whose practical shrewdness had been demonstrated in 1893, when she negotiated for a $1,000 instead of a $500 fee in payment for the grandiose *Columbian Ode* delivered at the Chicago Exposition, then sued and won $5,000 more from the *New York World* for having printed the poem prematurely and without permission. Blessed by valuable family connections with the city's upper strata and her own ability to make contacts and earn money by writing art criticism for the local papers, she devoted much of her time to travel. It was after an eight-month trip around the world in 1911, which had entailed an extended London stay, during which she dined with the Meynells ("my old friends") and was introduced by novelist May Sinclair to Elkin Mathews, Pound's innovative publisher, that she decided to provide an American forum for the neglected geniuses of poetry.

A basic and very astute element in her strategy was to reach out to all the "interesting" poets in England and America through a circular announcing her plan and asking for contributions and subscriptions: "All kinds of verse will be considered—narrative, dramatic, lyric—quality alone being the test of competence. Certain numbers may be devoted entirely to a single poem, or a group of poems by one person; except for a few editorial pages of comment and review." She had studiously prepared for the task by spending most of the summer in the public library, reading "recent books by the better poets" and "all the verse in American and English magazines of the previous five years." The poets thus approached through the mails, more than fifty of whom also received personal letters, represented almost every level and style imaginable, varying from Floyd Dell, Amy Lowell, Edith Wharton, and Robinson through the Georgians to Noyes, Yeats, and Pound. The latter replied with alacrity and customary enthusiasm, volunteering to keep the magazine in touch with developments in Paris and London, an offer that resulted in his appointment as *Poetry*'s unsalaried foreign correspondent.

In this capacity, Pound set about trying to obtain verses from Yeats and Rabindranath Tagore, whom he labeled "the very great Bengali poet," a rare major misjudgment, and forwarded some poems by Aldington, which were printed in the second issue. Meanwhile, he continued to bombard the responsive editor with advice and exhortations and in October enclosed a set of poems by Hilda Doolittle. At Pound's suggestion, when Doolittle's work appeared in the January 1913 number, they were attributed simply to "H.D. *Imagiste.*" His brief essay "Status Rerum," in the same issue, reported a lack of significant poetic activity in London, except that generated by the "*Imagistes*" and Yeats, whom he was helping to sculpt a more conversational idiom.

Unfortunately, Aiken was isolated from the battles whirling around him in London, having no access either to Pound and his group or to the opposing camps. Armstrong attempted to aid him and might have introduced him to Drinkwater at this time, but he himself had only recently published a first collection, *Exodus and Other Poems,* aptly characterized by Louis Untermeyer as "wholly without distinction," and was not yet in a position to supply the required entrée. To worsen matters, Aiken's sole submission to the *English Review,* "Leicester Square," an endless narrative poem about a streetwalker derived from his experience with Irene, was rejected by Hueffer, despite its Masefield echoes—*The Everlasting Mercy* had first seen print there. The arrival of *Poetry* increased his frustration, emphasizing the presence in the United States of the poetic ferment already agitating London's artistic community and the enviable rise of Pound. "Status Rerum" was especially galling in its casual dismissal of contemporary English poets, traditional but naturalistic, whom he most admired and was busy emulating.

His solution was to write Harriet Monroe a cagey letter of complaint in January from Florence, where they had gone to escape London's gray, drizzly weather after pleurisy had forced Jessie to spend a week in bed. Aiken launched a frontal assault, charging Monroe and Pound with propagandizing through the new magazine. By the second paragraph, Pound alone is the enemy, damned for arrogantly pronouncing Whitman and *vers libre* most important to the future of poetry. Pound's greatest sin, however, implicitly undermining Aiken's own borrowed aesthetic, lay in his presumptuous declaration that "there is no new poetry in England at the present—worthy of study." After warning against native insularity and praising Marsh's anthology, claiming that America possessed no young poets to match its roll of talented contributors, Aiken gives the game away by confessing that he, like Masefield (a Pound target), may come to be reviewed with his own volume of Chaucerian stanzas.

Both genuine and self-serving, as befits a poet, the letter was never printed because of lack of space rather than malefaction. In a December letter to the Old Bird, upon whom he depended for intelligent and appreciative reactions to his creations, he had described the immense amount of poetry composed since his honeymoon journey commenced, which encompassed at least five narrative poems, all over four hundred lines, "a number of short poems, lyric and philosophic (?)," and "a long narrative under construction" (already six hundred lines) about a burglar caught in the act by a housemaid, who then has a love affair with him. Aside from two cast in six-line stanzas, the narrative verses were indeed in Chaucer's seven-line stanzas and blatant in their Masefield effects.

Masefield's loudly heralded success had only confirmed what Aiken had previously heard in Robinson, a modernist note sounded amid a symphony of inherited forms through a concentration on lower-class characters and situations and the use of street language. The same letter to McCouch outlines the philosophy behind the constant stream of poetry, an endeavor "to make poetry of the commonplace and sordid. My idea is to keep an even tone of rough and ready realism in all the subordinate parts of a story, rising to the lyric, or impassioned when the event demands: at such moments permitting myself all the beauty I'm capable of. I allow myself slang, and all blunt, ordinary words that have meanings—do not at all restrict myself to the poetical vocabulary."

Apart from the marathon narrative poem alluded to, tentatively entitled "The Unregenerate Dust," December had witnessed the completion of "Earth Triumphant" as well, a long poem that uses the octosyllabic couplets of *The Everlasting Mercy* and not a little of its structure, although Poe, Robinson, and his own "Clerk's Journal" figure strongly in its romantic plot. A young man who has exhausted "one by one / Each creed, each weird philosophy" and abandoned a cloistered, bookish quest "for truth" down "devious sombre ways" in favor of immersions in both nature's sensual reality and urban nightlife meets and falls in love with the perfect young woman, "his earthly queen." Doom stalks their love, of course, and she reads glum fate in his palm with unintendedly comic portentiousness:

> "If you should ever love, have fear!
> Near death is written plainly here,
> For her or you I cannot say;
> Else, why should this line break this way?"

Unlike an archetypal Poe heroine, the narrator's dream girl weds him before she expires "sharp at ten o'clock," and he glides glibly into absolute despair:

> A loneliness, a loneliness,
> An absence of all loveliness,
> Came down upon his heart like rain,
> Insistent, gentle fall of pain,
> With not a pause, and not a let,
> No chance was given to forget.

Despite a congenial mood and topic, much of the poem is similarly fatuous, clotted with obvious rhymes and a melodious rhetoric that emulates Keats and Shelley at their weakest, climaxing not in religious redemption such as one would find in Masefield but in a pantheistic embracing of nature's cyclical regenerations:

> Earth sang, and trembled; down went sun,
> The dark poured out, the day was done . . .
> So, in a year's time, triumphed earth,—
> This May, at last May, brought him mirth.

It is a cynical coda delivered by a voice reveling in its naughty negativism, a pale Nietzschean voice. Aiken lifted Masefield's formula to confound his Christian message without understanding that the Englishman's models at least had the rough texture of working-class life and language to deter them from sliding off into affected silliness—plus a smooth narrative drive naive enough to convey conviction. Regardless of motive, Aiken's voice is that of a self-dramatizing outsider, an aesthete intruder among the lower orders.

But the poetry was flowing—he and Jessie had erased Spain from their itinerary to avoid damming the creative flood—and Florence granted them several glorious, sun-filled days. The plan now was to stay a few weeks and then move on to Rome, which they did, finding a small apartment overlooking the Spanish Steps. Ruth McIntyre, who was touring Italy with a girlfriend, showed up in Rome at the same time and was invited to visit: "We had dinner, and Conrad read us some of his poems, and Jessie said that he was perfectly remarkable: he sat down at the typewriter and typed a little, and there was a poem. She said, 'I can't understand it!' "

Unaccountably Aiken would ruin the pleasant evening and lose Ruth's friendship afterward when he escorted her back to her hotel. "He told me something he shouldn't have told me," Ruth remembers. "I believed him, and I shouldn't have believed him. I was a little naive about everything, so it was a question of making a choice, and I made a choice. . . . After that, I didn't see much of Conrad, except incidentally, I mean, I didn't talk to him, I didn't hear from him." In *Ushant,* in which Ruth is called "Kay," Aiken is reticent about the incident, noting simply that "Kay had been told of Wild Michael's philanderings (with the inevitable result, and Michael's threatening letter)" (177). After reading this, Ruth demurs: "He did not tell me what he says he did. He told me in Rome that Tom and a friend of mine I will call 'The Charmer' were engaged. This hurt me, I admit, because I had known them both so well since I was about twelve. Foolishly, I believed Conrad and I wrote to Tom, who hit the roof."

When Ruth forwarded McCabe's denial to Aiken in Sicily later, Aiken would write back insisting that he had seen the ring, which might be true. Ruth continues, "Tom cabled, 'Ring is at bottom of Charles River.' No use going into details. I add only that I broke completely with Conrad and Jessie. I could take my choice. It was awkward to meet Conrad on the street and cut him dead, but I did and I really loved Jessie." The exact springs of this curious episode are obscure, but it is evident that Aiken deliberately meant to wound Ruth, whom he knew was attracted to McCabe, and through her McCabe himself, whom he must have still detested. Why he chose to strike at this moment, at a time of personal happiness and productivity, is difficult to judge, though his behavior again points up the suppressed rage lurking behind his stoical, usually genial façade, which could erupt abruptly, often without overt provocation. It would contribute to his reputation as a potential savage, despite a real gift for friendship (male) and generous gestures.

In any event, the Rome stay was serene and fertile. Aiken wrote poetry as well as lengthy letters to friends and relatives in the United States, studied an Italian book on counterpoint, and related his fabulous dreams to Jessie each morning over breakfast—he pretended that the two narrative poems dealing with his experience with Irene were dreams refined. In a reply to a letter from McCouch admiring his poetry but not his philosophy, Aiken was grateful but insisted that "mere putting of life on paper, in words, does not justify itself to me any longer." He proposed, instead, a grand future design: "I have vaguely in mind the composition of a whole cycle of tales, as varied as possible in tone and subject, for the mere purpose of putting forth a very tangible philosophy of life *in terms of life itself.*" This vaunting ambition overlooked his inability to grasp any philosophy except that grounded in experience, a version of "life for life's sake," and made clear a germinal interest in the concept of linked sequences and reflexive reification. Because of Santayana and his grandfather, *thinking* poetry remained the ideal.

The Old Bird provided encouragement, however repulsed by secular cynicism, which somewhat blunted the blows delivered with every rejection slip, McCouch having dutifully passed his poems on to the unimpressed *Atlantic Monthly*. In December another well-wisher with poor taste had been recruited; Aiken had made the acquaintance of Lucien Bainbridge Crist, a novice composer from Boston, where he had practiced law for six years before deciding to complete his musical education in Europe. Crist, who was studying theory with C. Landi and singing with William Shakespeare in London, had reacted to his new friend's voluminous poetry with unrestrained praise, causing Aiken to contemplate, at the edge of bitterness, actual popular success: "Mr. Crist, the American composer here, whose tastes are soundly plebian, calls them MAGNIFICENT! GREAT POETRY! . . . If he represents the great unwashed, there is hope." Armstrong, too, rarely stinted in his approval, supplementing the positive reinforcement offered by the loyal Jessie. The problem, as "Earth Triumphant" shows, was that he had indeed deluded himself into believing he could have it all, à la Masefield, both a critical and a commercial victory.

In spite of a cold snap, Rome in February 1913 was refreshing, as was Palermo, Sicily, cold yet sunny when they went there the next month via Naples, but Aiken was growing restless, wanting to be, always, where he was not, even home. London's weather, real and social, had been too forbidding by far, and Italy was "no place for a live man" because "no one thinks, not even the philosophers; they dream." Cambridge's familiar streets beckoned, as did "good grey Boston." The crucial factor was whether Eliot would still be there to supply the intellectual excitement and fun he had in the past. He needed Eliot and had written to him from Rome to learn of his plans for the coming year, wondering if he would stay in Cambridge.

Eliot's return letter, affirming his intention to remain in pursuit of his doctorate, erased any lingering doubts about the wisdom of going home, which received an additional boost when Jessie missed a period—she appeared "very tired and not very well." They sailed back to Rome from Sicily to consult a doctor, who confirmed that she was pregnant. There was no question that their first child must be born in America. While in Rome, Aiken tirelessly finished another long narrative poem in the Masefield manner, "Youth," and dispatched it immediately to McCouch with an explanation: "You will be pleased to observe that whatever philosophy lurks in it is expressed not on the author's part but in the person of the protagonist himself. . . . The poem is nevertheless a kind of philosophy as a *whole*—an allegory, if you like, merely a pessimistic remark to the effect that Youth is a glorious affair while it lasts . . . and then when the shouting is over, well well, you are old and tame, but what does it matter—youth and age are equally useless, life is useless, sorrow and joy are useless, but thank god there are one or two things that can delude you into still thinking that life is beautiful, and above all that usefulness is beautiful—the main delusion of this kind being love."

Aiken would claim that Freud stood behind everything he did from 1912 on, but the two-pronged threat of Freud—a reduction of literature to day-dreams and wish-fulfillment and of mankind to rats trapped inside a maze of unconscious conflicts and urges—had neither been truly assimilated nor neu-tralized. In "Youth," which owes nothing to Joseph Conrad and differs little from its companion piece, "Earth Triumphant," the main character, Jim, is a Nietzschean superman, like Jack London's Wolf Larsen, though closer to Masefield's Saul Kane, strong and alienated, impelled by utter contempt for the ordinary human beings surrounding him. His amorality is predicated upon the Darwinian milieu (enlarged by Spencer and Huxley) of ceaseless struggles for survival and domination, unable to accept either a deity or a feminine ethic of Christian meekness, selflessness. Like Kane, Jim engages in a fight with a friend and fellow hood (named Jake), though he kills his adversary with a knife and has to flee to the mountains to hide. There he encounters another innocent but sensual stereotype of womanhood, a child of nature and of the farmer who gives Jim a job. Instead of becoming the latest victim of his seductive wiles, she captures his heart and acts as the flesh instrument of his salvation, her healing powers exerted in conjunction with the balm of nature's bucolic beauty.

The final Chaucerian stanza is romantically skeptical without relief, Freud-ian to the extent of defining civilization as repression of animal instincts, returning to the evolutionary celebration of earth's indifferent cycles of growth and death that had shaped the climax of "Earth Triumphant":

> And life made slave of him . . . Meanwhile, the earth
> Still through the starlight danced her endless song,
> Turning her lord's love to slow death and birth,
> Still changing grey to green, the weak for strong;
> Life's cry she heard not, knew not right or wrong;
> Youth rose, youth fell; she smiled to sun, danced on,
> Smiling the same smile, dancing, dawn to dawn.

The portrait of Jim, his crude psychology, has a certain rightness, perhaps because Aiken was fingering several basic strings in his own psyche, including the childish egotism and compulsion to debase females through seduction, though muted by an extravagant 1890s idea of lyric drama. He was making-the mistake, common to tyros, of thinking he could replicate the abstract melodies of music through a sonorous reliance upon assonance and lilting rhymes, thematic repetitions, and relentless iambic rhythms. He should have read Pound, who knew that the "musical phrase" in verse never resides in superficial imitations of song and ballad sounds.

More important, at the level of belief, where the poet requires a meta-physic, however spurious, Aiken had not yet recovered from the devastation wreaked by Freud upon his imagination and self-image at Harvard. He could only retreat behind a pose of adolescent cynicism, the sedition of Nietzsche fused to a Keatsian Romanticism. It did permit him to write poetry, even if that poetry signaled a step backward from the daring, albeit flawed, realism of "The Clerk's Journal." In submitting his art so totally to the naturalistic con-ventions championed by Masefield and copied by Gibson, Masefield's shadow, he retarded his development as a modern poet but located a viable method for dealing with an amoral universe that let him continue composing. The orthodox prosody and rebellious stance governing his personas' actions and minds, a chest-beating delight in the brutal details of meaningless exis-tence, aligned him with Brooke, Harold Monro, and other Georgians in their implicit antagonism toward the revolution being wrought by Pound and Eliot on separate continents, though his effort to keep track of Eliot and ability to recognize the merits of "Prufrock" demonstrate that he intuited the ultimate weakness of his position.

There would always be a sharp division between the critical and creative spheres of Aiken's vision during these years of stressful personal growth and cultural agitation, when the avant-garde had resurged against realism's rock shore and "such phrases as 'the new age,' 'the new era,' 'the boom in poetry,' were cliches in the little magazine and in the established literary journals." Psychologically, there was a compelling force to immerse himself in the art of a master, but his tendency to identify so often with inferior contemporaries, excluding Eliot, whose approval he courted like a cunning farm girl, might suggest that elemental insecurities could brook no genuine mastery. He identi-fied with poets like Masefield and, later, John Gould Fletcher because their talents operated in the realm of his own thematic and technical interests with-out dominating them, masters whom he could unconsciously relegate to a category of accomplishment somewhat below the level he thought himself capable of attaining.

Also, the critical function, since divorced from the emotional center of his need to articulate and rehabilitate a crippled psyche, could afford to weigh the relative merits of other poets objectively without serious risk of self-diminishment. This rephrases a truism, to be sure, but in Aiken's case the gulf between theory and practice would widen dramatically over the next several years as he sought to isolate and exploit his obsessions, evolve an individual voice, and protect himself from being swamped by the waves of new bards cresting all around him, threatening to leave him beached almost before he began. It was his peculiar misfortune (and rare opportunity) to be engaged in the onerous process of devising his own aesthetic at a time when various contrary forces were converging to bring about a major literary upheaval.

For the moment, he was still removed from the tempest, in itself a source of frustration, as the letter to Harriet Monroe stresses, and could maintain his faith in Georgian practices and a private Nietzschean code of cynical romanticism without undue strain, proud of his capacity for seeing truth plain, nature red in tooth and claw, man as nought but Pascal's thinking reed ripe for harvesting: "I have been feeling lately that the power of the individual over his destiny has been absurdly exaggerated." Zola would have approved, as would Stephen Crane, Howells, London, Robinson (with reservations), and Theodore Dreiser, whose *Sister Carrie* had been published in 1900, though withheld from circulation. In the poetic arena, however, such a naturalistic perspective was already obsolete, despite the ostensible success of the English Georgians. At best, in America, it would culminate in the naive popularism of Vachel Lindsay and Carl Sandburg, an easily exhausted minor movement at variance with the complexity of feeling and voice that an authentic modern poetry would have to manifest to satisfy the demands of a cultural awareness convoluted by Darwinian, Freudian, Marxist, and Einsteinian insights, not to mention World War I's exposure of the grave ethical faults underlying Western civilization.

As Robert Frost would convincingly demonstrate, it was possible to project a modernist sensibility within a traditional praxis, but it had to entail more than unidimensional narratives of lower-class existence oscillating between aesthete excess and Romantic identifications. Writing to Eliot from Rome near the end of February, Aiken asked if his friend had an extra copy of "Prufrock" that he could have to savor again. Hence he was conscious of a superior alternative to his Masefield line, of Eliot's achievement and the new vistas offered by French sources. And yet he felt persistent unease and hostility as well. In the same letter he admitted to having authored a caricature of Eliot entitled "Decadence." A portion of "Decadence" would survive as "Parasitics: To Certain Poets" in Aiken's first collection, in which he lumps Eliot among other wanly loitering ghosts, versifiers fatally detached from life: "There is no warm blood in your veins, / You know no human joys and pains."

The ambivalence toward Eliot continued to stem partially from Eliot's calculated failure to show sufficient enthusiasm for Aiken's poetry. He was altogether too neutral for comfort, with good reason in light of his chum's blatant lack of originality, remarking of "Youth" only that its protagonist was not as innocent as he seemed and probably carried "rubber goods" in his pocket. But Aiken, as always, paid close heed to whatever Eliot had to say or write. In a March letter, also from Rome, he expressed genuine pleasure over Eliot's decision to stay at Harvard and to jettison Bergson, whom Aiken found irritating and preciously subtle. Eliot's disaffection was to be expected because Bergson's entire philosophy of organic (psychical) evolution and inert matter's contrasting decline rested upon Darwin's godless scheme, but Aiken's subsequent pursuit of expanding human consciousness as a prime poetic motif contradicts any rejection of the French thinker's foundational premise, which involves an interesting merger of pre-Socratic notions of universal flux and theories about the mind's power over phenomena.

Aiken's confusion on the matter, a reflection of his difficulty in absorbing abstract discourse, was more evident later in the letter, when he reiterated impatience with subjective theorists such as Bergson. He told Eliot he was now of the opinion that all philosophy should start with a study of biology, morphology, and *The Origin of the Species,* especially the latter. By and large Bergson would concur, which once more underscores Aiken's intellectual limitations, though it also reaffirms his commitment to Darwinian reductionism at this point in his career.

The day after sending off his Eliot rejoinder, March 14, he received a letter from McCouch that included a note from Ruth McIntyre, to whom McCouch had forwarded Aiken's recent poems, unaware of the break between the two. Afraid of sounding as furious as he must have felt, Aiken still permitted some anger to slip through: "Your letter and Ruth's came this morning, and with Ruth I am annoyed beyond measure; I should use a stronger word about R. if I didn't like her so much." In explaining her disapproval of the poems, which she found unfinished and too derivative of Masefield, Ruth expressed the sensible fear that Aiken might mistake "money-getting literature for true greatness." Aiken's response confirms his familiarity with Freudian theory and the necessity of overcoming the creative sterility it had instigated: "And what is greatness that I should sacrifice my comfort for it? I have long since proved beyond all doubt to myself that art is an abnormal thing, a perversion, an illusion like all the other illusions that make life worth living. For over a year I could write nothing on this very account."

Regardless of personal factors, Aiken's rage arose from the maddening accuracy of Ruth's criticism, which boded ill for future public reception of his work, especially since it struck at the heart of his precarious recovery from the onslaught of Darwin and Freud, more evasion than recovery. His counterthrust is lame in the extreme:

> I write these poems in a spirit of impatient amusement,—they amuse me, but I cannot attach to them honestly any such importance or seriousness as would warrant my taking greater pains with them—or as Ruth says, with a kind of virtuous scorn, working them over once they are done. Why the deuce should I? The philosophy behind them is worth far more to me, as you know. If the poems irritate people, if people see this philosophy, if I could make a few folk temporarily angry with me or unhappy or discontented with their very smug little selves, and art, and christianity—that would afford me lots of fun, much more than to have the poems merely praised or condemned as poems.

Despite a measure of truth in the bravado concern for blasting an audience out of its social and religious smugness, the insistence upon a noble devotion to philosophic realities cannot hide the intellectual dishonesty at work here, a desperate rationalization that ignores both the ultimate sincerity of Aiken's verses and his ache for recognition. A young poet, unless either a fool or an inept poseur, never writes out of a "spirit of impatient amusement" or is indifferent to praise and condemnation. Poems, even bad poems, sometimes particularly bad poems, are the self's most vulnerable extensions. No assaults upon their erstwhile faults, however sound and constructive, are ever perceived without a substantial amount of covert anguish and defensive anger. Objective excellence is rarely the crucial issue, though the possibility that Aiken's acute critical faculties might have propelled him, at some subliminal threshold, to accept the veracity of Ruth's reaction would have only intensified his hostility. Also, as a mournful complaint at the end of the letter confirms, he was flailing away at an attitude of condescension too often evinced by relatives and friends toward his immaturity, his impulsiveness, his very choice of professions:

> I *was* peeved with Ruth, because in her remarks on my stuff, so extremely well meant, I recognized a complete expression of the amused tolerance, the paternal concern, which so many excellent friends of mine have always considered me with. I do hate to be considered a dreaming irresponsible! It seems as if my worthy friends were not going to let me grow up!—or if I am grown up, as I persist strangely in thinking, they will never, never admit it, because only as a kind of absurd child do I fit in with their ideas of what a poet should be. Isn't it distressing?

Undaunted, Aiken never pondered a different course. When he and the pregnant Jessie returned to Cambridge in June, the sole important question was how to live cheaply enough to assure unfettered dedication to the pursuit of his Muse. This meant renting a house at 73 Reservoir Street on "the wrong side of the tracks," much to the dismay of Aunt Grace and the Potters, because it provided seven rooms and a bath at the reasonable rate of $28 a month. It was there on October 10, 1913, that his first child, John, was born.

Not long before that, he had had to endure another death, Uncle William, who suffered from angina, succumbing to a heart attack on August 22 at the age of fifty-nine. He was buried among his ancestors at the Rural Cemetery in Fairhaven, across the river from and in sight of New Bedford, a special project of Cousin Julia's, who was determined to reunite the scattered clan. Aunt Grace would sell the house at 27 Everett Street, where Aiken passed through adolescence, and move into Boston. However mixed his feelings toward the Tillinghasts, specifically toward his aunt, their removal from his view and the place where they belonged must have reinforced fears of the universe's implacable flux.

It must have also added to the pressures engendered by the approaching specter of fatherhood. One of Jessie's sisters, and perhaps Mrs. McDonald herself, had come down from Montreal to help, and it is indicative of Aiken's agitation and unappeasable sexual appetite—death's surest somatic antidote—that he took this opportunity to try to seduce the sister. Successful or not, the pass was never reported to Jessie. And the dramatic birth process, which entailed unpleasant complications, threw him further off balance.

Aiken described the ordeal in a letter to McCouch: "Jessie had only slight pains during the day, and they didn't become acute till about eight o'clock; from then on she paraded the floor with me pressing the base of her spine. She took to bed at nine, but was driven to her feet again by the anguish, and we paraded some more at greater speed, finally rousing John to action, at about nine thirty. The actual birth then took place pretty quickly, being all over at ten ten."

A doctor and nurse were in attendance, which proved fortunate because the afterbirth took another hour to descend, and then, while Aiken held the ether cone, Jessie had to be anesthetized to let the doctor stitch up the damage inflicted by the birth trauma: "It took just an hour to get her under; for as soon as she was unconscious all her former self-control gave way, and she ran through the whole scale of human emotions in her sleep, all the while keeping so rigid that we could do nothing with her." To Aiken, it "was the most horrible experience of my life, as I continually felt certain she was strangling to death, and had no great confidence in the doctor." The blood and mess also tinged his view of Jessie, disgusting to his prepubic idealization of her, yet making her emotionally more central to his life. She recovered quickly, bothered only by the strict diet prescribed by the doctor, and the infant, slightly over six pounds at birth, drew them together: "We are both fonder of this queer little animal than we thought we would be . . . he is full of delightful sounds and gestures."

The birth of a son and return to neighborhood scenes was a tonic, although several familiar faces were missing besides Uncle William's. Bassett had earned a graduate degree in June and was off to teach French and Spanish at the Iowa State College in Ames, and Harry Wehle had returned to Minneapolis to enter the museum field. Tinckom-Fernandez also surrendered his post at the *World* in the "forlorn hope" of exchanging the journalism of New York for that of London, Eliot having come down to the Boston docks to see him off. McCabe was still around, pursuing an A.M. degree at Harvard, but their paths did not cross. McCouch had contrived to keep them apart after Aiken's return, fearful that McCabe would carry out his written threat to assault his friend. According to *Ushant* (177), they did meet one last time without violence, McCabe cravenly slinking away after uttering another empty threat.

Bill Taussig remained in Belmont, easily reached, and Jake Wilbur was at the Harvard Medical School, intent on an M.D. diploma, though he continued to regard himself as an eccentric exponent of Freud's "strange and revolutionary not to say abhorrent discoveries." He and Aiken took flings at analyzing each other. But it was Eliot whose company Aiken most frequently sought: "In the last close years between Eliot and Aiken—fall 1911 to summer 1912, and fall 1913 to summer 1914—they conversed once or twice every week on everything, from the practical question of where and by what means to live while they continued to write, to the question of which attitudes from the intellectual tradition of the West were sympathetic to them."

A regular feature of their interchanges was Thursday night dinner at the Parthenon, an inexpensive Greek restaurant on Kneeland Street in Boston, where they were joined by George Boas, a very bright, often irreverent philosophy student attending Harvard Graduate School. Inevitably, Boas and Eliot carried the bulk of the philosophic side of their bull sessions, which must have become quite heated on occasion in view of Boas's general impatience with metaphysics and with the Scholastic tradition in particular. An outgunned Aiken attempted to follow and contribute as best he could. He later conceded that in the matter of F. H. Bradley, the British neo-Hegelian at Oxford whose *Principles of Logic* had a profound influence, positive and negative, on the early thought of George Moore and Bertrand Russell, he had to depend upon

Eliot for translation: "I tried reading Bradley, but mostly I absorbed him from Tom. It was one of the most important experiences of my life."

Besides Bradley, a recurrent topic of debate and humor was the absent Santayana, to whom Aiken remained loyal. Eliot now claimed to discern the lineaments of a "charlatan" in Santayana's systemless system, and Boas denigrated what he viewed as a lack of logical rigor in his theories. Eliot dismissed both Santayana and Bergson for having reduced philosophy to mere "psychology," which, ironically, was the same charge Santayana leveled against Bergson, but the three young men in lighter moments also enjoyed speculating as to whether the former Harvard don was actually a homosexual. Aiken's participation in these conversations—and he must have felt besieged listening to the verbal disembowelment of his favorite philosopher—consisted mainly in advancing his interest in literary wellsprings, the relationships between artist and art as illuminated by Freud.

Earlier in their friendship, when Freud's study of dreams was yet vibrating in his mind, Aiken had suggested to Eliot "that Freud followed Aristotle by implying a notion of art as cathartic, 'a universal language of healing,' by the construction of wish-fulfilling illusions." As he remembered and told Joseph Killorin near the end of his life, he had asked, "Couldn't the artist himself provide the analyst with the context of his life insofar as it required *this* illusion?" And Eliot had replied, "Perhaps so. The private worlds of artists are the only significant truths, but they are that *only* to their creators." As observed in his subsequent introduction to Marianne Moore's *Selected Poems*, Eliot grasped the pivotal import of poets choosing "whatever subject matter allows us the most powerful and the most secret release; and that is a personal affair." To Aiken, the inescapable truth of this Freudian remark was not yet within his power (or desire) to execute because he had not puzzled out a way to combine the demands of naturalism with his own Nietzschean cynicism and rational allegiance to Santayana's philosopher-poet.

Over the course of that "delicious year," he would begin to synthesize many of these ideas into a coherent mental set, integrating Bradley's notion of serial, finite selves with the ego model already constructed from acquaintance with Bergson, Freud, and Nietzsche. But none of it affected his poetry, which remained Romantic in spirit and naturalistic in design. By the time of John's birth he had completed a series of sonnets that would be revised and published in his first collection as a narrative poem called "Romance" and another narrative poem in what was becoming a sequence about "earth" (natural processes), subsequently entitled "Earth Tedium." "Romance" details a shipboard affair in which a presumably sophisticated young man seduces a virgin and then abandons her casually when they dock, unaware of her previous innocence—a foretaste of Aiken's own behavior in many voyages ahead. She falls prey to tuberculosis, punishment for both of them, and he mourns at her deathbed with liquid excess that only an O. Henry enthusiast could appreciate:

> And many days the memory came returning
> Of her last kiss,—quivering, wet with tears,—
> Her clinging hands, her brimmed eyes dark with fears."

Worse, the final stanzas essay an apostrophe to Keats's season, "O Autumn! bringing to old adventures death," and expire in the familiar embrace of arch irony: "Yet beautiful is that death with sudden flame, / Ere it goes down to darkness, whence it came!" At least "Romance" has a story, admittedly trite, to relieve its weepy lyrics, a safety net that "Earth Tedium" lacks. Perhaps stung by Ruth's criticism, Aiken was engaged in a conscious effort to erase as much of Masefield's overt influence as possible. Accompanied by gobs of exclamatory rhetoric and precious anachronisms, the poem founders in a sea of clichés about personified youth and his Nietzschean struggles to transcend a Darwinian dynamic. Little positive can be said of its slush verses, except to note that the tight technical control supplies a certain degree of soporific lyricism, ending, as usual, with a Victorian moral tag: "Love has its secret sadness, like this rain, / And in all fruitlessness there lurks a pain."

Aiken was regressing as a poet, still unable or unwilling to transfer his growing knowledge of depth psychology into art despite the contacts with Wilbur and shared psychoanalytic texts and the appearence of Walter Lippmann's first book, *A Preface to Politics,* which daringly interpreted the American scene in terms of Freudian constructs. Maybe Eliot's erudite espousal of Bradley's philosophy, topic of his Ph.D. thesis, forestalled any move in that direction, since the finite centers of consciousness which Bradley depended upon to reach some comprehension of the self in relation to the world were not easily digested and not easily disengaged from the philosopher's arbitrary metaphysical commitment to the "Absolute" beloved of Eliot and Royce. More to the point, the ideas deluging Aiken during those invigorating Thursday night dinners with Eliot and Boas had to contend with a host of contradictory schemas siphoned from other thinkers, as well as with the embattled conviction that a naturalistic aesthetic best suited his antithetical realistic and Romantic inclinations. Also, the poet in Aiken might have feared being buried under the sheer brilliance of his Harvard comrade, reacting with unconscious antagonism to the species of modernism Eliot exemplified.

Aiken's poetic career received a boost when a letter arrived from Martin Armstrong a few weeks after his son's birth, enclosing a letter from Harold Monro about "Earth Triumphant." Armstrong had been acting as Aiken's London agent, much as McCouch had done in America a year earlier. Monro was interested in the poem but thought it needed alterations and wondered if it was in final form. On October 22, Aiken wrote to him directly, declaring his opposition in principle to making changes upon request, though he said he was willing to alter offensive words and perhaps delete a line or two where necessary. He claimed that several people had read the poem without asking for major revisions, except to suggest that he cut the repetition near the poem's finale, and conceding that Armstrong himself felt the wife's death was announced too suddenly. In defense of "Earth Triumphant" he also revealed that Macmillan had judged it acceptable before rejecting it on strictly financial grounds.

Aiken rose to eloquence in explicating the ego and pride that cause an artist instinctively to refuse editorial demands. In essence, he championed a flawed but beautiful work that was sincere to its author's intentions and character. The pat truth of his stand is undeniable, yet such a position tends to encourage inferior art as well, and Aiken's defense erects a high principle around poems that could benefit from a dispassionate critical eye, though Monro was not the one to focus it. Publication did not follow, but that was secondary to the political advantage of having made contact with a prominent Georgian.

A similar situation developed with Harriet Monroe about the same time. Aiken had submitted "Decadence" on September 23, followed ten days later by "The Unregenerate Dust," which was rejected. Unseen by Aiken, Monroe wrote across the top of his accompanying letter: "Masefield in his most boring mood." Her reaction to "Decadence" was less incisive, and she asked for changes. Again, Aiken protested while agreeing to yield in certain areas, but *Poetry*'s response was simply to reject the poem. Convinced that Monroe would never accept any poems under his own name, he had a Washington, D.C., friend of Crist submit "Discordants," a small series of more effective lyrics, on his behalf, signed with the initials R.F.D. When Monroe accepted the group shortly after the turn of the year, he saw it as a sign that he had been right, though he agreed to have the poem appear under his real name. Through the early months of 1914, Monroe continued to reject whatever he sent, resulting in another letter of protest and much grumbling.

As winter turned to spring and Europe lurched inexorably toward war, Aiken found himself infected with an increasing urge to flee to London, an urge abetted by the knowledge that Eliot would be heading for Germany in the summer and might not return. Aiken had arranged with Edmund Brown, shadowy publisher of Boston's Four Seas Press, to print a collection of his poems later in the year under Macmillan's imprint, a deal in which the author guaranteed all costs. The arrangement was hardly unique. When Tinckom-Fernandez met Rupert Brooke the preceding year in New York—Brooke was on a world tour that included a stop in Chicago, where he charmed Monroe, as he did almost everyone he encountered—the English poet admitted that "he had paid for the publication of his first volume in London," a volume that enjoyed considerable success.

Knowing that a book of his was on the horizon, Aiken became even more restless. Amy Lowell, after reading H.D.'s poems in *Poetry* and discovering that she too was an Imagist, had made her pilgrimage to London the previous summer, where she met Pound and let herself be enchanted by his "reticent praise" of her work, enlisting herself firmly in the Imagist ranks. Upon her return in September she wrote Monroe, who had provided the introduction to Pound, to thank her for the opportunity: "I feel that in him I have not only gained a personal friend, but, through his kindness, a little wedge into the heart of English letters." A "little wedge" into London's literary community was precisely what Aiken yearned for. His frustration was not lessened by the February appearance of *Des Imagistes,* Pound's pamphletlike anthology of poems by himself, Lowell, Fletcher, Hueffer, H.D., and others, which was published in New York and rapidly became both a commercial smash and a *succès de scandale*. As American critics assailed and parodied it with glee, they guaranteed its literary reputation and helped establish Lowell as Boston's leading iconoclast poet.

Imagism held few charms for Aiken because it ran counter to his desire to perfect an expansive, traditional methodology. But Lowell's sudden domination of his own bailiwick and Monroe's parallel mastery of Chicago's literary scene left no front garden space for his modest career to take root. London seemed the answer, and he fretted once more to assail its ramparts. The problem was Jessie and John, the encumbrance of family life, although in Cambridge it had not been a heavy burden; except for visits to relatives, he pretty much excluded his wife from his daily social rounds. His dinners out and drinking bouts with friends or Uncle Alfred, his excursions into Boston for concerts and vaudeville shows, his continued contacts with Harvard and with former classmates at the Harvard Club on Commonwealth Avenue were bachelor habits from the recent past that he refused to surrender. The burden for their son and large apartment was placed almost entirely on his wife's shoulders.

Jessie appeared to enjoy her lot, being far more domestic by nature than her husband, as daughter Jane would observe decades later, and Aiken's friends were not always her sort. She thought Eliot, for instance, peculiar—a tortured young man who made her uncomfortable—but the exclusion from her husband's social and intellectual pursuits was not yet a source of marital discord. She knew of his traumatic childhood and sympathized, realizing that literary achievement was essential to him and probably glad to act as nursemaid to his Muse, although it is hard to judge how aware she was of Aiken's various and potentially severe neuroses. Daughter Jane recalls that her mother "used to say that her mistake in her dealings with him was that she felt he was owed *everything* because of his disastrous childhood, and he's the most likely person to have suggested this to her."

As summer approached, Jessie again found herself pregnant and was happy to agree to take John for a visit to her family in Montreal while her husband sailed to England for the summer to breach London's literary cliques and investigate the feasibility of a permanent residence there for the family. Aiken's joy at the prospect was sharpened by the knowledge that this time he would not be a victim of either shyness or lack of formal access. He had secured a letter of introduction to Pound from Hermann Hagedorn and other letters to Brooke, W. H. Davies, James Elroy Flecker, and Edward Thomas, friend of Robert Frost, then living in England, from a casual acquaintance identified in *Ushant* only as a "freckled English girl, from Bedale's and Cambridge," who, years later, drowned "herself during an attack of puerperal fever" (203). He already was in touch with Harold Monro, of course, and confident of attaining a foothold. Early in June 1914 he wrote McCouch: "I think I will be happier if I waste no time in getting to London. There I shall do as much work as I can, and as much selling and self-advertising; in fact, I am hoping to obtain an opportunity of reading some of my works aloud at the Poetry Bookshop Readings, as I am taking letters and already know by correspondence the Prince of the place."

Along with his own poetry, Aiken toted some verses of Eliot's, which he hoped to place in London: "With me also was the typescript of *Prufrock* typed by its author with meticulous care on a Blickinsderfer which produced only italics, and *La Figlia che Piange.*" Eliot himself sailed in June, intending to explore parts of Italy and Belgium before moving on to Germany and Marburg University's summer program for foreign students, where he would spend July and August. Assuming he would eventually teach in its philosophy department, Harvard had granted him a Sheldon traveling fellowship, which he planned to use to study Aristotle under Harold Joachim, Bradley's disciple, at Oxford's Merton College beginning in October.

Aiken also sailed in June but directly for Liverpool, then was met in London by Armstrong, who had secured him a room at a cheap boardinghouse in Bloomsbury's Bedford Place. From there he sallied daily to conquer the heights denied him during his honeymoon visit. Monro's influence had grown greatly in the interim, assisted by the establishment in 1913 of his Poetry Bookshop, which became a central meeting place for English Georgians and radicals alike. Aiken wasted little time in taking advantage of its strategic position, his letters of introduction paying dividends from the first. Later he would recall, "The Poetry Bookshop was a fascinating place to drop into—

there was always somebody interesting there, and while I found it to begin with rather difficult to approach any of these extraordinary beings, by degrees I conquered the shy Monro and got to know practically all of the poets of that period."

Apart from Pound, the poet he most wanted to meet was Brooke, Cambridge's pet, an inveterate Romantic whose touch of realism in his verses did not obscure his nostalgic loyalty to a rural, upper-class past. Aiken presented his letter of introduction at the Raymond Building in Gray's Inn, where Brooke shared rooms with Edward Marsh, the affluent anthologist and private secretary to Prime Minister H. H. Asquith, but the poet was unavailable.

Shortly thereafter Aiken experienced a pleasant shock when Brooke "came and called upon me in my dreary little boarding house. . . . Suddenly, this angelic creature walked into the room and took me out to the Vienna Cafe for coffee and cakes." Over their cakes, Brooke spoke easily and learnedly about John Webster, whom Aiken already admired from his Harvard days, and about his appreciation of Lascelles Abercrombie, whom he would soon reread with much less enthusiasm. Brooke was modest about the limitations of his own work and told Aiken he had "decided to give up poetry, thought it was not his true *metier,* felt he was not in the same street with Abercrombie, had been soaking himself in Webster . . . and wanted more than anything else to write plays" (198). His eccentric world tour now completed, after having seen Tahiti and America, Brooke appeared serious about playwriting.

His kindness included an invitation to his rooms for further conversation, which Aiken gladly accepted, though the visit, in spite of excellent sherry and more fine chatter, had its embarrassing moment when he was asked to inspect some very large pictures of the handsome poet. He would see Brooke several more times before August and was present at a reading he gave at the Poetry Bookshop during which Amy Lowell shouted from the back for the soft-spoken Brooke to read louder.

Another popular literary figure who responded congenially to Aiken's letter of introduction was W. H. Davies, so-called "tramp poet"—literate tramps were irresistible social lions in Edwardian England—whose memoir, *Autobiography of a Super Tramp,* written at the Sevenoaks cottage of Edward Thomas and boasting an introduction by Shaw, had been an enormous success in 1908. Born in Wales in 1871, Davies was a bartender's son and had only a brief education before entering the picture-frame business, which he abandoned when his grandmother died and left him an income of two shillings a week. At the age of twenty-four he convinced the trustees of his grandmother's estate to advance him the fare to go to America, where he mastered the techniques of begging and train-jumping and spent the next six years covering most of the continental United States, as well as traveling eight or nine times between Baltimore and Liverpool in cattle boats. In 1901, after reading about the Klondike, he set out from Newport for Canada but fell off a train in Ontario, injuring his right leg, which had to be amputated at the knee. He saved up his allowance until he had 120 pounds, sufficient to take him first to Newport, then on to London. The metropolis proved no more hospitable than America's wide open spaces, and he lived in cheap boardinghouses and spent countless hours in local libraries, writing ballads and poems in the manner of William Burns. In 1905 Davies had a book of these naive but honest verses printed, and he peddled the book in the streets until he was discovered and aided by Shaw.

Davies had sent back a note in reply to Aiken's, asking him to drop by his second-floor room on Little Russell Street. Like most visitors, Aiken was enchanted by the unpretentious Welshman, who said he never read newspapers because they were too literal and had a negative effect on the imagination, a habit that would change drastically when the war commenced and he limped down to the corner stand every morning to buy two papers. He also told his American guest that his note of introduction had been a mystery to him because he could not remember the girl who wrote it, explaining that he had probably met her at some large gathering and forgotten it. Davies immediately became and would remain a warm acquaintance, a source of ready amusement and another connection with the literary stars in the Georgian firmament.

Edward Thomas was no less quick to respond to Aiken's letter, inviting him to visit when he could, but the war was fated to intervene; Thomas would be killed at Flanders in 1917. The letter of introduction to Flecker was never delivered. Aiken discovered that the poet and diplomat was in a Swiss sanatorium, suffering through the final stages of the consumption that would fell him the next year. But the "Poetry Squashes" at Monro's Bookshop, combined parties and poetry readings, were putting him in touch with almost every Georgian "name" he had ever wanted to meet. At one of these affairs he tried to interest the host in his friend Eliot's poetry and gave him a copy of "Prufrock," which Monro returned at once, claiming it was "absolutely insane, or words to that effect." Unfazed, Aiken took advantage of yet another Bookshop gathering to approach Monro on Eliot's behalf: "Later, at a party, during a discussion of symbolism, with H.M. and Flint, and thinking of the pertinence of 'La Figlia,' a copy of which was in my pocket, I produced it, only to have Harold thrust it back at me, with the remark, 'O I can't be bothered with this.' He so obviously thought I was seizing the opportunity for showing something of *my own* that I put things right the next day by sending it to him, with Eliot's address in Germany, and—of course that was rejected too."

Monro's initial reaction to Eliot's work would change after the American poet was championed by Pound and had acquired a degree of fame. Monro's instinctive rejection of Eliot was typical of the Georgians' conservative bias, and Aiken's success in penetrating their constellation still left him cut off from the more fecund, ultimately more crucial alternate current generated by members of the avant-garde wing. *Les Jeunes,* Heuffer called them. They had "for three or four years, culminating in the London season of 1914 . . . made a great deal of noise in a city that was preparing to reverberate with echoes of blasts still greater. . . . They stood for the Non-Representational in the Arts; for *Vers Libre;* for symbols in Prose, topage in Life, and Death to Impressionism." Though atuned to Romantic naturalism and leaning toward Impressionism (the Jamesian variety), Aiken knew that the young radicals were starting to have an appreciable impact on contemporary sensibilities and could not be ignored, as had been clear in the publicity accorded *Des Imagistes* back home. He knew also that Pound was their London fulcrum.

Bearing Hagedorn's letter, he literally bearded the reputed wild man in his Kensington den, the small second-story flat with its tiny triangular sitting room and odd clutter of works by Henri Gaudier-Brzeska. Pound was in another frenzy of organizational activity that summer, having borrowed a new aesthetic doctrine, "Vorticism," from Wyndham Lewis, a Canadian artist and satirist of dour disposition and fierce negative energy. He and Lewis were busily putting together a magazine, *Blast,* and planning a series of lectures at the Rebel Art Centre in Great Ormond Street to promote the Vorticist cause. It was a valid, if minor, advance over Imagism, at least doctrinally, transforming that mode's stripped-down metaphorical precision into a more open field for psychological probings, another variation on Symbolist shorthand.

The real or imagined advantages of the new movement were perhaps less important to Pound than the chance it gave to tap his frenetic drive for change, further challenges, the means to exert control over the cultural history of his era. The bold affectation that characterized his appearance—from floppy hat, pointed beard, single blue earring, and pince-nez down to the flowing cape and ubiquitous cane—manifested the calculated assertion of an unmistakenly American, unmistakenly bookish (*Yellow-Bookish*) concept of Bohemian sophistication, groomed in Pennsylvania and points west but more at home in Harvard's literary clubs, Pre-Raphaelite in its exaggerations, adolescently egocentric, a tinge archaic for all its playful radicalism. Aldington, who had gained much from him, discerned the "contradictions and perhaps a real disharmony" in Pound that made him "one of the problem children of modern poetry." He also espied the partial outlines of a psychological truth that does much to illuminate Pound's dictatorial manner and carelessness in politics and scholarship: "I think he lacks fundamental originality and self-confidence, which explains why he has put up so many stunts. He has tasted an enormous number of books, yet I doubt if he has ever read one with concentration from cover to cover."

Despite the inevitable insecurity behind the gaudy façade, behind the insatiable quest for the "new" and the provincial prejudices that would sour into paranoid, anti-Semitic delusions of grandeur, Pound was also that rarest of necessary creatures, as described by Lewis, "a man of letters, in the marrow of his bones and down to the red-rooted follicles of his hair. He breathed Letters, ate Letters, dreamt Letters." In that hot, sunny, portentious summer of 1914 he was a man of letters under siege by a formidable opponent, Amy Lowell of Boston. Lowell and her companion, Ada Russell, had arrived in June and occupied the same lavish suite at the Berkley Hotel, facing the Ritz and Green Park, that Lowell had occupied the previous summer. From there she had immediately set about fomenting a palace revolt against the autocrat whose generous aid the year before had ushered her into the movement that was responsible for her recent prominence.

Shrewd and lean as any Cassius inside the ponderous body that genetics had built around her sensitive spirit, she would claim that education was all she was seeking from Pound, a definitive explanation of the new poetry. But the aristocratic self-assurance gifted her by the Lowell name and money, which made her as politically conservative as she was poetically liberal, could not abide the antagonistic will of the equally high-handed Pound, who had no intention of relinquishing control over Imagism, despite his espousal of Vorticism. Beyond the charisma of his personality and obvious blaze of genius, Pound's hold upon his followers was tied to his valuable contacts with *Poetry* and similar journals, demonstrated most forcefully through his editorial management of the first Imagist anthology.

As the rich frequently do, Lowell appreciated the practical fashion in which power operates, and her plan was simple and efficient. She approached Aldington, H.D., and several other original contributors to the anthology and offered to arrange to have a second Imagist volume published as a cooperative venture in which each poet, including herself, would be given an equal number of pages to fill, regardless of merit. Her sole involvement would be executive, seeing to the book's publication and making sure that every poet received his or her royalties. It was an irresistible scheme to young authors avid for attention and a termination of Pound's regime, not to mention his keen critical ax.

At first Lowell felt the need to try to win Pound over, possibly a ploy, more likely a genuine effort to continue friendly relations with a man whose talents she had never underestimated. When Aiken showed up at Pound's flat and was treated with cordial informality, "served tea not so exquisitely among the beautiful Gaudiers," Lowell had yet to make her move, and Pound was secure on his imaginary, spider-legged throne. At the ebb of his life Aiken was prepared to concede that Pound had been "extraordinarily generous to me and kind, and took me in hand and began my education perhaps," but it would be unrealistic to expect the independent-minded Aiken to take warmly to his fellow American's blatant love of the mentor role. "Ezra was a hard task master," he said. "He evidently believed I should join the pack and obey the rules and didn't approve of my stepping out of the sacred clan here or there. I think Brooke was one of my mistakes from Ezra's point of view . . . he was very strict about that sort of thing, and I ventured too far afield too often to be regarded with complete trust after that."

Their relationship was seriously strained when Aiken did not attend the *Blast* dinner held on July 7—climaxed when Pound left the table and returned wearing a tin pot to express his contempt for Lowell and a few others—in defiance of Pound's scrawled direction on the circular he had sent over to Brook Street: "You'd as well take this in. It may be amusing or even interesting." The "thin-skinned" Pound would never forget or forgive Aiken's casual defection from the cause, though it is unlikely that the two men, so set in their arrogant ways, could have maintained a personal or professional association under any circumstances. Pound in short order came to count Aiken among the hostile horde of reactionaries who were always deriding experimental verse in the name of stuffy orthodoxy.

And yet contact with Pound was stimulating and increased Aiken's confidence at having alit at almost every influential base in London's literary whirlwind. Moreover, Pound could be useful, if not to him, then to Eliot, whose poetry Aiken continued to hawk. Eliot's two long letters from Germany in July were filled with familiar discontents and playful references to his host country's health-conscious inhabitants, whom he liked, in the main, talk of intellectual constipation alternating with allusions to a complex work-in-progress. Tentatively titled "Descent from the Cross" and sparked by religious paintings studied in Italy and Belgium, this work was an ambitious, suitably anguished sequence of several individual poems, vividly contrasting in tone and procedure, one of which, "The Love Song of St. Sebastian," he forwarded for Aiken's comments, denying that his sensual portrayal of the saint who had been martyred by arrows had anything homosexual in it. Aiken's reply is apparently lost, though the traffic in "crucifixion" imagery must have evoked an empathetic reaction. Having no luck in placing "Prufrock" elsewhere, it was only natural he show it to Pound, perhaps the sole intelligence in London at the time capable of appreciating its virtuoso mixture of Laforguian praxis, fin-de-siècle weariness, and deft psychological analysis, of understanding at once that Eliot, alone and unaided, had metamorphosed himself into a modern poet.

Pound's memory of the historic moment, telescoped by the perspective of a bitter old age, was less than charitable toward Aiken and skewed by an obvious chronological error: "Aiken tried to sell me Robinson, and I didn't fall. This was in London too. I then dragged it out of him that there was a guy at Harvard doing funny stuff. Mr. Eliot turned up a year or so later." That Aiken would have aired the virtues of Robinson, still a contemporary master in his eyes, is not surprising, but it is highly improbable that he required encouragement to display Eliot's work. Further, the subsequent meeting between Pound and Eliot would occur in a month or so, not a year. Details are secondary, however, to consequences. Pound would pass "Prufrock" on to a reluctant Harriet Monroe at *Poetry,* and it would see print in the June 1915 issue and forever change the shape and gait of mainstream American poetry, to the rejoicing of many and the utter despair of others, among them William Carlos Williams and Hart Crane.

In the middle of July, Aiken was invited to lunch with Pound at the Hotel Imperial in Russell Square to meet the representative of the newly founded *New Republic,* who turned out to be Walter Lippmann, "the darling of English 12" (201). Repeatedly throughout his career, Aiken was to discover himself in similar situations, validating the widespread impact of Harvard upon American literary history over the next several decades and underlining the advantage of having attended the right school (with the right "old boy network") in a country where an Anglo-Saxon elite still exercised a pervasive, if subtle, influence. Pound's kind attempts to widen Aiken's circle of literary friends were frustrated in a few cases, as with Yeats and Hueffer, who "were never, never in" (205). He did have tea with the Meynells, protectors and nourishers of his admired Francis Thompson before his tragic death from drugs in 1907, although he was upset by Alice Meynell's cruel dismissal of Brooke's poetic practices. And he gained an acquaintance with Aldington, who had wed H.D. a few months earlier.

Brooke might have supplied a golden key to unlock the doors that led to the society of the affluent and powerful personages surrounding his roommate "Eddie" Marsh (an intimate of Winston Churchill, first lord of the admiralty, and of the Asquiths and their glittering crowd) or to Lady Ottoline Morrell's salon in Bedford Square, as well as to the more intellectual group already coalescing around Bloomsbury, though Brooke had isolated himself from the latter in a fit of paranoid suspicion. But larger events were against it. Probably through the offices of the ever helpful Armstrong, he did secure the friendship of Lieutenant Colonel W. F. Wright (*Ushant*'s "Noble Lord"), secretary to

Keir Hardie, Labour party leader in the House of Commons, and cultivated devotee of music and the fine arts. Wright's comfortable apartment, in the same building where Marsh and Brooke lived, became another pleasant resting place and potential antechamber to some ambiguous seat of real authority, where evenings could be passed in civilized conversation or listening to the colonel's player piano. Though not yet as successful a Yank in England as, say, Robert Frost, who had taken a house in Gloucestershire near Abercrombie and Gibson in the spring of 1914 and whose first two volumes, *A Boy's Will* and *North of Boston,* had an appreciable effect upon the Georgians and their audience (and upon the astute Pound as well), Aiken could be excused for concluding that his conquest of London was proceeding with a certain implacability.

Added to the excitement had been his supposed "first infidelity," the first of many as recounted in *Ushant* (15), an awkward, amusing, practically innocent pursuit of a woman ("Felice") who had captured his attention by boldly undressing in front of her unshaded window. After numerous hesitations, Aiken invited her out for a beer by waving a sign in his own window, and the pair got together in Bedford Square, Felice asking if he would prefer to go to White City or the cinema. They went to neither but instead dined at the Brice in Wardour Street, his favorite restaurant, and then took a bus to Hyde Park for a walk past the Serpentine, seeking shadows where they could embrace. Afterward, walking home, his arm around her shoulder, hand idly caressing her breast, he discovered—as he would rediscover many times—that women refuse to conform to male plans for them. They would always ask too much of him.

Felice revealed that she was pregnant and that her husband was aboard a tanker in the Pacific, where he would safely remain for three months. Further, her home was in Surrey, not London. She had come to the city only to buy furniture, and she wondered if he would enjoy helping her shop and paying an extended visit to Surrey. She clearly envisioned his keeping her occupied until her husband's return, as other women would keep him occupied when he was separated from any of his three wives in the years ahead. Disappointed and in a panic, all thoughts of a summer dalliance with a promiscuous stranger abandoned, he escorted her back to her boardinghouse in Montague Street, kissed her goodnight, and vowed to himself never to see her again. He honored the vow, though it involved changing from a back to a front room to avoid her searching eye.

The aborted affair and Aiken's amassment of stock in London's cultural exchange were growing irrelevant as July dwindled down to a few hot days and rumors of war solidified into reality. By month's end, banner headlines proclaimed "GERMANY AND RUSSIA AT WAR OFFICIAL" and "BRITISH

ARMY MOBILIZED." Germany's invasion of Belgium soon made Britain's participation in the widening conflict inescapable. Early in August, Colonel Wright managed to get Armstrong and Aiken into Parliament, the rotunda between the two houses, where they listened to bits of feverish talk before returning to the colonel's flat "to play a Brandenburg Concerto (the second) on the player piano . . . and to look at the Noble Lord's collection of posters" (199). Aiken was astonished by the spectacle of London going wild, and when the colonel asked if he believed the people truly wanted war, he answered in the affirmative without pause. His description in *Ushant* (200) of the mounting war hysteria, the convulsions of an entire city rushing headlong into what would emerge as Europe's first bloody confirmation of Freud's most pessimistic theories, is a small masterpiece of on-the-spot journalism.

Aiken himself was not completely immune to the excitement, and time and again, after a rest at his boardinghouse, would plunge back into the street to be borne along by the noisy mob as it surged through the city in quest of news. Joined by Armstrong, Crist, and a music teacher, he led them to the Brice for a hurried dinner before they allowed themselves to be swept along to the Palace and Downing Street several times more. Again, they were able to enter Parliament, despite the colonel's absence, when Aiken murmured Keir Hardie's name at the door with cool authority. Somewhat later, back under the sway of the mob, the fact of war was at last established at Downing Street, when a black limousine moved slowly through the crowd and Asquith was seen leaning forward to inform the people.

August 3 was the date that sounded the knell of the extraordinary Edwardian era and Britain's global supremacy. It also marked the finish of Aiken's hopes for locating a second home and nurturing a London career. His major concern now, like that of the drove of German nationals congregating around their consulate not far from his domicile, was to find a ship to take him back to his native land. It would be almost a full month before he succeeded, during which time Eliot would escape from Germany and rent a room in his boardinghouse before departing for Oxford, their last close union for many years. Amy Lowell was also struggling to obtain a berth on a liner but in the meanwhile offered her services to the American ambassador, who had her meet all incoming trains from the Continent, wearing a sandwich sign over her ample form that read: "AMERICAN CITIZENS APPLY HERE." The indignity could not have been too bothersome because her private battle to gain control of the Imagist anthology had been victorious. In a sulk, Pound refused to submit his own poems and would dub the enterprise "Amygism."

When Aiken did finally secure passage home near the end of the month, he left in despair over the folly of mankind's aggressive drives and the squandering of June dreams, the "plans for the immense, the wonderful future" shared with Eliot (201). The generational change predicted by Brooke, last glimpsed by Aiken on August 3 from the top of a Fleet Street bus as he strode past the Cock Tavern, "bare head golden in the pale sunlight," was descending like Poe's silent pendulum to sever him from what appeared to be his own bright future.

One cannot violate the promptings

of one's nature without having that

nature recoil upon itself.

Jack London, *White Fang*

.   .   .   .

POETRY WAS EVERYWHERE

While Brooke sailed off to make a piecc of the Aegean "forever England" and died futilely from "acute blood-poisoning," Aiken sailed back to Cambridge under imaginary clouds of disappointment and the literal menace of war, which forced his ship, after leaving Glasgow, to return and wait in ignorant suspense for days before attempting the crossing without an escort. An odd feeling of exile, which suggested that England had already assumed the maternal guise of home in his unconscious, would eventually mature into the Panglossian realization that "there were elements in the Boston scene which were to prove invaluable to him" (216).

He was indeed to become aware of a significant cultural shift as the war began decimating England's young—a shift reflected poetically in the movement from Brooke's idealistic patriotism to the savage ironies of Wilfred Owen, Siegfried Sassoon, and Harold Rosenberg. The raucous American "renaissance" signaled in 1912 by the flagship founding of *Poetry* was now multiplying into a veritable armada of similar magazines and consequent literary groupings anchored in New York, Chicago, and Boston. Amy Lowell, by dint of a fierce, one-woman campaign to establish Imagism (and thus her own verses) as poetry's evolutionary apogee, seemed intent upon shaking Boston free of its nineteenth-century staidness.

The renaissance was literary, despite much concern with and dramatic advances in the other arts, and largely poetic in format: "By 1917, the 'new' poetry was ranked as 'America's first national art,' its success was sweeping, its sales unprecedented." It was an age of poetry, comparable to the era in England that had produced the Romantic revolution more than a century earlier, though the nurturing political and social environment in the United States resulted more from a pioneer civilization ripening into power and a fuller expression of hidden reflective strains than the revolt against classical restraints and aristocratic imperatives that had characterized the Wordsworthian rebellion. The America that Aiken returned to was on the verge of tremendous change.

The major signs of this revolution ranged from a steady loosening of sexual mores, influenced by Freud and the increasing availability of Henry Ford's assembly-line Model T's, along with a growing awareness of sexual hygiene, to a constantly spreading dependence upon the advertising business, which also owed a debt to Ford's innovative production methods. When Rupert Brooke passed through New York the year before, he was struck by a peculiar transformation of priorities: "Business has developed insensibly into a Religion, in more than the light, metaphorical sense of the word. It has its ritual and theology, its high places and its jargon, as well as its priests and martyrs. America has a child-like faith in advertising."

Brooke wrote of Boston, which seemed "homey" after New York, its "crowd curiously English," that it "used to lead America in Literature, Art, everything. The years have passed." Boston was the least sensitive of the urban centers to the inevitable cultural dislocations induced by generational gaps, a closed frontier, growing global weight, and the continued importation of sophisticated European notions, although no less inundated by a steady stream of new arrivals from abroad—unlimited except for imbeciles, paupers, prostitutes, and Orientals. This tide of immigration, mostly from southern Europe, satisfied an increasing demand for cheap, unskilled labor and swelled lower-class neighborhoods already crowded by Irish immigrants, stiffening the resistance of the Boston aristocracy and middle class to any alterations in the status quo.

In spite of Boston's entrenched conservatism, an attitude not in evidence among its lower classes or in the fast social scene of younger affluent natives, an unmistakable drift was evident toward a sharper division between urban and rural America, traditional enemies ceaselessly seeking to mandate the behavior of the entire nation. In the period between, say, 1910 and the end of the war, the cities appeared to dominate, at least to the extent of imposing their more liberal lifestyles on whatever national consciousness could be glimpsed. The supposed wave of loose morality washing over the country would have a logical legislative climax in the counterrevolutionary Mann and Volstead acts and subsequent antilabor laws.

"This dynamic country subjects its inhabitants to more extreme contrasts and abrupt changes during a lifetime or a generation than is normally the case with other great nations," Erik H. Erikson has written. These extremes are accentuated by cyclical financial swings, with the result that "the functioning

American . . . bases his final ego identity on some tentative combination of dynamic polarities." Nowhere was such a psychological balancing act more persistent than in Boston, which retained a Puritan distrust of experimentalism and a contrasting faith in Unitarian concepts of progress, so that a young poet such as Aiken, well educated and socially well connected but aware of the need for an open stance, oscillated between the exclusive male sanctuary supplied by the Harvard Club and the Bohemian freedom offered by less conventional contemporaries in the arts, who gravitated to the shabby haunts associated with the adversary small magazines, galleries, and theater groups sprouting in Boston, Chicago, and New York. Like many ambitious colleagues, he was soon making the familiar trek along the trade route linking the three cities in a quest for attention, outlets, and potential allies.

The "poetry renaissance," as its avid participants enjoyed characterizing it, was chauvinistic and self-conscious, decidedly idealistic but both self-serving and brassy in the worst manner of advertising excesses. It was also rife with suspicion and betrayal. Yet the genuine consciousness of a new dawn in American literature cannot be discounted, the liberating perspectives that caused Sherwood Anderson to abandon his Ohio family and respectable position and head for Chicago and an uncertain future as a writer: "All over the country indeed there was an outbreak of new poets. Something which had been very hard in American life was beginning to crack. . . . Something seemingly new and fresh was in the very air we breathed." Another rebel against middle-class restraints, a gentle former chess prodigy named Alfred Kreymborg, who had matured in the Germantown section of Manhattan without benefit of a college education, remembered the impact of *Poetry*'s appearance with vivid portentousness in his third-person autobiography: "The early poems of Pound, Sandburg, H.D., Lindsay and others, in the pages of the Chicago journal, thrilled him to an extent he had never known before, mainly because they were discovered in his generation and indicated endless possibilities across the vast continent."

However disappointed by yet another involuntary flight from London, Aiken forced himself to plunge back into the struggle for recognition soon after his return, renewing his special relationship with Harvard figures and making himself known at the offices of the *Poetry Journal,* Boston's answer to Harriet Monroe's more prestigious magazine. The *Journal* welcomed his work and eventually requested that he assume its editorship, a post he declined, as he had declined Cousin Ed's similar offer at the family newspaper in New Bedford. He also became friendlier with Edmund Brown, whose Four Seas press and bookstore occupied two floors of an old building near Scollay Square, and he established contact with Robert N. Linscott, an amiable editor at Houghton Mifflin. Malcolm Cowley, a Harvard undergraduate at the time, later described Aiken as almost "anti-careerist" in his cool eschewal of cliques and literary politics, but this was never strictly true and was assuredly inaccurate regarding the period between the start of the war and the early 1920s, when he entered the fray with all flags flying. Without ever compromising sturdy professional standards, Aiken openly sought and cultivated people who might advance his reputation.

The September publication of *Earth Triumphant,* the initial salvo in his bid to secure a firm beachhead on local soil, proved a dud in most respects. Forearmed by the prepublication criticisms of Monroe, Ruth McIntyre, and his friend McCouch, he attempted to defuse invidious comparisons with Masefield by adding a Preface in which he frankly admitted his debt to the latter but insisted that in writing "Youth," "Earth Triumphant," and "Romance" he had made "a deliberate effort to excise all echoes." His substance and his philosophy, "whatever their merits, and despite superficial resemblances," were entirely his own, he said, "and entirely different from those of Masefield." The stratagem did not prevent the majority of critics from either denigrating patent borrowings from Masefield and Keats or, more disheartening, ignoring the book. One of the few significant positive responses came from William Stanley Braithwaite, Boston's "indefatigable encomiast."

A small, slender, always dapper, light-skinned black man, Braithwaite had been born in 1878, son of a man of mixed Barbadian and French blood who immigrated to Boston from British Guiana. His father died when Braithwaite was seven, forcing his bright offspring to quit school five years later to help support the family. At fifteen he fell in love with poetry, developing a special fondness for the late English Romantics and Pre-Raphaelites. He eventually wed a Boston girl, who bore him seven children, and settled down at Ellsworth Street in Cambridge to live off his pen. With incredible industry he managed to do this in fairly comfortable fashion. Besides his own gatherings of Edward Dawson-like verses—*Lyrics of Life and Love* (1904) and *House of Falling Leaves* (1908)—he edited several successful period anthologies and earned the bulk of his income as a regular contributor of reviews and articles to the *Boston Transcript.*

Within modest limits, Braithwaite's taste was not deficient, despite a regrettable tendency to boost the native product, and his widespread publishing activities were transforming him into the single most important force in the local literary arena, causing Harriet Monroe, whose judgments he had questioned, to crown him "the Boston dictator" and Amy Lowell to pursue him shamelessly, inviting him often to her Sevenels estate in Brookline. In *The Anthology of Magazine Verse for 1914* (he had begun the annual series the year before, publishing the volumes at his own expense) he reprinted "Romance" intact. Although he did not include Aiken's collection among the "10

Books for a Small Library" or "25 Books for a Larger Library" listed at the back, he did have it head the roll of 45 books for "a Larger Library," granting it the additional honor of an asterisk denoting "special poetic distinction." Moreover, his comments on *Earth Triumphant,* lifted whole from his original *Transcript* review, were generous in the extreme, claiming its verses "suggest comparison with the longer poems of John Masefield, but have a firm independent technique of their own . . . reveal the heart of modern life in various phases of youth, and contain a reading of earth which differs from that of Meredith. . . . It is a distinguished first book of poems."

Aiken was delighted by both the *Transcript* review, which carried much weight with the hometown cognoscenti, and the anthology appearance but did not get around to writing to Braithwaite until February 25, 1915, when he expressed relief on being, for a change, linked with Meredith instead of with Masefield. George Meredith's *Modern Love* (1862), a sardonic sequence of fifty poems about the destruction of a marriage, had indeed been a prime influence. He also voiced surprise that Braithwaite preferred his shorter pieces, explaining that his second book would contain seven talks in verse, symphonically scored, and almost no short philosophical works. He and Braithwaite would keep in touch and occasionally meet over the next few years, though relations between them would never be close because of Aiken's subsequent attacks on the magazine anthologies and perhaps a trace of condescending racial prejudice in his attitude toward their editor.

The shift to symphonic formulas would fully materialize only after Aiken had submitted himself to another contemporary success, Edgar Lee Masters's Browingesque monologues. Though the *Spoon River Anthology* would not be published until 1915, many of its individual poems had appeared earlier in *Reedy's Mirror,* arousing intense interest. Less than a month after the publication of *Earth Triumphant,* Aiken was laboring over the title sequence of his second collection, *Turns and Movies.* The generally unenthusiastic reception accorded a maiden volume—in particular the nagging allusions to his Masefield debt—had shaken him far more than he conceded. He was desperate to locate a fresh model, another vehicle of proven popularity among the avant-garde and pseudo-avant-garde groups saluting Amy Lowell's Imagist campaign. Acceptance remained central, without altering a basic trust in the necessity for bringing a modern, realistic focus to bear.

Lacking Masters's small-town background, and wishing to avoid new charges of being derivative, he turned to the human drama nearest at hand, material urbane enough to make Spoon River seem remote yet common enough to permit sensational treatments of erotic and naturalistic motifs. The vaudeville shows in downtown Boston, which continued to attract him, were too rich in human types to ignore, as well as in tune with the fad to glamorize

the lower classes. Further, the idea of giving voice to a series of tawdry performers ironically enlarged the relationship between art and artist, assuring
him a modernist theme.

And yet, however well he adapted to the reality of his situation, Aiken had
not surrendered notions of an eventual return to England. The war could not
last forever, and Eliot and Armstrong maintained mail contact. A September
30 letter from Eliot told of meeting Pound, who insisted that he bring out a
collection after the war, and of looking forward to meeting Yeats before his
departure for Oxford, which must have pierced Aiken's heart with envious
pangs. Eliot once more raised the perplexing question of a permanent home,
yearning for Paris yet intrigued by England, in spite of the poor food and the
dreadful climate, scorning America as a fit environment for sensitive souls. In
the meantime, he had dined with Armstrong on several occasions, enjoying
his company, and managed to end with a satirical war poem.

Two weeks later Armstrong wrote, apologizing for not replying sooner to
Aiken's gift of *Earth Triumphant,* citing business chores and his enlistment as
excuses. He lauded his friend's collection with garlands of praise ("I never
doubted it would be good, but dammy if it isn't twice as good as I suspected")
and lamented that the war would prevent it from getting much attention in
England. Armstrong's candid view of Eliot, whom he found "an excellent
person," reveals enigmatic aspects of his personality that never surface in
Eliot's own relaxed, playful missives to Aiken: "Occasionally he says very
penetrating things, but so far as I can get at it, there seems a cynical intellec-
tuality about his outlook, which is rather chilly for one his age. He weaves
strange theories which seem to me good mathematics but quite unrelated to
real life, and when you steal up and try to catch hold of him, off he goes like a
sand-eel and begins twisting again a few yards further on: but the twistings are
always extremely interesting."

In November Aiken had two letters from Eliot within a single week, dated
the sixteenth and the twenty-first, which suggested an increase in unhappiness
(and accompanying psychosomatic ailments) at Oxford, where the writing of
verse was in other, less capable hands, though he thought the town itself
superior to American university towns. He was dissatisfied with the poetry he
had been writing recently, the St. Sebastian material, accusing his correspondent of being too easy on it, and felt he was not likely to produce good work,
that is, the equal of "Prufrock," for years because of the academic life he was
leading. In the second letter he asked Aiken to send some red or pink roses to
Emily Hale—a dear friend and probable former sweetheart—when she came
to Cambridge in December to perform in a play, and averred that he had loved
Earth Triumphant, the title poem in particular, an opinion he claimed was

shared by Scofield Thayer, to whom he had loaned the book. At least and at last, Aiken had garnered positive criticism, if only in private, from the source he most respected.

Whatever pleasure this might have engendered was overshadowed soon after the turn of the year when Jessie gave birth to a dead infant, a son, strangled at birth by the umbilical cord. Writing to McCouch about the tragedy a week later, on January 15, he noted that Jessie had taken it "extremely well," had gotten off easier physically "than last time, if anything, and is mending very quickly." A postscript was more poignant: "It was an excellent *boy.* Looked very like his father." The infant was buried, nameless, in Mt. Auburn Cemetery, with "Innocent" engraved on his small stone.

Jessie's real feelings are unknown, and it is difficult not to believe that she was putting up a brave front for her husband, whom she tended to mother. Perhaps the first fine crack in the foundation of their marriage had its genesis here in the unvented anguish of a woman who had carried a normal fetus for nine months only to deliver a dead infant, anguish that had to be hidden from a sensitive but self-involved husband. To Aiken the loss was genuine and touching but somewhat autistic, the death of a miniature self, a poet's loss rather than a husband's or father's.

Neither role was suitable, probably not even possible within the constrained perceptual and emotional field of his egocentric personality, the neoteny that made him charming and witty, a dedicated artist, though rarely a family force. "I remember Conrad," his daughter Jean has observed, "as the most entrancing person to be with, but not much as someone functioning as a parent." Aiken's unspoken concept of marriage was true to the Victorian paternalism and double standard of his era and background, which made few awkward demands upon his limited consciousness of Jessie as an individual, a distinct, complex human being. His sensitivity to the personalities of male companions was more sympathetic, though not much deeper.

Aiken still spent his time as he pleased, writing his poems in his exercise books with steady concentration. Most of the composition took place in his head. Afterward, he read the poems to a properly responsive Jessie, who continued to type them up and help send them off to various editors. The work had not ceased flowing, and it was the work alone that captured his pith energies, emotional and otherwise; his wife's existence, compartmentalized as mother to their son and liaison with Cambridge's formal amenities, was secondary to the shared task of promoting his career. Besides countless evenings on the town, attending vaudeville shows or concerts with Julius Clark, drinking bouts at the Harvard Club, and afternoons devoted to movies or pursuing the *Poetry Journal* crowd, he also plied the triangular trade route to Chicago and New York on his own when the need or mood struck him, never hesitating to engage in whatever sexual adventure came his way, easily keeping the naive Jessie in the dark.

It is clear that Aiken's marriage was a one-way street, abetted by Jessie's love of domestic routines and tolerance of his selfish behavior as the inevitable fruit of a blighted youth and creative spirit. Marriage, however, meant the middle-class regularity he cherished, indeed required. Unable to countenance disorder, he could never abide the Bohemian lifestyles of so many fellow poets and depended upon the home Jessie's conventional instincts and conditioning provided to certify his normalcy. Though committed to the obsession to master his art and be recognized for it, which would assert his identity in a public forum, Aiken was essentially bourgeois-oriented. Contradictions thus prevailed but were made to conform. In the sexual sphere, for example, his unbridled lust contrasted with a Puritan dislike of being touched or wearing a bathing suit; he regarded the new dances as dishonest forms of fornication (his persona in *Blue Voyage* discerns "something essentially horrible" in the sex act). Even his scholarly appearance—he favored the tweed jackets and buttoned-down shirts worn at Harvard and was rarely without a pipe—presented an image of stuffy respectability, augmented by impassive features and a taciturn shyness, well-mannered politeness.

This fundamental conservatism—a highly developed, intricately integrated series of defense mechanisms—extended into his distaste for Imagism and the entire free-verse movement, which he believed encouraged the second-rate to luxuriate in technical carelessness and sheer exhibitionism under the banner of the avant-garde. Never a blind opponent of authentic experimentalism, he reacted with an aesthete's outrage to the collapse of standards he detected all around him. He also recognized that private protest was insufficient. Consequently, 1915 was the year that witnessed his emergence as a critic, though with only two outlets for the moment, the *Poetry Journal* and the *New Republic*. His initial statement appeared in the *New York Times*, most reactionary of the New York papers, a letter written in response to a column by a Dr. William D. Goold. The doctor had mourned the absence of high-quality poetry and called for a return to the beauty once offered by the "Immortal Trio, Tennyson, Longfellow, and Whittier."

Aiken's response was a balanced blend of common sense and acute insight into the deficiencies and achievements of his contemporaries. After regretting the doctor's penchant for the sentimental, he distinguished between sentimentality, "emotion banally expressed," and poetry of the first order, where the doctor's "desire for the emotional would be quite as well satisfied, and this time legitimately, because the emotion would be given a beauty of expression more nearly proportionate to its intensity." Aiken agreed that something was missing:

> If there is anything that is conspicuous in current American poetry it is the lack of human warmth. Anyone who judged us as a nation by our verse might reasonably conclude that, though clever, we were as cold as seaweed. For our magazine verse is, with sincere apologies to Mr. Braithwaite, not worth a fig. All magazine verse may be divided into two classes: The prettified-sugary, artificial, decorative; and the modern, which may or may not be in *vers libre,* and which seizes in passionate embrace the locomotive, steam-shovel, and such. Neither sort has anything to say to the Average Man about his own life in his own language.

Using Lowell, Vachel Lindsay (Harriet Monroe's favorite), Robinson, Percy Mackaye, and George Woodberry as examples of the modernist trend, Aiken charged them with being "intellectualists," which he said was "a serious charge against any poet," though he conceded the first three had a "certain exuberance" and novelty. "But has any of them that emotional power, simplicity, above all, warmth, which will lay hold of what Ford Madox Hueffer calls the peasant intelligence?" he asked. Eschewing "an all-round estimate of the five poets in question," he summarized what they exemplified as a crucial failure of the American imagination: "It seems to be almost a national characteristic; we are conventional and derivative on the one hand, word-specialists and theorists on the other; but never, no matter whether we are old-fashioned classicists, or Imagists with Ezra Pound, do we feel things profoundly, or if we feel things profoundly, then it never occurs to us to say so."

As in the letter to Monroe the year before, the validity of Aiken's major criticism is vitiated somewhat by the self-interest necessarily propelling his assault upon competitors, specifically Lowell, as he would be the first to admit in a later essay: "We know what we like, and we know that what we like is the best." His own verses to this point were hardly models of intense emotions profoundly articulated, despite a naturalistic ethos, and it was Pound who said that "emotion alone endures." Aiken did venture upon a foundational issue, his literature's generic call for total immersion, self-candor, an expenditure of psychic energy that was intellectual solely in stratagem. Though poetry is "the scholar's art" (to quote Stevens), intelligence and knowledge are never sufficient in themselves. Aiken was canny enough to intuit that the modernist fervor sweeping past, over, and through him was encouraging the hacks, the politicians, the aping cultists—a majority in any revolution—to hide a lack of courage and skill behind the gimmicky constructions favored by an experimental climate. The entrenched conservatives, for whom Dr. Goold spoke, embodied no serious threat because their existence was the donnée of all rebellions, the mainstream Establishment which every sincere poet could and did oppose.

Aiken's campaign against the Imagist credo commenced in earnest with the publication of his satirical "Ballade of the Worshippers of the Image," followed by a caustic review of *Some Imagist Poets*, the anthology affirming Lowell's control, in the May 22, 1915, issue of the *New Republic*. Incensed, as usual, by a direct challenge, Lowell on May 26 wrote to Herbert Croly, the magazine's chief editor, to protest the review's "hostile and ignorant attack," intimating a conspiracy by claiming Aiken "has been in direct communication with Mr. Pound since our split" (a falsehood) and charging Croly's staff with harboring secret enemies. Another editor invited her to reply in print. Instead, she convinced Braithwaite, not an Imagist enthusiast but also none too thrilled by Aiken's dismissal of magazine verse, to do so on her behalf. His brief piece, "Imagism: Another View," was duly published in the *New Republic* of June 12; it belittled Aiken's condemnation of *vers libre* as a "fad," citing Remy de Gourmont in its defense, and declared that Imagism manifested the "first note of pure romanticism in English poetry of the last decade."

Enjoying the controversy, which was bringing him more attention than his poetry, Aiken returned to the battle in the July *Poetry Journal* with "Imagism or Myopia," a combined review of the Imagist volume and John Gould Fletcher's *Irradiations*. His animadversions were sound (if intemperately phrased) attempts to chart the inescapable barriers erected by an aesthetic so narrowly based. Unfortunately, however, the debate over Imagism had the negative effect of branding him a staunch conservative, a brand he would never be able to eradicate. It also earned him a potent enemy in Lowell, though their clash was probably predestined. In addition to gathering headlines as the combative champion of the "new poetry" in Aiken's own bailiwick, she had dismissed his beloved Georgian poets as "caged warblers" and "phonograph poets," and she regarded Freud as "trite, shabby and fundamentally medieval."

Another powerful figure dismayed by his strong anti-Imagist stand was Harriet Monroe, and in the September issue of *Poetry*, the same issue that carried "Discordants," she devoted her editorial to defending Imagism against Aiken's onslaught. Briefly restating his arguments to date, parading the harsh tags he had attached to the movement—"myopia," "synaesthesia," "super-refinement," "over-civilization"—and to its disciples, she delivered a personal thrust that was not without psychological truth: "Why all this excitement? Can it be possible that Mr. Aiken has taken a 'culture' from the imagistic poison and is feeling some discomfort until it gets into his system? How otherwise may we account for the difference between the pseudo-Masefieldian narratives of the earlier Aiken, and the more athletic lyricism which the later Aiken may hope for if he keeps advancing in the direction of his offering to our readers in this issue?" She could not resist concluding with a rhetorical flourish that chided Aiken and "other belated and provincial Victorians" for blocking the quest after "the Chinese magic" as "we dig deeper into that long-hidden, far-away mine of jewels."

Aiken's shrewd response, dated September 4, which Monroe did not print in the magazine or mention in her autobiography, was no less contemptuous, accusing the editor of having misinterpreted his articles. In a more placating tone, he emphasized that it was the Imagist *platform,* "precisely construed," that he felt constricting, incapable of magic when slavishly obeyed. He also praised Fletcher, Lowell, and Aldington and outlined his convictions that genuine radicalism was never merely a matter of technical innovations but that intelligence and instinct were the sole basis for genuine originality.

As proof of his liberality, he mentioned that he had been largely responsible for the appearance of "Prufrock" in *Poetry*'s June issue. It is a fair letter, certainly valid in the sense that Aiken had, since Harvard, been open to the influence of new trends, to the poetry of Robinson, Eliot, the French Symbolists and Parnassians, and others, if not quite honest about his devotion to the 1890s and Georgians underlying a strict allegiance to formalism or the true extent of his rejection of *vers libre,* Eliot to the contrary notwithstanding. More pertinent, the reference to Fletcher has to be read in the context of the master-pupil relationship that had evolved between them through Aiken's instigation during the spring.

Fletcher was a Lowell pet and had been a good friend of Pound before she lured him away. Like Aiken, Eliot, and so many other pivotal shakers in the poetry renaissance, he had been at Harvard, though he left the school in disgust four months before graduation. Born in Arkansas in 1886 to affluent parents, he found Harvard a cold and unrewarding place after he entered in 1903, as did many undergraduates who were from outside New England. His elderly father's death in his junior year gave Fletcher financial independence, whatever its emotional toll, and the following year, deciding that travel was more crucial than a degree, he accompanied an archaeological expedition to western Colorado. A return to Boston convinced him that America had minimal cultural stimulation to offer, and in the summer of 1908 he sailed for Italy, determined "to acquire an education, to learn something concerning aesthetic, moral, and spiritual values."

In 1909, like Pound, Fletcher left Italy to take up residence in London, where he believed his poetic ambitions and self-education project had their finest chance and where he would remain until the outbreak of war. His somewhat sour personality, which included paranoid tendencies, prevented him from making productive contacts, though his investigation of the arts led to an intelligent appreciation of modern music and Impressionist painting. In May 1913, discouraged by the British journals' rejection of the work he considered his best, he had five small volumes of poems published simultaneously by four different publishers at his own expense. If nothing else, this bold move gained him immediate attention, although the reviews naturally "varied from harsh to encouraging." On the bright side, A. R. Orage of the *New Age* promised a solid future for him, and poet Edward Thomas was sympathetic in the *Bookman*. The most bracing notice came in the *New Freeman,* where Pound unexpectedly praised the poet's "determination to fight out his own rhythms" and his courage for "daring to go to the dustbin for his subjects."

Oddly enough, Fletcher did not meet Pound until he took a trip to Paris soon after the multiple publication, but the relationship was an instant success. Fascinated by the technical aspects of verse, Fletcher had yet to mint a final style—his five collections demonstrate an amazing variety of voices, ranging from Georgian nature studies to imitations of Baudelaire and the French Symbolists—and was drawn to a man who shared his obsession and could more than match his European erudition. Aside from furthering his education in modern art and French culture, Pound was instrumental in introducing him to the "men of 1914" (Wyndham Lewis's pompous phrase for himself, Pound, Yeats, and Joyce) and others in London's revolutionary circles, although less successful in enlisting him in the Imagist cause. He also talked Fletcher into providing funds for his new literary review when he took over the *New Freeman* and renamed it the *Egoist.*

Pound brought Amy Lowell within Fletcher's purview during her first English visit, a strategic mistake because she cultivated her new acquaintance with sly charm, as she did all the members of the Imagist group. After returning to Boston she wrote Monroe suggesting that *Poetry* publish an article about Fletcher's poetry: "He writes in a style entirely his own, a sort of rhythmical prose, dropping now and then into rhyme, and which he manages so skillfully that it is capable of extraordinary versatility." It was not long before Fletcher deemed Lowell a "steadfast friend." He was growing more and more irritated by Pound's dictatorial ways and would eventually break with him. Like H.D. and Aldington, he saw in Lowell's scheme to take over the Imagist anthologies an opportunity to escape Pound's reign. Caught on the Continent when war was declared, Fletcher scurried back to America, settling in Chicago for a few months after visiting Lowell in Boston, then returning to Arkansas for an extended stay.

While in Chicago he stopped off at *Poetry*'s Cass Street offices, where Monroe recalled his telling her "in the falling cadences of his precisely rounded English, about his enthusiasm for Japan and Japanese prints." The interest in Japanese art and literature was not unusual among students of the Imagist school because the haiku and tonka forms seemed to epitomize the lyric compression of metaphoric means they were striving to achieve. It was an interest that Fletcher would pass on to Aiken, who became an avid student and collector of Japanese prints. After visits to Little Rock and New Orleans, Fletcher opted for Boston as home base, to be near Lowell, who was responsible for getting *Irradiations* into print. He still did not view himself as an Imagist, though willing to be published as such, and persuaded Lowell, whose knowledge of versification was never as certain as she thought it was, that his exploration of "polyphonic prose" was akin to Imagism in its refusal of inherited restraints and focus upon vivid details, its dumping of traditional rhetoric in favor of an almost stream-of-consciousness flow of musical phrases.

What captured Aiken's attention in *Irradiations* was not the shards of Imagist intensity, but, as indicated in the *Poetry Journal* review, that its author appeared "completely possessed by the subconscious." He even predicted that "the best theme for him will be one which is the least definite." Robert Linscott at Houghton Mifflin, publisher of Fletcher and of Aiken's second volume, introduced the two men, giving him a chance to convince himself that Fletcher had much to teach him. A month later, sometime in May, Aiken moved his small family to the top floor of a rundown boardinghouse at 11 Walnut Street in Boston, on the "wrong side" of Beacon Hill, to court Fletcher, who lived next door. In his autobiography, *Life Is My Song*, Fletcher notes that although Aiken "lived next door, we both ate our meals under the same roof, a fact which led to my seeing a good deal of him."

His early impression of Aiken is worth repeating: "I had known him chiefly as a shy and remote, sandy-haired figure, blinking behind his glasses, who lived next door, cherished an ambition to write poems combining the sensuous lyricism of Keats with the stark realism of Masefield, disliked imagism and all its works, but confessed to a paradoxical admiration of my own poetry." A love of Keats and Shelley bound the pair, along with a passion for translating the abstract constructs of music into viable poetic nodes, where a common pool of Romantic discontent might find appropriate melodic chords. Neither realized that the ultimate effect could be the very vagueness Aiken foresaw as Fletcher's major theme, a disastrous drift into imprecise mood pieces and symbolic ruminations upon images unable to bear the weight.

In any event, Fletcher's companionship was a boon because they also shared a desire to master their craft and were filled with curiosity about parallel technical developments taking place in the other arts. Music, for instance, remained one of Aiken's purest pleasures. As had Clark, Fletcher acquainted him with the finer points of symphonic structure, and he and his neighbor often discussed the variables of modern art and the special qualities exhibited in the stylized lineaments of Oriental art. Aiken would later purchase a painting entitled "Blue Mountain" by Marsden Hartley, a young artist and critic from Maine who lived in Manhattan, for the parlor wall of his small Cambridge apartment, the first of many thoughtful purchases made in the field over the years.

It is extraordinary that the relationship between two such difficult men—Fletcher with his brooding bouts of paranoia, Aiken ever pugnacious in defense of his opinions and dignity—lasted as long as it did. An explanation may be found in Aiken's determination not to lose his valuable catch. He regarded Fletcher as a sympathetic, possibly useful mentor. There were problems, of course, brief flare-ups, unavoidable arguments, but none proved fatal. One of the more revealing disagreements is recounted in *Ushant* (231), where Aiken's mediator guise—unusual for him, except when dealing with Eliot—is paramount. A few days before, Fletcher had narrated the incidents that had culminated in his rupture with Pound to Aiken and Jessie in their "eyrie," describing how he stormed angrily into Pound's flat and demanded back all the books he had loaned the poet, a signal that their friendship was ended.

In the meantime, Aiken was in the midst of his acrimonious paper war with Lowell and the Imagist faction and mentioned his intention to answer a recent defense of Imagism by Edward Storer in the *New Republic* with a blast of his own. Unknown to him, Fletcher took offense, convinced that Aiken's planned diatribe represented an attack on his work as well, and after a period of sullen reflection decided he must disassociate himself from Aiken and secure new quarters. When he suddenly appeared at Aiken's door one night to ask for the return of books he had loaned him, Aiken perceived the danger.

The next morning, when Aiken went down for breakfast, he was informed by the landlady that Fletcher had told her he must move out unexpectedly. He hurried up to Fletcher's room in the house next door and found him in the middle of packing. Fletcher greeted his arrival with a toneless monosyllable, gaze averted, as he went about shoving his clothes into a suitcase. Aiken tells us that he leaned against the doorjamb, and after a prefatory disclaimer about his intentions in the proposed article, "began to outline it in detail," demonstrating that it was "a very moderate, and carefully *raisonné,* inquiry into the whole question of free verse" (231). He told Fletcher his article might also suggest that in poems such as "Portrait of a Lady," Eliot had already created a form that might be exactly what they were seeking, a freer version of blank verse open to a wide variety of metrical and rhyme possibilities.

Aiken's reasonableness, plus his obvious wish to mend the break, was irresistible. The packing, which had been slowing down, came to a standstill. Fletcher grinned apologetically and suggested that they have lunch at the Parthenon, knowing that had been his and Eliot's favorite dining spot, where they could discuss the matter "over martinis and a bottle of wine" (232). They did and the relationship was restored to its former closeness. This event occurred in the winter of 1915, and soon thereafter the restless Fletcher sailed for England, with instructions from Aiken to get in touch with Eliot.

During the initial months of their companionship, which entailed almost daily contact, discord had been held to a minimum by Aiken's humble eagerness to heed Fletcher's solemn strictures on the ways in which poems could emulate symphonies, using poetic devices to echo musical orchestration. Influenced by Mallarmé and Debussy, Fletcher experimented constantly in an effort to wrench language out of its discursive and denotative prisons, to "develop this essentially musical quality of literature, to evoke the magic that exists in the sound-quality of words, as well as to combine these sound-qualities in definite statements or sentences." His impressionistic art, tuned as much to painting as to music, incorporated Imagist objectivity as merely one possible approach within the larger confines of his verbal harmonies.

It was the apparent answer to Aiken's quest for a formula that would permit his love of technique and music to address the problem of consciousness (and unconscious designs) he was beginning to discern at the core of his concerns as a poet. His literary submission to Fletcher, commencing when Fletcher was composing the "Dreams in the Night" section of his symphonically organized *Tree of Life,* was complete. Dreams were elemental to both of them. Aiken was still ravaged by nightmares redolent with death images and the screams of his mother's crucified pig and committed to Freud's dream theories. The dreams Fletcher was pursuing with heavy-handed abstractness in his poetry were easily viewed as adits to unconscious instincts and desires, to a hidden self, even if Fletcher himself, possessor of a mystic streak Aiken could not abide, failed to see them in quite that fashion.

According to *Life Is My Song,* after finishing *Turns and Movies,* Aiken started work on *The Jig of Forslin,* which Fletcher says "was directly written under my influence, and read by me in manuscript" as his pupil "began to develop in the direction of his own peculiar bent towards a combination of keen psychological analysis and romantic disillusion." The date is in doubt; Fletcher also claims it was written at Walnut Street during the summer, at a time when Aiken was in Vermont. The collection was subtitled "A Symphony" and arranged in a symphonic "program," with much varying of technique to encompass the entire spectrum of verse from traditional meters to irregular *vers libre.* It came in a rush and was under the spell of Fletcher's "music" though its largest debts are to the "Freudian psychology" (jacket blurb) and Eliot's example. Immediately after its completion, again according to Fletcher, Aiken began yet another "symphony," to be called *The House of Dust,* which his mentor avers, "moved me even more strongly than did the first."

The awesome facility of Aiken's poetry writing attested, in part, to the reassurance Fletcher's help provided. It also attested to a profound insecurity that was making him, in Braithwaite's somewhat biased eyes, an imitative artist: "In verse he jumped from one fashion to another, to whatever was in popular acclaim." A January 29, 1920, letter to poet Eunice Tietjens would confirm as much, when Aiken confessed that her reservations and others' had frightened and depressed him out of one style and into another. The normal maturational progress from imitation to originality, which often includes struggles against former models—Harold Bloom's Freudian schema of literature's primal father-son paradigms—is skewed in the case of Aiken. His mimic phase would endure well into his thirties as a result of the crippling effects of Eliot's superior achievements and the unresolved conflicts polarizing and inhibiting the growth of his ego. Distinct manic-depressive tendencies, probably inherited, were in league with the complex of environmentally induced neuroses warping his psyche since (and perhaps before) his parents' deaths, distortions amplified by cultural factors and the lack of an adequate, stationary maternal replacement during adolescence.

"I'm one of those talented fellows," Aiken's alter ego in *Great Circle* announces, "who combine all the madnesses in one—paranoia, dementia praecox, manic depression, hysteria." Reaffirming a number of previous Freudian assumptions, recent research indicates that the loss of a parent by death during childhood "influences the symptomatology of any psychiatric disorder from which a person may subsequently suffer," as well as triggering "a persistent, though perhaps disguised, striving to recover the lost person." More injurious, the cardinal trauma—and Aiken's was a cataclysmic loss at puberty's threshold—consigns its victim to an endless, vicious cycle of guilt, anxiety, depression, and suicidal impulses, contradictory expressions of an unformed infantile self. Today, Aiken might be diagnosed as a borderline personality, Heinz Kohut's narcissist model in whom overt and extravagant egocentric attitudes conceal a terrifying absence of ego.

Creativity in this situation, as Aiken would learn after shaking free from Eliot's steel talons and experiencing several near breakdowns, is a way of holding off the night, a form of salvation (a "reparation" dynamic to adherents of Melanie Klein's theories), not clinical healing, in which repressed ambivalences and instinctual energies are both tapped and converted into compensatory emotive abstractions. Poems mining obsessional depths, whether seeking to recover the ambiguous mother or, in Jacques Lacan's schema, reconstituting the missing father, become parental substitutes, positive linguistic nodes for negative feelings. They serve as models and mirrors for the psyche's struggle to create viable personae capable of reciprocal exchanges. This is why Keats could, sincerely and at different times, deem a poet "the most unpoetical of any thing in existence; because he has no identity" and "the fine writer" as "the most genuine Being in the World." By subjecting his imagination and praxes to Fletcher's literature, Aiken was saving himself from potential extinction while at the same time paradoxically retarding his poetic evolution.

None of this can be detached from the surface experiences forever at work upon the yeast of individual consciousness. Financially, aided by low rent and Bill Taussig's advice, the Aikens were on solid enough ground to be able to purchase a Ford, and Aiken never seemed to want for pocket money. The war in Europe was sparking prosperous conditions in the United States as far as jobs and wages were concerned, though the prices of food staples had started to rise. Except in German and Irish sections, sentiment was by and large pro-Allies, assisted by an efficient British propaganda machine and the general incompetence of its German opposite. The latter was in the hands of a literate group that included Hugo Münsterberg of Harvard and Manhattan's George Viereck, the Munich-born prodigy who had achieved fame with the fin-de-siècle verses of *Nineveh and Other Poems* (1907) and was currently coediting the *Fatherland*. Overseas, Henry James assumed the chairmanship of the American Volunteer Motor Ambulance Corps in France, an organization also aided by his friend Edith Wharton and later home to such literary-minded young Americans as John Dos Passos and Malcolm Cowley, who eagerly awaited America's entrance into the war. The sinking of the *Lusitania* on May 7, 1915, which impelled "a group of fifteen romantically indignant Harvard graduates" to send a telegram to the president "demanding that adequate military measures, 'however severe,' be taken," stirred further animosity against the Central Powers, but Wilson, echoing the sentiment of the nation's pacifist majority, proclaimed, "We are too proud to fight."

On the literary front, the sole front seriously impinging upon Aiken's consciousness, the war served to accelerate revolutionary fevers, reinforcing the increasingly popular notion that American culture was proving superior to the civilization dismantling itself across the ocean. Frost had returned in February, and the American publication of *North of Boston* certified his blossoming reputation. It and *Spoon River Anthology* were adjudged the "two great successes" of 1915 by Braithwaite, although a truer gauge of the American temper at the time was to be gained from Lippmann's *Drift and Mastery* and Van Wyck Brooks's *America's Coming-of-Age*.

Retaining his faith in Freudian doctrine, Lippmann was concerned with elucidating the specific heritage—"a rebel tradition"—of his generation, which he contrasted to the "absolutism, commercial oligarchy, and unquestioned creeds" being pressed upon it by a corrupt older generation. Brooks, whose acquaintance Aiken would renew, was striving to build upon Emerson's call for a native literature and culture divorced from European origins, even while dismissing the social effectiveness of Emerson's "Transcendental idealism." Reexamining the literary past, he espied defeat and ascribed it to "the failure of Americans in general to develop and express their personality in and through their work," which meant a failure to mature beyond either idealistic tenets or the materialism that a Puritan inheritance had somewhat sanctioned, indeed encouraged: "Plainly enough during what has been called the classical period of American literature, the soul of America did not wish to be moved from the accumulation of dollars."

The climactic simile Brooks used to convey an overall picture of contemporary currents is fascinating and appropriate—fascinating for its unspoken debt to an intellectual Freudian gestalt and appropriate in depicting the psychological state of the nation: "America is like a vast Sargasso Sea—a prodigious welter of unconscious life, swept by ground-swells of half-conscious emotion." Randolph Bourne, educational reformist and a friend of Brooks, whose sharp analytical mind was trapped inside a deformed dwarf's body, went further along the Emersonian path, charging that "timidity is still the reigning vice of the American intellect, and the terrorism of 'good taste' is yet more deadly to the creation of literary art than is sheer barbarianism." He ventured far enough to skirt nationalism's dangerous border: "By fixing our eyes humbly on the ages of the past, and on foreign countries, we effectively protect ourselves from that inner taste which is the only sincere 'culture.' "

Besides preparing the soil for the regionalized literature surfacing in Frost's tragic country people, Masters's lost souls, and the tortured grotesques limned by the Anderson stories later gathered into *Winesburg, Ohio,* the commentary by such astute observers as Lippmann, Brooks, Bourne, and H. L. Mencken validates the endemic impact of Nietzsche and Freud upon the noetic atmosphere of the day, an impact shared to a lesser extent with Bergson. Floyd Dell, who had departed Chicago in February 1913 for Greenwich Village, where he helped to edit the *Masses,* wrote: "Everybody in the Village had been talking the jargon of psychoanalysis ever since I came." He himself would undergo analysis between 1917 and 1918 without completing the process. Mencken's first two books had been *The Philosophy of Friederick Nietzsche* and *The Gist of Nietzsche.* And Bourne avowed in an essay that "Nietzsche stands for the splendid liberation from alien codes, the smashing of inequalities and cowardices," while maintaining allegiance to the thought of Thorstein Veblen and Freud, though the latter was replaced by Alfred Adler

in his rating scale because his emphasis on the power leitmotif better complemented Nietzsche's "will-to-power" concept.

Thanks to Mencken and others, Nietzsche was easily available in English,
and translations of Freud's works and related material were keeping pace because of loyal American followers such as A. A. Brill, whose *Psychoanalysis:
Its Scope and Limitations* was published in 1915. Jung's *Theory of Psychoanalysis* was also published that year, as was James J. Putnam's *Human
Motives* and a series of articles on Freud by Max Eastman in *Everybody's
Magazine*. The American Psychoanalytic Society, organized by Ernest Jones,
had been a going concern since 1911 with Putnam at its head, as had been the
New York Psychoanalytic Society, which Brill founded. More relevant to
Aiken and other writers, Susan Glaspell's play *Suppressed Desires*, "probably
the first drama in America to capitalize specifically on Freudian concepts,"
was produced at the Provincetown Playhouse.

When transmuting Fletcher's symphonic methodology into the Freudian
program of *The Charnal Rose*, which he said was written before *The Jig of
Forslin*, contrary to Fletcher's account, Aiken was not only responding to
private need and personal exploration of psychoanalytic ideas; he was also
riding the currents of thought that permeated the journals and books of the
period. Intellectuals were embracing Freudianism with the same religious passion they would lavish upon Marxism in the 1930s, discovering in its secular
rubrics of human behavior a convenient—often misunderstood or misap-
plied—implement for dealing with large social, political, and aesthetic issues
that no longer seemed amenable to dethroned rational approaches or their
philosophical analogs and antitheses. John Dewey's "instrumentalism," for
instance, would prove inadequate to the ethical demands of a state of siege,
and Dewey shifted from a pacifist to hawk position in 1916.

Aiken differed from most contemporaries in having come earlier to psychoanalytic theory and in having maintained a dialogue about its possible uses
with medical men in immediate touch with its evolving literature and practice,
first with McCouch, who continued the discussion by mail, and now more
intensely with Wilbur. He had also read heavily into the figures who anticipated Freud, such as Havelock Ellis and translations of R. Krafft-Ebing as
they became available. He was still both drawn to and made uneasy by the
aesthetic and personal implications of the entire Freudian apparatus, not yet
likely to subject his own psychosexual development to its harsh discipline,
either the initial trauma or consequent nightmares, which left him divided and
obsessed with death and insanity fears. He was, however, willing to begin
formulating a plausible critical hypothesis from its major equations. More
important, at the thematic and structural levels, he contemplated ways of
using it in imaginative works, as in *The Charnel Rose* and *The Jig of Forslin*'s

sequence of dream scenes, predicated upon the theory of vicarious wish-fulfillment.

For the time being he was content to play apostle to Fletcher and do battle with Lowell and the Imagist crowd. In June 1915 an uproar occurred at the Harvard commencement at Sanders Theatre when its *magna cum laude* speaker, Edward E. Cummings, gave a rousing speech titled "The New Art" in which he celebrated the appearance of post-Impressionist and Cubist painting and read two poems by the college president's notorious sister. Cummings would remain for another year to get his master's degree and organize the Harvard Poetry Society, whose founding members would include Malcolm Cowley, Robert Hillyer, S. Foster Damon, and John Brooks Wheelwright, a distant Lowell relative—a group that Aiken, as a published alumnus and familiar local presence, would have no trouble in cultivating. In the same month McCouch earned his M.D. degree but planned to stay on at the University of Pennsylvania, serving his two-year internship in the university's hospital.

Perhaps the most surprising news of the month was that Eliot had wed Vivienne Haigh-Wood, a high-strung English girl of impeccable social standing, and had surrendered all plans for a Harvard teaching career. Eliot's last letter to him on February 25, after consoling Aiken for his loss, had reiterated a dislike for Oxford's climate and food, which he blamed for continuing colds, indigestion, and the old constipation problem. He thought that he might be satisfied working at the London Museum, though he doubted if he could ever come to like England, a country whose disgusting food implied a lack of civilization. In the end, he admitted that he did not know his own mind, whether to get married, have a family, and live in America, where he felt he would have to compromise and conceal his opinions, or to retain his bachelor status and save his money for an early retirement. Obviously, he had decided on neither, making a bid to install himself in a cultured world that might gain him entry to its upper strata and have an Ezra Pound around to nurse his literary ambitions.

At least he was wedded, that much more integrated into a stable social establishment, although his wife would soon experience the first in a lengthy series of illnesses and mental demoralizations that would characterize their married life. Bertrand Russell reported "a disastrous 'pseudo-honeymoon' at Eastbourne, with Vivienne not far from suicide." A short period before his marriage Eliot had spent ten days at the home of Jim Clement, Harvard friend and fellow clubman, without mentioning the impending nuptials, then departed and never again, for no apparent reason, spoke to or saw Clement. Aiken regarded the incident as further proof of a sadistic tendency he had always sensed in Eliot. In any case, it was beginning to look as though Eliot and he were destined to advance their careers separated by an ocean, the war having deteriorated into a series of trench encounters.

Instead of a missed opportunity, Aiken's American return indeed seemed more and more like a fortuitous escape. Literary matters in England were at a relative standstill, at least as far as local outlets and review space were concerned, though Dorothy Richardson's stream-of-consciousness novel *High Windows* was to be the underground triumph of the year. If no longer hub of either the universe or America, Boston was proving congenial to his literary aspirations in spite of massive competition from Lowell.

But summer meant a flight from the city to the cooler hills of Cuttingsville, Vermont, for the Aikens, to the home of Rudolf and Adelaide Welcker, where they would pass the next several summers. Adelaide was Jessie's best friend from Radcliffe days, her husband a bright engineer given to good-natured teasing, which Aiken, whose zest for puns and one-liners was irrepressible, must have enjoyed. It was during one of these summers that Jessie felt she was falling in love with the handsome, unwed Jake Wilbur. *Ushant* captures the aftermath of the infatuation with rueful affection: " 'I've just had a conversation—!'—so Lorelei One [Jessie] had cried, one summer morning on the mountain road in Vermont . . . she was walking between Jacob and D., and she had been reading *Varieties of Religious Experience,* not to mention Freud; and, the day before, she had confessed her love of Jacob; but now she wanted to feel that she had dispossessed herself of that so inconvenient love, and, by an effort of will, to reconvert herself to D." (298).

The effect on Aiken was profound, even if *Ushant* is merely allegorizing what might have been the alembicated essence of his intuition that Jessie was entranced by the virile and articulate Wilbur. The mother complex that had sexualized and embittered his feelings toward all women left him no less vulnerable to its polar extreme of intense jealousy, fears that the mother surrogate would betray and leave him. It is no accident that the passage in *Ushant* detailing Jessie's lapse from expected fidelity—a fantasy flight at best for a woman mourning a child and strapped down by a Victorian marriage—glides into a lament, an elegiac meditation upon the abandonment of other homes to come, the houses that would reshape the empty house in Savannah enclosing his mind and imagination. But Jessie could no more contemplate disloyalty to him or their home than she could murder her child. She was too stable and maternal in her basic acceptance of the nesting instinct that middle-class society had reinforced into an almost automatic nurturing of family penates and lares. When betrayal invaded their hearth, it would be at her husband's initiative.

After the summer hiatus, during which Aiken kept the Imagist controversy churning and negotiated with Houghton Mifflin to publish his second collection (he agreed to reduce the volume by half and pay all costs, plus $50 for advertising expenses), he returned with his family to Walnut Street and a resumption of the pattern that had governed their lives to this point: a household revolving, often happily, around the campaign to establish his reputation. There were diversions, of course, such as family dinners at the Potters and elsewhere and the flow of neighborhood gossip, the most sensational example of the latter involving his former friend McCabe, who had wed Esther Freeman of Boston. Less than a month after their marriage, while on their honeymoon, a Canadian camping trip, their canoe overturned in rough water and Esther drowned, despite McCabe's vigorous efforts to save her. Spurred by a family seance, an unfounded rumor circulated that McCabe had killed his wife, presumably because he had been forced into wedlock by his in-laws. It is a measure of Aiken's own maliciousness and dislike for the man that he recounts the rumors and describes the drowning in *Ushant* as a response to the question of whether "there was a streak of murderousness" in McCabe, "a sadism, and cruelty, that made him capable of calculated murder" (159).

Gossip, politics, and the tribulations of old comrades still took a backseat to Aiken's preoccupation with writing poetry and securing a foothold among the cliques and journals intent upon identifying him with poetry's right-wing factions (in a letter to Harriet Monroe in connection with *Poetry*'s annual awards to contributors, Pound had cautioned against "an award to Amy, [Constance Lindsay] Skinner, Fletcher, Lindsay or Aiken"). He focused his attention on the first issue of Kreymborg's *Others* magazine, a July 1915 publication, and the November appearance of Braithwaite's annual anthology, which contained no Aiken poem but did have, in the Introduction, its editor's angry reply to his *Times* letter. Braithwaite took Aiken and Zoe Akins to task for lacking "both independence and judgement" in their attacks upon fellow American poets— and thus on themselves—and wrote that "it is an unseemly manner they pursue going about seeking their own self-effacement." The contents of the early issues of *Others,* which had been branded "the little yellow dog" by the New York press, included work by Lowell, Pound, Eliot, Sandburg, Williams, and Wallace Stevens—enough to convince him of its significance—and he began bombarding Kreymborg and his helpers with submissions, all of which were rejected. As with *Poetry,* even while submitting poems and suffering rebuffs Aiken poked fun at the magazine's extreme radicalism, eventually, according to Kreymborg, achieving renown as "one of the foremost opponents of the Imagists and *Others.*"

Other invaluable channels for gaining attention were the various poetry clubs and societies springing up everywhere. The most famous of these was the Poetry Society of America in New York, founded in 1910 by a group of local literati dominated by George Viereck and Jessie B. Rittenhouse, its main force and secretary, whose best-selling anthologies of contemporary poets would be traditionalist but never closed to obvious modernist successes. From its organization until quite recently the society maintained a well-earned reputation for conservatism and middle-brow taste, the bulk of its members newspaper poets such as Joyce Kilmer and Arthur Guiterman and a flock of equally slight female warblers, resulting in Mencken's delicious reference to its "dessicated ladies of both sexes." Kreymborg had been invited to join a year after its establishment but was banished—unofficially since his name remained on the rolls—when he ridiculed one of its *precisue* meetings. There were, however, a few talented and/or modernist members, such as Frost and Louis Untermeyer, though they formed a distinct, impotent minority, along with several older "name" poets such as Edwin Markham, who could not be excluded. Aiken had no problem entering their lists.

To her credit, and no doubt pleasure, Amy Lowell had left Boston on two occasions in 1915 to face them in their own hall at the National Arts Club, first on March 31, when she read "Bath" to outbursts of laughter and derisive comments, then in November, when she gave a lecture titled "Modern Metrics and the Poets Who Write Them," occasioning vehement objections from the floor. Needless to add perhaps, as Kreymborg notes, nowhere was Pound's "name held up to greater derision than in the columns of the New York press and the chambers of the Poetry Society."

It was inevitable that Boston, with its countless literary clubs and ladies' organizations, should emulate New York and inaugurate a similar body for its numerous poets and poetasters; just as inevitable that Aiken would be in on the birth, although it emerged as Lowell's triumph. The Boston Authors' Club was the founding group and home to all future meetings of the New England Poetry Club, which had an enlarged committee gathering in May at the Chilton Club to choose its first president. Aiken was there, as were Braithwaite, Lowell, Frost, and thirty or forty others. "All the significant poets," Braithwaite recollected, "but Mrs. Marks (Josephine Preston Peabody) didn't come." Peabody was a well-liked society matron who versified and was Lowell's major female competition, though neither conceded any antagonism in public.

As the meeting noisily progressed, it was soon evident that in the contest between the two nominees for president—Lowell and Peabody—Lowell was doomed to lose. What ensued next, vividly recalled by Braithwaite, provides an amusing insight into Lowell's petulant will and childlike insecurity: "When Amy Lowell realized that she was not going to be elected president, she dashed out of the room, out into the courtyard, into and down Dartmouth Street. . . . She had gone out of the room and out of the building before we realized what she was doing. When we did, Edward O'Brien, myself, and Conrad Aiken ran after her. And she had gotten halfway down to the Copley Plaza Hotel . . . before we caught up with her. Even then she sort of forged ahead and got into the hotel, by the Dartmouth Street entrance, and then, what a tirade!" She made it icily clear that she would have nothing to do with any organization that did not want her as president.

It was a dramatic demonstration of her Boston status—she was a Lowell, after all—that none of the three men considered leaving her to sulk. Instead, they wrangled a compromise, resolving to make her president. "We'd make Josephine honorary president; you see, Josephine was much too ill to be very active anyway, and of course Amy Lowell was well and active. And that seemed to mollify her . . . so we went back, and we put the proposition before the floor of the meeting." The motion carried easily, and Lowell had her victory, though two years later a revived Peabody would wrest control of the group from her. The first meeting of the New England Poetry Club with Lowell as president convened on December 1, 1915, and "all was most decorous." Aiken, however, "unable to abide Amy's publicity-seeking manner, attended two meetings of the club and then quietly withdrew," a step he never considered at the Poetry Society of America, whatever the moral cost.

The enmity between him and Lowell, which entailed no face-to-face debates, was strong and sincere, as could be expected of two such tenacious spirits. That same winter Fletcher, who remained a Lowell favorite, often defended his next-door neighbor at Sevenels. But Lowell was certain that Aiken's opposition to Imagism and free verse represented the natural outrage of a traditionalist, a mediocre traditionalist, and she rejected Fletcher's contention that his extraordinary technical gifts, especially his rhyming ability, betokened genuine talent. Unaware of this contretemps, Aiken plowed ahead with his poetry, immediately plunging into *The Jig of Forslin* after completing *The Charnel Rose* in November. By the start of 1916 he had finished more than a thousand lines.

Over the next two years, his facility would verge on the miraculous, these "delightful years 1916–7 in Boston." Public success, the publication of two books, and a gradual widening of his literary network were to highlight a year bracketed by two historic passings, the deaths of Henry James and Jack London. James died in London on February 28, 1916, a few days before *Turns and Movies* was published. London's death came in November and was a fittingly controversial event that encompassed charges of suicide and foul play. Significantly, near the end, London, self-made Horatio Alger hero, had read the newly translated *Totem and Taboo* of Freud and Jung's *Psychology of the Un-conscious* and had begun to glimpse the endopsychic conflicts that had fueled so much of his passionate ethnocentricity, to sense that the fierce archetypal configurations his best fiction projected were buried, still alive, in the uncon-scious past of his own difficult existence. If James, American apotheosis of European civilization, had pared the human mind down to some spool heart of subtle complexities, London had managed to snare the confused clashes of instinctive survival drives characterizing the pioneer ethos James fled.

Made insecure by his own masked fears, Aiken remained poised on a high wire somewhere in between, always appreciative of James, though still half-convinced that George Moore might be his equal, yet committed to the natu-ralistic impulse first gleaned from Robinson and now seen confirmed in Mas-ters's recent breakthrough. Like London in his last year, however, he was being steadily pointed toward a more complicated vision of humanity and self that was bound eventually to affect his aesthetic. For the moment, he emulated those he believed were hovering closest to the bone of his technical and the-matic interests—Fletcher, Masters, and Eliot. A definite improvement over *Earth Triumphant*, his earlier collection, *Turns and Movies and Other Tales in Verse*—named after the heading for the schedule of movies and vaudeville shows listed by the *Transcript*—never transcends, with a few bright excep-tions, the material it imitates, either the frame narrative of portraiture lifted from *Spoon River Anthology* or the stale cellar air of 1890s decadence heavily scenting every line.

The title sequence, character sketches of vaudeville performers, usually in a third-person simulation of a monologue (with a few actual ones thrown in), rarely eludes their author's taste for sentimental climaxes and a mauve-soft-ened, fin-de-siècle erotica and violence, justifying Horace Gregory and Marya Zaturenska's accusation that "Aiken became one of the many spokesmen in a reawakened search for Beauty," an American revival of England's *Yellow Book* decade. After her death a female dancer explains why she had to kill her lecherous partner by stabbing him in the eye before killing herself—Poe resur-rected—and the third male member of "The Apollo Trio" muses upon the sins of his two homosexual partners, who "eat up cocaine," brooding in a tavern—Robinson *redux*—over the girl he loved and the brief period when he was a star. Again and again, as if limned by Beardsley or voiced by Wilde, the women are evil fulcrums of carnal desire and icicle remoteness. Occasionally the excess strikes a nerve, as in the climax of "Aerial Dodds," a melodramatic discovery of homosexual sadism, when the protagonist, reflecting upon the loss of a young boy he has raised and trained, conveys the loss with studied sensationalism:

> And he would never touch again that skin,
> So young and soft; or have against his mouth
> Those curls . . . or feel the long-tongued venomous whip
> Curl around those knees, and see the young mouth tremble.

But the two strongest poems in the sequence, "Gabriel De Ford" and "Duval's Birds," intimate how the mode could best encapsulate its narrative and ironic potential. In the former the ventriloquist hero, another artist substitute, achieves life in the anticlimax, throwing his voice into his father's coffin at the funeral, causing a stampede of mourners, a humorous and imaginative counterweight to his mysterious refusal at present to talk at all. If the poem had dared to cease here, it would have replicated De Ford's special world and still retained enough mystery to satisfy literature's avid need for ambiguous intensities. Lacking confidence in himself, his audience, or both, Aiken insists upon a sentimental resolution, the witnessing by Zudora, a fellow performer, of De Ford weeping alone at a staging of *Carmen*. "Duval's Birds" happily avoids that mistake and is the single unalloyed success in the series, precisely because the climactic thrust depends upon understatement, a short-circuiting of the reader's expectations:

> When they were stubborn, she tapped them with a wand,
> And her eyes glittered a little under the eyebrows.
> The red one flapped and flapped on a swinging wire;
> The little white ones winked round yellow eyes.

Next comes "Discordants" and the undeniable potency of "Music I Heard with You," an Elizabethan ballad rephrased: "And bread I broke with you was more than bread." It tends, however, to underscore the inadequacy of the other four sections, their debts to Eliot and French Symbolism and to a pervasive 1890s naughtiness bred out of Keats: "O lamia silked and scented, / Art of the slumbrous magic of your eyes." Divided into six sections, "Evensong" also never escapes "the pale mauve twilight, streaked with orange, / Exquisitely sweet" with which it commences, swinging from a balcony in a dreary, weary, cliché circle back to "The perfect quiet that comes after rain." "Exquisitely" is the tipoff, a word and attitude almost anomalous in a modern poem.

The ensuing "Disenchantment" sequence, subtitled "A Tone Poem" and dedicated to Lucien Crist, who had returned from Europe to teach music in Boston and live in a house on Cape Cod, has only biographical interest to sustain it, the musical analogy too intent upon sonorous sound effects for much authentic drama, swelling lines beyond the edge of meaning. The narrator's disgust with life is focused on the realization that he no longer loves his wife as he once did, though she is unchanged and as beautiful as ever. Perhaps this theme can be related to similar stirrings in Aiken's breast under the daily burden of marital intimacy, a normal reaction to the normal decline of passion and passion's illusions concerning the love object that requires maturity to handle.

This twilight vision, a mating of Housman with every lyric poet who ever wrote—

> All lovely things will have an ending,
> All lovely things will fade and die,
> And youth, that's now so bravely spending,
> Will beg a penny by and by—

extends into a final narrative poem from 1913, "The Dance of Life," sequel to "Earth Triumphant." Its protagonist forsakes his wife, his earlier rescuer from corruption, and their tedious farm life for the garish pleasures of Manhattan, where the limits of Aiken's own sophistication are embarrassingly mapped:

> And niggers clogged in cabarets,
> And in the alleys round stage-doors,
> The rich Jews lounged and spat by scores,
> Each waiting for his chosen queen.

Love again redeems him, a musical reminder of guilt, of his deserted wife. Cut from the same cloth as "Earth Triumphant" and its yards of Masefield configurations, "The Dance of Life" preserves the same occasional virtuoso turns amid familiar defects, sensuality described with lulling, loving regularity as evil's painted visage and set among unreal female extremes.

"The fact is," Jay Martin has written perceptively of *Turns and Movies*, "that Aiken is still emerging from the nineteenth century and has scarcely gone either into the twentieth or back to the sixteenth and seventeenth centuries." Eliot, who had enclosed three more "King Bolo" stanzas in his letter of January 10, 1916, and informed Aiken of his plans to teach at Highgate School (secondary), was more definite in his reaction when he wrote again on August 25. After covering local news, such as his wife's peculiar clutch of ailments and the absence of so many companions to the war, and writing various philosophical pieces and review chores secured for him by Russell, he admits to liking the book—some poems more than others, of course—and praises its advance in craftsmanship over the first collection. He judges the title sequence best but cannot say he likes them, believing their author would be more flattered by the emotion they aroused, an extreme existential malaise. It is a remark Aiken remembered all his life. "He disliked them, I think, intensely."

Eliot's letter continues in a semiserious vein, the easiest way for two Harvard alumni to proceed, suggesting a comparison to Guy de Maupassant and questioning Aiken's cynicism and bulldog materialism. He concludes with a paragraph of absurd humor about an imaginary King Artaphernes, childish irreverence designed, clearly, to keep intact an old relationship and madness at bay. It was not the endorsement Aiken hoped for but treated the book with respect and, more important, reaffirmed Eliot's fondness for him. He required the bolstering.

As 1916 progressed, Aiken pursued the triangular trade route with increasing frequency, brief one-day hops and stops for the most part, designed to permit him to engage in shop talk, make whatever contacts (politic or amorous) he could, then return home as speedily as possible. However provincial, Boston was generally immune to the frenetic, often inhuman clamor and change associated with the more populous Chicago and New York. Randolph Bourne, who never considered permanent removal from the creative ferment of Greenwich Village, was enchanted during a visit: "Boston seems so smiling and restful and yet modernly intelligent. I lose all that hectic, anxious note of New York."

Though in agreement with Bourne, Aiken realized that his home city could not match the explosion of ideas and electric gatherings of artists and writers generated by the less refined metropolises, that the small magazine revolution accompanying the poetry renaissance was largely a New York and Chicago phenomenon despite the efforts of Lowell and such local boosters as Braithwaite. Lowell established a new magazine in May, the *Poetry Review,* with Braithwaite as editor, but it would last less than a year. In an August 25 letter to Braithwaite from Vermont, Aiken, who was published in its pages, coolly pinpointed the causes of the journal's failure as too few poems and too many amateurish reviews, with the former lacking edges and heft. Besides evidencing Aiken's adept critical scalpel, the letter stands as a prime example of the way he strove to separate personalities from professionalism, nourishing ties with people like Braithwaite even as he disparaged their views. It might appear naive in retrospect, but he had little choice if he wished to preserve his integrity and forward his career at a time when new poets, magazines, and movements were as unpredictable as a spun kaleidoscope.

He could and did compromise, at least with private standards, in approaching the magazines and the cliques clustering around them in Chicago and New York. For such a self-conscious man, the process could be painful and humiliating. *Ushant* recounts his attempt to penetrate the sanctum of Margaret Anderson's *Little Review,* sitting stiffly with the lady editors and discussing Marsden Hartley, whom he had already met in New York. On leaving, he had heard behind him, as he descended the stairs, "peals of uncontrollable and derisive

Conrad Aiken as a pensive young author (ca. 1914).

female laughter" (218). Anderson was inanely proud that her magazine had published only two or three unsolicited manuscripts in its entire history. Other Chicago figures were more receptive, and he made friends with A. Burton Rascoe, spirited newspaper reviewer and columnist, and Thomas C. O'Donnell, editor of a magazine called *Cartoons*. He also introduced himself at the *Chicago News* and reforged brittle links with Harriet Monroe.

It was in New York that Aiken located the richest sources of new acquaintances and possible outlets. The *Dial* had recently moved there from Chicago and was essentially a literary review, and by the end of the year he would be one of its contributing editors. He also reopened lines of communication with fellow Harvard alumni such as Brooks, Reed, and Seeger, who had been drawn to the more radical *Masses* (later the *Liberator*), which in turn led to encounters with other editors and poets from the left, among them Dell, Eastman, Waldo Frank, Mina Loy, and James Oppenheim. Another *Masses* editor Aiken enjoyed conversing and arguing with was Louis Untermeyer, the articulate, well-groomed, mostly self-educated poet and critic, whose prodigious energy permitted him to run a family jewelry business by day and write and socialize at night. Married to would-be poet and singer Jean Starr, Untermeyer was a curious mixture of hard-nosed entrepreneurial skills, instinctive insights into the modernist achievements, and personal naiveté. His dear comrades Lowell and Frost manipulated him to their own advantage without his full awareness. Aiken, with good reason, had no respect for his poetry but found him stimulating and congenial.

Yet the cultural circle that he most wanted to crack was the group of artists and writers associated with *Others,* orbiting around Kreymborg's small flat on Bank Street in the Village. Having been rejected by the magazine, he engineered a less direct offensive. Fortunately he was friendly with an artist who had been the first love of Gertrude Lord, Kreymborg's wife, for whom she still carried a torch, and dropped in on her at their apartment during one of his flying visits. Kreymborg returned home to discover "a sandy-haired gentleman" sitting beside his wife as she fed him "what looked like a chocolate cookie." Sensing the tableau had been prepared for his benefit, he asked, "Who is this accursed intruder?" In response, the "gentleman arose and murmured with an exaggerated drawl: 'I've come down from Boston in answer to some correspondence we've had from time to time.' " It was established that Kreymborg had rejected his work, and Gertrude teasingly begged her husband to guess the identity of their visitor, which he instantly did: "Then you must be that confounded conservative, Conrad Aiken!"

Kreymborg was won over by his guest's "genial spirit," and a "fellowship developed between them which was never threatened, not even by the admiration they eventually arrived at with respect to each other's work." Kreymborg, "a quiet, small man and fond of good talk," was easy enough to like, particularly since he was also "a fiery tennis player and a gregarious baseball buff," but whether Aiken ever really respected his verses, despite a few amiable reviews and supporting their inclusion in several anthologies, is doubtful. Their experimental playfulness epitomized the formless self-indulgence he despised. Nevertheless, the next day the new friends "took a long walk and gossiped about artists they knew," Kreymborg urging Aiken to stay in town another day, "but the Bostonian could never endure New York for more than twenty-four hours at a stretch."

For Aiken the encounter with Kreymborg, so carefully arranged, was probably the most significant social breakthrough of the year. While living in a shack in Grantwood, New Jersey, which he shared with artists Man Ray and Samuel Halpert, Kreymborg had published Pound's *Des Imagistes* anthology as an issue of the *Glebe,* his own journal. There, and later in the Village flat, he attracted the cream of the radical movement, playing host to writers as diverse as Marianne Moore, Orrick Johns, Carl Van Vechten, and Walter Conrad Arensberg and artists ranging from Hartley to Stieglitz. William Carlos Williams drove over frequently from Rutherford or from the uptown hospital where he was interning, as did the tall, "shy and sensitive," yet "broadshouldered" Wallace Stevens from Hartford. Aiken had reacted to Stevens's elegant poems in *Others* and elsewhere with immediate enthusiasm. Kreymborg was also on close terms with many of the young publishers in the city, including Allan Norton, an editor at the time; the Boni brothers, Albert and Charles, his first publishers; and Alfred Knopf, who had started his own firm (with Blanche Wolf) in 1915 on West Forty-second Street and was to publish *Others* as an anthology beginning that year.

Artists intrigued Aiken as much as writers, and the interaction with Hartley he especially relished, as he did contact with Kreymborg's Village friend Carl Schmitt, painter and pious Catholic devoted to Dante's poetry. Schmitt, who would become an early admirer of Gerard Manley Hopkins, loved having poets around. Most of them, like Aiken, Padraic Colum, and Ridgely Torrence, were "conventional in a literary sense," although Schmitt became the teenage Hart Crane's guardian in December. Aiken later met Crane at Schmitt's studio but was indifferent to him and his poetry.

Another interesting, if never very helpful, relationship that developed through the offices of the affable Kreymborg was with the handsome, highly affected Maxwell Bodenheim, still in his early twenties and fresh from Chicago, where he had fought with Anderson and Monroe, convincing himself that the entire Chicago scene was arrayed in a conspiracy against him. Bodenheim's frank self-absorption and martyr complex as Bohemian genius under siege, which entailed "often bitter outcries against those who had befriended and helped him most," had their sources in a miserable childhood as the only child of a Jewish businessman whose failures encouraged a nomadic family existence and a strong, sharp-tongued mother who vented her frustrations upon both her passive husband and their rebellious son.

Expelled from Hyde Park High School in Chicago, Maxwell had run away from home in 1908 to join the army, changing his name from Bodenheimer to Bodenheim, perhaps to elude his parents and a Jewish heritage. The regimentation was more than he could handle. He went AWOL, was picked up and brought back, swallowing some lye in a panic, and spent the remainder of his service time at Fort Leavenworth, Kansas. After a period of roaming the South he returned to Chicago in late 1912 and soon was acclaimed as the city's golden boy. His poems decorated *Poetry* and the *Little Review,* earning him the companionship of the ambitious cynic Ben Hecht, who has depicted him as "a golden-haired youth with pale eyes and the look of a pensive Christ." His sarcastic sneers and relentless egomania were accepted as intrinsic to his melancholic temperament and poetic function, accessories to talent. The more mature writers metamorphosizing the city from a cattle terminus into a mecca for culture-hungry midwesterners, including Anderson, Sandburg, Masters, and Dreiser, welcomed his presence.

Kreymborg had exchanged "poems and confidences" with him since 1914. When Bodenheim felt his position in Chicago was no longer tenable, he wrote to Kreymborg, proclaiming that he was migrating to New York to meet "the one man who seemed to have genuine elements of friendship." With characteristic kindness, Kreymborg rented a room for him in his own building on the floor above. Happily for the depressive Bodenheim, Kreymborg's generosity was matched by Gertrude's maternal patience, and he was treated like a precocious child: "Then they would sit down and talk—or rather Bogie [Bodenheim] would talk, since he rarely listened to anything anyone else might say. If one had a hard-luck tale to tell, it reminded him of something that had befallen him. And his misadventure, always beautifully embellished, but precise and accurate in the skeleton of the plot, made one feel one's mishap was gloriously fortunate by comparison."

Aiken soon met and enjoyed Bodenheim, amused by his victim-genius pose and his linguistic acrobatics, and Bodenheim in turn "appreciated Aiken's affability and his seeming stability, but not his art." Over the course of the year, after Kreymborg and Gertrude moved to seven comfortable rooms on Jane Street, Bodenheim paid several visits to Aiken, as he too plied the busy triangular trade route.

The initial visit was shortly after Bodenheim had assisted John Coffey, a professional fur thief with philosophic pretentions, to escape from Blackwell Island Jail, and the three lunched in Cambridge. In the meantime, Aiken finally had some verses accepted by *Others,* the consequence of a hoax similar to the one perpetrated on Monroe. During a period near year's end, when William Carlos Williams was editing *Others* for Kreymborg in Rutherford, "a package of imagistic poems, concise and picturesque, came in from an address in Connecticut with a strange name at the head of each sheet." Williams responded positively to the submission, as did Kreymborg when he dropped by, but the latter recognized the typewriting from earlier letters and had the poems printed under Aiken's real name, "much to Conrad's enjoyment of the turn of the hoax."

Some time before, Aiken had been able to give Kreymborg pleasure of a different variety. The move to more spacious quarters had not prevented the quiet disintegration of the Kreymborgs' brief marriage, a sad, affectionate breakup occasioned primarily by the return of Gertrude's old flame. It was decided to have a final dinner together on the day of their first anniversary, and Bodenheim, who had retreated from a recent foray into Boston to reside with them, was told that he would have to leave. After the pensive meal, "Bogie drew forth his old corncob and Krimmie his old briar and they sat in the gathering darkness and smoked without interruption." Aware of the impending split, Aiken traveled down from Boston to console Kreymborg, whose account of the episode reveals much about his calm, unfailing sense of humor:

> A day or two later Krimmie, now alone, received another visitor. Had he had any power in choosing a companion for this last day on Jane Street, he would have picked the very man who sat nearby and assumed a jocular mask his friend copied gracefully. As he had a delicate mania for analysing and caricaturing his own misadventures with life, Conrad could easily join in the mood Krimmie had determined upon as the one to carry him through packing material things in rooms echoing with spiritual ones. As the Bostonian was expert in the field of psychological detachment, he was able to help Krimmie talk about many an irrelevent theme.

Aiken's strength, as usual, was in an intimate zone where his self-mocking wit and phlegmatic composure, enhanced by that scholarly appearance and languid Harvard intonation, rarely failed to make a favorable impression, to beguile and surprise those familiar with him only at a distance or through his critical writings, which had caused many to think he wore "a perpetual chip on his shoulder." Though still averse to large gatherings, to formal dinners, dances, and sprawling cocktail parties, where he faded into the woodwork or made jokes from the sidelines, he was able and willing to insinuate himself among small groups with divergent tastes. If this also advanced his career, that was part of the game he had mastered at Harvard.

None of this social activity intruded upon his campaign against the Imagists and Lowell, whom he "tore assunder at every opportunity," nor interfered with his critical writing. It was probably his work on the poetic symphonies and the relative scarcity of outlets—his reviews were not a regular feature in the *Dial* until 1917—that explain why he published only five prose pieces for the year, all in the *Poetry Journal*. One of these was a review of Masefield's *Good Friday and Other Poems,* its title, "The Declining Masefield," indicative of disenchantment with a former idol; another treated Pound's *Catholic Anthology* with relative gentleness, using the opportunity to celebrate Eliot's achievement publicly. Though rankled by the collection's blatant bias, he judged the selection "an interesting one," if "only for the inclusion of *The Love Song of J. Alfred Prufrock* and the *Protrait of a Lady.*"

Aiken's analysis of Eliot's two poems underlines his sensitivity to his friend's special skills and why he believed his and Eliot's poetic aims were not dissimilar at heart: "Mr. Eliot uses free rhyme very effectively, often musically; and with the minimum of sacrifice to form conveys a maximum of atmosphere. Both poems are psychological character-studies, subtle to the verge of insoluble idiosyncrasy, introspective self-gnawing. Those who are constitutionally afraid to analyze themselves, who do not think, who are not psychologically imaginative, will distrust and perhaps dislike them." It is an equitable appraisal and, at the same time, another defense of Aiken's own art.

In *The Jig of Forslin,* scheduled to appear from Four Seas in October 1916 but not published until December, his Preface explains that the book "has been guided entirely by the central theme. This theme is the process of vicarious wish fulfillment by which civilized man enriches his circumscribed life and obtains emotional balance." He is careful to warn that "the range of vicarious experience, here of necessity only hinted at, or symbolized by certain concrete and selected pictures, is suggested on a completer and more comprehensive plan than will be found in any specific individual." As in "The Clerk's Journal," Gautier is used as well, his story *"La Morte Amoureuse"* structuring a vampire narrative in the fourth section. With Aiken's aid, Houston Peterson outlined the genesis of title and protagonist: "The 'jig' goes back to Aiken's old obsession with the Dance of Death. 'Forslin' he derived from the name of one Forsling, a Boston tailor. It recalled the Italian 'forse' meaning perhaps, and the Latin 'fors' meaning chance, while the dimunitive 'in' ending suggested weakling."

Freud stands foursquare behind the sequence's dream mechanism, manipulated to suit Aiken's Romantic purposes. The Old Bird complained of the manipulation in a letter, also painting the book as obscene. Aiken replied: "What I aimed at was rather the presentation of a typical cycle of adventures, vicariously experienced, not solely as the individual would achieve them incoherently and abortively by his own imagination, but also, and preponderantly, as they would be supplied to him by society: that is, already worked up and rounded either as works of art, or as the gossip of the smoking-room, or as the smutty story. And to some extent I merely took the sum-total of this idea as an adequate theme for musical development: an excuse for writing a poem!"

This is an open, accurate description of artistic intent that cannot, of course, relieve the sequence of demands for poetic intensity or conceal its ultimate lack of success but does confirm a remorseless quest for an efficient modus operandi to couple Aiken's passionate attachment to verbal music with the substantial body of psychoanalytic knowledge taking possession of his mind and imagination. Poe's euphonious "City in the Sea" and "A Dream within a Dream" are present—"He does not know if this is wake or dreaming; / But thinks to lean, reach out his hands, and swim"—and Eliot's "Prufrock" more so—"Let us drown, then, if to drown is but to change / Drown in the days of those whose days are strange." The lesson of Fletcher, however, dominates the sequence's narrative and musical range.

Peterson insists that *The Jig of Forslin* and the other "symphonies" anticipated and might have influenced *The Waste Land,* although it was Eliot, as the title sequence of *Nocturne of Remembered Spring* will verify, who was impressing and practically petrifying Aiken's imagination at the time. The point is moot, if historically interesting. That Eliot could have, consciously or not, "stolen" certain felicitous images or architectural motifs from the work of a friend seems reasonable. *The Waste Land* would be, however, a direct outgrowth of Eliot's earlier verses, an elaboration and amalgamation of material he had been wrestling with for years, its dramatic orchestration (largely Pound's doing) and austere, elliptical, Laforguean stanzas evincing a diametric contrast to Aiken's love of smoother rhetorical strokes and plot devices. More relevant, in practical terms, when one abandons straight narrative in any extended poem, what is left but some form of recurrent musical analog? With pragmatic opportunism, Aiken and Eliot and contemporaries like Pound were simply tackling the inherited problem of absent or discredited frames by applying a logical solution from their common arts background, the replacement of lost epic nodes and slack Victorian models with lyric sequences and frequent recourses to cyclical constructs.

The Jig of Forslin, which converts nightmare threats of death and perversion into willed dreams of eternal creativity without really confronting their etiology—foreshadow of Aiken's "consistent view" in his major works of the late 1920s and early 1930s—is an impressive failure in a year that witnessed the publication of H.D.'s *Sea Garden,* Sandburg's *Chicago Poems,* Lowell's *Men, Women, and Ghosts,* and Robinson's *Man Against the Sky.* It varies its voices as much as possible, though tonally limited by a prevailing fin-de-siècle weariness and despair, enabling Aiken to experiment further with a variety of lines and narrative effects inside a partial stream-of-consciousness approach. The failure stems from the character—the lack of character—of Forslin himself. By attempting to make him an individual *and* an Everyman, a familiar tactical error in all the symphonic sequences, Aiken was evading his poetic responsibility, his art's requirement that private obsessions be milked, the hidden self expended, whatever the cost. As Eliot had dared expose certain repressed facets of his own psyche through the medium of Prufrock's timid soul, so Aiken would have to locate a method and/or persona that would allow the maximum ventilation of unconscious energies.

For now, *The Jig of Forslin* augmented his technical control and circled around—still in an 1890s mask—the fundamental fear of death and an absent bottom self, intermingling sex and horror in an ambiguous, murderous Freudian context. Reviews were favorable in the main, or neutral at worst, and cemented Aiken's reputation as a significant literary force. Even the conservative *New York Times* saved most of its review space for explicating the book's grand aim, dubbing it a "much more ambitious effort than *Turns and Movies.*" Braithwaite was typically encouraging in the *Transcript,* observing that "the coarseness of the picturesque novel is introduced, and yet there are sections of mystical beauty and lyrical intensity. . . . As a poet Mr. Aiken gains immeasurably with this poem." And the *Review of Reviews'* anonymous reviewer was equally enthusiastic: "To the persons who like the newer schools of verse and enjoy the study of the processes of the mind, and to all poets, one heartily commends *The Jig of Forslin.*" Firkins of the *Nation* labeled its author "a born metrist," while Henry Turner Bailey's sour reaction in the *New York Call* offered a sobering dash of valid complaint: "The evident purpose is to render man's vicarious satisfactions of the tabooed impulses. The thing will be done some day; but it will take a greater knowledge of life and man and Freud than this poet seems to possess."

Unfortunately, regardless of positive notices, *The Jig of Forslin* had cost its author money to publish, as had the first two volumes and as would the next, already set for a 1917 publication date. Aiken had earned back only a little over $50 for *Turns and Movies.* He was in a position similar to that of William Carlos Williams, who had published his first three collections with Four Seas and paid "something in the neighborhood of two hundred and fifty dollars" for each, never receiving a cent in return. To pay for the printing of *The Jig of Forslin,* Aiken was forced to sell the family car, a move that could hardly have endeared him to Jessie, who was doubtless beginning to suspect that marriage to a poet was little different from marriage to a work-obsessed businessman, except that a poet can rarely provide the material comforts that console neglected spouses. There were few extras in their life together, however pleasurable the interchanges of ideas and the conviction that a creative talent was being nursed into greatness, a weakening conviction as Jessie no longer seemed fascinated by her husband's work. Eventually, many years hence, it would erode to the extent that she concluded he was a better critic than poet.

Their legacies kept them solvent, but the financial burden of rearing a child in an economy in which food prices were rising steadily to double prewar levels had to wear against Jessie's good nature. She is faintly damned as "the practical Lorelei" in *Ushant*, a wife beginning to show less patience with her husband's careless ways. On the credit side of the ledger, John had long crossed over the six-month stage—an invisible barrier Aiken decided existed between the time an infant held no interest for him and the time it neared individual status—and he began enjoying the antics of his towheaded son. If absent too often and reluctant to assume a parental guise, he did delight in playing with John and listening to his spontaneous chatter.

Approval outside the home came from having two poems, "Miracles" and "Evensong," reprinted in Braithwaite's annual anthology, listed as "among the best of the year," and three others in the *New Poetry*, Monroe's first gathering of verses from her magazine. Aiken did not look back. He rapidly finished *Nocturne of Remembered Spring* and immediately began another "symphony," to be entitled *The House of Dust*, under the inspiration of "the alarums and excursions over the problem of the 'group mind' and crowd psychology, and some rumors of [Gustave] Le Bon's famous book [*The Crowd*]," which "suggested to him a new theme . . . to capture the soul of a city, to contrast the sort of multicellular awareness of a mass of people with the multicellular awareness of the individual." By March 1917 the new volume, almost a thousand lines, was completed. More than four decades later Aiken claimed that as early as 1915, with the creation of *The Charnel Rose*, "the general project was already pretty clear to me, as well as much of the method." That is, the symphonies commencing with *The Charnel Rose* and *The Jig of Forslin* and evolving through *The House of Dust* and *Senlin* to *The Pilgrimage of Festus*, executed by 1920, represented the consummation of a master plan to explore human consciousness from various angles with every weapon in the poet's considerable arsenal.

True and not true. This is retrospective schematization, valid in essence and design, in the love of sequential musical arrangements and in an early determination to be a poet of ideas, yet giving too much weight to a young Aiken's specific reading of future goals. Consciousness intrigued him, as did Freud's model of the unconscious, but the "consistent view" posited by *Ushant* as an ultimate stance was still a vague tidal drift in his imagination at the time of the symphonies' actual composition. He intimated the general direction his art was taking him, an art aptly characterized by Frederick Hoffman as projecting "*no* intellectual substance," without having yet learned how to escape from the pressure of superior example or how to concoct (and believe in) a metaphysic worthy of his analytic ambitions. Put simply, he did not know himself and thus could not, would not, emotionally satisfy his poetry's programmatic demands.

This might explain why his next published volume, *Nocturne of Remembered Spring,* was a curious hodgepodge of old and new material. Aiken would rescue only one poem from it ("Episode in Grey") for his 1953 *Collected Poems.* The book proceeds backward in time, by and large, with "Dust in Starlight" from 1914, third and final part of "Earth Triumphant," terminating the collection, reassuring continuity and organic unity by reasserting the circular nature of experience and perception. The poem itself is not much of an improvement over the two previous sections but does, tersely, tentatively, alight upon several urgent images that would, a decade or so hence, help crystallize his three classic short stories, "Strange Moonlight," "Silent Snow, Secret Snow," and "Mr. Arcularis." At this way station on the path to Calvary, he was not yet ready to exploit the frightening subconscious shapes such eidolons released.

The opening scene, familiar from the Harvard poetry, precursor to the first poem in the mature *Preludes to Memnon,* presents a man alone in a room while the snow piles up outside. It is another tear-sodden tale of a husband who no longer loves his wife, his "golden-haired first love," as he once did. Before salvation can beckon, he must leave her and their home (a truly upsetting prospect for Aiken) and contemplate suicide, too self-conscious in its "exquisite" agony to evoke necessary despair and terror. He wanders through city streets, enters a movie theater in hopes that a woman will sit down next to him, gripped by sordid lust, not love. With real skill, the light cast by the projector's beam—

> Intense white stream, wherein a maze
> Of fiery motes whirled up and rose
> And dived and swam—

introduces the "light" motif that reappears later as moonlight, rays of redemption from distant stars. It will resurface in "Strange Moonlight," illuminating childhood's traumatic terrain.

Foreshadowing the fatal mirage—psychotic deliverance—that grants "Silent Snow, Secret Snow" its hypnotic spell, the young man lies alone in a rented room (perhaps masturbating), not knowing whether he is awake or dreaming:

> So in his mind, now, it was snowing,
> Silent, persistent: whelming deep
> A much-loved world in frozen sleep,
> Burying it, eternally.

The culmination is Christ's nativity: "A loneliness like silent night, / Come round him cold, come round him white." But the ramifications of this birth-and-death fusion are not investigated. Nor is the next association with Aiken's own childhood, as madness and loss of wife summon (portentiously) the memory scene that climaxes "Strange Moonlight":

> He called to mind how one night, late,
> They came home through the garden gate,
> And all the garden brimmed and spilled
> With moonlight, silver-grey, that filled
> The paths and lawns, and on the wall.

The ensuing lines intimate why the haunting recollection could not yet be fully tapped:

> His mother, too,—he saw her now,—
> Soft eyes, her wise and tranquil brow,
> Her mouth, so sweet, so warm, so sure,
> Her hands, so gentle, so secure . . .
> He would not see that face again,
> Nor feel its softness, soft as rain.

Sensuality reigns in the madonna mother, derived from memories of the protagonist's wife; the inner dynamic is lucid, ripe with physical desire for the lost taboo woman. The subtext's incest drive is irresistible, as he wonders what "soft hand stroked these sleepy things," these "longdead melodies." But interior connections between sex and death, between mother and wife, between a golden past and a lifeless present, within the confines of unresolved ambivalences and Oedipal threat, are deflected into masturbational fantasy, all "illusions turned to lust," rendering the poem harmless and dull.

Though lacking what Eliot might term its "objective correlative," another suggestive allusion occurs that has obvious biographical links to the aftermath of Aiken's parental deprivation:

> Bewildered, lost, a child again,
> Mutely enduring strangest pain
> Beyond all knowledge or all cry.

Again, the poem refuses the bait, swims away into the kind of cosmic voyage that "Mr. Arcularis" will take—"Catching in vain at star and moon / While all his senses seemed to swoon . . ."—without duplicating that artifice's brilliant synthesis of personal anguish and Freudian universality. Hiding from the terrible truth that the cosmic reference could reveal, the voyage deteriorates into a beached conflation of Nietzsche's shouts in the dark and Edna St. Vincent Millay (of "Renascence") swelling into a child's transcendence:

> He grew in stature, touched the sky;
> Commanded, with imperious eye,
> All earth and heaven, now so young
> While April's fires within him sing.

Imitation is evasion throughout the poem, and throughout the book, as the protagonist refuses to remain for long in Aiken's psyche, to take advantage of such productive strikes at subterranean ore as the vividly imagined death of his wife, "for all eternity, / Dishevelled, pale, unbreathing, cold." Light, now sunlight, redeems instead by sheer will, a return to the abandoned wife, loved as once she was, ominous nightmare converted arbitrarily into a didactic message of salvation; lust is defeated, transmuted into love, starlight promising "far-off, holier, higher things."

"Dust in Starlight" is the single most frustrating of Aiken's early performances, a veritable unspent treasure trove of precious motifs that reflect the very hub of his self and imagination, the dialectic animating and binding them together. By 1915, if not imprisoned by insecurity in the boxes of other men's styles, he had within grasp the basic elements of a possible breakthrough to his own voice and matter. True, he had yet to evolve the conceptual framework necessary for ordering unconscious obsessions into effective structures, but the subsequent experiments with symphonic formulas under Fletcher's influence, though assisting him in perfecting the technique of a final style, had shifted him further away from the veins of psychic energy laid bare by "Dust in Starlight." Self, persona, and protagonist remained far apart, too isolated from one another for reciprocal exchanges. He was willing to use Freud as an organizational principle, removing himself to the safety of an Everyman mask, was willing to trade analyses with Wilbur without "going all the way," and was eager to incorporate Freudian notions of reality and pleasure principles into his critical corpus. He was not yet ready, however, to invest himself in a psychoanalytic aesthetic.

Death haunts this poem, and most prior poems, but it is not a terror reified and set reverberating with symbolic discharges of obsessional power. It is, rather, death seen as melodramatic excess from a childhood vantage at the brink of Poe's hysteria and Swinburne's lyric density, death dressed up in the garish clown suit of the 1890s, where sex and love can be perceived as eternal opponents, dying itself a stage production enlarging the poet-hero's pity for self into a cosmic catastrophe at an unthreatening remove. Aiken's "facile diabolism" (Gregory and Zaturenska's just sentence) never broaches the genuine diabolism below Poe's tales with their trappings of Germanic supernaturalism because he is still detached from neurotic mainsprings buried in an unexamined past.

The rest of the poems in *Nocturne of Remembered Spring* are similarly artificial, repetitive to a numbing degree in their thematic concern with languishing young Werthers and fantasies of suicide and lost loves, scored with stock musical allusions and bleak winter landscapes, echoing Shakespeare, "forever, as all things must, / Into the grey and dreamless dust," and Eliot, "Take my arm, and let us drift," and Stevens, "These are the notes whereof my life makes music," as if borrowings and reconstructions could bestow literary worth upon trite material and attitudes and cliché plots. The two poems from 1917, "Nocturne in a Minor Key" and "Episode in Grey," fare little better, the former an address to a woman (who has rejected the speaker) in the mandarin manner of Wallace Stevens. "Peter Quince at the Clavier," which Braithwaite had reprinted in his 1915 anthology at Lowell's command, and "The Comedian as the Letter C" exercised a profound, durable influence upon Aiken. "Episode in Grey" revolves around the termination of yet another love affair, resorting to Tennyson's and Wordsworth's urbanized immensities, "vast self-generating laws." Its coda, predictably, confronts the realization that eventually the lovers will part, one of them discarding their love-hate relationship at last.

The title sequence's chief value lies in its demonstration of the incredible fashion in which Eliot's attainments were dampering Aiken's imagination. He borrows shamelessly, almost an act of sympathetic magic, though working with a character and situation worked with before:

> Let us return there, let us return, you and I,—
> Through the grey streets our memories retain
> Let us go back again.

The difference between Aiken's unsure but often impressive talent and Eliot's precocious genius is easily discerned in the intrusion of blunt "memories" and that superfluous last line. Section 2 returns to honeyed excess—"And remember, while rich music yawns and closes, / With a luxury of pain, how silence comes . . ."—and the third section resurrects many of the romantic clichés Aiken appeared afraid to surrender, a walk and talk of "foolish things, of life and death" amid a "net of silver silence" cast softly over "our dreams" until her "white face turns away" and he is "caught with pain." As usual, metaphor is yoked to genuine fears, in this case the fear of losing a maternal stand-in, but the worn image avoids deep emotion rather than acting as catalyst for its abstract realization.

Section 4 deals with snow, almost a logo, though it too fails to roam beyond a standard stage setting for a replay of a melodrama about lost love and melancholy youth: "I pursue your ghost among green leaves that are ghostly, / I pursue you, but cannot find. . . ." They are both ghosts that never lived, neither of them human enough to save the poem from pretentious allegorizing. In section 5 the narrator asks, "Do you foresee me, married and grown old?" The inquiry cannot move us as Prufrock's refrain does—"I grow old, I grow old"—because it is never welded to a figure (or his observer) with idiosyncratic tics sufficient to individualize him. And the closing section, recurrent, musically appropriate, has the former lovers meeting, pretending "serene forgetfulness of our youth," its climax—"And then we laugh, with shadows in our eyes"—more comic than tragic. The poem is best forgotten, as Aiken later did. That he could have essayed such a travesty of Eliot's accomplishment at this phase in his career emphasizes his imagination's refusal to pick up the Freudian challenge, as well as the fundamental insecurity engendered by Eliot's superior models.

Besides witnessing his continued poetic pursuit of identity masks in the symphonies, the year 1917 marked Aiken's maturity as a serious and important critic, one of the first to scrutinize the literary productions of contemporaries within the motivational grid of depth psychology. During the year he published some twenty reviews, all in the *Dial* and the *Chicago News,* except a crucial review of Nicolas Kostyleff's *Le mécanisme cérèbrale de la pensée* appearing in the *North American Review*—crucial because it seemed to proffer scientific support for a Freudian theory of the poetic process. After partially rejecting Freud's view of inspiration as the projection of unconscious complexes, erotic in genesis, as unable to elucidate large amounts of poetry not wish-fulfilling in nature, Kostyleff proceeds on the assumption that writing is a mechanical phenomenon in its farthest reaches, a series of associations ("verbo-motor" reactions) that take off from specific external stimuli and unleash entire chains of unconscious word stores, surging farther and farther away from the initial trigger. "In this manner," Aiken explicates, "we get a finished poem which far outruns, in emotional weight, the initial impulse."

He was entranced and mostly convinced, particularly by Kostyleff's conclusion that to "the factor revealed by Freud,—(the stimulus in the revival of psychic complexes,—) we see added another having an equally precise place in the organism,—an extraordinarily extended chain of verbal reactions." He was also alert to the reality that the plausibility of the Frenchman's main thesis did not resolve the basic problem of distinguishing, on an objective basis, between genuine poet and hack: "M. Kostyleff makes a good deal of the fact that the poet, both instinctively in childhood and deliberately in maturity, seeks by reading to enlarge his vocabulary and the richness of his prosodic sense. But of course the imitative poet does this quite as much as the original one, if not more." He is straying close to self-knowledge here. Aiken's solution was to identify inferior poets as those who "do not extend the field of our consciousness in any new direction."

The expansion of consciousness is thus already established in his mind as a desired literary fulcrum, but neither Freud nor Kostyleff could offer more than structural hints at the convoluted dynamic behind the typical artifice's pursuit of this worthwhile goal. His own verse symphonies, which must be characterized as failures despite brilliant patches and laudable ambitions, were hardly adhering to the prescription he would provide in a 1919 essay ("Magic or Legerdemain?") as part of his inquiry into "the state of mind of the poet during actual composition." There, healthy creativity is described as "a sort of dual consciousness, heightened no doubt on its ordinary plane, but conspicuously different from the usual state of mind in that the many passages which lead downward to the subconscious are thrown open, and the communications between the two planes, upper and lower, are free and full." Over the next few years he refined his theory of poetic inspiration to encompass Freud's binary dialectic of contending pleasure and reality principles, the former tagged as childhood's primal drive, so that his ultimate depiction of the mature, effective poet involves a balancing of these two antagonistic urges and conceptual stances.

As Claudia C. Morrison has noticed, however, the reason for the strength of his critical method was that, unlike many of the early psychoanalytic critics, "Aiken never argued for a specifically psychoanalytic approach to literature, but borrowed from Freud's system of psychology only such ideas as seemed to him relevant to the critic's basic function—that of evaluation." A case in point is his review of Alan Seeger's posthumous *Poems* for the *Chicago News*. He begins with Freud's vision of the artist as "one in whom the pleasure principle of childhood never gives way to the reality principle of maturity" and relegates Seeger to "that large class who never see the world as it is, who always sees it as they wish it to be," a neat, crudely valid simplification to buttress his dismissal of Seeger's trivial verses as "somewhat archaically romantic; mellifluous, always, in the effort to be sensuously decorative; a little self-consciously poetic." Worse, there "are no ideas to take hold of, no emotions so intense as to shake one's repose."

At the base of his astute critiques, aside from the natural yen to inculcate greater appreciation of Freud's message, lay a positive attempt to lift criticism out of the hands of mediocre impressionists and place it on a more secure, scientific plane less open to subjective manipulations by inferior sensibilities. It was a noble effort doomed to incomplete success by the absence of adequate research, but it enabled him to exert his own substantial analytic skills with a certain degree of objectivity.

To him, Braithwaite epitomized the second-rate, sentimental reviewer who invariably hides behind a cloud of impressionist rhetoric when faced by the difficulty of separating authentic talent from its imitator and generally makes the wrong choice. As a result, one of Aiken's sharpest, most intelligent 1917 reviews was of Braithwaite's *Critical Anthology,* a four-hundred-page compilation of *Transcript* pieces transmogrified, *à la* George Moore, into the form of conversations between Braithwaite and three others. After condemning Braithwaite's incomprehensible omission of Stevens, Eliot, and Bodenheim, along with a slighting of the radical *Others* group, he locates the source of the author's wrongheaded prejudices in a stubborn belief "that poetry is a sort of supernaturalism" that deteriorates into "a shrugging of the critic's burden from his own shoulders" onto "the shoulders of God." Consequently, he argues, "Braithwaite puts a clear emotional emphasis on work which is characteristically sentimental," overrating the effusions of poetasters on the order of Bliss Carman, Lizette Woodworth Reese, and Hermann Hagedorn.

Aiken inquires, as Wordsworth and Blake had implicitly inquired a century before: "Must poetry be all marshmallows and tears? Is it to be prohibited from dealing with ideas, or restricted solely to a contemplation of that small part of our lives which is, in a sentimental sense, beautiful?" Candor and personal sensitivity rather than ideological or psychological dogma are allied to beat back the counterrevolution represented by Braithwaite's limited taste, and a final question gives the essence of Aiken's own critical apparatus: "Shall we never learn that there is nothing mysterious or supernatural about poetry; that it is a natural, organic product, with discoverable functions, clearly open to analysis?"

The dilemma of a poet-critic, a fruitful dilemma if heeded, is that honesty eventually compels that the spotlight be turned inward. Even when deeply divided, as with Aiken, creative and critical functions find it hard always to maintain a safe distance from each other. Once committed to the critical road, he was forced to confront his own poetry from the outside to some extent. The offshoot was an anonymous review, negative in tenor, of *Nocturne of Remembered Spring* for the *Chicago News,* aptly entitled "Schizophrenia" and touchingly indicative of underlying insecurities. Unlike Whitman, Aiken is not intent upon public relations but on disavowing the recent past, as if requiring the ritual of print to assert that the dim master plan of the symphonies was geared to a more successful career than was evident to date: "Mr. Aiken himself seems to be somewhat uncertain as to his role—he comes to the rehearsal, so to speak, still fumbling in his pockets for his part. . . . This is a serious weakness. It points to a fundamental lack of conviction in Mr. Aiken's mind, as to poetic values."

He goes on to diagnose his failure in terms that suggest his general approach is pellucid, even if his format constantly changes, a left-handed self-compliment that has the psychological effect of keeping intact his grand project:

> If he is consistent as regards his material, sticking fairly closely to a preference for an objective psychological method in poetry, he is hopelessly confused as regards the problem of poetic form. In *Turns and Movies* he willfully sacrificed his ability to write in smoothly involute curves for a dubious gain in matter-of-fact forcefulness. In *The Jig of Forslin* he recanted, and, with occasional sops to downright and rigid realism, abandoned himself to a luxuriation in romantic virtuosity. And now, in *Nocturne of Remembered Spring,* he is more clearly than ever a schizophrenic.

The next long paragraph is a savage and acute dismembering of the last-named book's glaring weaknesses, its sterile mixture of modes and "a tendency to take refuge in an emotional symbolism which lies perilously close to the vague," though no mention is made of the derivative factors operating throughout to undercut intensity. The lapses dissected are mechanical, innocuous: "One gets tired of psychological variations, no matter how contrapuntal or subtle, if no element of suspense is introduced." It is easier to ascribe failure to tactical errors than to the absence of a near self, an inner imperative. When deriding "Dust in Starlight," he criticizes its octosyllabic couplets and lack of verse alterations and queries, with undeniable justice, "Can anyone remain interested for forty pages in the protagonist's vacillations between flesh and sentiment—except the protagonist himself?" He never asks why that protagonist does not permit highly charged material—allusions to maternal substitutes and obsessive snow images—to seek more fertile correspondences, the unconscious plundering he would envision as intrinsic to the creative act. Though willing, perhaps compelled, to expose the rotted beams bracing the shaky edifice of *Nocturne of Remembered Spring,* he was neither foolish nor wise enough to apply tough Freudian building codes as well.

The self-review is thus a species of contrition, and remarkable at that, but also a defense of his larger purpose and refusal to accept the logic of its press toward deeper levels of experience. As a comment on Eliot in a different review intimates, he had become aware of the necessity for such levels, however refracted through an abstract prism. Comparing Eliot to Wilfrid Wilson Gibson as another category of the "realistic" in modern verse, Aiken again alights upon "Prufrock" and "Portrait of a Lady" as exemplifying "psychological realism, but in a highly subjective or introspective vein." He says Eliot gives us, in the first person, "the reactions of an individual to a situation for which to a large extent his own character is responsible. Such work is more purely autobiographic than the other—the field is narrowed and the terms are idiosyncratic (sometimes almost blindly so)." He knew whereof he spoke, of course, in regard to the autobiographic features of Eliot's poems. More pertinent, as a critic he was demonstrating an awareness of how expenditures of self were a prerequisite to success, all of which stresses the continued gap between his critical acumen—confident and authoritative—and his unsure aesthetic, its reflexive timidity and self-deceiving penchant for adhering to the Santayanian idealization of poet as philosopher learned at Harvard, then reinforced by Reverend Potter's lectures.

Eliot was carving a minor niche in the obdurate wall of English letters, though still harassed by his wife's gnawing problems, mental and physical, and by forced economies. By 1917 he had surrendered his exhausting teaching chores for a post at Lloyd's Bank in London, closer to the war-thinned literary ranks. The publication of *Prufrock and Other Observations* had established his modernist credentials, and when Richard Aldington was drafted he assumed his assistant editor's position with the *Egoist*. For his career the war was a blessing because his American citizenship protected him from conscription. America's entrance into the war on April 6, barely four months after Woodrow Wilson had trounced Charles Evans Hughes on the basis of a firm neutralist policy, would not alter things much, although Eliot made a belated effort to enlist in the fall of 1918. The effect of American involvement on Aiken and his colleagues at home was also fairly minimal. As Floyd Dell exulted in his memoir, "The 'Renaissance' that had been predicted in 1911, that had begun in 1912, was still—fantastically!—going on. The war did not stop it."

Like the majority of intellectuals, Aiken was disgusted by his country's ensnarement in a struggle that did not affect national interests, though sympathizing with the plight of England. He never allowed himself to get embroiled in the patriotic madness that was causing Copey to pose as an unofficial recruiting sergeant at Harvard and Hermann Hagedorn to gather groups of local poets together into "Vigilantes." The sole intrusion upon his sane equanimity was a vague consciousness of a hostility toward the menace of Bolshevism, which the press reveled in exploiting, prodded by the Communist Revolution in Russia and that country's abandonment of the Allies. In most matters, he remained as apolitical and skeptical as ever.

In August, when Taussig wrote him in Vermont to inform him that he had enlisted, Aiken reacted with humorous cynicism, wondering what would happen to his precarious finances without his friend's expert guidance and poking fun at the peculiar human need to shed blood. Other friends were also drifting out of immediate reach. The peripatetic Fletcher had sailed for England the year before, where he married Daisy Arbuthnot, former wife of a photographer friend, and settled down to make London a permanent base. Aiken kept him apprised of local doings and in an April letter softened the blow of his review of Braithwaite's annual in which he had elevated Fletcher to "our major group" but accused him, Lowell, and Masters of "strange artistic blindness" and unpredictability of performance. He explained to Fletcher—a bit duplicitously—that he wanted to avoid the charge of nepotism.

The Old Bird, who had voyaged overseas to serve at a navy base hospital in Brest when his internship concluded in June, wrote after a long silence to tell of his engagement to Cecile, a Belgian nurse. After graciously congratulating McCouch for his good fortune and promising to write to Cecile separately, Aiken replied with the admission that "my sympathies are not much in this war (particularly as regards our own entrance) and I am personally determined to avoid a belligerent part in it as long as I can. If I am drafted, I shall go, but under protest." He touched upon their shared passion: "Are you expecting to get war-shock work? If so, it ought to be damned interesting as another aspect of this whole Freudian question. To that degree, I envy you your opportunity!"

Another partner in the Freudian enterprise, George Wilbur, was also soon removed. He had secured his M.D. degree in June 1916 and a year later married Mahila Joy Paxton of his native Kansas. On the same day as the ceremony, September 28, he entered the army as a first lieutenant, eventually being transferred to Fort Dix, New Jersey, where he would serve as a neuropsychiatric examiner until 1919. In the meantime, Wehle was still working in a museum in Minneapolis and would wed Kate Talbot Finkle on June 1, 1918, moving to Manhattan and the Metropolitan Museum of Art the following year. "The good Bassett" remained at his Iowa State teaching post, which he would not resign until 1918, when he returned home to work at the First National Bank of Boston.

The temporary absences and marriages of old friends—Taussig was to wed a Scottish woman, Beatrice Murray, in 1918—was compensated for by Aiken's circles of more recent acquaintances in Chicago and New York. Boston itself offered the frequent presence of Crist, Jules Clark, Uncle Alfred, Robert Linscott, and undergraduate poets such as S. Foster Damon, whose thesis on the Imagists he eagerly perused, and Robert Hillyer, who graduated in June, the same year his very traditional first collection, *Sonnets and Other Lyrics,* appeared. Harvard's literary clique had not lost its enthusiasm for an elitist aesthete stance, as Dos Passos remembered: "*The Yellow Book* and *The*

Hound of Heaven and Machen's *Hill of Dreams* seemed more important, somehow, than the massacres around Verdun." Hillyer was staying on at the college as an instructor and living in Cambridge.

Furthermore, by April it was known that Jessie was pregnant once again, lessening her appeal in bed but almost extinguishing the prospect of conscription. For sexual relief, Aiken had "Marian," an attractive young woman whom he had apparently picked up at a movie theater or vaudeville show and who lived at a boardinghouse on Brimmer Street in Boston. Marian was depicted in later years as short and pleasingly plump, "vivacious, a fun girl, a bohemian, a good cook, and genuinely interested in music." Their affair had commenced sometime before or soon after the move to Walnut Street and would continue to 1920: "From the passionate literary quarrels and debates with the farouche John, next door, or the choleric psychoanalytic discussions with Jacob . . . it was always to the bow-windowed room in Brimmer Street that he had gone, it was only to Marian that he could talk with his whole being, and *of* his whole being" (212).

Aiken seemed to have it all—free of a regular job, a second child on the way, engaged in exciting critical contests, publishing his poetry with increasing regularity and notice, acquiring influential friends, writing what he endeavored to convince himself was a major series of verse symphonies, a wife who put few obstacles in the path of bachelor perambulations among familiar Boston and Cambridge haunts, and an adoring, intelligent mistress to satisfy his feverish sexual itch and massage an ego that always needed attention. Better yet, he was fighting the good fight, the necessary fight against the second-raters, the "confectioners" and their reactionary cohorts: "These are the prettifiers, the brighteners of life, the lilting ones. They fill our standard magazines; they are annually herded by Mr. Braithwaite into his anthology; and now, taking advantage of the poetic decuman wave and the delusions of publishers, they are swamping the land with their sweet wares."

The war overseas, the most visible tokens of which were the trash cans spread around the Boston Common to collect the peach pits that were dried and used in gas masks, shrank to insignificance in comparison to his personal conflicts against the philistines taking over the literary revolution of 1912. Though still convinced that there was little poetry being written in the country "which we can hopefully put beside the recent work of the English poets," excepting Frost, Masters, Lowell, Fletcher, and Robinson, he again and again assaulted, with superb close readings on occasion, books by contemporaries he deemed grossly overpraised. For instance, of Sandburg's *Chicago Poems* he wrote: "Next to his deficiencies as regards form, it is perhaps Mr. Sandburg's greatest fault that he allows the poet to be outtalked by the sociologist." Toward Lindsay's *The Chinese Nightingale and Other Poems* he expressed "amazement at the author's solemn inclination to ambitions so childish, performances so amateurishly and stately inept. . . . Remember that it is the poet's office not merely to entertain, but also, on a higher plane, to delight with beauty and to amaze with understanding." Even when deprecating Williams's refreshingly original verses in *Al Que Quiere*—one of the few reviews the book received—as "more amiable than beautiful, more entertaining than successful," he could appreciate that the poetry "is at least real" and that there "is humor in it, too, which is rare enough in contemporary verse."

However wrong at times or unduly impressed by the conventional modes of English craftsmen, Aiken never hesitated to criticize those poets, editors, and fellow critics who he believed were responsible for nourishing exaggerated ideas of the worth of inferior native products, even though he knew their displeasure could have a negative effect on his own advancement. He was willing to maintain a relationship of "friendly enmity" with them as he did with Braithwaite and did so with surprising ease. Lindsay, for instance, counted him among his comrades, accepting his outbursts as the automatic reflexes of a pugnacious but well-meaning personality and suspecting that they contained much truth. The poets of the era, each wrapped in his or her own delusion of grandeur, expected to be stabbed in the back more than once by envious or incompetent soldiers-in-arms. Paranoia ranked second only to depression as the poet's commonest disease. Amy Lowell, with solid reasons, was one of the minority who saw in Aiken an implacable enemy whom she avoided whenever possible. Her feelings could only have been intensified when her *Tendencies in Modern American Poetry,* a critical study devoted to H.D., Frost, Robinson, Fletcher, Masters, and Sandburg, was published in November and promptly hacked to shreds by Aiken in the *Chicago News*.

Balanced, astringent, mostly on the mark, the review was often caustic: "It is, essentially, an adroit, though in the present reviewer's opinion erroneous, piece of propaganda. Posing as an impresario, an introducer of artists, Miss Lowell is really a Svengali; she is determined to have the art of singing develop in her own way . . . a certain intellectual unripeness and sketchiness, a proneness to hasty and self-satisfying conclusions without careful or accurate survey of the facts, make of Miss Lowell an amateur rather than a serious critic." The "propaganda" aspect—Eliot labeled her a "Director of Propaganda" in his *Egoist* review—lay in her scheme to posit Fletcher and H.D. (and by implication herself) at the apex of an evolutionary scale. Respecting the poetry of H.D. and Fletcher, with reservations, he had to reject as absurd the entire concept of imposing a Darwinian perspective, since "we have various different species of poet, and it is a falsification of the facts to say that one sort is necessarily in advance of another," grudgingly conceding, however, that "the papers on H.D. and Fletcher particularly are, despite bad arrangement, interesting and now and then illuminating." In fairness to Lowell, it should also be noted that in one of the final paragraphs she says of her six poets, "They represent all the trends in evidence in modern verse. Which of them will most influence the future it is impossible now to say."

Aiken's ability to separate art from politics and personalities was highlighted in the waning months of 1917 at a riotous, shameful meeting of the Poetry Society of America. The object of the uproar was Viereck, who had continued to champion his native Germany, despite America's entry into the war and the death in December 1916 (during a Radcliffe lecture) of his strongest ally, Hugo Münsterberg. Anti-German feelings were peaking, and the war was putting a tremendous strain upon democratic institutions as the "spy mania" swept the coast and government agencies infiltrated any organizations and journals that projected the slightest socialist or pacifist tinge, including the *Masses* and the *Seven Arts,* the latter a monthly founded by a rich patroness in November 1916 with James Oppenheim as its editor in chief and Brooks, Frost, Untermeyer, and Waldo Frank as associate editors. The angel behind the *Seven Arts,* Mrs. A. K. Rankine, withdrew her support under the pressure of adverse publicity in October, causing the magazine's collapse and probably contributing to her own suicide shortly thereafter. Frank, who had, along with Brooks, disapproved of Oppenheim's radical editorials and Bourne's brilliant series of antiwar essays, recollected: "Justice Department men came around the office pretending they were poets and writers and trying to see if they could turn up any sedition."

Aware at first hand of "the experiences and sensations of an American of German blood, facing a year or more the ecstatic Germanophobia of the rest of the population," Mencken had written in an April letter that "the position of actual Germans, of course, is very unpleasant. Some are already jailed." As would be true during World War II, and in spite of the leadership of a former Princeton president supposedly committed to democratic principles, the current hysteria was being abetted by the repressive measures of the very agencies established to protect individual rights. In August an issue of the *Masses* was barred from the mails, a prelude to the wholesale indictment of the entire staff under the Sedition Act less than a year later. Max Eastman would almost be lynched by a mob of soldiers. As Bourne wrote in "War and the Intellectuals" for the June issue of the *Seven Arts,* war entailed "the most noxious complex of all the evils that afflict men," leading him, in a final essay (appropriately titled "Twilight of Idols" after Nietzsche), into the rhetorical question that framed the entire national crisis: "Is not war perhaps the one social absolute, the one situation where the choice of ends ceases to function?"

Besides being entangled with the German Propaganda Bureau, Viereck made the mistake, with customary obnoxious bravado, of stridently defending Germany to the bitter last. He had already been expelled from the Authors' League, and now a resolution was introduced to banish him from the society he had helped inaugurate, although he and his wife had been among the brave handful of members to support Lowell's verse. Aiken was appalled, believing that the organization, as an artists' group, lacked the right to expel a member on political grounds, regardless of provocation. He, Masters, Markham, and a few others protested vigorously, "but it was not enough to carry the day." Aiken swallowed his outrage and remained a member of the society to the end of his life, an odd contrast to his behavior earlier at the New England Poetry Club.

War madness was not a pressing issue for his fundamentally insular mind, even when it posed a threat to academic freedom, as in the case of Columbia University denouncing Charles Beard, J. McKeen Cattell, and Henry W. L. Dana as subversive influences in October and forcing them off its faculty, a sign of the times that Bourne, a former student—but not Dewey, still on the faculty—vehemently protested. Aiken did not deviate from his position that art and politics were mutually exclusive domains, that a *littérature engagée* is practically impossible to achieve without sacrificing literary values, as his own maladroit "1915: The Trenches" in *Nocturne of Remembered Spring* attests. For him, the teacher at Columbia deserving attention was Joel Spingarn, an old Bourne nemesis since undergraduate days, who preached the doctrine of "creative criticism" in his English classes, an inevitable flowering of Pater's seeds which would later form the basis for the New Criticism of the 1930s and 1940s: "The poet's intentions must be judged at the moment of the creative act, as mirrored in the work of art itself, and not by the vague ambitions which he imagines to be his real intentions before or after the creative act is achieved." It was a statement any poet would resent, especially if in the midst of a grandiose project to link music with psychological realism and portraiture.

In *Creative Criticism,* a harvest of Spingarn's major essays, which Aiken read but did not review, the stress—echoing Brooks's previous fulminations against the suffocating didactic tradition in American literature—is always on paring away ethical and biographical extrania to enter and explicate the artifice as a self-contained, self-evident organism, proclaiming that the "poet's only moral duty, as a poet, is to be true to his art, and to express his vision of reality as well as he can." He is consciously aligned with Benedetto Croce, whom Aiken also read with mixed feelings and to whom the book is dedicated, crediting him with having "led aesthetic thought inevitably from the concept that art is expression to the conclusion that all expression is art." To Bourne, inextricably bound as he was to humanistic political and social touchstones, the crux peril of Spingarn's expressionist theories was that they permitted the gestation of monsters in their moral vacuums of technique, similar to the failure of Dewey's "instrumentalism" in the heat of the war's raging challenge.

Aiken, however, reacted warmly to the faintly 1890s notion that "the problem for criticism to attack is not the political ideals of the poet but the poetry which he had made out of them" and to Spingarn's credo that "the madness of poets is nothing more or less than unhampered freedom of self-expression. . . . To let one's self go—that is what art is always aiming at, and American art needs most of all." He could not abide the denigration of biographical criticism and the casual abrogation of a scientific (objective) platform for critical inquiry, which he thought he had located in his compound of Freud and Kostyleff. As a result, when he came to write "*Apologia Pro Specie Sua*" in 1919 he would lash Croce and Spingarn together as representative of a "sort of aesthetic solipsism" that replicated the fatal quicksands of relativity so clogging the less distinguished critical landscapes of Lowell and Untermeyer.

These were the issues that engaged Aiken, who was, like Pound, a man of letters to the marrow, never indifferent to social and political realities so much as confident that the questions and procedures of literature, such as his own exploration of mob psychology in *House of Dust,* could, if approached correctly, yield more foundational insights into the nature of mankind. Human problems were either private and temporal, geared to the unique individual, or massive and eternal, amenable to abstract laws of science; both were subject to the artist's fecund scrutiny and verifiable by psychoanalytic investigation. These were his cherished critical verities.

In the more relevant human calendar, the year swept to a pleasurable climax on December 4 when Jessie, again aided by McDonald relatives, gave birth to a healthy daughter, whom they named Jane. Doubtless this event somewhat relieved the distant, despairing retrospect of *Ushant*'s confession that the "consistent view" stayed out of reach during the clamorous war years.

If you are in possession of yourself

you will possess something you

would never wish to lose

and something

Fortune could never take away.

Boethius

. . . .

A CURIOUS REVERSAL

Frederick Lewis Allen, who had graduated from Harvard in 1912 with Aiken, would look back at the volatile period between the time of America's entrance into the war and the end of 1919 and discern chaos: "It was an era of lawless and disorderly defense of law and order, of unconstitutional defense of the Constitution, of suspicion and civil conflict—in a very literal sense, a reign of terror." Secular urban liberalism and evangelical rural conservatism clashed repeatedly, the fight for women's suffrage proceeding hand in hand to triumph with Prohibition, which had already been adopted by several farm states. The bull market surged into existence at a time when war-linked prosperity was squeezing prices into an inflationary spiral and swelling city rents, resulting in a severe housing shortage as the troops began returning. Against this background, aided by the manifold pressures of reluctant involvement in a European conflict and increasing labor unrest, the hysteria of the "Red Scare" mounted into paranoid proportions amid the government's repressive actions against left-wing organizations and sporadic demonstrations and acts of violence among communist and anarchist factions.

The ghosts in the country's closet—racism, misogyny, xenophobia, anti-Semitism—burst loose with a vengeance. Amy Lowell, for instance, reverting to her family's reactionary inheritance, could say to Braithwaite about the poet Leonora Speyer, who had wed Sir Edgar Speyer, financier of Robert Scott's polar expedition and Asquith's campaign for prime minister, "To think of her marrying that dirty little Jew for his money." And a Mencken, authentic champion of civil liberties, could write of the 1919 race riots in Chicago and Washington, D.C., that "the coons have fought back." When Floyd Dell participated in a demonstration for women's suffrage in Manhattan the next year, he was set upon by a mob of military men and punched for his troubles, escaping more serious injury only because of a female companion and the brave actions of a conscientious trolley car conductor.

Aiken, on the other hand, though disgusted by prejudice and the right-wing assaults on civil rights, would recollect these turbulent, harrowing years as a halcyon interlude of creative discovery: "As for my circumstances, mental and physical, during this period of gestation: all I can say is that I experienced during those four years a tremendous feeling of fecundity, excitement (the war here played its part) and well-being . . . everything was ripe at this period for my own perfect freedom for intellectual and emotional adventure into chaos. I attacked the thing with gusto, had the time of my life, felt an extraordinary energy and sureness of insight, and only began to distrust the latter when the books, one after another, fell dead." Poems were being written, literary battles waged, and that, as usual, seemed sufficient to keep insanity and the madding crowd at bay, including, in an emotional sense, the burden of a wife and two children.

In February 1918 Malcolm Cowley, Harvard junior and neophyte poet, impressed by the "symphonic form" of *The Jig of Forslin,* secured Aiken's Walnut Street address from Edmund Brown and wrote of his admiration. An exchange of letters led to an agreement to meet in the palm tree–studded lobby of Boston's Touraine Hotel, where Cowley was told to "look for a man in an orange necktie who wasn't a fairy," which he did: "On that unseasonably warm evening in February . . . I saw the necktie as he came in the door; it was brighter than his Valencia-orange hair. For the rest he wore the Harvard uniform of the period: white button-down Oxford shirt and brown suit. His forehead was high . . . his jaw square and his eyes were set wide apart. The impression he gave me was a mixture of shyness and pugnacity." The meeting went well and they had dinner together, probably "at Jake Wirth's beerhall, which, being German in spirit, had plenty of empty tables in those wartime days." They uncovered various common tastes: "We both liked Boston in decay, we admired the French symbolist poets, we wanted to achieve architectural and musical effects in our poems (I in theory, Conrad in practice), and we were fascinated by the political maneuvers of the poetry world, without wishing to take part in them."

Their conversation lasted far into the night: "We talked without pauses, talked with such excitement—at least on my part—that I didn't notice the streets through which we wandered before parting at the door of Conrad's lodging house on the unfashionable side of Beacon Hill." Destined to remain a loyal friend and supporter, Cowley found in Aiken what his closest friends, invariably men or undemanding sexual partners like Marian, found in him: "The shyest man I know, he is also the best talker. The shyness usually keeps him from talking in company, except for an occasional pun—there *are* good puns and Conrad makes them—spoken in a voice so low that most of the company misses it. Only quite late at night, or earlier with a single friend, does he launch into one of the monologues that ought to be famous for their mixture of flagrant wit and complete unself-protective candor." Cowley describes Aiken's speaking voice as "quiet, rapid, Old Bostonian without the broad A, and always correctly punctuated—with some words audibly underlined and some phrases preceded and followed by pauses like parentheses." Aiken apparently exercised the same care with the technical aspects of his speech as he did with his fluent poetry.

And the fluency of the poetry written during "the enormously productive years from 1915 to 1920," if not its worth, was beyond question. Cowley, who left for France in the middle of the year and would not return until June 1919, when he visited the Aikens at Cape Cod with his new wife, faithfully insisted that the reputation Aiken earned in these years as a facile poet was "undeserved." In the latter half of 1917, after finishing *The House of Dust*, Aiken had deliberately, to quote Peterson, "looked about for a traditional theme which he could elaborate along fresh lines, bringing to some synthesis his diverse psychological speculations . . . and happened to select the classic figure of Punch, bombastic clown of the *Commedia dell' arte*, who became the hero of the puppet stage." A clown was perhaps an inevitable mask in light of his emotional allegiance to the England of the 1890s and his great enthusiasm for "The Comedian as the Letter C" of Wallace Stevens; he did his homework studiously, working from the account in the *Encyclopedia Britannica* up to more comprehensive tomes in the Boston Athenaem library, securing a special pass to its restricted shelves. By the start of 1918 he had already completed the first two sections (almost half) of *Punch: The Immortal Liar*, but he unaccountably halted and devoted the next five or six months to writing "Tetélestai" and *Senlin: A Biography*, along with a series of pointed reviews.

Though he enjoyed the trips to New York and consorting with Kreymborg and his complex of *Others* contributors, as well as with many of the same experimental writers and artists gathering at Lola Ridge's East Fourteenth Street apartment beginning in mid-1919, Aiken's review of the second *Others* anthology was hardly panegyric. He coupled the magazine's experimental openness to Pound's "curiocollecting," which he said was "a delightful vein in verse" demanding no "great exertion of the reader." And he reiterated a "purist" stance by describing the "major tenet" of Kreymborg's "variegated band" of contributors as "the expression of a sensation or mood as briefly and pungently (and oddly?) as possible, with or without the aids of rhyme, meter, syntax, or punctuation." With expected disdain he passed lightly over "the studiously cerebral obscurantism of Marianne Moore, the tentacular quiverings of Mina Loy, the prattling iterations of Alfred Kreymborg, the delicate but amorphous selfconsciousness of Jeanne d'Orge, Helen Hoyt, and Orrick Johns" to pause "with admiration and delight before the 'Preludes' and 'Rhapsody on a Windy Night' by T. S. Eliot and 'Thirteen Ways of Looking at a Blackbird' by Wallace Stevens."

Excepting his dismissal of Moore, he was on the mark, his appreciation of Eliot and Stevens borne out by time and unhurried taste, an appreciation stemming in part from a perception of shared aims. Stevens's quest for transcendence through the luxurious reification of certain philosophical ideas about consciousness's creative facets, often playful and musically scored, matched his own forays into the same territory, and Eliot's psychological interests and reliance on traditional techniques, also musically construed, reaffirmed a personal bias: "It is significant . . . that Mr. Eliot uses rhyme and meter, a telling demonstration that the use of these ingredients may add power and finish and speed to poetry without in any way dulling the poet's tactile organs or clouding his consciousness—provided he has the requisite skill." More pertinent, after tagging the two Eliot poems as "in a very minor way, masterpieces of black-and-white impressionism," his acute final comment again points up the way in which Eliot was both helping and hindering his career: "Personality, time, and environment—three attributes of the dramatic—are set sharply before us by means of a rapid and concise report of the seemingly irrelevant and tangential, but really centrally significant observations of a shadowy protagonist."

Aiken, alas, would continue to depend upon vague interior monologues of a "shadowy protagonist" without duplicating the other positive qualities enumerated in the review: the "dramatic" element his verses lacked and Eliot's abundantly possessed, the conciseness and swiftness of effects that protect such protagonists from drifting off into disconnected fragments of imagistic extremes or into musical measures ultimately remote from the psychological processes being probed. Eliot himself is not always free of these flaws in the two poems, but the vividness of their jagged, strikingly juxtaposed tropes and the sheer force of their energizing despair carry them out of danger, as does their relative brevity. The problem is clearer in the second half of the review, in which Aiken is enraptured by *The Closed Door* of Jean de Bosschere, a Flemish poet residing in England. Once more the virtues celebrated in the de Bosschere collection reveal why Aiken's fluency had yet to locate an efficient form. After claiming that de Bosschere might have influenced "Prufrock" (he sees the Belgian as "in several respects . . . a maturer and more powerful Eliot"), Aiken isolates specifics: "These poems, in a colloquial but rich and careful free verse, occasionally using rhyme and a regular ictus, very frequently employing a melodic line which borders on the prosodic, seem at first glance to be half-whimsical and half-cerebral, seem to be in a key which is at once naive and gaily precious, with overtones of caricature; in reality they are masterpieces of ironic understatement and reveal upon closer scrutiny a series of profound spiritual or mental tragedies."

It is significant that he summons up "symbolism" and "a negative mysticism of disbelief and disenchantment" to describe de Bosschere's attitude and method, applauding him as a poet "who happens to be highly developed on the cerebral side, as well as on the tactile." This surely reflects Aiken's false picture of himself at the time, "a poet for whom the most terrible and most beautiful realities are in the last analysis ideas." In the review he quotes portions of a poem called *"Doutes"* to show that beneath its "idiosyncratic" narrative surface of a child's bitter discoveries of world and self "we have really an autobiography of disillusionment which is cosmic in its applicability"—the essential goal of his own symphonic tone poems, including autobiographical data clad in a distancing disguise. A few lines from the de Bosschere verses illustrate the correspondences:

> Nevertheless he still believes,
> Ax in hand, this burlesque of a man still believes:
> He will cut his dream, four-square, in the hearts of men.

The rhetoric, the Punch figure, the adolescent heroics, the taint of Pre-Raphaelite and Decadent posturing, all replicate Aiken's aesthetic, even down to the godhead quest, especially the "thoughtwrinkled" straining after philosophic weight.

Shortly after or simultaneous with the review, Aiken wrote "Tetélestai," which Martin declares "his first approach to the shortening of the symphonic mode." Its Christ center (and absent father) dovetails with de Bosschere's "doubts" of deity, though the poem evokes Shelley's "Ozymandias" and its desert air: "How shall we praise the magnificence of the dead, / The great man humbled, the haughty brought to dust?" Yet the presence of such potent personal configurations as the crucified Christ and intimations of a failing father, added to obsessive, child-magnified death fears—"Look! this flesh how it crumbles to dust and is blown!"—does not generate enough emotive drive to pierce a façade of grandiloquent Romanticism, despite a daring and prophetic shift behind the scenery in the last two of the five sections, where a protagonist nearer the poet is assumed:

The pencil dulls in my hand: I see through the window
Walls upon walls of windows with faces behind them,
. . . I am vanquished
By terror of life. The walls mount slowly about me
In coldness.

A buried life, Arnold would agree, but the final section, another defeat, projects empathy alone rather than a sudden stab of revelation or resistance, more flares of trumpets: "This, then, is the one who implores, as he dwindles to silence, / A fanfare of glory. . . . And which of us dares to deny him?"

Senlin: A Biography, which immediately followed, risks a further step into the chamber of his own psyche. It commences with a recognizable mirror image:

Senlin sits before us, and we see him . . .
He smokes his pipe before us, and we hear him . . .
Is he small, with reddish hair,
Does he light his pipe with a meditative stare,
And a pointed flame reflected in both eyes?

Interrogative distance enables the character to glide from reality into myth, another variation on Prufrock's timidity about disturbing the universe, offering a reply and an elaboration instead of mere contemplation, which is a definite advance. The varied, enjambed formula eases the line along, and a cosmic, speculative manner swings closer to Whitman, wanting a self that can amass more than self:

Or was I the single ant, or tinier thing,
That crept from the rocks of buried time
And dedicated its holy life to climb
From atom to beetling atom, jagged grain to grain,
Patiently out of the darkness we call sleep
Into the hollow gigantic world of light
Thinking the sky to be its destined shell,
Hoping to fit it well!—

As Aiken later explained, the name "Senlin" means literally "the 'little old man' that each of us must become," a thematic structure thus presaging Mr. Arcularis, a series of vicarious identities similar to the more extravagant scheme of *The Jig of Forslin*, erected upon the "perennially fascinating problem of personal identity which perplexes each of us all his life." *Senlin* is distinguished from its symphonic predecessors by the felicitous introduction of the concrete. Although Senlin hardly acquires three-dimensional density or

complexity, he does engage in specific actions, almost rotelike in their or-
dinariness, which prevent the poem from slipping away too frequently into the
lush image-making his creator was prone to appropriate as befitting a stream-
of-consciousness flow:

> I arise, I face the sunrise,
> And do the things my fathers learned to do.
> Stars in the purple dusk above the rooftops
> Pale in a saffron mist and seem to die,
> And I myself on a swiftly tilting planet
> Stand before a glass and tie my tie.

The poem's Freudian base, extended by ambiguous bows to Jung's animas,
racial memories, and a collective unconscious, does not schematize exces-
sively, as was true in *The Jig of Forslin,* and echoes of Eliot slyly avoid the
appearance of gross imitations. The symphonic arrangement, necessarily relying upon recurrent mood chords and syntactical repetitions, also blends in
more harmoniously with the thematic plan, again because the protagonist's
narrative gestures evade the mire of tedious introspective ornamentation.

But *Senlin* is not sufficiently intense to guarantee the staying power of a
"Prufrock," which is not solely the consequence of Eliot's superior metaphoric brush and dramatic-collage script. Time and again, Aiken's poem in-
terjects a crucial private memory or figurative touchstone, as in " 'Is it my
childhood there,' he asks, / 'Sealed in a hearse and hurrying by?' " and " 'Or
am I rather the moonlight, spreading subtly / Above those stones and times a
silver mesh?' " But the self-pursuit never dives further into the past or into his
own psyche. Instead, while tailing the banal Senlin through his day of wall-
building, it plays variations upon the idea of serial and diverse egos as a
single, mobile psyche at the brink of divinity. The confident handling of various conceits, such as the Whitman spider, which belongs to Frost's "Design"
as well, invites admiration and proffers distinct pleasures without touching the
heart. As anticlimax there is a retreat into Poe's melodramatic fears of an
unreal self, the past as Gothic stagecraft, which deftly encapsulates the
poem's perceptual convolutions while skirting a trapdoor dynamo:

> Yet we would say, this was no man at all,
> But a dream we dreamed and vividly recall;
> And we are mad to walk in wind and rain
> Hoping to find, somewhere, that dream again.

Since poet and poem tend to develop reciprocal lines of communication, it
seems reasonable to conclude that *Senlin* mirrored Aiken's growing awareness
of his identity's treacherous fluidity, confirming Bradley's bleak observation

that the self's only sure unity resided in the "immediate unity of a finite psychical center." If he also suspected that he was, like Kohut's superior narcissist, defending himself against the absence of an integrated ego— Nietzsche compared man to a rope stretched across an abyss—the knowledge helps to explain the poem's larger failure, its timidity. Reuel Denney believes "Senlin is too much like a woman to be a woman's lover. Yet the non-male in Senlin is not alive and active; it is, in every sense except recollection of it, dead." Sexual passivity, conventionally female or prepubic, suggests another intimidating polarity. In a candid letter to Allen Tate in 1926 Aiken would admit he lacked conviction during the composition of the symphonies, assessing their main worth in terms of thematic ambitions. Typically, he also viewed this as a refutation of Eliot, of his dictum that there were no major themes left for the modern poet to scale.

Regardless, except in some extended fragments and several graceful lyrics, he had never written as well. The interweaving of identity tropes within a lucid framework of familiar concerns—death and old age, alternative selves, Freudian dream strategies, and the like—implies that he was now consciously launched on a voyage of discovery toward his own *Preludes,* that the master plan of the symphonies was part of his imagination's interior map. From this point forward the fundamental problem would involve courage and will, not art alone. It would be years before Senlin could be metamorphosized into Arcularis, before he could abandon Crispin's desperate partial truth that what "counted was mythology of self, / Blotched out beyond unblotching." Unless nourished by the individual unconscious's original energies, no created identity can survive on borrowed mythic repasts. Made rigid by neurotic reflex, a mask easily cracks or shatters when thrust into a replay of a primal drama, as Aiken would sadly learn in 1920.

At least *Senlin: A Biography,* when published on October 28, 1918, with *The Charnel Rose* as a single volume, would bring a substantial taste of the critical acclaim he yearned for, which was not the case with "Tetélestai." William Carlos Williams, whose "run-over line" influenced its style, "could only find 'Tetélestai' absurd in essence, and it is said," Peterson reports, "he wrote an amusing prose parody of Aiken's 'pathetic glorification of the humble.' " Frost, a less open opponent, espying secret enemies everywhere, later dubbed its creator "Comrade Aching" in a letter to Untermeyer.

After *Senlin* was done, Aiken's life resumed its relative calm. Even the Work-or-Fight Act, promulgated in February and directed at people like himself who were not engaged in essential labor, did not disturb him. Because of Jessie and the children, he was already in the safe Class II category, and it was unlikely that the draft board would bother to alter his status. Of more pressing concern was the deteriorating housing situation. The attic flat was too crowded for the four of them, and later in the year he found more spacious accommodations at 6 Craigie Circle in Cambridge, which had the added advantage of a less urban environment and the proximity of the Potters. In the meantime, reviews of *Nocturne of Remembered Spring* were slowly dribbling in, causing him to regret having rushed into print and exacerbating the uncertainty always gnawing at him beneath his impassive exterior.

His Cambridge neighbor, Braithwaite, delighted at having a legitimate excuse for paying back a brash nemesis in kind, used one of Aiken's favorite terms of derision as a bludgeon in his March 20 *Transcript* review: "From the sentimental title, the sentimental conception of his themes, which is ever and eternally the sensual passion of love, to the sentimental language employed, these poems, written in musical connotations, are a continuous weariness of flesh and hectic wail of despair. The poet puts into his vague and incoherent utterances no will, no mind to give them substance." When his magazine annual appeared in the fall, Braithwaite did not include the book in his list "Some Important Volumes of Poetry" and reprinted none of Aiken's poems published in various journals. Also, his Introduction was devoted to tearing down Aiken's Kostyleff review-essay and Bodenheim's article "What Is Poetry?" in the *New Republic* (December 22, 1917), defending, in essence, the marshmallow impressionism Aiken had sought to undermine in his assaults upon the previous anthologies: "Mr. Aiken desires that judgement should be scientific. A poem should be analyzed with exactness, the process should be cold and calculating. . . . As a matter of fact the reality of poetry lies wholly in the abstract, and to reach that reality . . . is completely a matter of sentiment and not science." He relates Aiken's "mechanical performance" theory to Poe's earlier, unsuccessful flights into the same realm, though concluding that he has "nothing like Poe's genius for intellectual subtlety or logic"—an absurd statement in view of Poe's deficiencies in both areas.

Braithwaite's blast was somewhat counteracted by Fletcher's kinder review in the *Dial*'s March 28 issue, which burrows beneath the debris for omens of future victories: "In his more recent work Aiken contents himself with repeating his familiar cry. There is an atmosphere of boredom about it all, a hint of yawns, a trail of dust. . . . Conrad Aiken is developing, after all, and when he arrives in the country whither he is tending, I caution the dry-rotting celebrities of yesteryear in America to look out! They will find a poet." An anonymous *New York Times* (July 7) reviewer similarly stressed the potential for achievement implicit in the collection's failure. Aiken, this reviewer wrote, stubbornly "walks, like his own hero, 'in a pleasure of sorrow along the street.' He has in him the makings of a psychological poet of great keenness and originality. But in most of these 'Nocturnes,' 'Meditations,' and 'Sonatas,' the psychology is hidden too deep in the web of the flesh." None of the reviewers detected the large debt owed Eliot by *Nocturne of Remembered Spring;* they merely identified Aiken as a "psychological poet" and "sensualist"—tags he was proud to wear. Sensuality, like music, was a quality he thought contemporary American poetry sorely missed, which indeed it did and does.

When June arrived, the Aikens returned to Cuttingsville, their last season there, and he resumed work on *Punch,* laboring over its architecture and his "hills of Golden Bantam corn" (213), the simple physical demands of the latter removing him from a troubled world and nation. The first trial of the editors of the *Masses,* which had disappeared and was replaced in February by the *Liberator,* had begun on April 15. Although both trials, a year apart, would culminate in acquittals, more than a thousand International Workers of the World (IWW) members ("Wobblies") were not so fortunate, including Eugene Debs, earning stiff sentences of ten years or more. A week after the first *Masses* trial commenced, the government had tacked an amendment onto the Espionage Act that Mencken judged "astoundingly drastic" in its curtailment of individual freedoms. By June, American and Allied troops were invading Russia and the deadly Spanish influenza epidemic had started to sweep across Europe. Closer to home, word drifted through early in August that Joyce Kilmer had been killed at the Second Battle of the Marne on July 30, a loss to his friends but not to such a serious poet as Aiken, who appreciated that a poem like "Trees" was the epitome of a philistine antiart attitude and praxis (Vachel Lindsay would surmise with bitterness that "the American people hate and abhor poetry").

Affirmation of Lindsay's pessimism came via a notice to Aiken from his draft board, summoning him down from Cuttingsville to show cause why he should not either seek useful employment or allow himself to be conscripted (212). Before confronting the board he called upon Marian, and they arranged to meet afterward for lunch at the Westminster Roof Garden. The board insisted that he must locate other employment besides writing or be transferred to Class I, despite his dependents. It was an issue—aesthetic and moral tenets conjoined under social pressure—that brought out the best in Aiken.

As he explained: "The real principle at issue was not whether an artist should, *ipso facto,* be totally exempt (that I do not believe), but whether certain occupations having been decided to be less essential than others, the writing of poetry was to be included among the inferior occupations. This implication I should, in common with all other artists, vigorously resent." Asked if he had made any effort to secure other employment, he replied in the negative and "submitted that artists had in no way, it seemed to me, to be implicated in the Work-or-Fight Act." The board passed his objection on to higher authorities for a ruling, and a General Crowder in Washington eventually decreed that the author was in fact "usefully" employed, although the decision was not reached out of any consideration for the innate value of the arts but out of fear that reporters and other newspaper employees might also have to be reclassified. The ruling elicited much comment, "a little mocking, a little condescending, a trifle cynical" (214), with colleagues and the small magazines hailing it as another token of a new cultural maturity.

Harriet Monroe ran an enthusiastic editorial in the November 1918 issue of *Poetry,* lauding his stand, which she interpreted as demanding exemption for poets on the basis of their work's intrinsic worth, and Lindsay wrote to her on November 3: "I think you ought to get a more definite statement from Conrad Aiken about what he did in regard to deferred classification, and *since he has taken this stand,* persuade him to apply some of his wasted tartness on one very good issue . . . as an issue for boys yet unborn. Aiken is equipped with the proper vitriol to fight it out." Aiken's blunt candor did not have to be solicited. He wrote to Monroe on November 20 to correct her false impression: "It would have been indeed quixotically courageous of me to have asked military exemption on the ground that I was a poet. . . . The question was whether under the Work-or-Fight Law the writing of poetry was to be classed as non-productive—along with billiard-marking, setting up candle-pins, and speculation in theatre-tickets—and whether artists in general would have to change their occupation. . . . Was the consequent decision more commercial, perhaps, than idealistic in motive? *Hac itur ad astra!*"

Four days before writing the letter and five days after Armistice Day, under a banner headline ("LOADING POETRY WITH SHRAPNEL") and a large photo of Aiken ("The Poet Who Dared") spread across the front page of part 3 of the Saturday *Evening Transcript,* Braithwaite interviewed him. The war had produced "no more historic incident for America than in the event of bringing about the official recognition of the art of poetry," wrote Braithwaite extravagantly. Real frankness also surfaced:

We have been and are critical antagonists, as every one knows who has followed the fortunes of the art within the past few years. Our aims . . . have been the same—to win respect, appreciation, and support for poetry; our points of view and the method for attacking those aims have been antithetical. It has been a friendly warfare, in which neither side has refrained from using sharp weapons to pierce the arguments of the other. But nothing gives me greater happiness today than to publicly grasp the hand of my antagonist and commend him to the public for the splendid service, apart from his creative achievement, he has rendered the art of poetry in America and the future generations of American poets.

The inevitable question about the contretemps with the board yielded a modest explanation and disclaimer. Aiken requested that credit be given "where it belongs, to General Crowder." Of greater interest is his definition of poets as "those who, in whatever degree, extend the sphere of man's consciousness by being in some ways more conscious than their fellows, and by finding a more complex language to give this consciousness expression." This is pure monkish conviction, a commitment and vision that never changed, fueling the realization of his finest work to come. When specifically asked about his theory and practice, Aiken gave a brief outline of his progress: "I began with a kind of obsession that one should be tirelessly telling the truth; that effects of charm or beauty in poems should be purely ancillary to that purpose. Perhaps *Earth Triumphant* represents that Quixotic phase. The vaudeville sketches in *Turns and Movies* represented a weakening of the view (a use of the realistic genre solely for its own sake), *The Jig of Forslin* a complete abandonment of it, and *Nocturne of Remembered Spring* a somewhat temperate and romanticized return to it."

More honest is his admission that "I know so little about my own work that it would take me at least a volume to say it. . . . Poets, like potatoes, simply grow; they don't know what they're after. They can leave that to the psychiatrists." To a query about general "tendencies and achievements" in contemporary verse, Aiken noted its amazing variety, "a period of creative destructiveness, of restless exploration," and said he was glad to be alive at "a time when *The Congo, Men, Women and Ghosts, North of Boston,* and *Cornhuskers* were first published." But in reply to inquiries about "extreme radicalism" and the "future of *vers libre,*" he reverted to a more conservative posture: "I do not think extreme radicalism prevails even now, but that we have already seen literary bolshevism pass its height. Even those poets who went farthest towards artistic nihilism, whether in style or thought, are beginning to see the value of form and order."

Doubtless the interview impressed Boston with Aiken's increasing reputation, which must have pleased him, although his stand at the draft board was not well accepted by his relatives, particularly his angry in-laws, who condemned the public confrontation with the government as disgracefully unpatriotic. Nor did his unquestioned integrity extend into the sexual arena. In the same section of *Ushant* in which he recounts the struggle against conscription, he narrates a shameful episode that had taken place early in his relationship with Marian. He had presented her with a lovingly inscribed copy of one of his books, which had thrilled her, then regretted his action, fearful that she might use it to take advantage of him. As a result, one evening after careful planning, "he had torn out the incriminating page, while she was out of the room, and crumpled it in his pocket" (211). This action is remarkable evidence of his instinctive distrust of women, a predisposition to see them always as capable of betrayal, instant infidelity, however loving and generous in actuality.

The Charnel Rose, published with *Senlin* the same week that Braithwaite interviewed him, is equally revealing of the ambiguous, often hostile feelings females evoked in his mind and imagination, its prolix poetry less important than the nympholepsy it strives to embody and exploit. Thanks again to Peterson, we have the biographical scenario behind Aiken's attraction to the suggestive topic:

> In the wandering course of his youthful *Confessions* George Moore spoke of "a terrible malady the ancients knew and called nympholepsy. . . . And the disease is not extinct in these modern days, nor will it ever be so long as men shall yearn for the unobtainable." That passage and especially that exotic word, nympholepsy, fixed Aiken's attention, for he was himself an incorrigible nympholep made worse by early communion with Poe, fatally devoted to some lost Lenore, and he found the same theme gorgeously expressed in Strauss's tone poem, *Don Juan,* who was not a promiscuous sensualist or sadist but an insatiable and tragic dreamer, passing from love to love in quest of the absolute."

Aiken had described to Peterson how he mated "this loose theme" to the idea "of a single human consciousness as simply a *chorus:* a chorus of voices, influences. As if one's sum total of awareness and identity were merely handed to one progressively and piecemeal by the environment. As if one were a mirror." The Preface to *The Charnel Rose* is similarly intent upon the sequence's ideational system, the theme of nympholepsy approached "as that impulse which sends us from one dream, or ideal, to another, always disillusioned, always creating for adoration some new and subtler fiction," and as deliberate musical analog. "Beginning with the lowest order of love, the merely carnal, the theme leads irregularly, with returns and anticipations as in music, through various phases of romantic or idealistic love, to several variants of sexual mysticism."

Once again, Aiken had chosen a subject that should have tapped the fount of his repressed ambivalence toward women, the divided nature of his adolescent craving for their bodies and his contrary prepubic revulsion, an insatiable appetite for mastery and submission, for flesh and ideal, the paradox of a chaste consummation. Instead, another series of masks is forged and employed along the lines of vicarious psychological experiences projected into a safe rational mode, truly of a piece with the prior symphonic sequences. But the word and its connotations—hints of sexual anarchy, hidden forces—tend to expose more than anticipated. The private self or selves remain secreted, to be sure, yet occasionally, amid the Machenlike mist and Beardsleyan lamias, a nerve is jostled and genuine poetry spouts forth, as in this scene refashioned from "The Jolly Corner" of James:

> He was tired: he longed for death.
> He turned but met himself again in darkness,
> Pacing noiselessly, like a ghost, through darkness;
> And upon his face came softly his own breath.

Beyond sporadic lurches at netting a few death-obsessed nightmares, the strongest point of *The Charnel Rose* is the quest for a figurative language to convey censorious sexual material, as in Part 2 of the first section, where wet dream and masturbation are combined with high romance and terror:

> . . . High on his cliff, above high sands,
> He saw the moonlit ocean come
> In ever-inward rings of foam,
> Heard them break to shoot and seethe
> Ever inward far beneath:
> The ringed horizon rhythmic coming
> And in the moonlight silent foaming:
> But the dream changed: thick minutes dripped:
> Between his fingers a fleet light slipped:
>   Was gone, was lost:
> And on the sand, or in his brain,
> He saw red roses fall again:
> Rose-wreathed skeletons advanced
> And clumsily lifted foot and danced:
> And he saw the roses drop apart
> Each to disclose a charnel heart.

The passage is also a marvelous summary of key Aiken motifs: the sea and moonlight, recurrent dreams, sex without love, the ubiquitous dance of death. Freed by Freud, at least on the rational plane, from the overt embarrassments of an American nurture, Aiken treats his subjects in a surprisingly erotic fashion, ranging from straightforward copulation to the necrophilia that governs the sequence's imaginative progress. Ambivalent obsession with death fuses with a fierce love-hate conception of women, paradigms of the madonna-whore reductionism stifling his art. Characteristic too is the Manichean sundering of love from sex, which is both infantile and adolescent. Whores from the mauve decade (exaggerated and weary) alternate with doomed maidens (suffused with unearthly perfection and inner decay) from Poe's coffin climaxes, though the rose trope introduces and reverses Dante as well. There is also a Beatrice, the Beatrice of a paradisal rose and as guide to the ascetic redemption of *La Vita Nuova*.

Repetitive in metaphor and music, *The Charnel Rose* clothes psychoanalytic notions in literature (a danger Eliot warned against) in the twilight glare of Wildean decadence, again only partially venting unconscious pressures. Poe is the primary medium, and to understand the symphonies, what they are, and why they failed, it is necessary only to recall Dwight MacDonald's not unsympathetic recapitulation of Poe's methodology: "Few poets have taken their themes more directly from their own lives, and few have treated them in a more deliberately artificial style worked out according to a theory." *The Charnel Rose* did allow the schema of the symphonies to proceed toward its grandiose goal, a multifaceted exploration of human mental processes. Aiken would work on *The Pilgrimage of Festus*, last in the series, through 1919 and a portion of 1920. When all five symphonies were finally published together as a single work, *The Divine Pilgrim*, almost thirty years after their completion, he would revise *The Charnel Rose* considerably, confessing a need to carve out "its youthful exuberance and rhetoric, its Blue Flower romanticism and Krafft-Ebing decadence."

The necromania of *The Charnel Rose* had a gruesome appropriateness; the month it was supposed to appear, October, witnessed, in its first day, the peak of the Spanish influenza's onslaught against Boston. Only 3 to 4 percent of the people who contracted the disease perished, but the absolute numbers were staggering: the epidemic would kill half a million people in the United States and some 22 million worldwide, about twice the number of fatalities recorded during the entire war. Urban centers were hardest hit, of course, and Boston had experienced its first cases by September. At the end of the month, as the death rate continued to rise, filling the streets with a steady procession of black carriages and new high-topped limousines, city schools were closed. The governor ordered theaters and churches to lock their doors. The emergency would not be declared over until October had passed.

Aiken's closest brush with the scourge occurred when Bodenheim and a friend of his named Sonnenschein traveled up to Boston early in the course of the epidemic. Bodenheim came down with the flu, and Aiken was forced to nurse him, while Sonnenschein returned to Manhattan, where he also was stricken. Once recovered, thanks to Aiken's kind aid and the resources of his own young body, Bodenheim went back to New York, but his friend eventually succumbed to the pneumonia that often followed the flu. Another casualty was Aiken's *Dial* colleague Randolph Bourne, who died that December at the age of thirty-two.

Bourne had said, "Men stupid enough to resort to war are too stupid to make peace," a prediction tragically borne out by the events at the Versailles Peace Conference, where a vain, sick Woodrow Wilson would be manipulated into signing a vindictive treaty that ensured another world war, as Walter Lippmann (author of the "Fourteen Points") foresaw. The waning months of 1918, highlighted by a Socialist parade up Fifth Avenue in New York on Armistice Day that climaxed with a group of soldiers and sailors wading "into the procession, tearing down red flags, punching both men and women," were a time of continued satisfaction for Aiken. The move to Cambridge, the affair with Marian, the publication of another book, the flurry of publicity in connection with his draft stand, and the absorbing work on the last symphony conspired to promote a sense of well-being and accomplishment at odds with the disruptions and economic hardships stalking the land and disaffecting a growing band of young intellectuals and artists.

Snug inside the sanctuary of a poet's egotism, he was not indifferent to the schism wrenching the nation apart, merely unable or unwilling to test the social and political measure of its seriousness. Though a liberal, Aiken was mired in the white Anglo-Saxon tradition of New England Unitarianism that invariably underestimated human evil, perceiving outbreaks of violence as distasteful aberrations, momentary detours in America's implacable march toward the better life. He viewed the cancerous spread of the Ku Klux Klan and the red-baiting mobs that would pillage Socialist and union offices throughout the next year with disgust, but they could never be as important to him as a new collection of poems by Lowell or the victory of the Boston Red Sox over the Chicago White Sox four games to two in the 1918 World Series.

Aiken channeled extra energy into his reviews and letters, battling contemporaries and seeking to reinforce unsteady critical standards. His stubborn preference for English poets was expressed in a dual review of Masefield and Robert Nichols in the July 18 *Dial*. He dismissed Masefield's *Rosas* but overpraised the young Nichols's *Ardours and Endurances* as "one of the most remarkable of recent first books of verse—perhaps the most remarkable since *North of Boston*. . . . One can think of no poet in a decade or so who has come upon us with so richly prepared a sensibility, who takes such a gusto in sensation, or who writes of it with such brio." Glib superlatives about an arrogant visitor, "a sort of *literateur*-propagandist for the Allies," who had never hesitated to air his low opinion of American poets.

Aiken also used the *Chicago News* to review himself once more, *The Charnel Rose,* this time (December 4) relying on a dream formula to mock his colleagues without really considering the book. The frame is a letter to the editor (dated November 30, 1918) explaining how the following account of a dream was saved when the author found Aiken stuffing the manuscript into a lit fireplace: "Knowing how many masterpieces had already been sacrificed on the altar of his modesty I seized it." Excessive modesty is Aiken's sole charge against himself in the dream dialogue among contemporaries, though he reiterates previous criticisms of his poetry by having himself admit he feeds words into "a little machine," which "turns out the finest metrical verse . . . quite indistinguishable from the genuine article." For *The Charnel Rose,* he claims "that by mistake this little engine was fed a volume of Havelock Ellis," and for *Senlin:* "I am ashamed to admit it—it was *Alice in Wonderland.*" In tears, Aiken is then consoled by Amy Lowell, pictured throughout as floating on a cloud as if it were a divan: " 'Well, never mind, Conrad! Now that we KNOW you're not a poet, I think we're all going to like you much, much better.' (She taps him playfully with her fan: he collapses. The poets step away one by one over his prostrate body.)"

It is fun, if sharp-edged and malicious on occasion, each speaker true to his or her style and personality, Williams comparing his verses to "split B.V.D.'s, basted," Braithwaite bubbling over with hyperbole, Bodenheim losing himself in a fog of language, and Monroe refusing to confront him directly, scampering off when he appears. Pound defines Aiken's poetry in an equation of "Swinburne plus Fletcher minus Aiken equals Aiken," which Untermeyer counters with "Eliot plus Masters minus Aiken equals Aiken"—a shrewd thrust. But the heaviest satire is reserved for Lowell, whose speech approximates "polyphonic prose," as she is made to parody herself: "Aiken should let himself go! His technique is superb, but he is insincere. As for me—I sit on the dictionary and make poems—big words and little ones, flat words and then soft ones, pale words that writhe like vermicelli and round words with holes in the middle like doughnuts. I sit on a dictionary and make poems. What a pity that some words are pointed and blue like new tacks!"

Such lighthearted performances—lighthearted on the surface—did not prevent him from intuiting that the national spiritual crisis, a moral confusion and immaturity, was creeping inexorably into American letters. The loss of Santayana and Henry James, for example, their flights from the instinctive anti-intellectualism of a raw society to Europe's more respectful, less spontaneous complex of manners and mind, said much about the current cultural malaise at home. Except for himself, Van Wyck Brooks, and the Mencken of the *Book of Prefaces* (1917), which he esteemed as highly as he would George Moore's *Avowals,* criticism in America had reached a low ebb. Although 1918 had been invigorating in a literary sense, enriched by the appearance of Edna St. Vincent Millay's *Renascence and Other Poems,* Willa Cather's *My Antonia,* John Reed's *Ten Days That Shook the World,* and the initial installments of

Joyce's *Ulysses* in the *Little Review,* which the Post Office declared obscene and burned, the central text for the year again came from Brooks, his *Letters and Leadership,* the *cri de coeur* of a sensitive man who perceived in the multiplying wastelands of American villages and cities a metaphorical murder of Whitman's and Emerson's savior child: "Nature has been robbed and despoiled and wasted for the sake of private and temporary gains."

In Brooks's disillusioned eye, instead of narrowing the cultural gap between itself and Europe, America had lost "an army of gifted minds, of whom Henry James and Whistler are only the most notorious examples," had been shorn by an "ancestral faith in the individual" of "that instinctive human reverence for those divine reservoirs of collective experience, religion, science, art, philosophy, the self-subordinating service of which is almost the measure of highest happiness." One grave political consequence was insularity; another, the incapacity to respond creatively to demanding art. Americans had been happily embracing the most "difficult" European writers and thinkers, including Browning, Carlyle, Ibsen, and Nietzsche, without ever truly communicating with them: "They have said nothing real to us because there has been nothing in our own field of reality to make their messages real."

In native literature, the result had been a persistent outpouring of popular writing devoted to the doctrine that "the function of art is to turn aside the problems of life from the current of emotional experience and create in its audience a condition of cheerfulness." Among serious writers—to Brooks a peculiar mesh of Howells, London, and Dreiser—he observed a similar failure as they took refuge "in the abstract, the non-human, the impersonal, in the 'bigness' of the phenomenal world, in the superficial values of 'local color,' and in the 'social conscience,' which enables them to do so much good by writing badly that they often come to think of artistic truth itself as an enemy of progress." Embattled mother countries again seem the solution— "in Europe the great traditional culture, the culture that has ever held up the flame of the human spirit, has never been quite gutted out."

Regardless of Brooks's limitations, including ethnocentricity, Socialist rigidity, and a selective reading of contemporaries, his critique, like previous texts by Santayana and Henry James, is unmistakably true to the bleak gestalt that prevailed in postbellum America, a gestalt of hedonist excess, rampant reactionary politics, spiraling technological achievements, and an alienating despair that would soon drive many writers and would-be writers into expatriation with Pound and Eliot. Others would remain behind, of course— Stevens, Williams, Crane, and Moore—but their unique brand of art would be recognized much more slowly. Only practitioners of the "new decadence," gaudy retreats into fantasy, medievalism, and occasionally satiric 'art for art's sake' allegories as pursued by James Branch Cabell, Elinor Wylie, John Beer, Jean Nathan, and Carl Van Vechten would reap temporary success at home. Alfred Kazin has uncovered the desolation motoring their antiquated vehicles: "The vogue of the new decadence was to seem shoddy and vain soon enough, but it is easy now to see that it had its origins as a protest against the narrowness and poverty of even the most ambitious writing of the day."

Malcolm Cowley, whose social observations were always attuned to the ordinary music of daily existence that Brooks missed, would depict the decade after the war with painful accuracy in *Exile's Return,* portraying even Greenwich Village, chief generator of the country's Bohemian alternate current, as falling prey to the disillusionment of the era. The Village, Cowley said, was "full of former people," former anarchists, Wobblies, suffragists, conscientious objectors, German spies, settlement workers, strike leaders, poets, editors of Socialist dailies, though "the distinguished foreign artists who had worked in the Village from 1914 till 1917, and given it a new character, had disappeared along with the active labor leaders" as the rest of the nation adopted its libertine standards while ignoring its reformist ideals:

> Young women east and west had bobbed their hair, let it grow and bobbed it again; they had passed through the period when corsets were checked in the cloakroom at dances and the period when corsets were not worn. They were not selfconscious when they talked about taking a lover; and the conversations ran from mother fixations to birth control while they smoked cigarettes between the courses of luncheons eaten in black-and-orange tea shops just like those in the Village. People of forty had been affected by the younger generation: they spent too much money, drank too much gin, made love to one another's wives and talked about their neuroses. Houses were furnished to look like studios. Stenographers went on parties, following the example of the boss and his girl friend and her husband. The "party," conceived as a gathering together of men and women to drink gin cocktails, flirt, dance to the phonograph or radio and gossip about their absent friends, had in fact become one of the most popular American institutions.

Cowley also realized that as the Village died of its own success, "in other words, because American business and the whole of middle-class America had been going Greenwich Village," another Bohemian creed had to fill the moral and aesthetic vacuum: "But there was one idea that was held in common by the older and younger inhabitants of the Village—the idea of salvation by exile." For Aiken, voluntary exile was almost three years off in the spring of 1919, when the Prohibition Amendment was ratified by the necessary number of states and Congress moved swiftly to pass the Volstead Act.

The law that would alter the country's perception of legal authority and initiate an era of extraordinary criminal activity, granting alcohol a forbidden-fruit chic most people found irresistible, loomed on the horizon like an avidly watched tornado.

More important to Aiken were the mounting economic pressures, which must have increased family tensions. The inflationary surge, hastened by the conclusion of the war, was further worsened by a series of strikes across the nation, the result of inflation and the lifting of the "no strike" pledge given during the war. In consort with a speculative market, these factors would culminate in a mini-depression by 1920. Although still substantial, Aiken's main income (the legacy from Aunt Jane) was being diminished by the inflationary economy. It was already apparent that the Cambridge flat was too much of a drain, that he and Jessie would have to find a home farther away from the city, where prices and rents were lower.

None of his books published with Four Seas had earned anything back on their investment, and he had received only a little over $50 in royalty from Houghton Mifflin for *Turns and Movies*. Money from his reviews was fairly steady, if never a major source of income. He did, probably through Kreymborg's gatherings, make contact with Alfred Knopf, who agreed to bring out a collection of his essays and reviews toward the end of the year. Also, Untermeyer, whose critical volume *The New Era in American Poetry* he was to attack in the May 10 issue of the *New Republic,* was contemplating an anthology of contemporary American poetry along the lines of the Imagist and Georgian collections and would ask Aiken to participate in December.

Another sign of his career's positive thrust was an invitation to a prestigious series of poetry readings and lectures in Chicago. The list of invited poets leaned toward the Left, with Williams, Kreymborg, Untermeyer, Lola Ridge, and several other easterners involved. Bodenheim, who was not invited, wrote to Aiken in wounded outrage to complain that his former friends at *Others,* "the very people that have always ecstatically raved over my work to my face," had "unfairly" denied him a hearing. After expounding at length on the duplicity of such brazen hypocrites, he concluded: "I hope you will go to this Chicago lecture stuff with a delicate butcher's cleaver under your coat. Is your heart still an imperturbable Buddha masquerading as a dreaming youth?" Aiken enjoyed relating the anecdote of Bodenheim happening upon him in an avant-garde café in Boston and inquiring if he was not out of his "element," to which he had replied, "Max, I take my element with me."

Oddly, Aiken still managed to retain Bodenheim's affection, which went against the grain of the poet's self-hating tendency to antagonize all his acquaintances sooner or later, even the good-natured Kreymborg, which suggests that his mask of witty self-possession was too formidable for Bogie to dent. When he reviewed Bodenheim's first volume of poetry, *Minna and My-self*—Bodenheim had married Minna Schein in 1918—in the April 5 *Dial* with less than adulation, Bodenheim's blustery reply letter of April 7 would insist upon maintaining a personal tie: "I still place you among *the three or four real friends* I possess, but I intend to write a series of articles attacking your critical viewpoints and general outlook on literature. Outside of an earnest desire to destroy your theories you will find nothing personal or egotistically agitated in these articles. I still love you, you old scalywag!"

The Chicago trip, during which he roomed with A. Burton Rascoe, literary editor of the *Tribune,* would prove fruitful and somewhat surprising. In the latter category was a run-in with Nichols, the English poet he had praised so lavishly the year before. Rascoe gives an account of the incident in his autobiography, *Before I Forget:*

> Robert Nichols, the poet, returned to town after a lecture tour and uttered some inanities in that condescending manner which many Englishmen have. . . . Conrad Aiken, much superior to Nichols as a poet, had come to town . . . because a small lecture engagement had been arranged for him, and because Aiken was an American, he was shown none of the attention accorded Nichols. I brought Nichols and Aiken together at lunch. Later I showed Aiken a clipping of a newspaper interview Nichols had accorded. Aiken grew red with resentment. He seethed over the matter for a while and wrote a lampoon in verse, dedicated to Nichols, entitled "Verbum Saphead." I printed it. This caused Nichols to call upon me, with a wounded and humble letter in reply to Aiken, saying he had stayed up all night on a train to read Aiken's "Senlin," which he said was a poem to place Aiken's name beside that of Poe. Aiken was contrite, and so I published his letter of contrition.

Later, in England, Nichols would become a close friend.

While in Chicago, sometime in late February or early March 1919, Aiken renewed and strengthened his link with Thomas O'Donnell, editor of *Cartoons,* who asked him to send in poetry and who had printed a favorable review of *The Charnel Rose.* O'Donnell assured him in a subsequent letter that he had made many friends on his Chicago trip. He also had a pleasant interlude with Harriet Monroe, who requested verses and caught him off guard by asking that he review his own book for *Poetry.* He had been elated when his anonymous savaging of *Nocturne of Remembered Spring* caused Monroe to write the *Chicago News* to request the name of the reviewer, upset at discovering Aiken's ploy. Now she seemed determined to go him one better, but he realized that the opportunity to use *Poetry* for disseminating his theories and touting his own work should not be cast aside, assuming she did not renege or demand extensive changes. On March 18 he mailed her a review of *The Charnel Rose,* apologizing because it was neither what he intended nor what she expected, a general essay rather than a specific critique of his lengthy poem. It was also more kind than not about his idealistic goals.

In June, true to her word, Monroe printed the piece intact under the title "Counterpoint and Implication." In addition, she accepted and paid $50 for several selections from the unpublished *House of Dust* manuscript (Brown was again tardy—the book would not appear until 1920, although scheduled for October or November publication). Commencing with the premise "that it is the aim of every work of art to evoke, or to suggest," the ostensible self-review repeats Aiken's familiar division of poetry into realistic ("denotive") and impressionistic ("connotative") types, citing Masters and Bodenheim as respectable cases in point and noting the added complexity when an artist like himself is drawn to both, subject to uncertainty and Freudian dynamic, "obeying not merely a theory but, quite as often, the dictates of compulsions more unconscious." As for the "symphonic form" evolved through *The Jig of Forslin, The Charnel Rose,* and *Senlin,* Aiken admits that reality preceded theory: "It was partly a natural enough ambition for more room, partly the working of some complex which has always given me a strong bias towards an architectural structure in poetry analogous to that of music."

Ignoring the analytic possibilities of "unconscious" and "complex," he wastes an entire page on the manner in which musical analogies function, none of it relevant or very interesting because the technical discussion never expands into a consideration of the literary potency of theme and trope options that distinguish literature from music—there are no child prodigies in the former. Finally, after fumbling with the difficulty of separating out form and content, ticking off "emotion-mass" and "tone quality" like a grocer checking inventory, he makes the damaging confession: "Here I flatly give myself away as being in reality in quest of a sort of absolute poetry, a poetry in which the intention is not so much to arouse an emotion merely, or to persuade of a reality, as to employ such emotion or sense of reality (tangentially struck) with the same cool detachment with which a composer employs notes or chords." Swinburne or Edmund Wilson's Axel could not have said it more elegantly. *The Charnel Rose* is handled roughly: "The variation of tone has not been carried far enough: a little more statement and a little less implication would have been a good thing, for it verges on the invertebrate." Aiken spurns criticisms of himself as a Decadent, however, on the ground that the thesis of the work, and of a few passages in *Senlin,* impelled him to tackle decadent material. About *Senlin* he is vainer, conceding it "lacks here and there the opulence and gleam of parts of *The Charnel Rose,* but it makes up for it in precision, sharpness, and economy."

A final paragraph demonstrates his progressive awareness of the intrinsic limitations imposed by his obsessive quest for another art's abstractions: "One cannot, truly, dine—at least every evening—on, as Eliot would remark, 'smells of steaks in passageways.'" Eliot was still the measuring rod as well as the mountain Aiken had either to climb or to level. At the time, Eliot was undergoing a personal crisis that made him a poor correspondent, having to deal with the loss of his father, who died convinced his son had ruined his life, with haunting memories of Jean Verdenal, dead since 1915 and for whom he apparently harbored homosexual or at least homoerotic feelings, and with daily exposure to a neurasthenic wife frequently on the edge of hysteria: "It is terrible to be alone with another person." In search of salvation, he had returned, like a true Harvard offspring, to the Elizabethans, reading the sermons of Donne, Hugh Latimer, and Lancelot Andrewes.

The Woolfs' Hogarth Press published Eliot's *Poems* in May 1919. He spent that month and the next in part completing "Gerontion," a weary, vicious, anti-Semitic poem which adopts the guise of an old man that Aiken had also felt driven to adopt and rephrases the lurking stasis that any divided self has to face, as seen in many of Tennyson's lyric portraits and in James's late fictions. Further, the stasis tends to project undeniable features of a passive or female (albeit loveless) element that could be discerned in the psyches of both Eliot and Aiken, who would shrewdly isolate "Gerontion"'s Romantic theme as "the paralyzing effect of consciousness" in a 1927 review. Eliot was also, however, printing the early chapters of *Ulysses* in the *Egoist*, which gave him another example of how an interior monologue could be manipulated to simulate epic drama.

Aiken's parallel creation is "Counterpoint: Priapus and the Pool," published that year in *Coterie*, a minor English magazine. It entails a conflict between two voices that reinterprets the old antagonism between body and soul (at Harvard, Eliot had written a poem called "The First Debate between Body and Soul") as complicated by the artist's reflexive imagination, with a deliberate invocation of Keats's urn:

> Must we always, like Priapus in a wood,
> In the underbrush of our perplexities,
> Pursue our maidens,—pursuer and pursued?

Priapus was one of the Roman numias, "Cause of Fertility," an ancient phallic symbol whose statue often graced the gardens of the rich. In Eliot's "Mr. Apollinax" the fertility god serves to heighten by contrast the polarities in Bertrand Russell's character, "an embodiment of the paradox of man," as Lillian Feder remarks, "Fragilon and Priapus, inventive mind and wild, demanding body."

In Aiken's poem, which runs to several pages, the dichotomy between mind and flesh or instinct, God shaping man in "the image of Priapus," locates its counterpoint in the second voice's metaphoric pool:

> No one knows how deep it is.
> The ancient trees are about it in an ancient forest,
> It is a pool of mysteries!

Art's response—in other words, the artist's consciousness—can produce an allegorical pool to counter his mortal lust and the mind behind that lust. He questions "this sense of imperfections" fostered upon humans by intelligence but then is condemned to wonder if his mimic creation ever possesses humanity: "But can a pool remember its reflections?" There is no answer and Aiken had none at this juncture because he had yet to resolve the basic dilemmas of an unsure self and aesthetic. The result is a weak but intriguing poem that settles into failure, a puerile climax: "Was God then, so decisive as to shape us in the image of Priapus?"

Again, the poetry, which reflects the deadly circularity induced by un-synthesized psychic antinomies, stood in marked opposition to Aiken's public persona and discriminating taste. It was this taste that kept his criticism at a high mark of achievement, though he was naturally given to the grotesque mistakes and prejudices a strong critic is doomed to accumulate, such as an unrelieved preference for the conventional poetics of English contemporaries and his adoration of George Moore's archaic performances. The enthusiasm for Moore would attain its zenith when he reviewed *Avowals* for the *Chicago News* on October 22: "But of George Moore, from the very first moment, the moment of my casual and inadequate introduction to him by means of *Confessions of a Young Man,* I have always felt that here is a writer who has been, is, and will always be, as long as he continues to write, a great artist, one of the few consummate masters of English prose."

He defends the Anglo-Irishman's "audacity in dealing with sex" and celebrates his narrative prose, as evidenced in *The Lake, Celibates, Evelyn Innes, Esther Waters,* and *The Brook Kerith* (based on Christ's life), "the finest novel in the English language," before assessing the book under scrutiny. Aware of the carelessness of his idol's grammar, Aiken finds the ultimate secret behind the beauty of Moore's style in rhythm and texture, the language having "been winnowed again and again by the finest of temperaments."

Only once during the course of his survey of Moore's oeuvre does his critical blade reveal a more typical keenness, when considering his hero's "hostile notes" on Henry James, which included the absurd charge that the American did not understand psychology. Aiken attempts to extricate Moore from this untenable perch by appealing to a Freudian concept that relates as well to the covert struggle between Eliot and himself: "I prefer to think that this opinion is in the nature of a defense reaction—that Moore is a little frightened, in one, by *The Wings of the Dove* and *The Awkward Age* and *The Golden Bowl*—and that at bottom he perceives quite as clearly as any one the greatness of James, or would so recognize it, if he could read James again; and this time with faith in his own different genius not so easily shaken." His description of Moore as "despite a superficial brashness . . . at bottom full of quakings when he considers his own achievement" is also the mirror portrait of insecurity Untermeyer detected beneath Aiken's own surly front.

The intermittent love-hate relationship between Untermeyer and Aiken began in earnest in 1919 and was destined to endure for the rest of their respective lives. Aiken, the better poet and critic, always lost out to his inferior, who seemed able to pierce his congenial enemy's thick armor with greater precision than far abler minds could do. In *The New Era in American Poetry,* Untermeyer had dumped Aiken among a pile of disgruntled contemporaries "vacillating between a romanticism of which they have grown tired and a realism which they distrust" and had vivisected his career to date with infuriating exactitude: "Facile, energetic, critical, equipped with a strong feeling for verbal color and musical subtlety, it has seemed impossible for him to rise above either his own dexterity or his enthusiasm for some one else's discoveries. Each of his four successive books has held out promise of a succeeding coordinated and instinctive volume—a promise that has never been kept. The intrusion of outside influences, or his too-great affection for his masters, or a sex myopia, or possibly a hyperaesthetic astigmatism, has prevented him from seeing clearly what he tries so anxiously to reveal." After a brief analysis of each Aiken collection, tallying debts to Masefield, Masters, Eliot, and the Pre-Raphaelites, as well as to a Freudian schema, he ends by contrasting Aiken's "dreamy disillusion" with his compatriots' vigorous battles against the "rock of life" for beauty's rewards: "While an inexpressible world sounds its barbaric yawp, Mr. Aiken expresses himself in a refined and musical yawn."

Aiken and Untermeyer were rivals for the post of poetry critic at the *New Republic,* and this intensified their disagreements and brought Burton Rascoe into the fray: "I thought Untermeyer had been unfair to Aiken's work in a book of essays on modern poetry, so I attacked Untermeyer on this score." Aiken's response, excluding the review of Untermeyer's book, which was fairly well balanced, consisted of an exchange of letters and occasional talks over the year in which he skillfully defended the progress, coherent and subtle, of the maligned symphonic series, insisting that erratic publication out of sequence had made their evolutionary nature difficult for critics to discern. In December 1919 Aiken would write ostensibly to protest Untermeyer's review of *Scepticisms,* which had been favorable in the main, but in actuality to deny the accusation that his poetry had exhibited a "succession of styles rather than a development of one," a partial truth he did not wish to hear. His letter sounded the undertone of uncertainty taken before by other critics, and Untermeyer perceptively picked up on it: "But what distresses and—to stop this fencing—disturbs me far more is your self-doubt. . . . You almost talk as if I were glad of causing a fresh inhibition!" In return, refuting Aiken's charge of rationalizing his emotions, Untermeyer lays bare a piece of his own soul: "I am, as a disciple of Jung put it, an incurable extrovert—and, what makes matters worse, I hug my disease. . . . It has taken twelve bristling years to adjust my offensively yea-saying impulses to the dark introspectiveness of my wife. . . . Here, as you observe, I deliver myself into your hands—and only to prove that I refuse to let you outdo me at self-revelation."

The letter, dated December 26, closes with Untermeyer repeating his major objection to Aiken's verses, convinced he could admire them more if he felt "you were freer from your own program, less pre-occupied with form and musical analogies (ceasing to render unto W. C. Williams what is Prokioff's) and letting yourself go." Generously, he mentions the planned anthology— "no editor, no program, no preface except an introductory line or two"—and requests that Aiken participate in the project: "If you are not [in it], it will be more of a disappointment than you may believe." Aside from illuminating the fluid literary scene with colorful precision, the thrust-and-parry interaction between the two dissimilar men again throws into relief a prominent aspect of Aiken's complex personality: the ease with which his psychological defenses were breached by critical insights he could not emotionally accept. His response was to retreat into a contradictory submissiveness, blatant self-exposure, as he did with Jessie when describing the savage beatings administered by his father, which had lacked rational motivation yet provoked inexplicable guilt, feelings of diminished self-worth. He could not logically confound Untermeyer's strictures but had to keep whole his poet's foundation, while simultaneously making an implied plea for compassion through articulations of the damage these strictures were inflicting upon his psyche.

Work was the primary defense, however, and he devoted countless hours to the final symphony, *The Pilgrimage of Festus,* undeterred by adverse criticisms. He also maintained a high profile in the magazine field and engaged in several controversies. One of them embroiled him with the Kreymborg and Ridge circles in Manhattan, where Emanuel Carnevali, an Italian writer in his twenties who was being destroyed by encephalitis, had been a pet since he arrived in 1914. Aiken asked him to do an essay for the *Dial,* then returned the manuscript as unacceptable. Several members of the *Others* group descended upon the magazine's offices to protest, though Aiken held firm. The last issue of *Others,* which appeared in July, carried an editorial essay entitled "Belly Music" by Williams that decried "the stupidity of the critics writing today," naming Aiken, Fletcher, Mencken, Lowell, and Untermeyer, among others, an assault continued into the October issue of the *Little Review* as "More Swill."

Aiken's luck with the journals seemed to be running out. Two Harvard alumni, Scofield Thayer and Merrill Rogers, the latter the former managing editor of the *Masses,* reorganized and refinanced the *Dial,* costing him his position as a contributing editor, although the journal remained receptive to his reviews. Furthermore, he apparently lost the *New Republic* competition to Untermeyer. Compensation was later found when he secured the post of American correspondent for the London *Athenaeum,* which had been resuscitated in the spring under the editorship of J. Middleton Murry, literary critic and husband of Katherine Mansfield, whose short stories he greatly respected.

But this was also an unsettling time for Aiken as he prepared to move "into the country." Leaving Cambridge was especially painful because of its nostalgic connection to his youth and college days, the pain amplified by separation from old friends such as Louisa Bowen, that "most honest of women, the most loyal of friends, if also the most alarmingly and musingly outspoken" (344), with whom he frequently played tennis, and more recent ones such as Maurice Firuski, an ambitious young man of twenty-five who that year had opened the Dunster House Bookshop on quiet Dunster Street in Cambridge. Like Edmund Brown and other colleagues, Firuski had plans to venture into publishing and admired Aiken's work. The two would maintain close ties, the bookseller often supplying Aiken with books on credit, and Firuski's seventeen-year-old clerk, Richard Palmer Blackmur—"shy, introverted, good-looking, dark hair and brown eyes, a discerning face, ironic"— was equally amiable and devoted to literature, determined to educate himself and defy the poverty that had forced him to forego a college education. In time he would emerge as Aiken's most intelligent critic.

The question of where to live in the country had not been hard to answer, Cape Cod being within reasonable distance and connected by reliable rail service. As a resort area, its towns were empty enough for almost ten months of the year to ensure that prices would stay significantly below those in Boston. It was also remote from the violence still flaring up in the cities as the "doughboys" continued to return home to clash in the streets with the scapegoat radicals, blacks, labor organizers, and similar embodiments of "anti-Americanism" decried by press and government. Most alluring were historic links with the family. The village selected, South Yarmouth, boasted a Quaker churchyard burial field "full of Aikens," resting beneath their rows of identical plain stones, and provided the Lucien Crists as neighbors. Aiken's grandfather Potter had preached his first sermon in Sandwich, twenty miles away, and had taught school in South Yarmouth one summer. Less than ten miles from the town was South Dennis, home to George and Joy Wilbur, though they were at the University of Iowa's Psychiatric Clinic for long stretches, and to Gordon Bassett's mother, whose house her son lived in.

The cottage Conrad and Jessie purchased in South Yarmouth for about seven thousand dollars, had, unknown to them until years later, once been owned by a Cousin Abiel on the Aiken side. It was a sturdy white clapboard structure with a red roof set amid tall silverleaf poplars near the Bass River that flowed through the town and into the sea. Its scenic location was enhanced by large yards and numerous fruit trees, as well as by the traditional New England prettiness of the town and its inevitable white church, surrounded by woods and marshland. The price and mortgage were reasonable, and it seemed a distinct advance over the cramped boardinghouse rooms they had occupied previously. It would also be good for the children, though it necessarily entailed more work for Jessie, who could no longer depend upon nearby relatives and had to deal with a kitchen pump, kerosene burner, and Franklin stove. Aiken would take pleasure in planting lilacs in the sandy soil and tending the fruit trees after their June arrival, reinforcing the gardening habit developed in Vermont during the past several summers.

Bassett had been one of the final visitors at the Cambridge apartment, and Aiken would later recall telling him that the Marsten Hartley painting needed more room to be appreciated and should be hung in the tree outside the small parlor in which it was displayed. Bassett also walked from his mother's house in South Dennis "for their first Sunday of housewarming, and Lorelei's first scallop stew" (208). In retrospect, Aiken would wonder if "the Bassett, in fact, perhaps exercised some influence in their choice of the Cape, with his profound and inexhaustible knowledge of family lore there—D's as well as his own?" Eventually, this element was to be crucial, a spiritual integration with the family's rich New England heritage, part of the inner quest for hearth and identity. It touched upon "the snob element" that daughter Jane admitted was a facet of his personality and would include, as with Wallace Stevens, a subsequent search for genealogical roots and branches.

The summer in South Yarmouth was to prove more trying than anticipated, however, and deepen the "abyss" separating him and Jessie in Aiken's mind, which he presumably had first sighted when his wife conceived a momentary infatuation with Wilbur but, in reality, related more to his own inability to sustain the psychological weight of extended intimacy with a woman. On the credit side of the ledger were the children, John and Jane, especially Jane, an animated little girl with freckles and his own reddish hair, who became a favorite and stirred in him some of the emotions between father and daughter that Freudians love to calibrate. The children's demands on him were easily satisfied because they involved no mature adaptation to contrary personality differences or sexual antagonisms and permitted him to revert to a childish frame of reference and freedom congenial to his underdeveloped psyche. He could sympathize and identify with them much in the same way he empathized with cats and other creatures at the mercy of a world beyond their power to alter or control.

With Jessie, in contrast, too many negative undercurrents had been kicked into motion over the seven years of their marriage to allow for contentment to take hold. Instead of ripening into the friendship that characterizes most successful marriages in the gradual transition from passionate love to domesticity, their union had subsided into polite indifference, although it is unlikely that Jessie ever suspected the seriousness of her husband's alienation from her, possibly because she never suspected how central poetry was to his existence or how severe were the neuroses motivating so much of his behavior toward her.

For someone with Aiken's past and personality, the major disruptive factor had to be intimacy itself, the burden of constant exposure to his wife's physical reality, such as the shock in witnessing her giving birth and the trials of making love to a body no longer mysterious or challenging. In his novel *Great Circle,* more than once, Aiken's protagonist and component ego despairingly itemizes the elements in his marital baggage he could not bear: "The dirty stockings and the dirty sinks. Peeled potatoes. . . . The clipped fingernails on the floor. . . . Just ordinary human dirt and effluvia. . . . Sweat under the arms, gouts of pink toothpaste clotted on the toothbrush that hangs on the wall. The little crinkled hairs left in the bathtub, too—so telltale." Familiarity was breeding more than contempt.

Another novel, *Conversation,* written in 1939 but dealing with the tenure at South Yarmouth, also details the disintegration of their marriage with composite accuracy. The teasing, enchanting interaction with the children is faithfully preserved, as is the nagging realization that his wife did not grasp the terror that ensued whenever he had to confront a blank page, a terror that is transferred to the novel's alter ego, a painter: "He felt a little breathless, the familiar feeling of confused helplessness with which he always began a new painting—always, always—the panic of impotence." Few people, unless artists themselves, can ever comprehend the spider loneliness attached to spinning an artifice from self and imagination, but for Aiken, Jessie's failure to do so reeked of betrayal, maternal treachery.

Yet the portrait of Jessie sketched in *Conversation,* obviously softened by nostalgia, appears fair on balance, as husband and wife engage in a climactic debate. Her physical beauty is stressed, plus her bourgeois sense of genteel codes, which encompassed distress over swearing and an intense concern for the opinion of important neighbors, the Crists, the Wilburs, et al. Aiken's protagonist accuses her of turning into a prig like her mother. Her sensitivity also shines through, along with her affection for both her husband and children. Nor does Aiken neglect to let her defend herself, giving her version of their Cape Cod existence together and of his sly debate tricks: " 'I see. So if I'm unhappy, of course, it's a mistake to say so. I mustn't complain, on the penalty of making things still worse by alienating you. It's a very ingenious little system, isn't it? Oh, very. I'm just supposed to eat my heart out in silence. And if I hate this life here and hate all these people and hate being alone so much and hate the work and the dirt and the dishes and the everlasting social drabness and boredom of it, not to mention only seeing you half the week, and even then being pushed off by you because you want to work—.' "

She also outlines Aiken's later myth of a historic self and function and raises the ancient question about why the wife always pays the dearest price for her mate's nobility: "If I hate all this until I'm sick, and feel wretched day in and day out of the days on end when I'm alone, worrying about money and how to make ends meet, or to keep up appearances, I'm just expected to say nothing. Why? Why? What do *I* get out of it? Oh, I know, all that nonsense of yours about plain living and high thinking, about living the natural and honest life of our Pilgrim ancestors, and being independent." Jessie also resented being sealed off from her husband's literary universe, relegated "to the domestic entirely," a shallow creature who must restrict mind and interests to the household chores assigned her by convention. Further into the argument, the wife isolates the misogyny always intuited as there: "Women don't really exist, do they? Not for you, they don't! . . . your old superiority complex, I suppose, your feeling that the female isn't your intellectual equal."

The reply of Aiken's persona summarizes a poet's disappointment upon discovering that his labors are not as fascinating and relevant to others as they are to him and should be to everyone else, a horrendous lapse in the woman who was to play a second Muse and replace a lost, untrustworthy mother, the woman who had agreed during their engagement and early wedded years to dedicate their shared life to his art's tender nurture. Aggrieved by what his protagonist perceives as Jessie's breaking of their nuptial bargain—to nurse his career regardless of hardships—Aiken has him remind her of that original contract, which she claims expired because he has accomplished nothing. It is a low blow that detonates a furious response as valid as the wife's complaints: "Nothing! That's what you always say, isn't it? The truth is, and for me it's a bitter truth, that you never even bother to look at my work, you don't take any longer the slightest interest in it, except insofar as it might make money, you don't know what I'm doing. . . . I can remember when you used to *ask* to see what I was doing, in the first year or two—and when we were engaged you could think of nothing else." Worse, her doubts about his achievement are viewed as particularly treacherous "because of the very fact that I *do* myself feel unsure about it."

The novel concludes with a tearful reconciliation, as did many of the literal spats that contributed to the reconstructed argument, but the gulf between them was bound to widen on his side when uncertainty about his work merged with and intensified an abiding lack of faith in his very existence. Since the symphonies were not performing their envisioned therapeutic task, at least not under the scowls of an unsympathetic audience, his ever vulnerable self-image was eroding. A profound identity crisis lurked ahead, like an iceberg whose chill he could already feel—to steal a simile from "Mr. Arcularis." The bickering with and growing estrangement from Jessie, living symbol of his psyche's home aegis, tended to add to his unease, further undermining his confidence.

The incident that provided the plot for *Conversation* was the unexpected invasion of South Yarmouth in late August or early September by Maxwell Bodenheim and his pregnant wife Minna; John Coffey, successful fur thief and self-educated idealist; and Louise Bogan, age twenty-two at the time and caring for an infant, though in the middle of getting a divorce from the child's father. Using Coffey's plentiful supply of cash, they had rented a house not far from the Aikens' remodeled cottage and proceeded to scandalize the provincial village with their Bohemian ways. To compound the confusion, Peggy Cowley (née Baird) appeared and requested shelter for two months while her husband returned to Harvard and found them lodgings. The recently married Cowleys had been living in Greenwich Village under a severe financial strain, and Malcolm's decision to get his degree at Harvard, supported only by magazine hack work and a small scholarship, was the result of his awareness that a degree might prove economically essential. Peggy, who was in frail health, upset the Aikens and their neighbors with her Dutch-cut hair style—short-haired women were ipso facto radical—and casual notions of morality.

Of more concern, however, was Coffey's criminal reputation, which had preceded him and seemed confirmed by his obvious prison pallor. Crist, in particular, revealing an unctious smallness behind his air of sophistication, was outraged and threatened to have the law intervene. This would not have upset Coffey, who never hid his record or his intentions, which included a plan to use his inevitable trial for theft as a forum for testifying to the legitimate needs of the country's poorer citizens, but might have put Aiken in a shadow of sorts; he visited their messy communal abode on more than one occasion.

Dreading a scandal and the loss of her few cultivated friends in the area, Jessie was in a frenzy and demanded that her husband disassociate himself from the Village menagerie.

Aiken was mostly amused by the episode, admiring Coffey, the apparent sincerity of the Irishman's efforts to use his ill-gotten gains for commendable goals, though angry at Bodenheim and the rest for taking advantage of him. Eventually, a fierce row erupted between Aiken and Bodenheim in which he accused Bogie of tagging along with Coffey out of a desire to bathe in the Romantic, Rimbaud-like atmosphere of the scene rather than from any respect for Coffey's ideas, for his brave prophet stance. In his second novel, *Crazy Man* (1924), Bodenheim would present Coffey as a fusion of Christ and Robin Hood.

The entire incident was reduced to a comic anecdote when the Coffey group decamped after a brief stay to return to the Village, convinced that survival was impossible under such primitive conditions, followed near the end of September by Peggy Cowley's departure. Their wake left the Aiken marriage badly shaken. Fundamental conflicts in temperament and social perceptions had been exposed, old wounds reopened, although Aiken never considered abandoning either his wife or his children. He needed both as barriers against the flood of internal chaos lapping at his restless mind. Jessie's apparent transformation into a pillar of middle-class respectability, her prim suspicion of the artist's subversive motives and self-indulgence, made him more and more susceptible to the emotional turmoil that would accompany his trip to England in May of the next year. The tensions in his home life, which did not interfere with a constant pursuit of squalid sexual conquests (poet Robert Sanborn, associated with the *Others* crowd, spread the rumor in Manhattan that Aiken spent his summer days canvassing dark movie theaters for willing female victims) were throwing him back into an early adolescent stage of psychosexual development, not far from the center of his imagination's storehouse, where he waited for a maternal heroine to cherish from afar, erotic but uncorrupted.

The move to South Yarmouth did have the positive effect of removing the family from the agitation that shook Boston for three riotous days, when 1,117 members of the city's 1,544-strong police force walked off the job on September 8. Although 1919 was a year of strikes and the policemen were underpaid, working twelve-hour shifts, the frightening uniqueness of a police strike and the violence it engendered caused a wave of public revulsion. On the first night, crowds gathered in the vicinity of Scollay Square and its honky-tonks, flophouses, and burlesque theaters (Aiken's slumming district and home to Brown's office), where they milled around aimlessly, breaking windows, assaulting women, and blocking the trolley tracks with mattresses and wooden ties. The second evening, abetted by professional criminals, the mob clashed with the State Guard, which was forced to open fire, killing three men, and then cleared the Common with fixed bayonets. During the night two others were killed, and it was discovered that a sailor had been murdered amid the fracas at the Common. The following day Governor Calvin Coolidge, who had shamefully avoided acting earlier, restored order by calling out the rest of the Guard and reinstating Edwin Curtis, the police commissioner (his appointee), whom Mayor Andrew Peters, a Harvard man and Democrat, had suspended. Peters actually threw a punch at Coolidge in tearful frustration. Curtis fired all the strikers, raised the minimum wage, and began recruiting a new force, while Coolidge, in reply to Samuel Gompers's telegraphed plea for intervention and arbitration, wrote the statement that guaranteed him the vice-presidency in 1920: "There is no right to strike against the public safety."

Five days before the Boston police strike President Wilson suffered a stroke, and on November 19 the Senate defeated the treaty that he had struggled so hard to pass by a 55 to 39 margin. The national slide toward conservativism and isolationism had turned into an avalanche. In the literary wars of the period, alliances and allegiances were less certain. Two days after the defeat of the treaty, Aiken received a letter from William Carlos Williams, apologizing for asking a favor after recently berating him in print and requesting that he intercede on his behalf with their common publisher, the elusive Edmund Brown. Aiken, whose personal liking for Williams was to remain steadfast, generously invited him to South Yarmouth to meet Brown, who had responded to none of Williams's inquiries about the publication of *Kora in Hell.* The matter was cleared up by December 11, however, when Williams wrote to decline his offer and inform him that Brown had finally contacted him—the book would not be published until September 1920.

In November, Aiken's more reliable new publisher, Alfred Knopf, brought out *Scepticisms,* the volume he hoped would firmly establish his credentials as a critic and also counter what he believed were the mistaken impressionistic dogmas preached by the Lowell and Untermeyer critiques. He had carefully selected and arranged those essays and reviews he thought most representative of his more scientific approach to evaluating contemporaries and had penned a new essay for the collection, "*Apologia Pro Specie Sua.*" The essay dealt honestly with the self-serving bias sure to infect any poet-critic's attempt to survey an era "of uncertainty, of confusion and conflict," in which his own literary vanity and set of values were at stake:

> New ground has been broken in a good many directions, or ground which, if not new, has been at any rate so long unused as to have that appearance, at least, and to inspire a certain amount of scepticism as to

the resultant crops; and it has been engagingly natural, under these circumstances, that each poet should claim the most astounding properties
for his own plot of soil, and become a little willfully cynical as to the
claims of rivals. . . . Those poets who, like himself, are critics as well,
have had an almost unfair advantge in this situation. . . . Our utterances
are apt to sound authoritative and final. But do not be deceived! We are
no surer of ourselves at bottom than anybody else is. We are, in fact, half
the time, frightened to death.

Merging private insecurity with public doctrine, Aiken does not flinch from
identifying the fear as welling from severe competition, especially evident
during the "second stage" of a poet's career, when he "begins to exert himself
in the most audacious and exhausting task of his life, namely, to convince
himself, his public, and his fellow-poets that there is nothing accidental about
his success, that his work has about it a certain uniqueness of distinction
which should commend it for perpetuity, and even that it may have, somewhat, the qualities of greatness." A sentence later, personal terror, the repressed anxiety that might be traced back to Savannah and continuing existential despair, is laid out on the operating table under his remorseless knife:
"And it is precisely of the ghastly possibility that his impression of himself
may be wrong, that his undertaking, and indeed his life,—since the two are
nearly synonymous,—may be only dust in the nostrils, that he is so secretly
and so profoundly afraid."

"*Apologia*" paints a damning portrait of relativist criticism leading to "the
abyss that lies between one individual and another," the fact that our "tastes
are mathematically determined by the sensibilities and temperaments with
which we are born." The sole solution offered is an old one, the taste of a
select audience functioning over an extended time span. It foreshadows his
ultimate vision of consciousness's historic role in human affairs without
touching upon the problem of transitory cultural influences. But Aiken is wise
enough to concede that the basic enigma of taste pondered in connection with
a synchronic field is best left to "the behaviorist-psychologist or the Freudian"
for a satisfactory explication. True to theory, he proffers his book as, "in sum,
just as clearly an ideograph of Aiken as *Tendencies in Modern American Poetry* is of Amy Lowell or *The New Era in American Poetry* is of Untermeyer."

And yet the specter of relativism haunted him, and he added an Appendix
essay, "A Note on Values," that asks: "In what way,—when I write a critique, largely laudatory, of John Gould Fletcher, or of Maxwell Bodenheim,
or of Jean de Bosschere,—do I clearly advance any interest of my own?" He
perceives the saving possibility of disinterestedness in the appreciation of
aims and achievements at variance with his own aesthetic, though confessing

the issue is "far too complex" for such a "curt" resolution and confronting, at last, the psychological matrix: "All human judgement or tastes reduce themselves under pressure to the terms of the pathetic ego which stands as judge . . . we like a work of art only because it reflects ourselves, or because it gives expression to some part of us inarticulate, or consciousness to some part of us which was unconscious." If true, this would not obviate the existence of universal motifs, of course. The logical outgrowth of such an understanding would be, he agrees, an excursion into "the realm of autobiography . . . a second book longer than the first, a book of which the nature would be psychological rather than literary," since it would have to incorporate awareness of the critic's moods at the time of composition and knowledge of his relationship with the poets under discussion, as well as of his fundamental attitude toward life and art. And so relativism must remain the ghost in his critical machinery, however candidly avowed.

Aiken cannot leave off without demonstrating his intransigent loyalty to the English scene and tradition, invidiously juxtaposing "The Congo" and "Patterns" with Meredith's *Modern Love,* Abercrombie's "Emblem of Love," and Thompson's "An Anthem of Earth" to exhibit their "artistic incompleteness" as "characteristic of contemporary American poetry." Despite the familiar blemish, which denotes another aspect of the psychological dilemma he was grappling with, *Scepticisms* was and is a remarkable gathering of urbane, frequently accurate criticism, superior to anything comparable from its era and extraordinary in the bold frankness of its speculations about human motivations, necessary conditions of self-limiting subjectivity. Naked and reflective, he was putting himself on the line in a manner that he had not been able to duplicate in his verses. But, as should have been anticipated, the book's reception was far from intelligent. Bodenheim wrote on December 16 to thank him for "the miracle of a book which mentions me frequently and favorably," before declaring, "We are not all afraid, in the way you suggest," and expressing his intention to depart "very soon for California, and from thence to the most remote and uncivilized part of the world I can find." This Gauguin-like delusion, the fruit of a ruminative visit with William Carlos Williams in New Jersey, would culminate in a trip to England the next year.

An early, surprising review would come from Marguerite Wilkinson in the February 1, 1920, issue of the *Times,* who saw in *Scepticisms* "a nicely adjusted intellect at work." Aiken's style "is adroit and sharp and restrained," she wrote. But Braithwaite's *Transcript* notice ten days later used Aiken's sincerity against him by insisting that "the average reader will be inclined to discount his own argument because he cannot be sure of the critic's motives." The poets and the books "that he makes an intellectual flourish of judging," Braithwaite insisted, "have, for the most part, their fundamental purposes and qualities befogged and perverted by such critical charlatanry, no matter how brilliant the execution may be." Mary Terrill would launch an even crueler attack in the *Bookman* of April 1920: "It makes good sedative reading after you have got tired of Mencken, Cabell, Powys and some few others of the real brains of America." A more tempered stand by C. K. Trueblood would appear the same month in the *Dial*: "One's quarrel with Mr. Aiken will be with his limits, not with his accomplishment within his limits. . . . It is because he has done so much carefully that dissatisfaction arises at the incomplete significance of the whole work."

Aiken's suddenly exposed anxieties had to multiply when he was faced with this bewildering, sometimes malicious, often parochial affirmation of his worst fears. But the deleterious effect of those anxieties still lay in the future as he contemplated South Yarmouth's bleak winter vistas and commenced to dream about and plan for another return to England and Eliot, another "curious reversal" in his concentric career.

The human soul, it seems to me,

orientates itself afresh every

now and then. It is doing so

now. No one can see it whole,

therefore.

Virginia Woolf

·   ·   ·   ·   ·   ·   ·   ·   ·

THIS MERCILESS WARFARE

Despite its scenic charms and innumerable historic associations, South Yarmouth did not, could not, instill the peace Aiken envisioned—no single place ever could, divided as he was at every strata of his psyche. Though within a couple of hours of Boston and Cambridge, the resort town closed in around itself during winter, accentuating the provinciality of its permanent inhabitants and deepening Jessie's sense of isolation, which Aiken evaded by convenient "business" trips into the city. The handful of friends in the area capable of supplying the intellectual exchanges he thrived on were seldom available. Gordon Bassett was to sail for Buenos Aires on March 11, 1920, to work in the Argentine branch of a Boston bank, and Jake Wilbur, after the summer hiatus, had departed with Joy for Iowa. The Wilburs' returns to South Dennis were irregular and of uncertain duration. Lucien Crist was still in residence but made daily trips into Boston during the week to give music lessons. Grayson McCouch, after being invalided home with diabetes, was well again and had traveled with Cecile to England, increasing Aiken's urge to do likewise.

Early in the year Aiken's relationship with the young woman who appears in *Ushant* as "Marian" was dissolved. On January 16, 1920, Prohibition would go into effect nationwide, and the night before became a second New Year's Eve as hordes of customers stormed their favorite taverns in and around Boston to drink themselves insensible. Preserved in both *Ushant* and a short story called "The Night before Prohibition," Aiken's memory of the hectic evening was sharpened by what happened in his personal life. Jessie and the children were to be away in Montreal visiting the McDonalds, and Aiken took the opportunity to invite Marian to the Craigie Street apartment (apparently the Aikens were still using the apartment or the incident occurred earlier because Aiken clearly labeled the story "autobiographical"). Simply by taking her to the apartment he was exposing an unconscious animus against his wife, who is named Daisy in the story. In both the story (in which she is "Eunice") and *Ushant,* Marian is presented as a nurse, although in reality she was a voice teacher living at a boardinghouse full of nurses, her roommate among them. The literal events leading up to the crisis are the same in both accounts.

Aiken jocularly gives himself the name Walter Coolidge Swift in the story. After seeing his wife off at the railroad station, Swift telephones Eunice and asks her to meet him at the Avery, not remembering it is the last night of legal drinking. Once at the hotel, he realizes his mistake: "It had been almost impossible to get into the bar. Everybody was already drunk, fighting drunk. Tin horns were being blown in the streets as if for a holiday." After dinner and drinks they hail a cab and head for the "salt-box bridge" that crosses the Charles into Cambridge, Swift wondering, "Was it right to take Eunice to his wife's apartment?" It is an ethical question in tune with the tale's didactic evasion of psychological ramifications, typical of the moral dimensions forced upon too many of Aiken's stories, usually to their detriment.

It is also clear in the story that the idea of bringing Marian into his home (somewhat distanced from him by references to "Daisy's apartment") adds a dose of extra excitement, childish sin, to the erotic adventure, a "sharp edge given to their delight by the fact that they were using Daisy's apartment and that Eunice was secretly and wickedly, as it were, usurping Daisy's place." Eunice herself is intrigued by a not unnatural desire to see "the home of her supplanter! Every nook and cranny" (in the fiction, Swift had known Eunice before marrying Daisy). The act of love that ensues, presumably in his and Jessie's bed, benefits romantically from the substitution of Eunice for a staid wife, as Aiken chronicles "the profound simple happiness at being together again, after all these months, and in spite of the shadow of Daisy—or perhaps even more because of it."

What happens next differs in the two accounts only in coloring, not incident. In "The Night before Prohibition" the protagonist experiences a sudden detachment from Eunice as he lies beside her in silence, "remote, alone with himself . . . more and more self-conscious; the impulse to make love to her seemed to have come to an end." This detachment climaxes in an unsubtle rejection of her, as he accompanies her to Harvard Square to put her on the last trolley to Boston, "the owl-car" packed with "the dregs of humanity," rather than permitting her to stay the night or escorting her home. The episode is explained in embarrassed retrospect as "one of those freaks of psychology," a delicate "pang of conscience, some shadow of Daisy, some vague distaste for duplicity, which had dictated the whole fiasco, and brought to an end the loveliest relationship with a human being which he had ever known." But in *Ushant,* where the quest is for truth as self-knowledge, the feelings experienced during the cruel episode are more honestly shaped: "He had put her on the last car from Harvard Square, the only woman in a bedlam of drunken rowdyism, for the terrifying midnight ride to Boston, and then walked back to Craigie Street with a feeling of relief which amounted positively to elation" (209). The "elation" might also be ethical in origin, guilt's release, though it is clearly far stronger than the circumstances warranted.

Ushant, however, cannot hide behind the story's flimsy moral barricade to meaning. It must instead confront the peculiar emotions that had overwhelmed him that night, providing at least the rudiments of a credible response: "Disenchantment—it was that notion of the composer's, derived, he said, from a passage in Strauss's *Don Juan,* the theme of sexual disgust (*post coitum tristis est*) which again, as so many times before, had interposed its poisonous self-consciousness" (208). It is credible, indeed perceptive, for Aiken to link Strauss, himself a monster, with Don Juan compulsiveness and the extreme self-consciousness that prevailed throughout Aiken's life and that would certainly function with additional intensity during the period of indifference and/or revulsion common to males immediately after copulation. Yet in *Ushant* the overt ethical structure of the story and the intrusion of Jessie's "shadow" are ignored.

In *The Armed Vision,* Stanley Edgar Hyman noted that the "pattern of major American literature has involved a related pattern of sexual maladjustment, and every attempt to study the literature and blink the problem has been inevitably foredoomed to failure." This observation applies with no less force to Aiken's unstable love life and hostility toward women, which governed his choice of Decadent themes and imagery. Like so many other earlier American writers, as delineated by Leslie Fiedler's brilliant *Love and Death in the American Novel,* Aiken in his poetry and fiction tended to project a juvenile sexual identity at odds with their cosmopolitan formulations, retarding his artistic progress and restricting his imagination's reach. More pertinent, the precise, self-circumscribing vagaries of his immature sexual stance, which he would trace back to his mother without exploring all its implications, were to be blurred to the end of his life, in spite of a psychoanalytic background and frank discussions with Wilbur about his vivid dreams and personality quirks. The courage and intelligence manifested in subsequent forays into autobiography, when he began—first in the fiction, then in the poetry—to accept the challenge to confession implicit in the symphonies' ambitious schema and mandated by the lyric quality of his talent, would always stop short of complete exposure. Possibly Aiken feared the disintegration of his frail ego under the mounting pressures of introspective candor, especially unaided by professional guidance.

Besides a compulsion to cheat on his wife, which would be true through three marriages, there are allusions in *Ushant* and "The Night before Prohibition" to difficulties in sexual performance. A portion of Eunice's attractiveness stems, in the story, from her willingness to accept Swift's (Aiken's) "ineptitudes in making love," and in *Ushant*, there is a reference to "the occasional erotic mishap" (118). Aiken would also endure "sporadic impotence" during the early stages of his affair with the woman destined to become his second wife. Another element in Eunice's allure for Swift is touched upon solely in the story, when he tries to dissect the reasons why he was able to converse more freely with her than with his wife: "Partly, perhaps, because he had felt an intellectual and social superiority; though God knew he attached little importance to either."

The central factors are a Don Juan drive to seduce and master women without surcease (an obsession Jung no doubt would attribute to a son's "mother complex") and the sexual tensions induced by an unconscious urge to "save" fallen women, thereby debasing the mother's image, yet paradoxically defusing attendant guilt. A Freudian might ascribe this to an unresolved Oedipal complex, the failure of a boy to transcend that phase in his childhood when mother as love object (and father as castrating rival) focuses previously polymorphous and narcissistic sexual energies. Whether one accepts or rejects either Jung's or Freud's diagnostic systems, however, it seems likely that Aiken's problems with women relate back to childhood conflicts, the violent loss of both parents at the age of eleven, and the threat to his identity that this tragedy had instilled. Marian, who surfaces in at least two other stories, "Field of Flowers" and "The Last Visit," attesting to her firm subliminal grip on Aiken's imagination, was the victim of the hatred and insecurity she engendered as Anna's inferior totem, the treacherous aspect of the undead mother. This internal scenario was brought to a climax of rejection by Jessie's increasing disenchantment with him and his labors and by Marian's allowing him to sleep with her in his wife's bed and home, ultimate sources of love and betrayal. Many years later, when informed of Aiken's heart attack, the original of Marian would comment bitterly, "Really? I didn't know he had a heart."

Marian had served as a safety valve in his interior romance, the easily dominated antithesis of Jessie in her status as a stranger, her sexual availability, and her lack of critical reserve—she did not sit in judgment of him—and in her Bohemian code and its leftist freedom, which included subscribing to the *Daily Worker*. His unkind treatment of her, which he soon regretted, was not only reprehensible, it was a mistake on a selfish plane because the rejection left him open to further blasts of uncertainty and demolished an essential sanctuary of erogenous maternal reassurance and relief from a marriage grown cold. In despair, he would attempt to rebuild the bridge burned behind him that memorable night, but Marian refused to answer his pleading letters or to meet with him. She would no longer be around to soothe his agitation during moments of crisis, as she was the night of Jane's birth, when he rushed to see her afterward and they embraced daringly in the rear garden of the boardinghouse, forced there by the presence of her roommate (118)—or as she was when he returned from what would prove a final visit to his ailing grandmother in a Watertown nursing home, an event later translated into an inadequate story in which their sex roles are, interestingly, reversed.

If the pattern of Aiken's skewed interactions with women was pursued to axis depths, a pattern which also involved frequent altercations with wives of friends, it might dive down to the mirror image behind the mother, his female self or *anima*. And in his best work he would pilot this circular voyage to the heart of his search (inner or outer) for the flux corpus of consciousness, though ironically he was careful not to let it intrude upon his own biography. Rationalizing the unconscious was a basic necessity for his aesthetic, he would discover. It was an aesthetic predicated upon the ego's self-devouring awareness of self in performance of its Romantic chore, but the Freudian process appeared inimitable to the maintenance of a public persona, the surface artist whose identity myth subsequently evolved into *Ushant*. In the latter, as in many prior artifices, wives and mistresses are transfigured into Loreleis and *Leibeichens*, Rhineland sirens luring the hero to destruction. Dr. Aiken used to whistle *Lorelei* to one of their cats, convinced it annoyed the animal.

The immediate pleasures of Aiken's break with Marian were apparent. It granted him temporary ethical satisfaction, however troubling on reflection, and simplified his existence during a hectic period of transition. Further, it enabled him to expend a significant amount of hostility toward Jessie without the risk of losing her and the home she had created, defiling her bed and then, in symbolic effect, shoving her defiler and alter ego into the street. But the end of any close association entailed peril for him, a reminder of parental abandonment, and this association, because of Marian's love and maternal passivity, had meant more to him than he realized at the time. Marian later married a lawyer, not the stuffed shirt given her in "Field of Flowers"—her sister wed such a man and moved to Grosse Pointe in Detroit—and Aiken would not see her again until 1928, their last encounter.

Aiken was fretting to get away, not only from Marian but from America. He convinced Jessie that a trip to England might enable him to locate an English publisher, relieving their tight financial situation a bit, and to search for a permanent residence there for the family. By early March of 1920 he was writing to Martin Armstrong to ask if a previous offer to let him share his rooms at 37 Great Ormond Street whenever in London was still standing, since he contemplated a voyage to England in April, perhaps for a stay of several months. On March 16, Armstrong, who had surrendered a post at the Ministry of Pensions the year before to engage in free-lance journalism and pursue his own poetry, wrote back to reassure his American friend playfully that the invitation remained open, despite Aiken's "many bad qualities," such as "your ungovernable pride, your hateful tactlessness, the inordinate size of your boots, and your revolting habit of blaspheming in your sleep." He also reassured Aiken that his flat was "even more lovely than when you last haunted it, and you will have it to yourself for the better part of the day. Only towards evening, when you are thoroughly exhausted by the ardors of composition, shall I return and you will have my parrot-like and disjointed chatter to cope with, and our respective Muses can tear each other's eyes."

The generous offer and immediate resumption of a teasing, affectionate relationship was all the encouragement he needed to set his plan into motion, planning an April 21 departure date. The prospect was exciting, particularly the thought of seeing Eliot again and getting together with McCouch and Fletcher, who were in London, even if it meant separation from Jessie and the children for several months. He also looked forward to renewing his acquaintance with Colonel Wright and Harold Monro and any other members of the "Georgian" crowd still in evidence, as well as making contact with John Middleton Murry and John Collings Squire and securing more English outlets for his poetry. An English publisher would mean a financial gain, probably slight, but the most meaningful benefit from the visit lay in reestablishing his name among the London literati. South Yarmouth's genuine shortcomings in the winter months were daily adding luster to the notion of settling in England.

As for his work, the wintry isolation assisted his efforts at putting *Festus,* his newest Everyman, through his final paces. Aiken was unaware of Philip James Bailey's *Festus,* an unreadable Victorian epic of over forty thousand lines, and his choice of his protagonist's name was, as usual, designed for a specific intellectual purpose. "I think there was a vague underhand reference to Faustus," he would later recall, "and as a matter of fact I hadn't then heard of Mr. Bailey's *Festus* . . . I just wanted a good, slightly Latin-sounding, abstract name for my philosophic hero, who was set on a pilgrimage of his own—a rather internal pilgrimage—in search of the meaning of meaning, to anticipate Mr. Ogden and Mr. Richards." Faust was indeed in the background, as he had been for Bailey, and Aiken's thoughts must have been turned in that direction by the publication in 1919 of James Branch Cabell's *Jurgen,* which was suppressed in New York and which he had reviewed, with somewhat unfair harshness, in his second "Letter from America" to the *Athenaeum* (December 12, 1919), along with Joseph Hergesheimer's romantic novel *Linda Condon.*

In distinct contrast to his penchant for making correct choices, perhaps because he was intent upon distancing himself from the Decadent label often pinned to Cabell's fiction, Aiken preferred the Hergesheimer book, after spending several paragraphs demonstrating that the literary renaissance in America over "the last half-dozen years" had not included fiction. The "relatively brilliant" volumes of the period, he said, had been *The Education of Henry Adams,* Spingarn's *Creative Criticism,* Mencken's *Book of Prefaces* and *The American Language,* Masters's *Spoon River Anthology,* Frost's *North of Boston,* Robinson's *Man Against the Sky* and *Merlin,* and Fletcher's *Irradiations* and *Goblins and Pagodas,* and he made a respectful bow to Kreymborg, Bodenheim, and Stevens. Although he wrote of his "respect" for Dreiser as well, he took no notice of either *Winesburg, Ohio* or *My Antonia,* a sign that Aiken was unaware of the gradual shift already under way from an age of poetry into an age of fiction.

Cabell's novel, his strongest and one in a series about a mythical medieval land called Poictesme, is concerned with a middle-aged, poetical pawnbroker who is banished by the Devil and struggles to return home, getting magical aid and having many amorous adventures along the way with various legendary personages, including a spell in hell wedded to a vampire, which should have appealed to Aiken. Jurgen gains back his kingdom, resumes his prosaic married life, and discovers that past desires are lost illusions. The novel annoyed Aiken far beyond its worth. He detected large debts to Arthur Machen's *Hill of Dreams* and Anatole France's *Penguin Island* and accused its author of battening "rather on literature than on life" and of reducing a work with a larger aim to a mere "recital of the erotic exploits of its hero."

Aiken ends by dismissing *Jurgen* as "a prize for the Freudians," which would enrage Burton Rascoe, to whom the novel had been dedicated. Rascoe thought the review "smug and misinformed about Cabell's work." To understand Aiken's willful blindness in this instance, it is necessary to grasp the threat to his psyche that *Jurgen* represented. Apart from the Faust idea, the novel offers a merciless mirror image of what he himself had been attempting, down to the very cynicism he charges Cabell with possessing. The acerbic quality of his review reflects the self-disgust and dread he would experience more intensely after *Festus* was finished and he was off to England. In damning as unreal the allegorical visage adopted by Cabell's inferior art, he was in essence revealing, however unconsciously, the weaknesses undercutting his own poetry. Each stab at Cabell was a dagger punching holes in the elaborate fabric of Aiken's symphonies.

He would describe his own reworking of Faust material in a prefatory "Argument" as an imaginary pilgrimage: "It is a cerebral adventure, of which the motive is a desire for knowledge." It is also a schizophrenic journey in which an "alter ego" appears to Festus "in the shape of an old man," laying "the prospect of further experience and understanding pleasingly before him," so that Satan has been replaced by an alternate self, a future self nearer death, the skeleton of Mr. Arcularis, here inert since removed from private experience by a rational screen of philosophic design. And the knowledge quested after, not yet obsessional, is burdened not by sin (the myths of Faustus and *The Pilgrim's Progress,* that precious childhood text, are being intersected, redefined) but by the heavy chains of Bradley's (and Kant's) view of the self's solipsistic limitations: "It occurs to him that the possibility of knowledge is itself limited: that knowledge is perhaps so conditioned by the conditions of the knower that it can have little but a relative value."

Aiken's theoretical machinery, which would also serve as his metaphysic, was assuming its final configuration. The last turn of the screw came with the publication of Brooks Adams's *Emancipation of Massachusetts* and Henry Adams's *Degradation of the Democratic Dogma,* which he made the subject of his third "letter from America" to the *Athenaeum* (February 20, 1920). Having already absorbed *The Education of Henry Adams,* a best-seller when it was published in 1919, he was familiar with the Adams brothers' predilection for theory, "for the scientific attitude (particularly when it runs counter to the orthodox)" and their "manifest" brilliance. He charts the maturation of the strain of "degradation" or decline that sounds the "key-note" of their thought from a previous commitment to a Darwinian "ascent" motif through a concept of man's moral dualism, "idealism as against physical necessity, self-interest as against the interest of the social organism," to the gloomy prediction of "gradual or rapid degradation for man" and his civilization. Oswald Spengler and kindred prophets of doom had been fervently embraced by a war-weary Europe.

The metaphoric sextant for charting this inexorable decline is located in Henry Adams's theory of phase, which had been worked out in a 1909 essay, "The Rule of Phase Applied to History," in terms of entropy, the second law of thermodynamics governing a closed system's steady loss of energy (heat). This Aiken admiringly characterized as Adams's "magnificent engine of pessimism." The harnessing device is Willard Gibbs's "Rule of Phase" from chemistry and physics, which Adams slyly broadened to encompass cultural history by stressing the physical properties of human thought, then plotting the stages of intellectual decline that mankind has already experienced—the "leap of nature from the phase of instinct to the phase of thought" and thus through the Religious Phase (500–1600) and the Mechanical Phase (1600–1900) to the present critical juncture. Adams had mathematically arrived at the prediction that thought would reach its final or "ethereal" phase in 1921, said Aiken, summarizing. "This phase will last perhaps four years, perhaps fifty. After it will begin the long decline."

It is easy to see why the Adamses' negative dogma was so appealing to Aiken because it neatly complemented Freud's deterministic vision and conformed to his era's pessimistic mind-set. Henry Adams himself alluded to the West's pessimistic drift, an increase in collective melancholy, "invaded consciousness." He insisted that "civilization and education enfeeble personal energy . . . they aim especially at extending the force of society at the cost of the intensity of individual forces," hoisting Freud on the petard of his own repression. Moreover, the Adamses' doctrine would appeal to a misogynist and a New England puritan's love of order, although the books were important to Aiken primarily for the notion of a contemporary ultimate phase, an evolutionary acme of human consciousness and a subsequent fall, which reinforced his readings in Nietzsche. As *Ushant* illustrates, Aiken—with Bergson's assistance—converted this idea into a positive modality, "the flowering of an ultimate phase . . . in man's thinking, a final brilliance of consciousness, as of the world itself coming to self-knowledge, even to the point of then coming apart" (219).

The apogee, of course, is to posit this expanding consciousness in the poet's *malebolge* depths, deifying him in the process, a coupling that generally coincided with the completion of Aiken's symphonic sequence, first in *Punch: The Immortal Liar: Documents in His History* and now in *The Pilgrimage of Festus*, the last version of which was sent off to Robert Linscott for his reaction on April 14, 1920. The Punch and Festus countenances are allegorically akin, and the mock-heroic structure of their stories-in-verse is also similar, but in *Punch*, the earlier of the two though it would not be published by Knopf until 1921, the division is symmetrically tidy between Part 1, four accounts of Punch's life and death, and Part 2, two accounts of Punch's interior monologues as dreams within dreams of the puppet-maker Mountebank (apt name)—an "Epilogue" or coda belongs wholly to Mountebank, the artist figure. The division of selves thus projected, carried throughout by an effective conversational style that rarely stumbles into the swamp of nineteenth-century rhetoric that hindered previous symphonies, permits the Don Juanism of the traditional Punch to play off against the more sympathetic Punch of

Mountebank's perception of him as a trapped, tormented soul, a weak dreamer all too aware of narrow puppet boundaries, "vainly struggling / To loose weak wings from the glutinous web of fate."

These lines reflect Aiken's self-pitying image of himself in the real world. The sins of Punch in the poem—bragging and outright lying, killing Judy, almost yielding to Polly Prim's seduction—are offered (rationalized?) as the inescapable reflex actions of a highly self-conscious and sensitive creature buffeted by psychological winds beyond his control. The most terrifying reality of all, epitome of Aiken's refraction of the generic artist through the prism of his own fractured psyche, coheres in the fading grace notes of Mountebank's consciousness, which insert the pathetic dimension of powerless self-knowledge, the self observing the selves it generates without being able to alter them or him. At book's end, the stasis is frightening and absolute, puppet-master turned helpless puppet:

> . . . There was silence a moment;
> And when he turned back, expecting, perhaps, to see Judy
> Leaning her small white elbows there on the box-edge,—
> No, not a sign. The puppets lay huddled together,
> Arms over heads, contorted, just where he had dropped them;
> Inscrutable, silent, terrific, like those made eternal
> Who stare, without thought, at a motionless world without meaning.

Art about art, mythic icon, foreshadow of Memnon, *Punch* is a modernist construct that accepts the late nineteenth century's conviction that poetry had to replace religion in the cultural order in a return to ritual roots. Its climax, however, is sad rather than tragic because the desolation evoked remains at an emotional distance from the private disturbances that dictated its narrative options. The story within the story, in other words, elicits sorrow and a measure of the despair the author must feel without alighting upon the precise, most efficient metaphorical correspondence between them and his own personality, one that would permit Aiken's Punch, like Eliot's Mr. Prufrock, to embody the intense nexus of psychological dislocation and attendant agony endemic in the family-based society precipitating its reification. *Punch* comes closer than any prior attempt, aided by a mask's shelter and preordained literary structure, but the poem ends before Mountebank and Aiken can reexperience—and thereby transcend—the traumatic original drama that gestated the mute puppets. Instead of causes, again only symptoms are reconstituted.

With the character of Festus, Aiken relaxes back into the Everyman vagueness of *The House of Dust* and *The Charnel Rose,* forgetting what he should have learned from the relative success of Senlin's concrete gestures and *Punch*'s narrative leanness and directness. Superficially, *The Pilgrimage of*

Festus echoes the grandiose chapter headings of *Punch,* such as "He Plants His Beans in the Early Morning," but, as the prefatory "Argument" demonstrates, the emphasis is on a mental struggle, which almost vitiates the potential for achieving dramatic intensity. This is true despite a closing section that is almost all dialogue between protagonist and a future self, possibly revealing a minor debt to Millay's avant-garde Pierrot play performed in New York that winter.

Houston Peterson believes that several sections of *Festus* "rank with the best of Aiken's work," an understandable misjudgment that undoubtedly reflects sympathy with Aiken's propensity to concentrate on the grandeur of his thematic design at the expense of more fundamental poetic values. The biblical stanzas, for instance, are impressive, frequently transfigured by powerful tropes, but they rely on a cosmic-obsessed portentiousness that soars above the art's pervasive search for experiential nodes capable of eliciting an audience's most profound emotions:

> Festus, planting beans in the early morning,
> Far in his heart, in a solitary plain,
> Has a vision: the sun, like a golden monster
> Heaving his crimson flanks from the streaming darkness,
> No sooner seeks to rise than he is slain:
> Out of a vast sarcophagus of cloud
> Pours the black death of rain.

Such an imaginary microcosm, emulating the allegorical world of John Bunyan, cannot sustain the attention of a modern sensibility unless propelled by characterizations so specific and authoritative that they replicate a universal human entity or by original metaphors intense enough to align fantasy with the reality of contemporary existence. The narrative itself is not complex or unpredictable to a degree that could maintain interest solely through curiosity.

Aiken is here—an inner Aiken of obsessions with meaning and self and an outer Aiken who smokes a pipe and enjoys a garden—but never often, never sufficiently at risk to give his philosophic sincerity the urgency of a compulsion or the impact of poetry. Even in the section that is most clearly autobiographical, reviving the shock and horror he felt when accompanying Dr. Aiken to an operating room, Aiken's luxuriant language and his setting are inadequate to the task, a relapse into mannered decadence. Imitating a megalomaniac tyrant, Festus orders surgeons to vivisect "a princess from an eastern province" on a marble table while she is awake and while six or seven musicians play nearby:

> . . . The surgeons bend
> Intently to their work, shadows of clouds

Darken the room, darken the leaning faces,
The rose-bowl's butterfly of reflected brilliance
Pales on the ceiling, and you, too, gentle princess,
Grow pale, grow paler still, but in the shadow
Of clouds how more gigantic! Your white mouth
No longer utters cries, your golden head
No longer turns from side to side, your eyes,
Immense and dark with pain, amazed and silent,
No longer search our faces for an answer
To riddles black as these!

The moment is neither raw enough for pornography, although bound to that subgenre's sadism by a misogynist impulse, nor human enough for literary success—the princess is another puppet. The poet is too ready to concede that "riddles black as these" cannot be solved. Also, the cosmological interpretation of death and the primal revulsion against flesh limits are centered in a prepubic frame of reference that resists separation from the supposedly mature, omniscient puppet-master voice behind its inception. The thematic tactics guiding the scene's admittedly skillful contemplation of a love object's vulnerable physical aspects, and guiding the sequence as a whole, shine a potent psychopathic fantasy on a one-dimensional screen where its obvious germinating logos—desire for meaning merged with desire for a viable self—blunts and distorts the psychology animating it.

Similarly, Aiken's habitual Madonna-whore reductionism, which had always been poetically supported by his immersion in Poe's Gothic sea, surfaces in the first section of Part 2 of the five-part sequence, when Festus, after climbing "the colossal and savage stairs of the sunlight," confronts the "Grim Sphinx" as the "Woman of the bitter desert," addressing her as the witch spirit present in destructive females like Helen of Troy and Cleopatra (a favorite target), as if the violence of history, usually male-inspired, were somehow explained by the eternal malignancy of her kind, "Desolate and heartless woman!" Nowhere is there a hint of irony to suggest that the composite mythical figure depicted must be related to the perverse conceptions of her imposed by a patriarchal culture as well, that the violence afflicting humankind demands a much more complicated allegorical portrait. Instead, her equally unreal antithesis is resurrected and appealed to with a child's romantic prayer:

"Beautiful woman! golden woman whose heart is silence!
Azure pool of the eternal in which my soul bathes timidly!
Pity me, smile upon me, tell me the way
To the hold treasure which will unlock your love of me."

Significantly, at least for a biographer, the next section begins immediately after this plea to the mother's chaste shade with Festus waking under the shroud of night, aroused by his dreams and the return of an alternate self, the old man: "All my dark dreams return, sadly reproach me / With unfulfilments." One of the "unfulfilments"—for author and reader—stems from the allegory's movement away from the dreams and the truths they might elucidate, substituting philosophy for psychology. And in the final section of the poem, which follows Festus's refusal of the deification that will signify the ultimate permutation of Aiken's schema—"I will not have a god who is myself!"—there is a return to the crepuscular depression of impotent Mountebank, an image reminiscent of Stevens: "O small weak foolish brain that dared, that dared / To dream it could ever shape a world more singing out of this dust, ourselves!" The serene, meditative calm of theoretical reconciliation seemingly demanded by the sequence's superb orchestration has found instead an uneasy respite, more truce than peace, amid a concluding dialogue between protagonist and aged alter ego.

It is a climax writ large to climax all five symphonies. Music stirs in the forest during their conversation, provided by a band of butchers still clad in their blood-spotted white aprons, now green, hence fertile in paradox, beneath the moonlight. The closing speech by Festus resolves nothing, reiterating the pathos dominating sequence and symphonies:

> Thus ends our pilgrimage! We come at last,
> Here, in the twilight forests of our minds,
> To this black dream . . . Better it would have been
> To have remained forever there in the rain,
> Planting our beans together in the wind-worn plain! . . .
> Let us return . . . Are you content? . . . Let us return! . . .
> Where are you? I am alone . . . I am alone.

A coda section is an exact repetition of the volume's opening section, asserting the circular destiny of man and music, reasserting the tautological prison of self no amount of imaginative or philosophic battering can raze. Yet the symphonic or abstract validity of this arrangement denies the psychoanalytic truth it should be processing. Major motifs, such as an implicit father-son-mother triangle and the poet-as-divinity concept, which musically of course need not force a reification of their fertile essences, are left to perish in the extravagant masks donned for the concert. Their philosophic ramifications are pieces of an artistic jigsaw puzzle locking into some intellectual unity of expression, but their psychological vitality is allowed to dissipate, once again simulating only partial expenditures of repressed forces, antipodal conflicts.

Aiken would shortly suspect that the symphonies had failed, though he was too caught up in the dazzling afterglow of composition in April and May of 1920 to ponder that dire prospect. After all, the completion of *The Pilgrimage of Festus* was legitimate cause for celebration, the crowning achievement of five years of almost steady writing, an ambitious, honorable attempt to pick up the gauntlet flung down by Santayana and construct a secular quest epic in the daunting wakes of Dante and Goethe, while retaining his faith in science and the material world, in art and self as recast by the deterministic molds of psychoanalytic theories and his own skeptical American temperament. If still unable to surmount the treacherous defeatism of the Adams brothers or to transmute the James brothers' contradictory visions of pragmatic positivism and elusive multiple egos into a consistent, efficient, adequately complex aesthetic, he had never let a desperate foraging among alien modes—Eliot's or anyone else's—deter him from steadfastly pursuing a master strategy at odds with the narrower praxes of most of his contemporaries.

The slate crux of honesty that made him an effective critic also enabled him to complete his grand project from deep inside a pit dug by doubt and hostile public reaction. That same honesty, aided always by a narcissistic fear of an inner void, would compel him to contemplate the possibility that he had wasted his talent on "a series of grandiose failures," to ask himself in *Blue Voyage* the modern artist's ultimate question: "What if . . . in choosing this literary method, this deliberate indulgence in the prolix and fragmentary, I merely show myself at the mercy of a personal weakness which is not universal, or ever likely to be, but highly idiosyncratic?" *Ushant*'s longer view recalls the "self-doubt" that, at Freud's apparent command, undermined belief "in the social role of the writer," so that Aiken "had deferred, and temporized, had shied off, and gone round; he had waited, so to speak, to see; and, while waiting to see, had too often, alas, written with his eyes shut" (248–49).

Critical wisdom is retrospective and relatively painless when conceived from the outside. And yet the symphonies failed primarily because of the stranglehold of Eliot and Freud that had begun to smother Aiken's ever-fragile confidence at Harvard. The former had destroyed his trust in a Romantic heritage that ranged from Poe's instinctive grasp of pathological dynamics to Swinburne's and Thompson's lyric recapitulations of Keats's stubborn supernaturalism; the latter loosened the foundation stones of his faith in himself. Freud appeared to have this effect initially on most writers. Joyce, who was acquainted with Freud's and Jung's work from at least 1912, defensively condemned psychoanalysis as "neither more nor less than blackmail," and Mann, who conceded that *Death in Venice* "was created under the immediate influence of Freud," had serious reservations: "As an artist I have to confess, however, that I am not at all satisfied with Freudian ideas; rather, I feel disquieted and reduced by them."

Aiken's difficulties with Freud, which were not stated explicitly until *Blue Voyage* and never satisfactorily resolved, are summarized in his remark that the notion of "wish-fulfillment" could be equated with Aristotle's doctrine of tragic "cartharsis," Freud himself having related the idea to his abreaction method, the interactions between analyst and analysand. Such a comparison reduces the separation of artificer from artifice, experience abstracted and formally arranged to ritualize (and thus relieve) pent-up unconscious energies from the bifocal experience of the arranger. More relevant, however therapeutically true, boiling down "catharsis" to the thin pot bottom of a simple sublimination technique betrays a defense mechanism at work, willful blindness to the convoluted exchanges necessary between symbolic objects and community, as well as to Aiken's own more profound consideration of the problem in subsequent writings.

Eliot's durable impact, which would be reinforced when Aiken returned to London to find him nesting snugly among the Sitwells, the Lady Ottoline crowd, and the Bloomsbury set, was intensified at the literary level by an awareness that they still shared a common goal in wanting (à la Browning and James) to concentrate on psychological portraiture, albeit by different routes. He would never free himself from the pressure of Eliot's example, especially after the extraordinary success of *The Waste Land* in 1922 assured that his own career would remain permanently in the background, nor would he forget Eliot's ambivalence toward him and his poetry. But still he would salvage his conceptual blueprint, an imperative metaphysic and a private credo, from the wreckage of the verse symphonies, and he would eventually fashion major literature from the volatile material they had squandered. Beginning with an argumentative review of *The Sacred Wood* in 1921, he also would oppose Eliot in the critical sphere with growing acerbic certainty.

Recently given final shape by Adams's theory of civilization attaining its last phase of thought, Aiken's master design might be described as an amalgamation of Freud, Bergson, Nietzsche, and what he had learned about Bradley from Eliot's Harvard thesis, "Meinong's *Gegendstandstheorie* Considered in Relation to Bradley's Theory of Knowledge," which he read with sincere admiration. These he had welded to both Santayana's vision of the epic poet's philosophic task and his personal recognition of the poet's function as enlarger of human consciousness in a secular but Romantic context—that is, "religion without revelation," to use Kant's phrase, an antecedent of Emerson's and Grandfather Potter's sophisticated Unitarianism. Aiken was probably unaware of his "consistent view's" philosophic origins in Kant's seminal acceptance of the relative, finite conditions of phenomena as real, if incomplete, to any perception except God's, a form of discovery "that is at the same time a concealing." Hegel later expanded this notion to include the idea that the mind's transcendence of natural conditions was a divine process, humanity's progressive discovery of the world proceeding in tandem with God's progressive forming of the world, moving always toward a dialectical reconciliation.

Aiken's master design had a more immediate base in the English Romantics and their European allies, in an artistic revolt best configured intellectually by Kierkegaard's claustrophobic absorption in self, which entailed consciousness seen in despairing separation from godhead. Nietzsche's critical, fundamentally reactionary, and impressionistic role in this design was a determined dilation of Kierkegaard's exclusive emotional focus on the ego's dilemma as sole arbiter of self, reality, and meaning. Aiken borrowed Schopenhauer's interpretation of power as human will and coupled it with Kant's god-man conjunction and Hegel's dialectic to postulate a species of positive pessimism. The Lucretian myth of progress was reversed, with salvation sought in the unconscious (Dionysus) and a predicted race of supermen "beyond good and evil" whose ancestors are Plato's philosopher-kings and Carlyle's profiles of the hero. Devolved from an exciting mix of broad philosophical knowledge and adolescent egomania, Nietzsche's haughty splashes of insight were central to Aiken precisely because they were grounded in an ironic, rebellious experiential field that prefigured so much of Freud. Aiken's ultimate superman configuration would be the poet who embraces his neuroses or complex, exposing his own deepest workings to the abstract light of literary structure, and manufactures the endless series of mirrors (mirrors within mirrors) essential to the evolution of human consciousness into godhead.

In the 1960s, when talking to D. G. Bridson, Aiken avowed his commitment to Santayana's concept of "animal faith" and admitted, "I've always rather subscribed to the notion that we are, as it were, the 'becoming of God,' and I think Hardy somewhat held that view that we were God's consciousness— I think he went so far as to say that, or that our consciousness is the coming to consciousness of God." *Ushant*'s memory of the pursuit of an aesthetic program, which is presented as paralleling a search for "the artifact of civilization," identified it as "the unremitting quest for an equivalent *finesse* and logic in understanding, a quest which had led him from Darwin to Nietzsche and Bergson, for instance, and Santayana, and from these in turn to [Flinders] Petrie and Freud" (303). But the intellectual order of the ascent seems suspect, since it was Nietzsche and Bergson who were most crucial to Aiken's struggle to integrate (and thereby neutralize) threatening Freudian material and Bradley's finite epicenters with a more positive poetic stance in line with the redemptive aspects of Emerson's and his grandfather's writings.

Nietzsche, who respected Emerson, had revolted against the Western philosophical tradition from the start, characterizing Plato's Socrates and Aristotle as representatives of a "decadent" mode in Hellenistic thought, dangerous technicians who smothered instinct with rationality and fatally severed the union with the world achieved by pre-Socratic philosophers. Philosophers such as Heraclitus had at least envisioned themselves as part of nature's flux. Labeling himself "the first tragic philosopher" because of his Dionysian link with "the psychology of the tragic poet," Nietzsche proudly used the term "psychologist" for himself and as a pennant of praise when unfurled elsewhere. He sought to expose the ways in which Plato's separation of the ideal from the real and Aristotle's scientific methodology introduced a schizophrenic disassociation of self from self that could engender the foulest of evils, however necessary to technological and material development.

To wit, the mind in the laboratory that can contemplate the agonized behavior of mice whose hind legs have been cut off in an effort to study traumatized motor responses and perhaps save human lives is remote in degree, not kind, from the mind of a Nazi doctor in a concentration camp hospital busily recording the death throes of prisoners injected with disease viruses. At the pith is madness: once the ego learns to fracture itself deliberately in the name of objectivity, it is capable of assuming an infinite variety of monstrous shapes. Philosophy, Nietzsche insisted, must return to its poetical and religious roots, must function as a psychology of being, where the unconscious—our umbilical cord to nature—might again vent creative energies without fear of separation from the universe's germinal dynamic. Most pertinent to Aiken was Nietzsche's unwavering loyalty to the poetic function. In *The Birth of Tragedy,* Nietzsche had illuminated the special relationship between self and art in a lyric poet: "The lyrical poet . . . himself becomes his images, his images are objectified versions of himself. Being the active center of that world he may boldly speak in the first person, only his 'I' is not that of the actual waking man, but the 'I' dwelling, truly and eternally, in the ground of being. It is through the reflections of that 'I' that the lyric poet beholds the ground of being."

That "ground of being," which gives the poet contact with the "eternal recurrence" of things Nietzsche insisted pulse at the core of the universe, could easily be connected to Bergson's "*elan vital*" to bestow universality (hence divinity) upon poetic reverie, especially after interlacing Bergson's "creative evolution" with Emerson's similar conversion of Darwin's natural selection theory into the "ideal development" and "spiritual evolution" preached by Louis Agassiz, famed professor of natural history at Harvard. Like his friend Reverend Potter, Emerson's benevolent façade concealed cold girders of purpose, which included an awareness of nature's menacing Heraclitan flow and acute readings of human psychology, whether dealing with compensatory reflexes or power drives. Yet, like Arnold, he remained convinced that knowing oneself, the Socratic ideal he refused to abandon regardless of uncomfortable theological implications, was both pivotal and moral—despite grave reservations, Melville had fancied Emerson because "I love all men who *dive*."

Aiken could now, in a noetic sense, begin to counteract Freud's dissection of mankind's irrational components and its correlative reduction of the creative impulse by an appeal to Nietzsche's no less psychological elevation of the poet to divine status, superior in suffering and vision. Bergson, however, helped front the other major threat to an individual identity, Darwin, by giving further intellectual credence to a psychologically perceived ego, *contra* a mere rationalist or empiric self. He posited a consistent, evolutionary "I" below the serial selves that experience tells us is the rule of ordinary experience, "below the self with well-defined states, a self in which *succeeding each other* means *melting into one another* and forming an organic whole." The problem was, as Bradley saw, that such a conception requires an act of faith, a metaphysical reordering of felt experience and scientific data, to make the transition from the series of discrete selves that psychology framed to an evolutionary system.

For Aiken, to whom Bergson was a fruitful discovery in spite of subsequent hostility, the key Bergsonian premise dealt directly with his (and Eliot's) insidious felt knowledge of the ego's endless fragmentation and self-deceptions. "Consciousness, goaded by an insatiable desire to separate," he said, "substitutes the symbol for the reality, or perceives the reality only through the symbol. As the self thus refracted, and thereby broken into pieces, is much better adapted to the requirements of social life in general and language in particular, consciousness prefers it, and gradually loses sight of the fundamental self." The search for his "fundamental self" amid gaudy surface shards and dimmer psychoanalytic selves was at the heart of the verse symphonies and of everything Aiken was to write thereafter, a basic but complex stream of sentience beneath Freud's irrational psyche, ever conscious—even as it manipulates its alter egos—of itself and them.

What Bradley did for Aiken, via Eliot, who had to cast off both Bergson and Bradley in his panic-stricken search for a mystical path to permanent redemption, was to reconfirm the elemental validity of Bergson's schema and reinforce his own skepticism, his need for rational verification. Committed to the Hegelian injunction that "you must put your whole self, your entire will, into the will of the divine," an injunction that would not have endeared him to Aiken, Bradley never accepted the unphilosophical idea that religious submission obviated the intellectual responsibility of his calling. He was fiercely logical in his tenacious analysis of the self, the unity of which seemed far from apparent, Bergson to the contrary, since empirical evidence indicated otherwise. Consequently, the sole despairing conclusion to be reached, though never despairing to Bradley, safe in the arms of Oxford and the church, was that no single satisfactory theory of self was tenable or plausible, that our perception of self at any given moment represented appearance, never reality. "Personal identity," he confessed, "is mainly a matter of degree."

This theory explains Eliot's defection, though he never lost respect for the man and his mind, and Aiken's positive response to Bradley's thought, impressed by the obstinate honesty of his efforts to corral the ego's elusive enigmas. In reference to Aiken's improvised metaphysic, Bradley supported Bergson's description of a disconnected string of symbolic and symbolizing selves, which meant that his poetic ambition to capture the various selves in actual flight had strong philosophic backing. Also, the consciousness on display could simultaneously remain outside the process, observing and amassing the selves it generated into a continuous whole, which constituted man evolving into deity, ceaseless figures embracing physical and mental worlds beyond time's limits. It could thus expand his own ego, shoring up a battered psyche while providing mankind with a new cultural identity: the coming to consciousness of self and phenomena in a mimic rephrase of Henry Adams's brilliant last stage of human history.

The schema could not, of course, write successful poetry for Aiken, as the symphonies demonstrate, but this somewhat baroque carpentry did give him a solid pair of wings for the time when he would be capable of defying his father to seek the sun, aligning its thematic architecture with obsessive designs below consciousness to reconnoiter the country of his ravaged youth. First, like many of his generation and vocation, he would have to undergo a severe nervous breakdown, the impending psychic disintegration that Eliot was to confront in less than a year, before being freed, then forced to trace the fissures in his identity back to a family romance that had transformed him, forever, into an artist, the eternal narcissistic outsider. Afterward would come neurotic healing, the patching together of a relatively stable myth of self essential to survival and literature. The pattern was hardly new to his time and place, and it had been familiar to Mill, Tennyson, and other Victorians of the generation his own was endeavoring to conquer and incorporate, though Aiken's specific existential quandary was intensified by his inability, unlike Eliot, to betray a former self into its conservative antithesis or yield to a submissive spiritual urge he had always found demeaning. The myth of self that he would finally construct, as articulated by the Bible of *Ushant* and implicit in all the poetry from *Preludes for Memnon* onward, would be fastened to a traditional metaphysical impulse only by the tenuous vagueness of Santayana's "animal faith" and a familial identification with Reverend Potter's ethical courage, plus unconceded alliances with Jungian tenets concerning "racial memories" and a collective unconscious. Its main outline suggests the artist-saint projected by Pater and Arnold and sanctified by Nietzsche's *Ecce Homo,* the poet as *corpus vile* and grand synthesizer, crucified porcine victim and terrifyingly conscious prophet.

Emerson, Reverend Potter, and American history would supply much of the social and narrative mortar for the erection of this ultimate self and myth, as had Henry Adams by his example and theory and as had (and would) Henry James and Melville by the witness they bore to American literature's need to assemble alternative vehicles of consciousness. But it was probably the partnership, in Aiken's mind, of Freud and Bergson that was most important, if only because the latter ameliorated the former's determinism and reductionist threats while concomitantly aiding the conversion of Darwinian savagery into a spiral of moral and rational progress. In the spring of 1920, however, buoyed by the completion of *The Pilgrimage of Festus* and not yet ensnared in any postpartum depression, Aiken could think of little but his planned trip to England, which was being delayed by red tape. His confidence in the recently finished symphony is reflected in his desire to have a section of it appear in Louis Untermeyer's forthcoming miscellany.

His touchy relationship with Untermeyer had not been improved by the publication of *Modern American Poetry,* first in several series of contemporary verse anthologies that would make Untermeyer preeminent in the field, which, Aiken complained, was riddled by incompetents and sluggards who rarely bothered to read all of a poet's work before making their selections, content to imitate the taste of prior anthologists. Aiken argued with several of Untermeyer's choices and omissions, particularly his omission of Eliot, and with his introductory comments on Aiken's own career, which had again criticized him for not developing a mature, individual voice and for lapsing too frequently into vague, if melodious, rhetoric. Like other anthologists, Untermeyer chose "Music That I Have Heard with You" and two monologues from *Senlin.* Aiken's letter of complaint is not extant, but Untermeyer's reply is—a letter dated January 11, 1919, though actually written in 1920—in which he apologizes for slighting Eliot and asks his correspondent to "bear in mind that this hesitant collection is part propaganda, an effort to combat the entrenched prejudices of the average teacher of Litrachoor. And Win him over—gradually."

He openly mocks other of Aiken's objections, and Aiken's defense of two excluded favorites by Moody brings forth more cheerful derision: "The spectacle of the author of *Scepticisms* poring over 'The Daguerrotype' is something worthy of a Max Beerbohm cartoon." As of his repeated assaults upon Aiken's poetry, Untermeyer is no less certain: "If you will look up my printed and private remarks, you will discover that what I implied—and said—was that your work revealed not, as you have put it, 'a progressive decay,' but a succession of styles *instead* of any definite progression." He goes on to discuss the planned miscellany, a biennial, "on the order of the Georgian anthologies, only more full of poetry and less crowded with poets." Each contributor would be allotted "from two to twenty pages of new poetry," the idea being "to present something quite distinctive and fresh—something as far away from the Braithwaite bunk as possible." At this point, besides Aiken, the writers involved were Frost, Sandburg, Lindsay, Lowell, Sara Teasdale, James Oppenheim, the Untermeyers, Robinson, if he had something available, and possibly Fletcher.

It was a representative, fairly talented group, excluding Untermeyer and his wife, and Aiken knew that the volume's financial success was almost assured by its editor's entrepreneurial skills. Interestingly, in countering Untermeyer's charge of a lack of evolution in his verses, he once more stressed that the symphonic series had been published out of sequence—*The House of Dust* had appeared earlier that year, but *Punch* would not see print until the next year, followed in two years by *Festus*. He would also tell Jake Wilbur that he had deliberately arranged to have the sequence published out of order to confound the public and the critics, wary of their discerning personal information, because he had intended for the symphonies to be autobiographical. The truth is that no one, not even one of those closest to him, was ever likely to unearth many confessional references, buried under tons of allegorical cosmetics and abstracting layers of music analogies.

Aiken was not lying. Autobiography was a definite element in the symphonies' theoretical stagecraft. But the patent absurdity of his thinking again points up why the symphonies failed to achieve their ambitious goals: his refusal to accept his schema's imperative to burrow deeper into his own life for sources of conscious motivation. Only then could his plan to spotlight the artist in the naked act of mining ego and art culminate in moving, powerful, relevant poetry. Only then could that art fulfill the saving function that art always executes in its eternal struggle against oblivion. The matrix of autobiography and meaning that he feared might be detected in the symphonies was missing in their flawed expression—not merely private gossip and family history but such material in creative contact with psychological patterns generated by its disjunctions. If poetry was to rescue him from potential dissolution, it would have to use the beautiful schema his intelligence and learning had diligently hammered whole to sail into unknown reservoirs of the unconscious. As such contemporary philosophers as Ludwig Wittgenstein were discovering that the demands of their era required retreats into language, so Aiken would have to face the reality that literature's endless campaign to recapture ground lost whenever a word or image netted a meaning or meanings and excluded others would now have to refine the seine of figurative insight to encompass strands of self weaved by Freud.

None of this could he discuss with Untermeyer or other critics, which was another reason for returning to England and Eliot. He had yet to work out all the implications of his theoretical stance. The problem of his basic insecurity and a schema he did not really want to requite was exacerbated by the continued strain placed on his marriage by the move to South Yarmouth. Jessie's discontent and loneliness, only minimally relieved by visits from the Untermeyers and Linscotts, were increased by a growing awareness of the negative effect of the rural environment on the children. She was shocked when she heard John and Jane begin to acquire the local dialect and appalled by the crude behavior and language of neighborhood toughs, particularly upset to think that John would soon be attending the Cape's primitive public school system. Her strong maternal instincts and middle-class orientation, part and parcel of the supposed "innocence" that prevented her from recognizing her husband's infidelities, could not abide the prospect of her children maturing in such a limited cultural milieu. When Aiken finally sailed in May, he had her earnest blessing.

But the slow disintegration of their marriage, about which he was sensitive to a degree unsuspected by her—when Robert Taylor visited near the end of the year, he would notice "quite a bit of static" in his brother's household—left him emotionally vulnerable to the charms of another siren he would encounter on the voyage, someone to replace the lost Marian, who had evaded all his attempts to track her down. He was still regressing toward an earlier stage of existence, longing again for a Poelike heroine and lamia to pursue.

The heroine was Reine Ormond, beautiful and aristocratic niece of the artist John Singer Sargent, associated with Edward Burne Jones and the Pre-Raphaelite coterie. He had spotted her at the New York dock when he sailed for England in 1920 and had been stunned by the mixture of adoration and fear she inspired: "What was it, about her, that had so agitated him from the outset, when he had seen her climb up the gangway, slowly, then turn about on the deck [?] . . . she had, from the beginning, produced a peculiar change in him: She had made him shy, she had stripped him of his defenses, she had taken ten years from his age and made him a callow and awkward youth of seventeen." The quotation is from *Blue Voyage,* which Aiken called "a self-portrait pure and simple" and which is based on a second trip to England undertaken a year later. Ormond, as "Cynthia," dominates the novel as she dominated Aiken's mind and emotions during the crossing, casting a spell over him that only a boy in his early teens infatuated with an older cheerleader might fully appreciate. Three days passed before he had an opportunity to meet her, avoiding her in the meantime out of concern over the devastating effect she had on him. A friend of his introduced him when informed by Ormond that she was seeking a fellow chess player to relieve the tedium of the voyage.

The chess games inevitably gave rise to an easy acquaintance and mutual flirtation as he learned that she was binational, having lived part of her life in America, and possessed a highly cultivated background. Her beauty and regal bearing, her upper-class assurance, her schooled intellect and intimate associations with the near-legendary Pre-Raphaelites, "her exquisite old-worldliness" all combined to metamorphose her lovely form into a hovering Lenore, chaste and desirable. His self-conscious passion for her, which he never dared confess, obviously evoked childhood memories of Anna Aiken, the lost, unfaithful mother, the idol image—half madonna, half Circe—he retained of her from Savannah, with her gay parties and aristocratic aura. *Blue Voyage* confirms that he was soon conscious of this psychological association, his torturous, unrequited love for Cynthia acting as a springboard for recollecting Savannah and his mother, whom he imagines Cynthia seeing through the lens of his memory: "Surely you like my mother sitting there with her parasol?" Near the end of the novel, in his mind, he concedes that Reine Ormond had struck "more numerous and deeper responses in me than any other woman has done. It must be that you correspond, in ways that only my unconscious memory identifies, to my mother."

Perhaps Ormond physically resembled Anna Aiken as well, as did Jessie, but she was immediately superior to Jessie in not having yet let him sexually violate her, in not having let him observe her as a real human being. Also, unlike the banished Marian and other exploited women he identified with a social order somewhat below his, Ormond incarnated not the whore image but that of the Blessed Virgin on a pedestal, remote, uncontaminated, yet radiating maternal sympathy and sublimated sensuality, prepubic in her plaster perfection. Lust was not absent, merely filtered through a boy's imagined consummation with a delicious swell of curves that did not bleed, stink, sweat, or in any gross way betray flesh boundaries, fornication with the beautiful mother, who is without sin and incapable of bestowing guilt. Reine Ormond synthesized the polar caricatures of womanhood that had bedeviled Aiken's life since Savannah, qualities he had undoubtedly convinced himself Jessie had represented before marriage set in.

There was also social ambivalence, the upper-class façade that Aiken so admired, even as his democratic soul rejected its validity, and there were the woman's literate interests, which meant that his artistic achievements, his strongest weapon, could be appreciated in the schoolgirl way his wife had once appreciated them. Her cool distance, her self-confidence, the automatic command and gentle hints of intrinsic superiority attracted him as well, a tug of relentless oppositions, the son again questing for maternal firmness and love in an ambiguous, frightening world. Behind it, the blatant fact that she was beyond reach intensified the callow worship of her that began to obsess and diminish him. In *Blue Voyage* he uses Adler's term "inferiority complex" to explain the difficulties the protagonist encounters when interacting with the character who is Ormond. He is always tense and uncertain in her company, though relishing their time together and apparently making a good impression on her, asking himself: "Why was it that he never could be at his ease with those who were socially his equals—only at ease with his 'inferiors'?"

Further, he admits to "a passionate attachment for the fine and rich," although aware that "every so often he wanted a good deep bath in the merely vulgar. An occasional debauch was imperative,—whether it was only a visit to a cheap vaudeville . . . or a shabby little clandestine adventure of his own, in which his motive was largely, if not entirely, curiosity." Curiosity was hardly the compelling motive beneath the affair with Marian or "the brief, violent, disgusting Helen Shafter affair," his very language here steeped in infantile revulsion. Aiken was not being totally honest, even in a novel intent upon Joycean candor, in which his marital status is obscured. But he was voyaging closer to a variety of home truths as the liner docked in Liverpool. He became increasingly frantic over the possibility that he might never see Reine Ormond again, though he knew she lived at fashionable Cheyne Walk and had welcomed the notion of his calling on her.

He met her and her aunt, Sargent's wife, at Euston Station, where he was introduced to her father, whom he liked instantly, but the night before, which he spent in the Northwestern Hotel, panic had descended, "when I had one nightmare after another all night long, trying to find her," until morning brought the discovery of the two women alone in the dining room having breakfast. During the train ride into London he went to her compartment to give her a copy of the *Nation,* which she was delighted to receive. Later she came to retrieve him and they returned to her compartment for a long conversation while the aunt dozed across the way from them.

Once in London, however, though happy to see Armstrong, who had lost none of his teasing affection for him or their shared zest for extravagant flights of fancy, Aiken experienced an acute sense of loss. He spent the first afternoon in Hyde Park among a flotilla of deck chairs, wondering when he dared make his first call on her, concluding glumly that he could not properly do so before a week or two had passed. Two days after his arrival, reverting to a typical childhood pattern, he actually ventured to Battersea Bridge and located her genteel cottage, staring at it with shy longing from a distance. By the third day the anxiety was unbearable, and he worked up sufficient courage to ring the bell, which turned out well because she gaily invited him inside and, over the next several weeks, would accompany him to various concerts and museums. But the enchantment of being in her presence, of touching her hand or hearing her laugh at one of his witticisms, did not erase the heartache that her companionship also brought, "that frightful and inescapable and unwearying consciousness of the unattainable." He never told her he was married.

London did provide other pleasures to salve his wound, the tension induced by trying to maintain a relaxed, casual relationship with an adored woman outside his reach, but the depth of Reine Ormond's impact upon him can be gauged from the fact that by June 10 he had written four poems about her, first in a series that would eventually portray her as another ice queen, a Beatrice as dead to him as Lenore had been to Poe. The hope of finding a British publisher was also proving an illusion, Brown's English agent having stood him up twice. There were consolations in his roommate's company, the meals shared at old favorites like the Gourmet, the Brice, and the Chantecleer after Armstrong returned home each night, their visits to Colonel Wright's flat to hear pianola concerts, the colonel also introducing him to the inexpensive art of buying Oriental prints. In addition, they attended the poetry squashes at the Poetry Bookshop, where he renewed his acquaintance with Harold Monro and F. S. Flint and came to meet Richard Aldington, whose wife, H. D., was off in California with Winifred Bryher, Edward Shanks, Georgian poet and assistant editor of Squire's *Mercury,* and John Cournos, the Russian-American novelist and former newspaper editor, a thin, dark man with aquiline features and a relaxed openness that offered a pleasant change from the guarded manners of so many of his English colleagues.

One English friend Aiken made and was destined to keep was John Freeman, self-educated poet and highly successful insurance executive with the Liverpool Victoria Friendly Society, who as a child had had scarlet fever, which left him with a weak heart and scant chance of surviving much beyond his forties—he was now forty. Described by friends as "a slight man, with large eyes, somewhat long but well-kept hair, an expressive mouth, and a receding chin," Freeman owned a pleasant home in Anerly, where he lived with his wife, Gertrude, and their two daughters and which he said was always open to Aiken. In *Ushant,* Freeman is gifted with Shakespeare's adjective "gentle," and his kindness to his American friend, whose poetry he liked, was unstinting. His own poetry was traditionally mellifluous and primarily rural in theme, unmemorable in every respect, though his recently published *Poems New and Old* had won the Hawthornden Prize. He seconded Aiken's inordinate fondness for George Moore, the subject of his next book in 1922, and admired Herman Melville, whose life he would write in 1926 as a volume in the English Men of Letters series at the request of John Middleton Murry, another Melville enthusiast. The first collected edition of Melville's works was to be an English enterprise in 1923–24, the English having recognized his achievement (as they did Whitman's) before his native country did, although the next several years would see him receiving serious attention at home as well.

Eliot, who was busy working at Lloyd's Bank, putting together his initial collection of essays, dealing with an ailing wife, and establishing himself more securely among the people who mattered, seemed glad to see Aiken. There was, however, a new distance between them, and neither suspected that the other was going through a difficult period. In a June 10 letter to Jessie, to whom he wrote once a week and whose sense of isolation had been lifted by the arrival of her family, Aiken tells about lunching that day with Eliot and finding him reserved, albeit amiable, the old bantering tone of their intercourse muted to a few flashes of humor. Eliot encouraged him to send for his family and stay the winter and introduced him to a few of the younger writers, such as Aldous Huxley, who had left a post at Eton the previous year to come to London to work on the *Athenaeum* and write poetry. Aiken would have enjoyed meeting Pound again, but Pound was as busy as ever, soon involved with seeing *Hugh Selwyn Mauberly* into print and with preparations for moving to Paris.

One distinct success of the 1920 London visit, which would last till August, was meeting Jean de Bosschere. After the two dined together on a warm early June evening, John Cournos took Aiken to the Belgian poet's flat, where they encountered Maxwell Bodenheim and his wife, Minna, and two other couples. Minna had managed to borrow enough money to get them to England in May after Untermeyer, who had given generously in the past, turned down her husband's arrogant "request" for a $350 loan. Aiken was intrigued by de Bosschere—a small, gnomish man of about forty-five, pale, almost Napoleonic—although, as usual, he felt uncomfortable and awkward among strangers. Finally, he was able to steal an opportunity to speak with him alone for about fifteen minutes and was not disappointed. Fletcher had shown de Bosschere Aiken's approving review of *The Closed Door,* which created an immediate rapport, and de Bosschere asked him to visit again when he returned from a brief trip to Paris, promising to give Aiken copies of his earlier work.

The presence in London of such American friends as Eliot, McCouch, Bodenheim, and John Gould Fletcher, who was living in a grand house at a fancy address, aided Aiken's efforts to conquer the literary scene and encouraged his tentative plan to settle in London by winter. The more affected groups that circled around the *Athenaeum* and Bloomsbury and Lady Ottoline's temporary salon at her friend Ethel Sands's house in The Vale (Chelsea), however, proved less convivial. The familiar problem of Aiken's stiff self-consciousness came into frequent conflict with English formality and un-spoken class distinctions, keeping him in a limbo of uncertainty regarding his future chances as an expatriate and resulting in a fervent wish that England were populated solely by Americans. He lunched often, for instance, with Murry and other members of the *Athenaeum* staff and attended the journal's weekly dinners but was never accepted as an equal, at least in his own eyes. He surrendered his "American Letter" column in a fit of pique, preferring instead to write for and deal with Squire's *Mercury* and its "hearty simplicities."

The November 1920 *Mercury,* which would contain a poem by Aiken entitled "Flight," commented on the fifth number of *Coterie* that "the most interesting things are a poem by Conrad Aiken and a story by Aldous Huxley," and a review of Untermeyer's *Miscellany of American Poetry* by Squire himself praised Lindsay's contribution and "good work also by Conrad Aiken and Robert Frost." Shanks's "London Letter" in the June 1920 *Dial,* which included another Aiken poem, "Asphalt," about the darkness at the core of the world, argued with an Aiken essay in an earlier *Athenaeum* that had claimed the British persisted in viewing America as "a nation of barbarians—uncouth, restless, sharp at a bargain; enormously conceited and naked of culture." Shanks denied the charge, expressing gratitude for the United States's "larger appetite for would-be good, and especially for experimental literature," even as he confessed that his country's perception of American literature was comparatively low. Aiken had already begun to verify at first hand the reality of his protest.

But June was a time for adolescent dreams, and London never appeared friendlier, in large measure because of his continued contacts with Reine Ormond. Early in the month, while preparing to take her for tea as planned, Aiken was interrupted by the maid's announcement of two lady visitors, whom he asked to be shown upstairs. It was Ormond and Claire Mackail, Burne-Jones's granddaughter. *Blue Voyage* records the joy and embarrassment their surprise visit instigated: "I hurried dressing. . . . It was she and that artist's daughter. . . . 'What a lovely room!' she cried, 'and how extraordinary to find it in *this* street!' " She asked if he would prefer to attend an afternoon concert at Wigmore Hall, a Bach concerto, instead of having tea, and when he said he would, she told him to meet her in front of the theater.

After the concert they went to her house for tea, and a week later he escorted her across Waterloo Bridge to the Old Vic to take in a revival of ancient native dances and music, which they abandoned before the final curtain out of boredom in favor of a visit to the National Portrait Gallery in Trafalgar Square. Soon, however, she disappeared from his life as abruptly as she had entered it, leaving for an extended stay in France. Her departure only increased his desire to move to England, a desire he persuasively justified in his letters home by speaking of lower rents and generally cheaper prices, plus a refreshing scarcity of Bolshevism. The next decision was where they could settle if London proved too expensive. McCouch, whose wife was in the hospital for an operation, sang the praises of Oxford as a permanent residence, promising to take him to the famed college town when Cecile recovered. McCouch himself was busy with neurological research at Maudsley Hospital and managed to convince Aiken to serve "as *corpus vile* for some experiments" during the course of the summer.

However darkened by the loss of Reine Ormond and by his lack of success with both British publishers and high society, Aiken's months in England were far from dull. Though he did pass many days occupying a penny chair in Hyde Park awaiting Armstrong's afternoon returns, he also explored the city on his own and accompanied Colonel Wright on his print-hunting expeditions. One dealer in Holborn was impressed by his interest and taught him how to recognize the signatures of important Japanese artists. Other days were given over to sallies into outlying villages in search of the ideal domicile; Aiken hoped to locate an inexpensive rustic retreat within reasonable distance of London that was not as narrowly provincial as South Yarmouth.

At the end of his nearly four-month sojourn he had visited Windermere, Rye, Chichester, Keith Hill, Arundel, and Oxford, the last in the company of McCouch as knowledgeable tour guide. Except for a week's holiday in the Lake Country, most of his excursions were one-day affairs, diverting but exhausting. Cournos and Armstrong had been particularly insistent that he investigate Rye, which they believed would be a perfect choice because of its antiquity, the beauty of its harbor and marsh, its easy access to London (a two-hour train ride), and its resort-type charm that had always attracted writers and artists, alleviating inevitable small-town rigidities. The presence of Lamb House, Henry James's former dwelling, was enough to lure Aiken. Armstrong, his *cicerone* on the Arundel trip, took him for a weekend to the Sussex coast at the confluence of three small rivers where sat Rye and Winchelsea. In Winchelsea, the lovely town perched on a hill across the inlet from Rye, they had lunch and then walked down to the shore before returning to their inn. In Rye they climbed the Strand, the cobbled main street, passing the ancient house that the Aikens would purchase in a few years on their way to Lamb House.

By September 1920 Aiken was back in South Yarmouth, still torn and uncertain, happy to be back among his lilac bushes and poplars and the surrounding pine woods and salt marshes, yet far from content. Nothing had been resolved, and the anguish over losing Reine Ormond, whom, of course, he had never *had* in any fashion, gnawed at his imagination. Before leaving London he had received a note from Eliot, who was then at a Windermere hotel preparatory to departing for a Paris holiday—a trip Aiken had originally intended to make with him—expressing sincere regret that he was not going to remain for the winter. In a bitter reply, which is undated but must have been written after August 4 and before the fourteenth, the date of Eliot's departure, Aiken stresses the mixed feelings his impending return to South Yarmouth was eliciting. He said he preferred the Cape's crude but open manners to the glacial reserve of the English, especially the sterile, scheming reserve of English literary figures at *Athenaeum* functions. His negative reaction was shared by Virginia Woolf, who had also recently parted company with the journal and who wrote on September 15 in her diary: "Thank God, I've stepped clear of that *Athenaeum* world, with its reviews, editions, lunches, and tittle tattle."

And yet Aiken closes by conceding that a return in 1921 was possible. In *Ushant* (292), where a retrospective analysis of his career is phrased in the context of "this merciless warfare" that "had been proceeding, both in England and America, ever since," he recalls an *Athenaeum* luncheon at which he was seated between Woolf and Katherine Mansfield, whose fiction he thought second to none, except his adored Chekhov. The two women seemed to regard each other with "feral enmity" while exchanging pleasantries. The next day he visited Mansfield for tea at her Hampstead home. After discovering a shared love of rain, his hostess drew out his opinion of Woolf's writing, which he cagily deemed "interesting," until she finally got him to add a note or two to her "grace-notes of animadversion" (293). When, at last, he uttered the word "sterile," she instantly sprang to her feet "like a panther, her eyes flashing, and cried—'*Sterile*! But of course—!—*Sterile*!' "

Aiken could not know or anticipate the genuine affection that was to develop between the two talented women—the luncheon had been their first meeting—beneath the defensive thrusts and counterthrusts, a consequence of unavoidable friction between two substantial but vulnerable egos. One belonged to a colonial outsider never quite comfortable in English drawing rooms, the other to an inbred, sensitive, high-strung intellect always in the process (like Aiken's) of doubting its own considerable powers. Nor could he sense, then or later, that Woolf's accomplishments would mature beyond Mansfield's ken. What he could appreciate was that the revolving galaxy of the arts, especially among literature's sublunary orbits, reflected the remorseless competition evident whenever and wherever human beings sought to establish power structures, regardless or because of that power's illusory nature. Every gravitational pull and repulsion was stretched tauter by the special character of the psyches involved and by an unadmitted awareness of how impossible it was to predict the absolute significance of contemporary achievements, Aiken's claims for a "scientific" critical apparatus notwithstanding.

With familiar dry incisiveness, Eliot later summed up the matter: "As things are, and as fundamentally they must always be, poetry is not a career but a mug's game. No honest poet can ever feel quite sure of the permanent value of what he has written: he may have wasted his time and messed up his life for nothing." But Aiken was the Poet of White Horse Vale, too wrapped up in an exalted conception of his calling to accept the struggle for recognition that went with it as a mere "mug's game," too emotionally committed to it as an escape from the briar patch his parents had thrown him into, a means for imposing his ego upon the world, which he secretly feared. "*Apologia Pro Specie Sua*" had made clear that the "second stage" of a poet's career meant to him a public battle to convince hostile critical forces of the worth of what he had wrought. Until he could emotionally comprehend that the second stage of a poet's career actually commences with the realization that mastering the profession has priority over tangential endeavors to court attention and public approval, he would be unable to slake the ambitions of his noble schema. Nor would he find anything approaching personal peace. If choosing between life and art is the sole option, as Yeats suggested, then the sacrifice is without justification unless the poet matures enough to embrace the ultimately selfless dedication demanded by his constant raids upon the inarticulate. Not that fame, money, and the high opinion of supposed peers are ever unimportant or undesired—there is not sufficient praise in the universe to stuff the black hole of a poet's vanity—but they have to assume a subsidiary position.

In Aiken's case, the squabbling and hypocritical backstabbing among the frightfully correct literati in England seemed, at least for the moment, somehow worse than similar warfare waged by their American counterparts because the ostensible personality of the British appeared geared toward snobbishly crushing those born outside the gates of their public-school culture. Having encountered similar attitudes at Harvard and in Cambridge, and not entirely free of aristocratic conceit, he would exempt many English friends, like Armstrong, from such a gross generalization. Also, the London literary scene of the period was not nearly as rigid as it had once been, thanks to such interlopers as Pound, Eliot, Lewis, and Joyce, who, with the aid of more native insurgents—Hueffer (now Ford), Lawrence, and Wells—were forcing new modes of artistic consciousness upon the city, although Pound was bound for Paris—site of the next upheaval—and Joyce remained in Italy. But their relative success did not resolve Aiken's need to secure a toehold in the treacherous terrain of a restricted marketplace, where destructive rather than constructive criticism, often as malicious as gossip, held sway.

A few weeks after dispatching his sour note to Eliot, Aiken experienced a taste of such criticism when *House of Dust* was reviewed anonymously in the *Times Literary Supplement* (August 26) and by Huxley in the *Athenaeum*. The *Times* reviewer labeled the poetry "delicate and imaginative" but damned with very faint regret: "He is not easy to understand, and some minds would doubt whether a drift of phenomena so irrational as this, however delicately and imaginatively it is described, can be worth describing, except from the point of view of scientific interest." Huxley, who became an Untermeyer-like *bête noir* to his career despite a congenial personal relationship, granted Aiken "many poetical merits," then bemoaned that "he has the defects of his qualities. His facility is his undoing; for he is content to go on pouring out melodious language—content to go on linking image to bright image almost indefinitely. One begins to long for clarity and firmness, for a glimpse of something definite outside this golden haze."

Huxley's attack, which he subsequently elaborated on in an essay entitled "Subject-Matter of Poetry," extolled him as perhaps "the most successful exponent in poetry of contemporary ideas" but complained that the "trouble with Mr. Aiken is that his emotions are apt to degenerate into a kind of intellectual sentimentality, which expresses itself only too easily in his prodigiously fluent, highly colored verse." Variations on this charge were to be repeated by others over the years and were accurate enough to magnify intrinsic insecurities but never sufficiently cognizant of his work's telic shape, as he would soon complain in *Blue Voyage:* "The criticism is deserved, of course; but I have often wished that the critics would do me the justice to perceive that I have deliberately aimed at this effect, in the belief that the old unities and simplicities will no longer serve." Nonetheless, Aiken had yet to grasp that a reflexive, convoluted, stream-of-consciousness technique has to simulate effective replacements for the "old unities and simplicities" to avoid a habitual drift into glib analogies and the "intellectual sentimentality" scored by Huxley. Clever plotting, as in *Blue Voyage*'s own bell-curve structure, and fascinating conceptional goals do not eliminate literature's (especially poetry's) demands for compression, for archetypal conflicts, for an emotive strategy with dramatic impact, even if undercut at every turn by irony, as in Eliot's more expressionistic verses.

A warmly positive, though not uncritical, English response to *House of Dust* came from John Freeman, who wrote in late September 1920 inquiring about Aiken's precise aim in the book and noting a monotony in certain sections, specifically where feminine endings predominated. In his reply of September 28 Aiken outlined the sequence's governing design, the progress from a crowd to the individual, its poetic focus sharpening under crisis, with a parallel and gradual extension of consciousness until—in the third movement

of Part 4 ("Palimpset")—the climax consists of the individual's labor to ingest all consciousness. Of more import as a mark of ripening self-awareness is
his acknowledgment of the resultant monotony, which he had always feared,
and the further admission that his concern with verbalizing pure music neces-
sitated the absence of a thematic center. Tone was the means employed, he
explained, to fuse episodic segments together.

By the time Aiken answered a second Freeman letter on March 2, 1921, he
did so under the additional weight of two negative American reviews, in the
Dial and the *New Republic,* which again charged him with an excess of
"rhythm" and "harmony," an indictment he waved off, ascribing the failure
to appreciate his work at home to a native predilection for realism and the
persistent dearth of sophisticated criticism. Queried about his feelings toward
George Moore, he promised to send Freeman a copy of his laudatory review
of *Avowals* and indicated that he had purchased an expensive new edition of
Memoirs of My Dead Life only two days earlier. Moore, of course, was another magnet in his slide into an autobiographical praxis. Aiken's low opinion
of American reviewers was almost matched by his disdain for their British
brethren. In a final letter to Freeman before his departure for London in October 1921, he would once more lament the absence of solid American criticism, excepting Brooks, but agree with his correspondent that the English
publications were little better. The *Times Literary Supplement* was good, if
"somewhat sclerotic," and the always hospitable *Mercury* had no satisfactory
literary critics to offer, since Murry was too self-absorbed to be either fair or
astute, as a recent book on Dostoyevsky had demonstrated.

The decision about returning to England was left in abeyance in the fall of
1920, however, because Aiken had to participate in another family tragedy,
the slow and painful death of his grandmother in a Watertown nursing home.
His last visit to her, which may have occurred more than a year earlier, had
been a grueling experience. Emily Akin, who had forged a new identity for
herself after the death of her overbearing husband and who had aided her
grandson's efforts to resurrect and polish the memory of his father, was reduced to a skeletal husk, bedridden and helpless, when he saw her. At one
point during their one-sided conversation, as related in "The Last Visit," his
grandmother had ceased responding to his small talk: "She made no comment. But presently her eyes again, slowly, filled with tears, became intolera-
bly bright, and suddenly she cried out, weeping: 'I can't die! I can't
die! . . . I want to die and I can't!' "

It is no wonder he had fled from "the forlorn nursing home on Palfrey Hill"
to "one of his clandestine meetings with Marian" (104) for a session of passionate lovemaking; no wonder that he never returned to bid his grandmother
farewell. Sometime in October 1920 he received word that his grandmother's

death was imminent and wired his brother Robert the news. Robert, who had finished his senior year at Cornell in September 1919 after being discharged from the army, was working at a steel company in Pittsburgh when he learned of his grandmother's condition. "I left for Watertown on the night train," he recalls. "The next morning, I visited with my grandmother. That same afternoon, I took the train to the Cape, at Conrad's suggestion, and spent the night at their South Yarmouth cottage, and met their two kids."

Aiken did not have much in common with his brother. The gap between them had widened considerably since their separation, Robert having acquired his stepfather's formal manner and businessman's philosophy. In fact, he had visited Aiken only once since his brother's marriage, during the first year, when Conrad, apparently at Jessie's urging, sent a note to him at the Milton Academy asking him to lunch with them. "They had a small apartment on the back side of Beacon Hill (that is, behind the capitol, facing the Common). It was well furnished, and the table handsomely set. Conrad asked me how I liked the candlesticks, and I said they were very nice, or something to that effect. 'You, Kemp, and Elizabeth gave them to us as a wedding present.' I recalled Elizabeth had tagged me for cash for the present, but had never seen it." Robert did not mind the teasing and found Jessie "charming," later remarking how fortunate the children were to have her for their mother, although he noticed that whenever Conrad let his verbal fantasies wander off into the upper stratosphere, his wife firmly but gently brought him back down—not an auspicious omen for the marriage.

Subsequent contact between the brothers had consisted solely of an erratic exchange of Christmas cards as Aiken maintained a stoic distance from the siblings he had been deprived of through his father's insanity and Frederick Winslow Taylor's thoughtless cruelty. Kempton, who would not graduate from medical school until 1925, subsequently claimed that since childhood "I probably did not see Conrad more than ten or so times," though he was somewhat more sympathetic to his brother's literary aspirations than Robert and would himself write poetry in his declining years. Only Elizabeth, whom Aiken saw more often, particularly at Harvard, touched one of his buried emotional nerves. She too visited them at the Cape and convinced him that the Taylors were driving her to the edge of madness, the madness precipitated by the loss of her parents and breakup of the family.

In later years Aiken said that his sister had been insane since about the age of twenty-two, but she was not to be committed until her early thirties. Either he sensitively espied nascent signs of instability or memory deceived him. After the death of Frederick Winslow Taylor in 1915, which left Aiken's siblings more affluent than ever and perhaps provoked new spasms of envy, he had increasingly viewed his sister as a helpless victim of her stepmother's and grandmother's snobbish domination. "He thought nothing of those Taylors," a relative has testified. "He used to say he thought their stuffy atmosphere sank poor Elizabeth." Robert also recollects that after her stepfather's death, Elizabeth "was in Roxbury with a foster mother and foster grandmother, and they were always picking at her . . . she had no place to go otherwise—I think she went up to the Cape once to visit . . . just an escape to get out from under the pressure." Actually, Elizabeth was more mobile and independent than this description might intimate. Robert further recalls that she had an apartment of her own in Philadelphia for a while and "visited with her cousin Anna Taylor in Germantown" and with other close friends "on her way or returning from her Grandmother Spooner in Plymouth, Massachusetts."

But the visit to South Yarmouth brought Elizabeth's plight into guilt-honed relief in the inscape of Aiken's mind, as Jane remembers: "Conrad always maintained it was the breakup that did it for her—rather awful Taylors . . . there was some holiday she spent on the Cape, and he felt, suffered, feeling he ought to have been able to do more for her." Nearest to him in age, safe from overt rivalry by reason of her sex, Elizabeth was an unprotected extension of his ego's most vulnerable aspect, a female self as well as the bearer of an early sexual impulse: he would tell his second wife, half in jest, that he should have married Elizabeth instead of Jessie. Thus, apart from being another example of a female psyche's essential unsteadiness, her descent into schizophrenia represented an acting out of a profound fear, one of the two roaming the nightmare corridors of his unconscious—the dread of inheriting his father's mental illness.

The other, fear of oblivion, was lying in ambush for the time when his defenses would be laid waste by self-doubt and sexual restlessness. Death would come as a welcomed friend, not a nemesis. He probably already suspected that the right psychological conditions could transform destruction into desired release, that what we most fear can easily become what we most seek. Freud was discovering the fundamental mechanism in Vienna that year, shaken by the January death of his daughter. On February 4, 1920, defining himself as "a confirmed unbeliever," he confessed: "Deep down I sense a bitter, irreparable narcissistic injury." By December he had completed *Beyond the Pleasure Principle,* taking cues from Sabina Spielrein's work and Wilhelm Stekel's discussion of a "death instinct" in his *Causes for Nervousness:* "I had defined anxiety as the reaction of the *life instinct* against the upsurge of the *death instinct.*" But Freud, who was growing disenchanted with the therapeutic possibilities of psychoanalysis, tending more and more toward metapsychological investigations of human nature and history, expanded the concept into universal dynamic, ceaseless oscillations between Eros and

Thanatos, the survival imperative and "the instinct to return to the inanimate state."

Aiken was not yet in danger of being hypnotized by death's promise of release, though the "static" that Robert detected in his relationship with Jessie and the death of his grandmother, in addition to the frustrations stirred up by his infatuation with Reine Ormond, were contributing to a general dissatisfaction over the course of his life and career. If not in crisis, his mind was hardly at peace. Motion was needed, creative motion and some signals of success, reassurance. In the interim, rational work—writing criticism—was the stopgap answer. He had a congenial outlet in the *Freeman,* which had been founded in 1920 by Van Wyck Brooks, A. J. Nock, and several others as a liberal weekly devoted to political and artistic criticism, an organized response to the wave of conservatism sweeping the country. In his capacity as literary editor, Brooks frequently called upon Aiken for reviews, their mutual respect for the other's work undimmed since that year at Harvard together. The *Freeman* was Aiken's primary prose conduit in 1921. The magazine published six of his eight reviews during that year, the other two appearing in the *Mercury* in the format of "A Letter from America."

Aiken's review of *The Sacred Wood* in the March 2 issue of the *Freeman* underlined the chasm, or apparent chasm, that had grown between Eliot and himself over the controversial topics of personality in literature and critical methods. I say apparent because it is clear that he failed fully to grasp Eliot's aesthetic stance, although he was one of Eliot's most sensitive and intelligent critics. From the point of view of Aiken's psyche, that buzzing cluster of contradictory extremes, the review was healthy and purgative, a necessary lurch toward independence. As usual, however, fairness prevailed, an authentic, mostly reliable objectivity willing to praise excellence. Aiken wrote that Eliot's book "is severe and analytic, and we can think of no two qualities in criticism which are at the moment more desirable." In particular, he applauded Eliot's endeavor to apply the "scientific method," even though the results seemed to him a failure because of a reliance upon imprecise terms, such as "feeling" and "personality," which he believed were used in vague or conflicting ways to occlude meaning. The central essays, those on *Hamlet* and "tradition and the individual talent," caused most of his concern, and the most miscomprehension.

Joseph Killorin has revealed that against Eliot's statement that "the more perfect the artist, the more completely separate in him will be the man who suffers and the mind which creates," Aiken wrote in the margin of his copy: "This might be *exactly the other way.*" And in his review he quotes Eliot's description of poetry as "not the expression of personality, but an escape from personality" to stress a regrettable trend toward ambiguous phrases, without giving any sign that this might distill the quintessence of Eliot's poetic strategy: tradition as the self's ultimate refuge from self-indulgence and destruction; objective correlative as the surest means for a self to reify universal configurations. What Aiken intuits, and implicitly rejects, is that his former classmate had moved away from a thorough psychological or philosophically logical (regarding Bradley) exegesis of a literary performance toward an approach closer to that of Spingarn and Croce, the approach he abhorred as antithetical to any Freudian-oriented construct free of irrational mysticism: "Mr. Eliot . . . has been infected by modern psychology, and he uses the terms of it not infrequently; but the basis from which he employs it shifts. . . . Not with impunity can one mix the James-Lange set of terms with the terms of Freud: Nor again the terms of de Gourmont (who was an amateur psychologist, and often a misleading one) with those of Kostyleff."

It is a peculiar review, accurate in assailing Eliot's slippery vocabulary yet never able to force the obvious disagreement over psychology versus aestheticism into a distinct break. Aiken was content to berate Eliot for his vague platform, such as his witty characterization of *Hamlet* as "the Mona Lisa of literature," which he stiffly reduces to an algebraic demonstration to support the notion that "charming" material can generate the most potent art, without bringing a foundational disparity into the open. Aiken was still a little intimidated, fearing to look foolish, perhaps sensing that Eliot was the better critic, and so he concentrated upon the elements easiest to denigrate in the event that history proved Eliot correct. In addition, he might have been truly uncertain of *The Sacred Wood*'s intellectual weight; the collection offered the serious respect for and extensive knowledge of literature that usually pleased and impressed him. The origin of the major misunderstanding between them, which illuminates his subsequent disavowal of Eliot's monastic retreat into Symbolist detachment and mystical orthodoxy, was in Eliot's deft manipulations of modernism to express his psyche's damage through poetry with minimal autobiographical candor, and hence of the treacherous subjectivity he and Babbitt detested. Like Pound, his main longings were for a classical revival, the neoclassical modes of Dryden and Pope, in which satire and formulaic restraint can shield the ego from excessive revelation.

In the dissertation on Bradley that he would refuse to publish until 1964, and then only when prodded by his second wife and the submissive urges of a second childhood, Eliot had taken care to emphasize that "we know that those highly organized beings who are able to objectify their passions, and as passive spectators to contemplate their joys and torments, are also those who suffer and enjoy the most keenly." Aiken could not accept the psychological concession contained in this acute observation, as well as the distinction Eliot insisted upon between the two halves of the schizoid artist, because it encouraged the hated New Criticism's dispassionate disjunction of art from biography and, for Eliot, would culminate in a religious conversion he felt was intellectually sterile. Yet it seemed to simulate the very program he was now trying to evade. In effect, by denying the viability of Eliot's insight, he was also discarding the aesthetic behind his own symphonies, the failure of which he was beginning to comprehend lay in the absence of a specific "I" 's individual experience.

Valid or not, Aiken's review was a positive ventilation of much repressed hostility toward the oppressive talents of an older brother that commenced to mark off the theoretical sectors where he and Eliot parted company. Eventually he would envision their separating courses as a matter of courage, would see Eliot's flight from his "brilliantly analytic and destructive thesis in epistemology" to "Canterbury" (215) as a cowardly retreat from chaos, a surrender that was in sharp contrast to his own brave descent, like Ulysses, into the heart of darkness, his psyche's interior chaos. How accurate was Aiken's assessment of their divergent paths? Though distressful from a public perch, Eliot's adoption of obsolete religious, political, and social dogmas was not very different, in a survival context, from Aiken's improvising of his grand metaphysic. Both supplied the means for establishing relatively stable identities and myths of self while permitting them to write the type of poetry their personalities and backgrounds dictated, despite paying the "exorbitant price" in ordinary happiness that every neurotic must pay.

Aiken's schema was a far more valid reading of cultural evolution and intellectual history than Eliot's conservative resurrection of abandoned pieties, a reflection of his awareness that Nietzsche's translation of philosophy into psychology was pivotal to an understanding of civilization and aesthetics, that the sole legitimate "progress" evident in the recorded development of the human mind and its cultural products resided in an expanding consciousness—this, after all, is what distinguishes Picasso's imitations of primitive artifacts from their models. It is also one of the reasons why Aiken has to be considered a major force in the shaping of an American poetic tradition and intellectual focus. Even his steady advancement into the self's complex realities over the next few years was in tune with the "preoccupation with the nature of the self, separate from community and society," that Hoffman has characterized as typical of the 1920s.

And yet the review of *The Sacred Wood* was partly motivated by its author's unadmitted hostility and suffers therefore. Though there is measured praise, Aiken spits acid repeatedly at a dear friend and secret foe: "Mr. Eliot is forever abandoning *us* on the very doorstep of the illuminating. . . . He is meticulous without being clear . . . the evidence of thought is weighty, but the value of it is not." Unknown to Aiken, the disapproving reviews of Eliot's first collection of essays contributed to Eliot's drift into a mental breakdown as he grappled with *The Waste Land,* a poem he had been planning since 1919, and dealt with the implications of a looming psychotic climax. Aiken's psychological health was improved by the assault. Two other events in the spring of 1921 cheered him, sweetening the taste of despair and inadequacy left in his mouth from the rough treatment accorded *The House of Dust* and his disaffection with England: Knopf published *Punch* in February to generally favorable reviews, and he secured an English publisher—the London firm of Martin Secker contracted to bring out *Punch* in November and *Senlin* and *Nocturne of Remembered Spring* early the following year.

The latter event made the idea of settling in England once more appear feasible, and plans went forward for an autumn departure. Meanwhile, Aiken savored the *Punch* reviews as they materialized, including one in the April 23 *Literary Review* that accused him of failing to establish "a coherent picture or reading or 'imitation' of the Punch that he apparently set out to draw for us," but proffered a just encomium: "Yet his aesthetic feeling for the King's English and his ear for subtle beauties of rhythm are most exquisitely in evidence." His friend Padraic Colum discerned "the breaking of new ground" in a *Freeman* notice (April 13), though Colum felt that "the story is not developed so as to give us the whole story of Punch's personality," a reasonable qualification. His newer friend, Malcolm Cowley, was more critical, if no less reverential, in the June *Dial:* "There is a certain monotony of effect about the volume, but the monotony lies in Aiken's attitude toward his subject and not in his technique. The melody of his verse is apparent as never before."

Best of all, a stunning surprise, was the enthusiastic reaction of Amy Lowell, who wrote him a magnanimous letter of admiration for his accomplishment, which she felt was his finest to date, promising to try to place a review of *Punch* with the *New Republic.* As might be anticipated, she was successful, and the review that appeared on September 28 seems a blurb writer's cornucopia: "The drama of the man Punch becomes the tragedy of blind, yearning, cheated humanity. The poet rises to his climax inevitably and with a high seriousness new to his work. . . . As to the verse itself, Mr. Aiken has never done better, he has sustained his technique surprisingly throughout. His expression is simple, natural, and reads with that ease which is the aim and despair of all writers." A month earlier, another amiable adversary, Untermeyer, had been almost as panegyric in a *Bookman* review: "There are lyric interludes in this volume as insinuating as anything he has conceived with the exception of Senlin's 'Morning Song.' It is even a richer music than he had hitherto found."

Braithwaite had avoided reviewing Aiken's previous three books in the

Aiken and Jessie with John and Jane in South Yarmouth (ca. 1921).

Transcript, although he wrote in late August to request permission to use four poems in his next anthology of magazine verse. Aiken declined on August 29, saying he wished to save them for possible inclusion in Untermeyer's second *Miscellany.* Braithwaite's reply, reiterating his plea for the poems, claimed that his conscience had been bothering him in regard to the lack of *Transcript* attention, soliciting his help in a valiant fight to preserve Aiken's reputation against the opinion of others. Again refusing to grant reprint permission, Aiken dismissed Braithwaite's suddenly tender conscience and mocked his pretenses at championing his cause, asking that he stay a "good enemy" instead. He also suggested that they seal the pact by a common agreement not to have any Aiken poems in future anthologies. It was the last communication between them.

The decisive rupture with such a locally prominent figure as Braithwaite affirms the seriousness of Aiken's intention to make England his permanent home. Arrangements had been made to rent the cottage, and he planned to sail alone in October, with Jessie and the children to follow a month later. Jessie was delighted, the situation at South Yarmouth not having improved and John already enrolled in the local public school. Her husband set about writing to overseas friends inquiring about the best, least expensive places to settle. Freeman thought his own village of Anerley would be more than suitable, a tempting idea that Aiken rejected, concluding that he could secure cheap temporary lodgings in London for the family and then explore more rural areas at leisure.

The reasons for the move were many and compelling, economic as well as social and political. The election of Warren Harding to the presidency in 1920 had initiated a conservative regime of mean-spirited retrenchment not to be equaled until the advent of the reactionary Reagan government six decades later. A recent upsurge in bombings, raids, deportations of "undesirables," and various other frightening signs of the times, offshoots of the Red Scare campaign then at its zenith, enhanced the attractiveness of England's less explosive conduct of public and private affairs. Nor would Aiken be the exception in his voluntary exile from a country that seemed to have lost its ethical bearings. Hundreds of American artists and intellectuals were absenting themselves from a depressing situation in which fundamentalists, philistine conformists, and thoughtless lotus-eaters appeared to have assumed control of the nation's impoverished culture. But the daydream motive beneath all the sensible reasons for his going abroad was more compelling than any of them—his yearning to continue the vain pursuit of Reine Ormond.

In the depths of every heart there is

a tomb and a dungeon, though the

lights, the music, and revelry

above

may cause us to forget their

existence, and the buried ones, or

prisoners, whom they hide.

Nathaniel Hawthorne

. . . .

UNINTERMITTENTLY CONSCIOUS

Socrates, Aiken's prototype of highest man, had proclaimed that "knowledge is virtue," thus justifying Adam's sin, whatever wounds science and art might inflict upon an expanding consciousness. This did not, however, ameliorate the poetic task. Aiken was still embroiled with the pressing chore of locating an effective method for freeing familial corpses imprisoned in his own haunted mind's dungeon without sacrificing internalized ethical imperatives or the fierce linguistic quest of a symbol-making creature for beautiful abstractions and universal intensities. Unlike Arnold, who could, with Marcus Aurelius, simply "dig within" to tap a secret reserve of goodness, Aiken was a modernist poet quite aware of anxiety's major role in the genesis of imaginative works, Spengler's discovery that "cosmic fear is surely the most creative of all primordial feelings." He was equally cognizant of the human drive to seek community and completeness, morality's ultimate energy source.

Aiken yearned to be Emerson's Socratic "Man Thinking," but he could not yet fuse the anguished, unresolved contradictions in his psyche that had first made him the Poet of White Horse Vale. Now he was poised on the threshold of a dive into self capable of destroying or saving him. In effect, he had not managed to transcend the mirror stage in development that Lacan has postulated as a necessary preliminary to the processing of Oedipal strife, a stage in which language paradoxically distinguishes self from world and masters phenomena through reflections of the ego in other beings and things. During this growth phase, which is a potential artist stage for every psyche, moral and fantasy needs are entwined vines of the same innate urge to define and thereby protect the nascent self from an annihilating sun of nothingness. Assuming his structurally slanted divisions are valid in a Freudian context, Lacan's maturational trinity—the real, the symbolic, and the imaginary—are too intermeshed at such a stage to project a unified ego through the prisms of invented artifacts. Recently turned thirty-two and racked by doubts, Aiken had not only retarded his career as a poet because of neurotic insecurities and a consequent dependence upon imitations but had also refused to scrutinize his own productions closely enough. He had not isolated their major obsessional motifs with sufficient objectivity to be able to plug them into the emotional dynamo of his angst-ridden identity quest, literature's primal theme since *Gilgamesh*.

His bearings were sound, however, as he would recognize many decades hence when questioned about the symphonic series. "Naturally," he said, "the young man who was doing this didn't quite know where he was going, and he was as much under the influence of Freud on the one hand as under that of Bergson on the other . . . a musical form of the nature of flux, of fragmentation. . . . It was the direction that I was really ultimately to go, and it was the proper first step I think." The poetry written in 1921, which included expanding *Priapus and the Pool* into a sequence and composing a number of independent lyrics, reveals the familiar mixture of virtuoso technique and rhetorical elegance characteristic of his progress to date, self-conscious manipulations of mythic material combined with Gautier's "*l'art pour art*" decadence. Arthur Lerner has described it with unsentimental precision: "Except for a veil of romantic allegory which is always sketchy and transparent, the reader is face to face with the author in *propria persona*—an extremely introspective author holding an endless dialogue with himself."

In "Exile," for instance, which reflects the weight of Eliot's "Gerontion" and continuing paralysis under his example, an aged exile in a vague, distant land, betrays a passiveness akin to that of Tennyson's early verse portraits and is metamorphosed into a reflexive image of alien, spiderlike neighbors:

> I'll spin a web
> Between two dusty pine-tree tops, and hang there
> Face downward, like a spider, blown as lightly
> As ghost of leaf.

Ostensibly, artificer as spider has been summoned to perform for us. This is another poem about a poet separated from humanity, lacking Yeats's magical bird, "Birds of a golden color, who will sing / Of leaves that do not wither," but, underneath is the threat of death and decay suggesting anterior stasis as an aspect of self. "Samadhi," built around the use in Tchaikovsky's *Danse Arabe* of a persistent horn call and the "Sanskrit word for the absorption of thought into the supreme being, the ultimate stage of consciousness," also dwells in a mythic kingdom where a giant tree, perhaps of life or Norse legend, centers existence and experience, haunted by the music of a cynical bird hopping amid its huge branches and the promise offered by the horn's echo, "Half-mute nostalgia from the dark of things."

If this represents ultimate consciousness, the target of Aiken's quest—and its mythic trappings are unconvincing—failure and death are our sole reality. All the musical tropes and theatrical forest images come together at the end of a climax stanza light years away from the apocalyptic vision of "The Second Coming" prophesied by Yeats:

> Walk softly through your forest, and be ready
> To hear the horn of horns. Or in your garden
> Stoop, but upon your back be ever conscious
> Of sunlight, and a shadow that may grow.

The absence of Priapus is significant, that sexual element essential to the self's processing of moral and mirror or creative impulses, nature's somatic command. Thanatos prevails, and a child's existential fears, which have insisted upon a symbolic paradisal retreat.

The failure of the two poems as art and as fantasy responses to an identity vacuum, as intimations of mortality, is carried over into "Seven Twilights," a more ambitious sequence of seven sections, four of which—"Battersea Bridge," "Twilight, Rye, Sussex," "The Figurehead," and "Midnight"—had appeared as separate works in the June 1921 issue of the *Century* magazine. England supplies their narrative body, though their heart belongs to Reine Ormond:

> "This is the hour," she said, "of transmutation:
> It is the eucharist of the evening, changing
> All things to beauty."

She reincarnates the madonna side of the evil mother so often evoked in the features of Cleopatra, Helen of Troy, Circe, et al., the goddess beyond reach who promises her son a resurrection of the Eden stolen from him, Eros idealized, whether as a ship's exterior figurehead, "smiling still, unchanging, smiling still," or as the "pale goddess" under wood to whom the speaker prays at the end of the last section:

> Whose breasts are cold as the sea, whose eyes forever
> Inscrutably take that light whereon they look—

> Speak to us! Make us certain, as you are,
> That somewhere, beyond wave and wave and wave,
> That dreamed-of harbour lies which we would find.

Ambivalence obviously remains, but the stress is on positive facets of the witch-turned-savior, the plea to her a moving one (outside the poem's allegorical pretentiousness).

Permanence is what she promises the persona, "old as the world," who has presented himself as "a ragged pilgrim" pursuing "the road to nowhere" in the initial section, following "the human track," which goes backward, repeats what went before, to the point that nature is an animistic extension of the child's psyche:

> O trees! exquisite dancers in grey twilight!
> Witches! fairies! elves! who wait for the moon
> To thrust her golden horn, like a golden snail,
> Above that mountain!

Inevitably, the circular path must return, in section 3, to the "old ghostly house" where now he is only a guest and where he is told, in "a voice not human," that "Houses grow old and die, houses have ghosts." In the fifth section the persona, passive as ever, is in his own room surrounded by winter and twilight—an anxious signature scene—which he attempts to erase by drawing "chill curtains," pausing for a moment to study a single star before the curtains obliterate it. He is left alone with his books, their tiers of futile history and knowledge. What they illuminate as lanterns of human knowledge is no more than "One hanging strand of cobweb; / A window-sill a half-inch deep in dust."

The tombstone message is plain: for a sensitive soul, death and love are indivisible in their felt manifestations, necessary counterparts, though the force of the former tends to overwhelm the latter. As poet and persona, Aiken has stopped stock-still, writing the same poem in the same lush language he exploited so frequently in the past. And yet the map of inner turmoil sketched darkly between liquid lines intimates an approaching crisis, a massive movement of interior continents to uncover the earthquake fault (existential menace) first experienced in Savannah, where the fatal mother, an idol perfected in a child's telescopic gaze, must be begged to rescue him from the void yawning beneath his feet. Except for fitful lyric interludes, the poetry is stale and inert, petrified under the spell of Eliot and Yeats, but the habitual, compulsive penchant for aping circular forms, which ironically negate surface quest narratives, shapes the road his career would eventually justify: the archetypal journey of an aged child into Dante's dark wood (consciousness as a sinner's hell and heaven, as burden and potential salvation) to defy the father and restore the mother's sensual corpse, a missing self in her resuscitated configuration and mission of forgiveness, closing life's remorseless cycle of desire and death.

Aside from a traumatic instigation of existential dread, similar to the psychic impact of Freud's daughter's death on Freud, Reine Ormond had wrenched the gaze of Aiken's imagination from the evil mother to her redemptive double, as was already evident in "Coffins" from 1920, a poem in which mortality's savage destruction of every human value and vanity is tallied via a gallery of pathetic female victims:

> Jean, whose laughter flashed over depths of terror,
> And Eloise, who desired to love but dared not;
> Doris, who turned alone to the dark and cried,—

The final stanza has a heroic poet, "with death in his eyes," for its standard-bearer, seeking "immortal music, and spring for ever," but the weakness of the verse is less relevant than the air of forgiveness suffusing the varied women with equal softness.

The positive side of Ormond's effect is most notable in the poems added to the original "Priapus and the Pool" to form a sequence, twenty-two in all, the majority of them written in Armstrong's paneled rooms on Great Ormond Street (its very name seems to signify the portentiousness of their encounter). They are love poems in the tradition of the sonnet series pioneered by Petrarch's cycle and brought into English literature by Sidney and others. Ormond is constantly being compared to higher creatures or subtly vilified for remaining out of reach, true to the tradition, although the psychic agitation on display is uniquely Aiken's, at least in the maternal and existential implications adumbrated:

> I shut my eyes, I try to remember you.
> But as a diver plunging down through sunlight
> To meet his azure shadow on the wide water
> Shatters through it and is gone.

Mother as self's reflection does not cohere, cannot as yet be reassembled.

The thirteenth entry, strongest in the sequence, can stand for the rest, a marvelous demonstration of the way Aiken could, on rare occasion, meld metaphoric talent and orthodox Romantic material with his obsessive insecurities to create a memorable performance:

> Now over the grass you come,
> Gravely you come with slow step

Into the azure world I call my heart:
Tardily you approach me.

Butterflies of the sun flicker about you—
Who could have forseen it?
Moths of the moon at your finger-tips
Melt like flakes of snow.

Is it not too late that you come?
Are you not merely a ghost?
Behold, before you once speak my name,
Wind whirls us apart like leaves.

Never again, after this dream, shall I have peace.
In my heart is nothing but the crying of the snow.
The grass over which I seek you is white with frost.
You have left upon it no footstep.

I place my most secret thought
Like a bough of magnolia
Where perhaps you will find it and remember.
It withers, and you do not come.

This passage epitomizes Aiken's extraordinary mastery of technical resources, ranging from the adept handling of a very loose blank verse to genuinely original metaphors, as in the transition from moths to snowflakes—all in service of a song that appears almost Greek or Oriental. However conventional in conception and execution, the verse conveys a quiet passion appropriately draped in a cloak of ancient mystery.

It also, at a latent level, binds together mythic associations and private references without obscuring surface effects, the sonnetlike anticipation of the idolized beloved's treachery. Elemental signs—grass, snow, sun, flowers—bear additional layers of meaning with unforced ease, although a psychological perusal of their deployment reconfirms the manner in which a maternal substitute is welded to death and betrayal. "Bough of magnolia" suddenly introduces a Savannah setting, the original garden. More pertinent, as in the other twenty-one verses, the inner pilgrimage, the inner quest to repossess the mother in her idealized state, leads to disappointment. In poem after poem, an anguished persona experiences the loss of his inconstant goddess lover, conscious of her "dream" quality, her ephemeral distance, leaving him imprisoned in the "hated room" of his restless mind.

Dante is a surrogate spirit in the eighth poem as the poet,

walking once by the muddy river
Watched the inscrutable angel pass him by,
Shutting her flower-like heart. . . . He turned his torment
To torture of a world let slowly die.

But the outcome of his own Beatrice's elusiveness is a twofold disaster: Freudian insight into the inextricable relationship between art and agony and glum acceptance of his tragic fate. As a poet he is doomed to stride amid "the damned, unknown, unseeing," hell on earth, must give voice to the mute suffering of the underworld's condemned multitudes.

The Priapus sequence is superior to the bulk of the symphonic experiments because it brings about a more potent interaction between traditional Romantic allegories and its author's fractured psyche, the result of Reine Ormond's catalytic influence. The year or so since their last meeting had lent religious enchantment to her well-remembered charms, in part at least a consequence of marital discontent and Aiken's customary lack of confidence in his artistic achievements. Though chained to Jessie by the propensity to forge anxious attachments common among children who have lost parents at an early age, as well as by increasing affection for John and Jane, he yearned to resume his vain pursuit of the aristocratic Ormond. When he sailed for Liverpool on October 15, 1921, he knew he would have several weeks alone in London in which to reestablish contact with the young woman his fantasies had altered into a modern madonna; Jessie and the children were not scheduled to arrive until the middle of November.

As recorded in *Blue Voyage,* the first chapter of which was to be written in the winter of 1922, the crossing acquired a nightmarish cast with the discovery that the tall and beautiful Miss Ormond was traveling on the same ship, though literally and figuratively removed from him by money and social distinctions—he was in second class, she in first. Worse, when he did sneak up to the restricted upper deck with a companion and bumped into her as she was taking the night air with her mother and another young woman, she informed him that she was about to get married. In *Ushant* the crushing realization that his "dedicated angel" was truly lost to him is compared to a war injury: "He was wounded: if not mortally, then at any rate *im*mortally"—and related to the trauma endured in the mountains of Vermont when he had learned of his wife's infatuation with the virile Wilbur (140).

The grave extent of the damage to his vulnerable ego, which was intensified by the embarrassment of his second-class status and the memory of her not answering his last two letters or acknowledging the copy of one of his books he had dared send her, is depicted in *Blue Voyage* with painful accuracy, despite inevitable invokings of poetic license. "Mrs. Pauline Faubion," too, a "dark-eyed, vulgar, wonderful, forthright" fellow passenger who "had felt savagely for his feet under the table, the last night of the voyage, and later knocked emphatically at his stateroom door" (47) to consummate their shared lust, is exaggerated in a novel intent upon maintaining the childish polarization of womankind into whore and virgin stereotypes that had always blighted Aiken's imagination.

From the safe perspective of *Ushant,* it was easy to concede that the honest Faubion would have proved better for him than the refined Ormond, but *Blue Voyage*'s often brilliant stream of consciousness leaves scant doubt that the abrupt dashing of Aiken's unrealistic expectations regarding the capture of Sargent's niece inflicted a psychic wound of awesome proportions. Her casual puncturing of his obsessive Romantic dream represented a symbolic reenactment of Anna Aiken's assumed unfaithfulness to his father and cruel abandonment of him. It dragged him back into the past, summoning up the gauntlet of conflicting emotions that had thrashed him into the weak, shallow, restless, oversexed, and contradictory personality he seemed to be: a detached poet egotistical enough to filter out irrelevant stimuli at will, yet ready prey to the depressing suspicion that he might not even exist and that his grand work was nothing but a sham defense, a serious error in judgment.

With hawk-circling insistence, *Blue Voyage* makes clear that Ormond's enchantment was maternal in origin and force, a repetition of the vortex enchantment exerted by his mother as she sat under her parasol in Colonial Park while he played nearby. His alter ego, Demarest (roughly "man of the sea"), addressing Cynthia in his interior monologue, confesses, "The fact that I tell you this story . . . puts you in the position of the mother, and me the child." Similarly, her abrupt rejection of him simulated a repetition of his mother gently easing him outside the radiant circle of her love into a room of his own, bearing sibling rivals to keep him at a distance, and then, through her imagined treachery, causing his insane father to destroy all three of them. The refurbishing of his father's image with Emily Akin's assistance was also brought into question by Ormond's defection, his grandmother's prince once again seen as the vicious tyrant who had physically and mentally tormented his oldest son, petrifying him into a terrified hare and robbing him of his mother.

Whatever fragile balance he had achieved over the years, whatever neurotic adjustments had enabled him to survive as a poet and relatively stable human being since the Savannah tragedy, were now in ruins. Internal pressures began to impel him toward the brink of disintegration, though automatic psychic defenses, the artist mask of philosophical detachment from self and experience perfected by adversity, enabled him to continue functioning. There was no overt collapse and certainly no visible sign of despair. His angry pride prevented that, even when, at the end of the eight-day voyage, Ormond and her companions, who included John Sargent, pretended not to notice him as they bumped into him in customs, on the train to London, and in Eustace Station. Aiken's humiliation was complete. But a mind, however divided and self-consuming, is never so easily overthrown, particularly one schooled since childhood in handling identity threats. The artist ego, at its anhedonic remove, can contemplate almost any loss as a creative opportunity, grist for imagination's mill, as long as the traumatic material does not jam elaborate, time-tested defense systems. Like the art of psychoanalysis, the artist's expertness cannot abreact away clinical madness, though it can perhaps keep it at bay for a longer period than might the neurotic manipulations of a less gifted individual.

A fresh disappointment lay in store for Aiken soon after reaching London. He had anticipated another, more leisurely session of passion with Pauline Faubion, who had agreed to a rendezvous, but she wrote him from Cheshire to say that her aunt's illness prevented her from coming (47). It was their last communication. But he had sufficient practical tasks in hand to prevent dangerous brooding, such as locating suitable lodgings for the family, visiting his new publisher (Secker was bringing out *Punch* in a week), looking up old friends, and trying to reacquaint himself with literary London.

Eliot was not, alas, available. He was vacationing in Margate for three weeks preparatory to leaving for a Swiss sanatorium, after dropping Vivienne off with the Pounds on his way through Paris. He had secured a three-month leave from his bank post on October 2, the result of a consultation with a nerve specialist in late September, when the departure of his family—his mother, sister, and brother had paid a summer visit—left him in a state of near breakdown, a victim of the *aboulie* (inertia) he claimed as a persistent affliction and the unhappy marriage he could neither save nor abandon. The psychiatrist who would treat him, Roger Vittoz, a pre-Freudian, muscular Christian, could do little to dissolve the plots of familial and sexual ambivalences clogging his will and his sense of self, but the rest and a series of prescribed mental and physical exercises (*sans* a sick wife's oppressive, guilt-inducing presence) would at least permit him to reassemble battered defenses.

Aiken keenly regretted his absence. Except for Armstrong and Fletcher, his London contacts were proving difficult to approach and maintain, especially the English ones, and his depressive condition made him often wonder why he had foolishly believed the failure of 1920 would not be duplicated if he committed himself to a permanent move. Though still a correspondent for the *Mercury* and on a friendly footing with Shanks, Flint, Monro, Squire, and others, he again found the native literary figures impossible to deal with or comprehend. Their polite reserve frequently left him in a condition of secret terror and embarrassment, eager to flee at the first opportunity, a condition too reminiscent of the fear once instilled by Dr. Aiken. As he complained in a letter to Linscott, Martin Secker himself, although an agreeable man who obviously respected Aiken's work, never invited him to cross the barrier and sit down with him or did anything else to put him at his ease when he called.

Aiken had much better luck with the practical task of locating family lodgings, settling for a six-room flat in a typical townhouse complex in Notting Hill, northwest London, beyond Kensington. Cheap rent compensated for its unfashionable address. Unfortunately, the apartments in Colville Gardens were colder than most city apartments, which is saying much at a time when central heating was rare and winter promised to be harsh. Aiken was at the dock to meet Jessie and the children when they arrived in early November, and Jessie began to pine for a rural retreat as winter set in with a vengeance. She and her husband were in accord as to the necessity of escaping from the city, but the children, despite debilitating colds, enjoyed the novelty of their new home. John recalls: "We spent the winter in an apartment near Paddington Station . . . which we adored in all its fog-bound bleakness." Jane's memory is naturally less precise, except for a recollection of "playing on beaten mud paths in the central garden."

The recurrent cycle of depressions initiated by Reine Ormond's rejection received added fuel when, a month after publication, *Punch* had garnered few sales and no reviews except a brief note in the London *Times*. Aiken could not or would not want to explain his gloomy frame of mind to Jessie, though in a November 9, 1921, letter to Maurice Firuski, responding to the bookseller's confession of melancholic problems, he reveals: "I have had trials, crucifixions myself—bewilderments of pain, outrageous dislocations of the soul, and one of them, not a trifle, since I saw you. But I'm becoming a very Buddha of callousness." The covert allusion to Reine Ormond's assault upon his psychic integrity was treated more openly in a letter to Linscott several weeks later, but there he explained her cutting of him solely as a dismayed reaction to the news that he was traveling second class and would have his family in tow that winter, omitting any mention of his emotional entanglement with the Ormond clan and castigating Reine's mother as an extreme version of a Beacon Street snob. His wound was still festering, however hard he labored to squeeze behind his Buddha-like wall of indifference.

The same letter shows awareness of Eliot's breakdown and looks forward to his anticipated return in January 1922 and passes on the rumor that Katherine Mansfield was fatally stricken with tuberculosis and in seclusion at Davos. Mansfield's fate was cause for sincere sorrow because he had come to regard her as a contemporary master of the short story. He had reviewed *Bliss and*

Other Stories in May 1921 and would review *The Garden Party* the following
month, both for the *Freeman,* with respectful enthusiasm, though he was conscious of Chekhov's influence and superior range and of the narrow boundaries imposed upon Mansfield's material by the lyric (hence, subjective and
egocentric) quality of her imagination: "Thus, in Miss Mansfield's short stories, as in the poems of a lyric poet, it is always Miss Mansfield's voice that
we hear, it is always Miss Mansfield that we see. How it is that limitations of
this sort impose themselves on an artist, in childhood or infancy, we leave
psychology to discover."

The insight is important because it applies to Aiken as well, and he had
started writing short stories that winter, mailing the first three—"The Disciple," "The Dark City," and "Soliloquy on a Park Bench"—to Linscott for
him to place with American magazines if possible. None of the three was
more than competent, but he would soon develop a highly professional style
and adept control of his terse narratives, reflecting what he had gleaned from
the techniques of O. Henry, Chekhov, and Mansfield; his deeper connections
with the literature of Poe and Henry James were more evident in matters of
psychological interest and thematic stance. As was the case with his criticism,
Aiken's short fiction and novels would remain professional in every way,
without eliciting the staying power present in his best poetry, with the exception of "Strange Moonlight," "Silent Snow, Secret Snow," "Mr. Arcularis,"
and certain sections of *Blue Voyage* and *Great Circle.* As a lyric narcissist,
like Mansfield, he was incapable of empathizing sufficiently with alien sensibilities to reproduce and thus use their interior voices (he would concede the
"autistic" limits of his fictional reach to his second wife).

But the poet's story, when attached to the convolutions of an alter ego or
egos involved with processing fundamental obsessions and conflicts, can
achieve an extraordinary field of perception and simulated drama, as demonstrated in the fictions of Joyce and Woolf, who took full advantage of their
era's concern with self, with explorations of psychic intensities, substituting
streams of metaphoric depths for linear breadth. In any event, their special
genius and stricter fictional focus were not his; he would not produce a similar
piece of sustained literature until he harnessed his lyric talents to the schema
of a conflicted yet dynamic and divine consciousness in the myth-oriented
Preludes for Memnon. For the moment, he was enduring a poetic dry spell—
he always exaggerated the length of these brief periodic blocks—and believed
that fiction could provide some of the financial rewards poetry did not. He also
later claimed that he had deliberately planned to write poetry until age thirty-
five and then, reversing Hardy's career, switch to prose.

As 1921 came to a close, the unhappiness occasioned by the humiliating
termination of his fantasy pursuit of Reine Ormond had not abated apprecia-

bly, encouraged as it was by minor irritations such as the miserable weather, a perpetually freezing flat, English manners or the lack of them, and the absence of Eliot. But in a New Year's Eve letter to Firuski, whose bookstore had gone into publishing on a small scale, he instructed his similarly sad friend on how best to weather emotional storms: "Did I advise you to sink heart and soul? Good advice! and not difficult to take. All you have to do is wait a little and daily life will sink them for you quite without charge. . . . I'm not sure that they exist. We have a sensibility, designed, as far as one can tell, chiefly for the feeding of the ego. Keep that well fed, all is well. The fatal thing is to feed it without knowing it or starve it without knowing it."

Though aided by the consumption of much stout, these grudgingly cheerful comments reflect a tentative recovery of surface equilibrium, perhaps the onset of the manic phase in Aiken's inherited streak of manic-depression operating in concert with neurotic defenses and the simple realization that his situation was far from lamentable. He was in London, which he would always view as the most civilized city in the world, and he did not have to earn a living outside of writing—income from his inheritance, Jessie's legacy, rent from South Yarmouth tenants, and various poetry and review payments kept him in a fairly solid financial position. Moreover, he still had the bachelor freedom supplied by Jessie to cultivate his friendships with Fletcher, Armstrong, de Bosschere, Freeman, and the Georgians who clustered around Monro's Poetry Bookshop. Although Joyce, the writer he most wanted to meet, was in Paris with Pound, along with Ford and the steady stream of young American writers descending upon Gertrude Stein's atelier and Sylvia Beach's Shakespeare & Company bookshop, he had "at last a card to George Moore, and am expected there any day."

He was also perusing a two-volume edition of William James's letters, edited by a nephew, and pondering the original achievements of Dickinson and Melville, the last named of whom he now ranked with Hawthorne and James as America's three best novelists. This rekindled interest in his country's past, specifically in writers such as Dickinson and Melville, who had been ignored and misunderstood by their contemporaries, helped him to conclude somewhat cynically that the greatest blessing America bestowed upon its most talented literary children had been philistine indifference, which had permitted them to develop their unique gifts without interference, unhindered by pressures to conform or the problems of success that a more sophisticated society might have imposed. And yet, as James had indicated in his seminal analysis of Hawthorne's limitations, thereby justifying his own flight into exile, the absence of a highly evolved and appreciative cultural setting can also play havoc with an artist's maturation process, causing him to waste precious time and energy solving problems of craft that had already been handled and to isolate himself from the currents of community that nourish an art's richest flowering. It was a dilemma Aiken would never really resolve to his own satisfaction, another case of polar oppositions apparently prevailing with equal force, mirroring the bundle of paradoxes that snarled his psyche's every impulse.

He needed someone sympathetic and intelligent to talk to, someone who had experienced the antagonistic tugs of American and European scenes in the context of a common fascination with literature's complex machinery. That someone was Eliot, of course, and his return in January 1922 led to a partial renewal of their former closeness as they lunched together two or three times a week at a pub near Lloyd's Bank, "thus resuming a habit we had formed many years before, in Cambridge. . . . And of course we discussed the literary scene, with some acerbity and hilarity, and with the immense advantage of being outsiders (though both of us were already contributing to the English reviews); discussing also the then-just-beginning possibility of *The Criterion*, through the generosity of Lady Rothermere."

This quotation from an account written more than forty years later is accurate enough with respect to the "acerbity and hilarity" shared at these lunches but gives an impression of mutual warmth and trust that was not always in evidence, at least on Eliot's part. Eliot was reticent about the magazine venture in its early stages and is described in *Ushant* as having already commenced to disappear behind "splendid ramparts" since Aiken's last trip to England. Intrigued by Eliot's psychological difficulties, Aiken was oddly blind to the protective nature of the man's elaborate mask, to the anguish and rage so like his own behind that sardonic, immobile façade of pedantic tendentiousness and mandarin manners. During one of their lunches, for instance, Eliot candidly complained of a writing block, telling Aiken "that although every evening he went home to his flat hoping that he could start writing again, and with every confidence that the material was *there* and waiting, night after night the hope proved illusory: the sharpened pencil lay unused by the untouched sheet of paper. . . . He asked me if *I* had ever experienced any such thing. And of course my reply that I hadn't wasn't calculated to make him feel any happier."

Aiken subsequently mentioned Eliot's perplexity, violating his confidence, "to a very good friend of mine, Dilston Radcliffe, who was at that time being analyzed by the remarkable American lay analyst, Homer Lane," with the result that Lane unprofessionally conveyed the message through Radcliffe that Eliot's block was the consequence of his fearing to put anything down short of perfection because he thought he was God. Eliot's reaction when informed of Lane's remark was predictably acid, as Aiken should have known it would be: "For when I told Eliot of Lane's opinion he was literally speechless with rage, both at Lane and myself. The *intrusion*, quite simply, was one that was intolerable. But ever since I have been entirely convinced that it did the trick, it broke the log-jam. A month or two later he went to Switzerland, and there wrote *The Waste Land.*"

Aside from the admission that he himself did not encounter writing stoppages, which belies frequent claims to the contrary, and the error in chronology (*The Waste Land* and Swiss treatments were already behind Eliot when they met), Aiken's bit of reminiscence underlines the ambiguity of his feelings about his guarded school chum. Genuine admiration and affection are, as usual, intermingled with involuntary flashes of unspoken hostility toward the man who had always forced him into the self-abasing role of pursuer, the man altogether uncomfortably like himself in his contrasting mix of arrogance and secret passivity, yet possessed of a magical genius and surface command he could only either weakly attempt to emulate or downplay. From Eliot's vantage, as he endeavored to recover from a nervous breakdown and the emotional handicap that seemed to have triggered it, his friend's treachery must have approached the monstrous, since Aiken was perhaps the one person in London he would have trusted with this piece of personal information. His compulsive sense of privacy naturally recoiled from Aiken's lack of discretion, and the answer passed on from Lane, an insult and naive to boot in its glib dilation of Eliot's obvious anal-retentive trait, could hardly have influenced his return to writing. At the time, he was apparently contemplating a sequel to *The Waste Land,* which might have been one way to combat postpartum depression.

Aiken's motivations, complicated and conflicting as ever, stemmed largely from an unconscious desire to hurt and discredit an old antagonist and paternal authority figure, as well as a retrospective need to gain attention from his association with Eliot and his famous poem. When the brief memoir was written in 1965, one of Aiken's surest roads to public recognition was his friendship with Eliot, a sad commentary on his own relative neglect. More important, I think, was Aiken's unstable mental state at the time of their luncheon meetings, leaving literary historians with a comic-tragic sketch of two seriously disturbed fellow poets fencing each other over their grilled rump steaks and pints of Bass while struggling to hide grave psychic wounds behind the mein of imperturbable Harvard wit. Empathy and sympathy were almost unimaginable between them under the circumstances. Still reeling from Ormond's profound ego-thrust, Aiken, who read Eliot as well as anyone (which is why he intuited how most to offend him), could not afford to perceive himself refracted through the agony and tension easily deduced from his luncheon partner's prickly stiffness, especially now, when faced with an uncertain future in a cold clime.

But he and Eliot, like an old married pair harnessed together by common memories and ambitions, needed each other, and so the rendezvous continued through the early months of 1922. The extent and contour of Aiken's inner turmoil can be gauged from two contemporaneous poems, "Poverty Grass" and "Psychomachia," both conceived at the pessimistic extreme where inherited Romantic modalities can stray when convictions of art's eternal paradisal dream falter under the remorseless onslaught of consciousness's terror of annihilation, which remained, at least for Aiken, the negative side of Freud's picture of humanity's buried links with nature. From the moment of inception, which can be regarded biologically as nought but a by-product of an evolutionary mechanism, consciousness must defy the very membrane of nature that nourished it, individuality itself ("I am") unalterably opposed to the amoral indifference of a system predicated upon the survival of the species and a cosmic plot of endless regenerations. Nature had been the enemy from the beginning, engaging the best minds in every discipline and generation to combat its blind brutality, until Darwin and Freud once again reasserted mankind's inability to dissociate (and thus free) self from the Eros and Thanatos drives of an ecologically closed cycle. Not only was Freudian man subject to childhood dislocations and unconscious motivations, he was tragically retethered to nature's tireless horses of sex and aggression, his mind again seen at the mercy of instinctual commands.

One of the more attractive current answers was to follow Nietzsche's lead and return the sacred to the profane by rediscovering, with Yeats, Lawrence, and other Blakean mystics, the unity with nature's will that had supposedly been achieved by pre-Socratic philosophers, or aspire, with Eliot's brand of Eastern mysticism, to attaining the consciousness of the *Bhagavad-Gita*'s karma, "the ultimate Reality," which is where *The Waste Land* tends: "Shantih shantih shantih." But none of these responses to what Max Weber called "the rationalization of Western culture" could elicit complicity from Aiken, who was bound to his grandfather's Emersonian ethic and convinced that an artist must confront the chaos (inward and outward) Henry Adams had so tellingly limned in his *Education:* "Since monkeys first began to chatter in trees, neither man nor beast has ever denied or doubted Multiplicity, Diversity, Complexity, Anarchy, Chaos. Always and everywhere the Complex had been true and the Contradiction had been certain. Thought started by it." Needless to add, there is a horse-cart question whether Aiken's psychology left him much real choice in the matter.

The problem at this point, however, was the insufficiency of his aesthetic to tackle the grand schema he had managed to construct in his mind, as demonstrated by the two ineffective poems. In "Poverty Grass," a strident, Poe-like fantasy, the speaker is a prophet with divine powers who orders the people of earth to erect a crystal coffin for himself, significantly *inside* the coffin of a house, where he will await death. Invection (a nihilistic rage) and desolation are the poem's singular energy sources, damning man as corrupt and corrupting and demanding that the audience feed on him, "This bloodless carcass that contains your secret." And the secret that he possesses is the knowledge that "this singing world of yours / Is but a heap of bones."

Mood and essence belong to Eliot's "Gerontion," again, though a "personal grouse" has definitely not been translated into successful allegory; a further intent involves a deliberate, fearful denial of even Stevens's secular imagination, which affirms how upset Aiken was by the Ormond fiasco and ensuing suspicions of his inadequacy as man and poet. "Poverty Grass" seems animated by a bout of hysteria, a manifestation of frantic despair akin to the "state of mind" his perceptive review of *The Friend of the Family* for the *Freeman* a few months earlier had located in Dostoyevsky. The latter's haunting sense of evil was viewed as projecting itself through either a "monstrous symbol of pain" or "the symbol of the sense of horror and futility which arises from too acute a consciousness of the blank, empty, and indifferent determinism in which the human consciousness finds itself enmeshed." Once more, Freud's menacing merger of art and sickness was being used to analyze literature, arguing against critics like Murry, who would discard biographical material and seek ontological subsumption in the literary performance, which they treated as if it were a religious artifact. In the review Aiken described Dostoyevsky's novels as "dreams in a Freudian sense, since they are projections, again and again, of his own difficulties in life." Freud himself, in an October 19, 1920, letter to Stefan Zweig, had cited Dostoyevsky in observing: "Hysteria springs from the psychic constitution of itself and is an expression of the same organic basic power which produces the genius of an artist."

But Aiken could not yet, like Dostoyevsky, "exploit his disease." He was still compelled to write "analytic" rather than lyric poetry, to emulate the kind of poet that Reverend Potter and Santayana might respect, rejecting Dostoyevsky's involuntary approach: "Dostoevsky is perhaps the supreme instance of the compulsive nature of the artist's ideas." The hysteria of "Poverty Grass" is carried over into "Psychomachia," a more substantial effort in three sections, although the tone is softer, less melodramatic. A speaker is addressing an unknown male presence, probably a god, from whom he seeks the "mystery, a message learned, / A word flung down from nowhere, caught by you." The reply, which echoes the desolate conclusion of "Poverty Grass," alludes to ghosts, torn flesh, and "nothing, nothing, but a welling up of pain," since "you know this road, he said, and how it leads / Beyond starved trees to bare grey poverty grass." But the mystery, a raison d'être clearly related to the literary divinity established by Stevens's poetry, is pleaded for, "A word you have / That shines within your mind," until the stranger warns him to stay with his landscape of nerves and voices, because leaving it—presumably Aiken's psychotic inheritance as artist—would mean "death . . . call it sorrow."

In the second section Aiken offers a vision of a naked plain over which a cloud hangs like a bird. A figure suddenly shapes itself into a man and light pours down on him, but soon he is grappling with a beast or monster that is ever-changing,

> now was like an octopus of air,
> Now like a spider with a woman's hair
> And woman's hands, and now was like a vine
> That wrapped him.

For a climax, the Adamic creation destroys his nemesis and buries it in sand, dancing on the grave, surrounding himself with paradise, but the cloud bird darkens and covers him as he dances. This parable of human history and loss, of art's romantic powers and fated doom, culminates, in the third section, with the mysterious presence reiterating the message Aiken had decoded in Stevens:

> Thus draw your secret sorrow forth,
> Whether it wear a woman's face or not;
> Walk there at dusk beside that grove of trees,
> And sign, and she will come.

A split is desired, in other words, a rendering of Ormond and Anna from the female Muse in his psyche, so that his poetry can save him from the void that his consciousness could not help confronting and manufacturing, can save him from the "blank, empty, and indifferent determinism" enmeshing Dostoyevsky, the "blank desertion" Wordsworth had transcended in his *Prelude*. The poem does not end here, however, for the spirit directs him to bury her, when she comes to him, "All writhing, and so cover her with earth. / Then will the two, as should be, fuse in one." The language merges sex and death with admirable vividness. Moreover, once she is safely interred, his grief planted, his sterile landscape thence metamorphosized into Eden, he will find himself "at peace."

Yet doubts persist, resist an anima-animus convergence. The narrator inquires if it will indeed be better to have his self-created topography lit by her entombed fire than to retain her "single beauty fugitive in my mind?" A cryptic restatement of the status quo is the sole reassurance given, her nerves and voices as his landscape, his possession of her. At the allegorical level (bred out of China and New England), where design has an autodidactic purpose, suggestive of biblical tales or Arthur Waley's translation of *One Hundred and Seventy Chinese Lyrics* or the nightmare Arab's plight and message in Wordsworth's *Prelude,* the moral instructs the poet to remain in the country his imagination has invented to replace a lost mother and her punishing descendant, fusing madonna and bitch while quarrying poetry from the psychotic suffering they have induced. Psychologically, the wrestle with the mother's reincarnation on a mythic battlefield has mandated a primitive plot and *mise en scène,* almost a transcribed dream, in which rhetorical heaviness again distances reader from text, revealing how subtly aware Aiken was of his internal crisis and its tangled matrix of causes and how far away still from transforming knowledge into communal experience. That was the crux, of course, the tragedy of his riven condition. As *Festus* had striven valiantly to demonstrate, knowing is never enough, since solipsistic semantic boundaries adamantly bracket experience and any epistemological endeavors to encompass an amoral cosmos too dense to penetrate.

Though committed to attaining a poetry of expanding consciousness, of mating Freudian knowledge with experience and universal dream material, Aiken was intellectually faced with the skeptical reality, as spelled out in *Blue Voyage,* of both a "poisonous sophistry" and the similarly discouraging realization that "consciousness being finite, it can only in *theory* comprehend, and feel with, all things." Unlike Emerson and Reverend Potter, he could not take a lesson from the East and simply convert angst-blighted knowledge of a temporal and inhuman world into models of transcendental Platonism, although he clung (as also articulated in *Blue Voyage*) to the desperate artist hope of his age that all "this agony can be projected, and being projected will be healed." He still refused, however, to adopt the strategy dictated by his ambitious master plan, to inject the figurative blood shed by his obsessions more directly into the corpus of his imagination's elaborate disguises. This is why the poetry, in spite of his psyche's fertile state of unease, failed to yield ripe fruit.

With Secker's January 1922 publication of *Nocturne* and *Forslin,* which sold poorly but gained Aiken some respect among London peers, prospects for an English career seemed brighter. But he was growing more and more disgusted with the petty infighting that characterized and cheapened the ephemeral relationships in his chosen field. Dunster House's limited edition of *Priapus and the Pool* appeared in March, and he was delighted by the tasteful craftsmanship of the slender volume, though the reactions of close friends were far from overwhelming. "There are no comments on the book here," he would write to Maurice Firuski on June 7, "but it's not the custom to comment. Fletcher, with an evil gleam of the eye, remarked that the book was a beautiful piece of printing etc.—Armstrong said he liked the 'last poem' in it the best—etc. tutti frutti. More and more I detest poets and literati and 'literature' and the arts." Aiken had accepted Eliot's denigration of literary types as "shits" as applying to himself as well: "I sometimes wonder whether I shall ever be able to outgrow the disease, and become normal."

The situation at the Aikens' cold and grim flat had not improved, and Jane came down with the measles. Aiken was determined to locate a rural retreat before summer, if only for the sake of the children and peace at home. The area that most interested him was Sussex, in particular the attractive harbor he had visited in 1920 with Armstrong, where the two ancient hill towns, Rye and Winchelsea, faced each other across a semicircular inlet amid the wheat-fieldlike vistas of Romney Marsh. Further, Robert Nichols, the poet and would-be playwright he had encountered in Chicago during the war, was residing in Winchelsea with his wealthy wife, Norah, and they encouraged Aiken to move to the region.

When Aiken discovered that for a very reasonable rate he could rent a small but quaint house called Look Out Cottage perched just inside the entrance to Winchelsea, with sweeping views of the harbor and surrounding marshland, he leaped at the chance. By late May 1922 the family had moved in and seemed comfortably settled, finding the cramped quarters a distinct improvement over the roomier but less charming Colville Gardens apartment. The children were enchanted by the picture-book strangeness of their new neighborhood. Jane remembers "arriving at the little local station for Winchelsea, a mile from the village, into green grass and buttercups and complete delight," though the tininess of the cottage meant that baths were taken "in a tin bath by the kitchen fire." And John recalls that "we adored the move to Winchelsea . . . [and were] entranced by local place names like Appledore and Hamstreet." Jessie, too, was pleased by the scenic contrasts the town provided to the grim suburban bleakness of Notting Hill. It was prettier than South Yarmouth yet not as isolated, although both Winchelsea and Rye were also resort villages with local populations that rarely exceeded several thousand souls during the winter and maintained their own style of provincialism.

Since London, some sixty miles away, was within reach and the area supplied in abundance the seaside environment he loved best, Aiken was also sanguine about the move. South Yarmouth had taught him to appreciate the psychological and physical benefits of gardening and living among rural creatures and customs at some distance from the intense competitiveness of urban centers. Although the villagers were inevitably stratified and rigid in their ways, given to gossip and small-town prejudices, more cultivated circles were available. Besides the Nicholses and a smattering of London literati who owned homes in or around the two villages, including the novelist E. F. Benson, who had taken over Lamb House, there were several talented artists in the vicinity.

One of them, Paul Nash, simply "Paul" in *Ushant,* "swum up out of nowhere to knock on the door of the cottage" at Winchelsea ("Inglesee") and introduce himself (278). A slender man with "raven black hair, vivid blue eyes," and "finely chiselled aquiline features," whose taste for the good life and "immaculate, rather ambassadorial appearance and debonair manners" had earned him the title of "the last civilized man" from his friends, Nash was a successful painter of landscapes at this juncture in his career. He had been an artist at the front during the war and had been befriended by Edward Marsh and championed by Roger Fry, with whom he had worked on the restoration of the Mantegna frescoes at Hampton Court in 1914. Like his early idol Rossetti, he was drawn to literary people, and Marsh had introduced him to Rupert Brooke and W. H. Davies, the "tramp" poet Aiken was so fond of and an early purchaser of Nash's art. Another important literary contact, with T. E. Lawrence, came through Nash's wife, Margaret, daughter of Bishop Odeh, who had been chaplain to the Anglican bishop of Jerusalem and had taught Lawrence Arabic. John Drinkwater, playwright, biographer, and occasional poet, had also been a friend and patron since 1917.

The Nashes had a large house, Pantile Cottage, in Dymchurch, about fifteen miles down the coast, where they spent their summers. Aiken and Nash hit it off from the start, as could be expected from a shared taste for biting humor and cosmopolitan repartee and certain psychological parallels in their biographies that had resulted in Nash perfecting a unique surrealist technique that permitted him to inject disturbing dream motifs into his almost primitive landscapes.

As also could be expected, Aiken's relationship with Margaret Nash was not as warm. She was an intelligent, strong-willed woman, an Oxford graduate and early suffragette, whom he saw as dominating a childless marriage, his ingrained male chauvinism bridling over her feminist stance and her casual assumption of sexual equality. His hostility toward Margaret, which he tactfully avoided expressing in her company, did not extend to Norah Nichols, who maternally indulged her emotionally childish husband's every whim and appeared to accept his constant philandering with amused patience. Nash, too, engaged in extramarital affairs, which Aiken's implicit double standard had no trouble accommodating as a male artist's prerogative. Jane Aiken recollects her father once telling her that there existed an "aesthetic in morality" which should be pursued, but this never applied to the matter of amorous conquests, however cruel they might prove to his female partners. Sensitive women always intuited this sadistic strain in his otherwise benevolent character, as had Jessie, and no woman would ever be his friend in any meaningful sense.

Nash would supply valuable contacts with other artists and professional people who traveled the elite cultural and social paths Aiken could not help regarding as essential to the aristocratic side of his divided self, a blessing of the highly civilized ethos England profusely possessed and America lacked. Malcolm Cowley has observed that "during the 1920's many, and perhaps most, of the serious American writers felt like strangers in their own land." Years later, in an essay entitled "Why Poets Leave Home," Aiken stressed the superiority of London, "the deepest, richest, darkest, profoundest, meanest, ugliest, most sinister and beautiful of cities," over New York, "brilliant and superficial by comparison," and characterized his own migration as the consequence of "an appetite for more complexities and refinements than, at the moment, Boston seemed to provide, and for a civilization in which literature was more honorably a living thing." Without alluding to his oft-repeated wish that the mother country were populated by Americans, he went on: "It may have been an illusion, it may have been simply because I was young and impressionable, but at all events it appeared to me that the people I encountered casually in London, or elsewhere in England, were subtler and keener, and more in the civilized habit of making fine distinctions, than the people I encountered casually in America. If I acquired from them a feeling of inferiority, I also acquired an education."

Aiken viewed the shift to East Sussex, away from the squabbles and treacheries endemic among London cliques, which he could not abjure totally from a career standpoint, as especially fortuitous, even nourishing. In comparison to the American approach to living in the "country," English countryside life seemed unpressured: "Here too there are a few cocktail parties, for those who want them, where the cocktails are very bad and the gin very good; but they are not a desperate necessity, a *sine qua non*, as with us; one gets along without them just as one gets along without a car or telephone. It is not considered necessary to get mildly drunk every afternoon or evening. Instead, one goes for a walk through charming country, where footpaths make it admirably easy to avoid roads, and where the absence of undisciplined, ragged second-growth trees makes it an almost universal characteristic of the English landscape that one is always aware of distances."

His love for the terrain in the region was genuine, though he did not avoid the cocktail (invented that year)—Winchelsea's New Inn became a favorite hangout—and got "mildly" or more seriously drunk frequently. Nowhere does he mention the need periodically to return to America and bathe in the vulgarity its cities' seamier neighborhoods channeled into burlesque palaces and speakeasies or the inveterate restlessness that made him one of the London train's loyalest customers. Wandering around the Sussex landscape, however, was a pleasure that enabled him to grow closer to his children, whom he frequently took along when walking the two and a half miles to Rye or the mile to Winchelsea Beach or exploring the Salts and various parts of Romney Marsh. John and Jane were attentive companions whom he enjoyed amusing with stories spun spontaneously from his dream-fertilized imagination. "I think it was as early as this," Jane says, "that Conrad told us the long entrancing story of 'The Jewel Seed' as he walked us about the marsh. Written by John into little notebooks and lost in one of the family moves. Alas. And, yes, inspired by it, I told 'The Playlanders' aloud to John. A good time." The reference is to an "epic" poem Jane wrote in Winchelsea, though she was only five at the time, which Aiken would reprint near the end of *Ushant*.

No wonder he doted on the precocious Jane, who, like many of her sex, spoke readily and at length from an early age, although John was never aware of his sister receiving special treatment: "I don't recall any feeling of discrimination in favor of Jane: He was very fond of us both and a wonderfully stimulating and inventive father: when there." Aiken could sincerely sympathize with John's shyness, a genetic bond, leading his son to conclude subsequently: "I believe that Conrad's shyness and refusal to make public appearances . . . was innate and had little to do with the parental tragedy, since I inherited a good deal of this, certainly not from my mother. He spoke to me very freely about his social inadequacies when young, I think to try and help me overcome mine." Except for rare occasions, neither child could recall their father playing the strict disciplinarian. Jane remembers "being spanked by Conrad after behaving very badly indeed at a tea party. With John, of course." More typical are her memories of "the red berries on a yew tree and being told not to eat them. We had a cat called Nettle because she scratched, and a loganberry bush in the garden, and Martin Armstrong used to come to stay, and we woke him in the morning by bouncing on his bed." Nettle was the first in a long line of feline family members, for Aiken had passed on his love of cats to his children.

If this sounds idyllic, the main reason is not nostalgia so much as the ability of Aiken, "when there," to concentrate upon being his children's entertainer and playmate, relishing them and their antics like a fond grandfather who resided elsewhere. The more mundane daily grind of raising the children was of course left to Jessie, whose love and strength of character John and Jane came to accept as the bulwark upon which their growth and personalities must ultimately depend, even while she went about the difficult task of integrating the family into a local scene not given to embracing outsiders. Her sole social diversions were occasional weekend guests such as Armstrong, whose steady sense of fun kept them all amused, and more formal visits with people such as the Nashes. She also had to deal with a very modest budget—it was a "frugal era" in Jane's reckoning—and the not always benign neglect of a husband at war with himself and a hostile world, who was busier than ever in his tireless quest for a place in England's pale literary sun.

A month before the move to Winchelsea Aiken had begun sending letters of inquiry to a small group of fellow American poets, seeking permission to reprint portions of their work in an anthology of modern poetry he was putting together for Secker. The idea came originally from Louis Untermeyer, who had written the previous April suggesting that Aiken edit an anthology of contemporaries that would be more selective than his own *Modern American Poetry* volumes. Such a collection might prove profitable to Secker, who had lost money on the three Aiken books published thus far, and could perhaps combat the contemptuous attitude toward American writers prevalent among English critics, a contempt parroted by Eliot in his May 1922 "London Letter" to the *Dial* in which, as Untermeyer grumbled, "swelling the English chorus, he damns all American work, singling out Frost for particular condemnation" and excluding only Sandburg with "a patronizing shrug." Aiken had little use for Sandburg and could never persuade Eliot that Emily Dickinson was "one of the most remarkable of American poets, and that her poetry is perhaps the finest, by a woman, in the English language."

As outlined in letters to Fletcher and Frost, Aiken's plan was to devote most of the anthology to ten major contributors Frost, Fletcher, Masters, Robinson, Lowell, Eliot, Stevens, Kreymborg, Lindsay, and Dickinson, the only dead invitee—and the rest to six or so "lesser" talents, among them H. D., Bodenheim, Millay, and Williams. The profits would be divided equally between Secker and the poets, his editorial fee a mere five pounds per each thousand copies. By excluding his own verses, Aiken forestalled charges of self-interest and underscored his commitment to promoting the art and the country that defined his strongest self. Recent delvings into Melville and ruminations on the diverse achievements of nineteenth-century American literature, pursued in tandem with readings in current American writing for his *Mercury* articles, had enlarged and refined his perception of native achievements, somewhat diminishing his persistent overestimation of English colleagues, though he continued to champion and seek outlets in the United States for Freeman and Armstrong.

The stubborn honesty behind the anthology project was exemplified by the omission of the Untermeyers, despite the danger of possible repercussions, and Aiken's willingness to include Lowell and Pound, although both the latter and Masters had to be left out when reprint permissions were not forthcoming. Responses from the poets involved were generally positive, often revealing.

Vachel Lindsay, for instance, two of whose collections had appeared in England, one with an introduction by Nichols, wrote to Aiken from a hotel in North Carolina, where he was in the midst of another debilitating reading tour: "I was pleased and flattered to get your letter today and answer at once, as I wait for the 4:30 A.M. train to take me further south." He asked that Aiken not choose "The Congo" and "all poems of that type," which had "utterly mispresented my point of view and distorted my whole public life," insisting that he had never been "much interested in poems to be recited, or in reciting" and was again making his "pen-and-ink pictures the first consideration." Lindsay had studied and lectured on art for many years and was the first literary critic to take movies seriously. With melancholic weariness he lamented: "But my dear friend—no one buys my books. I have to lock myself up to escape the crowds determined to make me recite. . . . I expect to continue next year . . . reciting in every state in the union—and for every English Department that will let me in. It is my sole source of income. No one will buy my books."

Aiken was impressed and touched by Lindsay's lack of animosity toward him, the reviewer who had, only the year before, detected signs of a "final" decay in the poetic powers of the author of *The Chinese Nightingale*. "You are that rare combination—a man of honesty, courage and true fighting instinct in the critical field," Lindsay wrote. Amy Lowell was also flattering in her April 18, 1922, response to his request, after convincing her publisher not to charge for the reprinting of her work: "I think this anthology of yours is an excellent thing, and you have the distinction of being the only American resident in Europe who has lifted his finger to help his countrymen in the eyes of the English." Kreymborg, who was vacationing in Pallanza, Italy, with his second wife and two children and who had recently disassociated himself from *Broom,* the magazine he had launched the year before, respected the variety of styles Aiken's gathering would incorporate, though ruing Pound's absence: "I'm sorry Ezra is not to be in the Anthology, as he has advised me. He carries his American antipathy to a ridiculous degree, as I've advised him. It is certainly not a disgrace to appear among the names you have selected. They are distinctly varied individuals, each one fighting an honest, palpitating battle of his own, regardless of isms, and no one of them, with the possible exception of Amy, has had an easy time of it, nor ever will have."

Aiken replied immediately, listing the thirteen poems he wanted to use and alluding to the various sicknesses that had been snapping at the family's collective heels since London's bitter winter had taken hold. Kreymborg's sympathetic return letter points up the good-natured centrifugal force in Jessie's character that had swung her husband into her orbit in the first place: "We're awfully sorry to hear about your serious illnesses. Maybe the spring—if ever it shows its rose—will heal you all. Jessie must be exhausted—even her energies, the most chipper I've ever witnessed, must need a rest." Stevens, Frost, Robinson, and other contributors or their publishers proved similarly cooperative, and the anthology manuscript was ready by the July 1922 deadline, which would enable Secker to publish *Modern American Poets* in October.

Relations with one of the excluded poets, Louis Untermeyer, were less congenial. Inner agitation and doubts still made Aiken liable to overreact when criticized, and he had never recovered from Untermeyer's accusation that his poetry exhibited a lack of development. When he felt that an Untermeyer article in the *Nation* had implicitly slighted him, he rushed off a harsh letter, charging its writer with "log-rolling" and deploring Untermeyer's attack upon Armstrong and Freeman. Typically, Untermeyer's May 9, 1922, response neither backed down nor permitted Aiken's somewhat paranoid assumptions to go unanswered or unanalyzed:

> In the first place, why you should take my ignorance of Armstrong for granted is something beyond my meagre comprehension. I have before me as I write, his *The Buzzards and Other Poems* and, with the exception of the title poem, 'Hymn to the Ideal Beauty' and one or two others, I can see nothing in his poetry other than the traditional properties of English country verse dished up in the current Georgian manner. Two of Freeman's books have been published here by Harcourt (one of them a curiously voluminous affair) and his chief difference from Armstrong lies in quantity rather than quality. But, aside from your gratuitous accusation, what have either to do with my complaint? (Your suggestion that I have gone 'out of my way' to injure them or that I have singled them out because of their 'connection' with you—a 'connection' of which I was, of course, wholly unaware—is altogether absurd.) Are you developing an enlarged thymus gland or a swollen persecution complex?

Once more, however, Untermeyer did not allow Aiken's diatribe to sever communications between them: "And it is in saluting your own honesty that I cannot be outraged when you insist on coddling your own particular preferences. And it is because of this that I am not going to let our friendship break up or even become strained because of your logical, at least to you, decisions"—a reference to his exile from the Secker anthology. In his labors as critic and anthologist Untermeyer had learned that abuse from a poet was standard fare, and after denying he had been acting as Pound's agent—"I haven't heard from Pound, except by way of friends who have relayed his sneers to me, for three years"—his closing reverts to the amiable personal tone he favored in their up-and-down relationship: "How much longer do you expect the children to live on London fog? And where are the corrected proofs for the Miscellany?"

His remarks on the weakness of Freeman's and Armstrong's poetry were just, but Aiken's friendship with the two Englishmen prevented him from accepting Untermeyer's strictures, especially since he was striving to persuade Firuski to publish two of Freeman's stories in a limited edition and feared a negative press might frustrate the plan. More relevant, the excessive heat of his reaction and uncharacteristic critical denseness in the exchange of acrimonious letters with an important literary figure seem symptomatic of the self-disgust and uncertainty keeping him off balance. The precariousness of his psychological state intensified in August 1922, when a pamphlet entitled *A Critical Fable* was printed anonymously in the United States, a long poem in clever couplets poking fun, sometimes viciously, always shrewdly, at him and a host of American contemporaries.

Patterned after James Russell Lowell's nineteenth-century satire of the same title, *A Critical Fable* was obviously the work of Amy Lowell, although she endeavored vigorously to dispel that notion by pointing a finger at other suspects. Besides the overt imitation of an ancestor, her authorship was confirmed by the marshaling of attitudes well known as her own and by the special kindness accorded herself in the poem.

Arch mockery flails all and sundry, but the sharpest whacks are reserved for Aiken and Eliot, with the latter firmly handcuffed to Pound: "Each one is a traitor, but with different treasons." The assault on Aiken, "this extremely irascible gentleman," who is seen forcing his way into the speaker's presence, reiterates the pugnacious quality of his personality throughout and dismantles his poetry with distressing skill:

> Mr. Aiken's a poet so cram full of knowledge
> He knows all about poetry that's taught in a college.
> His versification's as neat as a pin,
> His metre so fine it becomes finikin.
> I say nothing of rhythm, for he's something fanatical
> Anent the advantage of the beat mathematical.
> Within his set limits, the pulse of his verse
> Is often most subtle, and even his worse
> Attempts are by no means either jejune or lacking
> In form, one can hardly imagine him slacking
> In pains or desire. He's all that a poet
> Can make of himself when he sets out to do it
> With his heart, and his soul, and his strength, and his mind.

For years now, he's had a most horrible grind
With his work, with the public, but what stands in his way
Is the awkward necessity of something to say.
A man of sensations, of difficult cheerfulness
Which the fog in his brain has tormented to fearfulness,
Possessed of much music and little idea,
Always steeping his soul in the strange undersphere
Of the brain. Since all thought in him tends to grow hazy
When his sentiment's roused, he is lost in a mazy
Vortex where he swings like some pale asteroid.
Seeking orientation, he's stumbled on Freud.
With the Austrian's assistance, he's become neurological,
A terrible fate to befall the illogical.

Lowell pinches more than one nerve, but she clearly had no understanding of the ambitious concert of aims that orchestrated Aiken's poetry. She hits home frequently enough, however, to destroy whatever confidence he might have had left in his success to date, though she tries to give his virtues their due:

He's built a basilica surely in "Senlin."
At least in that "Morning Song," which, until lately,
Was the sole, single fragment he'd done adequately.
Till "Punch," ah! with "Punch" now he should achieve fame,
But there's nothing so dogging as a once-come-by name.
If this were his first, he'd be up like a rocket.
Now I think he'll burn steadily on in his socket
Making beautiful poems though the public won't stand 'em
Because he can't drive style and tale in a tandem.
Since the books as they are stick so hard in the gizzard,
The sensible thing is to have each one scissored.
Cut out from each volume the one or two scraps
You might like on a third or fourth reading perhaps;
Paste them into a scrap-book, and some rainy day
Just glance over the lot and I think you will say:
"By Jove! What a fellow he is in his way!"
And I'll thank you for that as a true leaf of bay.
If he, the arch-sceptic, finds other folk doubting,
He makes a mistake to be seen always pouting.
He has not his deserts, yet to publish the fact
Is a childish and most unintelligent act,
But everyone knows he's deficient in tact.

A man who can work with such utter devotion
Can afford to wait patiently for his promotion,
And that it will come, I've a very strong notion.
One thing we can say, he will certainly wait
And either get in or turn dust at the gate.
Since Fame is a very good hand at the shears,
I shall not be surprised if he gets his arrears,
For quality counts in the long run of years.

The occasional lightning streaks illuminating a few of the shadowy corners in Aiken's psyche probably hurt most.

Although he had enjoyed pummeling Lowell in the past, their exchanges since the publication of *Punch* had been mutually complimentary and respectful, which only enhanced the shock, as did the timing of the satire's appearance. Fletcher remembered Aiken "indignantly" protesting about *A Critical Fable* to him, and the situation was made more annoying and ludicrous because a section of the American literary group immediately assumed he was the culprit. Critics such as Untermeyer had no difficulty in detecting Lowell's trademark, predicting she would own up to her signature before the year was out, but Linscott wrote playfully to Aiken on August 28 to confirm a consensus among many critics, including Burton Rascoe, that Aiken alone could have the intelligence and poetic capacity to produce such a professional grim burlesque. The rest of the letter continued in the same teasing vein, Linscott unaware of how disconcerted and hurt Aiken had been by a poem that picked apart his art and self with sly ease and foresaw a bleak future for his career, however kind about history's ultimate judgment of what he had already accomplished.

Two earlier letters to Firuski, written near the end of April 1922, hint at the depressed state of mind that caused him to bristle under Lowell's onslaught, forgetting that he had once parodied her as a monumental egotist floating on a divanlike cloud. After thanking Firuski for *Priapus* in the first letter and suggesting English journals to which it should be sent for review, he admits: "Personally, I find my opinion of the book confused and uncertain: I like one or two things that I almost left out, and another few I wish now I *had* left out." He also mentions his swim in Melville's Elizabethan ocean—he had read *Pierre, Moby-Dick,* and *Mardi*—and the physical ailments reinforcing inner ills: "Jane has the measles, and I have a sore throat and haemorrhoids!"

Responding to a "cryptic" note from Firuski concerning the bookseller's continuing problem, apparently amorous, Aiken again plays the role of spiritual adviser, airing some proven techniques for fighting off depression: "One can wring certain pleasure out of it! Take it, for example, to the art museum, and while meditating before a Sargent watercolor of Corfu or a Dodge Mack-night barn in snow, or, better than either, a Sung dynasty painting of an arhat playing with a pet tyger, . . . listen alternately to the ground bass of your grief and the ecstatic melody of beauty." He also counsels a more extreme remedy in the event of a deeper disturbance, counsel he himself could have benefited from: "You want to run away? well, why *not* run away for a few weeks, if you feel inclined? or, on the other hand, if you feel a considerable part of your difficulty is psychotic, and if you are a little worried for fear it may be deepening, then I beseech you, Maurice, go to see Dr. John Taylor, who is a kind of psychopathologist, at the Mass. Gen. Hospital, and who is A 1. He did wonders for a friend of Jessie's who had a nervous disorder absolutely wiped out every trace of a scar."

Flight, art, psychoanalysis: they were his own best tactics, forms of self-defense practiced previously with a degree of success, though the last-named procedure had usually entailed nothing more than discussions of his dreams and work with Wilbur. The trick was to prevent stasis, a lack of diversions, any prolonged retreats into melancholic introversion, as when he was momentarily shattered by Reine Ormond's desertion—significantly, Sargent is mentioned twice in the letter—so that, "if the affair is one of a new and unrequited interest; then I'm damned if I know what to say! Write a book. Paint pictures. Take up fancy skating, or go shimmying every night with Jack Gardner. Keep moving, in other words." He was ill and trapped in London at the time, the letter affirming his growing disenchantment with literary politics and Eliot's Machiavellian maneuvers:

> We lead an incredibly quiet and secret life—hardly see a soul. Eliot, I hear in a roundabout way, is starting a new critical magazine next autumn, with a financial guarantee for three years. I lunch with him once a week quite regularly, but in all our talk he has never once mentioned the project! . . . Everybody's like that here. Literary people in London are a lot of agile, half-starved crabs, furtive, sidling, always timidly on guard, afraid to give themselves away, and all scavengering round on the chance of stealing a good idea. (I've lost several in that way—and to men whom I call my friends. They steal without knowing it.). . . . Even more exasperating are the professional stealers like Murry and Huxley, who, not content with the theft, then try to poison the person from whom they stole. Huxley is especially good at that. . . . He is a skunk. Murry isn't quite so bad—let's call him a worm.

The vitriolic sentiments, even if earned by their two crafty recipients, reflect the failure to regain his balance after the Ormond incident and the completion of the symphonic series. Winchelsea seemed to offer salvation for the moment, an opportunity to regroup scattered psychic forces. Its antiquity and soothing climate acted as balms for frazzled nerves, as did the distance from London's hectic grayness and squabbles. The effect on his family's health and spirits was thoroughly positive—"Jessie and the kids are flourishing," he would write to Linscott in November 1922—and his affection for England was returning in full measure, again convincing him that permanent exile was a feasible option, though he could not, like James and Eliot, bring a convert's zeal to the enervating chore of out-Englishing the English.

This did not mean an end to his wanderlust, a desire to replenish depleted emotional reserves by revisiting adolescent haunts and old friends in Cambridge and Boston. He had an ideal excuse for a solo voyage to America in September 1922, when the summer tenants would be leaving the South Yarmouth cottage. Though not happy about it, Jessie had agreed to his going, since he also pleaded the need to take care of various literary matters. The crossing was enlivened by an encounter with a young man named Robert Hale, who had been staying with Waldo Peirce in Paris and engaged Aiken in a string of stimulating chess games. After berthing, Conrad visited the Potters, stayed with friends, spent a weekend at the Linscott home, played tennis with Firuski and Taussig, and had meals with various people, including Lucien Crist and Julius Clark. The latter was now bald, reminding him of his own retreating hairline, and Crist told him he had decided to move to Washington.

The renewed contacts were pleasant, in the main, again making him wonder if England was indeed the answer, though Prohibition had transformed his beloved Harvard Club into something of a mausoleum during off-dinner hours. But the person he wanted most to see, Jake Wilbur, had left for Iowa with his wife and infant son. He had counted upon Wilbur to help him come to terms with his psychological problems, wanting to thrash out the reasons behind his gnawing discontent with his life and poetry, perhaps by talking over the symbolic significance of his dreams and the literature it appeared to generate. He wrote to Wilbur to see if he contemplated a return to the Cape. Wilbur replied on September 18, 1922, explaining that he and his wife, Joy, would not be back at South Dennis until the following July, when he hoped to learn if the Cape could support a psychoanalyst. In the meantime, Joy was taking courses in botany and recovering from a difficult delivery; he was enjoying teaching psychiatry and giving occasional lectures, persuaded that he was building a reputation in the field and gathering sufficient material for a book.

Aiken wrote back on September 26, hiding the true extent of his disappointment and refusing Wilbur's kind offer to send him a train ticket to Iowa, although tempted. He also notes the modest upswing in his London reputation, the result of the three poetry volumes and recent publication of the anthology—and alludes to Eliot's tormented mental state, passing on Lane's glib interpretation of his perfectionism as a species of self-deification. He asks Wilbur to be sure to inform him if he does decide to spend the winter on the Cape because that might encourage him to do likewise, which emphasizes the importance he attached to Wilbur's proximity.

That same night Aiken was to dine with Amy Lowell at Sevenels, a unique invitation that he obviously welcomed. Yet he could not dispel the lingering effects of *A Critical Fable,* which had reenergized his old hostility toward Lowell. It was probably during this dinner or soon afterward that he confronted her, bluntly inquiring if she was the perpetrator. When she continued to deny responsibility, he lost control and blurted out, "Well, since you didn't write it, I can say what I really think of it. I think it's damn rotten." Lowell's companion and other guests quickly intervened to prevent further recriminations, but the rupture between the two strong personalities was now beyond repair, another sign of the hidden tensions at work in Aiken. A happier experience was driving to South Yarmouth with Crist to check over the cottage and grounds for damage and pack away prints and books he had brought with him from England.

It was late October when he returned to Winchelsea after a grueling, storm-tossed voyage of ten days. Jessie's sole relief while he was away had been a week in September spent visiting John and Gertrude Freeman at their Anerley home, where John and Jane had the two Freeman children for company and Jessie had a rare chance to demonstrate her own substantial powers of conversation. When writing to thank her for her parting gifts, Freeman expresses the wish, shared by his wife, that Jessie and the children would come again, perhaps enabling them to get the four youngsters to bed "earlier in the dark evenings, and leave you free for conversation or what do you call it, disquisition."

Freeman's letter also refers to her "being alone at Winchelsea, when days are short and evenings long," but it was a condition to which she had grown accustomed. Visits from her sisters helped, and "she made friends easily," although she did have, as her son John has recorded, "some trouble with the English social scene, which seemed very sophisticated and strait-laced." But the human factors that drew people to her and made her "a very good mother indeed" to John and Jane—"she was a wonderfully warm, charming, intelligent woman, we all loved her"—provided the maternal indulgence that her husband continued to abuse. By November 5, 1922, he was back alone in London, living at a boardinghouse while he shopped for the family's winter clothes, "talked to the boys," and took advantage of whatever romantic adventures came his way. He had returned from America to discover that his anthology was both a critical and a popular success, which engendered mixed feelings because his financial gain from the project was small in comparison to the sums being gathered in by the featured poets. When Harold Monro gave a reading from the anthology on the night of November 8, he did not bother to attend.

Modern American Poets deserved its plaudits. It and several other anthologies to follow would not only supply its editor with a steady, if modest, source of income but also exert a positive influence upon the course of American literature, eventually leading Robert Penn Warren to observe in 1979 that Aiken had "held a strategic position in letters. And never got his due." In the Preface to *Modern American Poets* Aiken concedes that he had not attempted "to cover the entire field of contemporary American poetry," eschewing the "one-poem poet" in particular. Rather, he had intended "to compile an anthology in which the more important poets alone might figure, and in which they might, therefore, be more generously and identifiably represented." In addition, Aiken apologizes for the absence of Masters and Pound for reasons beyond his control, and of Sandburg, a sacrifice to his personal "taste."

There are questionable omissions and inclusions, but the choices of poets and poems betray a keen critical knowledge of those works most likely to endure, as well as an unwavering appreciation of the central significance of controversial poets such as Eliot and Stevens, without ignoring the more idiosyncratic verses of Williams and Kreymborg. Twenty-three poems by Dickinson constitute the rediscovery of a major talent—Aiken would perform a similar service for Anne Bradstreet in a later anthology—and the selections from the verses of Frost and Fletcher encompass much of their best labor. Millay's "Renascence" appears alone. Six of Lowell's poems are reprinted, though, oddly, "Patterns" is not one of them, and Arturo Giovannitti's lushly, morbidly romantic "The Walker" is included, perhaps because it was so reminiscent of Aiken's own early failures (it would be dropped when the anthology was published in America by the Modern Library in 1927). Another curious editorial decision is the presence of "The Monk in the Kitchen" and "Ere the Golden Bowl Is Broken" by Anna Hempstead Branch. Obviously Aiken had not yet wholly accepted Santayana's tart dismissal of her poetry.

The mixed blessings associated with the debut of *Modern American Poets* were nothing compared to the ambivalance Aiken experienced when the inaugural edition of the *Criterion* was published in October and contained *The Waste Land,* which would also see print in the November *Dial,* resulting in Eliot being the second recipient of that journal's $2,000 literary award. Reaction was immediate and intense, almost granting Eliot fame such as Byron had encountered upon his return to England after the publication of *Childe Harold.* Flustered and impressed in spite of himself, he wrote to Linscott on November 8 from London and mentioned the extraordinary reception that had greeted the poem, deemed "great" by various commentators: "Am I cuckoo in fancy-ing that it cancels the debt I owed him? I seem to detect echoes or parodies of Senlin, House, Forslin: in the evening at the violet hour etc, Madame Sosostris etc, and in general the 'symphonic' nature, the references to music (Wagner, Stravinsky) and the repetition of motifs, and the 'crowd' stuff be-ginning 'Unreal city.' However, that's neither there nor here: it's the best thing I've seen in years." Whatever the actual extent of Eliot's borrowings, Aiken was overlooking their common Harvard background and debts to the French Symbolists, *The City of Dreadful Night,* Browning, et al., and the fact that Eliot had often structured his psychological portraits upon a music-organized grammar in the past.

The bombshell that *The Waste Land* detonated under the feet of Whitman-inspired experimenters like Crane and Williams was not unlike the malignant practical and psychological impact it was to have on Aiken's career and inse-cure self-image. With a single burst of sustained creativity, his somewhat patronizing friend and old competitor seemed almost to have done him in, and at a time when he was starting to suspect that Eliot was in despairing retreat from the high intellectual ground they had once shared in their earlier discus-sions of Bradley and the poet's demanding vocation as cultural spokesman for modern complexities of feeling and thought. His critical antenna, acute as ever, scented the poem's masterpiece quality, however he might quibble with its presumed "arbitrary and rather unworkable logical value" when reviewing it for the *New Republic* in a few months, and he must have sensed that it towered over his own equally ambitious symphonic series. It suggested that Eliot's implicit domination of their friendship would continue and increase, keeping him in the hated, awkward role of pursuer, though Eliot, in his wary fashion, maintained congenial relations and would eventually get around to soliciting contributions from him for the *Criterion,* which he had to produce at night and without pay.

Considering the brutal sequence of beatings Aiken's psyche had absorbed, commencing with the suspected failure of the symphonies and extending through Eliot's recent surge into permanent ascendancy, it is amazing that he persevered and went on writing. Several months before, while loitering and fornicating in London a month before sailing for America, he had suddenly entered his usual stationer's shop, bought two notebooks and some pencils, and (as he later told Wilbur) returned "to the hated rooms where [I] boarded and wrote without conscious foreknowledge the first draft of *The Dance of Deth.* Had only the usual preceding tension." Winchelsea was the setting and inspiration for the long poem, written in the octosyllabic couplets that he had preferred since his exposure to Mansfield, which intimates a formal reversion to earlier paths, though Aiken insisted to Wilbur that he "intended the poem to conclude sharply a period of his life." It was deliberately aimed at creating a mythic climax for the symphonies' fascination with scrutinizing the multisided aspects of modern man through generic portraits painted by allegorical guises of an ongoing self-analysis. This was the ambition at least, and a worthy one, but, again, the consequences were far from satisfactory.

At the crux of *The Dance of Deth,* which would eventually be titled *John Deth: A Metaphysical Legend,* are the twin obsessions of Aiken's entire development: a fierce fear of death and a reactive need to debase and possess a maternal surrogate, although the intellectual libretto was designed to incorporate what he claimed had always been his target, to "disclose the psychic mechanism of the artist and human being—in the interest of furthering self-knowledge." He explained the arrangement of the poem to Linscott almost two years later, after having read Santayana's review of Freud's *Beyond the Pleasure Principle,* uncovering a basic linkage between love and death:

> Superficially, the parable can be said to state that a great part of the effort of life is an effort to die; that consciousness is a disease of Matter, an abnormality, and that a part of consciousness knows this, and, like Sibyl, wishes to die, to return into unconsciousness. A very simple and very comforting idea. In the poem, John Deth and Millicent Piggistaile represent the positive and negative poles of life (the terms should be reversed), and 'love,' or Venus, is the will or force that moves them. The other figure, Juliana Goatibed, in a sense contains them, is the sum of them, is their consciousness: it is through her that Deth and Millicent know their slavery and misery, and desire, by crucifixion of Venus, to obtain peace.

Without mentioning John Lydgate's *The Dance of Death*, Aiken later told D. G. Bridson the plot was "largely based on legends and histories in Winchelsea. The characters (John Deth, Millicent Piggistaile, and Juliana Goatibed) are actually names out of the first list of grantees of land in the Winchelsea Church book. And various other names are taken from the neighborhood, so that it is, in a sense, the most 'English' of all my poems—that is, strictly English based." Aiken's enchantment with the idea of a dance of death, which can be traced back to his 1911 trip through southern Europe with McCabe, appeared to have located an appropriate mythic context in the Winchelsea records and could be manipulated to revive another morbid scene (a crucifixion) that had long inhabited his imagination and nightmares. And all of it permitted him to continue his determined pursuit of a convoluted, archetypal praxis capable of reifying a reflexive stream of consciousness in creative flight.

Divided into five titled sections, *The Dance of Deth* opens with "The Star-

Tree Inn," with Deth and his "doxies" (Millicent and Juliana) entering town in rags, ironically in June, to have the dance of death performed at the inn. Deth plans to sleep this night with Millicent. Two gypsy spirits appear, inevitable light and dark females, "she who bore the shameful name" and the "golden-haired, who loved her lord," and depart, while Deth broods upon three other ladies sleeping in their graves, bidding them to arise at ten and join him at the inn. What ensues, Deth's female cohorts dancing with and kissing to doom a range of village characters, flits between archaic ballad horror and strained adolescent excess. Deth's attraction to the resurrected Elaine, who had died on her wedding night, persuades him to dawdle with her a while before Petronilla's mockery awakens him to his duty and he sends Elaine off to perform her vampirelike function. The innocent opposite of a vamp stereotype, she is ashamed when Doctor Lewd becomes her dancing partner.

Section 1 concludes fittingly with midnight peace and the reappearance of the light and dark gypsy shades at the churchyard wall. In the next section, devoted to Millicent, Deth finds in her the maternal essence that might offer an escape from mortality's vicious sway, as she invites him to rest his head

> on this exhausted breast,
> This breast that is a ruined world.
> Here rocks decay, and seas are whirled
> To nothingness; here God is not;
> And all things living are forgot

Their consummation of a sexual bond, a mating of son and mother, is viewed as the ultimate union of Eros and Thanatos, with her gift of life through death:

> All graves at last become one;
> And that grave shapes itself in me
> For you to grow on like a tree.

After their union is achieved, a violent plundering of female submission— "Here thrust and knot your roots"—he feels himself changing, as if impregnated by her—"Like clotting water felt it drip / Into his heart"—into a Tree of Paradise (favorite Aiken edilom), metamorphosized like Daphne. In the interim, Juliana has dropped her book, presumably the *Doomsday Book* or the *Book of Life*, or perhaps merely an image for her artist identity, and the tree is seen as growing around a tomb, flourishing, until it shrivels and dies. Upon waking, Deth and Millicent arouse the sleeping Juliana and the three depart.

In "The Falling of the Birds," section 3, Deth moves through nature with devastating power, a "golden cage of osier" in his hand. When all the birds of

376 / Poet of White Horse Vale

the forest have gathered around him on a hill, he offers one of them survival, a refuge in the cage for the bird who can tell him his secret, the secret of transcending death, "the light that flies." One bird after another offers a possible solution, giving Aiken the means for categorizing the various ways in which humans have attempted to evade mortality. The owl, for instance, voices the wisdom of Confucius, who is pierced in his grave by a tree, the Tree of Heaven: " 'Beauty is in the mind,' he said— / 'Beauty is in the eternal way.' " And Whistling Dick, a thrush, suggests beauty is she that can "grieviously dead earth to wake," memories of flesh beauty, while the cormorant more realistically rewrites Keats: "Beauty is food,—food, beauty! there / Is all we know, and all our care!" A sparrow speaks of Catullus's Lesbia, whose tomb is now under grass, happy in knowing that beauty still exists after we have passed, in contrast to the tale of Philomel about a king who built a palace to peace and Buddha that sank into dust with the rest of frail human artifacts and philosophies. Only the bat gives the correct reply, a vicious message to the effect that Venus Anadyomene is beauty, which can be possessed through her murder: "Strangle the goddess with her bright hair!"

The final stanza of the third section, in which Deth waves his wand at the rising flock of birds to bring promised oblivion by turning them into snow, projects one of the poem's most effective moments, metaphor and method brilliantly converging:

> Then fell the snow;
> The hill was white. And bent, and slow,
> His shoulders bright with frost, one hand
> Clutching the cage, and one the wand,
> Deth stooped down from the voiceless hill.
> The sun broke forth. The bat was still—
> Head downward in the cage he swung;
> The cage a bell and he the tongue.

With the aid of the bat, a vampire beyond death's rule, Deth and his two doxies seek out Venus in her cave in the fourth section. She surrenders after she discovers that neither birds nor foxes can save her, saying,

> Caught, as it was predestined, lord!
> In the beginning was the word.
> Hang the bat in the hemlock tree.
> Nail my hand. Crucify me.

Echoing the crucifixion in *The Charnel Rose* and the vivisectioning of the princess in *Festus,* the destruction of Venus as Juliana looks on smiling and Millicent, daughter of the goddess, shrinks back, covering her eyes, is the soft-porn climax of a drive to defile and plunder the madonna ideal, Anna Aiken plus icy Reine Ormond, as if she were her evil double:

> Venus in moonlight slept as dead.
> The palms were pierced. The feet were bound.
> Millicent heard the mallet pound:
> And the goddess cry; and, then, from Deth,
> Whistling, a sharply taken breath.

This is a primal male fantasy both debased and raised to a mythic level, which must have salved Aiken's wounded ego even as it summoned up guilt and moral revulsion.

The guilt, an approximation of salvation, and some rational mitigation of the poem's nihilistic design have to coalesce in the figure of Juliana Goatibed, who controls the last brief section, since Aiken intended her to apotheosize the medium of consciousness for Deth and Piggistaile, as well as for the poem itself, a consciousness come to divinity through acceptance and fusion of psychic dichotomies, returning to the biblical beginning of creation:

> Then Juliana Goatibed,
> Carving the rock beneath her head,
> Carved it vast, with hammering thought
> Out of terrific vision wrought.
> It was the world. Nought else there was. . . .
> No shape it had: it had no bound.

On her "ship of granite infinite" she is "the demon" who has to perform divine work, calling forth the "carver's self" from "out of nought," the artist self, as romantic as "The Potter" profiled at Harvard, if less blatantly fin de siècle:

> "Carve, now!" said she. And he, unhearing,
> Unhurried, old, and nothing caring,
> Conscious of stone and nought but stone,
> Stone to be cut by brittle bone,
> With tiny chisel and mallet smote
> The ancient base of rock.

Slyly completing the orbit enclosing dream and reality, Aiken carves the epitaph for Deth and Piggistaile and Goatibed, "the flame between" husband and wife, "who drove / Their anguish on, accursed Love." A final stanza has the moon going down "with red-tipped claw," watched by Juliana alone,

"Deth sleeping, but about to wake; / Millicent, weeping for his sake," though she lies beside them in the earth. There is another dream within a dream, the artist god's secular replacement, as the poem ends:

> "Peace now!" she cried. She dropped her head,
> Her mind grew dark. The world was dead.
> She dreamed. The Carver and she, alone,
> Would sleep forever upon the stone.

End and start are one, the word that began creation its single survivor, a Poe-like vision distinctly in the mauve tradition of the 1890s, but it is Wallace Stevens and "Sunday Morning" that govern *The Dance of Deth*'s notion of death mothering beauty, which is the sole religion left, transcendence of experience through relentless aesthetic consciousness.

But there is a pathology at the core of Aiken's poem that Stevens would have found abhorrent, less on moral grounds than as a violation of the rationalist imagination that Stevens posited as the primary processor of a reality endowed with opulent mines of untapped magic, irrational energies that an imaginative intelligence can extract and master, replicating nature's own creative powers, as was done by Wordsworth, not Coleridge. The last named's nightmare poetry was closer to the impetus and formula of *The Dance of Deth,* which uses medieval fable structures (Chaucerian) to reenact an allegorical parable that preaches the importance of Stevens's secular imagination but delights in the vicarious sadism of antifeminine fantasies, cultural myths predicated upon a persistent urge to ravage potentially rejective maternal archetypes. When Aiken discussed the poem with Wilbur the next year on the Cape, the psychiatrist would describe the second part as "a fantasy of copulation working out the sadistic concept of coitus (cf. his use of 'hostilities' for coitus), then the dialogue between the two parts of the ego so frequent lately in his poems." They would have a long conversation about this sadistic element, "the association of blood ('vascular' a favorite word) with fertility, manure—and with delivery and menstruation."

From this standpoint, as with so many previous poems, *The Dance of Deth* at least staved off a mental collapse, releasing some of the anger and sorrow roiling Aiken's psyche, anger and sorrow welling from and directed at Reine Ormond and the ghost of his mother superimposed upon her tall, regal, snow queen form. No sadistic impulses or compulsions are ever without masochistic undertones, however, a shifting of chairs in the game of male-female relationships, literal or literary; the poem also forced its author to endure again Ormond's well-remembered betrayal of the Virgin Mary robe he had loomed for her from the unraveled skein of Anna Aiken's idealized other face and the passive, childlike side of his own personality. Such self-inflicted punishment, conveyed in a vehicle associated with measuring up to and surpassing the father, can be positive as well because geared toward relieving guilt: every piece of genuine literature reconstitutes absent parental gestures and attitudes, remaking a violated childhood.

When Aiken began to write *Blue Voyage* upon his return to Winchelsea, he was moving deliberately nearer the traumatic material that had permanently frozen him in a prepubic phase of psychosexual development, leaving him an emotional cripple, destined forever to search for the missing self configured by his mother's ambiguous visage, forever on the frustrating verge of adolescence and possible freedom. He was also tacitly conceding the failure of *The Dance of Deth,* which he would impatiently revise within the year. "I finished it, I think, in 1922," he would later recall, "and couldn't get it published. Nobody would have it." By commencing a novel that was to start and finish with the 1921 ocean crossing during which Ormond's rejection threw him into the state of inner turmoil that had tracked him ever since, he was evincing awareness of the episode's vital connections with his youth. With it went the concomitant realization that his craft must more candidly confront the experiential dramas behind its obsessional focus if it were to produce effective artifices, requiting his schema's quest for a secular deification and reification of the artist's unique consciousness.

As reported by Killorin, Aiken would inform one critic that "*all the way* the aim has been to disclose the psychic mechanism of the artist and the human being—in the interest of furthering self-knowledge," a claim that Killorin cites (in conjunction with the Wilbur discussions and similar evidence) to hypothesize that "the *Dance of Deth* at last closed the period it had attempted to open, once Aiken had found the 'parable' or 'fantastic myth' or 'metaphysical legend' which was the subject of the poem." Killorin characterizes the switch to *Blue Voyage* as signaling the onset of a different kind of autobiographical campaign. The hypothesis is accurate enough on the plane of intellectual evolution, but too neat, insufficiently conscious of the fashion in which Aiken was deceiving Wilbur and himself. It interprets the career as a strategy chart for a series of smoothly executed curves of rising achievement, as Aiken saw and had to see it, without taking account of involuntary factors, countless false starts and imitative modes, the neurotic insecurity and familiar defense mechanisms distorting a poet's conceptual looking-glass. Nor does it take into account the deep-seated knowledge of failure particularly symptomatic of this period in Aiken's life and art, when he was writing under the pressure of increasing psychological agitation, the aftershocks of Ormond's rejection, Lowell's critique, and Eliot's great leap forward.

The shift to autobiographical fiction can and should be regarded as the exercising of one of the few options left to a modern lyric talent. Where else could Aiken venture, except into a verse version of confessionalism, historically unavailable to him, although in 1925 he would finally align a personal self with a poetic protagonist when composing "Changing Mind"? The shift also coincided with the literary and cultural constructs of the milieu nurturing his every act. He was, as always, very much a creature of his times, and the self had indeed emerged as the topical fulcrum of the 1920s, honing to a finer edge the scalpel the Romantics had applied to a consciousness ambivalently perceived as both suicidal and salvational. Along with *Ulysses* and *The Waste Land,* 1922 witnessed the publication of Yeats's *Later Poems,* often overtly autobiographical and marked by a more contemporary (conversational) style forged under Pound's astute tutorage, and Wittgenstein's *Tractatus Logico Philosophicus,* a milestone treatise that discarded centuries of metaphysical debris to begin anew, to establish philosophy as a tool for investigating the self's oldest semantic assumptions. Proust died in November 1922 and in Prague during the early months of that year, a young Jewish writer named Franz Kafka, fighting against physical and mental collapse, victim of a self-consciousness so intense as to render potential action virtually impossible, had wanted to write fiction and discovered: "Writing withholds itself from me. Hence project for autobiographical investigations. Not biography, but investigation and discovery if possible of the small components, which I'll use to reconstruct myself."

Constructing a self is what *The Dance of Deth* does *not* accomplish, though in tune with its era's probings of the instinctual drives and archetypal configurations defining the ego's less accessible reaches. It is, instead, another highly professional, noetically intricate refurbishing of ancient folklore with Romantic introspection and aesthete decadence, substituting Freudian parables and soliptical philosophical nihilism for the religious ethics of the original allegories. Although forced at times and distracting, the octosyllabic couplets appear to suit the poem's ballad technique. The imagery is frequently arresting, and the narrative manages to maintain reader interest, despite flaccid interludes. But Aiken's almost immediate dissatisfaction with the poem, which he ascribed to uneasiness over technical matters, suggests how remote *The Dance of Deth* was from a literary environment dominated by Eliot's and Joyce's masterpieces, how archaic by comparison, and, more important, how inadequate from the vantage of his own schema's epic aims. Melville was partially to blame, since *Mardi* is as crucially involved as Stevens's elegant verses in firing the antinomic contentions (Romantic versus skeptical temperament) crippling this very English poem.

Aiken would be revising *The Dance of Deth* over the next several years as he worked on the initial chapters of *Blue Voyage,* wrote an occasional story, and turned out reviews, although he found writing criticism more and more irksome and refused to do any further reviews for Brooks's *Freeman* after scanning Mansfield's *The Garden Party*. Because it touched upon the relationship between literature and psychology, which was at the forefront of his analytic focus, the most significant of his 1922 reviews was the one he did on Frederick Clarke Prescott's *The Poetic Mind* for the July 19 issue of the *New Republic*. In his "Letter from America" piece for the September *Mercury* the year before, which used Carl Van Doren's *American Novel*, or at least Mencken's inane praise of it, as whipping boy for another attack on the poverty of mature American criticism, he had decried both Van Doren's and Mencken's inability to deal intelligently with Henry James. Aiken judged their insensitivity typical of the native critical establishment when confronted with serious novels that favored psychoanalytic over social perspectives. The consequences had been the "prodigious success" of books such as Sinclair Lewis's *Main Street*, Sherwood Anderson's *Poor White*, and Floyd Dell's *Moon-Calf*. "What we see, then, in our critics," Aiken wrote, "is a kind of diplopia—they suffer from a doubling of vision by which they confuse the social value of the work of art with its aesthetic value."

Under the circumstances, *The Poetic Mind* should have received a much warmer reception from Aiken than it did, especially since it sought to convert the Freudian threat (artifice as pathological product) into an annealing node. Like many literary critics with a Romantic bias who had been seduced by psychoanalytic theories, Prescott was mainly interested in saving the creative act and its products from the taint of illness and mechanical reductionism, which was easy to accomplish when restricting literature to various forms of wish-fulfillment. But Aiken, who insisted that "criticism is really a branch of psychology," was upset by Prescott's announced abandonment of "the rigorously scientific method" as "inapplicable," noting in disgust that "of mere vague happy speculation we have had quite enough on this subject—from Plato to Sydney, from Sydney to Shelley and Leigh Hunt and Arnold. This is a kind of praise of poetry, a song in defense of poetry; it honors the religion; but it has added little to the total of our knowledge."

Prescott seemed no less worshipful, and by shielding himself from "the dry light of science" he had manufactured "an extraordinarily confused book" that belied his impressive erudition, Aiken wrote. "One feels ultimately that it is the author's intention not so much to discover dryly and accurately the 'why' of poetry, with the aid of the new psychology, as to show that even if reduced, by this dreadful psychology, to terms of 'wish-thinking' or whatever, poetry remains beautiful and mysterious, a mystic and prophetic expression of the 'general mind,' a throbbing vein which connects man with the luminous infinite."

Aiken's major objection to *The Poetic Mind*, which equated "poetic work" with "dream work" and accepted Karl Abraham's interpretation of myth as the dream of an entire people, centered upon Prescott's timid refusal to extend the boundaries of its inquiry. When dealing with the train of association set in motion by an unknown stimulus that eventuates in a poem, for instance, Prescott shrugged off scrutiny of the images accumulated, their tenuous connections with the past and consequential emotional coloring, as "a matter so complex and intricate that it is beyond the reach of critical analysis." This ruled out the psychobiographical criticism that Aiken thought fundamental and that he had recently applied to Dostoyevsky. In the question of the "madness" traditionally ascribed to poets, Prescott again took the path of least resistance, content to incorporate John Keble's "safety-valve" view of poetry into his schema, a way for the poet to dissect and understand his own conflicts while fulfilling a more noble prophetic task, securing "our spiritual inheritance." Nowhere in his review did Aiken himself discuss the issue of possible traumatic origins, although he was given to using "psychotic" as an adjective for creative activity in other critical pieces.

In spite of an unfair harshness, what makes his reading of Prescott important, for him and for us, is his deft disassembling of pseudo-modernism masking very orthodox Victorian ideas, his awareness that the author of *The Poetic Mind* was simply another spokesman for the Pater-Arnold approach to literature as a replacement for lost spiritual modalities, an ultimately impressionistic quest for ambiguous "beauty," now renamed as unconscious impulse to conform to the language of depth psychology. *The Dance of Deth* had already conveyed his own notion of "beauty" as a pathological labor to hold off the night (nullity and consciousness) by plundering female perfection, though his review is more concerned with the self in objective remove from a literary performance, with a dispassionate search for the genuine mechanics of that performance's genesis and nature. Like his grandfather, he wanted sincerely to embrace religion without surrendering reason, wanted to encompass psychoanalytic insights, imitate the methodology of the physical sciences behind their inception, and still retain his Victorian faith in poetry as religion's contemporary successor.

Other aspects of *The Poetic Mind* that annoyed Aiken were its support of the discredited belief in innate ideas and a neo-Platonic conception of poetic inspiration. "Prescott," he said, "appears to believe that the poet's 'vision' is an intense and shattering thing, a violent seizure which transfigures the poet, whirls him out of time and space, and is accompanied by a profound emotional disturbance." In rebuttal, he turned again to Kostyleff's more prosaic interpretation of inspiration as an almost automatic sequence of events leading from experience and stimulus into a rosary of tropes "which are *specifically verbal* and *prosodic,* positing that the poet is an individual in whom the variety of 'verbal associations' is particularly large, and particularly related to the poet's own sensibility." This leaves form and content indivisible and allows Aiken to broach the crucial subject of evaluation, since, "as Kostyleff remarks, the initial stimulus . . . is soon lost sight of in the wealth of other language associations which are evoked from the subconscious, and the greater part of the poem may therefore have little or nothing to do with what Professor Prescott calls the 'vision.' It follows from this that even a bad poem is 'inspired'—the badness is not caused, as Professor Prescott thinks, by the failure of the poet to evoke the subconscious. . . . The deficiency in such a case is primarily a deficiency of sensibility."

Near the end of the review Aiken attempted to supply an abbreviated resumé of the poet as "one in whom feeling and thinking are inseparably associated with language and prosody; and the influence of traditions or taste will therefore operate on thought and language as if they were one." But the attempt patently avoids the question of pathological influences and does not really address the problem of devising a viable scientific apparatus for rating and describing poetic artifices, which remained Aiken's basic critical aim and would not locate a sympathetic text until I. A. Richards's *Principles of Literary Criticism* appeared a few years later. In the interim, Prescott's thought-provoking work and his own ponderings were to climax in "A Basis for Criticism," which would be published in the April 11, 1923, issue of the *New Republic*. The essay represents the peak achievement of his writings on aesthetics, suitable companion for the theoretical program anent an expanding, immanently divine consciousness already evolved in his mind for his own poetry.

Arrogant yet sweetly reasonable, "A Basis for Criticism" takes care to demolish much of the pretentious chatter that had frequently characterized past efforts to demarcate the limits and potentialities of literary criticism: "It is natural to man to overstate that which he wishes to believe and wishes others to believe; he is never so unreasonable as when, with eyes as cloudily bright as the chimaeras they see, he gives himself up to the fine ecstasy of pure theory. . . . And the more we examine criticism, from Plato and Aristotle to Coleridge and Arnold and Croce, the more we perceive it to be riddled with theory." Admitting to the useful worth of moral, biographical, and historical criticism, Aiken narrows his sight upon "aesthetic criticism," which he says has, "at any rate until the last few years, when it has been taken into the psychological laboratory, [been] for all its great brilliance and its accidental accuracies, for the most part an intense inane."

The trouble with the aesthetic approach has been its assumption that "beauty," like God, is "something detached, independent, not to say absolute, something which would exist whether or not there also existed any creature to give it praise," Aiken wrote. Its adherents were immune to scientific progress: "Any attempt at scientific psychological analysis is a horror to them." Beauty, Aiken explains, "is the name we give to a pleasureable relationship which exists between ourselves and a given set of stimuli. It is, in short, if anything at all, a feeling—nothing more." Before moving on to define the "given set of stimuli" further, "keys to association," the essay swerves to denigrate aestheticians for emphasizing arrangement over content, taking a swipe at Eliot (though not by name) in passing: "Our out-and-out aesthetician will tell us . . . that the precise nature of the stimuli themselves does not particularly matter; style is everything, and it is urged that *Hamlet* is a popular play not because it is a great work of art (which the critic questions) but because it is 'the Mona Lisa' of literature." Divorce of content from form is of course what Aiken wishes most to combat, and this puts him in the ridiculous position of assigning hierarchal values to the apples and oranges of artistic expression: "But it is suggestive to notice that the arts are held in importance exactly in proportion as their freedom to play an association increases: painting is more esteemed than sculpture, music more than painting, literature more than music."

Fortunately, he recovers from this bit of absurdity to reiterate the essential inquiry about why mankind clings to "his mythological lamia of beauty" and answers: "One suspects at once that it must be because beauty is useful to him, performs some vital function in his life." He breaks off to defend biographical criticism from the attacks of the "idolators of art," sneering at their claims that the literature a writer spins has little or nothing to do with him or his life: "It is not of the slightest consequence that Clare was mad, that Hearn was myopic, that Nietzsche was a paranoiac, that Wilde was homosexual, that Carlyle was sexually undeveloped, that Dostoevsky was an epileptic—only quite accidental is it that Clare's verse is mad, Hearn's prose full of descriptions microscopically exact, Nietzsche's philosophy a philosophy of aggrandizement, Wilde's verse and prose epicene, Carlyle's prose harsh to give an impression of exaggerated masculinity, Dostoevsky's novels vehement with the vehemence of the 'epileptic equivalent,' his famous 'timelessness' and 'mystic terror' and passionate interest in pain and evil all precise symptoms of the epileptic." The categories are crude, implying an untenable one-to-one causal equation, but they introduce the significant element of a "wound" in the artist's psyche—as Kenneth Burke later wrote, writers naturally tend to be most concerned with their "burdens."

As for the morally oriented critic, such as Plato, Aiken concedes that he has touched upon another primal factor of the art experience, the "good" being as important as "beauty" and equally difficult to pin down, "moral beauty" perhaps being "another way of saying 'accommodation of the individual to the tribal law,' " which leaves the main functional question unanswered: "Why is it that man so desperately craves the feeling we call beauty, or moral beauty, or aesthetic beauty, that he has developed, developed with religious zeal . . . the activity known as art for the satisfaction of that craving." Aiken's definition mates brilliant general insight with personal experience: "And the real explanation will not be metaphysical but psychological. Let us rashly posit that the pleasurable feeling we know as 'beauty' is simply, in essence, the profound satisfaction we feel when, through the medium of fantasy, we escape from imposed limitations into an aggrandized personality and a harmonized universe. . . . And illusion is vital to us because of the restrictions, of every kind, that hem us in: we come into the world confident of omnipotence, and daily our power dwindles."

Subsequent experimental testing of Freud's theories about dreams, however inconclusive or negative in the area of distinguishing latent from manifest content, strongly suggests that fantasy *is* a fundamental human need, which reaffirms the artist's central role as physician to his society's psychic balance and justifies Aiken's sweeping conclusion, though with reservations. In the matter of literature's obvious "escape" quality, "The Basis of Criticism" is no less persuasive, accepting Freud's linking of art with daydream and the hypothesis that the flight is not from self but to search out a self, inquiring: "But what part of ourselves is it what we find?" The answer is again a felicitous merger of personal knowledge and psychoanalytic theory: "Is it not exactly that part of us which has been wounded and would be made whole: that part of us which desires wings and has none, longs for immortality and knows that it must die, craves unlimited power and has instead 'common sense' and the small bitter 'actual': that part of us, in short, which is imprisoned and would escape? . . . There can be little question about it, and it is precisely of the associations connected with these major psychic frustrations that we have evolved the universal language of healing which we call art."

The major hole in Aiken's frequently convincing argument has to do with his refusal to raise and amplify the objection made earlier to Freud's dream approach, that nightmares, for instance, can also be the expression of unvoiced, unconfronted anxieties, which would leave room for a literature of unease, as in the case of *The Waste Land*. Although the poem is a purgation and partial curative for Eliot, its power resides in its articulation of a profound generational malaise, the abstracted nightmare of a crumbling culture and self. More revealing, Aiken never pushes his concept of reclaiming an Edenic past into the kingdom of recovering lost parents and refighting lost battles for possession of a chrysalis ego, although his accent on the "wound" the imagination must salve, anticipating Edmund Wilson's mythic metaphor for the stricken artist, indicates he was aware of the course he should be pursuing—in her work with disturbed children, Melanie Klein noted, "We constantly find that drawing and painting are used as means to restore people."

But the model of creativity erected in "The Basis for Criticism" is impressive for what it does include: an effective means for both integrating a psychoanalytic perspective into a field hitherto at the mercy of metaphysical-minded philosophers and resisting the antibiographical revisionism seeping into the literary scene. At the same time, it preserves a Freudian rationalist ethic from being swamped by the sea of mysticism unleashed by Jung's revolt and Lawrence's recent *Psychoanalysis and the Unconscious* (1921) and *Fantasia of the Unconscious* (1922). Like Freud's, Aiken's disdain for mysticism was unstinting, however much he desired to construct a critical and imaginative machine capable of transcending its own operations. That he could not travel beyond the point of an incomplete wish-fulfillment system does not detract from the historic merit attached to his tactically sound advance or from the honesty and courage that he was expending in the effort to satisfy the demands of his elaborate schema. During the early months of 1923 in Winchelsea he was putting himself on the line in the first chapter of *Blue Voyage*, which included a graphic description of his alter ego's scary moments of depression, when "suddenly a feeling of unutterable desolation came over him, a nostalgia made only the more poignant by the echoes it brought of other voyages. Oh, that incredible longing for escape, for a spider's cable by which he might swing himself abruptly into space or oblivion."

Although Aiken disregarded Eliot's warning to authors composing under the enchantment of *Ulysses* in the September *Dial*—"the intelligent literary aspirant studying *Ulysses* will find it more an encyclopedia of what he is to avoid attempting, than of the things he may try himself"—his struggle to snare his floundering psyche in a Joycean net was forcing him to expose obsessional depths, such as the fascination with crucifixions and an admission of bedrock anguish at Romanticism's core: "To suffer intensely is to live intensely, to be intensely conscious." The aggrandized self he had postulated as poetry's intrinsic goal was not in evidence among the cloudy cross-currents detailed by *Blue Voyage*'s opening chapter, which was steering toward (and making rhetorical) a Wordsworthian query: "Is the child father to the man?"

Aiken was writing, writing well, for the most part, though poetry, excepting whatever time he devoted to recasting *Deth* into blank verse, was not a priority. Eliot *was*, as Aiken composed his review of *The Waste Land*, which he would title "An Anatomy of Melancholy" after the Burton miscellany they had shared at Harvard. For all its moments of understanding and appreciation, the review manifests the same blend of hostility and admiration typical of his earlier reactions to Eliot, along with a possibly deliberate refusal to see the mystical horizon that gave the poem its metaphysical justification and ultimate union of the jagged hellscape fragments hacked from a traumatized ego's self-disgust. To be sure, what Aiken likes in Eliot conforms to his own ideas about the part an expanding consciousness must play in any contemporary artifice: "Everywhere, in the very small body of his work, is similar evidence of a delicate sensibility, somewhat shrinking, somewhat injured, and always sharply itself. But also, with this capacity or necessity for being aware in his own way, Mr. Eliot has a haunting, tyrannous awareness that there have been many other awarenesses before; and that the extent of his own awareness, and perhaps even the nature of it, is a consequence of these."

This critique is mostly apt, as is a brief tracing of Eliot's line of descent from roots that "were quite conspicuously French, and dated, say 1870–1900." Fair, too, is the consciousness of Eliot's bond with Pound's aesthetic, "as if, in conjunction with the Mr. Pound of the *Cantos*, he wanted to make a 'literature of literature'—a poetry actuated not more by life than by poetry; as if he had concluded that the characteristic awareness of a poet of the twentieth century must inevitably, or ideally, be a very complex and very literary awareness, able to speak only, or best, in terms of the literary past, the terms which had molded its tongue." And Aiken's reproach, with which Williams, Crane, the Objectivists, and countless "plain style" American poets since would agree, is also valid: "This involves a kind of idolatry of literature with which it is a little difficult to sympathize. In positing, as it seems to, that there is nothing left for literature to do but become a kind of parasitic growth on literature, a sort of mistletoe, it involves, I think, a definite astigmatism—a distortion."

Where Aiken veers off the road, and he does celebrate the poem's genuine worth—"*The Waste Land* is unquestionably important, unquestionably brilliant"—is in his blindness to the elliptical methodology imposed by Pound's acute editing, which had the positive effect of making *The Waste Land* more open-ended, of paring away much pathological and satiric debris, even as it underlined Laforguean contrasts of tone and matter. However dramatic its impact, *The Waste Land* is a lyric sequence, a lyric reinterpretation of Dante's *Divine Comedy* as a series of intense moments at the brink of disintegration and paralysis, turning to the East for relief, potential salvation. Unlike *The Dance of Deth*, it begins to construct a new self, or at least the ghost shape of a new self. But Aiken insists upon viewing Eliot's allusive, disjunctive method as a failure, the very opposite of the *Divine Comedy*'s organic and coherent unity, a victim of "confusion," not complexity: "What we feel is that Mr. Eliot has not wholly annealed the allusive matter, has left it unabsorbed, lodged in gleaming fragments amid material alien to it. Again, there is a distinct weakness consequent on the use of allusions which may have both intellectual and emotional value for Mr. Eliot, but (even with the notes) none for us."

And yet in attempting to summarize his vision of the poem's principal handicap, Aiken is forced to concede and describe its unique power: "Thus the poem has an emotional value far clearer and richer than its arbitrary and rather unworkable logical value." In spite of psychoanalytic sympathies and allegiance to the practice of a poet encouraging the flow of unconscious material into his work, he cannot admit that the supposedly "arbitrary" nature of *The Waste Land* represents a coolly rational manipulation of unconscious energies, clusters of archetypal feelings and scenes, which have been restructured to create a cinematic series of discrete psychological moments that parallel, in mocking despair, the progress of Dante's masterpiece, everything reversed or debased by a corrupt contemporary reality and mind-set: "April is the cruelest month." In fact, he uses his private knowledge of some of the earlier poems that Eliot had reworked to include in *The Waste Land* as a means for supporting his contention regarding the poem's organizational deceit: "If we perceive the poem in this light, as a series of brilliant, brief, unrelated or dimly related pictures by which a consciousness empties itself of its characteristic contents, then we also perceive that, anomalously, though the dropping out of any one picture would not in the least affect the logic or 'meaning' of the whole, it would seriously detract from the value of the portrait. . . . In this sense *The Waste Land* is a series of separate poems or passages, not perhaps all written at one time or with one aim, to which a spurious but happy sequence has been given."

This is a valid and important reading of a significant modern text, which adds considerably to our understanding of *The Waste Land* as a direct descendant of the psychological portraiture exhibited at its zenith in "Prufrock." But it is also Aiken's stubborn, persistently hostile rejection of Eliot's metaphysic and demonstrable superiority as a poet, a mean-spirited quibble and a legitimate philosophical recoil from the poem's implicit onslaught against modern Western culture. If truly disinterested, the review would have devoted the bulk of its skeptical endeavor to probing the poem's questionable historical view and mystical retreat from the pathological genetics of the attitudes on display, assuming Aiken comprehended or wanted to comprehend their human ramifications. Like everything written to that time, it is marked by a clash of unresolved contradictions, critical integrity jostling for control with personal and intellectual animosity and enthusiasm until a more balanced, though somewhat constricted, vantage can emerge: "But when our reservations have all been made, we accept *The Waste Land* as one of the most moving and original poems of our time. It captures us. And we sigh, with a dubious eye on the 'notes' and 'plan,' our bewilderment that after so fine a performance Mr. Eliot should have thought it an occasion for calling 'Tullia's ape a marmosyte.' Tullia's ape is good enough."

In the flesh, Eliot was as elusive and as frustrating as his soon-to-be famous poem. Virginia Woolf's capsule depiction of him in her diary the year before (August 3, 1922) remained accurate: "Tom was sardonic, guarded, precise, and slightly malevolent, as usual." More than once, in letters home, Aiken would bemoan his devious avoidance of closer contacts between them, though never willing to own up to the many jabs he had managed to launch at Eliot's rigid public face.

His later memoir of Eliot deals with the period just after *The Waste Land* appeared in the *Criterion* and stresses the rage lurking near the surface of Eliot's professional pose, even as it labors a shade too hard at validating Aiken's innocent victim persona: "And once more, it was as we proceeded from Lloyd's bank to our favorite pub, by the Cannon Street Station, for grilled rump steak and a pint of Bass, that another explosion occurred. For I said, 'You know, I've called my long review of your poem "An Anatomy of Melancholy." ' He turned on me with that icy fury of which he alone was capable, and said fiercely: 'There is nothing melancholy about it!' To which I in turn replied: 'The reference, Tom, was to *BURTON's Anatomy of Melancholy,* and the quite extraordinary amount of *quotation* it contains!' The joke was acceptable, and we both roared with laughter." Adding to Aiken's ambivalence toward Eliot, to his covert envy and sincere desire for a warmer association, was the steadily mounting chorus of praise and, to a lesser extent, blame being lavished on *The Waste Land,* with Linscott writing, "I like *Wasteland* better and better, it's being taken too seriously over here. Everyone discusses it solemnly, even the columnists have taken it up, it's a delirious ragbag, the counterpart in verse of *Ulysses* and a consideration of the absurdity of existence." Untermeyer's more negative reaction was scant solace because Aiken did not trust his taste and had had to assure him of Eliot's genius in the first place. "I am reacting to 'The Waste Land' in pretty much the way you would expect," Untermeyer wrote. "I think it is principally a clever mosaic, with a few elevated and many altogether cheap spots; a pastiche of garbled cultures and malformed quotations not sufficiently 'lifted' by Eliot's method . . . which will undoubtedly infuriate you."

But Eliot's success and continued difficulties relating to "English literary types" did not retard Aiken's adjustment to Winchelsea's rural days and ways. A March 26, 1923, letter to Cowley, who was in Paris but contemplating a permanent return to America, praises the town's economic and scenic advantages, particularly for the children. Earlier in the year Jessie and he had agreed to take the cottage for another year and a half, their evenings together enhanced by the installation of a player piano. But the letter to Cowley, which includes the false claim that, thanks to the spell of Winchelsea, he had been able to resume writing verse after a lapse of several years, also portrays a familiar restlessness and ache for American extroversion.

One episode that had amused Aiken and brightened a January day came when he and Armstrong took a train from London to the cottage of W. H. Davies in Oxted, Surrey, where they served as witnesses to the marriage of the Welsh poet to Matilda, his young housekeeper. Davies was in a frock coat, and his bride-to-be sported patent leather boots. At lunch, after the ceremony, during which Davies mistook his bride's name for Elizabeth, the groom tickled Matilda's knee under the table and refused to drink beer at first, causing Aiken to recall the rumor that he was not yet recovered from a case of gonorrhea.

Despite protests to the contrary, Aiken's circle of English friends was slowly widening. Besides Robin Flower, who was a curator of manuscripts at the British Museum and translated Gaelic poetry, Laura and Harold Knight had been met and won over, probably through Nash, since both were painters, well known at the time, especially Laura, a diminutive, cheerful woman who was a member of the Royal Academy and whose reputation was beginning its ascent. Dame Laura (née Johnson) achieved fame for her paintings of circus life and ballet scenes, but after the 1940s her career experienced a near-total eclipse. The Knight home in St. John's Wood was a congenial oasis for artists and writers. Later, in Rye, Aiken would also find amiable neighbors in Margaret and Robert Mackechnie, another, less successful, husband and wife team of painters, and still later, in 1931, enduring friendship with Edward Burra, by far the strangest and most gifted of his artist companions. Artists, like psychiatrists, were easier to cultivate and interact with than colleagues.

The problems entailed in maintaining cordial relations with poets were numerous and varied. Though Aiken had, incredibly, kept in the good graces of John Gould Fletcher, Linscott was not so fortunate. When he had to write Fletcher, with regret, to tell him that Houghton would not publish his new collection in America because his previous books had lost money, the response was, as recounted by Linscott, a vituperative letter in which Fletcher called him a fool "no less than three times and says he's been patient with me long enough but the end has come at last, and he wants never to hear from me or see me in this world or the next." A postscript mailed two days later was more rational, forgiving Linscott personally but swearing never to give Houghton another chance to publish his work, "not even if they should approach me on bended knees." In his letter of attack, Fletcher attributed Linscott's "low and corrupt state" to his liking for *Ulysses*—Aiken had told him of the editor's admiration for Joyce's novel. Aiken's role in this dispute was as a mediator, arguing with Fletcher that friends were more precious than poems. In late spring Fletcher would take his wife with him on a publisher-hunting safari to America, only to learn that he could not place a single poem there.

A more distressing situation involved Robert Frost. With Firuski's assent, Aiken and Fletcher had decided to launch a poetry magazine, *New Leaves,* to be published by Dunster House, and they approached Frost and Robinson for their cooperation in planning the venture and enlisting other leading poets. Frost informed Firuski that he would not participate unless Untermeyer was also asked to join, a proposition that Aiken angrily rejected, believing Untermeyer's woeful incompetence as a poet would compromise the enterprise. In May 1923, he wrote to Firuski from Winchelsea: "I have just written Frost that I won't stand in the way, and that, if he will only come in provided that Louis does also, I will peacefully go out. I officially notify you to that effect, and beg you to act accordingly, and keep my stuff out if you hear from Frost or the others that Louis is to be 'in.' . . . I do feel deeply that there's no use being in such a thing if it is not run on a strictly impersonal basis."

Aiken was no doubt convinced that he was proceeding on the most ethical of principles, but his action suggested a personal hostility toward Untermeyer and growing antipathy toward literary politics of any stripe, since, as Frost pointed out in a May 12 reply to his ultimatum, the founding group had at his request already been enlarged to take in Kreymborg, Williams, and Stevens. Moreover, as he must have known his friend would, Firuski abandoned the entire scheme when confronted by Aiken's absence. Aiken placed the blame on Frost in a June 20 letter to Linscott: "New Leaves is dead: beheaded, as Emily somewhere puts it, by the blond assassin, Frost." Dickinson's verses were much in his thoughts, as he had recently put together a selection of 160 of them for publication by Jonathan Cape in 1924. But he was candid enough to admit that the guilt was not unshared, another example of the literary scene's petty jostlings for attention, blaming Fletcher and Kreymborg as well for their behind-the-scene machinations on Untermeyer's behalf.

A poet who seemed unscathed by his occupation's egomaniacal hazards was Robinson, who had been in communication with Aiken since the anthology project first materialized and who arrived in London for an extended stay near the end of April 1923. His *Collected Poems* had won the Pulitzer Prize the previous year, a volume Aiken discussed with approving comprehension in his June 1922 "Letter from America" for the *Mercury,* comparing Robinson, a bit dubiously, to Henry James in their common fastidiousness. "It amounts pretty nearly to a disgrace," protested Aiken, "that in England he still remains unpublished, almost unknown; and that he can be referred to, as he was referred to the other day in an English weekly, as 'one of the dullest poets' now alive." In a brief letter Robinson thanked him for his kind words, as well as for enshrining his work in *Modern American Poets,* and promised to look him up shortly after docking, which he did. Although at the mercy of a busy social schedule, Robinson took advantage of Aiken's invitation to visit him at Winchelsea in June. Highlighted by a side trip to Canterbury, which demonstrated Robinson's great capacity for whiskey, his sojourn at Look Out Cottage proved entertaining for the whole family. Aiken was delighted by this quiet, unassuming, conservative yet unflappable gentleman, who had been so instrumental in introducing him and his generation to modern poetry.

Robinson sailed for home on July 26, his "conscience and grey matter together" telling him "that it is time to get down to work again," and Aiken's urge to follow suit intensified once more. He planned to leave in September and would this time have the benefit of a consultation with Wilbur, who had written to assure him that he anticipated living on the Cape for several years at least after their summer return, giving his wife, Joy, a chance to practice her botany and him an escape from Iowa's provincialism. He also asked Aiken to pick up a copy of *Ulysses* for him, a repeated request from American friends as the novel's price tag climbed, now selling for $500 in a first edition, and mentioned *The Waste Land,* which he liked but wondered if it was a joke, detecting traces of King Bolo in its method.

Aiken apparently had no intention of moving back to South Yarmouth, assuming Jessie would agree, but he still yearned to talk at length with Wilbur. His habitual struggle with insecurities had not abated. The winter at Winchelsea had been productive, though the movement toward autobiographical candor signaled by his assault on the first chapter of *Blue Voyage* had already been discarded near the start of February, to his editor's regret. Linscott had high hopes for the novel and thought the short stories, especially "Strange Moonlight," were certain to find a market soon. The only other Aiken story written in 1923 was "Smith and Jones." Its inadequacy, when stacked against the metaphorically organized personal material of "Strange Moonlight," offers a striking demonstration of how ineffectively his imagination functioned when not feeding off the experiences at the archetypal bone of his obsessions.

"Smith and Jones," which reads like newspaper fiction, is a schoolboy's facile reworking of an allegorical good and evil split in the same self as concocted from Poe or Stevenson, except that neither half manifests much rectitude. The plot consists of a dialogue carried on by two men as they walk into the countryside and scheme how to kill each other. From the start, Smith and Jones, like their names, are presented as nondescript, shabbily dressed, and interchangeable, obvious polar aspects of the same personality. Smith, the animalistic side, has recently "realized" a woman named Gleason, one in a long line of conquests, which Jones, the intellectual, remote from experience, downgrades to simply another illusion. But Smith defends his erotic adventure, an all-consuming affair, as something beyond liking or disliking, a cancer that cannot be destroyed without destroying the host organism, articulating a vision of conscious existence that distills the adolescent insight of *The Dance of Deth:* "In birth, love, and death, in all acts of violence, all abrupt beginnings and abrupt cessations, one can detect the very essence of the business—there one sees, in all its ambiguous nakedness, the beautiful obscene."

On their road "from civilization into the wilderness, the unknown," which is the emotional chaos Aiken enjoyed exploring, the two men agree that if Smith is correct about "the beautiful obscene," then the aim of life, as voiced by Jones, should be "to live completely, to realize life in the last shred of one's consciousness, to become properly incandescent, or *identical* with life, one must put oneself in contact with the strongest currents"—a neat Nietzschean reversal of the Freudian rationalization ethic. And the core paradox cannot be resolved: "It involves, inevitably, a return to the center, an identification of one's self with the All, with the unconscious *primum mobile*. But thought, in its very nature, involves a separation of one's self from the . . . unconscious." Smith remarks how his most pleasant moments with Gleason were precisely those "in which I most completely lost my awareness of personality, of personal identity. Yes, it's beautiful and horrible."

At one point a piece of Aiken's Savannah past is inserted, when Smith remembers feeling "brilliantly alive" seeing "a Negro sitting in a cab with his throat cut. He unwound a bloody towel for the doctor, and I saw in the chocolate color, three parallel red smiles—no, gills." Jones, who had sat at home "drinking tea and reading Willard Gibbs" while Smith engaged in his three-day orgy with Gleason, must murder Smith for moral reasons, although he was the one who attempted arson and failed. "Good Lord, with half a dozen matches," Smith reminds and mocks him. "That's what comes of studying symbolic logic and the rule of phase." Even in the act of attempting to kill Smith with a rock, he blunders: the victim adeptly turns the tables and stabs him to death. After rolling Jones into a ditch, Smith marches jauntily back toward the city "with an amazing air, somehow, of having always been alone."

The unconscious has won, artist as criminal, as Lawrentian experiencer of existence at the extreme, where self is sacrificed to the biological impulse to cooperate with the mindless drives of being and thus transcend ego and reason. This is what Aiken feared and rejected, which is why he no doubt regarded "Smith and Jones" as a horror tale, a crime against the ethical constructs of self and world inherited from Reverend Potter. That he should write such a story at this point, paralleling the allegorical nihilism of *The Dance of Deth,* evidences the anguished struggle with Freudian logic still tearing him apart, while again permitting partial expression of his own pathological wishes. Calvin S. Brown, who has done a great deal to clarify Aiken's specific use of musical analogs, captures the thematic dilemma with persuasive accuracy: "The problem of personal identity, the impossibility of finally communicating anything, the simultaneous complication of thought and feeling—these are the problems which fascinate him." A moral fervor must be added, however, the Puritan side of his erotic urges that Jay Martin has discerned in "nearly all of his fiction," which investigates "the ego to reveal failures of honesty, kindness, and integrity" and strives to recall "the pain he has caused both to others and to himself."

The failure of "Smith and Jones" to engage the reader's emotions, which spells doom for any piece of serious literature, the failure to engage them not only passionately but beyond the temporal confines of the actual reading experience, stems from Aiken's familiar problem of trying to impose, before the fact, philosophical and psychological precepts upon the surge of his imagination. A professional writer, assuming he is sufficiently compelled, learns what buttons to press to evoke the strongest response from himself, thus bettering his chances of isolating and using (in some maximum fashion) the events and images of his own psyche most likely to provoke a similar response from his audience. This is why "Strange Moonlight" will be read and remembered long after "Smith and Jones" has disappeared into some bibliographer's graveyard.

"Smith and Jones" lacks tension and flesh density, a breath of human interest to simulate life, to capture subtle psychological gestures; its sole merit resides in a moderately intriguing philosophical conflict and stance, a Nietzschean sermon and Freudian assumption already delivered by the tedious narrative poems that Aiken had written in Masefield's wake soon after leaving Harvard. Its concern with distorting literature into a vehicle for ideas, pseudo-profound allegory, rephrases the aesthetic dilemma of the more efficacious *Deth,* substituting pathological impulse for thought, abandoning any effort to project complex emotional motivations and behavior. Regardless of apparent psychic convolutions, the story is a surface contraption of didactic design that is more sleek than true.

"Strange Moonlight," however, which Aiken admitted was purely autobiographical, never mistakes architecture for organic will or felt meaning, as it skillfully processes the highly charged material of a youthful episode—the death of a neighborhood playmate in turn-of-the-century Savannah—into a fluid concert of image-oriented motifs that distances experience from self, but not fatally. "Invention and synthesis coming to the rescue of disorder and early sorrow" is how Aiken characterized "Strange Moonlight" in later years. He would choose it to represent him in Whit Burnett's 1942 anthology *This Is My Best;* his brief preface explains: "This little story is largely autobiographical, as will be at once obvious to anyone, and that may be one reason why the author has always been fond of it. . . . 'Strange Moonlight,' thus, for me, constitutes the best memory I can command of a moment in childhood which had for me a very special magic."

Offstage, behind the layered curtain, lurks the impending disaster of Dr. Aiken's savage act, the loss of parents and a healthier self they might have bestowed. Aiken always believed the absence of this traumatic event seriously flawed "Strange Moonlight" because it would have given the climactic scene and mood (and the moonlight drenching them) a tragic dimension. Perhaps. But as it stands, the narrative does portend further dislocations; death and death tokens prevail, extend into a future conditioned by menace. The pivotal factor, as Aiken would also admit, is that "imagination takes a hand, to be sure, and transmutes it, but the material is deeply personal, and is allowed to remain so."

Two well-versed critics among the many drawn to "Strange Moonlight," Seymour Gross and Mary M. Rountree, have offered sensitive readings of the story, identifying several pertinent literary influences and techniques at work throughout, but neither penetrates to the radium hub of its psychological reactor. Gross perceptively details Aiken's salvaging of Poe's "Annabel Lee" to create a thematic contrast between the tale and the poem, though this leads him to conclude erroneously that the protagonist's solution to the frightening problem of how to deal with death, with his first death, is, like Poe's, "to wipe out its reality. That his solution is ultimately destructive to the moral and aesthetic resources of life is the main burden of 'Strange Moonlight.' "

Assisted by Aiken's own exegesis—"The story is sonata, or quarter, the motif is *gold:* goldfinch, medal, goldpiece, and, in a sense, Caroline Lee, with moonlight as the counterpoint"—Rountree accentuates the music analogy with exactitude and a clever expansiveness, "the symbolic counterpoint" evolved between "sunlight and moonlight, gold and silver, life and death," linking the boy's dream at the tale's thematic center, which "involves a journey of discovery," with the crucial battle between tropes of animate and inanimate worlds. She finally relates the whole business back to the Poe-pervaded fictions Aiken had written at Harvard. Her last paragraph deserves to be quoted: "Like the sonata, Aiken's four-part composition resolves its conflict with a poise and balance that points up the resonant complexity of its theme. As both his apprentice stories at Harvard and his note on the structure of 'Strange

Moonlight' make clear, Aiken learned that he could, through the discipline of his art, reach a state of poise and balance by turning his personal pain into tender and compassionate renderings of universal human experience."

Such critics have managed to illuminate the important technical aspects of the story without drilling beneath its harmonious, proficiently sculpted surface to mine the rich vein of psychological correspondences that give it distinction and timeless emotive power. Therefore, they are unable to appreciate it as the precursor of "Silent Snow, Secret Snow" and "Mr. Arcularis," first of what I have called elsewhere the "poet stories," in which Aiken is contending almost nakedly with the traumatic episodes that had aided his metamorphosis into an artist, the creature "with liberal notions under his cap" who stands outside his own daily existence, forever divided from self and life. The story is a direct assault upon the origins of the two major fears—terror of death and of insanity—that had and would continue to propel and define his career, a career that always mandates a tragic, permanent existential distance from other human beings.

In the first section of "Strange Moonlight," Poe's Gothic imagination is immediately coupled with the adolescent consciousness narrating the story (an adult-masked voice) by a family-romance tie: the boy takes a book of Poe's tales from his mother's bookcase. In the nightmare that ensues, his companion in hell is a huge batlike wing and disembodied voice, "placid and reasonable, exactly in fact, like his father's explaining a problem in mathematics." The father-companion seems a blend of Dante's Lucifer and Virgil, abstracted to suit the dream work. As in the two later poet stories, there is a mystery and a voyage toward it, a mystery "vast and beautiful" in the black-walled "infernal city," which has Hades for its domain, though Paradise contains it, pleasure and terror merging. The enigma persists into daylight consciousness, a nagging sense that its solution is imminent, but Prize Day at school intervenes and the boy is awarded a medal for scholastic achievement, which he unboxes in Colonial Park amid the ancient tombstones and crumbling vaults, to find his name engraved in gold as if on a grave marker: "It was an experience not wholly to be comprehended." Inexplicably, like Paul's miraculous snowfall in "Silent Snow, Secret Snow," it is also an experience "to be carefully concealed from mother and father," though the latter discovers the honor and rewards him with glory.

Medal, tombstones, and dream mystery are intimated to possess some subtle relationship that has been poured into the medal, summoning up inappropriate emotions. The boy experiences shame when he is discovered by his father. He puts the medal in a drawer, where its presence burns him "unceasingly," the price of an unknown sin. Section 2 supplies a time frame of a week, but the story doubles back on itself, and everywhere lurks "that extraordinary hint of the enigma and its shining solution." While the boy and his brother and sister, John and Mary, play with toy soldiers, refighting the Battle of Gettysburg, a goldfinch suddenly flies into the room and blunders about frantically before making its escape, gold again connecting the diverse elements in Aiken's music score, but its secret song is a dirge, when considered in light of the familiar superstition that a bird indoors presages death. Accordingly, the boy goes off by himself to lie down and recall Caroline Lee, a girl recently dead of scarlet fever, whom he had visited once at her brother's invitation. Her house is the necessary Freudian symbol for womb and vagina, "dim and exciting," the wallpaper beside the staircase leading up to her room "rough and hairy," and she herself a nubile Poe heroine par excellence, "extraordinarily strange and beautiful. . . . She was thin, smaller than himself, with dark hair and large pale eyes, and her forehead and hands looked curiously transparent."

From here to death's door is not far, from innocence through Poe fantasy to the depths of hell (a sexual identity) that death impresses upon prepubescent minds. The other symbols interjected are Caroline's possessions, her goldpiece, pink shell, and Egyptian necklace (*Book of the Dead* talisman), plot emblems of the governing thematic puzzle that tends to disguise rather than uncover subterranean corridors where dwell their real significance and Minator horror, the source of their ultimate meaning. These lucid signs contribute to the boy's idealization of "a vision that was not to be repeated, an incursion in a world that was so beautiful and strange that one was permitted of it only the briefest of glimpses," but Caroline's unwitnessed demise three days after he learned of her illness—magic number once more, from the grim fairy-tale machinery of Poe and Freud—brings home the narrative's centrific burden: "The indignity, the horror, of death obsessed him." Portentiously, the red quarantine sign on her door is replaced by a white notice of death, and as he watches her silent house, aware that her corpse lies inside, he thinks of the goldpiece he had almost stolen from her collection, as he will "filch" Poe's volume of tales from his mother, and feels that the mystery is "once more about him." Caroline Lee and his mother are mated in the house, sexual treasures, frightening yet desirable, ripe with destruction and perilous to his identity quest, weighted down by the stones of unreasonable guilt, as will be Paul and Mr. Arcularis.

It appears inevitable, thus, that section 3 commences with him in bed watching the moonlight bathe the "white outhouse wall" and deciding to rise to get a better view of its enchanting effect upon two trees. Instead, he is treated to the unsettling knowledge that his parents are sexual beings—*Great*

Circle suggests Aiken had witnessed the primal scene, or at least listened to parental copulation—one of childhood's inescapable traumas, as he peers down the stairs and sees his mother and father together: "His mother had just called his father 'Boy!' Amazing!" Worse, his father laughs in a "peculiar angry way," threatening his wife with another child if her behavior does not improve. What the boy next observes "filled him with horror. His mother was sitting on his father's knee, with her arms about his neck. She was kissing him. How awful!" The sight, for the prepubescent recorder frozen in time and sorrow, is "offensive." The parents are not behaving like parents at all, but "more like children."

What is happening here is central. It certainly conforms to the riddle-wrapped death images prevalent throughout, the punishing medal as well as the irrational shame and attendant terror and curiosity, but its ramifications are even more profound than Aiken was probably willing to concede at this juncture in his aesthetic growth, despite psychoanalytic sympathies and convictions. The piece of the puzzle that does not fit is the position given the parents, she on his knee, which is natural enough but seems at odds with the Oedipal tensions implicit in the boy's excessive reaction, a boy on the threshold of sexual desire, though too young to have yet resolved the complex Freud had postulated as an essential step in the ego's psychosexual maturation. *Ushant* renders the incident differently as "that mysterious episode which he had introduced into an early story, when he had looked down over the banisters to see his father sitting on his mother's knee, with his arm around her" (302).

This account squares more readily with the idea that part of the child's extreme response, unspoken envy and rage, welled from his instinctive comprehension of the father replacing him in the mother's arms, the father who is (in all three poet stories) ambivalently perceived as omnipotent god and rival, potential savior and annihilator. And his shame has invisible sources in the guilt (which also haunts "Silent Snow, Secret Snow" and "Mr. Arcularis") that he experiences below consciousness for wanting his mother and wishing his father absent, dead. In the story as it is arranged, disgust over parental sexuality is made to carry the entire thematic load, to integrate it with the enigma orbiting around Caroline's unearned death, the erasure of innocence, and the coin he had wished to take from her. Death itself, as an obsession, is in its embryonic stage; its symbolic displacements, reversals, inversions, and condensations are not yet capable of rational fusion. But the narrative maintains a dual perspective, and the boy's flight from the disturbing scene between his parents to the dead Caroline, whom he imagines holding a conversation with him, swings nearer to one when she tells him that death is far from

Dr. William Aiken (left) poses with Anna (far right) and a Mr. and Mrs. Billington in the Aiken drawing room, 1895. Dr. Aiken took the photo himself by stepping on an extension switch.

absolute: "You climb out of the earth just as easily as you'd climb out of bed." She is performing a maternal function, calming his animal fear; death and sex are thereby entwined, hopefully obviated.

A return to the family romance comes at Tybee Beach when the boy continues to puzzle over the mystery and its array of gold symbols, grasping at the straws of a web-frail bridge between the medal, now burning and buzzing in his pocket, and a dream he had of thrusting his hand deep into a seachest of goldpieces. It is the medal in the sand, where he lays it, that causes him to wish Caroline were alive and with him, her house *their* house. "Their house would be perfect," a union of self and death in an ideal family. He and his brother and sister bury their father in the sand, and the father abruptly certifies the plausibility of a resurrection when he leaps "out of his tomb, terrifying them, scattered his grave clothes in every direction," and races into the water, a divine figure who can inflict instant fear from beyond the grave, father rival yet conqueror of death. The ambiguous crux of the story remains intact, though it glides closer to some elemental resolution and meaning when the family rides the streetcar home. The ride is transformed by the moonlight into the voyage toward death as cosmic mystery that Mr. Arcularis would take, a crossing into the undiscovered country of the psyche's impossible-to-imagine erasure: "Where was it they were going—was it to anything so simple as home . . . or were they, rather, speeding like a fiery comet toward the world's edge, to plunge out into the unknown and fall down and down forever?" From infancy until old age, falling is the self's foundational fear, as well as the narcissist's daily dread.

Upon their arrival, the house is seen drowned in moonlight, transfigured into something "ghostly" and "strange," and the horror elicited is purest Poe, a strip of light simulating the same jolt imparted by the climaxes of his subversive terror tales: "It was like a vine of moonlight, which suddenly grew all over the house, smothering everything with its multitudinous swift leaves and tendrils of pale silver, and then as suddenly faded out." The fissure in Usher's self-divided abode appears an intended reference. It is while the father is slipping the key into the lock, opening the door to a solution and simultaneously violating the house, the mother, their shared home, that the boy falls prey to the moonlight's fatal touch, feels "the ghostly vine grow strangely over his face and hands." This eventuates in the insight that Caroline, unreal heroine and incestuously loved alter ego, was "a sort of moonlight, herself," deadly and beautiful, remote as death, yet strangling him as he climbs the Freudian staircase, enters self-knowledge.

Overt climax to the enigma's musical structure, the end of the story has him taking the medal and the pink shell out of his pocket, which lifts him into a new level of consciousness, his felt awareness "at last that Caroline was dead." The ostensible mystery has been solved, or at least sufficiently patterned to permit some release from the intensities attached to the narrative's memory base, but the story itself is the maze for the maze of the mystery's latent telltale heart. To reduce the finale to a didactic warning against Poe's solipsistic romanticism, as Gross does, is to forsake the larger maze's telic design and primal quest energy, to miss the important proximity of the fiction to Aiken's psyche. Rountree does better, detecting the artist's self-scrutiny, but she too veers off before discerning the dynamic fueling the "poise and balance" achieved by the sonata form's reassuring reciprocities. The Oedipal conflict at the core of the plot is, after all, charted for death, and implicit in the story's every action is the loss of ambivalently viewed parents that looms ahead, plus its subsequent trail of guilt, dread, fury, and unrequited love.

The major discovery of "Strange Moonlight" is that the death of Caroline, which must substitute for parental deaths to come, has ushered the sensitive protagonist out of the sphere of normal reality, focused him absolutely on and in the self he cannot pin down, trapped inside the phase of infantile neurosis that Freud and Aiken would agree typifies the artist's lot. Art as cathartic wish-fulfillment, another tenet they held in common, amplifies and explicates the story's two resurrections. The boy's realization that Caroline is indeed gone, his first death, has a fuller explanation in a relevant passage from *Ushant:* "To be able to *separate* oneself from one's background, one's environment—wasn't this the most thrilling discovery of which consciousness was capable? and no doubt for the very reason that as it is a discovery of one's limits, it is therefore by implication the first and sharpest discovery of death" (32). Nietzsche would assent.

In addition, *Ushant* insists that Aiken's "voracious egotism" was a legacy from his parents, a burden that was also a gift, the source of his art: "And, granted that the egoism, as in his own deplorable case, was a nuisance and a menace, wasn't it also the very material for the all-transforming smithy of artifaction?" (305). More interesting, anticipating Freud's *Beyond the Pleasure Principle,* "Strange Moonlight" 's interior rubric of unresolved, re-enacted Oedipal dilemma and consequent egocentricity attains a heightened effect through hints of a death drive in embryonic formulation, a symbolic birth of imagination under the prod of extinction. Its hero is sentenced to an existence detached from humanity's emotional placenta, from life itself, while ironically wracked by terrors of its end.

The puissance of "Strange Moonlight" emanates from the hold these re-shaped configurations of archetypal family dramas exert upon readers, regardless of individual and cultural differences, which has much to do with the mystery of literature itself—left as unresolved as the pathological perceptions governing the story's inception and development. But the success of the story, contrasting sharply with the competent slightness of other stories written by Aiken before and soon after, did not encourage him to press on with his fictional exploiting of radioactive personal ore. When he sailed for America in September 1923 *Blue Voyage* had been put aside and he was most concerned about the first revision of *Deth.* The meeting with Wilbur on the Cape in October apparently did little to change his immediate course, although their discussion helped to clarify certain psychological underpinnings of Aiken's poetic allegory; he avoided possible connections between *Deth*'s sadistic impulse and "his early parental experiences." Killorin notes that "the language and tone of Aiken's actual conversations with, and letters to and from, Wilbur" would appear in Demarest's soliloquies in *Blue Voyage.*

Though willing to admit a need to start anew, he was not yet prepared, in either poetry or prose, to explore the autobiographical technique demanded by his philosophic schema and so potently wielded by "Strange Moonlight." Allegory seemed safer, as well as less self-indulgent, and there is an almost atavistic aversion to exposure in most of us, as if fearful of giving power over our lives, our secret selves, to strangers. Moreover, "a 'borrowed' fantasy can be less guiltily used," psychiatrist Hendrik Ruitenbeek has claimed, "since it comes from the outside." Still off balance and unsure of the worth of what he had already achieved—therefore of his identity—Aiken had not altered his plan to tame and give universal form to the unintermittent consciousness perpetually at hand, but, as *Blue Voyage* would certify, he was beginning to wonder whether any method, including art's, could suture the massive wounds a violated childhood had inflicted.

We arm ourselves to our own

overthrow; and use reason, art,

judgement, all that should help us,

as so many instruments to undo us.

Robert Burton

. . . .

THE GHOSTLY SUMMONS

In August 1923 Knopf published *The Pilgrimage of Festus*, the last Aiken title to be published by that firm, although Alfred Knopf would not be able to remember why a half-century later: "I can only say I had the good sense to publish several books by Conrad Aiken and the poor judgement to let him go. . . . Poets were not a special interest of mine in those days." The reviews of *Festus*, several of which Aiken read while he was still in America, tended to be respectful and admiring, with a few infuriating exceptions. Maxwell Anderson's minor reservation in the *New York World* (August 19) waxed philosophic: "Mr. Aiken has a real and powerful imagination. He walks with sure steps among self-shaped fancies of staggering size and difficulty. . . . His conclusion is the old one—that the search is worthwhile for its own sake. This final optimism is a bit false. 'Festus' should have ended, at least, in tragedy."

Ted Olson's review in the *New York Tribune* (September 2) was a rave. "With a new perfection of elfin, unworldly music," Olson wrote, "Conrad Aiken has recorded the futility of man's eternal quest. The discovery is not particularly novel, indeed. But in achieving it he has given us a book packed with a rich and memorable beauty, which will go far toward proving him, if further proof is needed, one of the most gifted and individual of American poets." Mark Van Doren seemed more interested in explanation than celebration in his notice for the September 12 issue of the *Nation:* "In this most ambitious of all Mr. Aiken's poems music is still the medium through which the poet speaks and sees. Music, here as before, is more than an inspiration for his rhythm; it is the creator of his diction, the very source of his thought. Mr. Aiken has rendered 'Faust' in terms of abstract harmony."

403

Critical qualifications inevitably harped upon the obvious monochromatic properties of Aiken's rainbow style when he was forced to cover an extended field, linear and thematic. H. S. Gorman's review in the November *Bookman,* for example, praised the "dreamlike and beautiful melody" of *Festus* and "a certain high evenness of distinguished phrases" but grumbled that "it grows tiresome after a time; the reader wearies with the eternal melancholy fall of syllables." And in his review in the December 5 issue of the *New Republic,* H. P. Putnam wrote: "The most summary judgment to make . . . is in fact that it does not say much and what it does say is not said with the greatest possible clarity; but that there are decorations of beauty along the way which make the journey worth taking." But the most disturbing reaction came from John Gould Fletcher, whose brief critique, about three hundred words, appeared in a roundup review in the December 19 *Freeman.*

Aiken's former mentor, whose own experiments with verbal symphonies and emotional tone poems should have made him sympathetic to the psychological ambitions of *Festus,* joined Untermeyer, Huxley, and other detractors: "We read on and on, our sensibilities are titillated, but we reach no conclusion about life, because the author is unable to draw any conclusion. We are still waiting for Mr. Aiken to make use of his considerable talents in the construction of a poem not dependent on associations of the sentimental order, but in which the associations are related in an intellectual proportion to each other, coinciding towards a mentally-fixed conclusion." Anticipating Aiken's anger, Fletcher sent him a gift copy of *Tyll Eulenspegel* soon after the review was published.

Aiken's reply letter of December 28, 1923, made it evident, however, that their friendship was in serious danger as he castigated Fletcher and defended the epistemological goals of *Festus,* describing his attempt to articulate the emotional basis for the limits placed on human knowledge by unconscious dynamics. Fletcher responded with placating congeniality, but in his next letter, dated January 4, 1924, Aiken refused to relent, especially upset because Wallace Stevens and he, who deserved more respect at this point in their careers, had been dismissed in a group review. The Stevens allusion is to *Harmonium,* his extraordinary first collection, also published by Knopf— Aiken was among the select few who immediately appreciated its genius.

As could be expected, Fletcher exploded, claiming that his correspondent would not be satisfied if a volume were devoted to him. Aiken's January 13 letter to Linscott mentions that he and the "Tyger Poet" had parted company. Though it would be healed in time, the rift only added to his gloom and self-doubts that winter in Winchelsea as 1923 came to an end. The major excitement in December had been the marriage of Jessie's sister Grace to Oswald Sitwell, which occasioned an invasion of Sitwell relatives and doubtless contributed to a Christmas reconciliation between Aiken and his unhappy wife.

Aside from *Harmonium,* which received little intelligent attention, the literary year in America had been highlighted by the publication of Cummings's *Tulips and Chimneys* and Millay's *The Harp-Weaver and Other Poems* and the Broadway success of Elmer Rice's pessimistic *The Adding Machine.* In England, the death of Katherine Mansfield at age thirty-five was particularly disturbing to Aiken, who had continued to write his short stories under her influence.

And yet the piece of literature that probably had the most profound effect upon his mind and imagination was a book review, Santayana's critique of Freud's *Beyond the Pleasure Principle* for the November *Dial,* wittily entitled "A Long Way Round to Nirvanah (or *Much Ado about Dying*)." Somewhat surprisingly, Aiken's old teacher found Freud's excursion into meta-psychology and metaphilosophy convincing, and this could have only further encouraged Aiken's commitment to a psychoanalytic vision of history and creativity. More to the point, he had already sensed the validity of Freud's perception during the composition of the late symphonies and the initial chapters of *Blue Voyage,* a universal mirror for the death drive intuited as present in the contradictory lurchings of his own psyche.

By May 5, 1924, he would write Wilbur that he was considering a play in which the protagonist would be a Messiah figure with delusions of divinity supplied by a father complex. To simulate a Greek chorus, he intended to divide his protagonist into six component characters, each suitably masked. What he wanted from Wilbur was guidance to the structuring of the various selves and help with motivation: "Would a death-complex (I coin the idea on the spot) be out of order? What I have in mind is the notion of Freud in 'Beyond the Pleasure Principle'."

This grandiose play was destined never to be written, perhaps for the best, because it appeared headed toward closet drama of the dullest kind, but the idea of eternally conflicting erotic and death drives clearly played a part in the allegorical plot of *The Dance of Deth* and would eventually aid in the evolution of the more potent "Silent Snow, Secret Snow" and "Mr. Arcularis." And in his abbreviated *catalogue raisonné* of the play's thematic elements, Aiken reveals both the profound division in his own personality and his sedulous labors to neutralize the Freudian threat without abandoning its valuable insights, to construct moral monads from the neurotic polarities of a fractured ego for himself and his audience:

> The hero is an out and out psychotic (verging on paranoia) who not only has tendencies, very strong, to considering himself a god, or a son of a god, but also has rather extraordinary 'healing' (suggestive) powers. But, unlike Christ (on whom in many respects he is founded) he is also intensely conscious of the deterministic nature of things, and, with the

help of a psychoanalytic friend, glimpses the harrowing possibility that his belief in himself is of psychotic origin, and not only that, but that his 'doctrine' is equally so, and might well retard the progress of many by a thousand or two years.

Much of this material would insinuate itself into *Blue Voyage,* which he would return to in the summer to work on the third chapter. He wrote Linscott that he was enjoying the labor but feared Joyce's heavy hand. Publication in the fall of Bodenheim's *Crazy Men,* which Aiken deemed "tiresomely sentimentalized," would help as well, at least reinforcing the conviction that his own instinctive identification with Christ and crucifixion scenes in terms of a self-devouring, pathologically oriented consciousness was a legitimate modality for contemporary literature.

But personal needs, the firmer settling of an auriole of depression upon the thin shoulders of his inner man, were too exigent early in 1924 not to demand a more immediate tactic. Travel being out of the question, he contented himself with a bolder, potentially riskier substitute, the purchase of a house in neighboring Rye. Besides, the family needed the room.

Known as Jeake's Storehouse, or simply Jeake's House, after its seventeenth-century builder, Samuel Jeake II, prosperous merchant and astrologer, the tall attached building on Mermaid Street was an unoccupied wreck when Aiken noticed in early January 1924 that it was for sale. He quickly convinced Jessie that, despite the poor condition of the house, the 1,700-pound price tag was a bargain, representing about a $7,000 investment. The deal was already closed by January 13, when Aiken wrote Linscott to detail the dilapidated state of his impulsive buy. The wallpaper was in shreds, plaster dangled from neglected ceilings, and rats scurried everywhere as a host of Death Watch beetles ticked remorselessly inside the walls. A small rear garden was a haunted wood of black weeds and hollyhocks, and creepers had closed all the windows.

The location was priceless, however. The house was on one of the oldest streets in the world, and it had an upper-story window that offered a breathtaking view of the harbor and beyond. A few doors up and across the uneven cobblestoned street sat the historic Mermaid Inn, erected in the late fifteenth century and notorious as a retreat for smugglers and highwaymen. Still farther up and off to the right of Mermaid's steep incline was Lamb House, the porched Georgian structure dating from 1723 that Henry James had loved and that Benson, another bachelor, presently inhabited. Behind and above Lamb House lay the impressive parish church, St. Mary's, built sometime between 1150 and 1300, and beyond the church, on a gentle slope, the formidable stone fort called Ypres Tower, over forty feet high and the oldest extant build-

Jeake's House as it looks today. The photograph was taken by John Aiken's wife, Paddy.

ing in the town, ordered built by the king in 1249 to repel French invaders. It was to Ypres Tower that Henry James had slowly walked in August 1914 after learning of the war's onset—"a nightmare from which there is no waking save by sleep"—to gaze across the Channel in the direction of France, ailing and weary but still "that queer monster, the artist, an obstinate finality, an inexhaustible sensibility."

Though the Aikens would not be able to move in until May, the Jeake's House transaction had been completed on the morning of January 8. A day later Aiken was writing to Firuski, to whom he had sent a Melville first edition in partial payment of his long-standing account, about the daring purchase and three inches of new snow mantling Winchelsea: "The cat embraces the whole white world in an ecstasy; Jessie shivers in the bleak stony kitchen; John recovers from the flu; Jane reads aloud one emphatic word at a time; and as for me, I smoke Gold Flakes by the thousand trying to understand my rashness of yesterday." Rashness it was, ensuring a heavy financial burden for many years, but necessary to lighten the gloom and loss of confidence constricting his mental horizons.

Social diversions, such as the December trip to Brompton Oratory for Grace's wedding and Armstrong's recent weekend visit, did not help much because they did not impinge upon the internal drama set in motion by the humiliating break with Reine Ormond. To hector him further, a "horse-faced lady of the neighborhood" had fallen in love with Jessie, declaring "her passion 5 times a day." When Aiken suggested that the lady cease and desist, her husband threatened to kill him, and she herself derided the provincial puritanism of him and his American compatriots. Homosexuality remained a deviation he could neither grasp nor tolerate; it ran counter to the intense, mother-centered heterosexuality of his own persistent appetite for female flesh and contrasting spasms of Victorian prudishness.

The impulse is strong in all of us either to recreate childhood's fondly remembered household or, if our nurture had tragic separations, to create the ideal family abode that cultural archetypes design and imagination identifies with a lost Eden. But even the actual removal in late May to Rye and the ancient house he would attempt to renovate into a replica of his youth's Savannah home would not significantly ease the melancholia poisoning Aiken's days. Spring of 1924 was to be, as he subsequently informed Peterson, a time of "great emotional turmoil" during which he was "seized with a feeling of lostness, isolation, failure." Art's treacherous double edge was never more obvious or sharper. Entrenched doubts about his talent were fueling doubts about himself, the worth and reality of his existence, and vice versa; yet the depressive syndrome was also powering a steady procession of literary ideas and artifices. Jessie, who was again pregnant, devoted two days in May to typing an extra copy of *Deth,* which he mailed off to Linscott on the sixteenth, along with an explanation of its structure and a cogent analysis of habitual weaknesses, such as his inordinate fondness for parable structures.

In September he would tear apart and revise the poem completely. The ambitious psychological drama outlined to Wilbur was abandoned near the end of May. Aiken was desperate to evolve a "new style" and escape the walled alley where the symphonies had deposited him. Like Eliot during his moment of trial, he almost instinctively responded by turning to Dante and the Elizabethans, to Webster and Marston. He would name Dante as "grandfather" to the series of blank-verse lyrics written soon after the move into Jeake's House. Their supposed new style was simply an effort to push his predilection for the parable formula farther along the road of what he regarded as an analytic methodology, a methodology that inescapably—as he would concede to Wilbur by September—encouraged a greater symbolic emphasis. Committed to the somber blueprint vouchsafed from readings in psychoanalytic texts and the theories of self expounded by Bradley, he had few options, being of course hedged in by the prepubic quality of his imagination, which had to maintain its concentration upon the revelations (experiential and unconscious or dreamed) emanating from a narcissistic boiler.

The May 16 letter to Linscott is a veritable act of confession that underlines how far Aiken felt he had tumbled from the heights of promise and epic ambitions first nursed at Harvard under Santayana's prod, how fragile the vanity of his surface arrogance. His letter admits to egotistical literary aims, convictions of talent, and alternating feelings of doubt and disgust with himself. The latter condition had been painfully magnified by the reception accorded his last four volumes, resulting in fears of having wasted his powers upon a sequence of elaborate failures. The letter concludes with a humble, contrite statement of the writer's intention to start anew.

Self-scrutiny was still the obsessive aim, conducted within the ideological confines of his grand schema's absorption in consciousness as potential ethic and metaphysic and a related compulsion, no less intense, toward restoring allegorical nodes, as was the expectation of achieving health through self-analysis. The expectation was somewhat vain in light of his shadowy situation, which did not include enough meaningful knowledge of the real causes of his predicament or encourage the fierce autobiographical probings that would characterize *Blue Voyage* and eventually buttress "Changing Mind" in 1925. Support for the increasingly popular image of the artist as sacrificial specimen of and unacknowledged physician to society had emerged in "Poetry and Neurosis," five articles by Wilhelm Stekel printed in consecutive issues of the *Psychoanalytic Review,* January 1923 through January 1924.

Slightly amplifying and embellishing on Freudian orthodoxy, Stekel defined the creative hero as "fundamentally a neurotic individual who found release from his sufferings through his creations." In particular, he saw the poet evidencing "symptoms of hysteria, repression, incest fancies, anxiety states, perversions, feelings of disgust, predisposition to falsehood and phantasy making, flights to religion," although he also isolated hysteria as the artificer's primary disease, "that old, baffling disorder without which the race would not have attained the cultural level which today appears to us quite natural but which is really the greatest of wonders." His crucial observation, more valid than not and acutely in tune with Aiken's own emergent credo, coupled psychopathology with Romantic assumption: "Keenly sensitive to the sway of our passions and at the same time endowed with a conscience finely responsive and far above the rest of mortals . . . the creative artist struggles and suffers for humanity and pays with his agony for the happiness of others." Less persuasive but no less true to traditional psychoanalytic dogma was Stekel's conception of dream and poetry as "almost identical psychic mechanisms" because both depend upon repressed unconscious material.

Two of the poems written that spring, "Cliff Meeting" and "The Road," were transcribed dreams, according to Aiken, obviously affixed below consciousness to a pair of fundamental anxieties: loss of female love and fear of death, the approach of old age. In "The Road" the narrator confronts an old, bearded peasant, who appears from the darkness to ask him to come and see the road they are building:

> "Of human blood and stone
> We build; and in a thousand years will come
> Beyond the hills to sea."

He agrees and walks the road in sadness, a road cutting through wilderness to the west, while another elderly worker predicts that completion of the project to reach the sea, to join east and west, will have their exultant people meeting in the road to sing. Daybreak brings narrator and aged companions to the crest of the hill where the road has dwindled into a field. There peasants, bent under "unrewarded work, and grief, and years / Of pain," labor without cease, patently in the grip of a religious mania.

The fourth and final section strives to apply a sepia shellac of Poe's death terrors to a canvas intent upon a biblical summary of the artist's and mankind's tragic yet noble fate:

> Weeping, thinking of human grief, and human
> Endeavour fruitless in a world of pain.
> And when I held my hands up they were old;
> I knew my face would not be young again.

Puerile and didactic, prey to the reductionism parable constructs abet, "The Road" is more efficient than memorable as it glides toward its unctious goal, not quite able to transcend the Nietzschean sentimentality and self-pity left over from Aiken's Masefield period, looking backward, as well, at Edwin Markham's "Man with the Hoe."

The other dream composition, "Cliff Meeting," which Armstrong was to like best among the new poems, is also a thematic regression, back to the pursuit and loss of a beautiful but treacherous female deity that had provided the plot device for several of the verses in the "Priapus and the Pool" sequence, although a vengeance motif and misogynous fury predominate, as they do throughout the thirteen poems written between late spring and summer of 1924. Former lovers meet on a cliff above the sea, stare deeply into each other's eyes, then sit in the chilly sunlight. The woman's hand rests on the grass, a small flower between her thumb and finger as he scratches her bare arm "with a tiny fork of heather" from elbow to wrist. Violence, casually sadistic, thus accompanies erotic urge from the start. When they kiss she plucks the sea-pink "unmercifully," and when the sun goes down, she rises to leave, suggesting that they meet again tomorrow—an archaic lamia still haunted Aiken's imagination.

Revenge and reversal, a shift of mastery, occurs as she gazes into his eyes again, perceives that love has departed, which drains her to the point of physically sagging—"pathetic seemed she"—and he is discomfited, "leering upon her, angry / That I had thought I loved her," odd to think that she had once "captured me." The next day she does not appear; instead, she has left a mysterious letter informing him that she had gone down "to the village, darkness, gone forever." She has also left a blue cormorant that is starved, near death. He offers his own flesh, his hand, to the bird, but the finger he sticks into its beak only hastens its death. Carrying the dead cormorant, he searches for the woman in twilight, but she does not materialize even to say good-bye while he walks the cliff's edge into darkness.

As a detached, self-contained lyric experience, "Cliff Meeting" is superior to "The Road," its emblems less blatant, its allegorical frame less oppressive, though similarly smooth and swift in unfolding. As companion parables drawn from Aiken's fecund reservoir of peculiarly telic dream narratives, the two poems dramatize the remorseless circular pattern of their creator's decline into depression and infantile defenses, ambivalence alternating with flares of fierce sexual animosity. "In the sleeper," Freud's *Introductory Lectures on Psycho-Analysis* (1917) noted, "the primal state of the libido-distribution is again reproduced, that of absolute narcissism, in which libido and ego-interests dwell together still, united and indistinguishable in the self-sufficient self." But that shell of minimal selfhood had also to encompass absence of identity, negation, and suicidal despair because, as José Ortega y Gasset would observe in 1939, "unlike all other beings in the universe, man can never be sure that he is, in fact, a man, as the tiger is sure of being a tiger and the fish of being a fish. . . . Being man signifies precisely always being on the point of not being a man, being a living problem."

The hatred directed against Reine Ormond and the maternal penumbra softening and sharpening her sensual figure, as it did the more mundane figures of Jessie and unforgotten Marian, comes in "Cliff Meeting" to the lip of nothingness, the quagmire beneath Narcissus's pool, when Aiken's protagonist cannot suckle her symbolic self, the cormorant, back to life, following his lost goddess down into "the dark." Art triumphs, however, not dream. The poem's conscious craft, a continuing effort to advance control over pathological energies, creating ethical analogs for his culture's fierce contest against nullity, against death and identity anxieties, prevents complete surrender: the artifice endures, its own tombstone witness and survival mechanism. This must be stressed. Regardless of familiar faults, among them fin-de-siècle rhetoric and a defensive blindness to the unhealthy abhorrence of an elemental female archetype, the thirteen poems proffer a fascinating and unusually successful sequence of modern lyrics. They also prefigure and set the stage for Aiken's integration of his master design with a pliable blank-verse style and penchant for serial drama that would produce the major poetry of the *Preludes* some three years hence.

When read in the chronological order of their composition, as Aiken intended, the thirteen poems' delineation of the personal "I" 's descent into negation is always accompanied by a premeditated exploration of the mind's rummaging among imagistic verities of literary history for a salvational guise, at a moment in Western time when skepticism and secular sciences had left man naked on an arid plain of his own design. In 1924 the intersection of self and society was more visible to a poet's eye, if only because the investigations of other disciplines clustered around the same nadir rudiments after the collapse of traditional values in the flames of World War I. It is therefore apt that "King Borborigmi" begins the sequence. In the poem seasickness is given human form as Aiken mixes Eliot's crude King Bolo and a Christ delusion to articulate the pain that knowledge (of mortality and meaninglessness) always brings, even to a paternal persona at midnight:

> —King Borborigmi laughed
> Alone, walking alone in an empty room,
> Thinking, and yet not thinking, seeing, yet blind.

Midnight and empty room, crucial stage elements for Aiken since Harvard, have been melded with the gestures of Senlin (again betraying a debt to Stevens) to shape an ultimate configuration of humanity at the threshold of self and hopeless world. The ever-present void has seeped into the house, into the last room, refuge of consciousness, womb to sentience and family. Laughter, wit's heroic refusal of reality, is the sole feasible ploy, but what is unique about "King Borborigmi" is the overt depiction of and mourning over parental deaths, though the allusion is embedded in a grid of gruesome images reminiscent of the eighteenth century's "graveyard school" and Poe's morbid hysteria:

> He saw his father's bones, fallen apart,
> The jawbone sunken and the skull caved in.
> Among his mother's bones a cactus rooted,
> And two moles crept, and ants held carnival.

And yet the paramount horror that undoes him is Dante's paradisal conceit, "in the centre / Of corrupt change, one guileless rose," the king now laughing out of "puzzlement and sorrow." Man's persistent belief in innocence and art despite knowledge of their finitude cannot be handled by Borborigmi, who neither dies nor sleeps dreamlessly until the "cook's alarm clock wakes him"—a subtle allusion to Savannah on the eve of Dr. Aiken's savage deed. He sleeps instead

> . . . like Hamlet,
> King of infinite space in a walnut shell—
> But has bad dreams; I fear he has bad dreams.

Hamlet, as Camus would agree, had asked the fundamental question, and Aiken's royal prototype of thinking humanity escapes surrender to suicide by a retreat into personality's fetal extreme, nightmares and all. Thematically, the poems to follow *are* his dreams, which assume the close relationship between dream and imagination mechanisms that Stekel had elucidated.

"And in the Hanging Gardens," for instance, which stems from a dreamy death-poem by Stickney, has a regal family from a deck of cards to reenact the unconscious drama of the infantile thrust toward rebirth, sexual identity. It is after midnight in the hanging gardens wet with rain:

> The princess reads. The knave of diamonds sleeps.
> The king is drunk, and flings a golden goblet
> Down from the turret window (curtained with rain)

Dream appears within dream, literature mirrors literature, as the poem contrasts restless castle life with quotations from the letter the princess is reading, a letter in which her lover, like Keats, describes how he died in a foreign land. The princess retires to her room, weepy with sadness. But grief will not be her only burden because the "knave of diamonds" has the key to her room, walks softly along the corridor, "and slides the key / Into the door that guards her," a violation that her father, who had gone downstairs to retrieve his dropped goblet, knows or cares nothing about, pausing on the turret steps to drink a "drop of wine."

La Vita Nuova is patently being parodied, overturned, the knave possessing Beatrice's key to salvation, her purity at his mercy, with the king aping her and a priest in his quest for the last drop of wine, "the goblet upright in one hand." Not a very compelling performance, "And in the Hanging Gardens" at least extends the nightmare metaphor of "King Borborigme" into a pellucid redefinition of the artist's contemporary task, which differs from Dante's in having to transcend an interior hades without the possibility of divine aid. Ethics have fled with the Christian myths that preserved them. Consequently, "The Wedding," a vicious poem that should have given Jessie pause, must confront the misogynistic symptomology that anxiety has induced, mating the "Tithonus" of Tennyson with the classical tale of Arachne, victim of Athene, whom she had dared to challenge to a weaving duel (slapped for her talent and insolence, she hanged herself in shame). Like Tithonus, however, who had been granted eternal life but not eternal youth by Zeus at the request of his lover, Eos, the dawn goddess, she was condemned to perpetual misery as an insect, a spider forever hanging herself, and Tithonus was metamorphosized into a grasshopper by the sympathetic Eos when old age reduced him to making ceaseless pathetic pleas for death.

In Tennyson's poem, accurately described by Christopher Ricks as "Tennyson's subtlest and most beautiful exploration of the impulse to suicide," language and situation perfectly suit Aiken's mood and motif:

> I wither slowly in thine arms,
> Here at the quiet limit of the world,
> A white-haired shadow roaring like a dream
> The ever-silent spaces of the East,
> Fan-folded mists, and gleaming halls of morn.

But Aiken had not yet attained Tennyson's poetic maturity; nor could he accept the reconciliation implicit in the passive eroticism of the Victorian's yearning for easeful death. The early lines of "The Wedding" seethe with unrequited rage:

> In the white web—where seven flies hung wrapped—
> She heard his footstep; hurried to him; bound him;
> Enshrouded him in silk; then poisoned him.

Twice shrieked Tithonus, feebly; then was still.
Arachne loved him. Did he love Arachne?

Hubris dominates, the exorbitant cost of seeking divine power, which might be seen as self-criticism in a poet determined to expropriate the godhead's creative properties through enlarged consciousness, but the emotive puissance (X-ray negative) pivots on loathing of female duplicity. As a grasshopper, Tithonus is the spider's natural prey, and the dimension added by the poem's title also suggests a black widow devouring her mate, which is indeed the foreshadowed climax. That "Love" is the trap adds to the evil of Arachne, who was a sacrifice to her own beauty, and her wish for Tithonus's pathetic song a mocking comment upon the artist's precarious position. He pays with his suffering for the lyric gift that his pride (loving a goddess) had brought him. He also, like Arachne, surrendered his capacity for love, her small heart "Rusted away, like his, to a pinch of dust." The rest of "The Wedding" simply amplifies the two human insects' dilemma until she

> sunk her fangs in him. Tithonus dead,
> She slept awhile, her last sensation gone;
> Woke from the nap, forgetting him; and ate him.

Irony and vehicle are too heavy, weighted down by familiar shock technique; yet the nightmare allegory stays true to the depression-coerced scrutiny of the dream arena, where a cornered, diminished ego must parry self-inflicted wounds with childhood's instinctive opposing hostility, converting ambivalence and insecurity into passionate grievance. Tennyson, whose campaign to integrate the science of his age into verse (and thereby ameliorate Darwinian dangers) made him a natural ally, was far more successful in conveying the sensual agony of Tithonus. His apparent influence on "The Wedding" emphasizes Aiken's greater openness to a lyric line more congenial to his own talents, though he was still shackled to Elizabethan vengeance theatricality and 1890s Decadence. Unlike Eliot, he could not react with empathetic involvement to Dante's theological tensions, however much he admired him, which is why his function in the sequence is invariably symbolic and nostalgic, an antithetical shape used to point up absent heroic attitudes and moral tetherings. Tennyson never resolved the antinomies endemic to his era and personal psychology, which significantly resembled Aiken's in its depressive tendencies and enervating contradictions, but he had managed to translate them into imperishable soundings of humanity's psychic seas.

In the Aiken poem "God's Acre," however, Tennyson gives way to Hardy and the typically Romantic obsession with tombstone meditations and melodramas, enlivened, in this case, by folk ghost literature. A woman, clippers in hand, tends a seaside graveyard, perhaps in Winchelsea or Rye, and the start of the first stanza is a daring and effective linguistic simulation of a broken syntax and world:

> In Memory Of. In Fondest Recollection Of.
> In Loving Memory Of. In Fond
> Remembrance. Died in October. Died at Sea.

The clippers introduce a disturbing Fate image, a shearing off of lifelines that hints at castration as well when juxtaposed with a "broken column, carefully broken."

Underground are a Potter, pun-deflected, "rejected by the Pot," and Josephus Burden, a carpenter like Jesus and Jesus' guardian. As the woman clips, grass wet and gumming the blades, sardonic playfulness imagines the dead trying to lift heavy chains around one of the graves, then comments on an owl's arrival, but the mood cannot be maintained and deteriorates into "graveyard school" excess at the brink of hysteria: "The broken column; the worm at work in the skull." Life feeds on life. The mind is no defense against nature. Woman alone is impervious, her sad thoughts bearing fruit: she holds

> the world between her two knees, pondering
> Downward, as if her thought, like men or apples,
> Fell ripely into earth.

Her consciousness is Aiken's—aware that life is unchanging and the dead beyond reach—yet there is little doubt that she has goddess proportions, is in tune with nature in a way denied males, confirmed by a closing section of beautifully unforced restraint:

> She rises from stiff knees,
> Stiffly, and treads the pebble path, that leads
> Downward, to sea and town. The marsh smell comes
> Healthy and salt, and fills her nostrils. Reeds
> Dance in the eastwind, rattling; warblers dart
> Flashing, from swaying reed to reed, and sing.

This ending saves the poem, contributing apparent wholeness to a jagged experience and disintegrating self. Again, a woman is going down to the town and sea, but she is sympathetically drawn, at least on the surface, and provides traditional resolution of death fears via a nurturing archetype. If a lower layer of imagery, where her role is as reaper in Darwinian process and as Freudian castrator, contradicts the reconciliation and consolation dynamic, it does so without derailing the emotional thrust toward redemption, steering rage into less distorting rue. Acceptance or conversion of melancholy into a positive aesthetic is not yet feasible, but the ground has been leveled—it almost intimates a resurrection of Wordsworth's "sacred spot of ground" metaphysic. Next come the actual dreams of "The Road" and "Cliff Meeting," which bracket "Dead Leaf in May," structured around the walk between Winchelsea and Rye and a spring elaboration of the autumnal "God's Acre." The "I" of the poem sees in a dead leaf from last year, caught between two blossoms of a hawthorn tree, a "world of dead worlds" that cannot be dislodged or dispelled by his walking stick. Its impact is catastrophic:

> That was the moment: and my brain flew open
> Like a ripe bursting pod. The seed sprang out,
> And I was withered, and had given all.

This could be Ahab locating his "topmost greatness" in his "topmost grief," a heroic facing of the void where philosophies expire in the flesh and intellect is subverted by felt knowledge of mortality's toxic tenacity. Unfortunately there is a last stanza, which incongruously merges nineteenth-century rhetoric with Cummings's linguistic whimsy:

> Lock the dry oak-leaf's flimsy skeleton
> In auricle or ventricle; sail it
> Like a gay ship down red Aorta's flood.
> Be the paired blossoms with dead ribs between.
> Thirst in the There, that you may drink the Here.

Nothing has been added to the poem, though the last line is a clear swipe at willing salvation into being, embracing consciousness of death as life's surest validation and intensification mechanism. Presumably, it also connects east with west as dreamed in "The Road."

But "Cliff Meeting" reasserts a cyclical, tail-swallowing reversion to allegorical replays of the primal trauma, murderous mother brought low only to unhorse her lover-son once more. Repetition, like mere motion, is survival's ultimate defense, base of art and selfhood at their desperate nadir, which is the subliminal message the sequence is encoding even as its sadistic and nihilistic gestures seem to claim otherwise. Consequently, "Sea Holly" replicates the seaside scene—each of the thirteen poems dances on the razor margin between existence and vast oblivion—with the difference that the female character here, a young woman carrying a basket of eggs, is more than nature's agent at the world's edge where rocks mate with rocks, "gnashing together" in a gross imitation of orgasm. Nature seeps into her, as if making a fossil, and saving repetition rests upon loveless sexual foreplay:

> And on her cheeks, the cheeks engendered of rock,
> And eyes, the colour of rock. The left hand
> Falls from the eyes, and undecided slides
> Over the left breast on which muslin lightly
> Rests, touching the nipple, and then down

Boundaries separating contours of human flesh from rocky landscape and ejaculating sea have disappeared, as self-consciousness disappears when in the grasp of sexual climax. More important, nature has been identified as female at her rock pith where inanimate imitations labor to resist and paradoxically reflect the insistent, "fruitful sea," life's endlessly rocking cradle. Another female figure is described as well, another extreme, a "thistle-prodder, old woman under a bonnet." She is also as one with harsh nature, "hard hands on the handle, peering / With rock eyes from her bonnet." The climax of the poem, expertly manipulated to amalgamate and relieve tensions between sterile stone realities and erotic fantasy of escape, represents desire yielding to the mind's stark dead end: "It was for this, stone pain in the stony heart, / The rock loved and laboured; and all is lost." Under the surface beauties of nature, maternal, cold-hearted nature, the skeleton is rock, which denies her womb and nurture functions, and Aiken's handling of the central conceit—orgasmic conjunction of female form and sea-torn coasts—delivers his fatalistic sermon with chilling power.

Where does one go when the circle of consciousness closes? Ovid's *Metamorphoses* would suggest another transformation, a recycling of mythic identities, and "Sea Holly" had established, once more, that sensuality, the repetition nearest the physiological membrane where instinct enters thought, might stave off depression's rapacious night. But in "Elder Tree," that pitiful defense is also demolished—by a woman, of course: "Tall, thin, and bitter as an elder tree." The narrator, who admits that his brain, when challenged by hers, fell down, maintains that he can prophesy, without much success, since he loses his life in hers as she announces that never yet " 'has voice of man flown in / To break my chords of being.' " Night triumphs over both of them, however, and the brain that birthed them.

It is significant, I think, that an elder tree has replaced the laurel of Greek mythology that captured Daphne, saving her from the lust of Apollo, god of light and prophecy, among other attributes—he was pursuer and protector of Daphne, the laurel sacred to him. Instead of an alluring nymph, Aiken's tree spirit is thin and bitter, projecting the image of an anile, unattractive woman, which his speaker must embrace, intermingling their beings, to proclaim an unconvincing salvation from the mind's relentless self-destruction:

> Thus mingled, in the world. No speech we had.
> Till suddenly (as at the end of death,
> The darkness being silent) we stood up

It is ironic that Aiken has been forced by consciousness's tightening noose to imagine eluding the rope through a resort to the "blood" doctrine of D. H. Lawrence. His poem reaches for a spring annunciation from the grateful tree: " 'The trees, the grass, the brain, / Come back again from blood; and they are strong.' "

While in the midst of his blank-verse sequence, Aiken had also been reviewing Lawrence's two recent books, *Birds, Beasts and Flowers* (June *Dial*) and *Studies in Classic American Literature* (July 12 *Nation and Athenaeum*). "Disintegration in Modern Poetry" was the disapproving title he attached to the critique of Lawrence's verse, complaining of its hermetic Whitmanesque subjectivity and radical *vers libre:* "For the most part his structure is casual, slipshod, and rhythmless, or, as said earlier, a prose structure." Only partially motivated by a conservative prejudice, his attack upon Lawrence's nonconformist aesthetic related directly to his own cultivated self-image as objective artist, rational and self-disciplined in his commitment to energizing unconscious symbols and parables that would benefit society, though admitting that "no work of art, however 'objective' in appearance, can be anything but the artist's self-portrait." To him, as a reflexive ideal, the objective artist was "one who, in the production of his self-portrait, employs affective terms—symbolisms of theme and form—which are universally significant and intelligible."

This neat piece of self-defense, which plots a therapeutic course similar to the one Aiken had criticized in Prescott, allows him to drop Lawrence among other fallen contemporaries as victims of subjectivity's esoteric vanity: "At its lowest, there can be no distinction between this art and the art of the definitely insane. It is hardly a step from the compulsive iterations of religious mania to the stammerings of Miss Gertrude Stein, or Mr. Pound's 'Spring . . . Too Long . . . Congula'; and even so fine a poem as Mr. Eliot's *Waste Land* is not untainted." In his quest for the means to defuse the psychoanalytic time bomb ticking away inside his locker mind, Aiken was starting to inch, without specific volition, from the shadows of Freudian determinism into the moonlight of Jung's less constrictive analytic psychology, despite his distaste for its supernaturalism. In his essay "On the Relation of Analytical Psychology to Poetry," translated into English that year, Jung had explicitly rejected any rigid superimpositions of psychoanalytic schemas upon literary artifacts, as had Freud himself: "The golden gleam of artistic creation . . . is extinguished as soon as we apply to it the same corrosive method which we use in analyzing the fantasies of hysteria." He dismissed Freud's entire notion of symbols as inaccurate typology because they were really "*signs* or *symptoms* of the subliminal processes" that did not fulfill the function of a genuine symbol, which "should be understood as an expression of an intuitive idea that cannot yet be formulated in any other or better way."

According to Jung, when used to investigate literature, the Freudian apparatus reduced artistic creation to an expression of the artist's personality, a momentous error because the "special significance of a true work of art resides in the fact that it has escaped from the limitations of the personal and has soared beyond the personal concerns of its creator." Moreover, the work of art is "a creative reorganization of those very conditions to which a causative psychology must always reduce it." Unfortunately, the truistic veracity of this observation, to which Aiken had pledged his career, progresses to the threshold of the occult with Jung's linking of instinctual material, an "autonomous complex" orchestrating the artist's existence and every production, to his concept of archetypes as profound figurative projections of an inherited collective unconscious. Aiken could never be comfortable with such an unscientific leap, though the *Preludes* exhibit a similar mechanism in their assumption of emblematic transcendence.

Perhaps the statement in Jung's essay that best summed up Aiken's dilemma entailed very little alteration in the various hypotheses about creative individuals originally proposed by Freud: "The biographies of great artists make it abundantly clear that the creative urge is often so imperious that it battens on their humanity and yokes everything to the service of the work, even at the cost of health and ordinary human happiness." In his depressive condition, constructing grim parables of purgation and redemption, what Aiken needed and wanted was health, moral validation, precisely that Jungian metaphysic denied him by rational skepticism, so that his poetry could metamorphose fragmenting selfhood and the consequential suicidal urge into a positive dynamic, one that did not involve yielding intellect to a nebulous soul he had never quite believed existed. He still yearned to emulate the tough-minded Transcendentalism of his grandfather and Emerson, who, aided by such neo-Platonists as Plotinus and Proclus, had been able to reshape the self-diminishing scientific revolution of their own era into a manifest affirmation of human potentialities. But he could not accept their faith in the power of consciousness to supersede self via Emerson's "apocalypse of the imagination" and make contact with some mystical "Over-Soul" that seemed tied to Swedenborg's theosophic system (backed by German idealism) in which the human incorporation of the godhead predicates the sole purpose of all creation. He was moving in that direction, however, as was evident in his poetry's allusions to the "East" and his focus on China as a site of possible answers.

But for now, personal anguish and an introspective aesthetic were shoving him toward the pit that centered on and devoured his imagination like a collapsed star. Lawrence's "blood" philosophy, the philosophy that Keats felt on his pulse, was not sufficient, and the next poem in the sequence is "The Room," characterized by Houston Peterson as a "preparation for suicide." It is a familiar room, the last on earth and Aiken's plinth metaphor. Consciousness seems locked in its own closet mind with darkness, a struggle of "darkness against darkness," imitating the chaos that prevailed before creation commenced and wishing for death (identity's easeful oblivion), the agony to define a self finally alleviated when darkness is seen crushing darkness:

> It killed itself: slowly: and with much pain.
> Pain. The scene was pain, and nothing but pain.
> What else, when chaos draws all forces inward
> To shape a single leaf? . . .

Interestingly, this taut realization of a birth pang, which owes much to a Blakean breakthrough to the other side of experience, anticipates a very credible later cosmological theory about the genesis of the universe. But Aiken was engaging in deliberate wish-fulfillment, coordinating the internal campaign against his depression's shrinkage of identity with a recreation of life's violent onset, without mythology, when matter first encompassed consciousness—in his *Psychology*, William James had insisted: *"If evolution is to work smoothly, consciousness in some shape must have been present at the very origin of things."* The shaping of a single leaf and related elemental signs of nature's phenomenal fecundity would dominate the imagery of the *Preludes,* a slant return to the blood pulse of Lawrence and the Romantic tradition behind his mystical brand of modernism. Here the lunge at salvation is tentative, although secured (as will be the *Preludes*) to the Tree of Life, grown biblical by the second stanza, which has the "great tree" taking possession of the room, smashing down walls and its single window—tentative because the solemn proclamation at the end of the last stanza, as it beautifully echoes the King James version, does not heal the division between self and darkness: "I will be watching then as I watch now. / I will praise darkness now, but then the leaf."

Instead of a resolution, "The Room" climaxes in a passive oscillation between life and death, reinforced by the caesura implicit in each of the two lines. Sensible advice has been offered—accept suffering as the penalty exacted for creativity—but the persona is stuck fast in his observer role; the poem alone, by reordering pain into image and rhetoric, connotes survival. "Sound of Breaking," which again reminds one of Tennyson, proceeds with linear logic to "The first brute step of God!" A madman is the speaker, a clone of Poe, who listens to a woman crying, close to her, so close that mind and heart are still, and watches humanity parade past with contempt: "Stumbling, exhausted, in this wilderness / Of our conjoint destruction!" Exclamation points abound, deafening their own shouts, though the scene has a macabre persuasiveness. And the Adam and Eve pair—she has no reality except through him—are mirror reflections, animus and anima, like Siamese twins: "The hands meet back to back, then face to face; / Then lock together." Narcissus has entered his pool to find the female double, his mothering self, but is dismayed by the woman fished to the surface: "Bitter of heart and brain and blood, bitter as I / Who drink your bitterness—can this be beauty?"

His muse, his maternal lover, originator of his gift and associated sorrow and rage, does not respond, as his queries suggest (and Rilke had already articulated), that terror births beauty, births art: "Do you cry out because the beauty is cruel? / Terror, because we downward sweep so swiftly?" Dante's Paoli and Francesca are probably being parodied, while the poem shifts dramatically into Tennyson's daybreaking mourning "for the touch of a vanish'd hand" at shore's edge: "The world is breaking, the world is a sound of breaking." They, too, crumble, leaning their "two mad bodies together," a shuddering fall, symbolic and sexual, that does not prevent the poem from uttering, like Tennyson's, an unbearable elegy for a lost love, a lost self: "It is a sound / Of everlasting grief, the sound of weeping."

Recovery from such grief would appear nearly impossible to invent, yet invention is consciousness's sole weapon at the bottom of the pit that has ingested creation itself, the child becoming the old man in Yeats's Byzantium, which is the wheel that turns Aiken's "An Old Man Weeping." The initial weeping in the poem belongs to a woman, who fawns and cries over a "murderous graceful hand" made of gold, "with fingers of brass," that plucks at random, "murderously and harshly, among / The stretched strings of the soul." Three ensuing stanzas search for a musical analogy equal to the task of describing the artist's pain-induced chore, running from "a burning tree" manufacturing a melody out of the wind through music shaped "like an octopus, each arm a beak" to love as a vague monster: "Taloned, with red on talons, and redder mouth." The human form of love, Erato and Poe's risen phallic maiden, is a "hated woman of wormwood, body steeped / In Lethe, tasting of death!" And the East is not an authentic alternative because the statue of a priest (under gilded "coronet" and lowered lashes) murmurs woodenly from a "passive suffering mouth" that Tao is "the way, the way." Such an idol hardly inspires trust.

The "blood" solution is no better, pouring semen and brain into her, a mingling of "gross" thoughts and music, but it culminates in the grave, where only their bones can entwine:

> And moved the pathetic bones toward me sadly,
> And locked me in her heart, as one might lock
> An old man, weeping, in a rusted cage.

Donne had warned that the grave, however tempting, is not a place where lovers may copulate, and Aiken is striving with pitiful desperation to puncture the cul-de-sac mandated by the implications inherent in the English strain of *carpe diem* sensuality that had nursed the metaphysical poets into ripeness, refusing Donne's convenient conversion to Christian renunciation, intellectual humility. Like Lawrence, he wished to exploit psychoanalytic revelations without duplicating Freud's absolutist drive to rationalize experience, but he lacked Lawrence's innate capacity for translating conscious knowledge into emotional epiphanies, Blake-like modalities that render contradictory intensities harmless, mystical stepping stones to higher consciousness. His pathetic couple, whether seen as Dante's doomed lovers or as a mother and son pair, defy death and dogma at the end of "An Old Man Weeping," leaving the reader with no hope of evading the finite barrier that mind and flesh rear around love, except through an act of imagination, which cannot escape the dictates of childhood obsessions.

From a biographical vantage, the import of the final lines resides mainly in the vulnerable feeling emanating from the image of Aiken imprisoned in the torture chambers (old age and a mother's absent heart) that had always shadowed him, touching testament to the gravity of the dejection harrowing his days. The brinkmanship practiced throughout the sequence metaphorically replicates the narcissist's compulsion to seek his own image in any available glass, which combines powerful antithetical reflexes: self-admiration and necessary proof of the self's reality. Death and madness are the nightmare ogres that demand resistance, and poetry remains suicide's surest opposition. Yet poetry cannot subsist in a vacuum, must be *about* something, and recovery of a sort arrives with "Electra," coda poem to the sequence—"An Old Man Weeping" is the series' natural terminus. "Electra" certifies the artist's continued survival as Freudian interpreter of the ego's convoluted dimensions.

A classical and English education, in league with personal taste, again favored a reversion to the archetypal myths and dramas inherited from ancient Greece, since their emotional machinery, as Freud had discovered early, retained the fairy-tale ability to project and satisfy unconscious expectations. And Electra's story, which included ethical and revenge motifs congenial to Aiken's psychological self-portrait, had already acquired an extra tier of meaning through Sophocles' tragedy and Freud's mention of her as symbolic counterpart to the Oedipus of his crucible complex in humanity's psychosexual history. For both Sophocles and Freud, the Oedipus and Electra myths were foundational scenarios for understanding how instinctual forces achieved the difficult transition to civilization, ethical and rational control. In Aiken's version of "Electra," which is divided into six numbered sections, the emphasis is on the princess's unrecorded childhood. The first section sketches an eleven-year-old girl celebrating her birthday by dismembering a blue butterfly out of curiosity—the inhuman curiosity of an insane scientist—then frowning when she saw "cerulean dust upon each finger tip." As in "And in the Hanging Garden," reading draws her attention and inserts a literary context:

> This, being rubbed against a tulip-mouth,
> (A glutted bee dislodged) she sat demurely:
> Opened her book, on which leaf-shadows winked;
> And blew a dart toward a scarlet bird
> In bright green tropics of the Amazon.

This profile of Electra, which presents the actions of a "good little girl" as the cruel gestures of an incipient madwoman, darkens further when the second section retrogresses to a prior stage, the period between her seventh and ninth years, which was devoted to Electra's dressing a doll of red wax to resemble King Ferdinand, pressing him "against her thigh for nourishment" before she covered him "with a soiled green handkerchief / And closed his eyes: exchanging glass for wax." What followed, ritually impelled, was worse, a family betrayal between her eighth and ninth years:

> The doll was clasped between her knees. She held
> A knife in one hand, while the other lifted
> A paper bird. The neck of this was severed.
> And Ferdinand had passed from milk to blood.

Freudian romance, not Sophoclean fatalism, prevails, and the nurturing of a father totem, King Ferdinand—a reference to Columbus's patron, sire to America's sire?—seems driven by a penis-envy core of fury that reverses polar extremes, the sacrifice of bird neck to nourish a fantasy monarch as Electra's castration revenge, with daughter and mother merged.

Milk to blood evokes a savage progress. The doll is lifted from thigh suckle (Dionysus, Semele's son, was born from Zeus's side) to be pinioned between his young mistress's knees, below the cleft where her penis should have been, imaginary father fed by imaginary blood. In Sophocles' tragedy, Electra was willing enough to kill her mother and Aegisthus, usurper of her father's throne, though Orestes saved her the deed. Case history is Aiken's underlying structure, however, and the third section concentrates upon the sixteen-year-old princess's pathological condition. She is criticized by her father for possessing a small soul in a body that "waxes to ripe beauty," revealing his own role in her crippled emotional development as he does so:

> Your mouth
> Though beautiful, and, yes, desirable,—
> (Even to me, who like a wizard shaped it),—
> Is much too red; too cruelly downward curved.

He predicts that she will murder, but her immediate response, which is carried by one of the most striking, genuinely erotic stanzas in the poem, underscores the schizophrenic division in her character and the character of the paternal magician who had both fashioned and flawed her:

> She locked strong hands around his neck and kissed him.
> Lifting a naked knee to press him subtly
> She hurt him consciously; kissed till he laughed;
> Unlocked her hands, then, sobered; moved away;
> Shook down the golden skirt; whistled a tune;
> And read the morning paper, coiled like a cat.

Knife, tooth, knee—simulated phallic weapons turned against the symbol of them all. Thus Electra has gained possession of what she was denied by birth and patriarchal oppression but in the process has sacrificed her soul, her humanity, like a frustrated artist. The "morning paper" and contented cat hominess of the last line undercuts, with modern whimsy, whatever semblance of tragic grandeur still clung to her mythic biography. More telling, since the first section, when Electra's sadism aped divine powers, oppositions and reversals have dominated the sequence's anecdotal structure, so that persecutor and victim are seen as alternating features of the same unifying consciousness, an identity configuration (male and female) giving dramatic form to the contrary impulses, always excessive, of its sick, yet creative, instinctual self. Orbiting ego meets and mates and murders itself.

Categorical knowledge, its inadequacy, even when transmuted into poetry's animistic language, imagination's essential maneuver, is the target of the fourth section's opening lines:

> "Under this water-lily knee" (she said)
> "Blood intricately flows, corpuscle creeps,

The white like sliced cucumber, and the red
Like poker-chip! Along dark mains they flow."

The tonal daring behind this figurative mixture proclaims Aiken's growing maturity. The two kinds of basic knowledge, scientific and mythic aware-nesses, which must become self-knowledge to have value, clash in Electra's teasing play with the moon, "this naked breast," Diana's "secret" discernible in its "blue vein." Electra, age nineteen, finally hears the "singing of the blood" foretold by her father and is transformed into "a doll of wax" in her own hands, herself the Ferdinand she had once sculpted and nursed, as be-neath the moon, eyes fixed "on Diana's hieroglyph"—goddess also of the hunt, of chastity and antithetical childbirth—she makes love to her own beau-tiful body.

The climax, literal and literary, buckles into place the major cycle organiz-ing the minor revolutions set spinning throughout the sequence, masturbation as homing aggression (suicide) and incestual epicenter for a narcissistic pur-suit of self. Having forfeited her capacity for love, Electra cries. In the fifth section of the poem, which covers her twentieth birthday, the moon snares her stone house and crypt, "as she had trapped the fly," while in the room (mind's final retreat) she and her victim weep together. The fatal circular path of the sequence is stressed by her transfiguration into the Arachne of "The Wed-ding," eternal feaster upon eternal Tithonus, whose hand she presses against her side, "where once the doll was pressed, / Prince Ferdinand"—the king's earlier self, her looking-glass love object. Oblivion seems preferable to this living death, this Kierkegaardian sickness—" 'Better to die, than be / Con-jointly now, henceforth, a broken thing"—but appetite, survival's animal will, perseveres; still hungry, she clenches her husband "hard between her knees" and hears "the song of blood" again, as she had once held the father totem, demanding that Tithonus shut his eyes and kiss her, oral sex reversed by the *vulva dentata* into Darwin's life chain. Her last complaint, a reply to her mate's worst fears, sums up the sequence's debilitating knowledge of art's failure to replace absent religious and moral imperatives with sufficiently con-structive emotive nodes: " 'The web, alas, is cut as soon as woven.' "

Truth has been severed from Keatsian beauty, victim of the pathological reality uncovered by Freud, and brute repetition (rhythmic, sensual instinct) clings to existence by reinhabiting and redrawing ancient family vaults, ac-cepting mental illness—egotistical anhedonia and voracious self-loathing—as the single potent dynamic available to keep a suicidal void at bay. Bringing together the House of Atreus and that Savannah home of "Strange Moon-light," where tragedy, a personal consciousness of man's fall, had its rebirth, the last section of "Electra" descends into barren stasis as house and moonlight sing together:

> While blood beneath supplied the essence gross.
> Useless! for it was spilled as soon as brimmed.
> Prince Ferdinand was dead, Arachne dead,
> The blood unmoving, and the moonlight vain.

Narrative sense dictates a pessimistic reading: blood and imagination ("moonlight vain") at their entropic end: loveless and perverted lust, like the discrete moments of the felt self isolated by Bradley and William James ("Each pulse of cognitive consciousness, each Thought, dies away and is replaced by another"), is expended ("spilled") immediately when unnourished by love. Art can no longer alchemize base human metal into worshiped or divine figures of gold and silver. Despair has touched bottom, repeating itself into a sunless solar system of revolving corpses.

And yet, without question, poem and sequence represent an extraordinary triumph, since touching bottom, as Lawrence knew, means recovery is possible. If a surface survey of the thirteen poems written between May and the summer of 1924 charts familiar territory, further permutations of an obsessive mother-Medea equation and related Decadent and psychoanalytic motifs, this cannot conceal or devalue the sequence's crucial role in its author's struggle to locate an original voice and stance. By accepting the pathological mainsprings at work in the Turning Machine generating his verses, Aiken had quietly, if somewhat tardily, achieved one of those "great epochs" in his career that Nietzsche (in *Beyond Good and Evil*) adjudged indispensable to survival and success: "The great epochs of our life are at points when we gain courage to rebaptize our badness as the best of us." He could, at last, echo the defiant avowal of Stevens in "Notes toward a Supreme Fiction" that "I have not but I am and as I am, I am," though unsympathetic, by temperament, to the Hartford aesthete's arctic ethical climate. The tendency of his invention to throw up sadomasochistic archetypes and antithetical extremes had finally managed to produce a "creative reorganization" (Jung's phrase) of the neurotic impulses tearing him apart that promised a durable impact upon his readers' sensibilities. In a later essay entitled "Psychology and Literature," Jung would declare: "The creative process has a feminine quality and the creative work arises from unconscious depths—we might say from the realm of the Mothers."

In spite of obvious faults, several poems in the series—"King Borborigmi," "God's Acre," "Dead Leaf in May," "Sea Holly," "The Room," and "Sound of Breaking"—are memorable individual performances, ranking with the strongest lyrics that Aiken had ever produced. The sequence as a whole gathers impressive cumulative weight, admittedly inside a negative or antimatter moral sphere, that is almost irresistible. More relevant, it hacks away the dead trees—that is, epic Dantesque closures and fin-de-siècle sensationalism—preventing him from assimilating the buried forest and self where his talents had their iron roots, enabling him to defy Lawrentian instinct and incorporate the conflicted Tennysonian aspect of his persona into the intellectual schema fashioned years before but never effectively implemented. The touchstone modalities of the sequence, whether squeezed into "the room" of a reduced ego or projected as ritualistic rephrases of "the word" separating chaos from creation, were ready for the subsequent climb into the expanding metaphysical universe of *Preludes for Memnon*—in Greek mythology, Memnon was Tithonus's son—once his imagination believed it could mesh the patent sickness of its fierce infantile drives with the ethically sound, rationally cohesive evolutionary dynamic of Emerson and Reverend Potter.

Sad to say, when the sequence appeared in *Priapus and the Pool* in 1925, it would be blunted by the intercalation of several earlier verses— "Chiaroscuro: Rose," "Psychomachia," "Exile," "Tetélestai," "Poverty Grass," and "Seven Twilights"—logical thematic insertions that obscure and enervate the unique virtues of its serial assault upon Hamlet's momentous query. Few readers would be able to detect the subtle shift in attitude and aesthetic blazoned by its skillful reprocessing of traditional narrative material to wed Sophoclean tragedy with Freudian allegory in a psychopathic dreamland (doomed to totemic repetitions) that simulated the cave of self where consciousness must have first manufactured language as mirror and eternal death-deflector. In simple Freudian terms, which hardly exhaust the work's stock of symbolic batteries, Aiken's artistic charge forward, verse recognition of the Tithonus mask as a valid, if unhealthful, expression of his distorted psyche, brought him nearer the nugatory mode and suicidal surrender he had always dreaded. It also forced him to front the pre-Oedipal condition controlling his inventive faculty's predilection for splitting powerful idealistic and sadistic impulses into self-destructive antagonists. But this same process, which entailed a continued obsession with punishing mothers and treacherous bridal surrogates, was conversely helping him shake off, at least in his poetry, the insecurity that had pressured him into imitative postures in the past.

The sequence is original and important, a firm announcement that progressive explorations of the "egotistical sublime" unleashed by Wordsworth were his major aim, that an analysis of self, regardless of projected negative tics, was the topic he was destined and most competent to address. Unlike Pound and Eliot, he was rejecting modern poetry as an escape from personality, heading, instead, toward a hypostatized self beyond the bounds of neoclassical disguises and stratagems. Like Stevens, who would locate his ultimate artist persona in the "Major Man" of "Notes toward a Supreme Fiction," categorizing him as the closest "thing to God there is," Aiken yearned for a representative performing self that could sing, meditate, gesture, and emulate divinity, but he did not desire the objective distance (ironic or philosophic) mandated by Stevens's playful, hedonist, severely anticonfessional stance, wanted real sinner and willed saint fused into an Augustinian creator. His sequence's dive down to the mind's polluted depths, where myths grow from neurotic obsessions and unresolved primal ambivalences toward parental memories, left him free to use the very engine of pathological compulsions (automatic defenses) as the remedial, endlessly reflexive means and ends of a lyric formula.

A chapter of *The Varieties of Religious Experience* is devoted solely to "the divided self, and the process of its unification," which summarizes James's belief that the psyche's drive to resolve antipodal tensions between an experiential and ideal self characterizes every maturation case: "Now in all of us, however constituted, but to a degree the greater in proportion as we are intense and sensitive and subject to diversified temptations, and to the greatest possible degree if we are decidedly psychopathic, does the normal evolution of character chiefly consist in the straightening out and unifying of the inner self. The higher and the lower feelings, the useful and the erring impulses, begin by being a comparative chaos within us—they must end by forming a stable system of functions in right subordination." If not "decidedly psychopathic," Aiken was near enough the mark as clinical depression and accompanying introspection crashed through his stout network of neurotic defenses. On May 13, 1924, three days before a letter to the same correspondent would concede his fear of having somehow missed his way, he wrote to Linscott with bitter humor about the worminess of the world when scrutinized by introspection, threatening to organize a gospel society to commemorate every martyr to consciousness by killing a million children.

The sequence he had embarked on did not, then, miraculously ease the jumble of conflicts fueling his melancholic state. Nor did it, or could it, convert that devouring consciousness into its curative anode, the reflexive version of Kant's "Transcendental Ego of Apperception" marshaling *Preludes for Memnon*. It did, however, permit him to survive, to write another day. The conversion James saw as foundational to growth was still out of reach, but Aiken was at least able to recover the negative virtues preached by Nietzsche, to view himself as superman antihero, ennobled by suffering, the poet who "shamelessly" exploits his experience and approaches maturity as seeking "the seriousness one had as a child, at play"—*Beyond Good and Evil* is again the text, which also offered the solace of virulent antifeminism and exhibitionist reversals of an adolescent romanticism: "The thought of suicide is a powerful comfort: it helps me through many a dreadful night." A *döppelganger* reflection is, after all, better than an opaque pool to Narcissus, and Nietzsche had already shown Aiken the ruthless automaton of the artist self he had to activate: "A human being who strives for something great considers everyone he meets on his way as a means or as a delay and obstacle—or as a temporary resting place."

Nietzsche, intuitive monster and idol of Aiken's college forays into poetry and mind, stands behind the sequence, inadequate but durable replacement for the obsolete Dante, preventing Tennysonian polarities from immobilizing his verse persona. In this sense, Nietzsche is also Poe justifying an amoral art with the endless anguish, saintly pure, of a ruined biography. In time, after the purgation simulated by *Blue Voyage,* which decides the war against Freudian rationalism in favor of mythification, and after a traumatic "betrayal" and suicide attempt instigated by Ormond's replacement, his second wife, the Augustinian ascent to consciousness's City of God would be launched by the *Preludes* and eventually hagiographized in the later historical poems and *Ushant.* In the painful interim, writing the sequence kept depression from bubbling over into psychosis and suicide.

The actual removal to Jeake's House also aided the fight against depression, despite the heavy expenses involved in getting the ancient wreck into a habitable state. Jessie and the children, who would attend school in Winchelsea for two more years, were plainly pleased by their new situation. As John recalls, there was only one casualty of the move: "We were delighted with Jeake's House, a wonderfully exciting house for kids. . . . Our beloved cat Nettle, tho, didn't settle in Rye and was destroyed." Nettle was buried in the small garden, and Aiken subsequently incorporated him into the serial "Jewel Seed" tale he relished extending: "The plot was very complex and involved dragons and wizards (some action in China), also ifrits and a lot of faking— false jewel seeds, etc. Eventually, the real one was recovered and planted in the Jeake's House garden, watered as directed by the ghost of a cat (Nettle). Up it came with a crop of jewels." Contrary to Jane's account, John believes the saga did not commence until after the arrival at Rye and that Aiken was responsible for most of the narrative, "but with suggestions from us."

In any event, walks and talks with their father, explorations of the new house's eleven rooms and of a relatively unfamiliar neighborhood, and the weekday bus ride to their old village and beloved teacher (a Miss Lonsdale) enhanced a childhood the two children would always remember as halcyon, though John recollects that Lonsdale "was a dear old thing but intensely religious and, ably aided by Conrad, converted me to a free thinker." His father had also taught him chess and would evince far more concern about his education and future profession than he showed for either daughter, approving his sane desire to pursue a career in science—a son was obviously deemed more serious business. The pleasures of fatherhood were complemented by the pleasures of transforming Jeake's House into that house in Savannah where Eden once held and expelled Aiken.

The installation of his books and prints completed the recreation of a lost home and youth, with Hiroshiege's *Snow on the Kiso Mountains* dominating a central wall and his grandmother's patchwork quilt from Watertown used as a tapestry (her precious china set was another of her legacies transferred to Jeake's House). Aiken's spacious study on the third floor, which gave him a sweeping view of the Channel beyond the narrow inlet confluence of the Rother, Brede, and Tillingham rivers at the foot of Mermaid Street, echoed another fondly remembered nest, the aerie in Aunt Jane's New Bedford house. The obvious disadvantages of Jeake's—buckled floors, sooty drafts, the need to lug coal and wood up and down three flights of stairs for the three fireplaces and the small potbellied stove in the study—were secondary to the psychological relief provided by the reconstruction of houses once adored, forever mourned. Things mattered more than people when they fostered the illusion of permanence and symbolic return to the real and imagined security of a maternal cradle (complementing the poetry's reassuring repetitions and recycled myths) for a free-floating ego incapable of adult love—Stevens might have been speaking for Aiken when he acknowledged that life "is an affair of people not places" and had to admit: "But for me life is an affair of places and that is the trouble."

Another ally in the war against depression, besides the children and the joys derived from writing poetry and moving into a new home with nostalgic features, was alcohol, one of Rye's undoubted charms being its unusually large number of drinking places, "fifteen glorious pubs" (224). Aiken had developed the habit of downing a batch of martinis before lunch and dinner, often sipping beer afterward or going off on a pub crawl alone or with companions such as Nichols. Much has been written and said about the pernicious effect of liquor upon writers, particularly poets, but drinking has probably saved as many poets as it has destroyed because the dependency syndrome and physical ravages involved do not always outweigh real psychological benefits. Aiken, for instance, defends its value in *Ushant* (224) as "insulation" against the burden of consciousness, and the alcohol did minister to stress points in his psyche, numbing the pain inflicted by memory and a sensitive nature, aggrandizing a powerful ego attenuated by failure and insufficient recognition. Further, the extreme self-consciousness that tormented his every social encounter was eased and shyness dimmed, permitting the vanity side of its moon face to emerge and shine.

The convenient Rye taverns provided male havens, suitably traditional in decor and ambience, where he felt most comfortable, escapes from the confines of banal marital rounds and a chance to demonstrate his fluent wit and conversational skills—he still loved to talk far into the night. Aiken's pub crawls in fact gained considerable local celebrity, and visitors from London and abroad, whose numbers would increase with summer's arrival, were inevitably dragged along, sharing in their host's evident pride when all fifteen establishments were conquered in a single wet evening. Aiken's capacity for absorbing alcohol remained heroic, and the physiological damage done to his system by excessive drinking would not surface until the last decade or so of his life. Meanwhile, it fended off despair, as did the sating of other body appetites used to discourage mental contractions, such as the gourmet meals prepared by Jessie, an excellent cook, especially the seafood dishes associated in his mind with Savannah, Cambridge, and New Bedford, and whatever sexual escapades he managed to engineer. It also assuaged the oral exigency of his paradoxical personality, a regressive component bound to grow more voracious under melancholia's ego threat.

Adding to his depressive state, which would harry him with varying degrees of intensity over the next several years, was Eliot's frustrating elusiveness. In spite of vague promises, his former classmate had never managed a trip to Winchelsea, and none of Aiken's work had yet to appear in the *Criterion,* although Eliot had been holding "Psychomachia" and an Emily Dickinson essay for almost a year and a half. On April 8, 1924, he had written Aiken, after seeing the Dickinson piece in the *Dial,* to express regret at having lost the opportunity to publish it—the essay was to appear as the introduction to *The Selected Poems of Emily Dickinson,* which Cape was publishing in July—and explaining his recent silence as the consequence of his wife's bout of flu. He claimed to have an open spot in the October issue of the *Criterion* reserved for a critical essay by Aiken, if he was interested. Aiken's return letter apparently alluded to serious financial needs, and Eliot responded by noting that a payment awaited him at the journal whenever he wished to take advantage of it, charging him with being evasive about the requested critical essay. Three days later, with a measure of impatience, Aiken threw back the evasiveness charge, mentioning "Psychomachia" 's purgatorial delay and wondering if Williams or Moore might be worth a full article. As for Eliot's invitation to join him and several *Criterion* contributors at one of their fortnightly Wednesday lunches at the Cock, as well as visiting with him privately some other day, he was enthusiastic and agreed readily.

This was an opening Aiken eagerly sought, a way of reestablishing closer ties, social and literary, with an admired old friend and London's newest literary star: "The various cliques formed or fell apart, new coteries rose and fell;

but central among them, and in the end omnipotent, was the group that erratically and fluctuatingly arranged itself, or rearranged itself, round the Tsetse's quarterly" (232). He informed Eliot that he would probably make it to town for a week or two of diversion either in June or July. Eliot's reply (May 19), though returning the Dickinson essay, reavowed his intention to publish "Psychomachia," but he did not think Williams or Moore merited anything long, unless Aiken wanted to review the next book that either published; he was enthusiastic about an article on Henry James. Aiken, in turn, promised to beard London at the end of the month, after the move to Jeake's House, to which Eliot reacted amicably, agreeing to a meeting and sending along a copy of Sacheverell Sitwell's *Southern Baroque Art* for review.

Before the end of the year Aiken would get to see Eliot several times in London and review two other books for him—the October *Criterion* would carry "Psychomachia" and Aiken's critiques of Osbert Sitwell's *Triple Fugue* and Gilbert Seldes's *The Seven Lively Arts*. And yet Eliot seemed incapable of coming from behind his mask, which had hardened further with the continuing mental and physical decline of Vivienne, who had lost her father the previous year. Like Aiken, he had still not resolved the frightening identity crisis that had forced him into a sanitorium a few years earlier and resulted in *The Waste Land,* a spiritual autobiography at its jejune core which called for a Jamesian conversion he was, at this juncture, unable to accomplish. Isolated even from his wife, whom guilt caused him to treat kindly, albeit with a martyr's obnoxious patience toward her penchant for embarrassing him in public, he remained trapped behind the gaunt, anguished features—their cadaverous planes heightened by green face powder on occasion—of a besieged pedant. He was again beached by a dry spell as far as poetry was concerned. Significantly, when he did return to verse near year's end, it would be to put together the lyrics of "The Hollow Men," that desperate masochistic exercise in defeat and humiliation keyed to Conrad's *Heart of Darkness* and the scarecrow emptiness of his present artificial existence.

The thunderous "whimper" at the conclusion of the poem had unfortunate biographical parallels in the subtly whining self-pity and quiet outbursts of contempt that issued from the remote mask during lunches at the Cock and elsewhere. In *Ushant* (232), Aiken best remembers the sadistic power politics rife among the members of Eliot's inner circle, a circle he surveyed from the outer edge of its sun king's wintry affection, he and Fletcher, with whom he would be reconciled by December. They were maintained in orbit at a condescending remove, mostly used as reviewers, literary hatchet men, who did not quite belong.

Of course, Aiken's own insecurity during a difficult time, which found ready reinforcement in Fletcher's paranoic brooding, hardly made him a disinterested recorder, but Eliot's crafty maneuvers—balancing, always, a fierce conformist drive against a private need to vent pent-up rage and guilt—have been confirmed by too many other sources to be gainsaid. If *The Waste Land* had let its author transverse a nervous breakdown, it had not satisfied the primary quest for a new self with which to counteract the narcissistic isolation, the emotional retardation and unbearable loneliness, every poet lugs around with him like a diver's helmet as he performs at the brink of the frail psyche this isolation conceals. Now in their thirties, the leading members of Aiken's literary generation were confronting a period of trial and agonized reassessment, when achievement has reached a plateau that should justify the past and manifest a viable, worthy future. Aiken and Eliot were not the only gifted Harvard graduates of their era to encounter the quicksand of ego disintegration during midpassage.

Across the ocean, in their blighted homeland, Van Wyck Brooks was being torn asunder by irreconcilable polarities in himself and his culture. His 1920 biography, *The Ordeal of Mark Twain,* which affirmed a pervasive allegiance to Freudian tenets, had used Twain as a looking-glass for himself and his fellow writers, seeing in his schizophrenic conflicts and unhappiness a cautionary tale in which repressed guilt (internalized Calvinist heritage) and instinctual artistic impulses battled fruitlessly for control over his career, leaving Twain embittered, unsatisfied, "the effect of a certain miscarriage in his creative life, a balked personality, an arrested development of which he was himself almost wholly unaware, but which for him destroyed the meaning of life." Not surprisingly, the arch villains of this psychodrama were Twain's mother and wife, portrayed as authoritarian agents of the bourgeois puritanism (conformity, propriety, materialism) he simultaneously sought and despised. Twain's fractured identity reflected the major split in Brooks's own threatened self, and it was perhaps inevitable that he turn next to Henry James for his subject matter.

After finishing the Twain book, Brooks was hounded by the same malaise of doubt and self-disgust harassing Aiken and Eliot: "I was consumed with a sense of failure, a feeling that my work had all gone wrong and that I was mistaken in all I had said or thought." Early in 1923 he put aside the James manuscript in disgust, his behavior erratic enough to intimate the onset of a nervous breakdown as manic-depressive swings worsened, and he began slipping into Catholic churches on the sly—an appropriate action for a personality once exposed to Harvard's aesthete love of medieval forms. After five months and within a year, he was able to return to and complete *The Pilgrimage of Henry James,* which would be published in February 1925.

Despite its skewed critical stance and questionable technique of mixing fact with James's fiction, the biography was an essential fable for colleagues crushed between antithetical psychic and cultural forces, projecting the severe division in Brooks's endangered self upon James's specimen life and art in a subjective manner that still succeeded in saying relevant things about the impossible choices an American modernist had to make. For Brooks, Eliot, Aiken, and kindred spirits of their crepuscular generation, James epitomized the fundamental identity dilemma intrinsic to their literary ambitions. His flight across the Atlantic and into a staunch country squire role had not prevented alienation from both cultures, tormented awareness of European corruption, which he required, and of American innocence and crass pioneer energy, which he reluctantly abandoned at heavy cost to his psyche. What Brooks did not comprehend, regardless of his acquaintance with psychoanalytic theory, was that James, like most artists, produced his most potent fiction when unlocking the reservoir of ambivalent emotions created by intense estrangement, Brooks foolishly (if necessarily in a psychological context) insisting that the later work was inferior to the earlier because of James's increasing rootlessness: "He had emerged as an impassioned geometer—or, shall we say, some vast arachnid of art, pouncing upon the tiny air-blown particle and wrapping it round and round."

Wavering between untenable extremes, Brooks had to believe that James, the instinctual American who could not accept America, paid a high price for his expatriatism, as would the modern voluntary exiles then residing in England and pouring into Paris, whom he condemned (defying his previous European bias) for having deserted their native land at an inopportune moment, yielding to an American neurosis. He also castigated the aesthete faction led by Spingarn, a personal friend, for its sterile Crocean immersion in style— "to begin with the form, to seek the form, is to confess that one lacks the *thing*"—and various local Marxists for elevating scientific principles at the expense of literature. The folding of the *Freeman* early in 1924 had not helped ease inner tensions, and Brooks was tortured by fantasies of imprisonment, live entombment, reviving Poe's infantile insecurities. Conversion and salvation had moved from a literary sphere into the private dungeon of a sinking psyche's most profound aspirations. A year later, he would start a book on Emerson, one of the oases dotting Aiken's own internal desert, that he calibrated as "a sort of religious experience," an effort to reach the "sunny side" of existence, but nothing could halt the paralysis of will ushering him toward catatonic withdrawals, numerous suicide tries, and several hellish years in mental institutions.

To Brooks and to Eliot, who would dramatically fall to his knees before Michelangelo's *Pieta* during a 1926 trip to Rome and enter the Anglican church the next year, the search for redemption, a new self, would ultimately entail a reversion to conservative tendencies of perception and thought always present in their background and schooling. This would mean a reinterpretation of the whole modernist strain (of their own adolescent rebellions against a convention they must now embrace) as a destructive failure of taste. They would enlist, without fanfare, in the antimodernist crusade that had invariably accompanied American flirtings (especially at Harvard) with European notions of secular revolutionary activities begun soon after the turn of the century, which T. Jackson Lears has accurately described as galvanizing "the philosophical revolt against positivism and the artistic avant-garde's recovery of primal irrationality." When Eliot turned his back on the radical openness to experience implicit in his experimental aesthetic, discovering that Laforguean irony was not sufficient to neutralize his urgent need for a positive emotional reordering of self-destructive insights, and when Brooks, after his recovery in the late 1920s, devoted himself with a convert's zeal to retailoring the arras of American literature to emphasize traditional themes, they would be simply returning to the fold, the privileged WASP Old Guard Pound had never really abandoned.

But Aiken, whose intellectual integrity would prove superior to that of better-known contemporaries, though Stevens would not forsake his poetry's sophisticated merger of imagination's difficult sacred and profane tasks until a deathbed conversion to Roman Catholicism, could not bring himself to desert the "liberal notions" associated in his mind with the germination and growth of his persona as the Poet of White Horse Vale. Despite the steady accretion of fears and doubts harbingering a breakdown, he could not yield to the impulse to defy reason and wallow in a mystical revival, which seems inherent in the American psyche, thus squandering the precious horde of wisdom gleaned from the writings of Nietzsche, Bergson, Bradley, Santayana, Emerson, Reverend Potter, Freud, and other thinkers who had contributed to his comprehension of twentieth-century man's existential dilemma. He still yearned for a scientific critical stance and an analytic lyric mode that would permit autobiographical explorations of consciousness's (and hence imagination's) elemental mechanisms in a Romantic context of transcendental intensities. If no less avid than Brooks and Eliot to locate a metaphysic, which Schopenhauer had seen as intrinsic to the human animal, he was not about to cast aside every hard-earned conviction he held dear anent man's tragic fate as an irrational, perishable commodity in a Heraclitan cosmos. Perhaps he intuited that such a betrayal might be even riskier than the depression undermining his identity and nourishing his art because it would entail an erasure of the cynical self-image evolved after the Savannah tragedy to protect him from further wounds.

Most important, goaded by his psychological predicament, which would worsen as he approached 1925 and the age of his father at his death, Aiken was writing at a rapid clip. By summer he had completed the poetic sequence commenced in May, finished enough stories for a collection, to be entitled *Bring! Bring!* after its second strongest tale, and was engrossed in the third chapter of *Blue Voyage,* which was supplying the most direct contact with the anxieties and memories heaved to the surface by his fragmenting self, material that resisted literature's generic rage for order: "Impossible to present, all at once, in a phrase, a sentence, a careful paragraph—even in a book, copious and dishevelled—all that one meant or all that one was." But this is the writer's ancient protest against the frustration induced by what language must omit as it paraphrases reality and did not prevent Aiken from giving a syntax, however elided, to his anguish, averting a plunge into the madness transmitted to him by Dr. Aiken's example and deed.

He fought also to defend his career in more public ways, as in the pursuit of Eliot and his crowd, and was as sensitive as ever to criticism, probably more so under the threat of his loss of confidence. When confronted by Unter-meyer's anthology, *American Poetry since 1900,* early in April, which reiter-ated its editor's dim view of Aiken's development, he fired off an angry letter that found Untermeyer in Austria, where he was touring with his wife. Once again, Untermeyer refused either to swallow personal insults—"It seemed a deliberate attempt to break up our friendship"—or to let their prickly rela-tionship dissolve: "Partly to protect my pride, partly to keep our relations unsevered, I convinced myself that what you were saying was in a bitter but humorous vein. If I was wrong, it is not too late to say so. Although my skin is not as sensitive as, say Bodenheim's, it can be pierced. . . . You, surely, should be the first to assume (and allow for) the variations and preferences of varying temperaments." The rebuke was heeded. Aiken remained friendly with Untermeyer, which was to his advantage, because in 1925 the latter would publish another *Miscellany* installment—*American Poetry 1925*—after failing to produce one in 1924: "I had determined not to take on the burden (and the ungrateful aftermath) of another one. But most of the members wanted the biennial to go on. . . . But this time, I will flatly abandon the conference idea and come out boldly as editor. . . . As before, every poet will be his own editor to the extent that he will be given 20 pages (or less if he wishes) to fill as he thinks best." Aiken's choices for his *Miscellany* entry were "The Road," "And in the Hanging Gardens," "Sea Holly," "Psycho-machia," "The Wedding," "Poverty Grass," "God's Acre," and "The Room."

Although willing to risk Untermeyer's ire, in spite of his evident power as America's premier poetry anthologist, Aiken was less likely to imperil the closer ties recently forged with Eliot. When Harold Monro's snide review of his Dickinson anthology appeared in the *Criterion* near year's end, stupidly dismissing the Amherst poet as "intellectually blind, partially deaf, mostly dumb, to the art of poetry," Aiken's complaint (through clenched teeth) to Eliot was mild in the extreme, though also protesting Herbert Read's "Psychoanalysis and the Critic" in the same issue, which had been published after his own essay on the subject had been rejected. Eliot was still the older brother he had to court and impress, and his good opinion obviously meant more than literary politics might explain. That the *Criterion* did finally print "Psychomachia" undoubtedly delivered more emotional punch than any number of appearances in Untermeyer's prestigious and popular anthologies.

Another definite gain in Aiken's career was Secker's acceptance of the *Bring! Bring!* manuscript that Knopf had rejected in the United States and that Linscott had dutifully brought to Houghton Mifflin, which also rejected it. Boni and Liveright would publish the American edition in May 1925. Linscott's support and agenting activities were proving invaluable during a trying time, especially since Aiken, because of Jessie's condition, was not able to make his annual fall voyage across the Atlantic. It was Linscott's thoughtful critique of *The Dance of Deth,* which his fellow editors at Houghton had rejected, that caused Aiken to revise the poem into a free-verse exercise: "I find it magnificent but unsatisfying. Specifically the rhyme scheme—which in the first section gives a delicious speed and lustiness to the narrative—grows to me monotonous toward the end, and imposes too rigid a mould for the natural development of so complex a theme."

In the same letter of June 10, which apologized for the resistance of American journals to Aiken's verses, Linscott appended a P.S. to announce that *Vanity Fair* had sent back *The Tinsel Circuit* "with a memorandum of Crowninshields . . . stating that he does not consider the series usable as a whole because they are a little sentimental, not sufficiently clear, and lacking in satire, humor and wit, but that they will pay $20 for 'Vyo-Lylyn' alone." Thus rejections continued to outnumber acceptances by far, emphasizing the ceaseless struggle (and psychic blows) even a relatively well-established poet must endure, rejections bearing an additional sting because of Aiken's tight financial situation.

The birth of his third child was probably more corrosive than healing in this context, entailing another bloody bedside scene and serving to remind him that marriage, which he needed as a family mooring, was also a prison and a daily reminder of life's dull, rapid passage. It was around three in the morning, Thursday, September 4, when Jessie awakened her husband and asked him to fetch the doctor. But at precisely 3:25 A.M., five minutes before the sleep-dazed Aiken returned with medical aid, she gave birth to a healthy, seven-and-three-quarters-pound, red-haired daughter. Jessie was rather badly torn, necessitating an anesthetic sewing-up at eleven that morning. Aiken wrote to Linscott later in the day to detail briefly the chaos, including the hasty departure of Armstrong, who had been visiting. The new kitten (Nettle's replacement) went berserk during the turmoil and knocked all the pianola rolls off the piano.

John was caught off guard by the sudden arrival of another sibling: "I remember being awakened by her first yells. The whole thing was a complete surprise to me, but I don't remember being upset; tho, in Jane's and my opinion, Joan was more demanding, and more spoiled, than we had been." Aiken's letter noted that John and Jane were intrigued and that Joan was to have been named Ann or Nancy Delano, but Jane insisted her sister's name begin with a J. Joan Delano Aiken was to have only brief contact with her father during her childhood years, easy prey to the upset connected with the breakup of her parents' marriage and the trial of adapting to a stepfather, with the consequence that she and Aiken were destined to have a distant, somewhat strained relationship until late in his life. Not expectedly from a psychological vantage, she was also to prove the most talented of the three children, all of whom eventually engaged in writing of one sort or another.

However elated Aiken was by the arrival of his daughter, his gray state of mind could not have been lightened by the presence of a noisy, odorous infant at a time when money worries and grave personal and professional uncertainties were assailing him. The same letter to Linscott refers to the group of lyrics he had written in the spring and summer, which he had sent on to the editor, who perceived their new tact, and concedes a continuing gap between aim and attainment. He sensed the need for further experiments but felt constrained by money worries.

Circumstances were against him. Thirteen days after Joan's birth, which had seen Rye racked by a steady southwest gale, Aiken again wrote to Linscott, bemoaning the irksome activities of his domestic imprisonment, such as racing up and down drafty stairs to tend to smoking stoves and a crying infant. In passing, he touched upon the death of Joseph Conrad, who had had a Catholic funeral at St. Thomas's in Canterbury on August 7, and the joys of reading E. M. Forster's novels and stories, but the accent throughout is on the mentally debilitating aspects of his veritable house arrest, which did not prevent him from tearing apart and revising *Deth* or laboring to finish a review of Croce's *European Literature in the Nineteenth Century* that he had promised to the *Nation & Athenaeum* for an early October issue.

Part of the regret occasioned by his inability to make a trip to America that year was that it prevented him from consulting with Wilbur about his writing and psychological difficulties, but Wilbur, now settled in a new house on the Cape, contacted him soon after the above was penned. Aiken replied on the twenty-first, amused by his friend's avowed ambivalence regarding his new home because it echoed his own mixed feelings about England. Except for criticism, he was finding it much easier to write in England than he had in America. Oddly, he never thought to relate his depression to the recent flow of creative juices, which suggests that he remained, in some measure, protectively shielded from the knowledge about self stemming from *Blue Voyage* delvings and the reflexive aesthetic governing his lyric sequence.

Instead, reacting to Wilbur's interpretation of one of his dreams—he had dreamed that he had bad teeth and his psychiatrist friend appeared as a dentist, only to pull the wrong tooth—Aiken opted for a literary, supremely rational explanation of the dream's symbolic content. He accepted Wilbur's idea of a castration motive, along with a possible homosexual element, and expanded the interpretation to explain his problem with writing criticism in England as well. Boiled down, his theory equated criticism with analysis, which meant that Wilbur's presence encouraged him, when in America, to seek out and use the psychological awareness necessary for critical insights, even as Wilbur inhibited the cathartic flow of creative juices that produced poetry and fiction. Aiken admitted, however, that his theory was imperfect because he had finished a batch of lyrics that summer and was deep into *Blue Voyage*. Also, he anticipated a recognition of the new poem's more analytic qualities, which had engendered an increased amount of symbolism and resistance.

The letter to Wilbur is a shrewd piece of self-scrutiny that tells much about the manner in which Aiken was discovering that the mythic and parable disguises used in *Deth* and the lyric sequence were often screening him from the psychic realities buried in his unconscious, though presumably designed to do the opposite. And yet the casual adoption of a Freudian lexicon and undeniably valid insight into the gestation of his poetry and *Blue Voyage* fails to confront the psychopathological nature of what was being symbolized as literature's traditional tropes. He was, as usual, honestly willing to process the mechanisms of his art in terms of relevant psychoanalytic doctrine, but without always relating uncovered neurotic machinery directly to his life and personality, without grasping, for instance, how his current despondency had fertile links with the ambivalence toward his mother (and Jessie) reactivated by Ormond's rejection, although *Blue Voyage* was forcing him back into the past that had hurt him into an artist's repressed rage and self-obsessed detachment.

Blue Voyage might be cited to show the awareness of mission steadily dawning on Aiken as he filtered memories of Savannah through the fine cloth of a novel based on the journey that had witnessed Ormond's defection. But the antagonistic need for control, for rational contours, which had almost fatally distanced "Strange Moonlight," was disfiguring valuable reflections of his divided psyche under the guise of Platonic analysis. Exchanging Freudian

notions about his creative machinery with Wilbur through the textually sani-
tizing medium of the mail might have helped keep him tethered to earth during
a period of internal and external storms, but it left oblique certain aspects of
his emerging depressive crisis that boded ill for a successful resolution of
basic conflicts. The contradictions are probably too tangled to unravel totally,
and the important thing is that he plunged ahead with *Blue Voyage,* regardless
of emotional penalties, and with his conscientious endeavor to construct a
viable critical theory. Croce, who struck him, "more every time I return to
him," as "a fine case of highclass intellectual fake," offered him an opportunity to refine the latter.

Aiken's review of *European Literature in the Nineteenth Century,* which
appeared in the October 11 issue of the *Nation & Athenaeum,* condemned
Croce's massive study to the level of "a competent, if unexciting, survey of
twenty-five rather capriciously selected nineteenth-century figures," though
his major objection, as could be expected, centered on the fundamental misap-
prehension of aesthetics underlying the Italian's judgments: "This profounder
something, which alienates one's sympathies, is in part Signor Croce's persistently metaphysical view of art, a view almost religious in intensity, hostile
to all other views, and aimed primarily (so one feels) at a philosophical justification of art, not at a functional understanding of it. He begins with the hypothesis that art is something sublime, absolute, and autonomous; and his
purpose seems not so much to attempt an analysis of its causes and roots in
human nature as to assign it a metaphysical place."

To make matters muddier, Croce tagged his enterprise as "scientific," eliciting Aiken's contempt for his slipshod methodology, "a generous hypothesis
or two followed by an 'argument,' an elaborate logical structure, which as
often as not is pure verbalism, and often enough is not even good logic." By
relegating art to the ideal stratosphere of a "*supremely real*" absolute, where
it could sublimely resist any authentic scientific probing of its categorical
aspects and form-content distinctions, Croce cut himself off from precious
vantages proferred by other disciplines: "His 'view' will not permit him, on
the one hand, to employ psychology and biography in his study of a poet's
'behavior' or development; nor, on the other hand, can he sufficiently admit
the separability of form or literary class to devote himself to a minute testing
of the principles there at work, and of the extent to which those principles
control the writer or are controlled by him."

Innate skepticism and Emersonian toughness stood Aiken in good stead as
the review of Croce's prolix tome further clarified his own critical position.
And a distinct beacon amid the December gloom of a year fraught with angst
and proliferating financial worries was being asked to review I. A. Richards's
Principles of Literary Criticism. Richards, a British-born scholar in his early

thirties who had studied at Cambridge and authored *The Meaning of Meaning* (1923) with C. K. Ogden, was intent upon applying scientific techniques to the murky domain of aesthetics, a project Aiken heartily endorsed.

Accepting experimental science as a procedural good, a model of true (verifiable and predictive) knowledge, Richards realized that it was emotionally sterile because it had to focus on *how* rather than *what* or *why* questions. His ingenious solution, not always persuasive, was to redefine *what* and *why* queries as "pseudo-questions"—pseudo because not directed at the phenomenal world—and poetry as "pseudo-statement" (emotive and referential) designed to respond to such inquiries. Consequently, poetry and literature in general (fictive) appear to describe reality but are actually organizing the reader's feelings about it in a satisfying manner, which is why psychology must assume major status in any intelligent effort to dissect the art experience and promulgate aesthetic principles. In his scheme, which would eventually support the very approach Aiken rejected when discerned in Croce and Spingarn, the most efficient poetry tends toward communal therapy by organizing the maximum number of conflicted emotional impulses with a minimum amount of frustration and struggle; the poem also serves as a microscope trained upon the poet's psyche.

Aiken was not completely taken in by the appealing merger of science and literature in Richards's treatise. His review, published in the January 24, 1925, issue of the *Nation & Athenaeum* and reprinted in the *New Republic,* commences with a salute to Richards as a significant, if flawed, answer to his own prayer for a critic who has mastered more than literary history. But Aiken balks at what he perceives as an inability to evade a relativistic weighing of critical values, despite a resort to psychoanalytic scales: "Mr. Richards, in his definition of value, follows, a good deal more than he likes to admit, the Freudian lead. An experience, he says, is valuable in accordance as it organizes and uses without waste 'conflicting impulses.' The poet's experiences 'represent conciliations of impulses which in most minds are still confused, intertrammelled, and conflicting.' " As a result, "we confront implications which are rather excitingly relativistic, and it is the most serious failure of Mr. Richards' book that it is exactly this point which he does not squarely meet."

As in earlier essays and reviews, particularly of Eliot, Aiken wants an elastic yardstick of aesthetic performance—objective yet sensitive to varying artistic goals and audience requirements—that will rule out retreats into impressionistic vagueness and metaphysical abstractions beyond scientific evaluation, retreats that Richards does not seem to forsake completely:

> There being no universal of value (in an objective sense), then it follows
> that a poem in which x finds value (*i.e.,* a better organization of impulses

than he can manage himself) must be *good:* it arouses in *x* the feeling we loosely call beauty. To escape the staggering solipsism which must ensue here . . . he appears to assume (1) that *y* is a better judge than *x* if his mind is a finer (less wasteful) systematization of impulses; and (2) that as between two works of art that one is the better which is the more complex—is the resultant of an organization of a *greater number* of impulses. This is suspiciously like stating that a good critic is one who likes a good poem, and that a good poem is one which is liked by a good critic. It is an argument in a circle, and inevitably involves the surreptitious re-entrance of the 'absolute' value which we had been at such pains to exclude.

Evincing signs of the new maturity that had permitted him to compose the lyric sequence begun that spring and to return to *Blue Voyage,* a maturity of vision, not personality, Aiken decries Richards's recoil "from the purely social-psychological view of art because he dislikes the implications (which it leads to) that value in art must always be simply an equation between artist and audience." In place of "sensibility" refuges, he insists that the sole valid method is to concede "there *are* many levels in art, each suited to its audience (for which it *is* art, producing the desired effect); and then classify these, studying their history and laws, in terms of the simple-to-complex," which means that Richards's haloing of the artist as one "better organized" than his fellow men to capture, resolve, and communicate antagonistic feelings must be revised: "A safer ground here, perhaps, is the assumption that the artist is one whose mind is *less* efficiently organized for a life of 'action' than the average, and that his art is the process, analogous to the daydream, by which he seeks to maintain his balance. To those whose psychosis corresponds closely to his own, his work will be 'good'—it becomes *their* successful daydream."

This is orthodox psychoanalytic criticism, coupling fantasy and literature as dream mechanism, with Aiken again blurring psychosis and neurosis and again failing to mention his previous, worthwhile emendation of Freud's dream diagrams to incorporate anxiety (unresolved) expressions. But his scoring of Richards's weaknesses is accurate enough if not entirely appreciative of the extent to which those weaknesses would encourage the development of an interpretive apparatus (New Criticism) at odds with his attempt to broaden the discipline base of literary analysis by encompassing a "purely functional" perspective. What had not altered, the review elucidates, was the passionate conviction that literature, for author and reader, has a therapeutic or cathartic function, however pessimistic or self-diminishing its message, that poetry aggrandizes the poet's ego in the face of frightening knowledge inflicted by experience.

> Poetry has always kept easily abreast with the utmost man can do in extending the horizon of his consciousness, whether outward or inward. It has always been the most flexible, the most comprehensive, the most far-seeing, and hence the most successful, of the modes by which he has accepted the new in experience, realized it, and adjusted himself to it. Whether it is a change in his conception of the heavens, or of the law of gravity, or of mortality, or of the nature of consciousness, it has always at last been in poetry that man has given his thought its supreme expression—which is to say that most of all, in this, he succeeds in making real for himself the profound myth of personal existence and experience.

Written in 1931, while the first set of *Preludes* was nearing completion and Aiken was undergoing a breakdown, here is the avocational rock upon which his recovery and career were to be built, culminating in the lyrically arranged *Ushant,* in which the mythic artist-self achieves redemption. But the idea, its necessary belief, was already aiding his survival at the conclusion of 1924. In early December he toured London on a Christmas shopping trip and had pleasant visits with Eliot, Monro, Freeman, Armstrong, the Untermeyers (on their way home), and Fletcher. His own uncertainty must have been assuaged a bit when he learned that Eliot, in spite of public acclaim, was dissatisfied and unsure of his path as well. Eliot told him he was out of humor with almost all of his previous works but had been doing some new things—probably a reference to "The Hollow Men," which was kin to Aiken's lyric sequence in demarcating some ultimate level of despair.

But Eliot's conversion was a year off in 1925, and during the early months of the year Aiken continued to grapple with depression and the additional financial demands placed upon him by the purchase of Jeake's House and another mouth to feed. Debts piled up, and the steady trickle of money earned from reviewing and magazine appearances was hardly sufficient to reduce them. His main hope lay in the possible success of the short story collection due to be published this spring in England and America. He pushed on with *Blue Voyage,* since that too held the promise of monetary rewards denied poets, although its concentration upon the tainted flotsam of childhood's golden wreckage abetted an introspective feeding on self not always conducive to reinforcing an identity under siege. The hebephrenic dilapidation set in motion by his melancholia undoubtedly aided the novel's progress, however, because it polished the infantile lens trained on Savannah. In her diary entry of March 18, Virginia Woolf, who was preparing *Mrs. Dalloway* for spring publication, would write: "The past is beautiful because one never realizes an emotion at the time. It expands later, and thus we don't complete emotions about the present, only about the past."

For a neurotic egotist, past is forever present, and Aiken's quest for the mother sacrificed to his father's madness could not be relaxed until another Reine Ormond was met and mastered, Anna Aiken restored to that pristine smiling image he retained of her at rest in Colonial Park. In her newest maternal chores, Jessie was farther than ever from the perfection demanded of such a madonna figure, the Virgin Mary icon so fundamental to a Western imagination, which Henry Adams espied at Mont-Saint-Michel and Chartres—"One sees her personal presence on every side. Any one can feel it who will only consent to feel like a child"—and which *Blue Voyage* posits as the male poet's ultimate Beatrice sublimation and salvation: "This love of yours must be kept pure, precious, and uncontaminated."

Yet the same novel's narrator has to confess that "I have always been one in whose consciousness illusion and disillusion flashed simultaneously." The answer remained art, a father's lance and a mother's womb, and the culturally sanctified myth of the artist, which allowed Aiken to redraw failure and rejection into the heroic profile of the poet as a martyred Prometheus established by the careers of such admired Romantics as Poe and Keats. He also had unsought-for assistance from his own body. Intermittently over the last year or so, he had been physically ill, bothered most by a persistent case of hemorrhoids. Early in May 1925 he experienced another attack that confined him to bed for an entire week. The local doctor diagnosed his ailment as a "periurethral abscess" that was cancerous and added that it might prove fatal. In *Ushant,* Aiken recalls sitting amid Rye's natural panorama of spring events after learning of his apparent death sentence, thinking "what a marvellous synthesis it all made, the incredible beauty with its incredible core of death! Yes, death must come to a house" (261).

Ironically, physical sickness, which tends to impel the self inward, brought the preciousness of life to the fore as it threatened involuntary extinction. Survival reflexes counteracted the negation lapping at the shore of his shriven ego, at least partially, temporarily. The Rye doctor advised him to consult a London specialist, a Dr. Neligan, and then have an operation as soon as possible. The specialist, however, informed him that his situation was far less serious than his doctor had suspected, although an operation would become necessary sometime in the future. It was on the train ride home to Rye that Aiken read in a newspaper about the May 12 death of Amy Lowell, which touched him in an unexpected way. He wrote to Linscott on May 14 from Jeake's House to express wonder at how moved and saddened he was by the death of a woman he had always regarded as an enemy, feeling she had bested him again. Self-contempt is the letter's prevailing mood.

Lowell's death, as he would learn from Linscott in a subsequent letter, had been hastened by titanic labors to complete her massive biography of Keats, which seemed to combine the grandeur and absurdity often typical of her dramatic existence: "She had rallied somewhat from her last rupture [hernia] and one afternoon got up and dressed. At the stroke of five as she was sitting before a mirror watching a maid comb her hair, she suddenly leaned forward, regarding herself intently, whispered two words—a stroke—and fell dead. Odd to watch death leap at one like that. And characteristic of Amy to be so alert as to understand and interpret at the instant of death the meaning of that muffled explosion when the blood vessel burst within her brain."

Aiken's strong reaction to Lowell's passing owed much to a sense of guilt, as he recalled for Linscott his last contact with her in 1923, when, over the phone, she had (forgetting and forgiving his rude behavior at her dinner party the year before) asked him to come out to her house, even though he had three guests in tow, a request he ignored. Worse, he had recently sent off a brutal review of her two-volume Keats book to the *Dial,* which was to publish it in the June 1925 issue. Aiken was angered by her daring to claim the poet about whom he had always been possessive, and his long review was recondite and accurate without being kind or absolutely fair: "I think Miss Lowell signally fails in what might be called the 'finer' departments (as against the mere collating of facts) of biography. She has little tact; her taste is uncertain; her psychological perceptions are imprecise; her imagination is forced and hectic, not instinctively apposite. There are many admirable and graphic pages in her *John Keats.* She makes also many admirable points. But on the whole the effect is one of provincialism, a pervading unripeness which no amount of cocksureness and bluster can cover."

Aiken frantically cabled the *Dial* to ask if he could alter the review or add a memorial note, but the magazine did not respond—the issue was already in print. The result was more regrets, further guilt. Lowell's heavy shape was too near a prepubic concept of maternal swells for comfort, and his attack on her (on her offspring birthed in death) must have requickened the remorse attached to ambivalent inner and poetic assaults upon Anna Aiken's memory. The night after Lowell's death he had dreamed that "Jessie complimented Amy on a certain poem," but he had not even bothered to doff his hat in her company; in the dream she was last seen rolling down a hill in a monstrous cab, leaving him behind with his rue. Mother, wife, Lowell—they were recurrent forms of the ambiguous female archetype that he had to pursue and rebuff. His critique of the Keats biography, which does reflect an intimate knowledge of the poet's life and work, offered yet one more astute self-portrait as well: "It was a hierarchy of profound psychic schisms which ruled him, and it is scarcely to be wondered at, in the circumstances, that his fine mind was so seldom permitted to work uninterrupted, and that he regarded the poet as a 'chameleon,' without identity. . . . The Keats whose life was a feverish search for luxury as a replacement for his mother was also, of course, the Keats whose poetry is the most completely and consciously sensuous ever written." Obviously, unlike the more controlled Aiken, Keats had never leavened the erotic verse products of his mother's absence with a father's hardness and analytic skepticism.

But the poet Aiken was reading intently that spring of 1925 was John Marston, and he quoted lines from *What You Will* in the May 14 letter to Linscott: "How t'was created, how the soul exists,— / One talks of motes, the soul was made of motes." Because it embodied in language what humanity had always envisioned as consciousness's imperishable, transcendent miracle, the notion of soul was intriguing to him as the scalding material dredged up from his unconscious by *Blue Voyage* burned away layer after layer of an unanchored selfhood. Marston's poems and plays, regardless of Jacobean excess, supplied impressive proof of how negation and antisocial urges could be converted into a wide range of formal solutions, varying from satire and vengeance melodrama to lyric meditations upon weightier spiritual matters. And the sheer eventfulness of life at Rye kept Aiken from floating off into the void.

Besides the children, to whom he enjoyed reading the dream verses of De La Mare, he had the spring influx of visitors to keep him occupied and reasonably amused. These complemented the frequent visits of Martin Armstrong and occasional dinners and parties at the Nashes and elsewhere. Though supposedly not a social creature, he enjoyed having company around, however exhausting and hard upon a deflated purse. A June 9 letter to Firuski notes that Cousin Julia Delano ("astounding woman") had come and gone, as had a "prospective cousin-in-law, Rosalind Parker," and now he was busy entertaining his Aunt Edith and a spinster companion, along with the ubiquitous Armstrong. Meanwhile, "Fletcher is coming next week," and the Taussigs would arrive in the fall. But the visitor he most wanted to greet, Tom Eliot, who had promised to drop in after recovering from a bout of flu, never materialized.

Unknown to Aiken, the Eliot marriage had taken a turn toward the exit. As Eliot had explained in great agitation to Virginia Woolf on the night of April 28, Vivienne's psychoanalyst, sometime early in the year, had set her "off thinking of her childhood terror of loneliness, and now she can't let him, Tom, out of her sight. There he has sat mewed in her room these 3 months, poor pale creature, or if he has to go out, comes in to find her in a half fainting state." Eliot also told Woolf about his departure from Lloyd's: "Tom's long gaslit emotional rather tremulous and excited visit . . . which informed us of his release (But I have not yet sent in my demission) from the Bank." The last Aiken had heard from Eliot had been a letter dated February 13 in which he complimented the Huxley review, asked if October was too late to publish the story called "Hey, Taxi"—it was—and expressed an earnest intention to visit Rye for a weekend after returning from a planned leave.

On June 27, Aiken sent Eliot a note to remind him of the open invitation, but at the beginning of July, when no reply was forthcoming and *Bring! Bring!* was published by Secker to respectful reviews, he took the train to London for the day and stopped off at Lloyd's. A bank official informed him that Eliot would be gone for six months. Mystified and somewhat alarmed about his friend's health, he returned to Rye, where he received a letter from Eliot dated July 7 that made no mention of his extended leave. Instead, Eliot wanted to know if Aiken was disposed to take on David Garnett, novelist son of translator Constance Garnett, as well as reviewing *Mrs. Dalloway.* He also suggested that Aiken might want to put together a series of papers on contemporary British novelists for a book, which he thought he could easily place with a publisher. Private and scheming as ever, Eliot had commenced maneuvers to land a position with Faber & Gwyer as an editor and have that firm take over publication of the *Criterion,* maneuvers that would result in a temporary breach with Virginia Woolf, who was more amused than hurt by this "queer shifty creature." Woolf wrote in her diary of Eliot's treachery in attempting to steal authors from Hogarth: "The Underworld—the dodges and desires of the Underworld, its shifts and cabals are at the bottom of it. He intends to get on by the methods of that world; and my world is really not the underworld. However, there is a kind of fun in unravelling the twists and obliquities of this remarkable man."

Aiken was caught in the middle, unsure of his footing in a terrain never quite familiar to him, particularly at Bloomsbury, though the Hogarth Press was the English publisher that month of his expanded version of *Priapus and the Pool.* Despite Woolf's reluctance, Hogarth had also taken over publishing and translating Freud's papers the year before, and this must have elicited Aiken's approval. In his July 9 response to Eliot he described his fruitless visit to Lloyd's Bank and expressed a lack of enthusiasm for the notion of a book on British novelists, which he would probably have to offer first to Hogarth, to whom he had granted refusal rights on his prose. As for David Garnett and Virginia Woolf, they did not appeal to him as review material, he apologized, at least not at the moment. Aiken's first review of Woolf (of *To the Lighthouse* for the *Dial*) would not appear until 1927. In it he hailed her extraordinary triumph over a possibly circumscribed and artificial style: "The technical brilliance glows, melts, falls away; and there remains a poetic apprehension of life of extraordinary loveliness. . . . The tragic futility, the absurdity, the pathetic beauty, of life—we experience all of this in our sharing of seven hours of Mrs. Ramsay's wasted or not wasted existence. We have seen, through her, the world."

There was no written reaction to Aiken's letter, but he managed to see Eliot during a London interlude. Their peculiar relationship continued on an even keel, if never as close as it had once been, with Eliot making his break from Lloyd's official in the fall and securing an editorial post at Geoffrey Faber's new house, which did assume financial responsibility for the *Criterion* (renamed the *New Criterion*). Woolf's essay "On Being Ill" appeared there in December, marking the end of her private alienation from its editor. At the conclusion of his July 9 letter to Eliot, Aiken had lamented the relative sparsity of his own creative output thus far in 1925. There was no reference to *Blue Voyage,* but depression and physical illness, in consort with relentless money problems, were certainly hampering his productivity. He desperately needed movement, a trip home to America, the change of scenery that had always helped relieve buildups of internal pressure. His June 9 letter to Firuski notes, regarding the prospective Taussig visit, "These tastes of my native land only whet my appetite for the soil itself: the cobblestones of Boston and the sand of South Yarmouth."

In the same letter he had offered to sell his first edition of Lowell's *John Keats,* which Linscott claimed was bringing forty dollars a copy, and inquired how "the exchange of books and autographs against my account" was progressing:

> All this financial frenzy is part of a last spasmodic effort to scrape up dollars enough to reach Boston by steerage later in the year. I MUST see the state house this year. I'll *die* if I don't see the Frog Pond this year. . . . As for sitting under a tree with you and Bob [Linscott], or playing tennis with you, or enjoying the cool grandeur of your laroseate drawingroom, or sticking with you on a hot evening to a red leather divan in the Harvard Club—am I never to taste these delights again? Is it possible that I shall never again drop a dime into one of those lovely glasstraps in the subway? or rot my belly with a milkshake? My tears fall like rice-grains as I look across the Camber salts to the so-expensive sea.

A few days later a letter arrived from Linscott offering a hundred-dollar loan "without interest to be repaid whenever you happen to be flush" and seeking permission to borrow a like sum in his name from Firuski and Wilbur.

Upset by Aiken's last letter (May 27), which he said "quite fills me with despair . . . what an abyss of melancholy," Linscott also advised the selling of both Jeake's House, "even at a loss if necessary," and the Cape Cod cottage, then "buying an old farm house about 20 miles out of Boston where you'd have plenty of seclusion and quiet but could dash in quickly whenever you felt the need for society and the brisker life. You can buy places at that distance very cheaply and with a Ford (only $260. now) everything is perfectly accessible to you but you to no one except callers that you wish to meet." The darkness of Aiken's letter is reflected in Linscott's appeal for him not to cut his throat, proferring "help in any way" and agreeing to peruse *Blue Voyage* (unfinished) for him: "I'd be delighted to read the novel but I'm afraid my counsel would only lead you astray." Aiken, however, had no intention of essaying a permanent return, assuming Jessie cooperated, which is extremely doubtful.

When he sailed for America in late August of 1925, he was planning nothing more than a stay of several months, during which he hoped to renew familial and friendly ties and tend to business matters. Boni and Liveright, with whom he had argued in February through the mails, had *Priapus and the Pool and Other Poems* scheduled for a September 15 publication date. The usually congenial *Dial* was proving equally perverse. The magazine refused to publish two previously accepted stories before *Bring! Bring!* appeared, causing Aiken to waste precious funds buying one back. Aiken's letter of warning to the magazine elicited a nasty response.

Scofield Thayer departed from the *Dial* in June, and after Brooks refused the position, its editorship was turned over to Marianne Moore, a change that appeared to omen a slackening of his close (and profitable) association with the prestigious journal, at least initially, because she harbored no love for his poetry. Aiken would complain to Fletcher the following year that Moore seemed to be a distinct disaster as an editor, but she was amiable and encouraging when he met with her, asking him to contribute essays and stories, although she would reject "Changing Mind" before he returned home. In fact, none of his poems would see print in the *Dial* until the magazine published the first "Prelude" in June 1928. Moore's admiration for his reviewing skills and integrity was, however, sincere, eventuating in her characterization of him as "the one perfect reviewer." But he nursed a grudge against the magazine for having failed to review *Festus* and was therefore cheered to learn from Moore that she had assigned Malcolm Cowley to review *Bring! Bring!* for the December issue.

Cowley, who was residing with his wife, Peggy, in a small house on Staten Island, having abandoned his safe job at *Sweet's Architectural Catalogue* that spring to discover if "I could live for a year by writing," was one of the literary figures Aiken wanted to link up with again. Aiken wrote in mid-September and invited him to accompany him to the South Yarmouth cottage, which he intended to occupy for a month or so, but Cowley begged off, looking forward to seeing Aiken upon his return. He also asked about the propriety of the older poet, presuming he was willing, approaching Liveright on his behalf in connection with a volume of verse he wished to assemble, to which Aiken responded positively, adding that he should, as Cowley suggested, see the manuscript first. Cowley's maiden collection, *Blue Juniata,* would be published by Jonathan Cape four years later, only after Hart Crane had edited the book into shape and pressed for its acceptance. Aiken's letter, dated September 26, expressed an interest in reading Cowley's review of his story collection, even if it was negative, and recommended, further, that Cowley look at *Priapus*.

The decision to spend a month at South Yarmouth was sensible, as well as financially necessary, because it enabled Aiken to write in peace and discuss his psychological problems and theories with Wilbur. Perhaps it was at South Yarmouth that he composed "Changing Mind," the poem that represented his first stride out of the desolation governing the lyric sequence from 1924. It overtly challenged Eliot's domination of their competition— "*Changing Mind* was my answer to *The Waste Land*"—and committed him to an autobiographical exploration and deification of consciousness (later termed "a religion of consciousness"), a poetic assimilation of *Blue Voyage*'s Joycean stream and Eliot's elliptical montage.

Inevitably, a room is the initial setting and symbol, where the narrator is ordered to "Come down under the talk," under water (womb) and language, under a "four-voiced dialogue" uttered by a quartet of people peering down at him. He does so and locates Narcissus, both of them in the river below the two male and two female observers, one of whom is a "blue-eyed woman" (later identified as Alba), insisting, "I am not dead; / Let him forget me at his peril!" At this point, the experience is pleasurable, and the blue-eyed woman's hair encompasses him, even though she condemns him to psychoanalysis, the vivisection he had formerly inflicted upon women in his literature:

> "Whistle derision from Rome to Jericho;
> Sell him to Doctor Wundt the psycho-analyst
> Whose sex-ray eyes will separate him out
> Into a handful of blank syllables,—
> Like a grammarian, whose beak can parse
> A sentence till its gaudy words mean nothing."

And he finds it true—articulated at last: he has been fragmented by the Freudian mirror, he and his literary mask, Narcissus exposed to the void (lack of a self), his sickness always concealed. He realizes too that she—song, purity, sensual mother, Goya's duchess—who had doomed him can save him as well:

> Dissected out on the glass-topped table, . . .
> I am dispersed, and yet I know
> That sovereign eye, if once it glare its love,
> Will reassemble me.

But the other woman, "in blue muslin, tall and meagre," reminds the arrogant blonde that she is

> but one
> Of all our host . . .
> Us he remembers when he remembers you:
> The livid; the sore; the old; the worn; the wounded:
> Hating the smell of us, you too he'll hate.

Goddesses or not, women must, in other words, suffer the same fate (contempt and detestation) in the misogynist's snare. She herself knows because she is "the dead cormorant whom he so loathed / And buried by the sea," which couples "Changing Mind" to the 1924 sequence, specifically to "Cliff Meeting," and its fable formulas. But allegory's various disguises are seen giving way to the alarming reality uncovered by depth psychology as the first section of the four-part poem achieves a portentous climax with Dr. Wundt, face "like a star," talking to the narrator's father, his young visage also shining "like the evening star, inexorable," their shapes forming "one image on the moving water."

Father and analyst configure the same demanding, frightening, male authority perfection in the effect they exert upon his divided self, albeit cold and remote from him in their ascendancy into the heavens, casting down the law (his future) in a single word ("Inheritor!") that "hung / Smokelike above the stream"—flow of consciousness and Heraclitan flux. But they have surfaced as ultimate sages in a small parade of key historic personalities, a parade consisting of Socrates, Christ crucified, and Hegel and his dialectic, projected through the stream's constant motion, plus the absent Freud, who is represented by Wundt. Clearly, the reflexive and restless progress of the poetic ego is intended to incorporate the secular curiosity of Greek philosophy (Aristotelian science), the selfless sacrifice of Christianity's founder (ethical passion), the Hegelian resolution (Nietzschean conversion and Bergsonian evolution) of polar tensions, and the remorseless abreaction dynamic and mirror inherited from the paternal Freud, which threatens to bare (and thus dismantle) the psyche's baroque defenses, including the sublimation process manufacturing his narcissistic art and this particular performance. In contrast to the latter thrust toward prismatic disintegration are the more human (emotional) reactions of the two females. The lady in blue, "starved blue cormorant whom I betrayed," weeps as her blonde counterpart glares "on the water to assemble me."

In the second section, while Narcissus sleeps under water, "and beside him keeps / Conscious and yet unconscious my bright soul," Aiken's speaker envisions new gods and worlds rising and asks, "Is it from me they come— / From me to me?" The fundamental question, solipsistic and infantile, though as pivotal as Hamlet's at the other pole of existence's scale, is followed by a slack patch of purple, the poem not regaining much dramatic force until Mephistopheles, Faust's ingenious tempter, replaces the male figures staring down at him and Narcissus, holding these new shapes in his own hand. Suitably small and dark, he elicits laughter from "the tall man" and the two women as his voice pursues the speaker, takes over his narrative task:

> "Childe Roland, leaving behind him the dark tower,
> Came in the evening to the land of kites.
> Peril was past. The skull of the dead horse
> His foot broke; and the desert, where wild dogs
> Bay up the moon from tall grass, this he crossed
> In the long light. And in the kite country—"
> (Ha, ha, they laughed, merry descending scale)—
> "He saw the diamond kites all rise at once
> From the flat land. And on each kite was bound
> A weeping woman, the arms outstretched, the feet
> Nailed at the foot!"

The term "kite" mandates connotations of sails and toys and human predators, which makes for further permutations and paradoxes, and the Roland mask offered to Aiken's persona has behind it memories of the legendary Dark Age hero who was defender against and martyr to invading Saracen infidels. His plight, presumably postmortem, is as anguished witness to the women's crucifixions, climbing slowly "in twilight to the weeping-cross," where he commiserates with the victim, who is presented as two women sexually merged into one, madonna and whore meshed together in perverted lust, "faces fused in one." The kiteflyers return, and Roland's last experience is hearing "you, weeping, blown aloft in air!" All the while, as noted in a parenthetical sentence, the supplanted speaker is "helpless, bound thus, in my cave, asleep, / Bound in the stinging nerves of sound, these voices," so that the bifocal perspective is maintained, doubled, Narcissus and artist separate and united as Mephistopheles (another facet or profile of the creating self) activates the pathological energies (sadistic, incestuous, misogynist) of the reigning imagination. A final stanza denies that disease—mental and moral—has prevailed:

> But it was not of the kites, nor the kite country,
> The giant swimmer sang, who brought me news,
> News of the southeast! O believe, believe!
> Believe, grim four, believe me or I die!
> It is from you this vision comes; while I
> Dreamed that I swam, and with that swimmer came
> Into the southeast of forgotten name.

The messenger allusion to a "giant swimmer" is mysterious, perhaps another manifold reference and personification that might embrace Peter, Christ's "Fisher of Men," and definitely encompasses a version of Aiken's own nascent better (artist) self, its aborning myth, although Whitman's "The Sleepers" is probably the main inspiration, in which the prophetic poet's alter ego (during a surreal night journey) amasses other selves and creativities: "I dream in my dream all the dreams of the other dreamers, / And I become the other dreamers." A "beautiful gigantic swimmer" is at the center of the third section of Whitman's poem, courageous and naked "in the prime of his middle age," yet destined to fail and perish in his hopeless (unknown) quest:

> Steady and long he struggles,
> He is baffled, bang'd, bruis'd, he holds out while his strength holds out,
> The slapping eddies are spotted with his blood, they bear him away,
>   they roll him, swing him, turn him,
> His beautiful body is borne in the circling eddies,
>   it is continually bruis'd on rocks,
> Swiftly and out of sight is borne the brave corpse.

Anticipating the northern-bound corpse that will climax the first set of Aiken's *Preludes*, Whitman's dead other self, nude as a newborn infant but in middle age, had unmistakable appeal to the author of "Changing Mind," especially since it related dream machinery to poetic process and strove to convert obsessive death fears into their positive anode. In fact, Whitman's entire oeuvre discloses a battle against tenacious death terrors pervasive enough to intimate a desperate campaign to defuse suicidal tendencies, culminating in the creation of the mythic identity reified by *Leaves of Grass*. The Good Grey Poet of omniscient dimensions, metaphysical magic, was able to translate any experience, however instinctually inverted or rebellious, into a historic ukase and Emersonian affirmation. A swing back to Whitman was for Aiken a natural strategy in a work determined to present "a poem . . .

complete with the formative matrix, the psychological scaffolding, out of which it was in the act, the very act, of crystallizing" (246), because "The Sleepers" (in the swimmer episode) proffers a dual vantage in which a schizoid "I" (already refracted via dream work) can examine, celebrate, mourn for the ideal self he has produced and murdered, simultaneously witnessing his resurrection as a dramatic function of the artifice itself.

Furthermore, "Changing Mind" is not only preparation for a new direction in Aiken's career. It must also serve as museum for the false starts and wrong turns littering his poetic past; the Whitman echoes have a distinct place in the evolution of his final voice, which is what "Changing Mind" is supposed to record and epitomize. Hence its third section, shifting from a loose blank verse into prose, evokes the tawdry vaudeville realism of *Turns and Movies* as well as reminding the audience of the butcher orchestra in *John Deth,* just as the vivisectioning of the narrator had stirred recollections of similar scenes in the allegorical "symphony" series and the lady in blue reiterates a line of descent (ascent?) from the previous year's lyric sequence. Sadly, the description of the performance of the seven-man orchestra before thousands of faces "in rows like flowers in beds," which will be transformed into a prize fight with Narcissus as the perennial loser—"Narcissus daily dead, that we may live!"—lacks impact, making this section the weakest in the poem, though Aiken takes care to keep his multileveled and quartet motif intact: "And all this, mind you, was myself! myself still asleep under the four-voiced dialogue! the fourfold river of talk!"

Prose reverts to blank verse for the rest of the section, reaffirming the complicated perspective and fable structure of the whole:

> All this I was, but also those four strangers
> Leaning above me, leaning above the stream,
> The tall man, the small man, and the blue-eyed woman,
> And that other woman, whose beauty, on a kite,
> Rose to a beauty like the evening star.
> Golgotha, the skull, was the amphitheatre,
> The skull was my skull, and within it played
> The seven-man orchestra, while Luvic sang—

This deftly engineered passage demonstrates why "Changing Mind," despite Aiken's high hopes, is a boon for critics, not readers, more fun to interpret than to experience. It manipulates its neat sets of symbols and psychoanalytic parables with ingenious relevancy but without escaping the fatal distancing imposed by such a geometric reflexive pattern. More to the point, the deliberate focus on the psychological genesis (and symbolic resistance) of the emerging poem and persona (ego) cultivates the rebound possibilities inherent in the 1924 sequence, Aiken's neutralization of the Freudian threat, the felt discovery and use of a revisionary metaphysic provided by Jung. Ted R. Spivey has been virtually alone among Aiken critics in appreciating the Jungian nature of the solution supplied by "Changing Mind" to the problem of locating a transcendental aesthetic in a modern skeptical context. In addition, he has convincingly parsed the ethical grammar involved: "Suffering and death are seen in the poem as tests necessary for overcoming the illusion of basic separateness, which causes narcissism. . . . The mythic poet, finally, is identified with the man who fights every day, though always weak and sick."

The most significant of Spivey's observations sums up the conversion qualities of "Changing Mind," the transmutation of Freudian pressures into an archetypal balancing of contradictory psychic drives that Jung saw symbolized in the mandala, emblem of the individuation process achieving maturity, inner harmony: "When he descends into his soul the pilgrim receives the help of a god who aids him in overcoming Narcissus, symbol of the betwitching ego that traps part of the pilgrim's powers. The descent into the soul also brings into the pilgrim's view other powers. He sees the dark god Mephistopheles, symbol of the destructive powers, that archetype Jung calls the shadow. And the shadow shows him a crucified woman, symbol of wounded feminine powers within the soul. The shadow is the final force to be overcome each day." And in *The Psychology of the Unconscious,* which Aiken probably read, Jung himself writes of the "mother-imago" in terms of "water and submersion" as representing "the maternal depths and the place of rebirth; in short, the unconscious in its positive and negative aspects." Because he was consistently aware of the innate tendency in contradictory forces to assume their opposite, Jung better reflected Aiken's own conflicted sense of self, though his reliance upon "mythopoetic" procedures made him suspect in comparison with Freud and his more rigorous methodology.

No matter, since poetic tactics are necessary, pragmatic adaptations to the poet's quest for a metaphysical vehicle that will enable him to project an identity, to persevere. Jerome S. Bruner, who has perceived the crux function of mythology "as providing a set of possible programmatic identities for the individual personality," concludes that "when the myths no longer fit the internal plights of those who require them, the transition to newly created myths may take the form of a chaotic voyage into the interior, the certitudes of externalization replaced by the anguish of the internal voyage." This certainly applies to both "Changing Mind" and *Blue Voyage.* Water is the maternal medium of the descent quest, life and death intermingled in memory and unconscious tensions. Once "Changing Mind" traverses the father's realm of rational design, comes to the last and fourth section (the actual poem or "crystal"), potent literature ensues, commencing:

> My father which art in earth
> From whom I got my birth,
> What is it that I inherit?
> From the bones fallen apart
> And the deciphered heart,
> Body and spirit.

Severe, ritualistic formality stresses the passage from pathological preparation (unconscious givens reshaped) to the India of highest cultural achievement (conscious ethical and aesthetic arrangement) as the rhymed sestet addresses the man charged with starting the whole business, father (Freudian twin) to interior chaos. His mixed, if rich, legacy, a "deciphered heart" and stark awareness of relentless mortality ("bones fallen apart"), is vitally, invidiously different from the mother's, who is prayed to in the second stanza—to parallel "The Lord's Prayer" rather than, say, a "Hail Mary" hints at some antagonism toward her contribution—and condemned for infidelity, mind betrayed by transitory flesh: "From the thought come to dust / And the remembered lust." All four stanzas mirror one another in technique, and the third stanza is a woeful apostrophe to both parents, conceding the perishable limits of their literal (disintegrating) world and inquiring, "What is it that I can be?" A final denial—"Naught lives in thee"—enjambs into the last stanza, where the cascade of negatives flows into reality's sewer basin, a fractured psyche chained to rotting parental corpses and a history (his and theirs) that will not hold: "Where the past, underground, / Falls, falls apart."

The descent quest has found tokens of a scattered, yet narcissistic, identity. Working inside severe technical restraints exercises a salutary effect upon Aiken's style, as does the willingness nakedly to confront Anna and William Aiken's remains and his ambivalence about them and their death, accepting, finally, their uncertain blessings and the uncertain self they preordained. The terrible ambiguity of this reaction to them signifies that he is ready, the poet they created, to bring art to bear upon the specific crucible of his life and being, to obey, without conscious reserve, the Socratic and Freudian command to know thyself. In the fourth part of "Changing Mind," the sole section of the poem that Eliot selected "with competent irony" for his magazine, craft and poetry disarm content's horrific message, while the quartet structuring establishes the mandala plausibility of a Jungian resolution.

With this poem and in this plague year when parental deaths were once more at the fore, a sickly, quickly aging poet was announcing an important

Conrad Aiken in his middle thirties.

transition in his career and existence, though still wracked by doubts. He wrote to Cowley on December 10 about a nagging suspicion that his verses were blemished in ways beyond reckoning. But such falterings, now habitual, did not obscure or deter the evolution of his previous faith in an experiential (Bradley) and predetermined (Freud) self into a transcendent concept able, like Melville, to dive deep and, with Whitman, to swallow the universe. He was on the verge of sincere commitment to Emerson's subversion of nature, coupling metaphysical models borrowed from Hegel, Bergson, Jung, and others to the rationalization of unconscious chaos encouraged by psychoanalytic siftings of the ego—"Knowledge, in the mystical sense, is primarily self-knowledge," Philip Rieff has observed. In less than two years, after further harrowings, he would be able to share Coleridge's imagination as "a repetition in the finite mind of the eternal act of creation in the infinite I AM."

The progress of "Changing Mind" from matrix to artifice as benison, as seeming solution and sacrificial offering—*suffering is beauty's insidious sire* was to be his credo's Romantic cornerstone—validates the ideational maturation of his poetic existence. From here, the Damascene road was clear, although no less hazardous: his personal past and inheritances must entwine with America's, while deifying the act and action of consciousness—the endless becomings and concealings of language and psyche—until Saint Aiken could proclaim in *Ushant* that "it was only by obeying the ghostly summons of the poet of White Horse Vale . . . that he had been able to accomplish what essentially and profoundly all this time he had most wanted and needed to accomplish, the retention of that nursery floor, that room, that house at Savannah, that house and the vivid life in it" (300).

He was launched on the self's ultimate voyage of discovery, which sails forever backward, shedding the armor of childhood's White Knight persona in the very process of recovering childhood (and its deathless apparitions) for art and survival's sake. It would mean stepping down from that funereal Savannah stoop into a new messianic identity and myth as a literary "Cosmos Mariner." In so doing, in transforming himself into Reverend Potter's spiritual as well as literal descendant, he would have to write further versions of *The Pilgrim's Progress,* even as he contemplated the unhappy truth that the Slough of Despond planted in his soul by an egotistical father and faithless mother could never be entirely bridged.

NOTES

. . . . . .

Notes are keyed by page and line numbers to the beginning of the quote or sentence referenced. Full citations for any works cited in abbreviated form will be found in the Selected Bibliography at the end of this volume. The bulk of Aiken manuscripts and letters is located at the Huntington Library in San Marino, California, including numerous family photographs and the letters and literary remains of the poet's father, William Ford Aiken.

Substantial batches of other Aiken material, along with further letters to and from Aiken, are housed in the University of Texas's Humanities Research Center, Austin, Texas, the Harvard University Archives, Cambridge, Massachusetts—among the latter's holdings are Aiken's letters to his second wife, Clarissa Lorenz—the Princeton University Library, Princeton, New Jersey, the University of Chicago's Joseph Regenstein Library, Chicago, Illinois, and the Manuscript Division of the Library of Congress.

The main bibliographical guide to Aiken's publications is *Conrad Aiken: A Bibliography (1902–1978)*, ed. F. W. Bonnell and F. C. Bonnell (San Marino: Huntington Library, 1982). M. Catherine Harris has compiled *Critical Recognition of Conrad Aiken, 1914–1978* (New York: Garland, 1982) and also wrote "The Critics and Conrad Aiken: A Bibliographical Essay" for the Fall 1980 issue of *Studies in the Literary Imagination*. R. W. Stallman's "Annotated Checklist on Conrad Aiken: A Critical Study" is in *Wake* 11 (1952): 114–21.

To facilitate the matter of repeated references, the following abbreviations are used:

C	CA, *Conversation* (New York, 1940)
EB	Edward Burra
CA	Conrad Aiken
CP	CA, *Collected Poems*, 2d ed. (New York, 1970)
CSS	*The Collected Short Stories of Conrad Aiken* (New York, 1960)
WFA	William Ford Aiken
GM	Grayson McCouch
CL	Clarissa Lorenz (Aiken)
MH	Mary Hoover (Aiken)
BV	CA, *Blue Voyage* (New York, 1927)
GC	CA, *Great Circle* (New York, 1933)
HA	*Harvard Advocate*
GAL	George Arents Library, Syracuse University, Syracuse, New York
HL	Huntington Library
HUA	Harvard University Archives
JRL	Joseph Regenstein Library, University of Chicago
NL	Newberry Library, Chicago
PUL	Princeton University Library
TCA	*Twentieth Century Authors*, ed. Stanley Kunitz and Howard Haycraft (New York: H. W. Wilson, 1942)

TRC   University of Texas, Humanities Research Center
TSE   Thomas Stearns Eliot

PROLOGUE

xv:22 George Moore's *Confessions of a Young Man*—Susan Dick's excellent text is based on the first edition (Montreal: McGill-Queen's University Press, 1972)—was also an important influence on *Ushant,* as was Wordsworth's *Preludes,* but the *Leaves of Grass* model projected a mythic, morally sound, autobiographical persona at some calculated remove from actual experience and character. :28 *CP,* p. 1012. *xvi*:5 *New York Times,* Aug. 19, 1973, p. 28. :18 CA, *Ushant: An Essay* (London, 1963), p. 246. All future page numbers will be in parentheses in the text. 4:13 *BV,* p. 173. *xvii*:7 Quoted in Carol Scholz, "They Share the Suffering" (Dissertation, 1977), p. 91. :18 *BV,* p. 205. :21 *BV,* pp. 215–16. :32 Scholz, p. 89. :41 CA to Maurice Firuski, Jan. 7, 1952, HL, AIK 932. The latter call numbers will replace HL when used. Aiken wished to have this brief description of *Ushant*'s genesis used on the book's jacket cover; see *Selected Letters of Conrad Aiken,* ed. Joseph Killorin (New Haven, 1978), pp. 300–301—cited hereafter as *SL. xviii*:1 Harvard *Class of 1911 Report* (1961), p. 5. Cited hereafter as *CR,* with the year in parentheses, unless from a different class. :9 AIK 1941. :24 AIK 933. :33 CA to Kempton Taylor, Mar. 16, 1952 (AIK 1945). *xix*:1 CA to Kempton Taylor, Apr. 2, 1952 (AIK 1946). :25 Stevens to CA, Sept. 15, 1952 (AIK 826). :32 CA to Stevens, Oct. 17, 1952 (*SL,* p. 302).

CHAPTER I

1:4 *Savannah Morning News,* Feb. 28, 1901, p. 10. :10 Ibid. :14 Biographical information on William Lyman Akin and his wife is thin, which has meant a heavy reliance on *Ushant* and the William Ford Aiken material at HL. 3:4 Most of the data on Reverend Potter's life and distinguished career come from "William James Potter" in *Dictionary of American Biography,* ed. Dumas Malone et al. (New York: Scribner's, 1935), p. 135, and "New Light on an Old Subject" in *Bulletin: Old Dartmouth Historical Society* (Winter 1960): 1–4. :10 Robert Taylor, Aiken's youngest brother, alluded to her as such when I interviewed him at his Provincetown home Oct. 17, 1979. Unless indicated otherwise, all quotes are from this source. :31 In a Feb. 1, 1977, letter to the author, Malcolm Cowley notes regarding Rev. Potter: "Conrad always traveled with his sermons." See also *SL,* p. 222, and Ralph Hickok, "Conrad Aiken: Portraits of 'Unconquerable Ancestors,'" *New Bedford Magazine,* Summer 1981, pp. 46–47— cited hereafter as Hickok II. 4:28 William Ford Aiken's letters to his parents during his year abroad are among his papers at HL (AIK 2827–60). :35 Joseph Killorin, "Conrad Aiken's Use of Autobiography," *Studies in the Literary Imagination,* Fall 1980, p. 46. 5:11 *Savannah Morning News,* Feb. 28, 1901, p. 10. :12 Aiken later explained that his father had tried Charleston first, then decided on Savannah because Dr. Houston's advanced age made a position with him more immediately promising—see Andrew Sparks, "An Hour with Conrad Aiken," *Atlantic Journal and Constitution Magazine,* May 5, 1963, p. 8. :17 CL letter to the author, June 21, 1980; Steven Eric Olson, "The Vascular Mind" (Dissertation, 1981), argues: "There is no known evidence to support the newspapers' or Aiken's own speculations (in *Ushant*) that either side of the family had a strain of hereditary insanity" (p. 59). :27 See *Ushant*, p. 120. :36 AIK 3365; *SL*, p. 3. 7:15 "Conrad Aiken Talking," pp. 4–5, typescript of an interview conducted by D. G. Bridson (Apr. 1968) in Savannah for the BBC. Aiken had agreed to talk about his parents' deaths with the stipulation that the interview not be broadcast until after his own death. In a Feb. 28, 1977, letter to the author, Bridson claims the interview was never broadcast, though the typescript gives Aug. 29, 1973, as the "Playback" date, cited hereafter as BBC II. :40 *The Poetics of Reverie*, trans. Daniel Russell (Boston: Beacon, 1971), p. 20. 8:9 BBC II, p. 4. :34 Among the Aiken "Ephemera" (Box 1–41) at HL are several newspaper clippings about card parties given or attended by Mrs. Aiken, and the letters to her mother-in-law from the last year of her life (AIK 2901–13) are riddled with references to parties and other social events, including inevitable weddings and funerals. Children's birthday parties were often major productions. :39 See BBC II, pp. 3–4; *Savannah Morning News*, Feb. 28, 1901, p. 10; *The Annals of Savannah* 40 (1889): 516–17; ibid. 41 (1890):352; ibid. 42 (1891): 443; ibid. 43 (1892): 89. A compilation of items from the *Morning* and *Evening News*, the *Annals* were printed in Savannah commencing in the early 1970s and are readily available at the city's public library. 9:8 Alexander A. Lawrence, "228 Habersham Street," *Georgia Review* 22 (Fall 1968): 320. :28 Robert Taylor interview. :31 Lawrence, 319. :34 *Annals* 42 (1891): 89. :40 AIK 2815. 11:23 AIK 2816. 12:8 AIK 2817. Dr. Aiken mistakenly dated his letter "1893." :15 *Savannah Morning News*, Feb. 28, 1901, p. 10; William Lyman Akin's death certificate, which misspells the name as Aiken, and the *New York Times*, Dec. 30, 1893, p. 4, obituary list cause of death as Brights disease. 13:2 Lawrence, p. 321. :17 ibid., p. 319. :31 *Savannah Morning News*, Feb. 28, 1901, p. 10. :38 *Bulletin*, p. 2. 14:25 Lawrence, p. 319. 16:6 Killorin, pp. 45–46. :11 *CP*, p. 889. :21 Lawrence, p. 321. 18:27 *The Aeneid*, trans. Robert Fitzgerald (New York: Random House, 1983), p. 20. 19:26 AIK 2818. :37 *CSS*, p. 277. 20:7 Lawrence, p. 325n. :29 See *Ushant*, p. 87, and "Ephemera" (Box 1–41). 21:12 BBC II, p. 4. :15 *BV*, p. 127. :32 *BV*, p. 99. :41 Houston Peterson, *The Melody of Chaos* (New York, 1931), p. 24. 23:1 Lawrence, 318. :8 *BV*, p. 144. :23 See *Ushant*, p. 38. :29 see *Ushant*, p. 38. :35 See *Ushant*, p. 101. :40 AIK 2819. 24:26 AIK 2821. 25:6 AIK 2822. :27 *BV*, p. 125. :34 *BV*, p. 154. 27:8 *BV*, p. 125. :23 *BV*, p. 129. :26 *BV*, p. 130. :29 *BV*, p. 127. :33 Peterson, p. 26. Since Peterson wrote the sections on Aiken with the latter's full cooperation, his facts can be accepted as autobiographical—see also *SL*, pp. 143–47. 28:5 see Lawrence, p. 322. :12 *BV*, p. 128. Miss Waring's father was a doctor friend of Dr. Aiken's. :26 I have used the text in *A Quarter Century of Middlesex Verse*, ed. The Anvil (Concord: Middlesex, 1917), p. 3, because this seems to be the earliest extant version. :35 See "Strange Moonlight" in *CSS*, pp. 281–94. 29:15 Robert Taylor interview. :17 AIK 2823. :36 Lawrence, p. 325n; AIK 2908. In her letter, Nov. 28, 1900, Anna Aiken complains that growing deafness caused her "to give up lectures and everything of the kind as hopeless, although I take the keenest interest in all such things." 31:2 *BV*, p. 164. :24 *BV*, p. 163. :25 Lawrence, p. 318, identifies Hogan as Butch Gleason. :29 *Ushant*, p. 89, alludes to the difficulties of being a "Yankee" youth in the South and similar problems when attending a Cape Cod school (p. 8), but I have found no evidence of his ever attending a Cape school. :39 *BV*, p. 164. 32:9 *BV*, pp. 164–65. :15 *BV*, p. 166. :21 *SL*, p. 146. :27 *BV*, p. 147. :38 See AIK 2823. The Aikens accompanied the Tillinghasts to their favorite vacation area at Jackson, New Hampshire, while the children remained behind at Duxbury, though

Anna wrote separate letters to the three eldest in late September (AIK 2876, 2884, 2886). 33:7 AIK 2823. :18 See Killorin, p. 46. :25 *BV*, p. 166. :32 In this Eliot-influenced poem, which appears dedicated to redeeming the parade of maternal replacements clogging his unconscious, Aiken early on identifies the house of the title as "the house I lived in; / The house you lived in, the house that all of us know" (*CP*, p. 120). In his *New Poets from Old* (New York, 1940), Henry W. Wells characterizes the entire poem as "a morbid inversion of the optimistic poetry of *Song of Myself*" (p. 297). 35:1 BBC II, p. 6. :2 Peterson, p. 23. :13 *BV*, pp. 134–35. :22 In Thomas Hughes, *Tom Brown's School Days* (New York: A. L. Burt, n.d.), the sixth edition of which appeared in the early 1900s, the epigraph is credited to a "Ballad." Hogan played Flashman's part in Conrad's childhood, a role perhaps unconsciously assigned to Eliot at times in later years, just as Aiken at times appeared to play Ignatz to Eliot's Krazy. :24 *Ushant*, p. 108. Despite Hickok, II, p. 47, it was probably Rev. Potter's *Twenty-Five Sermons of Twenty-Five Years* (Boston, 1886), not his posthumously published *Lectures and Sermons* (Boston, 1895), that he copied—see Olson, p. 23. :38 Patricia Reynolds Willis, "Unabashed Praise of a Poet," *Georgia Review* 21 (Fall 1967): 374. Since Willis's article was published, the DeSoto has been torn down, replaced by a monstrously modern Hilton. Playing hooky must have been a relatively rare gamble in view of Conrad's success at school and the teachers' easy access to the Aiken household. 36:1 *BV*, p. 165. :4 Anna Aiken's letter of Nov. 28, 1900, mentions Conrad getting into two "scrapes" and not being "allowed to go away from the front of the house for 2 weeks in consequence" (AIK 2908). :15 41 (1890): 352. As Anna Aiken's final letters document, social debts and her own delight in card parties made the Savannah social scene irresistible. :21 See AIK 2827–60. :35 In a June 6, 1900, letter (AIK 2901), Anna Aiken reports on the pleasure and pride Conrad experienced over being taken to Barnesville to see the eclipse (May 28) and being named in Dr. Aiken's article—another example of the extreme fluctuations in his father's treatment of him at this point. 37:3 *Savannah Morning News*, Feb. 28, 1901, p. 10. AIK 2904 indicates July 21 as their departure date. :20 AIK 2826. :31 See AIK 2907. :37 *Savannah Morning News*, Feb. 28, 1901, p. 10. 38:5 Ibid. :19 Aiken later believed that Dr. Charleton's oddly unresponsive behavior might be explained by a drug or alcohol problem—his daughter Julie was Elizabeth's teacher this year (see AIK 2906). 39:10 *BV*, p. 147. :18 *Savannah Morning News*, Feb. 28, 1901, p. 10. :26 Summarized in ibid. :30 The story is reshaped in "Strange Moonlight." As shown in AIK 2902, Anna Aiken did attend the school ceremonies: "It was given him with quite an oration by one of the speakers of the occasion. . . . When Conrad went up to the platform to get the medal everyone clapped and cheered and I felt very proud indeed!" :36 *BV*, p. 187. :37 Jane Aiken Hodge was interviewed at her home in Lewes, England, Mar. 27, 1978. Unless otherwise indicated, all quotes are from this source. 40:11 *SL*, p. 310. :21 Letter to the author, July 23, 1979. :29 Robert Taylor read the letter during our interview. 41:4 *BV*, p. 127. :6 Confirming the intermittent quality of Dr. Aiken's breakdown, the children's lives remained undisturbed. Robert was ill again, but Conrad, Elizabeth, and Kempton were back at school, and Conrad and Elizabeth were also attending a dancing school three times a week—see AIK 2906 and 2907. :10 Clippings of the articles are among the "Ephemera" (Box 1–41) at HL, as is a report from the *Savannah Morning News* (June 3, 1900) about his theory, which also promises to publish his actual paper in a few days. :22 *Savannah Morning News*, Feb. 28, 1901, p. 10. Dr. Aiken's depression must have been intensified by the death next door of his friend Dr. Duncan from a stroke, the Duncan house having always been open to the Aiken children. Dr. and Mrs. Aiken went to the funeral in the middle of December— see AIK 2910. :31 *Savannah Morning News,* Feb. 28, 1901, p. 10. :36 Dr. Aiken's paranoia gained more fuel when Emily Akin mistook Anna's request for a record of Dr. Duncan's career as a request for information on her son. In a return letter, Jan. 26, 1901, Anna notes that the "mistake has caused us much trouble and distress," the same letter in which she mentions Conrad being "home from school for a week with a knee injury—hurt playing football" (AIK 2911). :41 See also Anna Aiken's letter of Feb. 14 (AIK 2912). 42:4 *Savannah Morning News,* Feb. 28, 1901, p. 10. :10 Letter to the author, Sept. 14, 1981. :13 Lawrence, p. 326. :17 See also AIK 2911. :20 *Savannah Morning News,* Feb. 28, 1901, p. 10. 43:11 "Ephemera" (Box 79). 44:1 *BV,* p. 147. :4 AIK 2945. The poem was printed uncut in the *Savannah Morning News,* Feb. 28, 1901, p. 10. :20 Olson, pp. 5–13, discusses the impact of his father's poetry on Aiken's imagination, concluding that a "somatic, vascular base is common to the erotic metaphors of both" (p. 7). See AIK 2919–82 for examples of other poems by Dr. Aiken. :24 See AIK 2913. Anna's last letter, which evinces nothing but compassion for Dr. Aiken's condition, also proudly proclaims that Conrad had achieved first place in his arithmetic and geography classes and "good marks in everything." :27 *Savannah Morning News,* Feb. 28, 1901, p. 10. 45:4 BBC II, pp. 1–2. 46:14 *BV,* p. 178. :18 *Savannah Morning News,* Feb. 28, 1901, p. 10. :36 *Children of the Mire* (Cambridge, 1974), p. 42.

CHAPTER 2

47:1 Arthur Schopenhauer, *Essays and Aphorisms,* trans. R. J. Hollingdale (New York: Penguin, 1983), p. 201. :3 *DV,* p. 99. :19 *DV,* p. 146. 48.9 *BV,* p. 180. :11 See, for example, *BV,* p. 173. :16 *BV,* p. 141. :35 *Savannah Morning News,* Mar. 3, 1901. :40 Killorin, p. 47. 49:2 *BV,* p. 144. :10 Lawrence, p. 331. :17 Letter to the author, July 23, 1979. :22 *BV,* p. 84. :33 Lawrence, p. 320. :39 See *Who Was Who in America, 1897–1942* (Chicago: Marquis, 1943), p. 1219. 50:20 *BV,* p. 179. :26 *BV,* p. 155. 51:3 Letter to the author, Sept. 21, 1981. :16 BBC II, p. 5. :21 *Ethics in the Dust* (Boston: Dana Estes, n.d.), p. 136. :25 *HA* (Jan. 26, 1910), pp. 112–14. 52:17 BBC II, pp. 2, 5. :37 Letter to the author, Sept. 21, 1981. 53:15 Quoted in Ralph Hickok, "Conrad Aiken: New Bedford Revisited," *New Bedford Magazine,* Spring 1981, p. 48, cited hereafter as Hickok I. 54:9 To supplement *Ushant*'s account of Aunt Jane's household, see CA, "The Whale-ship," *Dial,* June 1927, pp. 461–69. 55:2 Peterson, p. 23. 56:2 Hickok I, p. 51. :15 Jane Aiken Hodge interview. 57:3 *SL,* p. 180. :5 BBC II, p. 5. 58:16 *Collected Works of Edgar Allan Poe: Poems,* ed. Thomas Ollive Mabbott (Cambridge, Mass.: Harvard University Press, 1969), pp. 146–46. Paz observes that "one of the most powerful and persistent currents of modern literature" has been "the taste for sacrilege and blasphemy, the strange and the grotesque, the marriage of the commonplace and the supernatural, in short, the love of irony, that great invention of the Romantics," which he defines (in Friedrich Schlegel's sense) as a "love of contradiction which lives in each of us, and awareness of this contradiction" (p. 40). :27 Mabbott, p. 326. :33 *GC,* p. 245. :35 See *GC,* pp. 240, 247, 254, 272, 274, 275. :40 Michel de Montaigne, *Essays,* trans. J. M. Cohen (New York: Penguin, 1958), p. 385. 59:4 Jean Piaget, *Play, Dreams and Imitation in Childhood* (New York, 1962), p. 172.

. . . .

:19 *The Hazlitt Sampler,* ed. Herschel M. Sikes (New York: Fawcett, 1961), p. 164.
:30 CA, "King Bolo and Others" in *T. S. Eliot: A Symposium . . .* , ed. Richard
March and Tambimuttu (Chicago: Regency, 1949), p. 20. :39 *GC,* p. 185. 60:18 *Massachusetts: A Guide to Its Places and People,* Federal Writers Project (Boston:
Houghton Mifflin, 1937), p. 202. :28 *BV,* p. 140. :37 Scribner's published Briggs's
Original Charades in 1891 and an enlarged edition in 1895. 61:5 Richard C. Evarts,
"The Class of 1903," *Cambridge Historical Society Proceedings, 1967–1969,* pp.
132–40. All quotes about Peabody are from this essay. :12 See also *Conrad Aiken: A
Bibliography (1902–1978),* ed. F. W. Bonnell and F. C. Bonnell (San Marino, 1982),
p. 129. 63:17 *GC,* p. 186. :19 *GC,* p. 185. Clarissa Lorenz, Aiken's second wife,
reports in her memoir, *Lorelei Two* (Athens, Ga., 1983), p. 4, that her husband "refused to dance" and that he once told her: "I never got over being pushed into dancing
school" (p. 21). :31 "The Child in the House," which helped mold Aiken's "On
Moving House" and is available in *Selected Writings of Walter Pater,* ed. Harold
Bloom (New York: Signet, 1974), pp. 1–16, has Florian return to the vacated home
only to find it "touched him like the face of one dead." Pater's metaphoric linking loss
of home to death stemmed, like Aiken's, from a premature loss of parents, his mother
dying when he was only two and a half, his father when he was fourteen. 65:1 Ruth
(McIntyre) Dadourian's letter to the author, Feb. 23, 1980. 113:9 *BV,* p. 210. :26
Grayson McCouch was interviewed at his West Chester, Pennsylvania, home Apr. 4,
1977. Unless otherwise indicated, all quotes are from this source. :28 Ruth (McIntyre)
Dadourian was interviewed at her West Hartford, Connecticut, home Feb. 2, 1980.
Unless indicated otherwise, all quotes are from this source. :31 *BV,* p. 210. It was
Gallagher who oversaw the "water cure" administered to Aiken in his senior year—
see *SL,* p. 330. 66:3 *The Poet's Work,* ed. Reginald Gibbons (Boston: Houghton
Mifflin, 1979), p. 59. :9 *SL,* p. 326. :12 *SL,* p. 5. 67:13 BBC II, p. 6. :18 See Bonnells,
pp. 129–31. 68:27 AIK 2874; *SL,* pp. 6–7. 71:11 Jane Delano's death certificate lists
cause of death as "General Arterial Schlerosis." :23 *GC,* p. 254. :40 The estate's
financial details were supplied by Robert Taylor. 72:13 See AIK 4423; *SL,* p. 326. :22
See *Class of 1912 CR* (1962), p. 353. 73:8 *BV,* p. 210. CL testifies: "He remembers
dreams vividly. They stand out like daily events, rich and strange" (p. 5). In a letter to
the author, July 26, 1981, she recalls that she "could only agonize over his nightmares, too many to record." :29 CA, "Gigantic Dreams," *Listener,* July 18, 1934, p.
122. According to his article, Aiken's first ether dream, presumably in Savannah, was
influenced by Lewis Carroll, resulting in a chessboard world in which all moves were
preordained "as the moves of knights and bishops." 74:9 The poems are in the first ten
pages of the Middlesex anthology, which is not listed by the Bonnells. 76:37 *BV,* p.
165. :38 See *SL,* p. 321. 77:3 *GC,* p. 208; *BV,* p. 210. :17 *GC,* p. 268. :26 Jane Aiken
Hodge has attested to her father's admiration of O. Henry, whose *Collected Works* he
kept in his Rye library. :33 *An American Anthology* sandwiched Dickinson among
almost nine hundred pages of largely unmemorable verse, but it did mark the official
"discovery" of Dickinson that had begun a decade earlier with the posthumous publication of *Poems by Emily Dickinson* (Boston: Robert Brothers, 1890). :41 Although
the final break between Freud and Jung would not occur until 1914, as early as July
1906, in a foreword to *The Psychology of Dementia Praecox,* Jung aired his reservations about Freud's heavy reliance upon sexuality and the infantile sexual trauma,
seeing psychoanalysis as only one of several possible therapeutic approaches—*The
Freud/Jung Letters,* ed. William McGuire, trans. Ralph Manheim and R. F. C. Hull

(Princeton: Princeton University Press, 1974), pp. xvii–xviii and 13–16. 80:15 *SL,* p. 330.

CHAPTER 3

81:6 Van Wyck Brooks, *An Autobiography* (New York, 1955), p. 101. :8 Larzer Ziff, *The American 1890's* (New York, 1966), p. 308. :15 Ziff, p. 313. 82:2 Ziff, p. 323. :4 CA, *Scepticisms* (New York, 1919), p. 134. :15 Richard O'Connor, *Heywood Broun* (New York: Putnam, 1975), p. 21. :21 Scholz, p. 75. :37 Peterson, p. 30. 83:4 Francis Biddle, *A Casual Past* (New York, 1961), p. 245. :7 Lyndall Gordon, *Eliot's Early Years* (New York, 1977), p. 21. See also George Santayana, *The Middle Span* (New York, 1945), p. 156. :16 Samuel Eliot Morison, *Three Centuries of Harvard* (Cambridge, 1936), p. 490. :24 Biddle, p. 220. :27 Morison, p. 418. :31 Brooks, p. 160. :41 Biddle, pp. 224–25. :13 Brooks, p. 116. :14 See Biddle, p. 226. :18 Brooks, p. 105. :29 Gordon, p. 20. :32 Biddle, p. 224. :37 Ibid. 85:7 Biddle, p. 123. :10 *The Letters of William James,* ed. Henry James (Boston: Atlantic Monthly, 1920). 2:5, cited hereafter as *LWJ.* :18 Brooks, p. 123. :21 *LWJ,* 1:166— "psychology and philosophy were never divorced from each other in his thought or his writing." Morison, p. 8, notes that James ceased teaching psychology after the publication of *Principles of Psychology* in 1890, and Bruce Kublick's *The Rise of American Philosophy* (New Haven, 1977), p. 419, points out that James kept psychology under the speculative thinkers, not the experimentalists, near the end of his Harvard tenure, reflecting a steady drift into metaphysical seas. :26 *Writers at Work: Fourth Series,* ed. George Plimpton (New York: Viking, 1976), p. 27, cited hereafter as *W at W,* unless a different series. :35 Münsterberg rejected the idea of a subconscious as a contradictory, untenable explanatory construct but would abandon the lab in favor of applied psychology in later years (without abandoning a behaviorist bias)—see Kublick, pp. 201, 213–14, 420. 86:2 *LWJ,* 1:122. :15 Biddle, pp. 122, 233. :19 Brooks, p. 120. :23 Gordon, p. 22, describes President Eliot paying a surprise visit to Santayana's class to inquire about its exclusiveness. Eliot kept Santayana in the junior ranks until 1907, when he was finally made full professor at age forty-four—see Kublick, p. 365. :29 *LWJ,* 2:16. :31 Morison, p. 20. :33 Biddle, p. 236. :37 *W at W,* p. 27. 87:5 Santayana, p. 159. :18 Brooks, p. 107. :23 From a typescript (transmission date Jan. 11, 1962) of two interviews of Aiken conducted by D. G. Bridson for the BBC in early 1962, cited hereafter as BBC Ia and Ib. :29 Quoted in Brooks, p. 240. :31 Quoted in Brooks, p. 115. 88:3 Brooks, p. 108. :13 Published by Scribner's, Wendell's *History* praises Hawthorne, appreciates the genius of *Huckleberry Finn,* has strongly mixed feelings about Whitman, ignores Dickinson, and dismisses Melville in a single sentence, which, to be fair, represented a consensus view until the middle 1920s. :24 Biddle, pp. 209, 234. :27 *TCA,* p. 1495. :33 C. David Heymann, *American Aristocracy* (New York: Dodd, Mead, 1980), pp. 168–69. :37 E. J. Kahn, Jr., *Harvard* (New York: Norton, 1969), p. 237. :41 J. Donald Adams, *Copey* (Boston, 1960), pp. 1–2, 16, 103, portrays him as "a little man with a bulbous head, topped always by a derby (in summer, a stiff-brimmed straw)," who wore checks and plaids to simulate bulk and suffered from "hypochondria and the dread of death." 89:8 O'Connor, pp. 22–23. :15 Ibid., p. 21. :25 Biddle, p. 324. :26 Brooks, p. 122. :31 Santayana, pp. 172–73; Adams sums up: "He had a sharp eye for the lonely and the ill at ease, and having himself experienced their suffering, he set tirelessly and effectively about its alleviation" (p. 132). :34 Brooks, p. 123. 90:7 CA, *The Clerk's Journal* (New York, 1971), p. 4. :9 *W at W*, p. 26. :11 Ibid.; see also Adams, p. 154. :17 For biographical data, see Rollo Walter Brown's *Dean Briggs* (New York, 1926), written with obvious affection while its subject was still alive. :28 *The Clerk's Journal*, p. 3. :31 Brooks, p. 113; Biddle praises Briggs as "a superb teacher, shrewd yet kind" (p. 223). :36 Gordon, p. 19. :39 Quoted in Millicent Bell, *Marquand* (Boston: Little, Brown, 1979), p. 72. 91:10 Brooks, p. 123. :15 See Biddle, p. 235. :30 Brooks, p. 122. 92:11 Brooks, p. 123. :21 BBC Ib, p. 2. :33 *HA*, Oct. 9, 1907, p. 29. 93:15 *HA*, Dec. 19, 1907, pp. 92–93. :19 Brooks, p. 105, recalls: "Whiskey flowed in all the circles I knew." :22 *Harvard Monthly*, Jan. 1908, p. 150. 94:7 Heymann, p. 168. :11 *HA*, Jan. 31, 1908, p. 144. :26 *HA*, Feb. 28, 1908, p. 2. 96:1 *HA*, June 1, 1908, p. 139. :13 *W at W*, p. 25. :20 Ibid. :22 *HA*, June 1, 1908, pp. 90–91. 97:18 BBC II, p. 6. 98:5 See *SL*, p. 30. :6 Ibid., pp. 32–33. :27 A fairly full account of Mariett's brief life can be found in *CR* (1936), pp. 446–48. :31 The collection was printed by Mitchell Kennerley soon after Mariett's death. Lippmann, who would visit Mariett almost every day during the last months of his life, put together the book and helped pay for its publication—see Ronald Steel, *Walter Lippmann and the American Century* (Boston, 1980), p. 55. 99:2 March and Tambimuttu, p. 2; *SL*, p. 8. :17 Gordon notes in contrast: "To most students, however, Eliot was a bit of a recluse, studiously preoccupied in his room in Russell Hall, Holyoke House, or Apley Court" (p. 20). :32 Ibid., p. 14. Eliot gave this impression himself and undoubtedly believed it at some level or another—see Peter Ackroyd, *T. S. Eliot* (New York, 1984), p. 13. Ackroyd mistakenly dates the meeting as coming in the 1909–10 school year (p. 35). :40 Information on Eliot's childhood has been gleaned from the initial chapters in both Gordon and Ackroyd. Most pertinent, perhaps, is Gordon's remark: "T. S. Eliot acknowledged that his early training in self-denial left him permanently scarred by an inability to enjoy even harmless pleasures" (p. 8). 100:8 The typescript is at the Olin Library, Washington University, St. Louis. :13 See *W at W*, p. 27. 101:12 Photos bear out the truth of the observation. :19 See, for instance, Lorenz, p. 4. :28 The letters are at HL (AIK 4373–4406) but require permission of the estate to inspect or quote. Jane Aiken Hodge, who had secured the letters for HL in the first place, kindly provided copies, which naturally lack catalog numbers. 102:4 CA to Barbara Leighton Durant, n.d., but clearly belongs to June 1908. :8 *GC*, p. 270; see Lorenz, p. 185. :12 *GC*, p. 184. 104:7 See *SL*, pp. 9–12, for an abbreviated version of the letter that appeared originally in the *New Bedford Sunday Standard*, Aug. 16, 1908. :32 CA to Durant, Aug. 10, 1908.

CHAPTER 4

106:4 See *SL*, p. 13. :14 *W at W*, p. 27. 187:4 March and Tambimuttu, p. 21. 107:2 *Writers at Work: Second Series*, ed. Van Wyck Brooks (New York: Viking, 1963), p. 93, cited hereafter as *W at W: 2*. :17 Peterson, p. 30. :24 Gordon, p. 21; Ackroyd, p. 31. 108:1 Eliot himself never took a science course at Harvard. See Gordon, pp. 19–22, 49. :24 *SL*, p. 222. :25 *Letters of Ralph Waldo Emerson*, ed. Ralph L. Rusk (New York: Columbia University Press, 1939), 4:338. :29 Brooks, p. 112. :11 See Gordon, pp. 9–13. :32 *W at W: 2*, p. 93; Gordon, p. 23. :40 Gordon, p. 25. 109:8 Not surprisingly in light of his stunted psychological growth, Aiken was also revolted by the physical reality of copulation—see *BV,* p. 293, and Lorenz, pp. 21, 167—but this never interfered with his tireless pursuit of female flesh, because his sexual energies were more intense and heterosexual than Eliot's, or at least less inhibited by fixated repressive mechanisms, though they shared an antifeminine strain in their characters, a strain their common culture and educations reinforced. :12 Gordon, p. 19. :18 According to Ackroyd, pp. 35–36, Eliot would continue to write to Babbitt to the end of the latter's life, often addressing him as "Dear Master." :27 Santayana, who had earned his Ph.D. under Royce in 1889 and published *The Sense of Beauty* in 1896, was Harvard's embodiment of and spokesman for an 1890s stance, downplaying "will" in favor of contemplation (Schopenhauer's technique) and an aesthetic concept of value —see Kublick, pp. 352–65, for a persuasive discussion of Santayana's ideas in a psychological context. :29 CA, Prefatory Note, "Anatomy of Melancholy," in *T. S. Eliot: The Man and the Work,* ed. Allen Tate (New York. Dell, 1966), p. 194. :34 Though published in 1907, James's book actually deals with a tour undertaken in 1904—see *Henry James Letters,* ed. Leon Edel (Cambridge, Mass.: Harvard University Press, 1984), 4:226–28. :37 Santayana, p. 178. 110:1 Ziff, p. 134. :6 James had previously given his lecture ("The Lesson of Balzac"), his first such, in Philadelphia—see Grant C. Knight, *The Strenuous Age in American Literature* (Chapel Hill, 1954), pp. 159–60. :10 David Perkins, *A History of Modern Poetry* (Cambridge, 1976), p. 104. See *The Poems of Trumbull Stickney,* ed. Amberys R. Whittle (New York: Farrar, Straus and Giroux, 1972), pp. 3–264. :15 *HA,* May 7, 1909, p. 80. :20 *W at W,* p. 27. :36 *HA,* Oct. 2, 1908, p. 2. For the text of Shelley's "Mutability," I used *Selected Poems,* ed. Frederick L. Jones (New York: Appleton, 1956), p. 51. 111:12 *Opus Posthumous: Poems, Plays, Prose by Wallace Stevens,* ed. Samuel French Morse (New York: Knopf, 1957), p. 218. :15 T. J. Jackson Lears, *No Place of Grace* (New York, 1981), p. 191. :26 *HA,* Oct. 2, 1908, p. 9. 112:16 *HA,* Nov. 25, 1908, pp. 67–68. :36 *HA,* Dec. 18, 1908, pp. 109–12. 113:31 *HA,* Jan. 26, 1909, pp. 136–39. 114:38 *HA,* Apr. 28, 1909, pp. 52–54. 115:28 Jay Martin, *Conrad Aiken* (Princeton, 1962), pp. 159–60. 116:8 *HA,* Jan. 26, 1909, p. 130. :30 O'Connor, p. 15. 117:6 Adams, p. 103. :7 March and Tambimuttu, p. 21. :11 Quoted in Gordon, pp. 20–21. :16 *W at W:* 2, p. 94. :21 Brooks, p. 107. :23 *W at W:* 2, p. 94. :27 *The Clerk's Journal,* pp. 4–5. 118:1 *SL,* p. 222; see also p. 57. :16 *W at W:* 2, p. 93. 119:7 March and Tambimuttu, p. 21. :13 See CA to Kempton, Dec. 28, 1948 (AIK 1931). :25 *HA,* May 7, 1909, p. 80. 120:1 March and Tambimuttu, p. 21. :6 Jane Aiken Hodge interview. :14 *CR* (1936), pp. 674–75. His father, Frank William, would teach at Harvard for thirty-five years and was a prolific author; his *Principles of Economics* (1911) became a widely used text, earning him the title "parent of modern American economic thought"—see *New York Times,* Nov. 12, 1940, p. 23. :18 CL letter to the author, 24 July 1979. :20 Class of 1912 *CR* (1922), pp. 319–21. :22 CL letter to the author, 24 July 1979. :27 Class of 1912 *CR* (1937), pp. 785–86. :29 Class of 1912, *CR* (1922), p. 26, and *CR* (1937), p. 39. :38 On Peirce, see Class of 1907, *CR* (1932), pp. 515–17. :16 Gordon, p. 29. :21 Information on Aiken's second trip to England comes mainly from two letters to Durant, July 23, 1909, and Aug. 1, 1909. 125:6 Thompson died in 1907, and his Shelley essay did not appear until two years later, as did a separate edition of *The Hound of Heaven,* which was followed in 1913 by a three-volume *Works* (published in America by Scribner's)—see John Walsh, *Strange Harp, Strange Symphony* (New York: Hawthorn, 1967), pp. 221–22, the first biography since Everard Meynell's *The Life of Francis Thompson* (London: Burns & Oates,

1913), attesting to the extraordinary decline in Thompson's reputation after World War I. :19 See Kahn, p. 265, and Morison, pp. 449–50. :28 Peterson, p. 31. :39 *HA*, Mar. 25, 1910, p. 1. 126:4 *HA*, May 20, 1910, p. 43. :14 *Exile's Return* (New York, 1956), p. 35. :25 Ibid., p. 34. 127:6 Quoted in Holly Stevens, *Souvenirs and Prophecies* (New York, 1977), p. 82. :22 *SL*, p. 194. :27 *TCA*, p. 595. :31 See Hermann Hagedorn, *Edwin Arlington Robinson* (New York: Macmillan, 1938). :37 *W at W: 2*, p. 95. 128:1 Ibid. :9 *HA*, Jan. 12, 1910, p. 104. :18 *Axel's Castle* (New York: Scribner's, 1931), p. 25. 129:4 For a balanced account of Freud's trip and reception, see Ronald W. Clark, *Freud* (New York: Random House, 1980), pp. 262–73. :17 Ernest Jones, in his *The Life and Work of Sigmund Freud* (New York: Basic Books, 1955), 2:57, credited James with this comment, but in a letter about the meeting, James wrote that Freud "made on me personally the impression of a man obsessed with fixed ideas" (*WJL*, 2:328). :19 Claudia C. Morrison, *Freud and the Critic* (Chapel Hill, 1968), p. 10. 130:13 Scholz, p. 73. :26 Quoted in John K. Hutchens, "One Thing and Another," *Saturday Review*, Dec. 20, 1969, p. 2. :27 See *SL*, pp. 144–45. :40 Santayana, p. 155. 131:8 *Three Philosophical Poets* (Cambridge, 1910), p. 20. :10 *W at W*, p. 27. :14 Ibid., p. 25. :17 See Santayana, p. 103. :20 March and Tambimuttu, p. 21. :23 BBC Ib, p. 3. 132:16 See, for instance, *The Basic Writings of Sigmund Freud*, trans. A. A. Brill (New York, 1938), pp. 310–11. :36 Morison lauds Briggs's "happy compound of naturalness and fastidiousness, of precision, humor, and grace" (p. 76). 133:6 *W at W*, p. 26. :17 Adams, p. 144. :36 *HA*, Feb. 11, 1910, pp. 124–25. 134:11 *HA*, June 15, 1910, pp. 80–82. :28 *HA*, June 30, 1910, pp. 141–42. 135:4 *The Poems of Tennyson*, ed. Christopher Ricks (New York: Norton, 1969), p. 566. :16 *HA*, Mar. 25, 1910, pp. 8–9. :20 *HA*, Dec. 20, 1909, pp. 79–82. 136:18 Martin, p. 86. :29 See Brill, p. 374. 137:29 *HA*, Oct. 26, 1909, pp. 19–20. :37 *HA*, Feb. 11, 1910, pp. 126–29. 138:38 Brill, p. 280. :40 Ibid., p. 302n. 139:14 This externalization and conversion process is a species of literary "dream-work," to be sure, as well as a psyche's basic survival mechanism, which is why Freud could so smoothly reduce literature to a form of wish-fulfillment—see Brill, pp. 307–11. 140:12 The texture of the imagery suggests fusion with the Elizabethan "music of the spheres" notion as well. :40 *The Necessary Angel* (New York: Knopf, 1951), p. 61. In *Parts of a World: Wallace Stevens Remembered* (New York: Random House, 1983), p. 9, Peter Brazeau notes that Stevens regarded Santayana as his "mentor" while at Harvard. 141:2 Morse, p. 225. :5 See Masao Miyoshi, *The Divided Self* (New York: New York University Press, 1969), for a convincing treatment of the various ways in which major Victorian writers went about reintegrating riven egos. :16 *HA*, Jan. 26, 1910, p. 114. :26 From Eliot's Introduction to Marianne Moore, *Poems* (London: Egoist, 1921). :28 *W at W: 2*, p. 93; Gordon, pp. 30, 33. :37 March and Tambimuttu, p. 21. 142:3 Letter to the author, Feb. 23, 1980. :8 See "Circe's Palace," *HA*, Nov. 25, 1908, p. 114. 143:8 Gordon, p. 33. :15 *HA*, June 24, 1910, p. 100.

CHAPTER 5

146:27 See R. W. Stallman, *Stephen Crane* (New York: Braziller, 1968), pp. 66, 218–36. :36 W. G. Tinckom-Fernandez, "T. S. Eliot, '10: An Advocate Friendship," *HA*, 1938, p. 8. Without mentioning his expulsion, Tinckom-Fernandez writes that he left Cambridge "to become a cub reporter on the New York *World*." 147:2 Brooks, pp.

153–54. :12 Stephen Crane had also lived across the street a dozen years before—see Brooks, p. 156. :15 Yeats was an intimate of John Sloan, Robert Henri, and others associated with the "new realism" school of painting, a school destined virtually to disappear after the 1913 Armory Show—see Sam Hunter, *Modern American Painting and Sculpture* (New York: Dell, 1959), pp. 28–40. :18 Richard Ellman's *Yeats: The Man and the Masks* (New York: Oxford University Press, 1948), pp. 7–20, offers a brief but acute account of the difficult father-son relationship. :20 Hunter depicts the restaurant as having a "relaxed, slightly old-fashioned atmosphere" (p. 40). Yeats had lived rent-free at 12 West Forty-Fourth Street the summer before until evicted by the landlady's husband in her absence. The Petipas sisters, who ran the restaurant and the four-story brownstone boardinghouse to which it belonged, rented him an upstairs room, where he would remain to the end of his life twelve years later—see William M. Murphy, *Prodigal Father: The Life of John Butler Yeats (1839–1922)* (Ithaca: Cornell University Press, 1978), pp. 353–54. :35 CSS, pp. 510–19. 148:21 See *Henry James Letters,* 4:354–62, and *WJL,* 2:350. :33 Quoted in Leon Edel, *Henry James: The Master, 1901–1916* (New York: Lippincott, 1972), p. 347. 149:1 Ibid., p. 351. :12 See AIK 485–86; Gordon, p. 38. According to Ackroyd, p. 20, Eliot would give his mother a copy of Bergson's *Introduction to a New Philosophy* in 1912. :15 Gordon, p. 37; Ackroyd, pp. 42–43, 309. James E. Miller, Jr.'s *T. S. Eliot's Personal Waste Land* (University Park: Pennsylvania State University Press, 1977), pp. 17–21, provides the fullest account of what is known about Jean Verdenal. AIK 487, Eliot to CA, Dec. 31, 1914, refers to sexual feelings aroused in Eliot during his Paris days that he could not bring himself to act upon. :18 T. S. Matthews, *Great Tom* (New York: Harper & Row, 1974), pp. 32–34. :29 *The Clerk's Journal,* p. 1. :35 Macmillan was engaged in publishing English translations of *The Complete Works of Friedrick Nietzsche,* vol. 11 in the series being *Thus Spake Zarathustra,* trans. Thomas Common, which appeared in 1909. 150:13 AIK 4410; SL, pp. 32–33. :24 *Essays,* p. 194. :30 *The Poems of John Keats,* ed. Jack Stillinger (Cambridge, Mass.: Harvard University Press, 1978), p. 373. 151:10 HA, Feb. 17, 1911, pp. 133–35. :29 See *Poems of John Keats,* pp. 225–26. 152:7 Ibid., p. 75. :9 *Selected Letters of John Keats,* ed. Robert Pack (New York: New American Library, 1974), pp. 55, 91. :22 HA, Jan. 27, 1911, pp. 119–21. :27 *Heart of Darkness* had been published in 1902. 153:14 Tennyson's poem, which is in Ricks, pp. 246–47, has a biblical basis but moves from unconscious depths to consciousness's self-consuming surface. :19 See *The Fictional Father: Lacanian Readings of the Text,* ed. Robert Con Davis (Amherst: University of Massachusetts Press, 1981). :30 HA, Dec. 13, 1910, p. 80. 154:11 HA, Sept. 29, 1910, pp. 6–7. :28 "Endymion: A Poetic Romance"—see *Poems of John Keats,* pp. 102–220—was published reluctantly by Keats with the admission that "there is not a fiercer hell than the failure in a great object." An allegory of the artist's pursuit of ideal beauty, it undercuts (and thus intensifies) its own premise of immortality by frequent recourse to images of death and melancholia. In reviewing Amy Lowell's biography of Keats, Aiken would say of Keats: "Death, for him, had a profoundly erotic significance—it became a symbol for consumation; and love, just as significantly, meant death" (*CC,* p. 250). 155:3 HA, June 15, 1910, p. 72. :23 *The Clerk's Journal,* p. 1. :31 Keats had stayed with the Brawnes until a few days before departing for Italy and claimed that he could face death but could not "bear to leave her"—see W. Jackson Bate, *John Keats* (Cambridge, Mass.: Harvard University Press, 1963), pp. 653, 663, 668–69. :36 *The Clerk's Journal* gives a reading and a facsimile copy of the poem, including Brigg's comments—the original is at HL (AIK 2798). 157:6 *W at W:* 2, p. 94. :8 Hutchens, 24. :9 *W at W*, p. 28. :14 In *The Waste Land*, of course, Eliot also took advantage of the stream-of-consciousness technique he so admired in *Ulysses*. 158:10 *Ushant*, p. 170. :14 Ibid., p. 171. 159:13 *SL*, p. 14. 162:38 *TCA*, p. 41. 164:34 *SL*, p. 14. 166:18 Peterson, p. 34. :24 *Ushant*, p. 179. :31 The essays on Keats and Shelley appeared in *Essays in Criticism: Second Series* (London: Macmillan, 1894), pp. 100–121 and 205–52, as did "The Study of Poetry" (pp. 1–55), which developed Arnold's concept of "touchstones" and envisioned poetry as a "criticism of life" that had to be weighed in terms of "high serious" aims. 167:32 Gordon, p. 40; Ackroyd, p. 37. :40 Gordon, pp. 18, 19, 23; Ackroyd, p. 37. 168:21 Lorenz, p. 19. 171:25 Ibid., p. 166. 172:3 Arnold would doubtless disagree. In his essay on Aurelius—*Essays in Criticism: First Series* (London: Macmillan, 1893), pp. 344–79—he deemed the Stoic emperor "perhaps the most beautiful figure in history" because he rose beyond mere self, though "a man like ourselves, a man in all things tempted as we are." 173:27 *Ushant*, p. 133. :39 See Clark, pp. 102–3 and Frank J. Sulloway, *Freud: Biologist of the Mind* (New York: Basic Books, 1979), pp. 332–33, 410. 174:36 He was the library's main buyer of books—see Morison, p. 621. 175:22 *Art and Artist* (New York, 1932), pp. 428–29. :32 *W at W*, p. 26. 176:24 March and Tambimuttu, p. 21. :33 Ibid. :38 *Life*, Jan. 15, 1965, p. 92. 177:4 March and Tambimuttu, p. 21. :13 *SL*, p. 182. :21 In *The Sacred Wood* (London, 1920), p. 158. :22 See, for instance, *Ecce Homo*, trans. R. J. Hollingdale (New York: Penguin, 1972), p. 81. In her Introduction to *Thus Spake Zarathustra*, Mrs. Forster, Nietzsche's sister, avers "it was the idea of the Eternal Recurrence of all things which finally induced my brother to set forth his new views in poetic language" (*xv*). See also *Twilight of the Idols/The Anti-Christ*, trans. R. J. Hollingdale (New York: Penguin, 1968), pp. 202–3. :30 *Thus Spake Zarathustra*, p. 100. :38 BBC Ia, p. 10. 178:2 Peterson, p. 33; *W at W*, p. 29. :13 *SL*, p. 146. :18 Piers Gray, *T. S. Eliot's Intellectual and Poetic Development, 1909–1922* (N.J.: Humanities, 1982), pp. 97–105, 143–48, is quite good on Royce's importance to Eliot in his need to abandon Bergson and embrace the Anglo-American version of Idealism represented by Royce and Bradley. :30 *The Genteel Tradition: Nine Essays by George Santayana*, ed. Douglas L. Wilson (Cambridge, Mass.: Harvard University Press, 1967), pp. 37–64. 179:12 *Ushant*, p. 204. 181:18 AIK 4411; *SL*, pp. 16–17. :23 Joan Aiken Goldstein was interviewed in her Greenwich Village home Mar. 22, 1979. Unless indicated otherwise, all quotes are from this source. :36 Lorenz, p. 73. :39 Taken from a typescript of "An Old Grad Goes Back to Harvard," which Clarissa Lorenz had written about Aiken for the *Milwaukee Journal*, June 10, 1928. 182:6 Ibid. :34 AIK 4409; *SL*, pp. 17–18.

CHAPTER 6

184:5 *TCA*, pp. 924–26. :10 In 1912 *The Everlasting Mercy* and *The Widow in the Bye Street* were published together as a single volume by Macmillan. :22 *Georgian Poetry, 1911–1912*, ed. Edward Marsh (New York: Putnam's, 1913). :34 Armstrong's poems would appear in the last volume, *Georgian Poetry, 1920–1922* (New York: Putnam's, 1923), pp. 11–22. A wealthy man, Marsh gave half of the considerable profits from the anthologies to the Poetry Bookshop and divided the other half equally among the contributors—John Lehmann, *The Strange Destiny of Rupert Brooke* (New

York, 1980), p. 70. :38 See Malcolm Bradbury, "London, 1890–1920," in *Modernism: 1890–1930*, ed. Malcolm Bradbury and James McFarlane (New York: 1976), p. 185, cited hereafter as *Mod*. :41 *Ripostes* (London: Swift & Co., 1912). 185:11 *Mod.*, p. 193. :14 For a narrative of Pound's activities from 1908 to 1912, see Noel Stock, *The Life of Ezra Pound* (New York: Pantheon, 1970), pp. 53–114. :18 See *The Selected Letters of Ezra Pound*, ed. D. D. Paige (New York: New Directions, 1971), p. 90, cited hereafter as *LEP*. :32 Joy Grant, *Harold Monro and the Poetry Bookshop* (Berkeley, 1967), pp. 39–51. :38 "The Future of Poetry," *Poetry Review*, Jan. 1912, p. 12—this was the journal's first issue. 186:4 "Credo," *Poetry Review*, Feb. 1912, p. 73. :11 With much justification, Eric Homberger believes that *Poetry*'s brief leadership service as America's modernist outlet "was due less to the efforts of Miss Monroe . . . than to the labor and good taste of her foreign editor, Ezra Pound"—see his "Chicago and New York: Two Versions of American Modernism" in *Mod.*, p. 154. In her autobiography, *A Poet's Life* (New York, 1969), Monroe rates Vachel Lindsay as "perhaps the most gifted and original poet we ever printed" (p. 279). :24 See Monroe, pp. 117, 124, 139, 143. :33 Ibid., pp. 222–23, 243–44. :39 Ibid., pp. 251–52. 187:10 *LEP*, p. 9. :14 Ibid. Several years later, when Tagore won the Nobel Prize, Pound was less enthusiastic—see *LEP*, p. 106. :19 Ibid., p. 11. :29 *Modern American and British Poetry* (New York: Harcourt, Brace, 1923), p. 252. :39 Written in January 1913, the letter is quoted by Monroe (p. 307) and reprinted in *SL*, pp. 21–23. The original is at JRL. 188:13 AIK 4408; *SL*, p. 19. 189:4 Text from *Earth Triumphant and Other Tales in Verse* (New York, 1914). :37 Letter to the author, Oct. 6., 1980. 190:38 *SL*, pp. 23–24. 191:9 See Nicolas Slonimsky, *Baker's Biographical Dictionary of Musicians* (New York: Schirmer, 1978), p. 362. :16 AIK 4412; *SL*, p. 20. :27 CA to Eliot, Feb. 23, 1913; *SL*, p. 26. :36 CA to McCouch, Mar. 5, 1913; *SL*, p. 28. :40 AIK 4414; *SL*, p. 28. 192:13 "Youth" was in *Earth Triumphant*, pp. 69–131. 193:2 BBC Ia, p. 10, affirms his passion for Beethoven and Strauss's tone poems. :5 See Murray Schafer, "Ezra Pound and Music," in *Ezra Pound: Twentieth Century Views*, ed. Walter Sutton (Englewood Cliffs: Prentice-Hall, 1963), pp. 129–41. :25 See "Movements, Magazines and Manifestos" in *Mod.*, pp. 192–205. 194:14 AIK 4412; *SL*, p. 21. :30 *SL*, p. 26. :39 *Earth Triumphant*, p. 212. 195:2 BBC Ia, p. 5. :7 *SL*, pp. 29–31. :28 AIK 4412; *SL*, pp. 31–34. 197:8 Tillinghast's death certificate lists his age as fifty-nine. Morison notes that his library career covered thirty-one years, complimenting Tillinghast's "unstinted labor freely given in spite of failing health" (p. 616). :19 Jane Aiken Hodge interview. :25 *SL*, pp. 34–36. 198:11 Tinckom-Fernandez, 48. :22 Class of 1912 *CR* (1961), p. 780. :25 Killorin, 37. :30 George Boas was interviewed at his Baltimore home, Apr. 14, 1977. :36 In a letter to the author, Sept. 21, 1979, Boas recalls that "when Eliot was with us, we talked philosophy (to Conrad's chagrin!)." Another letter, July 20, 1979, concludes: "A. was not gifted philosophically." :37 Russell was at Harvard for a lecture series and had semiadopted Eliot—see Sandra Jobson Darroch, *Ottoline* (New York: Coward, McCann & Geoghegan, 1975), pp. 136–37; Ackroyd, p. 50. Eliot took a course in symbolic logic with Russell. 199:1 Quoted in Killorin, pp. 38–39. :3 In later years, Aiken spoke to Ted R. Spivey with deep feeling about Santayana's influence "on his thought and work and even spoke of an influence Santayana had at the time on T. S. Eliot but which Eliot was careful to cover up"—see Spivey's "The Life of Reason," *Southern Quarterly* 21 (Fall 1982): 152–53. :6 Boas letter to the author, July 20, 1979: "Since I didn't know the meaning of either the term or the acts it referred to . . . I wasn't much enlightened. (Eliot after some awkward questions on my part got me to read Havelock Ellis)." Kublick reports that Harvard students tended to regard Santayana as an "unconscious homosexual" (pp. 765–66). :19 Killorin, 37. 200:4 I have used the text in *Earth Triumphant,* pp. 167–82. :20 Lippmann's "Freud and the Layman" in the *New Republic,* Apr. 17, 1915, would be one of the earliest and most intelligent defenses of Freud's theories published in America. 201:2 *SL,* pp. 36–37. :24 CA to Monroe, Sept. 23, Oct. 3, 1914, at JRL. :25 in BBC Ia, p. 9, Aiken explains: "I inverted my name, called myself D'Arnoc . . . and had this group sent to Harriet Monroe in a roundabout way." A copy of the original submission is at JRL. 202:1 Tinckom-Fernandez, 7. :8 Monroe, pp. 275–76. :13 *Des Imagistes* was published by the Boni brothers as a special issue of Kreymborg's *Glebe* magazine. 203:17 AIK 4423; *SL,* p. 39. :24 March and Tambimuttu, p. 22. :41 BBC Ia, p. 6. 204:11 Ibid., p. 7. :24 Aiken's visit was recorded by Marsh in his journal—see Christopher Hassall, *Rupert Brooke: A Biography* (New York: Harcourt, Brace, 1964), p. 454. :27 Jean Gould, *Amy* (New York, 1975), p. 122. :31 *TCA,* p. 351. 205:32 Quoted in Grant, p. 101. :34 BBC Ia, p. 6. 206:6 Quoted in *Mod.,* p. 186. :18 Pound's essay on "Vorticism" first appeared in the *Fortnightly Review,* Sept. 1, 1914, pp. 461–71. :37 Richard Aldington, *Life for Life's Sake* (New York, 1941), p. 110. :41 Ibid., p. 104. 207:11 Gould, p. 125. :24 Aldington complains: "Ezra was a bit of a czar in a small but irritating way, and he had the bulge on us, because it was only through him that we could get our poems into Harriet Monroe's *Poetry*" (p. 134). :28 Gould, pp. 136–37. :38 See Monroe, p. 276. 208:3 BBC Ia, p. 7. :6 Ibid., 8. :16 Quoted in Ibid. The circular is at HL. :26 Eliot to CA, July 19, 1914 (AIK 488); July 25, 1914 (AIK 489). 209:5 *W at W: 2,* p. 47. :12 See *LEP,* pp. 40, 41, 50, 57; *The Autobiography of William Carlos Williams* (New York: New Directions, 1951), p. 146; and John Unterecker, *Voyager: A Life of Hart Crane* (New York: Farrar, Straus, and Giroux, 1969), p. 260. :17 Charles Norman, *Ezra Pound* (New York, 1960), p. 166. :32 Brooke condemned the Bloomsbury intellectuals as "dehumanized, disgusting people . . . mostly pacifists and pro-German"—see Lehmann, p. 118. 210:6 For a thorough account of Frost's career in England, see Lawrence Thompson, *Robert Frost: The Early Years, 1874–1915* (New York: Holt, Rinehart, Winston, 1966), pp. 392–468. Pound's reaction to Frost is in *LEP,* pp. 20–21. 211:32 Gould, p. 136.

CHAPTER 7

213:1 See Lehmann, pp. 141–49. :16 See J. B. Harner, *Victory in Limbo* (New York, 1975), pp. 42–43. :24 Dell, p. 213. 214:6 Samuel Eliot Morison, *The Oxford History of the American People* (New York: Oxford University Press, 1965), pp. 904–8, cited hereafter as *HAP.* :12 *Letters from America* (New York, 1916), p. 84. :16 Ibid., p. 86. :22 *HAP,* p. 897. :32 Knight, p. 196, charts the rise in American divorce rates from twenty-five thousand in 1886 to seventy-two thousand by 1906, twice the rate of the rest of "the Christian world," and affirms it as largely an urban statistic. :38 Erik H. Erikson, *Childhood and Society,* 2d ed. (New York, 1963), p. 285. 215:2 Cleveland Amory, *The Proper Bostonians* (New York: Dutton, 1947), p. 356, describes the Harvard Club as "a bulwark of Boston society." :19 Sherwood Anderson, *Memoirs* (New York, 1942), p. 241. :26 Alfred Kreymborg, *Troubador* (New York, 1925), p. 198. :35 Hickok I, p. 51. :41 Malcolm Cowley was interviewed at his Sherman, Connecticut, home Apr. 15, 1977. 216:20 Biographical information comes from the Introduction to *The William Stanley Braithwaite Reader,* ed. Philip Butcher (Ann Arbor, 1972). :33 Ibid., p. 1. :38 He would produce the volumes until 1929. 217:10 See Amory, p. 332. Aiken's letters to Braithwaite are at Harvard's Houghton Library (bMS Am 1344). :18 See Butcher, pp. 41, 86–87, 107, 109, 223, and letter to the author, May 15, 1981. Pound was more open in his prejudice, referring to Braithwaite in a letter to Monroe (Dec. 1, 1911) as "the coon"—*LEP,* p. 66. 218:6 AIK 487. :15 Armstrong to CA, Oct. 11, 1914 (AIK 47). :29 See AIK 490–91. 219:6 AIK 4423; *SL,* p. 39. 220:14 Lorenz, pp. 21, 167. :35 The letter is partially reprinted in *SL,* pp. 40–41. 221:29 "*Apologia Pro Specie Sua,*" *Scepticisms,* p. 25. The essay is also in *CC,* pp. 25–34. 222:5 *New York Sun,* May 9, 1915. :8 S. Foster Damon, *Amy Lowell: A Chronicle* (Boston: Houghton Mifflin, 1935), pp. 308–9. :20 *Poetry Journal,* July 1915, pp. 233–41. :28 Quoted in Heymann, p. 229. :36 Quoted in Monroe, pp. 308–10. 223:8 *SL,* pp. 41–42. :26 Biographical information on Fletcher comes from Edna B. Stephens, *John Gould Fletcher* (New York: Twayne, 1967), pp. 13–14, 17–27, and his autobiography, *Life Is My Song* (New York, 1937). :37 Stephens, p. 20. 224:30 Quoted in Monroe, p. 277. :41 Ibid., p. 322. 225:25 Fletcher, p. 208. :27 Ibid., p. 225. 226:21 Aiken was probably alluding to an editorial he published in the *Poetry Journal,* Sept. 1915, pp. 31–34, entitled "Fertilizing Poetry." 227:13 Quoted in Stephens, pp. 65–66. :32 Fletcher, p. 208. 228:3 Ibid., p. 226. :8 Butcher, p. 109. :9 The letter is at JRL. :22 *GC,* p. 241. :26 John Bowlby, *Sadness and Depression* (New York, 1980), pp. 289, 295. :29 See ibid., pp. 301–7. As Bowlby indicates in *Separation* (New York, 1973), p. xiii, along with "various forms of acute or chronic anxiety and depression" goes that restlessness and inability to love conceded by Aiken in *Blue Voyage* and elsewhere, "difficulties of every degree in making and maintaining close affectional bonds, whether with parent figures, with members of the opposite sex, or with own children." :32 See R. R. Grinker et al., *The Borderline Syndrome* (New York, 1968), and Otto F. Kernberg, *Borderline Conditions and Pathological Narcissism* (New York, 1975). In *The Analysis of Self* (New York, 1971) and *The Restoration of the Self* (New York, 1977), the controversial Kohut challenged prevailing psychoanalytic doctrine by stressing the value of narcissim when transformed into higher cultural activities and achievements such as creativity and, ultimately, wisdom. This view represents an impossible therapeutic aim and path for most post-Freudians, especially Kernberg, since they believe that narcissism cannot be separated from object relations without grave danger, that narcissism entails a libidinal investment in a pathological self-structure. Besides illuminating the dynamic of creativity, Kohut's major contribution perhaps resides in his recognition that the narcissistic borderline condition has emerged as our society's signature illness, excepting actual schizophrenia. In a final response to his critics, which can be found in the posthumously published *How Does Analysis Cure?* ed. Arnold Goldberg (Chicago: University of Chicago Press, 1984), pp. 1–46, Kohut tellingly designates "disintegration anxiety" as "the deepest anxiety man can experience" (p. 16). :37 Klein's work with children convinced her that creativity stemmed from the desire to repair damage (imagined or wished) done to the mother—see esp. her "Infantile Anxiety Situations Reflected in a Work of Art and in the Creative Impulse" in *The Creative Imagination,* ed. Hendrik M. Ruitenbeek (Chicago: Quadrangle, 1965), pp. 55–66 and in her *Love, Guilt and Reparation and Other Works, 1921–1945* (New York, 1984), pp. 210–18. She also concluded, *contra* Freud's psychosexual schema, that the Oedipal conflict began in the middle of the child's first year. Simon Stuart's *New Phoenix Wings* (New York: RKP, 1979) provides an interesting demonstration of how the Kleinian reparation paradigm can be applied to literary artifices, working best, I think, with Wordsworth. :41 See Neal H. Bruss, "Lacan and Literature: Imaginary Objects and Social Order," *Massachusetts Review,* Spring 1981, pp. 62–92, for a lucid survey of Lacan's efforts to integrate Freudian psychology with language acquisition and symbolic (literary) expression, particularly strong on the central part played by the "mirror stage," when language aids the child's escape from the mental prison constructed around his inability to distinguish between the real and the imaginary. 229:5 Pack, pp. 113, 178. :18 Elmer Gertz, *Odyssey of a Barbarian: The Biography of George Sylvester Viereck* (Buffalo: Prometheus Books, 1978), p. 126. :18 Ibid., pp. 67, 122–23. :27 Francis Russell, *The Great Interlude* (New York, 1964), pp. 10–11. :37 *Anthology of Magazine Verse for 1915* (Boston, 1915), p. xxii. :39 *Drift and Mastery* (New York, 1915). For the text of Brooks's volume, I used *Three Essays on America* (New York, 1970), which also contains *Letters and Leadership* (1918) and "The Literary Life in America" (1921). 230:14 In *Van Wyck Brooks* (New York, n.d.), p. 138, Raymond Nelson identifies 1918 as the year when Bourne would introduce Brooks to Freud and Jung, but this obviously does not rule out an earlier case of unconscious intellectual osmosis. :21 Quoted in Van Wyck Brooks, *Fenollosa and His Circle* (New York: Dutton, 1962), pp. 304–5. Brooks first met Bourne in 1918. :34 *Homecoming* (Port Washington, 1969), p. 291. :35 Dell's analyst was Dr. Samuel A. Tannenbaum, to whom he would dedicate *The Briary Bush*—see Clark, p. 414, and Morrison, pp. 31, 120–22. *HAP,* p. 907, tallies five hundred practicing psychoanalysts in New York City by 1916. Anent the impact of Freud on the radicals connected with the *Masses,* see Leslie Fishbein, *Rebels in Bohemia* (Chapel Hill: University of North Carolina Press, 1982), pp. 83–93. :39 Quoted in John Moreau, *Bourne* (Washington, D.C., 1966), p. 44. Mencken charged Nietzsche with having "poisoned" the German universities—*Letters of H. L. Mencken,* ed. Guy J. Forgue (New York: Knopf, 1961), p. 51, cited hereafter as *LHM.* :24 Morrison, p. 235. 231:9 The Jones organization was, in fact, formed in response to Brill's group, true to the factionalism and internal dissensions that characterized (and continue to characterize) the growth of the psychoanalytic movement—see Reuben Fine, *A History of Psychoanalysis* (New York, 1979), pp. 77–79, which also offers a reasonable explanation for the phenomenon. :12 Morrison, p. 17, n. 41. See also W. David Sievers, *Freud on Broadway* (1955; rpt. New York: Cooper Square, 1970), pp. 53–55. :13 Aiken first publicly gave the correct chronology of the five symphonies-in-verse in his Preface to *The Divine Pilgrim* (Athens, Ga., 1949), which contains all five. :25 "Instrumentalism" might be summarized as a pragmatic calibration of thought's function as an instrument for controlling man's environment, thus rating ideas in accordance with their function in matters of human progress and experience. The best single effort to anthologize Dewey's massive oeuvre is the two volumes of John J. McDermott's *The Philosophy of John Dewey* (New York: Putnam's, 1973). Dewey did initially defend pacifism but found it ineffective, and McDermott, 1:xxi, rightly portrays him as "a man of extraordinary personal integrity, who often risked his reputation in a defense of others." 232:4 Heymann, p. 224. 417:16 AIK 492. :34 Quoted in Gordon, p. 76. :39 CA to Tate, Mar. 3, 1965 (NL). 233:3 Pound was busy trying to find a publisher for Joyce's *The Dubliners*—see *Pound/Joyce: The Letters of Ezra Pound to James Joyce,* ed. Forrest Read (New York: New Directions, 1967), pp. 34–40, cited hereafter as *P/JL.* :40 Aiken's correspondence with Houghton over the publication of *Turns and Movies,* which extends from July 13, 1915, to July 31, 1916, is at HA. 244:9 Dadourian interview. :22 *LEP,* p. 64. :27 *Anthology of Magazine Verse for 1915,* pp. xvi–xvii. :31 Kreymborg, p. 205. :37 Ibid., p. 249. :40 See Jessie B. Rittenhouse, *My House of Life* (Boston, 1934). 235:8 Quoted in *The Letters of Robert Frost to Louis Untermeyer* (New York: Holt, Rinehart and Winston, 1963), p. 24, cited hereafter as *F/UL.* :9 See Kreymborg, pp. 156–58. :11 *F/UL,* p. 24. :16 Horace Gregory, *Amy Lowell* (New York: Thomas Nelson, 1958), pp. 140–45; Gould, pp. 173–75, 187–88. :22 Kreymborg, p. 205. :31 Butcher, p. 224. :40 Ibid. 236:15 Damon, p. 407, quotes a Mar. 30, 1917, Lowell letter: "You will be amused to hear that they have kicked me out of the Presidency of the Poetry Club and Josephine has practically come out as my avowed enemy." Lowell left and never looked back. :17 Heymann, p. 214. :19 Ibid., pp. 226–27. :34 *SL,* p. 144. :39 See Andrew Sinclair, *Jack: A Biography of Jack London* (New York: Harper & Row, 1977), pp. 220–22. 237:17 (Boston, 1916). Aiken would include only the title sequence in *CP,* pp. 3–17. :28 *A History of American Poetry, 1900–1940* (New York, 1946), p. 219. 239:25 Martin, p. 220. :28 AIK 492. :31 AIK 493. :38 BBC Ia, p. 5. 240:16 Quoted in *Fenollosa and His Circle,* p. 301. :24 Butcher, p. 257. The *Poetry Review,* with offices at 12 Chauncy Street in Cambridge, lasted from May 1916 to February 1917. 242:1 *The Little Review Anthology,* ed. Margaret Anderson (New York: Horizon, 1953), p. 21. :15 *TCA,* p. 775. :31 Kreymborg, pp. 248–49. 243:19 Kreymborg, pp. 208, 238–39. :24 See Jean Strouse, "Master of the Borzois," *Newsweek,* Sept. 27, 1982, pp. 71–72. :32 Brom Weber, *Hart Crane* (New York: Bodley Press, 1948), p. 24. :33 Ibid., p. 36. :35 For biographical background, see Jack B. Moore, *Maxwell Bodenheim* (New York, 1970), pp. 11–35. 244:13 *Child of the Century* (New York: Signet, 1955), p. 208. :16 Dale Kramer, *Chicago Renaissance, 1900–1930* (New York: Appleton-Century, 1966), is a good general history of the era and the city that nurtured it. :20 Kreymborg, p. 251. :21 Kramer dramatizes the verbal duels Hecht and Bodenheim conducted in Chicago: "Hecht was a vivid talker with flourishes of adjectives, adept at phrasemaking . . . Bodenheim was more the counterpuncher, but with a deeper hatred of the fixed order (any order) and a gift for the scaring thrust" (p. 258). In May 1920, just before leaving for London, Bodenheim would fling a charge of egocentricity back at Williams in a final letter between the two: "Like all exuberant megalomaniacs you have been ever the first to hurl the charge of self-centeredness at me"—see Paul Mariani, *William Carlos Williams* (New York, 1981), pp. 171, 793, n. 159. :34 Moore, p. 29. :39 Ibid., p. 28. 245:2 Kreymborg, pp. 248–50. :16 Ibid., p. 266. :35 Heymann, p. 265. 246:2 Ibid., p. 223. :6 *Poetry Journal,* Mar. 1916, pp. 74–77. :8 *CC,* pp. 171–72. :22 CA, *The Jig of Forslin* (Boston, 1916); *CP,* pp. 54–114. :29 In his essay on "Conrad Aiken and the Supernatural" in *Southern Quarterly* 11 (Fall 1982): 123, Douglas Robillard concludes: "For Aiken, the lamia is a vivid symbol. As woman and snake, she is at once desirable and dangerous, representing the carnal side of the dreams that men dream of the unattainable, or of the unwanted if attained." :32 Peterson, pp. 71–72. Brown, Aiken's publisher, renders a more prosaic, though not mutually exclusive, account of the name's origin, an account never disputed by Aiken: "Aiken used to come in pretty regularly, and when he was thinking about a name for *The Jig* which would not be a common name, he noted that there was a tailor on the first floor whose name was Forslin"—quoted in the Bonnells, p. 7. :40 AIK 4423; *SL,* p. 44. 247:18 Peterson, pp. 84–85. :22 Fred D. Crawford's "Conrad

Aiken's Cancelled Debt to T. S. Eliot," *Journal of Modern Literature* 7 (Sept. 1979): 416–32, isolates several specific borrowings made by *The Waste Land* and decides: "Many of Eliot's more memorable scenes, images, and lines owe much to Aiken, but the difference in Aiken's expression and Eliot's expression of the same ideas demonstrates the superior poetic genius of the latter." 248:18 *The Book Review Digest* (New York: Wilson, 1918), p. 6. :20 *Boston Transcript,* Dec. 20, 1916, p. 9. :23 *Review of Reviews,* Feb. 1917, p. 211. :26 *Nation,* Sept. 6, 1917, p. 245. :27 *New York Call,* Jan. 5, 1918, p. 15. :31 CA to Houghton Mifflin, July 31, 1916 (HA). :34 *CC,* p. 381; Mariani, p. 133. :37 *CR* (1921), p. 4. 249:5 Jane Aiken Hodge interview. :18 *Anthology of Magazine Verse for 1916,* pp. 110–18—not listed by the Bonnells. Published Feb. 28, 1917, by Macmillan, and also not listed by the Bonnells, Monroe's far too generous anthology would prove very popular. She had intended to omit Aiken, deeming him "not essential" and resenting his critical attacks, but included him at the suggestion of Edward C. Marsh at Macmillan—see Craig S. Abbot, "Publishing the New Poetry: Harriet Monroe's Anthology," *Journal of Modern Literature* 11 (Mar. 1984): 91–93. :23 Peterson, p. 85. The first English translation of *The Crowd* was in 1896, a year after its French publication as *La Psychologie des foules.* :30 Introduction to *The Divine Pilgrim.* 250:5 Frederick J. Hoffman, *Conrad Aiken* (New York, 1962), p. 86. :10 *CP,* pp. 21–25. 253:18 Lowell had been impressed by Stevens when she first read him in *Others* in 1915—see Gould, pp. 164n, 187n. 254:23 *Scepticisms,* pp. 32–47; *CC,* pp. 34–40. 255:14 *CC,* p. 43. :27 Morrison, p. 143—Morrison devotes an entire chapter to Aiken's criticism, full of appreciation and understanding, though also aware of the imprecision sometimes riding his psychological lexicon down vague alleys (pp. 142–60). :29 *Scepticisms,* pp. 133–35. See also Class of 1910, *CR* (1935), p. 219. 256:8 *Scepticisms,* pp. 126–32. :34 *CC,* pp. 120–22. 257:37 *Scepticisms,* pp. 203–4. 258:22 Ackroyd, p. 87. :27 Dell, p. 292. :32 See Morison, p. 453, and Kublick, pp. 438–42, 444–45, on the anti-German hysteria poisoning Harvard's philosophy department at the time, isolating Münsterberg from his friends and colleagues, which offers a shabby contrast to William James's sane, skeptical attitude during the Spanish-American War. See also Damon, p. 406. :40 *SL,* pp. 44–45. 259:5 *SL,* pp. 42–43. :13 *SL,* pp. 43–44. :41 *The Best Times* (New York: New American Library, 1968), p. 35. 260:9 CL letter to the author, Aug. 14, 1981. :25 *Scepticisms,* p. 179. :39 Ibid., p. 144. 261:1 Ibid., p. 158. :6 Ibid., pp. 184–85. :23 Published in New York by Macmillan. :27 *Scepticisms,* pp. 251–57. 262:10 See Untermeyer, pp. 31–44. :21 Quoted in Moreau, p. 162. :24 *LHM,* pp. 63, 130. :31 Resek, pp. 13–14. :35 Quoted in Moreau, pp. 155–56. The five antiwar essays Bourne published in *Seven Arts,* written as a response to a series of essays by Dewey in the *New Republic,* are in *War and the Intellectuals: Collected Essays by Randolph S. Bourne, 1915–1919,* ed. Carl Resek (New York: Harper and Row, 1964), pp. 3–47 and 53–64. 263:7 Gertz, pp. 151–52. Witter Bynner and Harriet Monroe also protested against Viereck's expulsion, and Padraic Colum and Shaemus O'Sheed resigned, but Theodore Roosevelt endorsed the action in a letter to the society—see George Sylvester Viereck, *My Flesh and Blood: A Lyric Autobiography with Indiscrete Annotations* (New York: Horace Liveright, 1931), pp. 297–300. *F/UL,* pp. 83–84, notes that Viereck was also dropped from *Who's Who in America.* :12 Moreau, p. 164. :25 *Creative Criticism* (New York, 1917), p. 22. All further Spingarn quotes are from this source. :40 See Moreau, pp. 128–29. 264:15 *Scepticisms,* p. 24; *CC,* p. 31.

CHAPTER 8

265:3 *Only Yesterday* (New York, 1931), p. 46. :6 The conflict between town and country was hardly a new phenomenon in America, but it had been heating up considerably, intensified by the oceanic influx of immigrants since the turn of the century, the majority of whom remained in the cities, which were streaming upward and outward to fashion modern metropolises. In his *Age of Excess* (New York, 1965), p. 365, Ray Ginger estimates that a million immigrants a year entered the United States in the period between 1900 and 1914, with the result that by 1914 "nativism was near hysteria" (p. 242). Further, increasingly, the cities "were regarded as sewers of vice, of immorality, of political corruption" (p. 288). :8 See Allen, pp. 1–45. :11 After the war, colleges were viewed as centers of communist radicalism. Even Dean Briggs was accused of letting his Radcliffe girls "go bolshevik"—see Brown, p. 228, and Morison, pp. 463–67. :17 Ginger, p. 289, thinks that the binary notion of rural purity (an old Romantic myth) and urban corruption was strongly reinforced by racial bias in the years between 1879 and 1914. :21 Quoted in Butcher, p. 228. Despite countless past services to the country, Sir Speyer had disgracefully been forced to leave England on twenty-four-hour notice because he refused to sign a loyalty oath as a matter of principle. :22 *LHM*, p. 152. In an earlier letter (Feb. 3, 1919), Mencken lamented: "Free speech is absolutely abolished in America" (p. 138). 266:2 Dell, p. 342. :9 *SL*, pp. 144–45. :20 "Biography with Letters," *Wake* 11 (1952): 26–31. 267:3 See also Lorenz, p. 6. :20 Peterson, pp. 174–75. :24 BBC Ia, p. 13. Aiken sees *Punch*'s goal as "a sort of psychological study of the pathological liar and mountebank." :33 *Scepticisms*, pp. 160–69; *CC*, pp. 136–41. 269:29 Martin, p. 98. :30 *CP*, pp. 195–222. :32 *Selected Poems*, p. 8. 271:11 When taxed by Bridson (BBC Ib, p. 11) about his use of the phrase "race memories" in connection with the hero of "Changing Mind," Aiken was patently uncomfortable. "Well, I suppose I'm using that in a somewhat Jungian sense; but not exactly. I don't know what more to say about that." :37 In BBC Ib, p. 4, Aiken insists that *Senlin* illustrates "within certain limits, the apparent disintegration of the soul or ego with which modern psychology has confronted us at a specific moment." 272:1 *Appearance and Reality: A Metaphysical Essay*, 2d ed. (Oxford: Oxford University Press, 1897), p. 404. :6 *Conrad Aiken* (Minneapolis: University of Minnesota Press, 1964), p. 13. :9 CA to Tate, Mar. 3, 1926, at NL. :23 Wallace Stevens, *The Collected Poems* (New York: Knopf, 1965), p. 28. :28 A second edition would appear in 1922. :31 Peterson, p. 194. :34 *F/UL*, pp. 104–5. 273:10 *Book Review Digest*, 1919, p. 7. :22 *Anthology of Magazine Verse for 1918*, pp. ix–xvi. :41 *New York Times*, July 7, 1918, p. 23. 274:11 On the *Masses*, see Untermeyer, pp. 31–34, 38, 171; Dell, pp. 294, 298, 310–13, 319, 231; Fishbein, pp. 24–26; 28–29. :18 *LHM*, p. 121. :19 Russell, pp. 2, 21. :21 The year before, Aiken had lumped Kilmer with the "sentimentalists, dabblers in the pretty and sweet, rhetoricians of the 'thou and thee' school"—see *Scepticisms*, p. 180. :27 Quoted in Rittenhouse, p. 122. :37 "Loading Poetry With Shrapnel," *Boston Evening Transcript*, Nov. 16. 1918, pt. 3, p. 1. 275:13 *Letters of Vachel Lindsay*, ed. Marc Chenetier (New York: Burt Franklin, 1974), p. 174. :19 This time Monroe did print his letter: *Poetry*, Jan. 1919, pp. 230–31. 277:14 Peterson, p. 44. :24 Quoted in Ibid., p. 48. :29 *CP*, pp. 1016–17. 279:12 Introduction to *Poems of Edgar Allan Poe*, ed. Dwight Macdonald (New York: Crowell, 1965), p. 14. :21 Preface to *The Divine Pilgrim*. :25 Russell, p. 28. :30 Ibid., pp. 2, 21. :33 Ibid., pp. 25–28. :35 Moore, p. 29. :41 *Fenollosa and His Circle,* p. 320. 280:3 Quoted in Moreau, p. 197. :19 Dell, p. 342. :32 *Scepticisms,* :37 Burton Rascoe, *Before I Forget* (New York, 1937), p. 357. Anderson describes Rascoe as being, despite his calm facade, "a highly nervous, sensitive man. He was easily hurt" (p. 252). :39 *CC,* pp. 122–26. 282:5 *Essays on America,* pp. 113–90. 283:4 *On Native Ground* (New York, 1942), p. 229. :12 *Exile's Return* (New York, 1956), p. 67. :18 Ibid., pp. 64–65. :33 Ibid., p. 74. 284:20 *Scepticisms,* pp. 258–71. :30 AIK 129. :35 Moore, p. 29. 285:1 *Scepticisms,* pp. 232–39. :4 AIK 130. :14 Rascoe, pp. 357–58. :32 O'Connor to CA, Apr. 26, 1919, at GAL. 286:1 CA to Monroe, Mar. 18, 1919, at JRL. :9 *CC,* pp. 126–30. 287:10 Quoted in Gordon, p. 78. :11 Ibid., p. 103. :22 *CC,* p. 183. :23 See Gordon, pp. 23–24. :27 *Coterie* 2 (Sept. 1919): 7–9. :39 *Ancient Myth in Modern Poetry* (Princeton, 1971), p. 125. 288:22 *CC,* pp. 303–6. 289:16 *The New Era in American Poetry* (New York, 1919), pp. 329–38. :34 Rascoe, p. 358. 290:5 AIK 840. :36 Mariani, p. 167. 291:2 Quoted in ibid., p. 164. :15 *CR* (1921), p. 5. :26 CL letter to the author, Jan. 24, 1982. See also Russell Fraser, *A Mingled Yarn* (New York, 1981). Like Aiken, Blackmur had attended Peabody but was expelled from high school after a quarrel with the headmaster in 1918. He is drawn by Fraser as "a lonely and unprepossessing young man whose family had come down in the world" (p. 4). :29 See, for instance, *The Expense of Greatness* (New York, 1940), pp. 199–223, and the Introduction to *The Collected Novels of Conrad Aiken,* pp. 5–11. 293:23 *GC,* p. 258. See also pp. 194, 259, 261. :33 *C,* p. 58. 294:6 Ibid., p. 231. :16 Ibid., p. 233. :25 Ibid., p. 235. :38 Ibid., p. 234. 295:20 The infant, Maidie, had been born in the Panama Canal Zone, and her father, an army officer, died in 1920, the same year Bogan would convince William Carlos Williams to write an article defending Coffey, who had been sent by a court to Matteawan, an insane asylum—see *What the Woman Lived: Selected Letters of Louise Bogan, 1920–1970,* ed. Ruth Limmer (New York, Harcourt, Brace, Jovanovich, 1973), pp. 3, 6n. :26 See *SL,* pp. 49–50—Killorin incorrectly dates the letter "1920." 296:10 See *SL,* p. 255. :25 *SL,* p. 50. :32 Russell, pp. 39–51. 297:22 AIK 911. :25 Mariani, p. 17. :34 *Scepticisms,* pp. 11–31; *CC,* pp. 25–34. 299:28 AIK 132. :35 *New York Times,* Feb. 1, 1920, p. 59. :38 *Boston Transcript,* Feb. 11, 1920, p. 6. 300:3 *Bookman,* Apr. 1920, p. 194. :6 *Dial,* Apr. 1920, p. 491.

CHAPTER 9

301:9 Class of 1912, *CR* (1937), p. 781. :14 *CR* (1936), pp. 427–28. :21 *CSS,* pp. 340–56. 303:24 *The Armed Vision* (New York, 1948), p. 121. :29 Fiedler, of course, was not without debts to D. H. Lawrence's *Studies in Classic American Literature* (1924). 304:16 See Jung's "The Mother Archetype" in *Four Archetypes* (Princeton, 1970), pp. 15–44. :20 In his 1910 essay, "A Special Type of Object Choice Made by Men," which is in *Sexuality and the Psychology of Love* (New York: 1963), Freud declares that "rescuing the mother acquires the significance of giving her a child or making one for her—one like himself, of course" (p. 57). See also "The Most Prevalent Form of Degradation in Erotic Life" (1912) in the same collection (pp. 58–70), since its discussion of "physical impotence" as an incestuous fixation on mother and sister compellingly helps explain the necessity for debasing the mother to the level of a prostitute, while also encapsulating the tragic plight of men like Aiken: "Where such men love they have no desire and where they desire they cannot love" (p. 62). :34 CL letter to the author, Nov. 5, 1981. 305:8 See *CSS*, pp. 22–32. :36 Robert Taylor interview. 306:5 AIK 48. :34 BBC Ia, p. 13. :39 *CC*, pp. 143–48. 307:33 Rascoe, p. 358. 308:4 *The Pilgrimage of Festus* (New York, 1923), pp. vii–viii; *CP*, 1023–24. :19 *CC*, pp. 115–20. Aiken's pun-sharp title for his review was "The Lucifer Brothers in Starlight." Eliot's *Athenaeum* review of Adams's autobiography resorted to a paraphrase of Arnold on Shelley: "He was seeking for education, with the wings of a beautiful but ineffectual conscience beating vainly in a vacuum"—quoted in Jay Martin, *Harvests of Change* (New York: Prentice-Hall, 1967), p. 296. :23 Knight scalpels to the psychological heart of Adams's *Education*: "At bottom it was an attempt to explain and minimize an inertia which troubled his New England conscience, a 'Hamlet' substituting the second law of thermodynamics for a father's ghost" (p. 145). :34 *The Degradation of the Democratic Dogma* (New York: Macmillan, 1920), pp. 188–89 and 211. 309:16 In Ibid., Adams sneers at women's intellectual capacity, deeming maternity their "great purpose," and warns: "As an intellectual being, as the modern feminist would make her, she has only the importance of a degraded boy, though she is far more dangerous to society than such a boy would be" (p. 112). :30 *CP*, pp. 300–363. 311:4 Millay's play, actually a play-within-a-play, was an antiwar allegory entitled *Aria da Capo*—see Jean Gould, *The Poet and Her Book* (New York: Dodd, Mead, 1969), pp. 105–6. :8 Peterson, p. 175. 314:20 *SL*, p. 92. :21 *BV*, p. 29. :37 Joyce's distaste for Freud and refusal to acknowledge any influence is recorded in Richard Ellmann, *James Joyce* (New York, 1982), pp. 85n, 546. In gathering material for this revision of his masterful biography, Ellmann discovered that Joyce had in his possession in Trieste three German pamphlets: Freud's *A Childhood Memory of Leonardo da Vinci*, Ernest Jones's *The Problem of Hamlet and the Oedipus Complex*, and Jung's *The Significance of the Father in the Destiny of the Individual*, all published (and probably read by Joyce) between 1909 and 1911 (see p. 340n). :40 quoted in Clark, p. 418. 315:33 Published by Faber and Faber (London) in 1964 as *Knowledge and Experience in the Philosophy of F. H. Bradley*. 316:1 Joseph P. Fell, *Heidegger and Sartre: An Essay on Being and Place* (New York: Columbia University Press, 1979), p. 7. See also pp. 4–12 for a concise, authoritative recapitulation of the struggle for rational verification of metaphysical meaning and identity in Western philosphy that began with Descartes's founding of modern ontological dualism—Descartes's crucial formulation came in his Second Meditation, which is in *Discourse on Method and Other Writings*, trans. F. E. Sutcliffe (Baltimore: Penguin, 1970), pp. 102–12. Aristotle's theological speculations provided an early model for Hegel's notion, since the "Final Cause" (or God) in his schema, that is, form without matter, entailed the belief that the "world is continually evolving towards a greater degree of form, and thus becoming progressively more like God"—see Bertrand Russell, *A History of Western Philosophy* (1945; rpt. New York: Simon and Schuster, 1960), p. 169. :19 There is no direct evidence that Freud read Schopenhauer before establishing his major psychoanalytic premises, but Jung (among others) detected obvious connections between his id construct and Schopenhauer's "World Will"—see Sulloway, pp. 253n, 465, and Jung's *Critique of Psychoanalysis* (Princeton, 1975), pp. 41, 74. :27 BBC Ib, p. 8. 317:1 This nutshell reprise of Nietzsche's main conclusions derives from a consideration of all his texts, but perhaps *Philosophy in the Tragic Age of the Greeks*, trans. Marianne Cowan (Chicago: Regency Gateway, 1962), which was left unfinished when madness intruded, best brings together many of his critical insights, esp. pp. 30–31, 40, 47, 54, 58, 62, 73, 79, 83, including a despairing realization that words were inadequate to climb over the wall of relations to "some sort of fabulous primal ground of things" (p. 83). :27 *The Birth of Tragedy,* trans. Walter Kaufmann (New York: Viking, 1967), p. 48; see also Killorin, 38. In *Philosophy in the Tragic Age of the Greeks,* p. 62, Nietzsche stresses art work or play as self-consuming oppositions, the artist necessarily inside and outside his creation. 318:5 Quoted in Edwin Haviland Miller, *Melville* (New York: George Braziller, 1975), p. 173. :13 *Time and Free Will,* trans. F. L. Pogson (New York: Macmillan, 1910), p. 95. :23 Ibid., p. 128. See also *Creative Evolution,* trans. Arthur Mitchell (New York: Henry Holt, 1911), pp. 199–200, which presents Bergson's theory of consciousness as the driving motive for evolution, working through matter via intellect and intuition, with man at the zenith of the evolutionary scale—Mitchell taught at Harvard and had been helped in his translation chore by William James. :37 Quoted in Eliot's review of *Ethical Studies,* which was reprinted in *For Lancelot Andrewes* (New York, 1929), p. 84. 319:6 *Appearance and Reality,* p. 73. 320:6 This contradicts the thesis of Leo Bersani's *A Future for Astyanax* (Boston: Little, Brown, 1976). Bersani traces the stages in the "deconstruction of the self" evident in literature from Racine down to recent pornography, predicating a literary assault upon any concept of a stable, logically structured self—see esp. the final chapter, "Persons in Pieces," pp. 286–315. By arguing against the civilizing value of sublimation, he seems to be aligning himself with the antirational Romanticism of Blake, Yeats, Lawrence, Jung, et al., but, in reality, his aim is much healthier than that at the societal level, since he is convinced that "an imagination of the deconstructed, perhaps even demolished, self is the necessary point of departure for an authentically civilizing scepticism about the nature of our desires and the nature of our being" (p. 313). What is missing, I think, from his elegant thesis and study is sufficient awareness of the performative self's tendency (under the awesome pressure of modern experience and knowledge) to manipulate fragmented or component egos as a personal *saving* gesture, confirmation of the creating self's ultimate distanced wholeness, despite existential dread. *The Waste Land,* for instance, did not diminish Eliot; it helped him survive a massive identity threat. :25 See *Modern American Poetry: A Critical Anthology* (1919; rev. New York: Harcourt, Brace, 1921), pp. 358–59. :31 AIK 838. 321:18 Killorin, 41. 322:27 Because of his work on Boston's public library, Sargent crossed the Atlantic a number of times between 1917 and 1921. Reine, whom he dubbed a "mysterious individual," and his sister Emily accompanied him on a 1919 voyage—see Charles Merrill Mount, *John Singer Sargent: A Biography* (New York: Norton, 1955), pp. 371–78. :31 *BV,* p. 77. :36 Quoted in Lorenz, p. 60. 323:5 *BV,* pp. 29–30. :18 *BV,* p. 179. :20 *BV,* p. 271. 324:9 *BV,* p. 29. :11 *BV,* p. 28. :21 See *BV,* p. 150. :26 *BV,* p. 151. 325:5 *BV,* pp. 166–67. :26 *TCA,* pp. 317–18. :30 Quoted in *TCA,* p. 317. 326:5 Virginia Woolf had come to feel an affectionate awe for Eliot and his "formal and even heavy" locutions—*The Letters of Virginia Woolf,* ed. Nigel Nicolson (New York: Harcourt, Brace, Jovanovich, 1976), 2:295, cited as *LVW* hereafter, with year of publication in parentheses if a different volume. :9 See *SL,* pp. 50–54. :37 Darroch, p. 235. Darroch also notes that Lady Morrell's friendship with Eliot was "probably the closest and most genuine" (p. 233). 327:14 *Mercury* (London), Nov. 1920, p. 10. :18 *Dial,* June 1920, p. 733. :31 *BV,* pp. 175–76. :41 See *SL,* p. 146. 328:8 *SL,* p. 55. 329:12 *The Diary of Virginia Woolf,* ed. Anne Olivier Bell (New York: Harcourt, Brace, Jovanovich, 1978), 2:66, cited hereafter as *DVW,* with publication year in parentheses if a different volume. :27 The Hogarth's second publication was *Prelude,* a Mansfield story, and comments in her letters after Mansfield's death intimate something of Woolf's real feelings for her rival—see *LVW* (1978), 3:8, 9, 17–18. A diary entry (May 31, 1920) depicts Mansfield as "of the cat kind: alien, composed, always solitary and observant" (2:44). 330:4 *The Use of Poetry and the Use of Criticism* (London: Faber and Faber, 1964), p. 154. :12 *CC*, p. 26. 331:8 *Athenaeum*, Aug. 20, 1920, p. 235. :16 *Collected Essays* (New York: Bantam, 1960), p. 96. :23 *BV*, p. 290. :37 *SL*, pp. 55–56. 332:7 Ibid., pp. 57–58. :18 Ibid., pp. 59–60. 333:4 Letter to the author, May 3, 1983. :13 Ibid. :28 Letter to the author, Aug. 1, 1980. :33 Jane Aiken Hodge interview. :36 BBC II, p. 3. 334:4 Letter to the author, May 3, 1983. :19 CL letter to the author, July 26, 1981. :32 *Letters of Sigmund Freud*, trans. Tania Stern and James Stern (New York: Basic Books, 1975), p. 358. :33 See Aldo Corotenuto, *A Secret Symmetry* (New York: Pantheon Books, 1982), pp. xvi, 16, 20, 21, 29, 49, 146, 147–49. :37 See Clark, pp. 430–33. 335:10 See Nelson, pp. 152–54. :19 *CC*, pp. 172–76. :36 Killorin, 36. 336:37 *Knowledge and Experience*, p. 169. 337:22 Karen Horney, *The Neurotic Personality of Our Time* (New York, 1937), p. 26. Besides calculating the "exorbitant price" a neurotic pays in terms of a fundamental impairment of the capacity to achieve and enjoy life, Horney defines two basic characteristics of all neuroses as "a certain rigidity in reaction and a discrepancy between potentialities and accomplishment" (p. 22). :34 *The Twenties: American Writing in the Postwar Decade* (1949; rev. New York: Collier, 1962), p. 234. 338:9 See *SL*, p. 62. :15 *Literary Review* (Apr. 23, 1921): 4. :19 *Freeman* (Apr. 13, 1921): 117. :23 *Dial*, June 1921, p. 700. :26 AIK 747. :31 *New Republic*, Sept. 28, 1921, p. 139. :37 *Bookman*, Aug. 1921, p. 547. 340:20 See *SL*, p. 60. :28 Arthur S. Link, *American Epoch* (New York, 1958), pp. 241–44. Link discloses that certain industrialists fanned the flames of the Red Scare to discredit strike leaders and break unions.

CHAPTER 10

341:1 According to Ashley Brown, "An Interview with Conrad Aiken," *Shenandoah* 15 (Autumn 1963): 36, Aiken had read and much admired ("A brilliant little book") *The Freudian Wish and Its Place in Ethics* (New York: Henry Holt, 1915) by Edwin Holt, a Harvard don, which limns the Freudian ethic as "a literal and concrete justification of the Socratic teaching" (pp. 140–41), insisting that "morals evolve and develop; they grow and are part of the general growth and evolution of the universe" (p. 148). :11 Quoted in J. P. Stern, "The *Weltangst* of Oswald Spengler," *Times Literary Supplement* (London), Oct. 10, 1980, p. 1149. Spengler's father had died at a young age and his mother, crippled from birth, was apparently a hateful hypochondriac, helping the son to realize early that the "fear of their waking state that overwhelms children is something no adult experiences in the darkest hours of his life." 342:15 BBC Ia, pp. 9–10. :25 *Psychoanalytically Oriented Criticism of Three American Poets* (Rutherford, N.J., 1970), p. 222. :33 *CP*, p. 370. 343:1 *CP*, pp. 371–72. :2 Peterson, p. 202. :21 *Century Magazine*, June 1921, pp. 198–201; *CP*, pp. 363–69. 345:11 *Coterie* (Easter 1920): 12–13. :28 I used the text in *Priapus and the Pool and Other Poems* (New York, 1925), pp. 99–136. 347:19 See *SL*, p. 64. 348:24 There is a Desmarest mentioned in *Moby-Dick* (New York: New American Library, 1980), p. 261, a naturalist mocked for getting his illustrations of "authentic abortions" from a "Chinese drawing." :25 *BV*, p. 275. 349:1 *SL*, p. 64. :22 Ackroyd, pp. 115–16. :29 Lady Ottoline had recommended Vittoz—Ackroyd, p. 115. See also "Abulia and the

Journey to Lausanne" in Leon Edel, *Stuff of Sleep and Dreams* (New York: Harper & Row, 1982), pp. 164–91. Abulia was another name for the inertia Eliot shared with Henry Adams and other members of his class, country, and generation—"like Hamlet—or like Henry James—he could not act physically" (p. 173)—but Edel's keen analysis of its roots is curiously timid at the individual threshold, though culturally accurate enough. 350:3 See *SL*, p. 63. :17 Letter to the author, May 29, 1983. :19 Letter to the author, June 6, 1981. :21 See *SL*, p. 63. :26 AIK 928; *SL*, p. 62. :29 *SL*, p. 65. 351:5 *CC*, pp. 291–93, 293–97. :10 *SL*, p. 64. :25 Lorenz, p. 37. 352:5 AIK 929; *SL*, pp. 65–66. :25 Ibid. :27 See *CC*, p. 49. :37 See Henry James, *Hawthorne* (London: Macmillan, 1909). This title in the English Men of Letters series was first published in 1879. 353:10 Tate, p. 194. :26 Ibid., p. 195. 354:4 Ackroyd, p. 108, accepts Aiken's mistaken sequence of events, but Gordon (p. 160n) does not; the time (winter 1920–21) seen as correct, though coming after the Lausanne stay and *The Waste Land*'s composition. :21 Gordon notes a desire on Eliot's part (as he informed his mother) to write a sequel to *The Waste Land*, "a more optimistic poem about the coming of the grail" (p. 117), but Ackroyd indicates that by mid-1923 he would be at work on "Sweeney Agonistes" (p. 135). 355:27 See esp. "Nature" in Ralph Waldo Emerson, *Essays: First and Second Series* (Boston: Houghton-Mifflin, 1883), pp. 161–88, where nature is reduced to a "vast trope." In "Compensation," Emerson proclaims: "All things are moral. That soul which within us is a sentiment, outside of us is a law" (p. 99). :31 *The Education of Henry Adams* (Boston: Houghton-Mifflin, 1961), p. 455. :39 *CP*, pp. 373–76. 356:12 *CC*, pp. 163–67. :25 *Letters of Sigmund Freud*, p. 332. Freud's own essay on Dostoevsky was written in 1928—see "Dostoevsky and Parricide" in *Character and Culture* (New York, 1963), pp. 274–93. :32 *CP*, pp. 377–80. 357:38 Aiken had reviewed Waley's translations in 1919, revealing a familiarity with two other volumes of Chinese verse as well—see *CC*, pp. 377–80. 358:19 *BV*, p. 224. :20 *BV*, p. 249. :25 *BV*, p. 241. :31 See AIK 933; *SL*, pp. 68–69. :38 Ibid. 359:23 Letter to the author, June 6, 1981. :26 Letter to the author, May 29, 1983. :28 See *SL*, p. 71. 360:4 The most recent biography of Nash is Andrew Causey's *Paul Nash* (Oxford: Oxford University Press, 1980). Lorenz portrays Nash as "a blue-eyed, black-haired aesthete wearing a fancy cravat and quizzical smile" (p. 89). :32 See Lorenz, pp. 89–90. :38 Letter to the author, June 6, 1981. 361:7 Cowley, p. 214. :9 *Scribner's Magazine*, Jan. 1931, pp. 84–86. 362:7 Letter to the author, May 29, 1983. According to John Aiken, the poem was found and is at HL. :16 Letter to the author, May 29, 1983. :25 Letter to the author, June 6, 1981. 363:6 See *SL*, pp. 66–67. :16 AIK 861. :22 See *SL* pp. 66–67. 364:4 CA, "A Letter from Vachel Lindsay," *Bookman*, Mar. 1932, pp. 598–601. :23 AIK 748. :30 AIK 2727. :40 AIK 2728. 365:16 AIK 861. 366:11 Amy Lowell, *Complete Poetical Works* (Boston: Houghton Mifflin, 1955), pp. 389–434. 368:14 Fletcher, p. 302. See also AIK 863. :17 See Linscott to CA, Aug. 28, 1922, at HA. :32 AIK 931. :39 AIK 933. 370:4 *SL*, p. 72. :13 See *SL*, pp. 69–71. :30 AIK 2111. :37 *SL*, pp. 69–71. 371:9 The incident with Lowell, which was probably only the second time they met, is covered in Gould, p. 324; Heymann, p. 263; and Damon, pp. 618–20. According to Damon, Lowell felt the pamphlet had made a "permanent enemy" of Aiken. :19 See *SL*, pp. 71–72. :24 *John Freeman's Letters*, ed. Gertrude Freeman and John Squire (London: Macmillan, 1936), pp. 17–18. :31 Letter to the author, May 29, 1983. :34 Jane Aiken Hodge interview. :37 See *SL*, pp. 71–72. 372:9 Letter to the author, Apr. 27, 1979. :11 *Modern American Poets* (London, 1922), pp. v–viii. 373:1 *SL*, p. 72. :12 Williams was convinced that French influences were wrecking American poetry and that "the world has fucked itself with Freud too long"—see Mariani, p. 181. :36 Quoted in Killorin, 33. 374:10 *SL*, p. 92. :25 BBC Ia, p. 14. 375:1 *CP*, pp. 397–442. :37 Chaucer's *The Parlement of Foules—The Complete Works of Geoffrey Chaucer*, 1, ed. Walter Skeat (Oxford: Oxford Univ., 1899), pp. 335–59—clearly influenced this section. Chaucer's allegory, framed by a dream, is concerned with all aspects of love. Nature and Chaucer observe the birds choose their mates, which occasions much debate. 378:23 Quoted in Killorin, 34. 379:11 BBC Ia, p. 14. :21 Killorin, 32. 380:18 Quoted in Ronald Hayman, *Kafka* (New York: Oxford University Press, 1981), p. 272. 381:1 See *CC*, pp. 293–97. :2 *CC*, pp. 46–49. :5 *CC*, pp. 49–53. 383:19 *CC*, pp. 53–68. 384:36 *The Philosophy of Literary Form* (Berkeley and Los Angeles: University of California Press, 1973), p. 17. 285:13 See *The Scientific Evaluation of Freud's Theories and Therapy*, ed. Seymour Fisher and Roger P. Greenberg (New York, 1978), pp. 1–76, esp. 40–48. 386:1 Ruitenbeek, p. 56. :19 *BV*, p. 3. :24 *Dial*, Sept. 1922. Pound had already made the same point in his Paris Letter in the May issue—see *P/JL*, p. 196. :29 *BV*, p. 15. :33 *BV*, p. 22. :36 *CC*, pp. 176–81. 389:6 *DVW*, 2:187. :7 See *SL*, pp. 74–78. :14 Tate, pp. 195–96. :25 AIK 711. :31 AIK 863. :38 *SL*, p. 73. 390:5 See *SL*, p. 77. :34 AIK 711. 391:12 AIK 934. :18 AIK 620. :25 *SL*, p. 78. :39 *CC*, pp. 341–44. 392:1 AIK 1585. :5 See *SL*, pp. 77–78. :11 AIK 1586. :13 AIK 2112. :35 *CSS*, pp. 196–207. 394:6 Calvin S. Brown, *Music and Literature* (Athens, Ga., 1948), p. 202. :10 Martin, p. 86. :36 See my "Conrad Aiken's Short Fiction: The Poet's Story" in *Southern Quarterly* 2 (Fall 1982): 111–17. 395:1 *SL*, p. 313. :4 Published by the Dial Press. :23 "The Reflections of Poe in Conrad Aiken's 'Strange Moonlight,'" *Modern Language Notes* 72 (1957): 185–89. :29 Aiken's letter is quoted on page 6 of Rountree's paper, "Symbolic Counterpoint in Conrad Aiken's 'Strange Moonlight,'" which was delivered at the 1980 MLA Convention in Houston, Texas. 397:39 *GC*, p. 265. 401:35 Killorin, 34. 402:2 "Psychoanalysis and the Study of Creative Imagination" in Ruitenbeek, p. 31. Louis Fraiberg notes that several analysts, including Kris, have suggested that "aggression plays a greater part in creativity than might be expected" (p. 232), which should surprise no one at all sensitive to the rage and anguish initially powering an artist's psyche into expression.

CHAPTER 11

403:3 Letter to the author, Aug. 25, 1981. :9 *New York World*, Aug. 19, 1923, p. 7. :14 *New York Tribune*, Sept. 2, 1923, p. 19. :20 *The Nation*, Sept. 12, 1923, p. 271. 404:4 *Bookman*, Nov. 1923, p. 332. :8 *New Republic*, Dec. 5, 1923, p. 18. :17 *Freeman*, Dec. 19, 1923, p. 356. :25 See *SL*, pp. 80–81. :29 See *SL*, pp. 81–83. The Fletcher to CA letters are at TRC. :35 Quoted in *SL*, pp. 85–86. 405:8 Reprinted in *The Dial Miscellany*, ed. William Wasserstrom (Syracuse, 1963), pp. 165–72. :19 *SL*, pp. 87–89. 406:6 *SL*, p. 93. :7 SL, p. 97. :22 See SL, pp. 85–86. 408:1 See Edel, *Henry James*, 5:511–13. :3 Quoted in ibid., p. 500. :11 AIK 936. :21 A letter of Jan. 25, 1988, from Jane Aiken Hodge notes: "This is a total travesty on my mother's relationship with Margaret Game and her solicitor husband, both of whom we children knew well. We have discussed and dismissed Conrad's allegation that she made lesbian advances. She was just a formidably intelligent woman, versed in his kind of psychotalk, and he couldn't take her." :36 Peterson, p. 220. Aiken's pressing psychological danger here, perhaps increased by the shock of Jessie's pregnancy, which tied him tighter to the family, was from what Freud designated as "introjection," a turning *inward* of hostility now being directed against Jessie, Miss Ormond, and his mother, which could push depression into suicidal self-hatred. In general, if sufficiently brave, poetry writing can deflect the latter by discharging a certain amount of accumulated anger, thus somewhat refilling a deflated ego. :40 *SL*, pp. 91–93. :4 See *SL*, p. 102. :9 See Peterson, pp. 220–21. :13 See SL, p. 99. :20 SL, p. 92. :36 See Morrison, pp. 48–51, for a lucid summary of the Stekel articles. 410:2 As reported in the *New York Times*, Sept. 23, 1984, p. 63, a one-year (1982–83) study by Dr. Kay Jamison at Oxford University of a group of painters, poets, and playwrights concluded that not only was there a strong link between creativity and mental illness (statistical), but that poets in particular were victims of the severest form of manic-depressive symptoms. Serious depression and manic-depressive illness average out to 6 percent among the general population but affected 50 percent of Dr. Jamison's study sample. :14 Less persuasive because poetry's rational design—its conceptual, symbolic, and moral modalities—is deliberately opposed to what seems to be a dream's essentially amoral need to discharge bound instinctual energies, even if not necessarily true to Freud's schema in simple terms of satisfying the id's repressed, disguised drives. In the Introduction to his anthology, Ruitenbeek discovers agreement among many analysts, such as Kris and Hanns Sachs, that "artistic works set feelings which rouse guilt and anxiety at such a distance from the person that they can be experienced vividly, yet with minimal pain" (p. 18). :17 Peterson, p. 221. :20 *CP*, pp. 452–53. 411:6 See *SL*, p. 95; *CP*, pp. 455–56. :36 *Introductory Lectures on Psychoanalysis* (New York, 1977), p. 417. 412:2 Quoted in Heinz Lichtenstein, *The Dilemma of Human Identity* (New York, 1977), p. 273. :23 See Peterson, pp. 220–21. :31 *CP*, pp. 443–46. 413:29 *CP*, pp. 447–49. See "Be Still. The Hanging Gardens Were a Dream," in Whittle, pp. 80–81. 754:1 *CP*, pp. 449–50. 414:13 *CP*, pp. 449–50. See *Poems of Tennyson*, pp. 1112–17. :16 See Edith Hamilton, *Mythology* (New York: New American Library, 1968), p. 288. :18 Hamilton, pp. 289–90. :24 *Tennyson* (New York: Collier, 1972), p. 129. 415:23 It was the pre-Darwinian fossil revelations in Charles Lyell's *Principles of Geology* (published 1830–33) that Tennyson had to incorporate, neutralize, becoming a uniformitarian in the process, though he reverted to a "catastrophist" (apocalyptic) position in his declining years—see A. Dwight Culler, *The Poetry of Tennyson* (New Haven: Yale University Press, 1977), pp. 14–15. :16 *CP*, pp. 450–51. 758:11 Geoffrey H. Hartman's perceptive essay, "Wordsworth, Inscriptions, and Romantic Nature Poetry," in his *Beyond Formalism* (New Haven: Yale University Press, 1970), pp. 206–30, covers the matter effectively. :37 *CP*, pp. 454–55. 417:33 *CP*, pp. 457–59. 418:24 The eternal allure of *Metamorphoses* for a modern sensibility—Shakespeare's, for instance—resides not only in its narrative riches but in the distance between urbane narrator and borrowed folk material already established, which prevents alienation and permits another level of meaning to emerge without sacrificing the collected myths' primitive power, at least not a fatal portion of it. :28 *CP*, pp. 459–60. :35 See Hamilton, pp. 114–15. 419:6 See Philip Rieff on Lawrence ("A Modern Mythmaker") in *Myth and Mythmaking*, ed. Henry A. Murray (New York: Braziller, 1960), esp. pp. 242–46. :11 *CC*, pp. 256–61. :14 *CC*, pp. 261–63. :38 Reprinted in *The Spirit in Man, Art, and Literature* (Princeton, 1971), pp. 65–83. 420:4 In 1915, linguist Ferdinand de Saussure's *Cours de linguistique générale* was published in Paris. It stressed the arbitrary nature of linguistic signs, noting the absence of an intrinsic link between the signifier or word and the signified (meaning), as well as their arbitrary (synchronic) relationship to the real world and history. :34 See Gay Wilson Allen, *Waldo Emerson* (New York: Viking, 1981), pp. 52, 282, 375, 484–85, 579, among others. Allen writes about Emerson's problems with Hegel in 1867, unable to read him "with satisfaction" (p. 631), but Hegel's ideas were a part of his intellectual heritage. He was friends with William Torrey Harris, America's Hegel expert, who got him to peruse Hegel in the first place. Allen also notes that Emerson anticipated Freud in certain areas—see pp. 161, 227, 306, 329, 331, 649. :39 Quoted in Allen, p. 271. In "The Over-Soul," Emerson conceded: "We can point nowhere to anything final . . . planet, system, constellation, total nature is growing like a field of maize in July; is becoming something else; is in rapid metamorphosis"—see *Essays*, pp. 251–78. He counted Swedenborg among those (Socrates, Plotinus, George Fox, et al.) blessed by trance-like prophetic inspirations, which implies a "certain tendency to insanity" (p. 264), reflecting his own rationalist unease. In *An American Procession* (New York: Knopf, 1984), which is keenly attuned to Emerson's pervasive influence, Alfred Kazin speaks of "the Emersonian legacy: the unconscious mind as oracle" (p. 254). 421:6 Pack, p. 89; *CP*, pp. 460–61; Peterson p. 221. :24 *Principles of Psychology*, 1:149. Emerson saw Agassiz's theory of the universe's "ideal" or "spiritual evolution" and Darwin's natural selection mechanism, which Agassiz rejected, as counterparts of the same machinery—see Allen, p. 573. 423:30 *CP*, pp. 464–68. :25 In "Female Sexuality," written after Aiken's poem (1931), Freud would confess to perplexing complications in trying to chart a female's psychosexual maturation course, believing "we are right in rejecting the term 'Electra complex' which seeks to insist that the situation of the two sexes is analogous" (p. 198)—see *Sexuality and the Psychology of Love*, pp. 194–211. 424:3 Lillian Feder's *Madness in Literature* (Princeton, 1980), pp. 35–97, confronts Greek myths and tragedies as communal exercises in learning how to control irrational forces. :34 With apt symbolic pathos, Semele had died from exposure to Zeus's light, necessitating his surrogate-mother action—see Hamilton, pp. 54–55. 426:4 Hamilton, pp. 31–32, 46. Diana's identity was various under different guises, as Apollo's twin (Artemis), for instance, or Selene, the moon goddess, being associated with healing, hunting, and childbirth, among other functions, some of them negative. 427:9 *Principles of Psychology*, 1:336. Later in the same chapter, James draws the then-radical conclusion that the "same brain may subserve many conscious selves, either alternate or coexisting" (p. 400). 427:25 *Beyond Good and Evil*, trans. R. J. Hollingdale (New York: Penguin, 1966), p. 86. :27 *Collected Poems*, p. 405. Stevens's climate was first allegorized in "The Snow Man," his "mind of winter"—ibid., p. 9. :34 *The Spirit in Man, Art, and Literature*, p. 103. 428:15 See *Priapus and the Pool and Other Poems*, pp. 11–98. 429:13 *The Varieties of Religious Experience* (1902; rpt. New York: Collier, 1961), pp. 143–59. :25 *SL*, pp. 90–93. :32 To Kant, "all human knowledge begins with intuitions, advances to concepts, and ends with ideas," a paradigm that helped him translate Descartes's ontological theorem into an objective, sensual self at one with phenomena, since the categories imposed upon experience by consciousness could be viewed as making internal and external events identical, thus collapsing the boundary between perception and reality (sensed) reared by materialists like Hume— see *Critique of Pure Reason*, trans. F. Max Muller, 2d ed. rev. (Garden City, N.Y.: Doubleday, 1961), esp. pp. 219–45, 412–13, 417–99. In *The Varieties of Religious Experience*, pp. 60–61, 350, James belittles Kant's refusal to view God, soul, freedom, and the like as proper objects for knowledge, although accepting belief or faith in them. He then proffers Kant's doctrine of a Transcendental Ego of Apperception as the "basis for modern idealism." :35 *Beyond Good and Evil*, p. 91 and p. 83. 430:1 Ibid., p. 91. :7 Ibid., p. 222. :11 In ibid., Nietzsche avows: "Profound suffering makes noble; it separates" (p. 270), and in a letter to the author, May 29, 1983, John Aiken recalls about his father: "He and I had a ferocious argument about Haydn vs. Beethoven, from which it emerged clearly that he believed strongly that an artist must suffer to achieve excellence." :18 Lichtenstein, p. 305, describes how the "use of coercive sexuality and aggression rather than pleasurable gratification in order to bring about well-being" can serve "as a defense against the possibility of encountering negation." :24 Letter to the author, July 28, 1983. 431:6 See Lorenz, pp. 82–83. :22 Quoted in Brazeau, p. 95. 432:23 See "Emily Dickinson," *Dial* (Apr. 1924): 301–8; AIK 499. :29 AIK 501. :33 *SL*, pp. 89–90. 433:4 AIK 943. :9 The review appeared in the July 1924 issue of the *Criterion*, pp. 486–89. :12 See *CC*, pp. 79–83, 141–44, 148–50. :20 A note in *Varieties of Religious Experience* posits the "main phenomena of religion" as "melancholy and conversion" (p. 28). :21 Ackroyd, pp. 114, 116, 123, 139–41, records Eliot's dependence upon Vivienne during this trying period, as well as her help on the *Criterion*. When Huxley met Vivienne for the first time in 1917, he thought "that it is almost entirely a sexual nexus between Eliot and her"—see *Ottoline at Garsington*, ed. Robert Gathrone-Hardy (New York: Knopf, 1974), pp. 206–7. :24 See Ackroyd, p. 136, and *DVW*, 2:190. :27 Eliot had wanted to begin *The Waste Land* with "Gerontion" and a quote from Conrad ("The horror!")—Ackroyd, p. 118—but Pound convinced him to drop both. See *The Waste Land*, ed. Valerie Eliot (New York: Harcourt, Brace, Jovanovich, 1971), pp. 2, 125. :31 Woolf captured the mask in a 1920 diary entry: "The odd thing about Eliot is that his eyes are lively and youthful when the cast of his face and shape of his sentences is formal and heavy. Rather like a sculpted face—no upper lip; formidable, powerful; pale" (*DVW*, 2:67). 434:15 Published by Dutton. :21 Quoted in Nelson, p. 137. :31 Quoted in Nelson, p. 180. :33 See Nelson, pp. 151–80. 435:17 *The Pilgrimage of Henry James* (1925; rpt. New York: Octagon, 1972), p. 130. :27 Quoted in Nelson, p. 160. :36 Nelson, p. 178. 436:9 Lears, p. xiv. Lears has also acutely analyzed the basic reversal dynamic: "Confronted with a sense of imminent nonexistence, Brooks finally reaffirmed 'masculine' activism and began a lifelong effort to deny his own ambivalence" (p. 257). 437:6 *BV*, p. 99. :19 AIK 864. :29 AIK 846. :40 *SL*, pp. 99–100. Read's essay, somewhat revised, is in his *Selected Writings* (New York: Horizon, 1964), pp. 98–116. 438:18 AIK 724. :36 See *SL*, pp. 94–95. 439:5 Letter to the author, July 28, 1983. :27 See *SL*, pp. 95–97. :41 See *SL*, pp. 97–99. 441:8 *SL*, p. 98. :11 *CC*, pp. 71–74. :39 See AIK 940. 442:22 *CC*, pp. 75–78. 444:3 *CC*, p. 80. :17 See AIK 941. :40 *DVW* (1980), 3:5. 445:9 *Mont-Saint-Michel and Chartres* (1905; rpt. Princeton: Princeton University Press, 1981), p. 178. In dissecting American males, Erikson discovered that behind a "fragmentary 'oedipus complex' . . . appears the deep-seated sense of having been abandoned and let down by the mother, which is the silent complaint behind schizoid withdrawal" (p. 296). :12 *BV*, p. 240. :14 Ibid. This statement spotlights the ingrained streak of skepticism Aiken had in common with Eliot, who was less able to handle its intellectual and religious implications. Ackroyd is especially fine on this quality in Eliot, though it causes him somewhat to misread *The Waste Land* as lacking in content, in structural (psychological) development (p. 119)—see pp. 49, 70, 76, 118, 160, 163, 172, 176, 181, 197, 200, 242–43, 291. Maud Bodkin's early interpretation of Eliot's poem in her *Archetypal Patterns in Poetry* (London: Oxford University Press, 1934), pp. 308–

14, as exhibiting a mythopoetic rebirth progression remains far more convincing. And Miller argues that "perhaps Eliot's most compelling motive in adding the notes was to give *The Waste Land* a shape, a form, a structure it had lost in Pound's revision" (p. 62), which makes the sexually mixed Tiresias the poem's consciousness. Jung similarly misread Joyce's *Ulysses*, dazzled by its virtuoso surface, which is not surprising in light of the influence Joyce's epic mother quest exerted upon Eliot—see " 'Ulysses': A Monologue" in *The Spirit in Man, Art, and Literature*, pp. 109–34. :38 *SL*, pp. 100–102. 446:4 AIK 727. :11 See *SL*, p. 101. :19 *CC*, pp. 238–53. 447:8 See *SL*, p. 102. :21 John Aiken letter to the author, May 29, 1983, recalls: "He brought us up on *Peacock Pie*." :26 AIK 943; *SL*, pp. 102–3. :36 *DVW*, 3:14. 448:1 AIK 509. :6 *SL*, p. 106. :10 AIK 510. :20 *DVW*, 3:41. See also p. 45. :32 *SL*, pp. 106–7. :37 *CC*, pp. 389–92. 449:18 AIK 943. :36 AIK 728. 450:15 See AIK 942. :26 CA to Fletcher, July 29, 1926, at TRC. :33 *Wake* 11, 56. :39 *And I Worked the Writer's Trade* (New York, 1978), pp. 61–62. :40 CA to Cowley, Sept. 26, 1925, at NL. 451:16 Quoted in Killorin, 36. :21 *CP*, pp. 276–88. :36 Wilhelm Wundt, a professor of philosophy at Leipzig, founded the world's first psychological laboratory in 1879. 454:16 *The Complete Writings of Walt Whitman*, ed. Richard Maurice Bucke, Thomas B. Harned, and Horace L. Traubel (New York: Harper & Row, 1902), 2:46–50. 456:2 "Conrad Aiken's Fusion of Freud and Jung," *Studies in the Literary Imagination* 13 (Fall 1980): 99–112. :23 *Symbols of Transformation* 2d ed., trans. R.F.C. Hull (Princeton, 1976), pp. 218–19. This is a new translation of the 1916 *Psychology of the Unconscious*. :33 "Myth and Identity" in Murray, p. 286. 457:26 Northrop Frye, whose structuralist criticism relies heavily on Jung, perceives literature's descent quest as increasingly in evidence among twentieth-century works, having been revived by the Romantics—see "New Directions from Old" in his *Fables of Identity* (New York: Harcourt, Brace and World, 1963), pp. 52–66. :23 CA to Cowley, Dec. 10, 1925, at NL. 459:10 Murray, p. 246.

SELECTED BIBLIOGRAPHY

· · · · · · · · · · · · ·

CONRAD AIKEN'S WORKS
(American and British Editions)

Earth Triumphant and Other Tales in Verse. New York: Macmillan, 1914.
Turns and Movies and Other Tales in Verse. Boston: Houghton Mifflin, 1916;
London: Constable, 1916.
The Jig of Forslin: A Symphony. Boston: Four Seas, 1916; London: Secker, 1922.
Nocturne of Remembered Spring and Other Poems. Boston: Four Seas, 1917;
London: Secker, 1922.
The Charnel Rose; Senlin: A Biography; and Other Poems. Boston: Four Seas, 1917;
London: Secker, 1922.
Scepticisms: Notes on Contemporary Poetry. New York: Knopf, 1919.
The House of Dust: A Symphony. Boston: Four Seas, 1920.
Punch: The Immortal Liar, Documents in His History. New York: Knopf, 1921;
London: Secker, 1921.
Priapus and the Pool. Cambridge: Dunster House, 1922.
The Pilgrimage of Festus. New York: Knopf, 1923; London: Secker, 1924.
Bring! Bring! New York: Boni and Liveright, 1925; London: Secker, 1925.
Senlin: A Biography. London: Hogarth Press, 1925.
Priapus and the Pool and Other Poems. New York: Boni and Liveright, 1925.
Blue Voyage. New York: Scribner's, 1927; London: Gerald Howe, 1927.
Costumes by Eros. New York: Scribner's, 1928; London: Jonathan Cape, 1929
Selected Poems. New York: Scribner's, 1929.
John Deth: A Metaphysical Legend, and Other Poems. New York and London:
Scribner's, 1930.
The Coming Forth by Day of Osiris Jones. New York: Scribner's, 1931.
Preludes for Memnon. New York: Scribner's, 1931.
Great Circle. New York: Scribner's, 1933; London: Wishart, 1933.
Among the Lost People. New York: Scribner's, 1934.
Landscape West of Eden. New York: Scribner's, 1935; London: Dent, 1934.
King Coffin. New York: Scribner's, 1935; London: Dent, 1935.
Time in the Rock. New York and London: Scribner's, 1936.
A Heart for the Gods of Mexico. London: Secker, 1939.
Conversation: Or, Pilgrim's Progress. New York: Duell, Sloan and Pearce, 1940;
London: Rodney, Phillips and Green, 1948.
And in the Human Heart. New York: Duell, Sloan and Pearce, 1940; London:
Staples Press, 1949.
Brownstone Eclogues and Other Poems. New York: Duell, Sloan and Pearce, 1942.
The Soldier: A Poem. Norfolk, Conn.: New Directions, 1944; London: Nicholson
and Watson, 1946.
The Kid. New York: Duell, Sloan and Pearce, 1947; London: John Lehmann, 1947.
Skylight One: Fifteen Poems. New York: Oxford University Press, 1949; London:
John Lehmann, 1951.

The Divine Pilgrim. Athens: University of Georgia Press, 1949.

The Short Stories of Conrad Aiken. New York: Duell, Sloan and Pearce, 1950.

Ushant: An Essay. New York and Boston: Duell, Sloan and Pearce, 1952; London: W. H. Allen, 1963.

Collected Poems. New York: Oxford University Press, 1953.

A Letter from Li Po and Other Poems. New York: Oxford University Press, 1955.

Mr. Arcularis: A Play. Cambridge, Mass.: Harvard University Press, 1957; London: Oxford University Press, 1958.

Sheepfold Hill: Fifteen Poems. New York: Sagamore Press, 1958.

A Reviewer's ABC: Collected Criticism. Edited by Rufus A. Blanshard. New York: Meridian Books, 1958; London: Mayflower Books, 1959. *Collected Criticism.* New York: Oxford University Press, 1968.

The Collected Short Stories of Conrad Aiken. Cleveland and New York: World, 1960; London: Heinemann, 1966.

Selected Poems. New York: Oxford University Press, 1961.

The Morning Song of Lord Zero. New York: Oxford University Press, 1963.

The Collected Novels of Conrad Aiken. New York: Holt, Rinehart and Winston, 1964.

Three Novels. London: W. H. Allen, 1965.

A Seizure of Limericks. New York: Holt, Rinehart and Winston, 1964; London: W. H. Allen, 1965.

Cats and Bats and Things with Wings: Poems. New York: Atheneum, 1965.

Tom, Sue and the Clock. New York and London: Collier Books-Macmillan, 1966.

Thee: A Poem. New York: Braziller, 1967; London: Inca Books, 1973.

Collected Poems, 1916–1970. New York: Oxford University Press, 1970.

A Little Who's Zoo of Mild Animals. London: Jonathan Cape, 1977.

The Clerk's Journal: Being the Diary of a Queer Man. New York: Eakins Press, 1971.

Selected Letters of Conrad Aiken. Edited by Joseph Killorin. New Haven: Yale University Press, 1978.

ANTHOLOGIES EDITED BY CONRAD AIKEN
(British and American)

Modern American Poets. London: Secker, 1922.

Selected Poems of Emily Dickinson. London: Jonathan Cape, 1924.

Modern American Poets. New York: Modern Library, 1927.

American Poetry, 1671–1928. New York: Modern Library, 1929.

A Comprehensive Anthology of American Poetry. New York: Modern Library, 1945.

Twentieth-Century American Poetry. New York: Modern Library, 1945. Rev. ed. 1963.

Selected Poems of Emily Dickinson. Reedited by Robert N. Linscott. New York: Modern Library, 1948.

SECONDARY WORKS

Ackroyd, Peter. *T. S. Eliot: A Life*. New York: Simon and Schuster, 1984.

Adams, J. Donald. *Copey*. Boston: Houghton Mifflin, 1960.

Aldington, Richard. *Life for Life's Sake*. New York: Viking, 1941.

Allen, Frederick Lewis. *Only Yesterday*. New York: Harper and Brothers, 1931.

Anderson, Sherwood. *Memoirs*. New York: Harcourt, Brace, 1942.

Biddle, Francis. *A Casual Past*. New York: Doubleday, 1961.

Blackmur, Richard P. *The Expense of Greatness*. New York: Arrow, 1940.

Bradbury, Malcolm, and James McFarlane, eds. *Modernism, 1890–1930*. New York: Penguin, 1976.

Brooke, Rupert. *Letters from America*. New York: Scribner's, 1916.

Brooks, Van Wyck. *An Autobiography*. New York: Dutton, 1955.

———, ed. *Writers at Work: Second Series*. New York: Viking, 1963.

———. *Three Essays on America*. New York: Dutton, 1970.

Brown, Calvin. *Music and Literature*. Athens: University of Georgia Press, 1948.

Brown, Rollo Walter. *Dean Briggs*. New York: Harper and Brothers, 1926.

Butcher, Philip, ed. *The William Stanley Braithwaite Reader*. Ann Arbor: University of Michigan Press, 1972.

Cowley, Malcolm. *Exile's Return: A Literary Odyssey of the 1920's*. New York: Viking-Compass, 1956.

———. *And I Worked the Writer's Trade: Chapters of Literary History, 1918–1978*. New York: Viking, 1978.

Dell, Floyd. *Homecoming*. 1933. Reprint. Port Washington, N.Y.: Kennikat, 1969.

Eliot, T. S. *The Sacred Wood: Essays on Poetry and Criticism*. London: Methuen, 1920.

———. *For Lancelot Andrewes: Essays on Style and Order*. London: Faber & Gwyer, 1928.

Ellmann, Richard. *James Joyce*. 1959. Revised edition. New York: Oxford University Press, 1982.

Feder, Lillian. *Ancient Myth in Modern Poetry*. Princeton: Princeton University Press, 1971.

———. *Madness in Literature*. Princeton: Princeton University Press, 1980.

Fletcher, John G. *Life Is My Song*. New York: Farrar and Rinehart, 1937.

Fraser, Russell. *A Mingled Yarn: The Life of R. P. Blackmur*. New York: Harcourt, 1981.

Ginger, Ray. *Age of Excess*. New York: Macmillan, 1965.

Gordon, Lyndall. *Eliot's Early Years*. New York: Oxford University Press, 1977.

Gould, Jean. *Amy: The World of Amy Lowell and the Imagist Movement*. New York: Dodd, Mead, 1975.

Grant, Joy. *Harold Monro and the Poetry Bookshop*. Berkeley and Los Angeles: University of California Press, 1967.

Gregory, Horace, and Marya Zaturenska. *A History of American Poetry, 1900–1940*. New York: Harcourt, Brace, 1946.

Harner, J. B. *Victory in Limbo: A History of Imagism, 1908–1917*. New York: St. Martin's, 1975.

Hoffman, Frederick J. *Freudianism and the Literary Mind*. Baton Rouge: Louisiana State University Press, 1957.

————. *Conrad Aiken*. New York: Twayne, 1962.

Howarth, Patrick. *Squire: Most Generous of Men*. London: Hutchinson, 1963.

Hyman, Stanley Edgar. *The Armed Vision: A Study in the Methods of Modern Literary Criticism*. New York: Knopf, 1948.

Kazin, Alfred. *On Native Grounds*. New York: Harcourt, Brace, 1942.

Knight, Grant C. *The Strenuous Age in American Literature*. Chapel Hill: University of North Carolina Press, 1954.

Kreymborg, Alfred. *Troubador*. New York: Boni and Liveright, 1925.

Kublick, Bruce. *The Rise of American Philosophy: Cambridge, Mass., 1860–1930*. New Haven: Yale University Press, 1977.

Kumar, Shiv. *Bergson and the Stream of Consciousness Novel*. New York: New York University Press, 1963.

Langbaum, Robert. *The Mysteries of Identity: A Theme in Modern Literature*. New York: Oxford University Press, 1977.

Lears, T. J. Jackson. *No Place of Grace: Antimodernism and the Transformation of American Culture, 1880–1920*. New York: Pantheon, 1981.

Lehmann, John. *The Strange Destiny of Rupert Brooke*. New York: Holt, Rinehart and Winston, 1980.

Lerner, Arthur. *Psychoanalytically Oriented Criticism of Three American Poets: Poe, Whitman and Aiken*. Rutherford, N.J.: Fairleigh Dickinson University Press, 1970.

Link, Arthur S. *American Epoch*. New York: Knopf, 1958.

Lippmann, Walter. *Drift and Mastery*. New York: Mitchell Kennerley, 1915.

Lorenz, Clarissa. *Lorelei Two: My Life with Conrad Aiken*. Athens: University of Georgia Press, 1983.

Lowell, Amy. *Tendencies in Modern American Poetry*. New York: Macmillan, 1917.

Mariani, Paul. *William Carlos Williams: A New World Naked*. New York: McGraw-Hill, 1981.

Martin, Jay. *Conrad Aiken: The Art of His Life*. Princeton: Princeton University Press, 1962.

Mencken, H. L. *A Book of Prefaces*. New York: Knopf, 1917.

Monroe, Harriet. *A Poet's Life*. 1938. Reprint. New York: AMS, 1969.

Moore, Jack B. *Maxwell Bodenheim*. New York: Twayne, 1970.

Moreau, John. *Bourne: Legend and Reality*. Washington, D.C.: Public Affairs Press, 1966.

Morison, Samuel Eliot. *Three Centuries of Harvard*. Cambridge, Mass.: Harvard University Press, 1936.

Morrison, Claudia C. *Freud and the Critic: The Early Use of Depth Psychology in Literary Criticism*. Chapel Hill: University of North Carolina Press, 1968.

Nelson, Raymond. *Van Wyck Brooks: A Writer's Life*. New York: Dutton, n.d.

Norman, Charles. *Ezra Pound*. New York: Macmillan, 1960.

Olson, Steven Eric. "The Vascular Mind: Conrad Aiken's Early Poetry, 1910–1918." Ph.D. dissertation, Stanford University, 1981.

Paz, Octavio. *Children of the Mire: Modern Poetry from Romanticism to the Avant-Garde*. Cambridge, Mass.: Harvard University Press, 1974.

Perkins, David. *A History of Modern Poetry: From the 1890's to Pound, Eliot, and Yeats*. Cambridge, Mass.: Harvard University Press, 1976.

Peterson, Houston. *The Melody of Chaos*. New York: Longmans, 1931.

Potter, William James. *Twenty-Five Sermons of Twenty-Five Years*. Boston: George H. Ellis, 1886.
_____. *Lectures and Sermons*. Boston: George H. Ellis, 1895.
Prescott, Frederick Clarke. *The Poetic Mind*. New York: Macmillan, 1922.
Pritchard, William H. *Seeing through Everything: English Writers, 1918–1940*. New York: Oxford University Press, 1977.
Rascoe, Burton. *Before I Forget*. New York: Literary Guild, 1937.
Rittenhouse, Jessie B. *My House of Life: An Autobiography*. Boston: Houghton Mifflin, 1934.
Russell, Francis. *The Great Interlude*. New York: McGraw-Hill, 1964.
Santayana, George. *Three Philosophical Poets*. Cambridge, Mass.: Harvard University Press, 1910.
_____. *Persons and Places: The Background of My Life*. New York: Scribner's, 1944.
_____. *The Middle Span: Persons and Places Continued*. New York: Scribner's, 1945.
Scholz, Carol. "They Share the Suffering: The Psychoanalyst in American Fiction between 1920 and 1940." Ph.D. dissertation, University of Pennsylvania, 1977.
Spingarn, Joel E. *Creative Criticism*. New York: Henry Holt, 1917.
Steel, Ronald. *Walter Lippmann and the American Century*. Boston: Little, Brown, 1980.
Stephens. Edna B. *John Gould Fletcher*. New York: Twayne, 1967.
Stevens, Holly. *Souvenirs and Prophecies: The Young Wallace Stevens*. New York: Knopf, 1977.
Untermeyer, Louis. *The New Era in American Poetry*. New York: Henry Holt, 1919.
_____. *Bygones*. New York: Harcourt, Brace, 1965.
Wasserstron, William, ed. *The Dial Miscellany*. Syracuse: Syracuse University Press, 1963.
Wells, Henry W. *New Poets from Old: A Study in Literary Genetics*. New York: Columbia University Press, 1940.
Ziff, Larzer. *The American 1890's: Life and Times of a Lost Generation*. New York: Viking, 1966.

RELEVANT PSYCHOLOGICAL TEXTS AND STUDIES

Bowlby, John. *Attachment and Loss: Separation*. New York: Basic Books, 1973.
_____. *Attachment and Loss: Sadness and Depression*. New York: Basic Books, 1980.
Erikson, Erik H. *Childhood and Society*. New York: Norton, 1963.
_____. *Life History and the Historical Moment*. New York: Norton, 1975.
Fine, Reuben. *A History of Psychoanalysis*. New York: Columbia University Press, 1979.
Fisher, Seymour, and Roger P. Greenberg. *The Scientific Evaluation of Freud's Theories and Therapy*. New York: Basic Books, 1978.

Freud, Sigmund. *The Basic Writings of Sigmund Freud*. Translated by A. A. Brill. New York: Random House, 1938.

————. *Beyond the Pleasure Principle*. Translated by James Strachey. New York: Norton, 1961.

————. *Sexuality and the Psychology of Love*. Edited by Philip Rieff. New York: Collier Books, 1963.

————. *Introductory Lectures on Psychoanalysis*. Translated by James Strachey. New York: Norton, 1966.

————. *Character and Culture*. Edited by Philip Rieff. New York: Collier Books, 1983.

Grinker, R. R., et al. *The Borderline Syndrome*. New York: Basic Books, 1968.

Holt, Edwin. *The Freudian Wish and Its Place in Ethics*. New York: Henry Holt, 1915.

Horney, Karen. *The Neurotic Personality of Our Time*. New York: Norton, 1937.

James, William. *Principles of Psychology*. 2 vols. New York: Henry Holt, 1890.

Jung, C. G. *Four Archetypes*. Translated by R. F. C. Hull. Princeton: Princeton University Press, 1970.

————. *The Spirit in Man, Art, and Literature*. Translated by R. F. C. Hull. Princeton: Princeton University Press, 1971.

————. *Critique of Psychoanalysis*. Translated by R. F. C. Hull. Princeton: Princeton University Press, 1975.

————. *Symbols of Transformation*. Translated by R. F. C. Hull. Princeton: Princeton University Press, 1976.

Klein, Melanie. *The Psycho-Analysis of Children*. Translated by Alix Strachey. 1932. Revised edition. New York: Delacourt, 1975.

————. *Contributions to Psychoanalysis, 1921–1945*. Translated by Alix Strachey. London: Hogarth Press, 1948.

Kohut, Heinz. *The Analysis of Self*. New York: International Universities Press, 1971.

————. *The Restoration of the Self*. New York: International Universities Press, 1977.

————. *How Does Analysis Cure?* Edited by Arnold Goldberg. Chicago: University of Chicago Press, 1984.

Lacan, Jacques. *The Language of the Self*. Translated by Anthony Wilden. 1968. Reprint. New York: Delta, n.d.

————. *The Four Fundamental Concepts of Psycho-Analysis*. Translated by Alan Sheridan. New York: Norton, 1978.

Lichtenstein, Heinz. *The Dilemma of Human Identity*. New York: Jason Aronson, 1977.

Lifton, Robert Jay. *The Life of the Self: Toward a New Psychology*. New York: Simon and Schuster, 1976.

Piaget, Jean. *Play, Dreams and Imitation in Childhood*. Translated by C. Gattegno and F. M. Hodgson. New York: Norton, 1962.

Rank, Otto. *Art and Artist*. Translated by Charles Francis Atkinson. New York: Knopf, 1932.

Ruitenbeek, Hendrik M., ed. *The Creative Imagination*. Chicago: Quadrangle, 1965.

CRITICAL ESSAYS

Aldrich, Jennifer. "The Deciphered Heart: Conrad Aiken's Poetry and Prose Fiction." *Sewanee Review* 75 (Summer 1967): 485–520.

Beach, Joseph Warren. "Conrad Aiken and T. S. Eliot: Echoes and Overtones." *PMLA* 69 (September 1954): 753–62.

Blackmur, Richard P. "The Composition in Nine Poets." *Southern Review* 2 (Winter 1937): 558–76.

———. "Conrad Aiken: The Poet." *Atlantic Monthly,* December 1953, pp. 77–82.

Blanshard, Rufus A. "Pilgrim's Progress: Conrad Aiken's Poetry." *Texas Quarterly* 1 (Winter 1958): 135–48.

Bollier, E. P. "Conrad Aiken's Ancestral Voices: A Reading of Four Poems." *Studies in the Literary Imagination* 13 (Fall 1980): 51–62.

Butscher, Edward. "Conrad Aiken's Short Fiction: The Poet's Story." *Southern Quarterly* 1 (Fall 1982): 99–118.

Crawford, Fred D. "Conrad Aiken's Cancelled Debt to T. S. Eliot." *Journal of Modern Literature* 3 (September 1979): 416–32.

Dillon, George. "Mr. Aiken's Poetry." *Poetry* 37 (January 1931): 221–25.

Gross, Seymour. "The Reflection of Poe in Conrad Aiken's 'Strange Moonlight.' " *Modern Language Notes* 72 (1957): 185–89.

Hagenbuechle, Helen. "Epistemology and Musical Form in Conrad Aiken's Poetry." *Studies in the Literary Imagination* 13 (Fall 1980): 7–25.

Hamilton, G. Rostrevor. "The Floodlit Mind." *Wake* 11 (1952): 32–48.

Killorin, Joseph. "Conrad Aiken's Use of Autobiography." *Studies in the Literary Imagination* 13 (Fall 1980): 27–49.

Lawrence, Alexander A. "228 Habersham Street." *Georgia Review* 22 (Fall 1968): 317–34.

Malin, Irving. "Introduction: Aiken Reflections." *Southern Quarterly* 1 (Fall 1982): 3–6.

Marten, Harry. "The Unconquerable Ancestors: 'Mayflower,' 'The Kid,' 'Halloween.' *Studies in the Literary Imagination* 13 (Fall 1980): 51–62.

Moore, Marianne. "If a Man Die." *Wake* 11 (1952): 50–56.

Murray, Henry A. "A Poet of Creative Dissolution." *Wake* 11 (1952): 95–106.

Olson, Steven E. "*Great Circle:* Conrad Aiken's Autoplastic Journey into Childhood." *Southern Quarterly* 1 (Fall 1982): 38–63.

Pinsker, Sanford. "The Artist and the Art Novel: A Reappraisal of Conrad Aiken's *Blue Voyage.*" *Southern Quarterly* 1 (Fall 1982): 28–37.

Rein, David M. "Conrad Aiken and Psychoanalysis." *Psychoanalytic Review* 42 (October 1955): 402–11.

Robillard, Douglas. "Conrad Aiken and Herman Melville." *Studies in the Literary Imagination* 13 (Fall 1980): 87–97.

———. "Conrad Aiken and the Supernatural." *Southern Quarterly* 1 (Fall 1982): 119–31.

Rountree, Mary Martin. "Conrad Aiken's Heroes: Portrait of the Artist as Middle-Aged Failure." *Studies in the Literary Imagination* 13 (Fall 1980): 77–86.

———. "Conrad Aiken's Fiction: 'An Inordinate and Copious Lyric.' " *Southern Quarterly* 1 (Fall 1982): 9–27.

Schorer, Mark. "The Life in the Fiction." *Wake* 11 (1952): 57–60.

Spivey, Ted R. "Conrad Aiken's Fusion of Freud and Jung." *Studies in the Literary Imagination* 13 (Fall 1980): 99–112.

———. "Conrad Aiken and the Life of Reason." *Southern Quarterly* 1 (Fall 1982): 148–57.

Story, Nancy Ciucevich. "Conrad Aiken: A Functional Basis for Poetry and Criticism." *Southern Quarterly* 1 (Fall 1982): 132–47.

Symons, Julian. "The Poetry of Conrad Aiken." *Wake* 11 (1952): 107–13.

Tabachnick, Stephen E. "The Great Circle Voyage of Conrad Aiken's *Mr. Arcularis*." *American Literature* 45 (January 1974): 601–7.

Tuttleton, James W. "Aiken's 'Mr. Arcularis': Psychic Regression and the Death-Instinct." *American Imago* 20 (1963): 295–314.

Voelker, Joseph C. " 'A Collideorscope!': Sigmund Freud, Malcolm Lowry, and the Aesthetics of Conrad Aiken's *A Heart for the Gods of Mexico*." *Southern Quarterly* 1 (Fall 1982): 64–81.

Waterman, Arthur. "The Evolution of Consciousness: Conrad Aiken's Novels and *Ushant*." *Critique: Studies in Modern Fiction* 15 (1973): 67–81.

Wheeler, James L. "The Ushant Dream of Conrad Aiken." *Southern Quarterly* 1 (1982): 82–98.

Wilbur, Robert Hunter. "The Acts of Consciousness: Conrad Aiken's Poetry." *Northwest Review* 2 (Spring 1959): 49–54.

Untermeyer, Louis. "Conrad Aiken: Our Best Known Unread Poet." *Saturday Review,* November 25, 1967, pp. 28–29, 76–77.

ILLUSTRATION CREDITS

* * * * * * * * * * * *

Page 6
Dr. William Ford Aiken, 1888. Courtesy of the Henry E. Huntington Library and Art Gallery, San Marino, California.

Page 10
Conrad Aiken at age two, 1892. Courtesy of the Henry E. Huntington Library and Art Gallery.

Page 15
Reverend William James Potter, 1890. Courtesy of the Henry E. Huntington Library and Art Gallery.

Page 17
Aiken's house on Oglethorpe Avenue East, Savannah. Family photograph.

Page 22
Conrad Aiken with his sister Elizabeth, 1895. Courtesy of the Henry E. Huntington Library and Art Gallery.

Page 26
Conrad Aiken at age six, 1896. Courtesy of the Henry E. Huntington Library and Art Gallery.

Page 30
Anna Aiken with Kempton and Robert, 1898. Courtesy of the Henry E. Huntington Library and Art Gallery.

Page 34
Anna Aiken with her four children (Conrad, Elizabeth, Robert, and Kempton) and their nurses, Selena and Clara, ca. 1896. Courtesy of the Henry E. Huntington Library and Art Gallery.

Page 45
Aiken's parents, Dr. William and Anna (Potter) Aiken, taken shortly before their deaths in 1901. Courtesy of the Henry E. Huntington Library and Art Gallery.

Page 53
Jane Delano Kempton's New Bedford house. Courtesy of the Henry E. Huntington Library and Art Gallery.

Page 56
Julia Delano's New Bedford mansion, ca. 1890. Courtesy of the Henry E. Huntington Library and Art Gallery.

Page 64
Conrad Aiken in 1903. Courtesy of the Henry E. Huntington Library and Art Gallery.

Page 69
Emily H. Ford Aken, ca. 1890. Courtesy of the Henry E. Huntington Library and Art Gallery.

Page 79
The Middlesex graduating class of 1907. Courtesy of Margaret McCouch.

Page 142
Harvard Advocate staff in 1910. Courtesy of the Harvard University Archives.

Page 180
Jessie McDonald as a graduate student, shortly before she met Aiken in 1911. Courtesy of Ruth Dadourian.

Page 241
Conrad Aiken as a pensive young author, ca. 1914. Courtesy of Clarissa Lorenz Aiken.

Page 339
Aiken and Jessie with John and Jane in South Yarmouth, ca. 1921. Courtesy of Clarissa Lorenz Aiken.

Page 399
Dr. William Aiken with Anna and a Mr. and Mrs. Billington in the Aiken drawing room, 1895. Courtesy of the Henry E. Huntington Library and Art Gallery.

Page 407
Jeake's House as it looks today. Photograph by John Aiken's wife, Paddy. Reprinted with permission from *Lorelei Two: My Life with Conrad Aiken* by Clarissa M. Lorenz.

Page 458
Conrad Aiken in his middle thirties. Courtesy of Clarissa Lorenz Aiken.

INDEX OF TITLES

· · · · · · · · · · ·

INDEX